From Memory to Written Record

ⅠB

For R. H. C. Davis, my friend and teacher (1918–1991)

From Memory to Written Record

England 1066–1307
Second Edition

M. T. CLANCHY

BLACKWELL
Oxford UK & Cambridge USA

Copyright © M. T. Clanchy, 1979, 1993

The right of M. T. Clanchy to be identified as author of this work has been
asserted in accordance with the Copyright, Designs and Patents Act 1988.

First edition published in 1979 by Edward Arnold Ltd in UK and by
Harvard University Press in USA

This edition first published by Blackwell Publishers 1993
·Reprinted 1994, 1995, 1996, 1997, 1998,1999 (twice)

Blackwell Publishers Ltd
108 Cowley Road
Oxford OX4 1JF, UK

Blackwell Publishers Inc.
350 Main Street
Malden, Massachusetts 02148, USA

British Library Cataloguing in Publication Data
A CIP catalogue record for this book is available from the British Library

Library of Congress Cataloging in Publication Data
Clanchy, M. T.
From memory to written record, England 1066–1307/M. T.Clanchy—2nd ed.
p. cm.
Includes bibliographical references and index.
ISBN 0–631–17823–6 (acid-free paper) — ISBN 0–631–16857–5 (pbk: acid-free paper)
1. Great Britain—Politics and government—1066–1485. 2. Written communication—
England—History. 3. Public administration—England—History. 4. Oral Communication—
England—History. 5. Public records—England—History. 6. Literacy—England—History.
7. Scriptoria—England. 8. England—Languages. I. Title.
DA176.C54   1993   92–20180
942.02—dc20   CIP

Typeset in 9.5 on 11pt Baskerville by TecSet Ltd, Wallington, Surrey

Printed and bound in Great Britain by T. J. International, Padstow, Cornwall

This book is printed on acid-free paper

Contents

Plates

(following on p. 345)

Preface to the First Edition

The title and subject of this book were suggested in my paper 'Remembering the Past and the Good Old Law', published in *History* (volume LV) in 1970. Since then I have benefited from discussing its themes with colleagues at the Medieval Society and the Historians' Discussion Group of the University of Glasgow and in other talks which I have given at the universities of Aberdeen, Dublin (UCD), Edinburgh, London (Institute of Historical Research), Manchester, Sheffield, and Stirling. I am grateful to all those who organized these talks or contributed to them. I also thank the University of Glasgow for travel grants and my fellow teachers of medieval history there for cooperating in a system of sabbatical leave which has enabled me to write. At an early stage I was encouraged by two scholars who have not lived to see this book. Max Gluckman helped me with anthropology and G. D. G. Hall with the history of law. From the confidence and enthusiasm of Mr John Davey, formerly of Edward Arnold Ltd, my ideas took publishable form.

In writing the book I have benefited from the comments of Dr Peter Davies, Professor Jack Goody, Dr Michael Richter, Mrs Felicity Riddy, Dr J. A. F. Thomson, Professor Ralph V. Turner and Mr C. P. Wormald, who have all read drafts of particular chapters. Mrs Katherine Thomson of the *Dictionary of Medieval Latin from British Sources* has advised me about the history of certain words, notably *rotulus*. The completed book was read in typescript by Dr C. H. Knowles and Professor S. E. Thorne. All these scholars have helped to eliminate errors and make positive improvements; they are not responsible for any of my mistakes.

In getting together the photographs for the plates I have had particular help from Miss Deborah Beevor, Mr Roger Custance, Miss Eleanor M. Garvey, Dr Edith Henderson and Mr Trevor Kaye. For permission to reproduce the plates I am indebted to: the Warden and Scholars of Winchester College (plate I); the British Library Board (plates II, III, IV, XI, XV); the Law

School of Harvard University (plates v, vi, vii, xvi, xvii, xviii, xix); the Controller of Her Majesty's Stationery Office (plate viii); the County Archivist of Berkshire (plates ix, x); the Houghton Library of Harvard University (plates xii, xiii); the Master and Fellows of Trinity College Cambridge (plate xiv).

Finally I wish to thank Miss Mary Brodie for typing, Mrs Glenna M. Satterthwaite for reading the proofs, and Miss Fay Sharman and the publishers.

M. T. Clanchy

University of Glasgow

Preface to the Second Edition

The text of the first edition has been preserved as far as possible, but the footnote references have been updated throughout. The following sections of the book are substantially new: the latter parts of the Introduction; the section on 'Documents and Bureaucracy' in chapter 2; 'Liturgical Books' in chapter 3; 'Wax, Parchment, and Wood' in chapter 4; 'Ways of Remembering' and 'Ways of Indexing' in chapter 5; 'What Reading Meant' and the introduction to part II; the section on 'The Writing down of French' in chapter 6; 'Word and Image' in chapter 8; 'The Symbolism of Seals and Crosses' in chapter 9. The new guide to 'Further Reading on the History of Literacy' indicates the amount published on this subject, particularly on the history of art and literature in medieval England, since the first edition.

I am grateful to all who have sent me amendments and suggestions, and particularly to my colleagues in London at the 'Earlier Middle Ages' seminar at the Institute of Historical Research, the 'Learning, Literacy, and Education' seminar at the Warburg Institute, and the 'Understanding Literacy' seminar at the Medical Research Council's Cognitive Development Unit. Drs Peter Denley and Uta Frith read sections of the Introduction; they are not responsible for my opinions. As with the first edition, I am most grateful to Mr John Davey of Blackwell Publishers for his encouragement throughout.

For permission to publish the plates, I am indebted to those acknowledged in the preface to the first edition, together with the British Library for the new plate xx.

M. T. Clanchy

Department of History,
University College London

Reprinting has enabled me to improve the index, update the bibliography, and make corrections.

M. T. Clanchy

September 1993

Abbreviations

Alexander & Binski	*Age of Chivalry: Art in Plantagenet England 1200–1400* ed. J. Alexander and P. Binski, Exhibition Catalogue (1987).
Anglo-Scottish Relations	*Anglo-Scottish Relations: Some Selected Documents* ed. E. L. G. Stones, reprint (1970).
Annales Monastici	*Annales Monastici* ed. H. R. Luard, Rolls Series xxxvi (1864–9).
Baronial Docs	*Documents of the Baronial Movement of Reform and Rebellion 1258–67* ed. R. F. Treharne and I. J. Sanders (1973).
Battle	*The Chronicle of Battle Abbey* ed. E. Searle (1980).
Becket Materials	*Materials for the History of Thomas Becket* ed. J. C. Robertson and J. B. Sheppard, Rolls Series lxxvii (1875–85).
Bennett & Smithers	*Early Middle English Verse and Prose* ed. J. A. W. Bennett and G. V. Smithers, 2nd edition (1968).
Berks. Eyre	*The Roll and Writ File of the Berkshire Eyre of 1248* ed. M. T. Clanchy, Selden Society xc (1973).
BIHR	*Bulletin of the Institute of Historical Research*

Bishop & Chaplais	*Facsimiles of English Royal Writs Presented to V. H. Galbraith* ed. T. A. M. Bishop and P. Chaplais (1957).
BJRL	*Bulletin of the John Rylands Library.*
BL MS	British Library (formerly British Museum) manuscript.
BM Facs	*Facsimiles of Royal and Other Charters in the British Museum* ed. G. F. Warner and H. G. Ellis I (1903).
Boase, *English Art*	T. S. R. Boase, *English Art 1100–1216* (1953).
Book of Fees	*The Book of Fees Commonly called Testa de Nevill* (1921–31).
Bracton	Henry de Bracton, *De Legibus et Consuetudinibus Angliae* ed. G. E. Woodbine (1915), reissued with translation and revisions by S. E. Thorne (1968–77).
Carruthers, *Memory*	M. J. Carruthers, *The Book of Memory* (1990).
CChR	*Calendar of Charter Rolls* (1903–27).
CClR	*Calendar of Close Rolls: Edward I* (1900–8).
Chaplais, *Docs*	P. Chaplais, *English Royal Documents: King John–Henry VI* (1971).
Cheney, *Chanceries*	C. R. Cheney, *English Bishops' Chanceries, 1100–1250* (1950).
Cheney, *Notaries*	C. R. Cheney, *Notaries Public in England in the Thirteenth and Fourteenth Centuries* (1972).
Cheney, *Texts & Studies*	C. R. Cheney, *Medieval Texts and Studies* (1973).
Cheshire Facs	*Facsimiles of Early Cheshire Charters* ed. G. Barraclough, Lancashire and Cheshire Record Society (1957).
Clanchy, '*Moderni*'	M. T. Clanchy, '*Moderni* in Medieval Education and Government in England', *Speculum* L (1975), pp. 671–88.

Clanchy, 'Remembering'	M. T. Clanchy, 'Remembering the Past and the Good Old Law', *History* LV (1970), pp. 165–76.
CLibR	*Calendar of Liberate Rolls: Henry III* (1917–64).
ClR	*Close Rolls: Henry III* (1902–38).
Court Baron	*The Court Baron* ed. F. W. Maitland and W. P. Baildon, Selden Society IV (1890).
CPatR	*Calendar of Patent Rolls* (1891–).
CuriaRR	*Curia Regis Rolls* (1922–).
Curtius, *European Lit.*	E. R. Curtius, *European Literature and the Latin Middle Ages* trans. W. R. Trask (1953).
De Hamel, *MSS*	C. de Hamel, *A History of Illuminated Manuscripts* (1986).
Dialogus	*Dialogus de Scaccario* ed. C. Johnson (1950).
Donovan, *de Brailes*	C. Donovan, *The de Brailes Hours* (1991).
Duggan, *Decretals*	C. Duggan, *Twelfth-Century Decretal Collections and their Importance in English History*, University of London Historical Studies XII (1963).
Eadmer, *Historia*	*Eadmeri Historia Novorum in Anglia* ed. M. Rule, Rolls Series LXXXI (1884).
Eadmer, *Vita*	*The Life of St Anselm by Eadmer* ed. R. W. Southern (1962).
EHR	*English Historical Review*
English Library	*The English Library before 1700* ed. F. Wormald and C. E. Wright (1958).
Essays to Poole	*Essays in History Presented to R. L. Poole* ed. H. W. C. Davis (1927).
Fälschungen	*Fälschungen im Mittelalter*, Monumenta Germaniae Historica: Schriften XXXIII (1988), iv.
Foedera	*Foedera etc. or T. Rymer's Foedera* ed. A. Clark et al., Record Commissioners' publications, I–III (1816–30).

Galbraith, 'Literacy'	V. H. Galbraith, 'The Literacy of the Medieval English Kings', *Proceedings of the British Academy* xxi (1935), pp. 201–38.
Galbraith, *Studies*	V. H. Galbraith, *Studies in the Public Records* (1948).
Gervase	*The Historical Works of Gervase of Canterbury* ed. W. Stubbs, Rolls Series lxxiii (1879–80).
Giraldus	*Giraldi Cambrensis Opera* ed. J. S. Brewer et al., Rolls Series xxi (1861–91).
Glanvill	*The Treatise on the Laws and Customs of the Realm of England Commonly Called Glanvill* ed. G. D. G. Hall (1965).
Glenisson, *Livre*	J. Glenisson, *Le Livre au Moyen Age* (1988).
Goody, *Literacy*	*Literacy in Traditional Societies* ed. J. Goody (1968).
Gransden, *Historical Writing*	A. Gransden, *Historical Writing in England c.550–1307* (1974).
HMSO	Her Majesty's Stationery Office publications.
JMH	*Journal of Medieval History.*
Jocelin	*The Chronicle of Jocelin of Brakelond* ed. H. E. Butler (1949).
Kauffmann, *Romanesque MSS*	C. M. Kauffman, *Romanesque Manuscripts 1066–1190* (1975).
Ker, *English MSS*	N. R. Ker, *English Manuscripts in the Century after the Norman Conquest* (1960).
Legge, *Anglo-Norman*	M. D. Legge, *Anglo-Norman Literature and its Background* (1963).
Lewis, *Matthew Paris*	S. Lewis, *The Art of Matthew Paris in the 'Chronica Majora'* (1987).
Matthew Paris	*Matthaei Parisiensis Chronica Majora* ed. H. R. Luard, Rolls Series lvii (1872–84).
MM for Stenton	*A Medieval Miscellany for D. M. Stenton* ed. P. M. Barnes and C. F. Slade, Pipe Roll Society new series xxxvi (1960).

Monasticon	W. Dugdale, *Monasticon Anglicanum* ed. J. Caley et al., (1817–30).
Mowbray Charters	*Charters of the Honour of Mowbray* ed. D. E. Greenway (1972).
MSS Hunt	*Manuscripts at Oxford: An Exhibition in Memory of R. W. Hunt* ed. A. C. de la Mare and B. C. Barker-Benfield (Bodleian Library, 1980).
Northants. Facs	*Facsimiles of Early Charters from Northamptonshire Collections* ed. F. M. Stenton, Northamptonshire Record Society IV (1930).
Orderic	Orderic Vitalis, *Historia Ecclesiastica* ed. M. Chibnall (1969–80).
Oxford Facs	*Facsimiles of Early Charters in Oxford Muniment Rooms* ed. H. E. Salter (1929).
P & M	F. Pollock and F. W. Maitland, *The History of English Law before the Time of Edward I*, 2nd edition (1898).
Parkes, 'Literacy'	M. B. Parkes, 'The Literacy of the Laity' in *The Medieval World* ed. D. Daiches and A. Thorlby (1973), pp. 555–77 [reprinted in M. B. Parkes, *Scribes, Scripts and Readers* (1991), pp. 275–97].
Patrologiae	*Patrologiae: Cursus Completus Series Latina* ed. J. P. Migne (1844–73).
PRS	Pipe Role Society publications (1884–).
R & S	H. G. Richardson and G. O. Sayles, *The Governance of Medieval England from the Conquest to Magna Carta* (1963).
Ramsey	*Chronicon Abbatiae Rameseiensis* ed. W. D. Macray, Rolls Series LXXXIII (1886).
RC	Record Commissioners' publications (1805–48).
Richardson, *Jewry*	H. G. Richardson, *The English Jewry under Angevin Kings* (1960).
Rot. Lit. Claus.	*Rotuli Litterarum Clausarum 1204–27*, ed. T. D. Hardy (1833–44).

Rot. Lit. Pat.	*Rotuli Litterarum Patentium 1201–16*, ed. T. D. Hardy (1835).
RRA-N	*Regesta Regum Anglo-Normannorum 1066–1154*, ed. H. W. C. Davis, J. Johnson, H. A. Cronne and R. H. C. Davis (4 vols, 1913–69).
RS	Rolls Series: *Rerum Britannicarum Medii Aevi Scriptores* (1858–97).
S.	Society serial publications.
SCCKB	*Select Cases in the Court of King's Bench under Edward I* ed. G. O. Sayles, Selden Society LV (1936); LVII (1938); LVIII (1939).
SCPWW	*Select Cases of Procedure without Writ under Henry III* ed. H. G. Richardson and G. O. Sayles, Selden Society LX (1941).
Smalley, *Historians*	B. Smalley, *Historians in the Middle Ages* (1974).
Smalley, *The Bible*	B. Smalley, *The Study of the Bible in the Middle Ages*, 2nd edition (1952).
Southern, *Medieval Humanism*	R. W. Southern, *Medieval Humanism and Other Studies* (1970).
SPC	*Select Pleas of the Crown* ed. F. W. Maitland, Selden Society I (1887).
SS	Selden Society publications (1887–).
Statutes	*Statutes of the Realm* ed. A. Luders et al., Record Commissioners' publications, I (1810).
Stenton, *Feudalism*	F. M. Stenton, *The First Century of English Feudalism 1066–1166*, 2nd edition (1961).
Stenton, *Justice*	D. M. Stenton, *English Justice between the Norman Conquest and the Great Charter* (1965).
Stubbs, *Charters*	*Select Charters* ed. W. Stubbs, 9th edition, ed. H. W. C. Davis (1913).
Study of Medieval Records	*The Study of Medieval Records: Essays in Honour of K. Major* ed. D. A. Bullough and R. L. Storey (1971).

Thompson, *Literacy*   J. W. Thompson, *The Literacy of the Laity in the Middle Ages* University of California Publications in Education IX (1939).

TRHS   *Transactions of the Royal Historical Society.*

Van Caenegem, *Writs*   *Royal Writs in England from the Conquest to Glanvill* ed. R. C. van Caenegem, Selden Society LXXVII (1959).

VCH   *Victoria History of the Counties of England.*

Walter Map   *De Nugis Curialium* ed. M. R. James, C. N. L. Brooke, R. A. B. Mynors (1983).

Walter of Henley   *Walter of Henley and Other Treatises on Estate Management and Accounting* ed. D. Oschinsky (1971).

Wattenbach, *Schriftwesen*   W. Wattenbach, *Das Schriftwesen im Mittelalter*, 3rd edition (1896).

WiltsRS   Wiltshire Record Society publications, formerly Wiltshire Archaeological and Natural History Society.

Zarnecki, *Catalogue*   *English Romanesque Art 1066–1200* ed. G. Zarnecki, J. Holt, T. Holland, Exhibition Catalogue (1984).

Introduction

This book is about the uses of literacy in the Middle Ages. It concentrates on England in the two and a half centuries from 1066 to 1307 (from the Norman Conquest to the death of Edward I) because these years constitute a distinctive period in the development of literate ways of thinking and of doing business. In the eleventh century literate modes were still unusual, whereas in the thirteenth century they became normal among the rulers. This formative stage in the history of literacy has received less attention from scholars than the invention of printing in the later Middle Ages, although it is no less important. Printing succeeded because a literate public already existed; that public originated in the twelfth and thirteenth centuries. Writing was not new in 1066, of course, either in England or elsewhere. In the royal monasteries of Anglo-Saxon England, as in other parts of Europe, an original literate culture had been created which was distinguished especially by its illuminated manuscripts of parchment. From these royal and monastic roots, new uses and forms of writing proliferated in the twelfth and thirteenth centuries and took shapes which would last for generations.

The particular argument of this book is that this growth in the uses of literacy is indicated by, and was perhaps a consequence of, the production and retention of records on an unprecedented scale (unprecedented, that is, in England). The difference between Anglo-Saxon and thirteenth-century England in this respect is marked. From Anglo-Saxon England about 2,000 charters and writs (including originals and copies and an indefinite number of forgeries) survive.[1] From thirteenth-century England, on the other hand, tens

---

[1] This estimate is based on P. H. Sawyer, *Anglo-Saxon Charters: An Annotated List* (1968); see pp. 28–9 below.

of thousands of such charters and writs survive; this estimate is no more precise because the documents have never been systematically counted. How many documents once existed (as distinct from how many now survive), either in the Anglo-Saxon period or in the thirteenth century, is a matter for conjecture and inevitably therefore for different opinions. An estimate further on in this book suggests that eight million charters may have been written in the thirteenth century alone for smallholders and serfs.

The increase was not merely in numbers of parchments, but in the spread of literate modes both territorially and socially. By the reign of Edward I royal or seignorial writs reached every bailiff and village in England, making writing familiar throughout the countryside. Similarly the use of charters as titles to property made its way down the social hierarchy – from the royal court and monasteries (in the eleventh century and earlier) to secular clerks and knights (in the twelfth century), reaching the laity in general by the reign of Edward I. This is not to say that everyone could read and write by 1307, but that by that time literate modes were familiar even to serfs, who used charters for conveying property to each other and whose rights and obligations were beginning to be regularly recorded in manorial rolls. Those who used writing participated in literacy, even if they had not mastered the skills of a clerk. One measure of this change is the possession of a seal or *signum*, which entitled a person to sign his name. In Edward the Confessor's reign only the king is known to have possessed one for authenticating documents, whereas in Edward I's reign even serfs were required by statute to have them.

The book is arranged in two parts. The first part describes the making of records of all sorts, because their gradual accumulation in archives and their distribution throughout the country prepared and fertilized the ground in which literacy could germinate. Through the spread of record-making the practice of using writing for ordinary business, as distinct from using it exceptionally for solemn religious or royal purposes, became first familiar and then established as a habit. Among the laity, or more specifically among knights and country gentry in the first instance, confidence in written record was neither immediate nor automatic. Trust in writing and understanding of what it could – and could not – achieve developed from growing familiarity with documents.

The second part of the book therefore describes the growth of a literate mentality. It traces the halting acceptance of literate modes by the rulers, both clerical and lay. The use of writing for business purposes was almost as unfamiliar to many monks in the twelfth century and earlier (except in the great houses under royal patronage) as it was to knights and laity. Elementary rules of business, such as the need to write dates on letters, were only learned with difficulty because they raised novel questions about the writer's place in the temporal order. Forgery was consequently rife. Despite the increasing use of documents (both authentic and forged) traditional oral procedures, such as the preference for reading aloud rather than scanning a text silently with the eye, persisted through the Middle Ages and beyond. There were also special problems to be overcome in England, such as the variety and different status of the languages in use after the Norman Conquest.

Outside the king's court and great monastic houses, property rights and all other knowledge of the past had traditionally and customarily been held in the living memory. When historical information was needed, local communities resorted not to books and charters but to the oral wisdom of their elders and remembrancers. Even where books and charters existed, they were rarely consulted at first, apparently because habits of doing so took time to develop. Unwritten customary law – and lore – had been the norm in the eleventh century and earlier in England, as in all communities where literacy is restricted or unknown. Nevertheless two centuries later, by Edward I's reign, the king's attorneys were arguing in many of the *quo warranto* prosecutions against the magnates that the only sufficient warrant for a privilege was a written one, and that in the form of a specific statement in a charter. Memory, whether individual or collective, if unsupported by clear written evidence, was ruled out of court. As written titles had only come into common use relatively recently and as few charters were sufficiently exact, the *quo warranto* prosecutions threatened to disfranchise nearly all the magnates. Although the *quo warranto* cases were rapidly suspended in the 1290s and the king's government had to concede that tenure 'from time out of mind' was a legitimate claim, the principle had been established for the future that property rights depended generally on writings and not on the oral recollections of old wise men. Hence the title of this book, *From Memory to Written Record*, refers to this shift in ways of thinking and acting, which made its mark between the Norman Conquest and the reign of Edward I.

The title is a variation of H. J. Chaytor's classic, *From Script to Print* (first published in 1945), which described the differences between the manuscript culture of the Middle Ages and the print culture of the Renaissance. Acknowledging its debt to Chaytor, *From Memory to Written Record* takes a step behind the conditions he described to the time when even important information was usually held in the memory alone and not in script of any sort. The shift from habitually memorizing things to writing them down and keeping records was necessarily prior to the shift from script to print, and was as profound a change in its effects on the individual intellect and on society. Literacy is also approached here from a different point of view from Chaytor. Whereas he was chiefly concerned with vernacular and literary works, this book (while not excluding literature) is primarily based on Latin business documents and legal records. The development of literacy from and for practical purposes of day-to-day business, rather than creative literature, is the theme of *From Memory to Written Record*.

A change as obvious as the growing number of records has not gone unnoticed by historians. V. H. Galbraith in particular has stated the general argument in various forms, for example:

Early society is ordered and governed by oral tradition . . . Then there is a long twilight of transition, during which the written record encroaches more and more upon the sphere of custom. In this way the volume of written evidence available steadily increases until we reach a time – *not I think earlier than the thirteenth century* – when most of society's

major activities find some sort of written record. More, however, is at
stake than the mere volume of evidence. As documents grow more
plentiful their whole meaning changes.[2]

Although this book differs from Galbraith in its interpretation of particular
documents, its general aim is to build upon his work and extend it from the
growth of 'public' records (that is, the documents of the king's government) to
all types of writing, and from the writings themselves to the people they
affected. Twentieth-century scholars of medieval England tend to be specialists in particular types of writing, because the records are so large and
complex, whereas medieval makers and users of documents would have seen
less significance in such distinctions as public and private, royal and
ecclesiastical, or historical and literary. Essential as they are for specialized
study, these distinctions can obscure the breadth and unity of medieval
experience.

  This book necessarily therefore draws throughout on the expertise of other
scholars and consistently uses a selective method, which needs explaining and
perhaps also justifying. First of all, because it is an axiom of the argument that
the number of documents markedly increased in the period 1066–1307, no
single scholar can claim to have studied them all or even most in detail. This
book proceeds by citing a limited number of examples, often in detail, in order
to illustrate a series of propositions. These citations (many of which have been
noted by previous authors in other contexts) have been selected from a large
body of material; they aim to be typical or particularly significant.

  An additional principle of presentation which needs explaining is that,
although this book is solely concerned with the making of manuscripts, it
generally cites printed editions of texts rather than the manuscripts themselves.
Even where manuscripts are referred to, the reader is normally directed to a
facsimile and not to the original document. This procedure has been adopted
because much of the argument is novel and some readers will wish to pursue
or verify translated citations or references as readily as possible. While
admiring manuscript culture and trying to convey to the reader its special
qualities, every author must acknowledge the advantages which printing has
brought to scholars by making uniform texts available in multiple copies.
Furthermore, generalizations cannot often be made directly from medieval
manuscripts, because each one usually requires detailed study and presentation by an editor (to establish the best text, assess the date, identify persons
and so on) before it can be adequately understood. Editing texts and
generalizing from them in books like this one are different endeavours.

  Although this book makes few original observations about particular
manuscripts, it is intended to provide a new general survey of the medieval
documents of England in the period it concerns. Chapter 3 on 'Types of
Record', for example, or chapter 6 on 'Languages of Record' aim to describe

---

[2] *Studies*, p. 26 (my emphasis). This argument was first put forward by Galbraith in 1935,
'Literacy', pp. 204–6, and finally in 1962: 'At the very outset of the thirteenth century, with
the beginnings of the official archives preserved in the Public Record Office, we pass from a
customary and largely oral society to an age of record', *The Historian at Work*, p. 3.

their subjects comprehensively though far from exhaustively. Such broad treatment is made necessary by the book's prevailing theme of literacy developing over time across many types of writing activity. This treatment has the added incidental advantage of bringing together areas of scholarship which are normally kept apart. Thus chapter 6 discusses all written languages used in England at the time (Latin, French, English and Hebrew in approximate order of frequency), whereas scholars often specialize in one language only. Likewise chapter 3 includes scholastic texts and works of literature as well as charters and rolls. The inevitable superficiality of this approach is counterbalanced, in theory at least, by the range of discussion achieved.

The purpose of concentrating on one place, England, and on a well-defined period, the years from 1066 to 1307, is to make the subject manageable. More general studies of literacy, particularly by anthropologists, have emphasized both the diversity of forms which literacy can take and the common recurrent features which distinguish all literate cultures from non-literate ones.[3] Descriptions of the development of literacy in particular places and periods (as in this book), on the other hand, provide a variety of readers with sufficiently detailed information to draw reliable conclusions for their own purposes. The shift from memory to written record, which occurred in England in the twelfth and thirteenth centuries, was not restricted to England, although it is most evident there. It was a western European phenomenon, as figure 1 at p. 60 suggests, which compares the number of letters extant from the chanceries of England, France and the papacy between *c.* 1066 and *c.* 1200. Comparable graphs could be drawn to show the growth of documentation in the medieval kingdoms of the Spains and of Sicily, or in Germany and the Italian city states, although the sources of information are more fragmentary in these instances. It is probable, moreover, that the letter-writing energies of the papacy, from the reign of Gregory VII (1073–85) onwards, set new standards of documentation – both in output and quality – which compelled secular governments to follow suit.

In the period 1066–1307 England was peculiarly open to continental influences because the monarchy was controlled first by the Normans, secondly by the Angevins and then in the thirteenth century by the Poitevin and other southern favourites of King John and Henry III. Edward I likewise was a ruler of European stature and interests. Nevertheless this combination of influences created in England over the twelfth and thirteenth centuries an amalgam of Anglo-Saxon, French and Latin culture which is a distinct entity rather than a mere accumulation of parts. Although English experience of literacy was far from being unique or self-contained, it presents itself as a relatively coherent whole in the period 1066–1307 because the country was dominated by a centralizing royal bureaucracy. Even though the day-to-day power and importance of the royal government has been exaggerated by 'public' record-oriented historians, it has left a formidable reminder of its

[3] Goody, *Literacy* and *The Domestication of the Savage Mind* (1977). See also S. Scribner and M. Cole, *The Psychology of Literacy* (1981) and the works cited by Roy Harris, *The Origin of Writing* (1986), pp. 159–63.

manifold activities in the hundreds of thousands of parchments now preserved in the Public Record Office in London. William the Conqueror's Domesday survey at the beginning of the period and Edward I's *quo warranto* prosecutions at the end were both countrywide inquiries, which aimed to record the most important rights of the king and his feudatories in writing. Nothing on this scale survives from any other European state. The Emperor Frederick II conducted a comparable survey in the kingdom of Sicily in the 1220s, but its details are now lost.

No inquiry by an medieval government ever exceeded in scope and detail the survey inaugurated by Edward I in March 1279, which immediately preceded the *quo warranto* prosecutions. Commissioners in each country were instructed to list by name and have written down in books all villages and hamlets and every type of tenement whatsoever, whether of the rich or the poor, and whether royal or otherwise.[4] The stated purpose of this survey was to settle questions of ownership once and for all. The returns have only survived in their original form from a handful of counties in the south Midlands (much of Oxfordshire, Huntingdonshire and Cambridgeshire and parts of Bedfordshire and Buckinghamshire) and they vary in their attention to detail.[5] Some exceed the commissioners' instructions and list every serf by name, while others are very brief. It may be more than a coincidence that the area producing extant returns lies on a line between the university towns of Oxford and Cambridge.[6] Only there perhaps were a sufficient number of clerks found to make the survey. Students, who had learned to note down their masters' lectures, could apply this expertise to the king's business. If this hypothesis is correct, it looks as if the survey of 1279 was too ambitious even for Edward I. Only in the clerkly area of Oxford and Cambridge was literacy sufficiently widespread to fulfil his aims.[7] Unlike the Domesday survey of two centuries earlier, the survey of 1279 excited little comment among chroniclers. They were by then perhaps long accustomed, and even weary, of the monarchy's preoccupation with making surveys and lists, especially when 'no advantage came of it' (in the opinion of the Dunstable chronicler).[8] The numerous surveys of Edward I's reign suggest that the bureaucracy's appetite for information exceeded its capacity to digest it. Making lists was in danger of becoming a substitute for action.

It is possible that Englishmen became exceptionally conscious of records as a direct consequence of the Norman Conquest. Making records is initially a product of distrust rather than social progress. By making Domesday Book

---

[4] Commission in *Patent Rolls*, 1272–81, p. 343; *Foedera* I, part ii, p. 567; *Rotuli Hundredorum*, RC, II, p. ix.

[5] Most of the returns are printed in *Rotuli Hundredorum* II, pp. 321–877. D. E. Greenway, 'A Newly Discovered Fragment of the Hundred Rolls of 1279–80', *Journal S. Archivists* VII (1982), pp. 73–7.

[6] W. Urry, *Canterbury under the Angevin Kings* (1967), p. 3.

[7] M. T. Clanchy, 'Power and Knowledge' in *England in the Thirteenth Century* ed. W. M. Ormrod (1985), p. 12; 'Handlist of Illuminated MSS Made in Oxford 1200–1270' in Donovan, *de Brailes*, pp. 201–5.

[8] *Annales Monastici* III, p. 263; H. M. Cam, *The Hundred and the Hundred Rolls* (1930), p. 240.

William the Conqueror set his shameful mark on the humiliated people, and even on their domestic animals, in the opinion of the *Anglo-Saxon Chronicle*.[9] The harsh exactitude of Norman and Angevin officials, with their writs and pipe rolls, caused churchmen and ultimately even laymen to keep records of their own. Thus it has been calculated that out of 971 papal decretal letters of the twelfth century whose destination is known, 434 went to England.[10] This statistic does not mean that the papal *curia* expended nearly half its energies on English business, but that English recipients were more careful to preserve papal letters than clergy in other European states. Similarly of 27 early collections of decretals compiled by canon lawyers in Europe as a whole, 15 are English.[11] The history of record-making and literacy in England merits separate study, provided it is understood that medieval England was part of Europe and not an island in the cultural sense.

BEING PREJUDICED IN FAVOUR OF LITERACY

A difference between this book and some previous studies of records by historians is that it tries to avoid being prejudiced in favour of literacy. Writing gives the historian his materials and it is consequently understandable that he has tended to see it as a measure of progress. Furthermore, literate techniques are so necessary to twentieth-century western society, and education in them is so fundamental a part of the modern individual's experience that it is difficult to avoid assuming that literacy is an essential mark of civilization. By contrast, anthropological studies of non-literate societies in the third world and sociological studies of deprived urban proleteriats in the west both suggest that literacy in itself is primarily a technology. It has different effects according to circumstances and is not a civilizing force in itself, although there is a relationship between national minimal literacy averages and the mastery of modern industrial technology.[12] Identifying literacy as a 'technology of the intellect', J. Goody has given examples of how 'writing is not a monolithic entity, an undifferentiated skill; its potentialities depend upon the kind of system that obtains in any particular society.'[13]

Only a minority of those who attend school can be proven to benefit, in either economic or cultural terms, from the acquisition of literacy. H. J. Graff asks: 'How important have literacy and schooling been to occupational and economic success? Traditional wisdom, modern sociology, the rhetoric of modernization, and nineteenth-century school promotion all celebrated the role of education in determining success. Yet not all the evidence, past or

[9] See ch. 1, n. 26 below.
[10] Van Caenegem, *Writs*, p. 366, n. 5.
[11] Duggan, *Decretals*, pp. 66, 124.
[12] C. M. Cipolla, *Literacy and Development in the West* (1969), is an introduction to modern mass literacy.
[13] Goody, *Literacy*, p. 3, cf. pp. 11ff, 198ff.

present, lends credence to this view.'[14] Graff shows that in the industrialized nations, schooling in literacy is primarily used for 'training in being trained'.[15] It is the schooling process which is significant and not literacy as such. Educational reformers in the nineteenth century – in Europe, America, and Japan – showed that schooling could produce an orderly, disciplined, and deferential workforce; the training of the classroom was transferable in this form to the factory floor.

Literacy has become the shibboleth of modern societies because the individual demonstrates through it his acceptance of, and success in, the industrialized schooling process. The word 'literacy', as it is used today, 'indexes an individual's integration into society; it is the measure of the successful child, the standard for an employable adult.'[16] A person who cannot sign his name is consequently now a social deviant, whereas in medieval society the most educated people did not often write (they perfected the art of Latin dictation) and neither did they put a value on their personal signatures: documents were ratified with crosses because the cross was the most solemn symbol of Christian truth. Signing with a cross became a symbol of illiteracy only with the secularization of western society after the Reformation. Through schooling, modern society makes those who cannot write into a potentially subversive minority, whereas in past cultures they were the norm. 'Whatever our assumptions may be about the conduct and meaning of literacy in our world, we must be cautious about applying them to the circumstances of earlier cultures.'[17]

For students of the Middle Ages, a warning was sounded in the 1950s by the Hungarian historian (and opponent of Marxist progressivism), I. Hajnal. In his fundamental study of writing and scholasticism, he asked 'whether we are right in wishing to contrast at any price spoken and written language as agents of civilization, considering the first as an obstacle to progress and the second as its active promoter'.[18] An example of what Hajnal warned against appeared in the 1970s in a history of English education. Its otherwise excellent summary of the period 1066–1307 concludes:

> Over the past two centuries literacy and education had certainly grown in extent and also become more secularized: England was far more civilized as a result. The vast rural majority, however, still passed their lives in mental confinement, limited by their own experiences in a small circumscribed world ruled by village custom and popularized religion.[19]

---

[14] *The Literacy Myth* (1979), p. 196, reprinted in *Literacy and Social Development in the West: A Reader* ed. H. J. Graff (1981), p. 233.

[15] Graff, *Literacy and Social Development*, pp. 258, 260. See also E. Verne, 'Literacy and Industrialization' in Ibid., pp. 286–303.

[16] K. O'B. O'Keeffe, *Visible Song* (1990), p. 10.

[17] Ibid.

[18] *L'Enseignement de l'écriture aux universités médiévales* ed. L. Mezey, 2nd edition (1959), p. 20. My translation.

[19] J. Lawson and H. Silver, *A Social History of Education in England* (1973), p. 39. Scribner and Cole, *Psychology of Literacy*, pp. 113–33, discuss literacy and schooling.

The first sentence equates literacy with education, and the growth of literacy with the extension of civilization and secularization. The second sentence assumes that literacy was the only medium for communicating educative ideas, and that it flourished in urban rather than rural environments.

These assumptions are inaccurate as generalizations about English or European cultural development before the nineteenth century. The most literate part of medieval Europe, at least from the thirteenth century (judging by the number of vernacular manuscripts), was Iceland, which had no towns. This was as true in the eighteenth century, when Iceland 'achieved near total diffusion of reading and writing skills among its population (it can still claim the highest ratio of bookstores to citizens in the world)'.[20] Literacy did not necessarily make medieval Icelanders happier or more prosperous, any more than the ability to read newspapers or sign their names makes people better off today. The medium is not the message. Where only a minority of a population are literate, those who are illiterate do not necessarily pass their lives in 'mental confinement'. It may be some modern academics, rather than peasants, who risk mental confinement within the 'small circumscribed world' of their field of specialization. Through the division of labour, all societies confine their members' minds within specializations. In the Middle Ages the 'vast rural majority' had to be knowledgeable about numerous aspects of their environment in order to survive – its flora and fauna, the cycle of the seasons, the hierarchies of persons and things. Whether they were better or worse off than modern labourers is a matter of opinion, not historical fact. Of course schooling, and reading and writing, can bring great benefits to individuals and societies, but they do not do so automatically. Everything depends upon the circumstances. What is learned in this or that school, and by whom? What is written and what read; by whom, and with what consequences?

Primarily and most obviously, it is language itself which forms mentalities, not literacy. Writing is one of the means by which encoded language is communicated; it can never be more than that. As medieval peasants have left few records other than material remains in archaeology, not much can be known about the details of their cultural values and mental experience. It is argued in chapter 7 of this book that, judging medieval literacy even by the narrow criterion of understanding Latin, a considerable number of villagers in thirteenth-century England had some experience of literacy without formal schooling. Whether a little Latin made them or anyone else more educated, in the broad sense of understanding and mastering one's environment, is a matter of opinion. Morally and psychologically, depending on the circumstances, literacy may liberate or it may confine. In the twentieth century, political dictators and newspaper proprietors have shown that they understood more about the potentialities of the growth of literacy than professors of education. 'Ideological assumptions haunt the use of the word "literacy". Behind its simple dictionary definition as the quality of being literate lies a morass of cultural assumptions and value judgements.'[21]

[20] R. Pattison, *On Literacy* (1982), p. 122. See also H. J. Graff, *The Legacies of Literacy* (1987), p. 230; R. F. Tomasson, 'The Literacy of the Icelanders', *Scandinavian Studies* XLVII (1975), pp. 66–93.

[21] O'Keeffe, *Visible Song*, p. 10.

Over the last hundred years, in the world's industrialized nations, schooling directed by the state towards universal literacy has reinforced ideological and cultural prejudices in competing populations and set them on collision courses. This is most evident in the history of twentieth-century European states. Xenophobia, racism, and militarism were all compounded by the schooling of whole populations in the literacies of dominant vernacular languages: English, French, German, and so on. For many individuals within these populations, speaking their mother tongue, or what was described by the state's teachers as a dialect, was forbidden in school. Mass schooling in 'literacy', meaning the reading and writing of a standardized national language, was the instrument by which the ideology of the dominant group was enforced in each state. The requirement of a uniform and universal literacy made minority languages in Europe (Basque, Breton, Catalan, and so on) into a social problem and a political threat. In modern nations everyone has to measure up to the standard of literacy required by the state, and they are graded accordingly. 'It is not enough to know how to read and write; the state insists that one know how to do these according to a uniform standard of correct form, and the punishment for those who do not is exclusion from its munificence, a severe penalty where the state is the chief employer'.[22]

Compulsory schooling in literacy brings all those who cannot read and write to the attention of the legislator. The British Mental Deficiency Act of 1913 defined 'feeble-minded persons' as those 'incapable of receiving proper benefit from the instruction in ordinary schools'.[23] These children, together with 'moral imbeciles', were to be segregated by schools at the earliest possible age and confined in institutions named 'colonies'. Because of the belief in hereditary degeneration, children and adults in Britain (and other industrialized nations) who could not read and write were deprived of their liberty. In Germany in the late 1930s scientists and doctors designed and operated the gas chambers and incinerators in the first instance for them. Because schooling in literacy enforces conformity on children day by day as they grow up, it has become the most powerful social instrument, for good or evil, in the modern world. Like the priests of the Roman and Catholic inquisition and the elders of the Protestant reformed churches, twentieth-century professors and state officials believed that their tribunals and assessment procedures regulated everything for the best. Literacy was seen as the saving grace of modern European society; no one withstood its devotees with impunity.

Through schooling in literacy, disadvantaged or dissident groups in unitary national states were classed as aliens. The United States of America restricted the meaning of its Declaration of Independence from British rule by imposing literacy tests on voters. Descendants of slaves and other racially disadvantaged immigrants were required to read aloud and comprehend 'any section of the Constitution of this state', to quote the Mississippi State Constitution of

---

[22] Pattison, *On Literacy*, p. 65.

[23] *Statutes*: 3 & 4 George V, ch. 28, article 1 (c). See also 'Report of the Royal Commission on the Care and Control of the Feeble-Minded' HMSO Cd4202 (1908); R. Fido and M. Potts, 'It's Not True What Was Written Down', *Oral History* 17 (1989), pp. 31–4.

1892.[24] Like a school teacher or professor, the Mississippi state official might choose whatever section of the Constitution was most likely to make difficulties for the examinee. In Ireland, following its revolution against British rule in the 1920s, the Irish Republic imposed a literacy test in the Irish language on all holders of public office. Compulsory schooling and literacy tests have proved an effective way of marking out minorities for discrimination. To consider instances only from the industrialized nations in the half-century 1930–1980, potentially dissident groups have been marked out by separate but compulsory schooling in Germany, Israel, Japan, South Africa, the UK, the USA, and the USSR.

It may be a consequence of mass literacy, rather than a coincidence, that the mass killings of the twentieth century have been done by the most schooled populations in the world's history. Conscription and compulsory schooling have marched together. 'Con-scription', as the word itself implies, is a process of literacy: school leavers get 'en-listed'; recruits 'sign up'; casualties are 'written off'. The skills of the traditional schoolmaster and his usher – in listing, marking, scheduling, and disciplining – which had long been instruments of intimidation for the individual pupil, were applied by the nation states of the twentieth century to terrorizing whole populations. The archetypal teacher of the Middle Ages had conventionally been depicted in the form of Lady Grammar, brandishing a birch rod and seated on a professorial chair above her cowering and half-naked pupils. In the words of Alan of Lille (writing in the 1180s), 'in one and the same action she is father and mother; by her blows she makes up for a father, by her milk she fills the role of mother.'[25] Schooling provides models for oppression as much as for enlightenment.[26] In the advanced nations of the twentieth century, Lady Grammar and her pupils graduated from the schoolroom to the drill hall and the prison camp.

MEDIEVAL, RENAISSANCE, AND REFORMATION LITERACY

The state schooling of the last 100 years has distorted our picture of how literacy developed over the preceding 10 or more centuries. In the commonest view, the perspective is foreshortened and the colour obscured in order to highlight the present. The medieval past is seen as a period of ignorance

---

[24] Pattison, *On Literacy*, p. 174.
[25] *Anticlaudianus* Bk. ii, lines 401–3, trans. J. J. Sheridan (1973), p. 85. Alan of Lille's description is contemporary with the sculpture of Lady Grammar on the Portail Royal of Chartres cathedral, illustrated by A. Prache, *Lumières de Chartres* (1989), p. 54.
[26] The oppressive side of schooling and bureaucracy is not discussed by J. Goody in his chapters on 'The State, the Bureau and the File' and 'The Letter of the Law' in *The Logic of Writing and the Organization of Society* (1986). Neither is it addressed in the monographs on literacy by Martin (1988), Oxenham (1980), and Street (1984) (the details of these monographs are given in 'Further Reading on the History of Literacy' below). 'Literacy: an Instrument of Oppression' is the title of a brief article by D. P. Pattanayak in *Literacy and Orality* ed. D. R. Olson and N. Torrance (1991), pp. 105–8.

(synonymous with illiteracy) and barbarism; these were the 'Dark Ages' awaiting the enlightenment of the Renaissance, the Reformation, and the progressive reforms of the nineteenth century. How could literacy have been widespread before the invention of printing, the liberalization of religious teaching, and the direction of schooling by democratic states? Medievalists have no short answers to these questions. They have no sociological data, covering large populations or periods in a statistical form, with which to measure literacy rates. They rely largely on individual cases, which cannot be proved to be typical, and inferences and estimates which will always remain controversial. This is why general histories of the Middle Ages do not address the development of literacy in any detail, even though this omission gives the impression that literacy was of little importance or was not widespread.

The Cambridge Illustrated History of the Middle Ages, 1250–1520 edited by R. Fossier mentions literacy only in the context of the invention of printing: the printing of the Bible meant that 'the *illiteratus* of the Middle Ages would henceforth be able to drink at the very fountain of knowledge.'[27] Certainly the printing press produced many more copies of texts. Whether this increase in volume motivated the illiterate of the sixteenth century to drink in knowledge is unlikely; there is no demonstrable relationship in modern schooled societies between the volume of reading material available and the number of literates. The Oxford Illustrated History of Medieval Europe edited by G. Holmes, in its few references to literacy, shows the difficulty of estimating numbers. For the early Middle Ages, T. Brown suggests that the level of lay literacy in Italy 'far exceeded other areas of the west: 77% of witnesses who appeared in Lucca charters of the 890s were able to sign their names'.[28] Although counting signatures does at least measure something consistent, it cannot be an adequate measure of literacy in medieval societies because more people (probably many more) learned to read than to write. The papyrus and parchment charters of early Italian cities like Lucca are indeed an impressive record of Latin legal writing.[29] Whether literacy levels in Italy exceeded those in other areas of the west is more doubtful. Reading and writing in the early Middle Ages may have been as common in Merovingian Gaul and Visigothic Spain, and likewise in both pagan and Christianized England and Ireland. In all these places vernacular and proto-vernacular literacies were developing in symbiosis with Latin, as the contributors to R. McKitterick's *The Uses of Literacy in Early Medieval Europe* demonstrate.[30] Although the language might be less classical than in Italy, and some of the writing materials (particularly the soft woods used for message-sticks) were less durable than parchment, they probably served well enough at the time. As Venantius Fortunatus, the sixth-century Italian-educated poet (and bishop of Poitiers), acknowledged:

---

[27] (1986), p. 496.

[28] (1988), p. 39.

[29] The earliest charters of Lucca are published in facsimile in *Chartae Latinae Antiquiores* ed. A. Bruckner and R. Marichal, xxx–xxxvii (1988–).

[30] I. Wood, 'Administration, Law, and Culture in Merovingian Gaul'; R. Collins, 'Literacy and the Laity in Early Medieval Spain'; S. Kelly, 'Anglo-Saxon Lay Society and the Written Word'; J. Stevenson, 'Literacy in Ireland: The Evidence of the St Patrick Dossier'. See also the articles in R. Wright ed., *Latin and the Romance Languages in the Early Middle Ages* (1990).

The barbarous rune may be delineated on tablets of ash-wood:
What papyrus does, a smoothed stick does just as well.

(Barbara fraxineis pingatur runa tabellis:
  Quodque papyrus agit, virgula plana valet.[31])

Estimating numbers is as problematic at the end of the Middle Ages. Concluding *The Oxford Illustrated History of Medieval Europe*, M. Vale puts no figures on his estimate that 'the proportion of literate people among the population of northern Europe was probably lower than that found in Italy by 1500.'[32] Vale's 'probably' indicates his awareness that the stereotype of more literacy in Italy than in northern Europe may be mistaken. Addressing the same question of what proportion of the population was literate, D. Brewer in *The New Pelican Guide to English Literature* suggests that in England 'probably more than half the population could read, though not necessarily also write, by 1500.'[33] More people could read than write. Even so, how could half the population have learned to read, when few boys were sent to school and even fewer girls? The answer depends on what was valued in reading. Medieval assumptions about functional literacy differed from modern ones. Literates were expected to function primarily as believers in Christian scripture. The emphasis in reading (and writing) was therefore put not on mass schooling for the state's and industrialists' purposes, but on prayer: collectively in the church's liturgy and individually at home with a Book of Hours. Instruction in reading was primarily domestic: by one individual to another, most typically by mother to child.

In fifteenth-century western European culture the ideal of the mother teaching her little boy to read was enshrined in the recurrent image of the Virgin Mary with the Child Jesus and a Book of Hours; for girls, there was the parallel image of St Anne (the Virgin's mother) teaching her to read.[34] Early reading, for purposes of prayer, was everyone's ideal by 1500. Maybe half the population could read, in medieval England and throughout Latin Christendom, if by reading is meant the ability to recognize the written words of the best-known prayers. The really significant point is not the proportion of the population which could read (in whatever sense), but the fact that the dynamic of literacy was religious. Until the introduction of compulsory elementary schooling in the nineteenth century, individual prayer (whether Catholic or Protestant) remained the foundation of European literacy. This is why, in the seventeenth and eighteenth centuries, the most literate societies

---

[31] Bk. viii, ch. 18, *Patrologiae* l.xxxviii, col. 256, cited by R. I. Page, *An Introduction to English Runes* (1973), p. 100. Runes and Oghams are discussed by E. H. Antonsen and R. P. M. Lehmann in W. M. Senner ed., *The Origins of Writing* (1989).

[32] (1988), p. 346.

[33] Ed. B. Ford, *Medieval Literature: Chaucer and the Alliterative Tradition* (1982), p. 23.

[34] This is the subject of my *Woman and the Book in the Middle Ages* (forthcoming); M. T. Clanchy, 'Learning to Read and the Role of Mothers' in *Studies in the History of Reading* ed. G. Brooks and A. K. Pugh (1984), pp. 33–9. See also pp. 112, 251–2 below; K. Schreiner, 'Marienverehrung, Lesekultur, Schriftlichkeit', *Frühmittelalterliche Studien* xxiv (1990), pp. 314–68; S. G. Bell, 'Medieval Women Book Owners' in E. Erler and M. Kowaleski eds. *Women and Power* (1988), pp. 149–87.

were rural and remote but conscientiously Protestant: Iceland (which has already been mentioned), Denmark, Scotland, and Sweden.[35] Likewise in colonial America, literacy was most widespread in the Protestant countryside of the North: 'the motive behind such Protestantism, whether or not it added schools (and therefore writing) to its programme, was that men – and often women – should learn to read the Word of God.'[36] At the same time, in South America and parts of Asia, Jesuit and other Catholic missionaries were pioneering literacies for reading scripture in non-Latinate vernaculars.

Before the twentieth century, in Europe and its colonies throughout the world, it was pastors and priests (rather than schoolteachers) who pioneered the diffusion of literacy among the masses. Missionaries had to teach reading and writing, because the Middle Ages had irreversibly established Christianity as a religion of a book: that is, the Bible and the mass of explanatory writings which stemmed from it. In medieval Latin, 'writing' (*scriptura*) and holy 'writ' (*scriptura*) became synonymous, as did office 'clerks' (*clerici*) and the church's 'clergy' (*clerici*). Exceptions to the latter rule are the notaries of the Italian city-republics. They were an elite of professional writers, who established a special status distinct from both ecclesiastics and laymen. They developed as 'writers' in every sense: scriveners, secretaries, law clerks, calligraphers, prose stylists, *litterati*, authors, journalists. When the writing of Latin became distinct from Italian vernaculars, in the thirteenth and fourteenth centuries, the smartest notaries added teaching the classics and expertise in rare books to their repertoire. The most influential group were the circle in later fourteenth-century Florence around the notary Coluccio Salutati. Poised between ecclesiastics and laymen, the notaries' programme of classicial studies became known as 'humanism' in the fifteenth century, and they as 'humanists'. They proved excellent propagandists for their classical curriculum; so much so that their idea of an Italian Renaissance has become a commonplace. The humanists claimed to be the true *litterati*, who had brought Europe out of the millennium of medieval barbarism into the classic light of knowledge and civilization.

As has often been pointed out, the Renaissance humanists' programme of studies was deliberately elitist and backward-looking. Their origins as clerks and middlemen, standing between the nobility and the people in the Italian city-republics, made them into courtiers and patron-seekers. They aimed to dominate the educational curriculum, not to bring literacy to the masses. In their limited and well-defined objective of educating their masters, the humanists succeeded. Their speciality of Latin and Greek prevailed in the schooling of upper-class men in western Europe for five centuries, from approximately 1450 to 1950. Their claim that the Middle Ages were a despicable period of barbarism subsists to the present day in the pejorative meanings of 'medieval'. Although they only targeted the elite, the humanists changed everyone's perceptions of literacy. This is most obvious in typo-

---

[35] Graff, *The Legacies of Literacy*, pp. 223–30. An extract from E. Johansson's *History of Literacy in Sweden* (1977) is in Graff, *Literacy and Social Development*, pp. 151–82. For Scotland, see T. C. Smout, 'Born Again at Cambuslang', *Past and Present* xcvii (1982), pp. 115–27.

[36] K. A. Lockridge in Graff, *Literacy and Social Development*, p. 187.

graphy: humanist script remains the model for printing and word-processing throughout the world. This replacement of medieval ('Gothic' was the humanists' opprobrious term) book-hands by italic and other classical letter-forms best illustrates what the Italian Renaissance achieved. The new script had been created by the professional writers in Salutati's circle in Florence, particularly by the exquisite calligraphy of the notary Poggio Bracciolini, and it was disseminated throughout Europe a century later by printed books.[37] In lettering, as in other areas of literate culture, the humanists achieved a fundamental change of style by repeatedly and provocatively challenging long medieval practice.

As far as the history of literacy is concerned, the humanists have been all too successful as propagandists, since the educated public (including many historians) continue to accept them at their face value. A writer on the social history of medieval Books of Hours in 1988 described medieval Europe as: 'a largely illiterate society; even by 1500, persons who could read were a small fraction of most nations (the more advanced of the early-Renaissance Italian towns were perhaps the only exceptions).'[38] Here are displayed the fundamental presumptions that humanist propagandists wanted their patrons to believe about their rivals, the ecclesiastics (who were accused of monopolizing literacy) and the lay nobility (who were dismissed as illiterates). Coluccio Salutati and Poggio Bracciolini would indeed have agreed that, by contrast with the unlettered nations north of the Alps, their city of Florence was in that cultural vanguard of the 'more advanced of' the early-Renaissance Italian towns'. Triumphing over contradiction and absurdity, the humanists advanced backwards towards their Renaissance, looking forward (in the words of Petrarch) to the time 'when the darkness breaks and the generations to come manage to find their way back to the clear splendour of the ancient past'.[39] Popular belief in progress and in the march of mind originated in the humanists' need to distance themselves from the dark Middle Ages.

Humanist schoolmasters propagated and reinforced all sorts of myths and dubious ideas about literacy, such as that it stems from schooling rather than the home, that it is the preserve of schoolmasters rather than mothers, that its inspiration is secular rather than religious, that it is elitist rather than inclusive, uniform rather than multicultural, and town-centred rather than rural. All these assumptions fed into the state schooling programmes of nineteenth-century reformers (who had themselves been educated in the classical curriculum) and thence into the beliefs of the schooled populations of today. Within their own terms of reference as propagandists and patron-seekers, the humanists were absolutely right; their peculiar curriculum of ancient Greek and Latin did require a special and exclusive sort of schooling,

[37] A. C. de la Mare, *The Handwriting of Italian Humanists* vol. i, fascicule i (1973); M. Lowry, *The World of Aldus Manutius* (1979).
[38] L. R. Poos, 'Social History and Books of Hours' in *Time Sanctified: The Book of Hours in Medieval Art and Life* ed. R. S. Wieck (1988), p. 33.
[39] *Africa*, Bk. IX, line 553. This deliberately colloquial translation of Petrarch's Latin verse is by J. Shiel in P. Burke, *The Renaissance* (1964), p. 2.

which was ultimately epitomized in the Victorian Classical Sixths of the English public schools and their equivalents in the other European nations.

The diffusion of literacy beyond the upper class, on the other hand, primarily through reading the scriptures and writing in vernaculars, did not have to meet all the conditions demanded by Renaissance schoolmasters. Before compulsory schooling in the nineteenth century, literacy in Europe and America was most widespread in remote rural Protestant areas, like Iceland and Massachusetts, (as has already been pointed out). In other words, literacy spread best in the places least influenced by the Italian humanist curriculum. Nineteenth-century school reformers were indeed promoters of widespread instruction in literacy, albeit at an elementary and minimal level; Renaissance humanists were not. Teaching in vernaculars was the foundation of modern European mass literacy, not the humanists' curriculum of dead languages. This is not to say that Latin and Greek were an unproductive curriculum, but only that they could never be the basis of mass elementary schooling. The humanists had made no such claims for them; they had aimed to be influential, not popular. Like his medieval predecessor, Lady Grammar, the Renaissance schoolmaster wielded a big stick to make his pupils love him.

Another assumption about the spread of literacy, which was successfully promoted by the humanists, is the belief that Rome (and by extension Renaissance Italy) was the apex of the world: culture diffused downwards and outwards from the capital to the provinces. The diffusion in the sixteenth century of classical architecture, or italic letter-forms in printed books, from Renaissance Italy as far as the Orkney Islands and Latin America appears to confirm the humanists' belief. But closer examination suggests that the reverse proposition – that innovation often originates at the peripheries and makes its way to the centre, where it is monopolized and redirected – has as much to commend it as a generalization about cultural diffusion. In this light, the first humanists themselves can be seen as provincials, making their way spiritually – and sometimes in person (as in the case of Poggio Bracciolini, the papal secretary) – from their colony of Florence to classical and papal Rome.

ENGLAND'S PLACE IN MEDIEVAL LITERACY

In *From Memory to Written Record*, the role of peripheries *vis-à-vis* centres is an important question because England is the focus of attention. Conceptually, England stood on the edge of the medieval world, which was centred on Jerusalem: England, the Anglo-Saxon Aelfric had declared, was on 'the outer rim of the earth's circumference'.[40] Innovation can be easier on the fringes of a culture, where cross-fertilization makes adaptation more necessary and the centre's dominance is less secure. Within England itself in the twelfth century, growing-points can be observed on the frontiers: notably in the region of Hereford on the Welsh border and Durham on the Scottish border. From the Welsh border came the most original and influential authors writing Latin for entertainment – Geoffrey of Monmouth, Walter Map, and Gerald of Wales –

---

[40] Cited by M. T. Clanchy, *England and Its Rulers 1066–1272* (1983), p. 22.

and the cathedral city of Hereford itself was an international focus for the numerate sciences of the medieval curriculum.[41] At Durham cathedral in the 1100s the greatest innovation in medieval church building (the rib-vault) took shape, as did Domesday Book (if P. Chaplais's hypothesis is correct), and England's twelfth-century Renaissance may be seen to originate there.[42] The Durham monks took over the Northumbrian heritage of Bede's Jarrow and Cuthbert's Lindisfarne, much as the Florentine humanists claimed classical Rome's past for their city; in each case artists, writers, and propagandists (including forgers) gave impressive form to a myth.

Hereford and Durham exemplify innovation at the peripheries within twelfth-century England. England as a whole, as far as literacy is concerned in the period 1066–1307, played a comparably innovative role *vis-à-vis* medieval Europe. England in 1066, with its Anglo-Saxon and Germanic civilization, stood at a meeting-point of languages and cultures. Across the Channel to the south were the nations of Romance languages writing in Latin. The seaways to the north, as far west as Iceland and east as Russia, were dominated by the Scandinavians writing in runes. To the west lay the Celtic lands of Wales, Ireland, and the highlands and islands of Scotland, writing in ogams and Gaelic. Much of this area had never been conquered by the Romans, and had experienced Latinization only through the church. Pope Gregory VII expected the Norman conquerors, headed by Archbishop Lanfranc as primate, to assert Latin uniformity over the whole of the British Isles. The conquest of Ireland was seen by the papacy as the justifiable process of bringing barbarians into line with Rome. Gerald of Wales praised Henry II as the western Alexander the Great, who by invading Ireland in 1171 had revealed marvels in the west to match those of the east.[43] In twelfth-century European literature the British Isles became a place of fascination and mystery, remote in time and place, the land of King Arthur, Morgan la Fey, and Merlin the magician and master of writing.[44] A journey to Britain, the islands of the Ocean Sea, was the equivalent of going to outer space in twentieth-century science fiction. In *Cligés* (composed in the 1170s) Chrétien de Troyes has his hero go from Greece to England, 'which at that time was called Britain', because he wished to win a reputation for courage. Britain itself was believed to take its name from Brutus, a defeated Trojan, who had been promised a new Troy in the western lands beyond the sunset. In his life of Thomas Becket, William Fitz Stephen identified this promised land with London, which he claimed was older than Rome and the birthplace of the Emperor Constantine as well as of Becket.[45]

---

[41] Clanchy, *England and Its Rulers*, pp. 177–8. In general see *Medieval Art and Architecture at Hereford*, British Archaeological Association Conference Transactions (1990).

[42] J. H. Acland, *Medieval Structure: The Gothic Vault* (1972), p. 83; P. Chaplais in *Domesday Studies* ed. J. C. Holt (1987), pp. 65–77. In general see G. Bonner, D. Rollason, C. Stancliffe eds, *St Cuthbert: His Cult and his Community to A.D. 1200* (1989).

[43] Giraldus, v, pp. 189–93; R. Bartlett, *Gerald of Wales*, p. 59.

[44] R. H. Bloch, *Etymologies and Genealogies* (1983), pp. 1–2.

[45] *Becket Materials*, iii, p. 6. The myth of the Trojan Brutus derived from Geoffrey of Monmouth, *History of the Kings of Britain*, Bk. i.

Because England stood on the periphery of Latin culture, its attitude to it was ambivalent. Its writers either excelled in their mastery of Latin learning and enthusiasm for things Roman, as Bede had done in the eighth century and John of Salisbury did in the twelfth, or they eschewed Latin, like the Old English poets and prose writers and the writers of French and Middle English after 1066. The practice of writing in some form of the English language, probably in runes, was well established enough at the time of Augustine's mission in 597 to ensure that the laws of Aethelbert of Kent were written down in Old English instead of Latin. This is an extraordinary instance of missionaries of the Roman church tolerating the writing down of a barbarian language. The practice of writing laws in the vernacular had become so well established in England by the time of the Norman Conquest that it probably provided the precedent for the so-called 'Laws of William the Conqueror' being written in the new vernacular of French in the twelfth century.[46]

French first developed as a written language not in France, but in England in the century after the Norman Conquest.[47] French was first seen as a distinct language when isolated in England, whereas in eleventh-century France it was no more than one of many unwritten vernaculars. In France writers were taught that Latin was the only proper way to write, whereas in England generations of monks as well as lay people had learned that English had a literature alongside Latin. France had great writers in the period 1050–1150 (Peter Abelard, Bernard of Clairvaux, Hildebert of Lavardin and many others), but they all wrote in Latin apart from the troubadour poets of the south. The pride of the Norman 'French' knights, who had sung the *Chanson de Roland* at the battle of Hastings, may have become self-consciously literate in England because of the need to compete with national epic writing in English like *The Battle of Maldon*. (These and other points about the writing down of French are discussed in chapter 6 below.) In the century after 1066 the writing of English was depressed and devalued by the Norman conquerors, even though Anglo-Saxon traditions were maintained in the great churches. Nevertheless in European writing as a whole, the twelfth century in England was a period of brilliance, distinguished by authors in Latin (John of Salisbury, Geoffrey of Monmouth and many others) and original writers in French (Gaimar, Hue de Rotelande, Jordan Fantosme, and others).

The Norman conquerors not only promoted the writing of French. England's peculiar circumstances also caused them to promote literacy in Latin by building a bureaucracy unprecedented since the fall of the Roman Empire (discussed in chapter 2 below). As Sir Richard Southern has pointed out, John of Salisbury's *Policraticus*, the *Dialogue of the Exchequer*, and the lawbook called *Glanvill* are all products of 'the intellectual stimulus provided by the work of government in the time of Henry II'. 'These books were not simply manuals or textbooks for office use like the contemporary collections of

---

[46] See ch. 6, n. 84 below.
[47] I draw this conclusion from I. Short, 'Patrons and Polyglots: French Literature in Twelfth-Century England', *Anglo-Norman Studies XIV: Proceedings of the Battle Conference 1991* ed. M. Chibnall. I am most grateful to Professor Short for letting me see this in advance of publication; he may not agree with my conclusion.

decretals: they aspired in some degree to invest the routine of government with an intellectual generality.'[48] Their authors were conscious of their originality in using learned Latin to discuss matters as mundane as the regulations of courts. 'I have done my best without teacher or model', Richard Fitz Neal wrote in concluding the *Dialogue of the Exchequer*, 'I have laid my axe to the virgin and rough wood and cut for the royal buildings timber that a more skilled builder may smooth with his adze.'[49] This was an elegant way of saying that he had laid down rules for the Exchequer which would be followed for centuries to come. Similarly the rules of law described in *Glanvill* remained theoretically in force until the nineteenth century.

The main contention of *From Memory to Written Record* is that lay literacy grew out of bureaucracy, rather than from any abstract desire for education or literature. The demands of the royal Exchequer and courts of law compelled knights in the shires and burgesses in the towns to create lesser bureaucracies of their own. The borough of Wallingford's rolls of tradesmen (see plates ix and x below) and Richard Hotot's estate book (see plate xv below) illustrate this process very well, as does the image of the benefactors of Crowland pressing forward to present their charters to the abbey (see plate xx below). However, emphasizing the growth of bureaucracy can obscure a parallel development in the history of medieval literacy whereby clerical habits and values were absorbed into lay households, not so much through knights and burgesses responding to tax demands and royal writs, as through their ladies acquiring prayer books for their private use. Judging from extant Books of Hours, this was a development of the thirteenth century in which England was to the fore, though under the stimulation of French and Flemish artistic influences (see the discussion of liturgical books in chapter 3 below).

The focus on England, throughout this book, rather than on medieval Europe as a whole, caused some reviewers of the first edition to wish for its range to be widened, or at least for more comparisons to be made between England and other places. The shift from memory to written record in the twelfth and thirteenth centuries was not an exclusively English phenomenon; it was at the least western European, as has already been pointed out. But specific comparisons between England and other places in western Europe – the cities of northern Italy, for example, or the monarchies of the Spanish peninsula or the bishoprics of Germany – are rarely made in this book because the evidence available is at present too disparate and uneven. After years of neglect, medieval literacy is at last being more widely studied (as the section below on 'Further Reading on the History of Literacy' shows). Nevertheless the evidence is not yet sufficient to make consistent comparisons, particularly in a statistical form, across western Europe. To take only one example, the charters extant in twelfth-century England have still to be listed and counted, let alone those in France or Italy. Tens of thousands of documents are involved here, some of them in rarely accessible archives. To overcome the difficulties in writing a reliable history of medieval literacy at a European level, this book provides instead detailed information from a single time and

[48] Southern, *Medieval Humanism*, p. 176.
[49] *Dialogus*, p. 127.

place; in due course this can be set into a larger picture. Concentrating on England is not intended to imply that Wales or Poland or Sicily was unimportant in the history of medieval literacy, but only that they cannot all be studied in detail by a single author.

This book selects one place – England between 1066–1307 – to investigate, much as an archaeologist digs an exploratory trench. To gauge the value and meaning of the subject matter, everything that comes out of the trench – however small or obscure – must be investigated, while the archaeologist recognizes at the same time that the contents of the trench are only an arbitrary cross-section. Where to dig the trench is a matter of judgement and luck; both historian and archaeologist work in the light of experience. England is not an anachronistic unit of study to have selected, as its kingdom was a distinct political and cultural entity by the eleventh century. The continuity of its monarchy and institutions have caused the printed and manuscript sources from the Middle Ages to be relatively rich and accessible, though it is possible that the power of the crown and its officers has distorted record-making in its favour. The researcher can be relatively well satisfied that he has seen a representative cross-section of the evidence. Restricting the period of this book to the years 1066–1307 is the equivalent of the archaeologist measuring to a fraction of an inch the length and breadth of his trench. Restriction defines the task. Although the years 1066 and 1307 designate political events, the battle of Hastings and the death of Edward I respectively, they were symbolic in the history of record-making. The Norman Conquest marked a new start with Domesday Book, and the death of Edward I terminates the reign of the most record-conscious king (as argued in chapter 1 below).

On the other hand, such sharp starting- and ending-points as the single years 1066 and 1307 are ill-suited to a history of literate culture, where changes must have been halting and intermittent. Indeed the title *From Memory to Written Record* is open to misunderstanding because it suggests a single and inevitable line of progress from illiteracy to literacy and, by implication, from barbarism to civilization. The concentration on written records, rather than literate people, suggests likewise that literacy is primarily a technology of which records are the end-product. Combining the idea of progress with that of technology leads to technological determinism of a utilitarian and mechanistic kind. The fundamental problem here is that modern literates, including the author and his readers, are conditioned by their own schooling to believe that literacy is the measure of progress and that those who use documents less are less civilized. Over the centuries the durability and conservation of writings has varied. The amount of writing done in western Europe in the first millennium AD has been hugely under-estimated, judging by such archaeological discoveries as the Vindolanda letters and the Bergen message sticks.[50] As the historian of the Anglo-Saxons James Campbell has written, 'one can too easily assume that the development of the Anglo-Saxons and of other peoples in northern Europe was from the

[50] A. K. Bowman, *The Roman Writing Tablets from Vindolanda* (1983); R. I. Page, *Runes* (1987).

chaotic to the orderly, from the *ad hoc* to the schematized, and from weaker rule to stronger.'[51]

Allowing for these disclaimers, *From Memory to Written Record* addresses an archaeological fact which demands an explanation: that masses of writings survive from twelfth- and thirteenth-century England by comparison with the preceding Anglo-Saxon and Roman periods. Probably this was because more documents were made, as well as more being preserved. This book argues that this accumulation of documents, and their bureaucratic use, made more people literate. The numbers of medieval documents can be measured to some extent, whereas the number of literate people cannot. This book is not intended as a general essay on modes of communication, although like all historical works it is a product of its own time and of contemporary interests. The proliferation in the second half of the twentieth century of non-literate forms of communication, like television and videos, and of electronic and photographic systems of storing and retrieving information may teach the historian to put his books and documents into perspective. The technology based on Greek and Roman alphabetic script, which has dominated European culture for more than two thousand years in its classical (papyrus), medieval (parchment) and modern (printed paper) forms, may be entering its final century. On the other hand, word processors and fax machines may reinforce the dominance of the written word and the proliferation of paper. The development of written record in medieval England or elsewhere was not a simple or irreversible advance in some march of progress and civilization, but it was a change of profound historical importance. This book aims to recover a little of what was lost by the growth of literacy as well as indicating what was gained.

---

[51] *The Anglo-Saxons*, ed. J. Campbell (1982), p. 241. See also J. Campbell, 'Was it Infancy in England? Some Questions of Comparison' in *England and her Neighbours: Essays in Honour of P. Chaplais* ed. M. Jones and M. Vale (1989), pp. 1–17.

Part I

The Making of Records

1

Memories and Myths of the Norman Conquest

Once the conquest of 1066 was achieved, King William 'decided to bring the conquered people under the rule of written law'. He therefore had a codification drawn up of Mercian, Dane, and Wessex law and, 'to give the finishing touch to all his forethought', Domesday Book was made so that 'every man might be content with his own rights, and not encroach unpunished on those of others.' This version of events, making William the Conqueror responsible for the transition from memory to written record, is preserved in an oral tradition told by Henry of Blois, King Stephen's brother, to Richard Fitz Neal, who recorded it in the *Dialogue of the Exchequer* around 1179.[1] As Henry was bishop of Winchester, he may have been transmitting an authentic local tradition emanating from the treasury at Winchester where Domesday Book had originally been kept. Like many legends, Henry's story oversimplifies details and shortens the time-scale in order to convey a fundamental and probably widespread belief. The Norman Conquest did mark a new start in the making of records and Domesday Book was its most awesome precedent.

Having accepted Henry's story, however, as a valuable opinion, it is immediately necessary to add provisos to it. For if the story were taken literally and whole, at least in the form in which Fitz Neal gives it, it could be misleading. Obviously, for a start, Domesday Book did not succeed in recording everyone's rights between its covers. Nor in the century after it was made was it frequently used to settle questions about such rights, although William the Conqueror may have hoped that it would be. More open to misunderstanding, though less obviously misleading, is the association of Domesday Book with law codes and the proposition that William the Conqueror 'decided to bring the conquered people under the rule of written

[1] *Dialogus*, p. 63.

law'. The Latin phrase for 'written law' here is *juri scripto legibusque*, which recalls the *jus* and *lex* of Roman jurisprudence. Fitz Neal, rather than the original tradition, may have associated William the Conqueror specifically with Roman law, since it was a fashionable academic subject in Fitz Neal's time. By presenting William as a maker of literate law, Fitz Neal was associating him with the emperors of antiquity and bringing England into the international fraternity of jurisprudence. The original tradition may simply have said that William, because he was a conqueror, aimed to put the laws and everyone's rights into writing so that there could be no further dispute about them.

Across a broader time-span, the idea of William the Conqueror replacing the uncertainties of memory and the spoken word by definitive written law is both illuminating and open to misinterpretation at one and the same time. The idea implies that nothing of importance had been written down before 1066 and also that William the Conqueror's records were decisive for the future. Neither implication is acceptable in that form. Important as his achievements were in the development of literate ways of doing business, it would be a misunderstanding of William the Conqueror's administration either to undervalue his debt to the Anglo-Saxon past or to exaggerate his contribution to later forms of medieval government. Like other historical legends, the story of William the Conqueror bringing the people under the rule of written law achieves its dramatic effect by minimizing both the past and the future. In historical fact England already had literate traditions extending back for centuries and conversely non-literate habits and methods of proof persisted in unexpected quarters for generations after the Norman Conquest. Bringing the people under the rule of written law, in the broad sense of decisively and irrevocably extending the uses of writing, needs more precise definition and description.

By way of introduction, the rest of this chapter therefore first looks back at Anglo-Saxon writing and then moves forward via Domesday Book to the *quo warranto* proceedings of Edward I. Separated by two centuries, Domesday Book and the *quo warranto* proceedings mark the two most ambitious attempts in medieval England to reduce government and property-holding to writing. The fact that such attempts needed repeating makes it clear that no sudden and single venture could succeed. Literate modes could not be imposed by royal decree.

ANGLO-SAXON USES OF WRITING

A reassessment of the place of Anglo-Saxon writing in the development of literacy requires a book on its own instead of a preamble to this one. Nothing less than a book would be adequate, since the period is long and the documents, though relatively few, are diverse and difficult. What follows is no more than an indication by a non-specialist of those areas of the subject which bear particularly on the situation at the time of the Norman Conquest. A possible misconception to clear away at the outset is any assumption that the Normans had greater expertise in writing than the Anglo-Saxons. On the whole, Norman administrators probably had less experience than Anglo-Saxon ones of written records, and the Normans before 1066 had not shown such a consistent interest as the Anglo-Saxons in recording their history and institutions in literate forms. There was nothing in Normandy comparable with the *Anglo-Saxon Chronicle* and the law codes. The Englishman Orderic Vitalis says that his fellow monks of St Evroul in Normandy 'shrank from bending their minds to the task of composing or writing down their traditions. So in the end I, who came here from the remote parts of Mercia as a ten-year-old boy [in 1085] have endeavoured to commit to writing an account of the deeds of the Normans for Normans to read.'[2] Although Orderic exaggerated his originality, as there already were histories of the Norman dukes, the general idea that Englishmen showed the Normans the usefulness of writing has much to commend it.

Nevertheless a Norman innovation, which may have contributed to the belief that William the Conqueror introduced Roman *jus scriptum*, was the replacement of Old English by Latin as the language of royal writs.[3] This was not an immediate change in 1066, but was probably a consequence of appointing Normans and other foreigners to bishoprics and abbacies. Latin made quick progress because it was the written language with which William's clerks (in both the ecclesiastical and modern sense), from Archbishop Lanfranc of Canterbury downwards, were most familiar. In the eyes of contemporaries on the European continent Latin was the only language of record; a person unfamiliar with it was illiterate. In this frame of mind the foreigners made a fresh start in assembling theological libraries for monasteries and cathedrals, both by gifts of books (like those made by Lanfranc to Canterbury and William of St Carilef to Durham) and by making new manuscripts. 'The century after the Norman Conquest . . . is the greatest in the history of English book production.'[4] In the new books, moreover, less emphasis was put on the illustrations and more on the text than was usual in Anglo-Saxon manuscripts.[5]

In increasing the use of Latin writing, the Norman Conquest brought England into the mainstream of medieval literate communication. At the same time, in the short term, the Conquest may have caused a reduction in literacy (in the modern sense of being able to read and write the language one speaks), because it divorced writing further from everyday speech. Although Old English in its standard written form was itself an archaic and learned language by 1066, it was obviously nearer to the vernacular than Latin. In these paradoxes the difficulties of assessing the effects of the Norman Conquest can be appreciated.

Even greater difficulties arise in estimating how much writing was done in pre-Conquest England and for what purposes. To take the question 'How

---

[2] Orderic, Bk. v, ch. 1, vol. iii, p. 4, M. Chibnall, *The World of Orderic Vitalis* (1984).

[3] D. A. E. Pelteret, *Catalogue of English Post-Conquest Vernacular Documents* (1990).

[4] Ker, *English MSS*, p. 1. See also M. Gibson, *Lanfranc of Bec* (1978), pp. 178–81; M. Gullick, 'The Scribe of the Carilef Bible' in L. L. Brownrigg, *Medieval Book Production* (1990), pp. 61–83.

[5] C. R. Dodwell, *The Canterbury School of Illumination* (1954), pp. 17, 26, 32.

much?' first of all. An estimate of the extent of writing activity in medieval
states is best approached through documents like writs and charters, rather
than books, as documents are more widely distributed and they can be
attributed to specific persons and times. A disadvantage of estimating by
documents, however, is that single sheets of parchment are less likely than
books to have survived for a thousand years. Some ephemeral memoranda
were probably thrown away as soon as their usefulness was expended.
Admitting these disadvantages, the number of writs and charters extant (in
either originals or copies) is the best measure of writing activity available,
inadequate though it is.

From Anglo-Saxon England rather less than 2,000 writs and charters
survive. P. H. Sawyer's list, which includes copies as well as originals and also
lost and incomplete texts, numbers 1,875 items.[6] To this for our purposes
should be added a number of purely ecclesiastical documents and a small but
significant group of miscellaneous memoranda, such as one concerning levies
of men for warships.[7] Conversely an indefinite number, even of the documents
listed by Sawyer, are forgeries made after 1066. The number is indefinite
because scholars' criteria for deciding questions of authenticity inevitably
differ. For example, of the 164 documents written in the name of Edward the
Confessor, 44 are likely to be spurious and there are doubts about a further
56.[8] Over all, the majority (1,163 items) of the documents listed by Sawyer are
grants and declarations made in the names of kings, and the next largest
group are grants by bishops (165 items). About half of all the documents listed
purport to date from the century immediately preceding the Norman Conquest, and it is among these also that forgery after the Conquest is the more
likely.

The 2,000 or so writs and charters extant from Anglo-Saxon England are a
small number compared with those extant from the period 1066–1307 and
particularly from the thirteenth century. A single collection (which is not the
largest) of mainly thirteenth-century charters, the so-called *Registrum Antiquissimum* of Lincoln cathedral, numbers 2,980 items in the printed edition.[9] A
single session of the royal justices in eyre in an average-sized county in
Edward I's reign used about 500 membranes of parchment and produced
more than 2,000 documents in four or five weeks.[10] Although statistics can
mislead – and medieval statistics above all – comparisons of numbers are
important because an axiom of this book is that the permanent growth of
literacy is related to the growth of documents.

The incalculable question, which becomes progressively harder yet more
important to answer the further back one goes in time, is what relation

---

[6] *Anglo-Saxon Charters* (1968). Anglo-Saxon charters are magisterially discussed by P.
Chaplais in *Prisca Munimenta Presented to A. E. J. Hollaender*, ed. F. Ranger (1973), pp. 28–107;
and by S. Keynes, *The Diplomas of King Aethelred the Unready* (1980).

[7] *Anglo-Saxon Charters* ed. A. J. Robertson (2nd edn, 1956), no. lxxii.

[8] See pp. 318–19 below.

[9] Ed. C. W. Foster and K. Major, Lincoln Record S. (12 vols, 1931–73).

[10] For the range of eyre records see *Berks. Eyre*, p. xvii; and D. Crook, *Records of the General
Eyre* (1982).

documents now extant bear to the numbers originally made. What proportion of the original whole are the 2,000 or so Anglo-Saxon writs and charters? The conjectures made in answer to this question for late Anglo-Saxon England are necessarily so large that there will never be agreement about them. Examples of such conjectures appear in two lectures given to the Royal Historical Society in 1974. In the first J. Campbell draws attention to miscellaneous memoranda in Old English, such as the one already mentioned concerning levies of men for warships, and suggests that they are 'survivors from a much larger number' and that their existence is one reason for thinking that there was 'a considerable degree of lay literacy' in late Anglo-Saxon England.[11] In the second lecture S. Harvey restates her argument that the Anglo-Saxon government had documents in its treasury upon which Domesday Book was based.[12] The conjecture which both lectures have in common is that many documents in Old English were lost after the Norman Conquest, because the Normans preferred Latin and also because many writs and memoranda may have been ephemeral in purpose in the first place.

The possibility that the Normans dispersed archives of documents and destroyed an extensive literate culture in Old English cannot be excluded, although in some monasteries the Conquest may have had the reverse effect as the English monks laboured to justify their practices and cults to the conquerors. Eadmer of Canterbury describes in the 1090s how he sees 'men of the present age anxiously trying to find out about the actions of their predecessors . . . yet they cannot for all their pains succeed in doing as they would wish because the elusive scarcity of documents [*scriptorum inopia fugax*] has buried them in oblivion.'[13] Even explicit mentions like this of lack of documents could be interpreted as signs of Norman destructiveness, despite William the Conqueror's claim to be the lawful successor of Edward the Confessor.

It is difficult to assess the implications of lost documents. Whereas Campbell argues for 'a considerable degree of lay literacy', C. P. Wormald reasserts that 'the traditional view of restricted literacy is substantially valid for the whole early English period.'[14] Harvey's contention is as controversial. She states that 'chroniclers and cartulary makers have long told us explicitly of the earlier treasury documents and how the Domesday survey using them as its *exemplar* sought additional and extraordinary material.'[15] The chronicle to which she refers is that of Abingdon abbey and the cartulary is Hemming's. A preliminary difficulty is that the words translated as 'documents' or

---

[11] 'Observations on English Government from the Tenth Century to the Twelfth Century', *TRHS* 5th series xxv (1975), p. 42. See also J. Campbell, 'Some Agents and Agencies of the Late Anglo-Saxon State' in *Domesday Studies* ed. J.C. Holt (1987), pp. 214–18.

[12] 'Domesday Book and Anglo-Norman Governance', *TRHS* (1975), p. 175.

[13] *Historia Novorum in Anglia* ed. M. Rule, RS LXXXI (1884), p. 1. R. W. Southern describes the monks' search for documents after the Norman Conquest, 'The Sense of the Past', *TRHS* 5th series xxiii (1973), pp. 247ff.

[14] 'The Uses of Literacy in Anglo-Saxon England and its Neighbours', *TRHS* 5th series xxvii (1977), p. 113.

[15] Harvey, 'Domesday Book', p. 176.

'records' in this context are *scriptura* in the Abingdon text and *cartula* in Hemming's. These words are feminine singular forms, not neuter plural ones: the Abingdon chronicler refers not to 'the records [*scriptura*] of the royal treasury' but to an individual 'writing', and Hemming likewise not to 'documents' but to an individual 'little charter' [*cartula*]. The difference between singular and plural is crucial when the quantity of documents is at issue. The texts which the Abingdon chronicler and Hemming cite in this context are connected with the Domesday survey. Whether they are earlier or later than Domesday Book is not explicitly stated.

The Abingdon *scriptura* is a list of the abbot's hundreds and hides in Berkshire, which accord with entries in Domesday Book concerning the time of Edward the Confessor.[16] In origin this *scriptura* might be any one of the following:

1 a memorandum extracted from Domesday Book itself;
2 one of the records made at the time of the Domesday survey, from which Domesday Book was compiled;
3 a record made in Edward the Confessor's reign and subsequently used in the compilation of Domesday Book.

Harvey prefers the third alternative, though the others are also possibilities, as the Domesday survey collected information concerning the time of Edward the Confessor and it kept these preliminary records in royal treasuries. The Abingdon chronicler's reference to 'another book of the royal treasury of the time of King William' does not exclude the possibility that the *scriptura* was extracted from Domesday Book, as the text cited from this other book contains details not included in Domesday.[17] The sense seems to be that both the *scriptura* and the other book were made in the time of King William. Hemming's cartulary likewise refers to records in the treasury of King William *senior* (in other words, William the Conqueror) and not to pre-Conquest documents. In his use of the word *exemplar* Hemming is not referring to a documentary precedent for the Domesday survey, but to an 'exemplifica-tion' or confirmatory transcript of some evidence concerning Oswaldslaw hundred. In this purely local context he is explaining that 'as confirmation of this business, an exemplification of it is written down in an authentic charter of the king, which is preserved with the descriptions of the whole of England in the royal treasury.'[18] The 'descriptions' mentioned here are most probably the preliminary records produced by the Domesday survey, from which the book

[16] Text ed. D. C. Douglas, 'Some Early Surveys from the Abbey of Abingdon', *EHR* xliv (1929), p. 623.

[17] D. C. Douglas (ibid., p. 619, n. 2) notes differences between this text and Domesday's, whereas Dr Harvey ('Domesday Book', p. 176) suggests that it is an extract 'from Domesday itself'.

[18] 'ad hujus rei confirmationen exemplar ejus in autentica regis cartula, ut predixi, scriptum est, que in thesauro regali cum totius Anglie descriptionibus conservatur,' *Hemingi Chartularium* ed. T. Hearne (1723) i, p. 288; V. H. Galbraith, *Domesday Book: Its Place in Administrative History* (1974), p. 214.

itself was compiled. These alternative interpretations illustrate the difficulties of distinguishing between references to pre- and post-Conquest documents and they also suggest that the case for the existence of earlier treasury documents has been overstated.[19]

Administrative documents were certainly used in late Anglo-Saxon England, since a few copies of them still exist. Whether there were once enough to be kept systematically in archives and to be commonplaces of business are still matters for conjecture. If there had once been many more documents, the forms of those surviving should be stereotyped (as is the case with thirteenth-century charters and writs) because bureaucratic routines would develop. The Anglo-Saxon sealed writ, with its economy of expression, comes closest to such standards. V. H. Galbraith has been the protagonist of the argument that the sealed writ goes back to Alfred's reign or earlier, and that 'long before the Norman Conquest the Saxon kings had a secretariat of their own, and the first great step had been taken towards bureaucratic government.'[20] But P. Chaplais interprets the Alfredian evidence differently and points out that 'no seal impression or trace of sealing of any kind prior to the Confessor's reign has been found', although that is not evidence that none ever existed.[21] The sealed writ is certainly pre-Conquest, but it may have been introduced no earlier than Cnut's reign; whether Anglo-Saxon writs usually carried seals authenticating them before the reign of Edward the Confessor cannot be definitely decided. Chaplais is likewise sceptical about whether the Anglo-Saxon kings had a secretariat of their own; as late as Edward the Confessor's reign the organization of the secretariat 'is a matter for speculation'.[22] Royal scribes are occasionally named and the consistent wording of writs suggests established drafting rules, yet at least one authentic writ of Edward the Confessor can be shown to have been produced in the *scriptorium* of Westminster abbey. Nevertheless by that reign sealing probably took place in a royal office; to that extent at least there was a chancery.

Whatever view is taken of the state of the evidence, it cannot warrant Galbraith's assertion that by the tenth century in the administration of England 'the whole structure was articulated by the royal writ.'[23] It is debatable whether bureaucracy had developed as far as that by 1150, let alone 950. Certainly the Anglo-Saxon vernacular writ, as it existed in the reign of Edward the Confessor, was the root from which later varieties of royal

[19] A. Freason, 'Domesday Book', *History* LXXI (1986), pp. 375–92, reasserts the view that Domesday Book used pre-Conquest records, as does M. Chibnall, *Anglo-Norman England* (1986), p. 107.

[20] *Studies*, p. 36. Cf. Galbraith, 'Literacy', p. 218. Galbraith's case has been sustained in the 1980s by S. Keynes. Keynes's work is brought together in his 'Royal Government and the Written Word in Late Anglo-Saxon England' in *The Uses of Literacy in Early Medieval Europe*, ed. R. McKitterick (1990), pp. 226–57. See also ch. 2, nn. 76–8 below.

[21] Bishop & Chaplais p. xii.

[22] Ibid. Chaplais reasserts his case in 'The Royal Anglo-Saxon "Chancery" of the Tenth Century Revisited', in *Studies in Medieval History Presented to R. H. C. Davis* ed. H. Mayr-Harting and R. I. Moore (1985), pp. 41–51.

[23] *Studies*, p. 36.

charters and letters grew, but the forms had to be changed before the writ could articulate the whole structure of government. From William I's reign, but not earlier (Chaplais argues), writs were used for giving instructions (injunctions) to named individuals.[24] Similarly the practice of keeping sealed writs as title-deeds, 'one of the most important phases in the general change-over from an oral procedure to a written one', was still in the process of happening in William I's reign.[25] Differences of opinion are therefore as large about the purposes for which Anglo-Saxon documents were made as they are about the numbers which once existed. It seems unlikely that England was governed by a bureaucracy using documents in its routine procedures before 1066.

THE USES OF DOMESDAY BOOK

The chief reason for suggesting that Anglo-Saxon government had not already brought the people 'under the rule of written law', in the sense of ruling through a bureaucracy, is that even the Norman conquerors did not succeed in doing this. The effects of Domesday Book are easy to exaggerate because it impressed contemporaries so much. In a well-known passage the *Anglo-Saxon Chronicle* says that King William had the investigation made so narrowly 'that there was no single hide nor virgate of land, nor indeed – it is a shame to relate but it seemed no shame to him to do – one ox or one cow nor one pig which was there left out and not put down in his record.'[26] This description obviously exaggerates in order to emphasize the frightening – and shameful – thoroughness of the Domesday survey. Similarly Fitz Neal explained a century later that the book had been called *Domesdei* 'by the natives' because it seemed to them like the Last Judgement described in Revelation.[27] The tremendous image of Christ in majesty, seated as a judge holding the book of the Scriptures or laws, would have been familiar to anyone entering a Romanesque church, either sculpted over the door-way or as a mural painting within. An earthly king evoked this image at his ceremonial crown-wearings.[28]

Fitz Neal is explaining that by his time Domesday Book was of symbolic rather than practical importance: 'That is why we have called the book *The Book of Judgment*, not because it contains decisions on various difficult points, but because its decisions like those of the Last Judgement are unalterable.'[29] For Fitz Neal Domesday Book was a majestic and unchangeable memorial of the Norman Conquest. The earliest copies of it likewise suggest that its function was symbolic rather than practical. Two multi-coloured editions were made: one in the twelfth century (the manuscript called *Herefordshire*

---

[24] Chaplais, *Docs*, p. 5, n. 4.

[25] Bishop & Chaplais, p. xi.

[26] *The Anglo-Saxon Chronicle: A Revised Translation* ed. D. Whitelock *et al.* (1961), pp. 161–2.

[27] *Dialogus*, p. 64. Revelation, XIII, 8.

[28] J. L. Nelson, 'The Rites of the Conqueror', *Anglo-Norman Studies*, ed. R. Allen Brown, IV (1981), p. 131; Zarnecki, *Catalogue*, pp. 23, 25.

[29] *Dialogus* p. 64. This argument is expanded at ch. 5, nn. 19–21 below.

Domesday) and another in the thirteenth (the Exchequer Breviate), the most elegant manuscript ever produced by the royal administration.[30] But the Breviate was of no practical value because it omitted all details of land use. *Herefordshire Domesday* has some marginal notes updating it, making it more useful than the Breviate, yet even here the work is left uncompleted. Embellished like liturgical texts, these manuscripts reinforce the idea that Domesday Book was seen as a sacred book of judgment.[31]

A surprising fact about Domesday Book is that it seems to have been used so rarely in the two centuries after it was made. There are only ten references extant specifically to the use of information connected with Domesday Book between the time it was made and the death of Henry I in 1135.[32] Nor do most of these references unequivocally refer to the book as such, but to writs (*breves*) or charters (*carte*). These writs or charters are probably the same as the 'descriptions of the whole of England in the royal treasury', which Hemming mentions in his cartulary.[33] As a consequence of the Domesday survey the king's government therefore possessed, perhaps for the first time, not only a great book but an archive of writings to which it could refer.[34] Nevertheless this archive was not carefully kept, as it disappears without trace. It is last mentioned by Henry of Huntingdon (writing probably in the early 1130s), who says that the information of the Domesday survey had all been written in 'charters' (*carte*), which were brought to William the Conqueror and 'are kept deposited in treasuries up to the present day'.[35] The disappearance of these treasuries of documents is an argument in favour of the hypothesis that earlier Anglo-Saxon archives had likewise vanished. But it also suggests that even in the middle of the twelfth century government had not yet developed to the point where archives were progressively accumulated.

After Henry I's reign there is no further evidence of Domesday Book being searched for specific information (although fair copies were made of it, as already mentioned) until a plea roll of 1221 notes: 'Remember to search Domesday for the bishop.'[36] Even this reference suggests that it was private litigants, rather than royal officials, who first realized that the book might be used to their advantage. In the 1250s, however, Henry III and his favourites begin to refer to it. In 1256 the king used it to show that the men of Cheshire were obliged to pay for repairing the bridge at Chester.[37] Three years later Peter of Savoy had Domesday Book cited in Parliament to prove that Witley in Surrey was not ancient demesne of the crown from before the Conquest, as his tenants alleged, because it had been held then by Earl Godwin and not by

---

[30] Balliol College Oxford MS. 350 and PRO Exchequer E. 36/284.

[31] I differ here from V. H. Galbraith, *Domesday Book* (1974), pp. 106ff, and E. M. Hallam, *Domesday Book Through Nine Centuries* (1986), pp. 41–7.

[32] *Herefordshire Domesday* ed. V. H. Galbraith and J. Tait, PRS new series xxv (1950), pp. xxv–xxvii sets out these references conveniently.

[33] See n. 18 above.

[34] S. Keynes, *The Diplomas* (1980), pp. 148–9, discusses Anglo-Saxon archival practices.

[35] *Historia Anglorum* ed. T. Arnold, RS lxxiv (1879), p. 207

[36] *CuriaRR* x, p. 68; Galbraith, *Studies*, pp. 119–20.

[37] *CLibR* iv, p. 282.

the king; Peter was therefore entitled to increase the rent.[38] Proving ancient demesne became a routine use of Domesday Book in Edward I's reign. For example, in a case in 1306 one counsel asks: 'Are we ancient demesne or not?' and another replies: 'We will send to the Exchequer to search in Domesday.'[39] Two generations earlier counsel's question would have been answered, not by searching Domesday Book, but by asking a jury of twelve knights to give oral testimony; there are numerous instances of the latter procedure in the plea rolls of Henry III's reign.[40] This change in the method of obtaining information – from hearing the testimony of reliable local men to looking up a book kept by the Exchequer – is one indicator of the transition from memory to written record. Once the new procedure has become familiar, that is, from the last quarter of the thirteenth century, relevant extracts from Domesday Book were copied into numerous cartularies and registers.

Two centuries thus elapsed before Domesday Book became a record which was regularly consulted or valued for its contents. Why was this so? One answer is that such a book would have been of only limited use at any time. It was founded on a misconception of how to use writing in administration. The Normans seem to have been so impressed by the way written record, in the form of charters, gave apparent durability to their individual acts that they assumed that a big book would give similar permanence to the government of the whole of England. A document could indeed make time stand still, in the sense that it could pass on a record of an event to remote posterity, but it could not prevent change. In Domesday Book lords and serfs, animals and ploughs, mills and streams, all stand in arrested motion like clockwork automata when the mechanism fails. But historical change has a self-sustaining momentum; not even William the Conqueror could prevent change, and so Domesday Book soon went out of date. Its only practical use was to answer questions about archaisms like ancient demesne. The qualities which make it an unrivalled historical record for us today detracted from its usefulness to medieval administrators.

Another answer to the question why Domesday Book took so long to be consulted is that it was too precocious. In the twelfth century a mythology seems to have grown up around it. The educated believed that it had brought the people under the rule of written law, and 'the natives' compared it with the Last Judgement. Both the educated and the natives were more accustomed to writings in the form of symbolic and sacred books than to business documents for mundane use. Practical questions were answered by oral testimony and not by reference to documents. Only gradually, as documents began to accumulate, did habits of consulting them and ultimately of depending on them become established. Domesday Book began to be consulted regularly in Edward I's reign and no earlier because dependence on records in general only became at all regular at that time. Through this

---

[38] *SCPWW*, p. 92, no. 76; *VCH Surrey* III, p. 63; R. S. Hoyt, *The Royal Demesne in English Constitutional History* (1950), pp. 175–7.
[39] *Year Books of 34–5 Edward I* ed. A. J. Horwood, RS xxxi (1879), p. 311.
[40] E.g. *Berks. Eyre*, nos 388, 596.

change Domesday Book ultimately became a useful but limited work of reference instead of an awesome relic like a Gospel book.

Although Domesday Book had not brought the people under the rule of written law in any specific sense, it had associated writing with royal power in a novel and unforgettable way. Of course there were precedents for it, from imperial Rome and the Carolingian polyptychs, but there is no firm evidence that anything of the sort had been attempted before in England. The organization which had made the Domesday survey possible was Anglo-Saxon – the grouping of local communities into shires, hundreds and vills; the practice of juries giving solemn oral testimony which was binding on their communities. The Norman novelty lay in using this organization to compile a written record which reflected the efficiency of Anglo-Saxon government. The unique event of the Conquest produced a unique document. Nevertheless, because Domesday Book was unique in scale and purpose, it could not itself form the first document in a continuing series. Bureaucracy begins with the pipe rolls of the twelfth-century Exchequer rather than with Domesday Book.[41]

EDWARD I'S 'QUO WARRANTO' PROCEEDINGS AND THE EARL WARENNE

Even in Edward I's reign documentary methods of proof were not as firmly established as his lawyers assumed in the *quo warranto* proceedings. The story of the Earl Warenne exhibiting a sword from the Norman Conquest instead of a charter before Edward's judges, saying 'This is my warrant!' shows that old oral traditions and attitudes persisted despite Domesday Book and the immeasurably greater increase in documentation in the thirteenth century. Some historians have found the Warenne story as unacceptable as Edward's judges may have done, because it seems so primitive and ill-founded by literate standards of proof. Thus it was removed in 1913 from the canon of Bishop Stubbs's *Select Charters*, which used to be the bible of history students.[42] The story is certainly inaccurate in details, but it has a value comparable with the myths Fitz Neal recorded a century earlier about the Norman Conquest and written law. Myth is not necessarily the 'purely fictitious narrative' of a dictionary definition. In oral tradition it can be a formulation of fundamental belief and experience handed down in a memorable way. The Warenne story recalls a non-literate tradition of the Norman Conquest, and, if examined as an evocation of dying oral culture, it indicates better than more formal records the change of attitudes which had occurred since the coming of the Normans.

---

[41] For differing views see E. M. Hallam, *Domesday Book Through Nine Centuries* (1986), ch. 2; and W. L. Warren, *The Governance of Norman and Angevin England* (1987), ch. 3.

[42] The reasons for removing the story are discussed by H. M. Cam, *Liberties and Communities in Medieval England* (1944), pp. 176–7, and G. T. Lapsley, *Crown, Community and Parliament* (1951), pp. 35–62.

The story appears in one version of the chronicle of Walter of Guisborough and runs as follows:

> The king disturbed some of the great men of the land through his judges wanting to know by what warrant [*quo warranto*] they held their lands, and if they did not have a good warrant, he immediately seized their lands. Among the rest, the Earl Warenne was called before the king's judges. Asked by what warrant he held, he produced in their midst an ancient and rusty sword and said: 'Look at this, my lords, this is my warrant! For my ancestors came with William the Bastard and conquered their lands with the sword, and by the sword I will defend them from anyone intending to seize them. The king did not conquer and subject the land by himself, but our forebears were sharers and partners with him.'[43]

Historians have rightly pointed out that the story contains inaccuracies and inconsistencies. Edward I's *quo warranto* prosecutions did not demand warrants for 'lands' but for franchises or privileged jurisdictions. Nor were the magnates' lands seized by the king, as he was not powerful enough to do that. Nor is there evidence from other records that the Earl Warenne protested in these terms, although he was harassed by *quo warranto* prosecutions. Moreover, the story is attributed to a different earl, Gilbert de Clare of Gloucester, in another version of this chronicle, and in the best version it does not appear at all. The story also oversimplifies the conduct of judicial proceedings in Edward I's reign. An earl had learned counsel to advise him and to speak on his behalf. Warenne would have known not to threaten royal judges in open court, and that a rusty sword was not going to help his cause at law, since claims without charters were inadmissible in many *quo warranto* cases.

At first sight so many inaccuracies suggest that the Warenne story is worthless for serious historical purposes. At best it is a popular legend; it is certainly not a precise account of legal proceedings. Nevertheless it is important and useful precisely because it does seem to be a popular legend. At the heart of the story is a memory which allegedly went back to the Norman Conquest and an archaic method of proof, the exhibition of the rusty sword, which had been superseded in Edward I's courts by written evidence and book-learned law. The story seems to be a desperate reassertion of the primacy of oral tradition over recorded history and of non-literate forms of proof over Edward I's lawyers and their demands for charters. Although Warenne's assertions were inadmissible at common law, they had generations of tradition behind them and they probably still commanded wide sympathy. Despite its inaccuracy of detail and the inevitable scarcity of evidence about non-literate beliefs, the heart of the Warenne story can be shown to be credible.

[43] *The Chronicle of Walter of Guisborough* ed. H. Rothwell, Camden S. 3rd series LXXXIX (1957), p. 216.

To consider first the memory of the Norman Conquest. The claim that an earl like Warenne was entitled to privileges by right of conquest was certainly circulating at the time of the *quo warranto* proceedings, as it is explicitly contradicted by a royal attorney in 1286 in an action against the earl of Hereford.[44] One justification for this claim was the notion that the earls (*comites*) were the descendants of the companions (*comites*) of William the Conqueror. Similarly the larger idea inherent in the Warenne story, that the descendants of the Norman conquerors were living memorials of that conquest, regardless of whether they had documents to prove it, was certainly a century old. In about 1175 the chief justiciar, Richard de Lucy, recommended Henry II to confirm the charters of Battle abbey (which were recent forgeries in fact) because 'even if all charters perished, we should all still be its charters, since we are enfeoffed from the conquest made at Battle.'[45] Richard meant that the king's companions should be Battle's testimonials because the abbey had been founded in thanksgiving for the victory at Hastings.

In emphasizing conquest the Warenne story may also be recalling a more general and ancient belief among the medieval nobility. That warriors were superior to writers and to all their works seems to have been part of the traditional ideology of the barbarians, who had conquered the Roman empire and replaced the constraining written law of Rome by flexible oral custom. Matthew Paris had recorded one formulation of this idea in a declaration allegedly made by some of the French baronage against the clergy in 1247. They declared that 'all of us, the king's chief men, perceive by applying our minds that the kingdom was not won by written law, nor by the arrogance of clerks, but by the sweat of war.'[46] To the Normans in particular, who were usurpers wherever they triumphed – whether in France, England, Italy or Syria – the righteousness of conquest was part of a mythology.

The most interesting part of the Warenne story is not the justification of conquest, however, for that is quite common in medieval political ideas, but his alleged production of an 'ancient and rusty sword' which purported to be the very sword used by the first Earl Warenne at the Norman Conquest. Whether this relic was authentic and whether it ever was shown to Edward I's judges are features of the story which cannot be verified. It is possible that such a revered weapon might have been kept and it is also possible that the earl might have shown it to the judges on some occasion less formal than a session of the court considering his case. Although at first sight the story suggests that Warenne was threatening the court with his sword, closer scrutiny shows that he was enunciating a familiar theory of conquest and supporting it by the most appropriate type of evidence, the symbolic instrument of conquest. The sword was rusty; it was a relic, not a practical weapon. Nevertheless Warenne was perfectly capable of threatening to fight a royal officer in what he deemed to be a just cause. The sheriff of Lincolnshire

[44] D. W. Sutherland, *Quo Warranto Proceedings in the Reign of Edward I* (1963), p. 83.

[45] *Battle*, p. 310. Battle abbey's forgeries are referred to at p. 318, n. 92 below.

[46] Matthew Paris IV, p. 593. Matthew attributes this declaration to the influence of the Emperor Frederick II.

had disarmingly explained to the king's judges in 1276 that he would have needed a force of 'around five thousand men' to execute a writ within Warenne's liberty of Stamford.[47] Perhaps it was in reaction to this writ that Warenne had displayed his sword before the judges.

The use of objects, including swords, as props in the theatre of memory was recommended in medieval academic treatises, since 'the remembrance of things is held by the images, as though they were letters.'[48] At a less exalted level it had been usual practice, before charters became common, to preserve the memory of a title to property in the object which had symbolized the conveyance. The earl of the story was producing something different, yet comparable, in the sword which symbolized his family's acquisition of their lands. To emphasize the importance of personal mementoes in evidence of title, an earlier Earl Warenne in a gift to Lewes priory in 1147 had given it possession by the hairs of his head; these, together with his brother's, were cut off before the altar by Henry of Blois, bishop of Winchester.[49] Such symbolic objects were retained by the beneficiary, but they have rarely survived because their significance could easily be lost when it depended on oral transmission only. Among recorded examples of such objects accompanying gifts of land are a cup given to Durham cathedral in *c*.1066 by Copsi, earl of Northumberland, which (according to a Durham author writing in *c*.1100) 'is preserved in the church and retains the memory of that deed for ever'; a gold and ruby ring given to St Paul's cathedral in the first half of the twelfth century by Osbert de Camera, which was affixed to his charter; a staff cut 'from the land' concerned and given to Ramsey abbey in 1121–2 by Wulfget, 'which we still have' (according to the Ramsey chronicler writing in *c*.1170).[50] Although specific records like these of such objects are rare, the practice was presumably commonplace. A comparable practice survives to the present day in the giving of wedding rings.

There was nothing necessarily unusual, then, in the Earl Warenne possessing a symbolic memento of the Norman Conquest, nor in objects serving as evidence of title to property. More strange was the form of the earl's symbol, a sword, and the allegation that he produced it before the king's judges. At least from the beginning of the thirteenth century, and probably from Henry II's reign, the king's court had refused to take cognizance of symbolic mementoes other than seals. Furthermore, it would certainly not have considered any object to be a sufficient title to a franchise unless it were supported by a charter. Instances of objects other than sealed writings being produced as evidence of title in royal courts are consequently very rare.

One interesting case made its way on to the royal records in 1213, however, when a litigant objected to the prior of Durham producing a charter against

[47] R. C. Palmer, *The County Courts of Medieval England* (1982), p. 265, n. 10.

[48] F. Yates, *The Art of Memory* (1966), p. 64 (citing Martianus Capella); Carruthers, *Memory*, p. 147.

[49] *BM Facs*, no. 25; *Early Yorkshire Charters: The Honour of Warenne* ed. C. T. Clay (1949) VIII, p. 84.

[50] *Symeonis Monachi Opera Omnia* ed. T. Arnold, RS LXXV (1882), I, p. 97; W. Dugdale, *The History of St Paul's Cathedral* ed. H. Ellis (1818), p. 6; *Ramsey*, p. 246, no. 264.

him, which 'is not made according to the custom of the realm nor is there a seal on it, but a certain knife which can be put on or taken off'.[51] This charter (one half of a chirograph in fact, dated 1148) is still preserved at Durham and from it hangs a knife with a polished haft of horn and a broken rusty blade.[52] This knife could indeed be easily 'put on or taken off', as it is attached by a strip of parchment which is threaded through a hole in the haft and then tied. Judging by the numbers of references to them in charters, knives like this were favourite symbols of conveyances in the Anglo-Norman period, although they have seldom survived.[53] It is possible that other charters of the twelfth century, which have empty parchment strips hanging from them, were originally authenticated by knives rather than seals. Most exceptional is a charter dated 1151 for St Denys priory near Southampton with two parallel slits in it, through which the blade of the donor's symbolic knife was once fixed to the parchment.[54]

Although knives were common enough, a sword is unusual as a symbol of title despite its being the most obvious symbol of knightly and secular power. A knight's oath at his inauguration was made by his placing a sword on an altar, just as other symbolic objects were placed in conveyances of property. Justifying this practice, John of Salisbury argued that this symbolic gesture by a knight was valid without any form of words in writing, such as a bishop or abbot needed at his profession, for 'who would demand of a non-literate [*illitteratus*], whose duty is to know arms rather than letters, that he should make a lettered profession?'[55] When Thomas de Muschamps became a monk at Durham, probably shortly before his death in *c.*1130, he invested St Cuthbert and the monks with the estate of Hetherslaw by his sword offered on an altar. In this instance investiture by sword was the symbol, not of the beginning of a knightly career, but of its ending.

In presenting his sword to the monks of Durham priory, Thomas de Muschamps laid down his arms and offered up his worldly goods in one symbolic gesture. Nevertheless this gesture did not prove as memorable as it should have done. Unlike the Earl Warenne, Durham priory neglected to keep the sword. Record of it survives only because the monks were obliged to get writs from King Stephen and Henry II, when Thomas's heirs repeatedly refused to surrender Hetherslaw.[56] In pursuit of this claim Absalom, the prior from 1154 to 1158, wrote a public letter to the sheriff of Northumberland insisting that he and another monk had actually witnessed the investiture with

---

[51] *CuriaRR* vii, p. 39. The word for 'knife' in this text is *cnipulus*, not *umpulus*; I am grateful to Mr R. E. Latham for this correction.

[52] Illustrated in black and white (actual size) by K. Major, 'Blyborough Charaters' in *MM for Stenton*, plate xv, and in colour (reduced size) by C. J. Stranks, *Durham Cathedral* (1976), p. 21.

[53] P & M ii, p. 88.

[54] *BM Facs*, no. 32.

[55] *Policraticus*, Bk. vi, ch. 10, ed. C. C. J. Webb (1919) ii, p. 25.

[56] J. Raine, *The History and Antiquities of North Durham* (1852), appendix, p. 141. *RRA-N* iii (1968), p. 92, no. 257.

the sword two or three decades earlier.[57] Ironically the day for settling this claim was fixed by Stephen of Bulmer, whose uniquely inscribed and labelled carving knife (recording an agreement with Lindisfarne) is now preserved as a title-deed at Durham.[58] Although Durham priory apparently failed in this claim and Thomas's sword was not kept, this dispute at least provides an instance, comparable with the Earl Warenne's, of a title to property depending, on the evidence of a sword.

There are, moreover, at least two English examples of early medieval swords being kept as symbolic mementoes. The better-known is the Conyers falchion, which is exhibited in Durham cathedral treasury.[59] This sword was the symbol by which the head of the Conyers family held the manor of Sockburn from the bishop of Durham. Each head of the family was obliged up to 1860 to show the sword to the bishop as evidence of title. Although this is a parallel with Warenne's sword, a problem is that the falchion does not seem to be the original weapon, as it dates from no earlier than the thirteenth century and has been associated (by the heraldry on its pommel) with Richard of Cornwall, the brother of Henry III. A closer parallel with Warenne is a sword (no longer existing), which was kept in the royal treasury 'to this day' according to the Ramsey chronicler writing in *c*.1170.[60] It was preserved 'as evidence of God's bounty and the royal victory' over the Scots by King Athelstan at Brunanburh in 937. St Odo of Canterbury had miraculously provided it, when Athelstan's own sword had slipped from its scabbard. The Ramsey chronicler is careful, however, to report this story with a cautious note, 'as is said'.

Closer in time to the Warenne story and perhaps for that reason a closer parallel is Edward I's use of the symbolism of arms and armour in a letter to the pope in 1301.[61] This letter put forward a battery of arguments, from both myth and recent history, to justify English overlordship in Scotland. Boniface VIII had argued in 1299 that Scotland belonged to the Roman church from ancient times and he challenged Edward to produce his titles and muniments.[62] Edward was thus obliged in effect to state by what warrant he claimed jurisdiction over Scotland, just as two decades earlier he had required magnates like the Earl Warenne to show warrants for their jurisdictions. Although Edward made it clear at the outset that he did not consider himself bound to answer the pope in this case, his lengthy explanation concedes that an answer was necessary. Placed in a similar situation to his magnates a little earlier, though with many more documents at his disposal, Edward and his

---

[57] 'et per gladium suum eundem sanctum beatum scilicet Cuthbertum investisse', Raine, *North Durham*, appendix, p. 141.

[58] M. T. Clanchy, 'Reading the Signs at Durham Cathedral' in *Literacy and Society* ed. M. T. Larsen and K. Schousboe (1989), pp. 175–7; see also p. 258 below.

[59] Illustrated by J. Cherry, 'Symbolism and Survival', *The Antiquaries Journal* LXIX (1989), p. 112, plate xvii.

[60] *Ramsey*, p. 16.

[61] *Anglo-Scottish Relations*, pp. 96–117.

[62] Ibid., p. 87.

advisers resorted to arguments from myth and symbolism almost as readily as the earl in the Warenne story.

Unlike the Earl Warenne, however, Edward did not possess an ancient sword as a symbol of conquest. Athelstan's miraculous sword, which the Ramsey chronicler had mentioned a century earlier, had either got lost or the chronicler may have been mistaken in his original information. Nevertheless Edward did attempt to compensate for not having Athelstan's sword by referring to a fissure in a rock near Dunbar, which had allegedly been made by a miraculous sword blow from Athelstan. This blow had been facilitated by the intervention of St John of Beverley (not St Odo of Canterbury this time) and, according to Edward's letter to the pope, 'may still be seen as an evident sign of this event'.[63] Edward had also a more recent and convincing argument from arms. After King William the Lion was taken prisoner by the English in 1174 he had offered his helmet, lance, and saddle on the altar of York minster as tokens of subjection, 'and they are kept and preserved in that church up to the present day.'[64]

These comparisons between the Warenne story and other sources suggest that it would not have appeared as peculiar or incredible to people in *c*.1300 as it has to some twentieth-century historians. The descendants of the Norman conquerors, particularly the earls, probably did believe in a right of conquest. Physical objects, especially knives, were kept as titles to property. Although the use of swords as mementoes is rare in England at least, the sword was the archetypal symbol of knightly as distinct from clerkly authority. Titles to authority or property could not always be proved by producing charters or citing precedents in writing. To justify English claims in Scotland Edward I's government had to resort to myth and physical symbols just as the earl did in the Warenne story. Taken together, these fragmentary details help to reconstruct ways of thinking and remembering which were widespread before the coming of written records. The growth of literacy did not occur in a cultural vacuum. It replaced non-literate ways, which seemed equally natural to those who were accustomed to them. The most difficult initial problem in the history of literacy is appreciating what preceded it.

A paradox of the Warenne story is that, although it is ill-founded by literate standards of proof, it is essentially more truthful than some of the pleadings based on charters which were duly recorded in the official rolls of the *quo warranto* proceedings. In producing an ancient sword instead of a charter as his title from the Norman Conquest, the earl showed greater historical awareness than an abbot who produced a charter of William the Conqueror. Many – perhaps most – charters of Edward the Confessor or William the Conqueror circulating in the thirteenth century were forgeries, including even those of Battle abbey founded by William himself, because title-deeds had been the exception rather than the rule in the eleventh century.[65] If Edward I's lawyers in the *quo warranto* proceedings had persisted in demanding titles in

---

[63] *Anglo-Scottish Relations*, p. 99.
[64] Ibid., p. 102.
[65] Forgery is discussed at pp. 318–26 below.

writing from 1066 or even earlier, using the argument that 'time does not run against the king', nearly all owners of property in England would have been disfranchised.[66] In 1290 by the *quo warranto* statute a compromise was made.[67] In subsequent case law the king was understood to have conceded that documentary proof would not be required henceforward from any date earlier than the accession of Richard I in 1189. The last decade of the twelfth century was a realistic date from which to expect written titles, as tenure by charter among the tenants-in-chief at least was beginning to be normal by then.

In the 1290s the earl of the Warenne story could therefore return his 'ancient and rusty sword' to its scabbard for all time, as it was now a mere historical oddity instead of being a living relic transmitting memory to future generations. 'Legal memory', that artificial memory which depended primarily on documentary proof and not on mementoes or mortal oral testimony, had been arbitrarily set at 1189 and remained there for the rest of the Middle Ages. This is the context within which this book aims to trace the shift from memory to written record between the Norman Conquest and the reign of Edward I. William the Conqueror had not brought the people under the rule of written law. Nor was Domesday Book the last judgement; rather, it was a symbolic new start. By contrast two centuries later, in the last decades of Edward I's reign, when the Earl Warenne allegedly produced his ancestral sword as testimony of the Norman Conquest, his claim (assuming that something like it was made) went unrecorded in the official rolls of the king's court because it was irrelevant. By then the province of myth and hearsay was the only appropriate place for a story which claimed priority for memory over written record in the king's court.

The growth of reliance on writing has been a continuing process without a precise beginning or end. In England it had started long before 1066 with Roman inscriptions and Anglo-Saxon charters, and would go on for centuries after 1307. This book concentrates on the two and a half centuries from 1066 to 1307 because it argues that these are the years in which the use of writing first became normal for government business and titles to property, not only in England but in western Europe as a whole. This change is marked by the increasing number of documents which were kept and by growing indications that landowners were themselves becoming literate. The difference between the uses of writing in 1066 and 1307 has been introduced in this chapter by comparing myths about the effects of the Norman Conquest, because myths can convey pre-literate beliefs.

In the twelfth century, when charters were still uncommon and bureaucracy had scarcely begun, William the Conqueror was credited with the impossible and therefore heroic feat of having made a definitive book of judgement by which to govern the conquered people. A century or more later the idea of bringing the people under written law had come closer to reality, with the expansion of royal and seignorial bureaucracies and the use of

---

[66] Sutherland, *Quo Warranto Proceedings*, p. 14; Clanchy, 'Remembering', p. 174; and Clanchy, *Moderni*, p. 688.

[67] Sutherland, *Quo Warranto Proceedings*, pp. 91–110; see also p. 152 below.

charters even by some serfs. Popular legend reacted then with the story of the Earl Warenne, who is committed to the equally heroic task of halting the *quo warranto* proceedings with his rusty sword. The Norman Conquest, which was identified with the threat of written record in the twelfth century, had become by 1307 in the Warenne story a symbol of the good old days of simple and forceful memory. Magnates like Warenne could indeed curtail the king's political power and they maintained a tradition of doing so from Magna Carta onwards, but they could not stop the advance of writing into more and more areas of ordinary life because that was caused by the massing of documents in archives and the spread of literate skills over the country.

2

The Proliferation of Documents

In 1170 Master David of London wrote from France to an unnamed agent in England, giving him directions about the safekeeping of his correspondence.[1] The year before, David had been a representative at the papal *curia* of Henry II and Gilbert Foliot, bishop of London, against Thomas Becket. As a consequence he had earned an annuity of £20 (paid partly by the king and partly by Foliot) and the enmity of Becket. The controversy had become so fierce in the last few months of Becket's life that David took steps to safeguard this new pension. He explained to his agent in England that he had obtained from Henry II two charters, one confirming the king's portion and the other Foliot's obligation. As Henry II's eldest son, Henry the Young King, had just been crowned, David also obtained a letter close from Henry II, commanding the Young King to issue similar charters for him.

The two royal charters, and the letter close promising two more, only safeguarded the principle of David's pension. In addition he needed writs detailing how the payments were to be made. The king's bailiff in Godalming, Ranulf de Broc, was therefore ordered in another royal letter close to pay David £15 a year at specified intervals. This letter, David explained, was intended to save him having to apply for a new royal writ to the bailiff every time he required payment. A similar letter was sent to the bishop of London concerning the remaining £5 of the pension. To ensure that the bishop was not charged twice, another royal writ had to be issued ordering the sheriffs of Middlesex not to exact the £5 from the bishop in future. Likewise the Exchequer (which accounted with the sheriffs) was instructed to allow the £15 from Ranulf de Broc and the £5 from the bishop, so that Ranulf and the

[1] Z. N. Brooke, 'The Register of Master David of London' in *Essays to Poole*, p. 240. This story is repeated by R. Mortimer in *Anglo-Norman Studies* xii (1989) ed. M. Chibnall, pp. 129–30.

bishop would not have to apply for writs acquitting them each time. Settling how David's pension was to be paid had therefore necessitated letters to various levels of the king's bureaucratic hierarchy ranging from the bailiff, Ranulf, up to the barons of the Exchequer. By these means David had acquired a series of 'standing orders' so that the payments due to him would be authorized automatically in future.

David was still not satisfied. 'To be on the safe side', he wrote, 'so that they cannot malign me, I have had sealed [by the Chancery] a transcript of that [writ to the Exchequer] and a transcript of the one which is to be sent to Ranulf.' David told his agent 'to keep these with my charters'; he was evidently rapidly acquiring an archive of his own. Even so, neither the king's letters nor the transcripts allayed his anxieties entirely. As an added precaution, he got two of the king's confidential ministers, Richard of Ilchester and Geoffrey Ridel, to write on his behalf to William St John and Thomas the Sealer (who were probably officers of the chief justiciar in England) 'so that things may be made to run expeditiously'. After all these letters, David had the temerity to conclude his instructions to the agent by telling him that he had not been able to obtain the one writ which the agent wanted for himself, because he did not wish to trouble the king with trifles when Henry was so worried about Becket.

To sum up, the documents which David needed to safeguard his pension comprised two charters from Henry II, two charters from the Young King and a letter close to the Young King; writs to Ranulf de Broc, the bishop of London, the sheriffs of Middlesex and the barons of the Exchequer; official transcripts of two of these writs; two letters from ministers to officials in England. Altogether eleven royal documents were to be produced and two letters from ministers. These letters would in their turn have created other correspondence. David had also, of course, to get the letter written to his agent and to keep the copy of it, which was preserved in his register and hence retained for posterity.

Master David's letter explains better than many generalizations how records proliferated, and it suggests the point this process had reached at the time of Becket's death, a century after the Norman Conquest. In England, with its extraordinarily centralized monarchy, the principal producer of documents was the king's government. Many, perhaps most, of the letters produced were written within the organization to other royal officials. The letters to the bailiff, the sheriffs and the Exchequer, and those from Richard of Ilchester and Geoffrey Ridel, illustrate this in Master David's case. Behind any solemn royal charter now extant there once existed numerous ancillary documents – petitions, drafts, transcripts, writs to officials, letters to other interested parties, and correspondence among the officials themselves 'so that things may be made to run expeditiously'. As the king moved continually from place to place within England, and often across the Channel as well (particularly in Henry II's case), he communicated with many of his officials by letters. Almost any royal order required some sort of writ to, or from, the Exchequer in London; the purpose of Master David's 'standing orders' was to reduce the repetitious issue of writs of this sort.

Moreover, all these officials had to be cajoled and encouraged by offerings and fees to produce the necessary documents. One advantage enjoyed by royal clerks was that they were not expected to make such offerings to each other and could therefore get the documents they needed free of charge, thus further enlarging the number of documents produced. On one occasion at Henry II's court, Thurstan, the king's steward, complained to Henry that Adam of Yarmouth, the spigurnel (the sealer of writs), had refused to seal a writ for him for nothing. It emerged that Adam felt aggrieved because Thurstan had not let him have two cakes when he was entertaining guests; Adam had refused to seal the writ in retaliation. The king resolved the dispute by making Adam sit down, with the writ and his seal, while Thurstan offered him two cakes on bended knee. This little piece of gossip, from Walter Map's *Courtiers' Trifles*,[2] illustrates how the king himself could get involved in the pettiest disputes within his household and the discretion his bureaucrats had to dispense or withhold favours. The proliferation of documents meant that government became more dependent on literates; it did not make it any less arbitrary or capricious.

In Walter Map's story and Master David's letter it is evident that the initiative for obtaining the writs came from the beneficiaries and not from the bureaucracy itself. David was anxious to provide against every conceivable mishap; so he took the trouble to obtain transcripts for himself, writs to other officials, and letters from persons of influence to expedite his business. Once the bureaucratic machine had taken shape, over-anxious users encouraged it to grow progressively more complex and extensive. On the other hand, neither Thurstan, the king's steward, nor David are entirely typical in their attitudes, as both were connected with the royal court and would consequently have had a special knowledge of, and interest in, forms of documentary proof. David had also attended the schools of Paris and Bologna, which would have made him literate in every sense of the word. By 1170 the king's government was much more dependent on documents than a century earlier, but it was still relatively primitive. It would be wrong to assume that the whole of England was bureaucratically controlled in Henry II's reign.

DOCUMENTS AT VILLAGE LEVEL

A century later, however, by Edward I's reign, the use of documents had extended down to village level. The English *Song of the Husbandman* (probably dating from the early fourteenth century) depicts the beadles collecting taxes from the peasants, 'the men on the earth' (*men utho mold*), by the authority of an Exchequer writ. The beadles say: 'You are written in my list, as you know very well' (*Thou art written y my writ that thou wel wost*).[3] The beadles may not have been exaggerating. The statute of Exeter of 1285 had required local bailiffs to supply the king's commissioners with the names, written down in a roll, of every village, half-village and hamlet within franchises as well as in the kingdom as a whole.[4] Furthermore, from at least the 1270s, seignorial

---

[2] Walter Map, Bk. v, ch. vi, p. 486.
[3] *The Political Songs of England* ed. T. Wright, Camden S. 1st series vi (1839), p. 151.
[4] *Statutes*, p. 210.

stewards and bailiffs were meant to have written on rolls the names of all males (excluding clerics) over the age of 12; these lists were read out twice a year when the sheriff or the franchise-holder visited the locality for the view of frankpledge.[5] In theory at least, Edward I's government thus had access to lists of every place of habitation, however small, and every man, however lowly his status.

By 1300 beadles and their like were accustomed to making lists; or rather, that was the practice recommended by writers of treatises on estate management in Edward I's reign. The book called *Husbandry* recommends the bailiff in the autumn to list everything that remains on the manor, such as tools and horseshoes, great and small, so that he will know what to buy for the coming year. The same book mentions in passing, as if it were a commonplace, *la respounse del issue de let* – the record of yields of milk from the cows.[6] Such a record may have been a notched wooden tally, and not a parchment. Even so, it shows that some manorial bailiffs and reeves used records, other than their memories, for day-to-day management. The editor of these treatises, D. Oschinsky, argues that 'it was probably within their power to write symbolic signs and figures', but she does not think that a reeve or his agents could read or write Latin.[7] P. D. A. Harvey likewise rejects the proposition that 'the peasant farmers who normally became reeves were able to read, let alone write their own annual accounts.'[8] Nevertheless one of the treatises, *Seneschaucy*, assumes that the bailiff or reeve can read (in French, if not in Latin), as it warns him to admit no one and hand over nothing from the manor to any person whatsoever 'without the warrant of a writ' under pain of repaying the loss from his own purse.[9] If the bailiff or reeve were unable to read such warrants when they were delivered to him, he would soon have been out of pocket. It is impossible to know how many farms in England in 1300 were administered with the degree of bureaucratic efficiency laid down in the rule books. At the least, however, the leading men in villages must have considered wooden tallies a commonplace and been familiar with written warrants in Edward I's reign.

The fact that many – perhaps most – people in thirteenth-century England had to read from time to time does not mean that they also wrote. In manuscript culture reading and writing were separate skills. Writing documents required clerical training and special equipment; parchment, ink and quill pens were not on sale at the village shop. Reeves and bailiffs employed clerks to draw up accounts and send letters to their superiors. In many villages, in addition to the priest, there would have been other peasants (both men and women) who had received some clerical training when young, either by serving in the parish church or in a lord's domestic chaplaincy. But writing was not required as often as reading. It may have been harder in a village to

[5] *Court Baron*, pp. 68–9.
[6] *Walter of Henley*, pp. 436, 430.
[7] Ibid., p. 223.
[8] *Manorial Rolls of Cuxham* Oxfordshire Record S. 50 (1976), p. 42.
[9] 'sanz garant de bref', *Walter of Henley*, p. 292. Parkes, 'Literacy', pp. 559–60 argues that reeves could read and write.

get ink and parchment than to find a clerk to use them. Like buying a ribbon or a needle, writing something down might mean waiting until an itinerant specialist appeared in the neighbourhood. Documents of one sort and another can have been no rarer in villages than ribbons and needles, but they were as ephemeral. Only very special ones have survived.

Even the lowest class in society, vagrants, were expected to carry certificates of good character. In Essex in 1248 five men from as far afield as Barnard Castle and Canterbury, after being acquitted of theft, were forbidden to return to the county unless they brought with them 'their testimonial of trustworthiness'.[10] That a written document is referred to here, rather than oral testimony, is suggested by two cases from Sussex in 1261–2. In one Robert de Parys of Battle, who had been arrested as a horse thief, obtained the bailiff of East Grinstead's permission to go away and fetch a testimonial of his trustworthiness, but he never returned.[11]

The other case from Sussex is more explicit about the testimonial being in writing. William of Badgeworth (in Gloucestershire) sued Peter de Turvill, the bailiff of the honour of Bramber (in Sussex), for wrongful imprisonment and grievous bodily harm. William's story, which was upheld by a special jury, was that he had come to Sussex to visit a relative when he was arrested by Peter on suspicion of theft. He asked Peter's permission to return to Badgeworth to obtain 'letters testifying to his trustworthiness' from his lord's court.[12] William was duly issued at his manorial court with a letter, sealed by the bailiff and suitors of Badgeworth, testifying that he was a trustworthy man. He then returned to Sussex and presented his letter to Peter in the honorial court at Bramber, but Peter reacted by imprisoning him in a dungeon and only released him because he was at death's door. Although this case shows that William's letter failed to protect him (initially at least), it also suggests that the sending of such letters between seignorial courts was a routine procedure. The bailiffs who had the letters written, the suitors or members of the court who sealed them, and the recipients who benefited from them, must all have been sufficiently familiar with writing to understand the import of a letter. Indeed William – mistakenly as it turned out – had such confidence in his letter that he thought it would save him from a dungeon when he returned to Sussex.

Comparable with testimonials of trustworthiness are the warrants of lawful purchase which accompanied sales of livestock. In Kent in 1241 John le Keche and others were acquitted of stealing oxen, but the jury noted that they had bought the animals foolishly and 'without the warrant that they could have had'.[13] That a written warrant was meant is made clear by a case from Oxford in 1258 in which a receipt (in the form of a letter patent) for the purchase of a horse is mentioned.[14] Similarly in 1292 a plaintiff told the king's

---

[10] 'warrantum suum de fidelitate', PRO JUST/1/232, m. 3. I owe this and the references immediately following to Dr H. R. T. Summerson, whose knowledge of the crown pleas MSS of Henry III is unrivalled.

[11] JUST/1/912A, m. 40.

[12] 'litteras testimoniales de fidelitate', JUST/1/911, m. 8.

[13] JUST/1/359, m. 29 (Dartford).

[14] KB/26/148, m. 8 (*Coram Rege*).

justices that he had been deprived of a letter issued in the name of Hereford corporation, stating that he was searching for a stolen horse.[15] The conclusion to draw from such evidence is that by the second half of the thirteenth century it was imprudent for anybody to wander far from his own village without some form of identification in writing, both for himself and for anything in his possession. Medieval society's savage laws against strangers and vagrants must have been a forceful promoter of literacy in the countryside.

Given these facts, it comes as no surprise to find that by 1300 serfs and villeins used documents. If they wished to advance themselves or provide for younger sons or daughters, they had to imitate their betters and exploit written procedures. A Latin poem written in *c*.1276 describes, from a hostile point of view, the efforts of the people of Stoughton to sue their lord, the abbot of Leicester. One of the rustics says: 'I will go to the king, I will bow to the king, I will hand him the case in writing' (*Ad regem vadam, coram rege cadam, causam scriptam sibi tradam*).[16] But these wretches, who had hoped to be *magistri* ('masters' in both the academic and the social sense), were quickly overawed by a smooth advocate at the king's court and returned weeping and empty-handed. In this case the serfs had achieved nothing with their document and were treated almost as a band of rebels. Occasionally, however, individuals were more successful. An action in the King's Bench twenty years later concerned a certain John son of Robert of Estgate, whose grandmother had been a serf of Robert de Mortimer.[17] Robert of Estgate had (according to the plea roll) 'subsequently increased in goods and by his trading improved himself so much' that he acquired lands by charters from the Mortimers. Robert is thus a real instance of that stereotype, the peasant of servile origins who bettered himself by trade. The charters from the Mortimers were intended to give documentary reinforcement to his eminent status.

The legality of serfs acquiring or conveying property by charters is complex. In the case just mentioned Robert had been obliged to surrender his charters to William de Mortimer, his lord, who argued on those grounds that Robert was his villein; but John, Robert's son, claimed to be a freeman and was adjudged to be so. Similarly the Peterborough abbey cartulary, entitled *Cartae Nativorum*, can be interpreted in contrary senses.[18] 'Natives'' or 'serfs' charters' might imply that these were illegal documents, which had consequently been surrendered to the lord, the abbot of Peterborough, just as Robert had surrendered his charters to William de Mortimer; if that is so, Peterborough abbey made a record of the charters because they concerned its own property. Conversely the title *Cartae Nativorum* might suggest that charters made by serfs were a legal commonplace; they were recorded in the cartulary to reinforce their validity, just as private charters of greater men were sometimes enrolled in the royal archives for further security. The former

[15] *Select Bills in Eyre* ed. W. C. Bolland, SS xxx (1914), p. 35, no. 55.
[16] R. H. Hilton, 'A Thirteenth-Century Poem on Disputed Villein Services', *EHR* LVI (1941), p. 95.
[17] *SCCKB* III, pp. 47–9.
[18] Ed. C. N. L. Brooke and M. M. Postan, Northamptonshire Record S. xx (1960). Cf. E. King, *Peterborough Abbey* (1973), ch. 6.

[handwritten marginal note, right margin:] A

[handwritten note, bottom right:] Serfs ① Don't have the vocab. to communicate ② Can't argue effectively ③ they are un-free peasants... so they can't dispute property rights

hypothesis, that the documents had been surrendered to Peterborough because serfs had no legal title by charter, is the more likely.

Whether or not the serfs who made these charters had a legal right to do so, the existence of the Peterborough documents (even in cartulary copies) demonstrates that in the latter half of the thirteenth century small properties were being conveyed by peasants using writing. Whether the persons and properties concerned were technically free or unfree, these charters are a landmark in the development of written record. There are, for example, 15 *cartae nativorum* from the village of Tinwell in Rutland; seven of these charters concern half-acres of land, another five one acre each, and the remaining three the rent and sale of some houses.[19] If in many parts of England, as is probable, and not just on the Peterborough abbey estates, single acres and half-acres were being conveyed by charter by 1300, the number of peasants' charters produced amounts to hundreds of thousands or even millions. Supposing that on average one charter was produced for each acre of arable once in the thirteenth century, the number of charters made would total at least eight million.[20] It is very unlikely of course that a charter was made for every acre, even of arable. On the other hand, the *Cartae Nativorum* show that numerous documents concerned less than one acre, and the same land might be rented or conveyed more than once in the century. Attempted partitions and short-term conveyances must have been common, because the population and hence the pressure on land had reached a peak by 1300. It seems reasonable to conclude that at least hundreds of thousands, and perhaps millions, of peasants' charters were made, although those who made them were the more prosperous smallholders and in that sense were not typical serfs (see the charter of William Benedict, plate vi).

Unlike papal or royal letters for the great monastic houses, peasants' charters would not have been kept when they went out of date; because the legal status of the charters was dubious, peasants did not make cartularies, and such small and fragile documents would have been difficult to preserve anyway. Nevertheless a few actual charters (as distinct from copies like those in the *Cartae Nativorum*), undoubtedly concerning unfree tenures, have been found and more are likely to come to light. R. H. Hilton describes a lease (dating from *c.*1230) between Gloucester abbey and a widow, Emma, who was to perform ploughing and other duties in addition to paying a money rent.[21] Even if she were not of servile status herself, some of the services prescribed are those of an unfree tenement. Her charter is in the form of a bipartite chirograph, which implies theoretical equality between the contracting parties, Emma and the abbot. The abbey's half of the chirograph (the extant half) is authenticated, as was required, by Emma's seal, which bears her name and a cross as a central device.

[19] *Cartae Nativorum*, pp. 131–6, nos 397–411.
[20] R. Lennard, *Rural England, 1086–1135* (1959), p. 393, estimates the arable acreage (excluding the northern counties and Middlesex) in 1086 at 7.2 million at least. Population and land-use had undoubtedly increased since then.
[21] R. H. Hilton, *The English Peasantry in the Later Middle Ages* (1975), p. 153.

The possessor of a seal was necessarily a person familiar with documents and entitled to participate in their use. The metal matrix of a seal like Emma's would not have been made to use once only. Even if it were mass-produced by casting and sold ready-made with a blank space around the border, as is possible, the owner's name had still to be engraved by hand. The name made the seal unique and hence legally valid. Possession of a seal thus implied that its owner could read his own name, as well as being prepared to authenticate documents with the impress of his 'signature'. Emma's chirograph therefore demonstrates that a holder of unfree land, even a woman (albeit a widow), might 'sign' a document as early as 1230. From the same date or earlier there survives a chirograph, made by the earl of Chester and Lincoln with the men of Freiston and Butterwick in Lincolnshire, which bears the seals of at least fifty of the men.[22] Most of these men were probably not technically serfs, but they were certainly smallholders.

In Henry II's reign his chief justiciar, Richard de Lucy, had smiled contemptuously when Gilbert de Balliol had mentioned a seal, saying: 'It was not formerly the custom for every petty knight to have a seal, which befits only kings and important people.'[23] Yet a century later not only knights, but some of the smallest property-owners had seals. So far from opposing this development, the statute of Exeter of 1285 actually required 'bondsmen' to have seals to authenticate their written evidence, when they served on inquests for which there were insufficient freemen.[24] The government was prepared to overlook the distinction between freeman and serf when it found it inconvenient. On the other hand, as with the surrender of serfs' charters, some lords attempted to enforce that distinction rigidly. In 1295 the customary tenants of Bromham in Wiltshire were fined 100 shillings 'because they made a common seal in contempt of the lord', the abbot of Battle.[25] Seals for individuals may have been tolerated more readily; a communal seal suggested an organized association against the lord. Perhaps too Battle abbey pursued a consistent policy against seals, as it was an abbot of Battle, Richard de Lucy's brother, whom Gilbert de Balliol had been opposing a century earlier. Despite the objections of some lords, seals like charters were probably possessed by the majority of landowners, however small their holdings, by 1300. The possession of any type of seal implied that its owner considered himself to be of sufficient status to use and understand documents, even if this were an aspiration rather than a reality.

---

[22] These and other peasant seals are illustrated by T. A. Heslop in E. King, *Medieval England 1066–1485* (1988), pp. 214–15. See also P. D. A. Harvey, 'Personal Seals in Thirteenth-Century England', in *Church and Chronicle: Essays Presented to John Taylor* ed. I. Wood and G. A. Loud (1991), pp. 117–27.

[23] *Battle*, p. 214. R. Mortimer, 'The Charters of Henry II', *Anglo-Norman Studies* XII (1989), p. 122.

[24] *Statutes*, p. 210, Cf. ch. 7, n. 39 below.

[25] G. C. Homans, *English Villagers of the Thirteenth Century* (1941), p. 332.

THE CHRONOLOGY OF CHARTER MAKING

By the latter half of the thirteenth century, charters and documents were evidently a commonplace in England. Although in legal theory it was not essential to have a charter to validate a conveyance of property, Bracton shows that the ceremony of livery of seisin (which had traditionally given legality to the conveyance) had itself become dependent on documentary evidence. He explains that the donor may take the livery through an agent, provided the agent has a procuratorial letter or writ from the donor, together with his charter, so that it may be said that the agent 'had both a writ and a charter'. Bracton records this phrase, 'he hadde bothe writ and chartre', in English.[26] This is exceptional at such an early date (perhaps as early as 1230); it suggests that documentary evidence had become sufficiently familiar to enter into everyday speech. Similarly the word *fet* in Anglo-Norman or *factum* in Latin, translated as a 'deed', comes to have its modern meaning of a 'title-deed' or charter from the late thirteenth century.[27] A 'deed' was no longer the physical act of conveyance, symbolized by a turf from the land and livery of seisin; instead it was a sealed document which the donor made.

Giovanni di Bologna, a notary on Archbishop Pecham's staff from 1279, would not have agreed with the generalization that documents were commonly used in England in Edward I's reign. He wrote: 'Italians, like cautious men, want to have a public instrument for practically every contract they enter into; but the English are just the opposite, and an instrument is very rarely asked for unless it is essential.'[28] Compared with Italy, and Bologna in particular whose university specialized in legal and business training, it was doubtless true that the English produced fewer documents. But Giovanni exaggerates the discrepancy between Italian and English practice. By the statute of Merchants of 1285 every important town in England was obliged to have a clerk to enrol recognizances of debt in duplicate and write out bills of obligation authenticated by a royal seal.[29] The making of this statute might suggest that written contracts had not been the practice hitherto, but in fact this legislation amended existing rules rather than introducing something entirely new. Even if the notion that an Englishman's word is his bond was already in existence, it was an established rule of the common law at the time Giovanni was writing that the only type of enforceable contract was one expressed in a sealed document; the sealing and delivery of the parchment made the contract. As early as 1235 a plea was adjudged to be void because the plaintiff did not produce either a charter or a chirograph; moreover, the clerk recording this plea originally wrote that the covenant itself was void,

---

[26] Bracton, fo. 40, vol. ii, p. 125. Whether the livery was made by the donor or his agent, the ceremony still required the conveyance of an object symbolizing the gift; see ch. 8, n. 24 below.

[27] P & M ii p. 220, n. 1.

[28] *Summa* ed. L. Rockinger (1863), p. 604, trans. Cheney, *Notaries*, p. 135.

[29] *Statutes*, p. 99; T. F. T. Plucknett, *Legislation of Edward I* (1949), pp. 138–44.

though he subsequently corrected *convencio* to *loquela* (a plea).[30] Being a notary, Giovanni may have not considered a common law contract under seal to be a valid public instrument, because it required no notarial authentication. Self-interest or ignorance may have led him to discount the importance of charters and chirographs in England, where anyone possessing a seal was considered competent to authenticate his own written acts.

It is true nevertheless that compared with Italy, and with later centuries, England in 1300 was not universally document-minded. Yet the point had been reached by then where charters and written instructions penetrated to every village. Giovanni di Bologna was generalizing from the great cities of northern Italy and comparing their merchants with English ones. If the use of documents in the countryside in Italy and England were compared, English peasants, particularly in the open fenlands where the *Cartae Nativorum* were made, were probably as familiar with writing as their counterparts in the plains of Lombardy. Moreover, comparisons need to be made not only across Europe, but across the centuries. Viewed chronologically, England was remarkably document-minded in 1300 compared with the situation in 1100. In the twelfth and thirteenth centuries, as far as titles to property among laymen were concerned in particular, the balance in England had shifted from memory to written record.

To generalize, in the eleventh century laymen of all classes and many monks gave and received tenancies often without any kind of documentary evidence.[31] In the twelfth century magnates used documents occasionally and they and the gentry made gifts for religious houses by charter because the monks wanted this. In the thirteenth century laymen began to convey property to each other by charter; in the latter half of the century this practice extended below the gentry class to some peasants. Laymen used documents among themselves as a matter of habit only when they became sufficiently familiar with literate modes to trust them. By 1300 even serfs, the more prosperous ones at least, were familiar with documents. These generalizations do not necessitate everybody being able to read by 1300, still less to write. Clerks did the writing throughout the Middle Ages; most of the reading was likewise done by them, as the custom was to read out loud. By these means laymen of all classes, who remained technically illiterate, could participate in the use of documents and were encouraged to do business with charters (see plates I, V and VI).

To these generalizations the bookland of the Anglo-Saxon past is the most obvious exception. Bookland was exceptional by definition, as it created a privileged status in land by virtue of the grant of a 'landbook' or charter. It is difficult to judge how widespread bookland had been or to assess its effects on the growth of literacy among laymen. As with other questions about the uses of writing before the Norman Conquest (which are discussed in chapter 1), there is room for conjecture and therefore for controversy. For Maitland,

---

[30] *CuriaRR* xv, p. 345, no. 1365; P & M ii, pp. 219–20.
[31] J. C. Holt, 'Politics and Property in Early Medieval England', *Past and Present* lvii (1972), p. 38.

bookland was 'an alien, ecclesiastical institution, from which few inferences can be drawn', whereas Stenton argued that the granting of bookland to royal thegns shows that 'the conception of the chartered landholder who is not a churchman was well established before the end of the ninth century.'[32] Although bookland had the theoretical potential to create a class of chartered tenants, both clerical and lay, it seems to have declined in importance in the century preceding the Norman Conquest instead of increasing. This may have been because the landbook itself was too unauthentic a form of document ever to have served as an adequate foundation for literate business.[33] Whatever the cause of the decline of bookland, written titles to property make a new start after the Norman Conquest on the basis of the autographed diploma and the sealed writ (see plate 1).

Another exception to the generalization that in the eleventh century laymen gave tenancies without any kind of documentary evidence is a writ in the name of Geoffrey de Mandeville, which purports to date from the reign of William the Conqueror or William Rufus. In this writ Geoffrey orders Edric, his reeve, and the men of Waltham in Berkshire to take nothing from Hurley priory without a *documentum* from the prior.[34] (Hurley was a daughter house, which Geoffrey had endowed, of Westminster abbey.) At first sight such an order suggests that documentary authority was common on the estates of Norman barons, whose officials like Edric were accustomed to receiving letters. But this interpretation is almost certainly mistaken. Firstly, the word *documentum* most probably means an oral instruction rather than a writing. Furthermore, the writ itself may be a forgery of the mid-twelfth century, as Westminster abbey produced a revised version of Geoffrey's foundation charter for Hurley (together with other audacious forgeries) at that time.[35] Whether forged or not, Geoffrey's writ to Edric is not what it appears to be, namely a letter from one of William the Conqueror's barons to his reeve, as it was almost certainly written by and in the interests of Westminster abbey. The real purpose of such a document was not to convey information to Edric, but to serve as evidence of Hurley's exemption from the authority of Waltham.

One way of investigating how extensively documents were used at the beginning of the twelfth century is to examine the extant charter collections of magnates in Henry I's reign. Even at this exalted level of society few charters (including writs and less formal letters) seem to have been made, and the majority of these derived from religious houses. Although the numbers are too small to be significant as statistics, they do indicate a common pattern. Information about four magnates, whose charters and other letters have been collected by modern editors and can therefore be counted with confidence, is

---

[32] P & M ii, p. 87; cf. ibid. i, p. 60; F. M. Stenton, *The Latin Charters of the Anglo-Saxon Period* (1955), p. 63.

[33] As argued by Galbraith, 'Literacy', p. 217 and *Studies*, p. 32.

[34] J. Armitage Robinson, *Gilbert Crispin, Abbot of Westminster* (1911), p. 135, no. 7.

[35] P. Chaplais, 'The Original Charters of Herbert and Gervase Abbots of Westminster in *MM for Stenton*, pp. 97–8, 105–8.

given in table 1.[36] Robert, earl of Gloucester, was Henry I's bastard son whom 'philosophy educated in the liberal arts.'[37] The other three magnates were among the new men whom Henry had 'raised from the dust';[38] Miles was the constable, Nigel succeeded to the Mowbray honour in the north, and Roger was at first chancellor and then chief justiciar. All four men were therefore products of the educated court of Henry I and would have been unusually familiar with documents. Yet the table shows that they each issued in their own names less than one charter per year, if extant documents are taken as the criterion.

Table 1 Charters issued by magnates of Henry I

	Year of coming of age	Year of death	Number of active years	Number of charters	Charters per year
Miles, earl of Hereford	c.1121	1143	22	10	.45
Nigel d'Aubigny	c.1107	1129	22	17	.77
Robert earl of Gloucester	c.1113	1147	34	17	.50
Roger 'le Poer'	1101	1139	38	31	.82

Obviously more charters once existed; references have been found for example to another 26 grants made by Robert, earl of Gloucester.[39] If these are added to his 17 extant charters, Robert issued 1.27 charters per year on average. Charters, whether extant or lost, comprised only a small proportion of the total number of documents issued. Master David of London's correspondence shows how many ancillary documents might accompany a royal charter. Figures based on the output of Henry I's scribes (which are discussed more fully below) suggest that the number of extant charters might be multiplied by 100 in order to estimate the total output of documents. Assuming a similar pattern for magnates, which is probably overestimating their output, the number of documents issued each year by the four men tabulated would be 45 by Miles, 77 by Nigel, 50 by Robert, and 82 by Roger. On that assumption, the conclusion is that such men wrote one or two letters a week.

At first sight it is hard to believe that these magnates wrote so few letters. It is true that Roger was described as 'almost illiterate' by William of New-

---

[36] 'Earldom of Hereford Charters' ed. D. Walker, *Camden Miscellany*, Camden S. 4th series xxii (1964), pp. 13–16; *Mowbray Charters*, pp. 5–19; *Earldom of Gloucester Charters* ed. R. B. Patterson 1 (1973); E.J. Kealey, *Roger of Salisbury* (1972), pp. 228–71. The statistics have been compiled by me and are not the responsibility of the editors cited.

[37] *The Historia Regum Britanniae of Geoffrey of Monmouth* ed. A. Griscom (1929), pp. 219–20.

[38] Southern, *Medieval Humanism*, pp. 212ff.

[39] *Earldom of Gloucester Charters*, pp. 169–75.

burgh'[40] but he at least produced more documents than Robert, who was said by William of Malmesbury to have drunk such 'a full draught of the knowledge of letters' that he readily understood a papal bull.[41] Literacy concerned being learned in Latin and would not directly relate to an interest in issuing charters. Neither Roger's alleged lack of learning nor Robert's abundance of it necessarily invalidate the figures tabulated. The most reasonable inference to draw is that the figures are substantially accurate, as the average number of extant charters issued per year correlates quite well between the four magnates at 0.63.

   Some editors of twelfth-century charters have argued that magnates possessed organized writing offices or chanceries. But the variety of hands and drafting styles in extant charters suggests that documents were usually written by the beneficiaries themselves, if they were religious houses, or by whichever chaplain or scribe was available. Haphazard methods are understandable if only one or two letters had to be written on average each week. Even bishops in England did not develop organized writing offices until *c*. 1200. A generation or two earlier their letters, like those of other magnates, indicate a variety of scribal practices.[42] Great men certainly employed clerics in their households on a regular basis, but that had been so for centuries; household clergy performed a variety of religious and learned functions, among which writing had always been one, though it was not done on a specialized and regular basis until the last decade of the twelfth century. M. T. J. Webber has examined the handwriting of the charters of the earls of Chester up to 1237; this is the largest series of documents of a lay lord extant from this period in their original form (comprising over 100 charters). She concludes that 'even in the early thirteenth century, it is difficult to speak of anything as formal as a writing office, still less a chancery'.[43] (By 'chancery' as distinct from 'writing office', Webber means a secretariat, headed by a chancellor, using prescribed rules to obviate fraud.) She illustrates the assured cursive hand of Thomas, the earl of Chester's clerk in the 1190s, who is twice described as 'chancellor' in charters he witnesses.[44] But, as in the royal administration, the use of the title 'chancellor' precedes the organization of writers into a 'chancery' department by many decades. It is generally true that magnates, whether bishops or earls, followed the lead of the king's government in their writing procedures. This is not surprising, as the Norman conquerors – through Domesday Book and the Exchequer – had established the monarchy as the greatest user of writing in England. The administrative reforms of Hubert Walter (on either side of 1200) led to another proliferation of royal record-making, to which magnates like Ranulf III earl of Chester (1181–1232) responded.

[40] 'fere illitteratus', *Chronicles* ed. R. Howlett, RS LXXXII (1984), I, p. 36. For the meaning of *illitteratus* see ch. 7, pp. 229–30 below.

[41] *Historia Novella* ed. K. R. Potter (1955), p. 23.

[42] Cheney, *Chanceries*, pp. 55–6.

[43] 'The Scribes and Handwriting of the Original Charters', *The Earldom of Chester and its Charters* ed. A. T. Thacker (1991), p. 147.

[44] Ibid., plate ii and pp. 143–4; *The Charters of the Anglo-Norman Earls of Chester c. 1071–1237* ed. G. Barraclough, Record S. of Lancashire and Cheshire CXXVI (1988), nos 247, 289.

THE OUTPUT OF ROYAL DOCUMENTS

In twelfth-century England only the king possessed permanently organized writing facilities, under the ultimate supervision of the chancellor, and even these were somewhat makeshift and of recent origin. Only the Exchequer, created by Henry I, had a stable existence. 'What is the Exchequer?' asked Gerald of Wales. 'It is the seat of the public treasury in England, a sort of square table at London, where royal dues are collected and accounted for.'[45] Its receipts on inscribed wooden tallies and audited accounts on great rolls of parchment, the pipe rolls, absorbed most of the record-making energies of the government, as they required numerous ancillary documents like the writs Master David of London had to obtain to ensure that his pension was paid. As David's correspondence also illustrates, there had in practice to be more than one writing office, because the Exchequer remained static while the king perambulated. A clerk in charge of the *scriptorium* sat at the Exchequer table and was responsible for finding and supervising the scribes who wrote the chancellor's roll and the writs and summonses. 'These duties', commented Fitz Neal in the *Dialogue of the Exchequer*, 'need but few words to explain, but demand almost endless labour, as those know who have learned by experience.'[46]

How many scribes laboured in this way, and how many documents they wrote, are matters for conjecture. As far as personnel are concerned, the problem is that some scribes or clerks performed duties as chaplains in the royal household as well as acting as writers. Moreover, there were different grades of clerk; some simply wrote and copied, while others (the predecessors of the Chancery Masters) composed and dictated the letters. Nor were all the king's letters produced in his *scriptorium*: royal charters, just like seignorial ones, might be written by the beneficiaries' clerks (see plate III) or by a scribe casually employed. T. A. M. Bishop has demonstrated that four charters of Henry II for Lincoln, written in a professional cursive hand which palaeographers would once have called a distinctively Chancery style, were in fact written by a scribe of the bishop of Lincoln.[47] Of the 750 or so royal charters extant in originals from the twelfth century, only 450 can be shown to have been written by identifiably royal scribes.[48]

Consequently estimates vary of the size and nature of the writing facilities which later became known as the Chancery. One of Becket's biographers, William Fitz Stephen, described him when chancellor in 1158 as having 52 clerks in his service.[49] Bishop, on the other hand, has identified the hands of 16 royal scribes in the period 1155–8, but only four of these can be shown to have been regularly employed.[50] The discrepancy between these estimates is not as great as it appears. Fitz Stephen's figure of 52 included the clerks of Becket's

---

[45] Giraldus, III, p. 28.
[46] *Dialogus*, p. 26.
[47] T. A. M. Bishop, *Scriptores Regis* (1961), pp. 9, 14. See also ch. 4, p. 129 below.
[48] Ibid., p. 3, 11.
[49] *Becket Materials* III, p. 29.
[50] Bishop, *Scriptores Regis*, p. 30.

entourage and those who dealt with vacant benefices and other ecclesiastical business. Bishop's number, on the other hand, is confined to scribes (that is, it does not include all clerks) and to those whose handwriting is still extant. As Bishop points out, surviving royal charters cannot give a reliable estimate of the output of the Chancery, because 'it was not simply with the object of parting with the lands and rights of the crown that Henry II maintained a Chancery writing staff.'[51]

An increasing number of executive orders to bailiffs and sheriffs and so on, concerning daily administration, were put in writing. The volume of writs generated by the Exchequer alone was considerable. The earliest pipe roll, that for 1130, refers to the issue of nearly 300 *brevia* authorizing expenditure.[52] These *brevia* comprise only one class of letter; the figure of 300 should probably be multiplied by 10 or 20 to estimate the average total output per year of royal letters of all sorts (charters, precepts, warrants, requests for information and so on) in Henry I's reign. Suppose the multiple of 15 is taken (as the mean between 10 and 20), then $300 \times 15 = 4,500$ letters produced each year. Bishop estimates that Henry I employed at least four scribes in *c*.1130. In that case each scribe wrote an average of 1,125 letters a year, or three letters each day. (J. E. Sayers reaches the same estimate for the output of the papal chancery: a rate of three letters per scribe per day.)[53] Three letters a day may not seem the 'almost endless labour' which Fitz Neal described later in the century, but three is an average for every day of the year and each letter had to be free from errors. The average number of charters extant (in originals or copies) per year from Henry I's reign is 41.[54] That figure may therefore need to be multiplied by 100 or more to appreciate the total output of royal letters each year. In other words, about 1 per cent of the original output has survived. A significant point is that the king's output of documents is ten, or even twenty, times as great as that of any of his magnates.

It must be emphasised that the estimates in the preceding paragraph are largely conjectural. Their purpose is to provide a context for specific numbers concerning the output of royal documents, which are set out in figure 1 and in table 2. Figure 1 (at p. 60 below) compares the number of letters extant per year of reign (in originals or copies, but excluding forgeries as far as possible) issued by the kings of England and France and the popes between the time of the Norman Conquest and the reign of Henry II. Table 2 (opposite) shows the average weekly consumption of sealing wax by Henry III's Chancery over nearly half a century between 1226 and 1271; it will be argued that the amount of wax used correlates with the number of letters sealed. Both Figure 1 and the table therefore indicate a marked and relatively steady increase in the number of documents issued over the years. The numbers rise 'in a sort of geometrical progression',[55] doubling every two or three decades: for the

---

[51] Ibid., p. 32.

[52] Ibid., p. 32.

[53] *Papal Government and England during the Pontificate of Honorius III* (1984), p. 51.

[54] The number is based on *RRA-N* as computed by A. Murray, 'Pope Gregory VII and his Letters', *Traditio* xxii (1966), p. 166, n. 46.

[55] Galbraith, *Studies*, p. 57.

reign of William Rufus an average of 15 documents per year are extant; for Henry I 41; for Henry II about 115. In the thirteenth century the Chancery's consumption of wax increased even faster, as the numbers in table 2 (which are averaged and summarized from the appendix at pp. 78–80 below) indicate.

Table 2 Sealing wax used by the Chancery

Approximately 5-year intervals	*Amount of wax per week (in lb)*
1226–30	3.63
1230–3	4.03
1237–40	4.78
1242–5	7.58
1245–6	8.56
1250–4	7.86
1255–60	13.02
1260–5	20.31
1265–71	31.90

Although the numbers in both Figure 1 and the table contain anomalies and uncertainties and are not acceptable as true statistics, at the level of generalization over decades and centuries they demonstrate how the mass of documents increased. No statistics from the twelfth and thirteenth centuries can be expected to do much more than indicate general trends.

Figure 1 makes no claim to use hitherto unnoticed information, as it is based on printed lists and summaries.[56] The numbers available are sparse and imprecise, because royal documents in this period do not usually specify the year in which they were made. The number of documents issued by each ruler per year has therefore been averaged over the whole of his reign; in the case of the papacy only pontificates of eight years or more have been included. The number of documents extant are not of course the same as the total number produced; it has already been suggested that those extant for England might be multiplied by 100 in order to estimate the number which once existed. It is known similarly that Pope Alexander III must have issued many more letters than survive.[57] The popes and the kings of France are included in Figure 1

[56] For England, from William I to Stephen, the numbers are those computed by A. Murray (n. 54 above); for Henry II's reign the estimate of a total of 3,500–4,500 originals and copies has been taken at the mean of 4,000 to give an annual average of 115; this estimate derives from Bishop, *Scriptores Regis*, p. 3, and R. Mortimer, 'The Charters of Henry II', *Anglo-Norman Studies* XII (1989), pp. 119–20. For France, the totals (including mentions of *acta* as well as extant copies) are those of R. Fawtier, *The Capetian Kings of France* trans. L. Butler and R. J. Adam (1962), p. 8. Concerning missing French *acta*, see M. Nortier in *La France de Philippe Auguste*, ed. R. H. Bautier (1982), pp. 430–3. For the papacy, the numbers are based on P. Jaffé, *Regesta Pontificum Romanorum* (1882); cf. R. W. Southern, *Western Society and the Church in the Middle Ages* (1970), p. 109 and A. Murray (n. 54 above).

[57] Duggan, *Decretals*, pp. 120–1, 144–5.

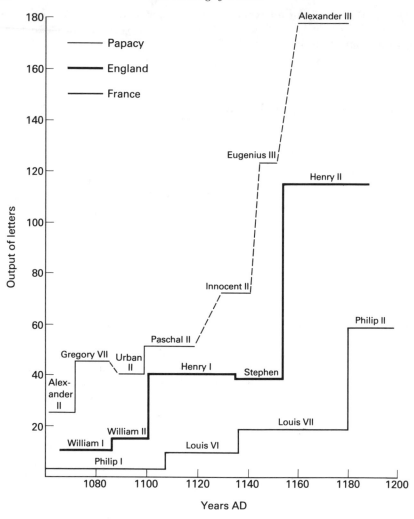

Figure 1 Number of letters extant per year of reign

for comparison and in order to show that the increasing use of documents was a general trend in western Europe. Two other increases in the period 1060–1180 also need to be taken into consideration: the population of western Europe may have doubled and the number of monastic houses multiplied at least tenfold. As many, perhaps most, royal and papal letters concerned monasteries and were preserved by them, monastic expansion may be the greatest single cause of the increasing number of documents up to *c*.1200.

In thirteenth-century Europe too the number of documents continued to increase fast. The average number of letters extant per year for the pontificate of Innocent III (1198–1215) is 303, whereas for Innocent IV (1243–54) it is 730. By the end of the century Boniface VIII (1294–1303) is estimated to have issued 50,000 letters a year.[58] Similarly more than 15,000 letters are known of Philip the Fair of France (1285–1314), compared with the 2,000 of Philip Augustus (1180–1223).[59] Registration of copies of letters by the senders means that comparisons of numbers between the twelfth century and the thirteenth are not very significant, however, as more record survives of the dispatch of letters from *c.*1200 onwards by the rulers of England, France and the papacy. On the other hand, registers are no measure of an office's total output because only selected letters were registered. In the case of the papacy in the thirteenth century, J. E. Sayers estimates that only about a quarter of all letters were registered.[60] The primary purpose of registration was to retain precedents for future reference, not to keep a record for historians of all letters sent out.

Table 2 (and the appendix pp. 78–80 below), showing the amount of sealing wax used by Henry III's Chancery, is intended to be a surer way of measuring the output of documents in the thirteenth century than counting extant letters. Although many letters were registered in the Chancery rolls from John's reign onwards, numerous routine documents (common law writs are the best example) were not enrolled. The weight of wax used should therefore give a better indication of the total volume of documents than either the Chancery rolls or extant writs and charters. It must be emphasized, however, that the figures concern the Chancery only; wax used by the Exchequer was accounted for separately and only its cost, and not its weight, was recorded. Because the Chancery had to account to the Exchequer, its records specify the weight used as well as the cost. This careful accounting has left the historian with a constant measure to apply over the years, whereas the cost alone is insignificant because of fluctuations. It is true that different quantities of wax were used for sealing various types of document (for instance, charters were authenticated by the great seal, whereas some letters close bore the privy seal), but there is no reason to think that on average either more or less wax was used per document in the 1220s than in the 1260s.

It is not possible, however, to enumerate how many documents were sealed with each pound of wax, mainly because it cannot be established whether common law writs were sealed with the whole great seal or only a portion of it. Although weight cannot be converted into a specific number of parchments, it is reasonable to assume that a rise in the weight of wax indicates a commensurate increase in the sum total of documents issued. Despite not being able to quantify the number of parchments, these figures have the advantage over all others that they were compiled at the time by an official, the keeper of the hanaper. Some allowance must be made for the honesty or efficiency of the official concerned, but at least the historian does not have to estimate an indefinite number of lost or unrecorded documents.

[58] R. Fawtier's estimate, reported by C. H. Lawrence in *History* LVIII (1973), p. 429, reviewing W. Ullmann, *A Short History of the Papacy.*
[59] Fawtier, *The Capetian Kings*, p. 9, n. 2; J. W. Baldwin, *The Government of Philip Augustus* (1986), p. 403, table 13.
[60] *Papal Government and England* (1984), p. 67.

The numbers derive from the liberate rolls which record authorizations for payments from the treasury, in this case to the spigurnels (sealers) or serjeants of the chapel royal 'for sealing the king's writs'. The average weight of wax used per week has been calculated throughout by dividing the weights recorded in the rolls by the number of whole weeks concerned. The years 1226–71 have been selected because the liberate rolls for these years are published, which makes it possible to verify the data. Anomalies in the figures suggest that they are generally accurate. The relatively low weights for June 1253 – February 1254 and for July 1262 – November 1262 may be accounted for by Henry III's absence in France at about these times. Conversely the exceptionally high weight of 31.69 lb per week for the period from October 1261 to January 1262 coincides with the apogee of Henry III's reassertion of power over the barons in the struggle with Simon de Montfort. More wax may have been required to summon the king's followers, issue safe-conducts and pardons, confirm titles to property, and so on. An anomaly which cannot be readily explained, however, is the low figure of 8.15 lb per week for the first half of 1259, as this was the period of legislative and reforming activity by the barons; perhaps ordinary government business was curtailed by reform, or the record may be incomplete in this instance.

DOCUMENTS AND BUREAUCRACY

By and large, both the graph of letters extant and the table of wax used suggest that the number of documents increased progressively, only being temporarily affected by political crises. In the graph the civil war of Stephen's reign shows a small recession, yet the numbers of letters are more than double those of William Rufus's time. Similarly the volume of wax used in Henry III's Chancery does not usually correlate with the frequent political crises in the years concerned, despite the exceptions discussed in the preceding paragraph. The weight of wax used, 17.1 lb per week, in the months of de Montfort's dominance between the battles of Lewes (May 1264) and Evesham (August 1265), is similar to the 16.87 lb used per week in the last months of Henry's personal rule before the parliament at Oxford in June 1258. Both king and barons depended on documents in order to assert their authority.

The increasing mass of royal documents tended to enlarge and stratify the bureaucracy which produced them. The origin and early development of English government departments has been described by numerous constitutional and administrative historians over the last century and does not require general repetition here. There was obviously a close connection between the growth in numbers of documents and of the functionaries who made them. This is best illustrated by a story, told by Fitz Neal in the *Dialogue of the Exchequer*, which can be taken to stand as typical. Fitz Neal describes how Henry II employed Master Thomas Brown, who had been the secretary of Roger II of Sicily, to keep a watching brief in the king's interests over the administration. In this capacity Brown made a roll 'of the laws of the realm and the secrets of the king'.[61] To make this roll Brown needed a scribe to sit at the Exchequer table. But his scribe could not be fitted on to the writers' bench at the Exchequer because it was already occupied (from right to left) by the treasurer, the treasurer's scribe (who wrote the pipe roll), the chancellor's scribe (who copied from the treasurer's scribe and made the chancellor's roll), the chancellor's clerk (who supervised the chancellor's scribe) and the clerk of the constabulary.[62] Brown's scribe was therefore given a place higher up, where he could make his copy over the treasurer's scribe's shoulder. As the pupil in the *Dialogue* comments, the scribe must have been 'lynx-eyed to avoid mistakes'.

This story, together with the numbers cited in Figure 1 and table 2, leave the impression that the proliferation of documents and functionaries was inexorable and almost subject to some mathematical law. Nevertheless there are significant exceptions to the rule that documents steadily multiplied. Even Fitz Neal's story about Thomas Brown's scribe can be interpreted in a contrary sense. After Brown's death or retiral in *c.*1180 the copy of the pipe roll which he had kept was discontinued, though his scribe may have stayed at the Exchequer as the earliest king's remembrancer.

A clearer instance of the bureaucracy being first enlarged and then curtailed appears in Fitz Neal's remarks about another of Henry II's confidants, Richard of Ilchester, archdeacon of Poitiers, who sat on another side of the Exchequer table. Richard's duties were to supervise the making of the rolls and to stop the treasurer from falling asleep.[63] As we have seen, Master David of London had hoped to expedite his business by getting a letter addressed to him. Richard introduced a system of keeping a copy of every summons sent to a sheriff in order to prevent him from altering it: 'so, when the sheriff was sitting at his account and the chancellor's clerk was reading the summons, the archdeacon's clerk, with his eye on the copy, watched him to see that he made no mistake.'[64] By this means a check was kept on both the chancellor's clerk and the sheriff. 'But', Fitz Neal continues, 'as time went on, and the number of debtors enormously increased, so that a whole skin of parchment was scarcely long enough for a single summons, the number of names and the labour involved proved overpowering.' The roll of summonses was therefore abolished. As Fitz Neal points out, it had not really been necessary in the first place, as all the debts summoned were already recorded on the pipe roll. This anecdote illustrates the speed at which record-making increased: the lists of debtors had become enormous within a decade or so; but is also shows that the advance of bureaucracy could, occasionally at least, be stopped. The formation of the royal bureaucracy was thus a complex process of experiment and makeshift; although the net result, when averaged over decades, was a constant increase in the production of documents.

[61] *Dialogus*, p. 35.
[62] Ibid., p. 18 and diagram of the seating arrangements at p. xlii.
[63] Ibid., p. 27.
[64] Ibid., pp. 74–5.

A significant point in the formation of the bureaucracy was Henry II's Inquest of Sheriffs in 1170. This was so called from its first clause, which inquired into financial peculation by sheriffs. However, the Inquest extended beyond these royal officers:

> Likewise inquiry is to be made concerning the archbishops, bishops, abbots, earls, barons, vavasors, knights, citizens, burgesses and their stewards and ministers as to what and how much they have received throughout their lands from every one of their hundreds, every one of their villages and every one of their men – whether by judicial process or without judgement – and they are to write down individually all these exactions and their causes and occasions.[65]

In the detail demanded, the Inquest was as massive an undertaking as the Domesday survey of 1086. As steps towards bureaucracy, two of its requirements stand out. Firstly, every responsible person (ranging from the two archbishops down to knights, citizens and burgesses) is to answer for 'every one of their men' – *de singulis hominibus suis*. Secondly, all those with responsibility are to write down their findings 'individually' – *scribant separatim*. The requirement to put the details in writing is repeated in a number of the Inquest's clauses: 'what they ascertain thereon, they are to write down carefully' – *quid inde inquisierunt, scribant diligenter* (clause 8); 'and this likewise is to be written down' (clause 6); 'and the whole thing is to be written down' – *hoc totum scribatur* (clause 12).[66]

Did the drafters of the Inquest of Sheriffs overestimate the writing abilities of the 'knights, citizens and burgesses and their stewards and ministers'? Were ink and parchment, not to mention scribes, available 'throughout their lands'? Would magnates be willing to put on record everything that they had received, whether legally or illegally? The Inquest was held just nine months before the killing of Thomas Becket, who had refused in 1163 to allow a payment due to the sheriff of Kent to be inscribed in the king's records.[67] Did Becket's officials in 1170 comply with the Inquest? Unlike the volumes of Domesday Book, no replies to the Inquest are extant in the form of fair copies written up in books or rolls. Nevertheless a few replies have come to light in the Public Record Office and they suggest that more must once have existed. From Castle Rising in Norfolk, for example, 39 burgesses are named, together with the sums that each of them has rendered their lord, the earl of Arundel: 'they gave all these sums to the earl of their own good will to redeem his land from the Jews; they gave them to the steward, Nicholas.'[68] From Fakenham in Suffolk, it was answered that the bailiff, Walter of Sapiston, had paid 40 shillings compensation to his lord, Robert de Valognes, for neglecting his hay

---

[65] Stubbs, *Charters*, p. 176, clause 3.
[66] Ibid., pp. 176–7.
[67] *Becket Materials* II, p. 374.
[68] *The Red Book of the Exchequer* RS vol. ii (1896), Appendix A, p. cclxviii, no. 2; D. C. Douglas and G. W. Greenaway, *English Historical Documents 1042–1189*, 2nd ed (1981), no. 49, pp. 473–4.

crop; Hugh Painter, the swineherd, had paid 5 shillings likewise for mismanagement, as had Gilbert Nep, the bee keeper.[69]

These replies are written in a variety of hands, in Latin, on separate pieces of parchment. They are presumably chance survivals of the individual writings sent in by the officials of the earl of Arundel and Robert de Valognes. One reply has been discovered which is written in French, the earliest piece of business French to survive in England.[70] The instructions for the Inquest had been issued in Latin and this was presumably the proper language in which to reply; the French document was perhaps intended as a draft which was sent in by mistake. None of the replies are in English, which is not surprising, as it was not a language of legal record at this time. Local people presumably made their oral replies in English and these were then converted into Latin documents, sometimes perhaps through French, by the clerks. The extant replies do not suggest that there was any shortage of writers capable of doing this. At Fakenham the earl of Arundel had a clerk as his 'minister' named Godfrey. Similarly in the bishop of Ely's hundred of Milford 'Achard the bailiff and Payn the priest, during the bishop's illness, increased the rent from £8 so that the men are so heavily burdened that, unless it is amended, they will all be paupers.'[71] Payn the priest had presumably done the writing here for Achard, though he is unlikely to have been the writer up of this complaint against himself.

The existence of clerks in the medieval countryside should cause no surprise; the mistake is to assume that the rural population was cut off from literate culture. The Ely Farming Memoranda, written in Old English early in the eleventh century, suggest that lists and informal notes were commonly made by estate managers, who had probably been doing this for centuries.[72] In the Inquest of 1170 Henry II was perhaps trying, like William the Conqueror in the Domesday survey, to channel these long-standing habits of seignorial record-making to the crown's advantage. The replies to the Inquest of Sheriffs have been cited at some length in order to show the kind of detail about individuals that Henry II's government was demanding and receiving. W. L. Warren has suggested that the Norman conquerors developed the practice of reaching down, through record-making, to a mass of named individuals in the localities because they neither understood nor trusted the Anglo-Saxon system of delegated jurisdiction. Anglo-Saxon kings had depended on bishops' and abbots' scribes in the countryside, whereas Henry I and his successors built up a centralized bureaucracy of royal clerks at Westminster.

> There is a break in continuity not at the Conquest itself, nor on the morrow of it, but within fifty years of it. The break occurred not because

[69] *The Red Book*, no. 46; Douglas and Greenaway, p. 478.

[70] H. Suggett, 'An Anglo-Norman Return to the Inquest of Sheriffs' *BJRL* xxvii (1942), pp. 179–81. Cf. p. 219, n. 86 below.

[71] *The Red Book*, no. 50; Douglas and Greenaway, p. 479.

[72] *The Golden Age of Anglo-Saxon Art*, ed. J. Backhouse, D. H. Turner and L. Webster (1984), pp. 147–8, exhibit no. 150.

the Normans did not wish to preserve the Anglo-Saxon inheritance but because they did not know how to. It may have been an involuntary breach, but it was nonetheless fundamental because the consequence was a transition from a sophisticated form of non-modern state, managed through social mechanisms, to a crude form of modern state organized through administrative institutions.[73]

This is the break that brought about Henry I's Exchequer system. Through the pipe rolls and other Exchequer records, the 'royal government learned that it was possible to deal with individuals instead of simply with communities', as the Anglo-Saxons had done.[74] The names of debtors were entered on the rolls and carried forward from year to year. Warren's description of a 'state organized through administrative institutions' is precisely what Fitz Neal describes in the *Dialogue of the Exchequer*, with its elaborate rules and hierarchy of officials.

The structure of the Exchequer accords too with Max Weber's characterization of the 'pure type' of bureaucratic state, in which 'administrative acts, decisions and rules are formulated and recorded in writing, even in cases where oral discussion is the rule or is even mandatory. The combination of written documents and a continuous organization of official functions constitutes the *bureau* which is the central focus of all types of modern corporate action.'[75] In Weber's terms, Warren is right to describe the Norman form of government as 'modern' though crude, by contrast with the Anglo-Saxon form which had been 'non-modern' though sophisticated within its own terms.[76] Warren's hypothesis here is that the Anglo-Saxon kingdom was managed through elaborate customary mechanisms, which did not depend on masses of record-keeping. In Weber's terms, Anglo-Saxon government was 'traditional' in form: 'the person or persons exercising authority are designated according to traditionally transmitted rules . . . the organized group exercising authority is, in the simplest case, primarily based on relations of personal loyalty, cultivated through a common process of education.'[77] In Anglo-Saxon England King Alfred had epitomized these 'traditional' values.

[73] W. L. Warren, 'The Myth of Norman Administrative Efficiency', *TRHS* 5th series xxxiv (1984), p. 132.

[74] Ibid. p. 131.

[75] *The Theory of Social and Economic Organization* ed. A. M. Henderson and T. Parsons (1947), Bk. iii, ch. ii, section 3, p. 332.

[76] Late Anglo-Saxon government is analysed by J. Campbell, 'Some Agents and Agencies of the Late Anglo-Saxon State' in *Domesday Studies* ed. J. C. Holt (1987), pp. 201–18, and 'Was it Infancy in England?' in *England and her Neighbours: Essays in Honours of P. Chaplais* ed. M. Jones and M. Vale (1989), pp. 1–17. See also: S. Keynes, 'Royal Government and the Written Word in Late Anglo-Saxon England' in *The Uses of Literacy in Early Medieval Europe* ed. R. McKitterick (1990), pp. 226–57; H. R. Loyn, *The Governance of Anglo-Saxon England* (1984); P. Stafford, *Unification and Conquest: A Political and Social History of England in the Tenth and Eleventh Centuries* (1989).

[77] Weber, *The Theory*, Bk. iii, ch. iii, section 6, p. 341.

Whereas King Alfred had typically settled disputes by informal personal negotiation, as in the frequently cited case of Helmstan (when the king gave his ruling while standing in his 'bower' washing his hands),[78] Henry II used a system of standardized writs to automate and depersonalize the legal process. 'Without being aware of it, Henry had achieved what Weber describes as "the routinization of charisma". The majestic power of the king, symbolized by his seal showing him seated on his throne, was disseminated throughout the kingdom in thousands of royal writs containing his orders.'[79] Henry's regal authority (his 'charisma' in Weber's terms) was depersonalized ('routinized') by means of the Chancery clerks and the operator of the great seal-press (the king's 'spigurnel'), who mass-produced royal writs in common forms for sale to plaintiffs. Earlier English kings, at least from Alfred onwards, had been familiar with seals and writs, and perhaps issued them in considerable numbers. The difference in Henry II's reign is in the scale and precision of Chancery production. The forms of the writs were standardized so that the clerks could copy them out without further authorization or drafting. The king's signing of each writ was entirely automated through the seal-press, which looked like – and was the precursor of – the printing-press. By using engraved plates for the common form of each writ, the press made it possible to automate the writing process as well as the sealing; but this was not done until the eighteenth century. Nevertheless, by increasing the number of clerks, Henry II's Chancery was capable of producing by hand hundreds of writs per week.

The fundamental and elementary idea was that of a core, or register, of writs in common forms which could be repeated in accordance with demand. The most successful ones in Henry II's reign were the writs of 'novel disseisin' and 'mort d'ancestor', which automatically arranged for jury verdicts to be given in the localities before the king's justices. The lawbook ascribed to the justiciar Glanvill (composed in the 1180s) is structured around the common forms of the new writs and explains how each of them is to be used.[80] The structure of Glanvill's book underlines Weber's observation that 'bureaucratic administration means fundamentally the exercise of control on the basis of knowledge. This consists on the one hand in technical knowledge which, by itself, is sufficient to ensure it a position of extraordinary power. But in addition to this, bureaucratic organizations, or the holders of power who make use of them, have the tendency to increase their power still further by the knowledge growing out of experience in the service.'[81] Like the *Dialogue of the Exchequer*, with which it is contemporary, Glanvill's work serves as an insider's handbook for the royal bureaucracy.

---

[78] D. Whitelock, *English Historical Documents 500–1042*, 2nd edn (1979), no. 102, p. 545. In general see S. Keynes and M. Lapidge, *Alfred the Great* (1983).

[79] M. T. Clanchy, *England and its Rulers 1066–1272* (1983), p. 156; Weber, *The Theory*, Bk. iii, ch. v, pp. 363–73.

[80] Glanvill, ed. G. D. G. Hall (1965); J. Biancalana, 'For Want of Justice: Legal Reforms of Henry II', *Columbia Law Review*, lxvii (1988), pp. 433–536.

[81] Weber, *The Theory*, Bk. iii, ch. i, section 5, p. 339.

Henry II cannot have known that his court was devising bureaucratic procedures which would remain in place for six and a half centuries; procedure by 'novel disseisin' and 'mort d'ancestor' was abolished in 1832, along with the unreformed House of Commons. It is not possible to establish precisely how far Henry II was responsible for the innovations done in his name. The likelihood is that he did have some personal part in them, as Walter Map (who was a royal justice) describes him as the 'subtle inventor of uncustomary and hidden judicial process', concerned in his literacy with 'utility' (*utiliatatem*).[82] The *Dialogue of the Exchequer* similarly claims to address utility. 'You are to write', says its prologue, 'not subtleties but useful things' (*Tu scribe non subtilia sed utilia*).[83] The subtleties referred to here are the academic books of Plato and Aristotle. Henry II, on the other hand, in Walter Map's description at least, concerned himself with managerial subtleties: those uncustomary and hidden devices, which proved to be the foundation of bureaucracy in the English common law down to the nineteenth century.

THE WORK OF HUBERT WALTER

1190–1210

From the point of view of posterity – by looking, that is, at documents which have survived – the most decisive increase in production occurred within a decade or so on either side of 1200. The earliest extant series of plea rolls, feet of fines, and Chancery enrolments of outgoing letters begin at this time. These are the years in which Archbishop Hubert Walter held office, first as chief justiciar (1193–8) of Richard I and then as chancellor (1199–1205) of King John. Whether Hubert invented all these types of record, or whether some had existed earlier but did not survive, are matters for conjecture. An explicit instance of deliberate record-making by Hubert is the earliest tripartite final concord, dated 15 July 1195. The document is endorsed:

> This is the first chirograph that was made in the king's court in the form
> of three chirographs, according to the command of his lordship of
> Canterbury [Hubert Walter] and other barons of the king, to the end
> that by this form a record can be made to be passed to the treasurer to
> put in the treasury.[84]

The reference to Hubert's responsibility for the innovation is reinforced by his brother, Theobald, being the plaintiff whom this chirograph concerns. The purpose of the third copy (which was the novelty), or 'foot of the fine', is explicitly stated to be 'to the end that by this form (*per illam formam*) a record' might be deposited in the treasury. Keeping a third copy was not entirely novel, however, as the practice had Anglo-Saxon precedents and within living

[82] Walter Map, Bk. v, ch. 6, p. 475. In general see P. Brand, 'Henry II and the Creation of the English Common Law', *Haskins Society Journal* II (1990) pp. 197–222.
[83] *Dialogus* p. 5; see p. 73 below.
[84] *Feet of Fines: Henry II and Richard I*, PRS XVII (1894), p. 21; P & M II pp. 97–100; C. R. Cheney, *Hubert Walter* (1967), p. 96.

memory Henry II had personally insisted in 1164 that a third copy of the chirograph recording the controversial Constitutions of Clarendon should be put 'in the royal archives'.[85]

Although there were precedents for Hubert Walter's action, the importance of the feet of fines should not be underestimated. For the first time, a form of record had been deliberately inaugurated as a continuing series for archival purposes. Furthermore the feet of fines gave private individuals the opportunity to have transactions kept on permanent record in the royal treasury. What had in the past been exceptional practice now became the rule; that is the principle underlying many of Hubert's bureaucratic reforms. Although the king's government already made regular records for its own purposes, it had not normally extended its archival facilities to private individuals. A few non-royal conveyances of property were enrolled in the pipe rolls and the *Cartae Antiquae* before 1195; but, unlike the feet of fines, this practice was neither systematic nor regular.[86] The use of feet of fines was of course confined to the more prosperous landowners, who were able to pay the fees and take the risks of litigating in the king's court. Hubert Walter could not, and probably did not intend to, benefit everybody. Nevertheless the extent to which these documents became widespread among landowners within a few years is indicated by a concord made at Westminster on 29 October 1198 between William de Bruce of Annandale and Adam of Carlisle concerning eight ploughgates in Lockerbie.[87] Lockerbie was (and is) in Scotland, though the fine was filed with those from Northumberland.

The success of the feet of fines archive may have been the cause which encouraged the government to enrol copies of royal letters during Hubert Walter's chancellorship. These rolls form three main series – the charter, close and patent rolls, extant from the first, second, and third years of John's reign respectively.[88] Like the feet of fines, the Chancery rolls benefited private individuals, who paid fees to have their royal grants recorded in them.[89] Had such rolls existed in Henry II's time, for example, Master David of London would have been able to have the various royal letters he obtained recorded there. These rolls also served the government as an official register. In 1201 (the second year of the extant charter rolls) Jocelin of Brakelond records that King John ordered an inquiry to be made 'through his register about what sort of charter' he had given the monks of Ely because the monks of Bury disputed its terms.[90] The contentious passage was duly found, as it still can be in the charter rolls, and letters protecting Bury were issued. The immediate consequence of this, however, was an armed raid by Bury on Ely and not a peaceful settlement.[91] Similarly, many years later, Henry III wrote to Pope

---

[85] 'in regum archivis', *Becket Materials* III p. 288 (Herbert of Bosham, Bk III, ch. 29).

[86] *Cartae Antiquae* ed. L. Landon, PRS new series XVII (1939), p. xv.

[87] *Feet of Fines 10 Richard I*, PRS XXIV (1900), pp. 53–4; G. W. S. Barrow, *The Kingdom of the Scots* (1973), p. 114.

[88] Chaplais, *Docs*, p. 4, n. 1.

[89] H. G. Richardson, *Memoranda Roll 1 John*, PRS XXI (1943) pp. xxxv–li, argues that collection of fees was the sole purpose of instituting enrolments.

[90] 'per registrum suum cuiusmodo cartam', Jocelin, p. 133, cf. pp. 157–60.

[91] *Rotuli Chartarum*, RC (1837), p. 91; Jocelin, pp. 133–4.

Gregory X in 1272 assuring him that some letters patent, which the prior of Christ Church Canterbury was exhibiting in a lawsuit at the Roman *curia*, were a forgery because 'no such letters can issue from our court unless they have first been registered [and] we have had our register searched about this case with the utmost care and diligence, and nothing whatsoever is to be found in it about the aforesaid letters.'[92] In fact the king was mistaken, as these letters had been enrolled in the patent rolls in November 1265.[93] It was easier to make records than to use them efficiently.

The twelfth century had been a great period of making documents, the thirteenth was the century of keeping them. From the viewpoint of the historian today, the formation of an archive seems an obvious and essential step, once documents were produced in any quantity. To medieval governments, however, neither the urgency nor the usefulness of archives would have appeared as compelling. Copying outgoing letters on to rolls was an immense labour, as Fitz Neal's anecdote about the fate of Richard of Ilchester's attempt to enrol the Exchequer summonses illustrates. Hubert Walter was not necessarily the inventor of the principle of enrolling outgoing charters or of filing incoming documents (returned writs, feet or fines and so on) on leather thongs, but he did create the principles of organization which made continuous royal archives possible. The French royal archive of the letters which it received begins in 1194, with the retention of a treaty between Philip Augustus and the future King John of England.[94] There may be more than coincidence in the development of royal archives in England and France in the same decade, as the two kingdoms were in almost daily contact because of the struggle between the Angevin and Capetian monarchies.

It would be rash to assume that such archives brought a return of information to the government which balanced the worry and expense of making them. Like Domesday Book, the Chancery and judicial rolls and writ files benefited remote posterity rather than contemporaries, since they provide minutely detailed information about the countryside and people of England as viewed by the king's government. The making of such records is an indicator of the efficiency of the government rather than its cause. They are a notable step in the transition from memory to written record because documents created more documents in their own image, not because they made for more effective government in themselves. The two examples cited in the preceding paragraph, of King John consulting his 'register' in 1201 and Henry III in 1272, suggest that the information provided, even when it was correct, did not help to keep the peace. The royal archives constituted a vast potential source of information, which could not be thoroughly consulted in the medieval period itself. Historians today are better equipped to search the rolls than the king's clerks were in the thirteenth century.

The creation of these central government archives (still extant in the Public Record Office) during Hubert Walter's years of office has been frequently described and has therefore been summarily treated here. Just as important in

---

[92] *Diplomatic Documents* ed. P. Chaplais, HMSO (1964), p. 304, no. 434.

[93] *CPatR* 1258–66, pp. 496–7.

[94] J. W. Baldwin, *The Government of Philip Augustus* (1986), p. 410.

the proliferation of documents at the time was Hubert's effect on local government, although very few local records survive from this early period. Within his first year of office as chief justiciar, in the instructions for the justices' visitation in September 1194, he instituted coroners in each county including a clerk; from this order stemmed the coroners' rolls.[95] From 1202 and 1203 comes the earliest evidence of the coroner's rolls being used to check oral testimony in county courts. In the Lincolnshire justices' visitation of 1202 the county was fined £200 because their oral 'record' differed from that of the coroners' rolls.[96] Likewise in Staffordshire in 1203 the county court and the coroners 'recorded' that Simon Pring had not been outlawed, whereas the rolls of the coroners (as distinct from their persons) and of the sheriff showed that he had. In the judgement against the county court and the coroners, preference was accorded to the written records.[97]

Hubert Walter's instructions for the justices' visitation in September 1194 also provided the first public local archives and official writers. The purpose of this legislation was to regulate loans made by the Jews.[98] Neither money-lenders' bonds nor royal intervention in Jewish business were novelties in themselves; what was new was the establishment of archives and supervised writing facilities on a regular basis. It was ruled that *all* debts and pledges of the Jews were to be put in writing: loans were to be made in designated places only, where two scribes (financed by fees) would be provided and supervised by a clerk appointed by the king's commissioners, William of Sainte-Mère-Eglise and William of Chimillé. The documents recording the loans were to be written in the form of bipartite chirographs: one part would be kept by the Jews, and the other deposited in a communal archive (*in arca communi*) or public chest, with three sealed locks, whose keys were kept by the Jews, the Christians and the royal commissioners respectively. As if this were not sufficient security, the commissioners' clerk was also to keep in a roll up-to-date transcripts of all the chirographs in the chest; furthermore a roll of receipts of money by the Jews was to be kept in triplicate. These regulations were not all immediately enforced, but within two decades 17 towns (mainly county towns) had archives of this sort.[99]

By these means the principles of producing authenticated documents, retaining them in archives and transcribing copies on to rolls for ready reference spread from the royal Chancery and Exchequer to provincial centres. It may not be a coincidence that the earliest extant borough records, the Leicester guild rolls of 1196, survive from this period, although Leicester itself was not a Jewish centre.[100] The king's government was not in this

---

[95] Stubbs, *Charters*, p. 254, no. 20. Some written records of crown pleas had been made before 1194, R. F. Hunnisett, 'The Origins of the Office of Coroner', *TRHS* 5th series VIII (1958), p. 97, n. 4

[96] *SPC*, p. 16, no. 38.

[97] Ibid., p. 28, no. 62.

[98] Stubbs, *Charters*, p. 256.

[99] Richardson, *Jewry*, pp. 14–19.

[100] The earliest borough records are listed by G. H. Martin in *TRHS* 5th series XIII (1963), p. 129.

instance primarily concerned with promoting record-making as such, but with taxing the Jews and their transactions as thoroughly as possible. Taxation had been the king's main motive for making records, certainly since the institution of the Exchequer at the beginning of the twelfth century and probably since Domesday Book.

The same principles, of making multiple records in the localities for taxation purposes, received their greatest extension in the plans for the carucage of 1198, which was required to finance Richard I's war against Philip Augustus in Normandy. This tax on every plough team necessitated making a survey of how many teams there were in each village. Such a survey was not novel in itself; as in the Domesday inquest, 'all these things were to be reduced to writing' (*in scriptum redigebantur*).[101] The innovation lay in requiring rolls to be made in quadruplicate. In each county a clerk and a knight were to act as collectors. Each was to have a copy of the carucage roll; a third copy was to be kept by the sheriff and a fourth by the baronial steward, whose lord's land was involved. Thus of these four rolls, only one was to be kept by a clerk; the three others were in the hands of laymen.

If these regulations had been enforced, every baronial steward would have possessed a list of his lord's plough teams, which comprised his basic resources in men and animals. Familiarity with documents, if not literacy itself, would have been compulsorily extended to knights and barons and their officers by legislation. It is doubtful, however, whether all these rolls were made, as Hubert Walter resigned from the chief justiciarship in the summer of 1198 at his own insistence (according to Richard I) because of 'the intolerable burden of work and his own incapacity'.[102] Perhaps the difficulties in making England a more documented kingdom had temporarily overwhelmed him. Yet he returned to record-making within a year as King John's chancellor.

Much of this chapter has emphasized the role of the king's government in the production and proliferation of documents. The main reason for this emphasis is that royal administration is the best-documented, and therefore the most measurable, example of the production of records in medieval England. Moreover, there is every reason to think that the king was by far the largest producer of documents at the time, as well as having the best archives to transmit them to posterity. In England, from the time of William the Conqueror's Domesday Book and Henry I's Exchequer onwards, it was not the church or churchmen as such who were the principal promoters of the documentary habit but the king's clerks. Although such men were technically clerics, they usually put the interests of the king before those of the church as an institution. Thomas Becket, chancellor and archbishop, is the most notable exception to this rule. More typical is Hubert Walter. 'Where did the archbishop come from?' asked Gerald of Wales in his denunciation of Hubert at the papal *curia* in 1199. 'From the Exchequer . . . This was the academy, this was the school, in which he had already grown old, from which he was

---

[101] Stubbs, *Charters*, p. 249.
[102] *Foedera* I, part 1, p. 71.

called to all the grades of his [ecclesiastical] dignities, like nearly all the English bishops.'[103]

Hubert was no theologian, nor probably even a canon lawyer; there is no real evidence that he was a graduate of Bologna.[104] *Illitteratus* (in the opinion of an unfriendly chronicler), or 'only indifferently endowed with book-learning' according to a more charitable estimate,[105] he had been brought up in the household of his kinsman, Ranulf de Glanvill, who became the chief justiciar. Both Hubert and Ranulf have been credited with the authorship of the lawbook ascribed to Glanvill, whose prologue regrets the impossibility of reducing the laws of England entirely to writing because of the ignorance of scribes and the confusion of the sources.[106] If either Hubert or Ranulf were accepted as the author, it would be possible to see where Hubert derived an ambition to put so much into documentary form. In that case the Jewish archives of 1194, the feet of fines of 1195, the rolls of plough teams of 1198, and the Chancery rolls of 1200 were all products of a consistent purpose in making records, pursued by Hubert throughout his years of office.

The Exchequer may well have been Hubert's school, as Gerald of Wales alleged, although he probably came to it only when he was grown up. As a member of the chief justiciar's household, Hubert could have learned about making records from the acknowledged experts, Richard of Ilchester and Richard Fitz Neal. The earliest known reference to Hubert 'surnamed Walter' is as a witness to a charter in *c*.1181, where his name accompanies those of the two Richards and of Glanvill.[107] Richard of Ilchester's innovations in record-making have already been mentioned.[108] Richard Fitz Neal, as author of the *Dialogue of the Exchequer*, had shown his aptitude for instruction by question and answer and his delight in the technicalities of documents. 'Master', asks his pupil, 'why do you not teach others that knowledge of the Exchequer for which you are famous, and put it into writing lest it should die with you?'[109] Even in that question the concern for putting as much as possible into writing is evident. The making of records was a difficult and technical business, not requiring book-learning nor academic training as such, but instruction by those with practical experience. Fitz Neal claimed to teach 'useful things' (*utilia*), not the 'clever things' (*subtilia*) of the scholastic masters.[110] Hubert became the legatee of all this expertise and put it to more ambitious uses. The proliferation of documents was a European and a continuing phenomenon, yet if it were to be associated in England with one man, he would be Hubert Walter.

[103] Giraldus III, p. 28; Cheney, *Hubert Walter*, p. 4.

[104] C. R. Cheney, 'Hubert Walter and Bologna', *Bulletin of Medieval Canon Law*, new series II (1972), pp. 81–4.

[105] Cheney, *Hubert Walter*, p. 181, n. 2 and p. 164, n. 2.

[106] Glanvill, p. 3. Attributions of authorship are discussed by R. V. Turner, 'Who Was the Author of Glanvill?' *Law and History Review* VIII (1990), pp. 97–127.

[107] *Cartae Antiquae* ed. J. Conway Davies, PRS new series XXXIII (1957), p. 56; Cheney, *Hubert Walter*, p. 19.

[108] See nn. 63–4 above.

[109] *Dialogus*, p. 5.

[110] Clanchy, '*Moderni*', p. 678. See also n. 83 above.

ROYAL INFLUENCE ON OTHER RECORDS

From the king's government first the bishops and then other magnates learned how to make records. The bishops of Winchester, who were the earliest barons to keep systematic accounts in their pipe rolls (extant from 1208), imitated the methods used in the Exchequer.[111] This is not surprising, as the bishops between 1174 and 1238 were successively Richard of Ilchester (Henry II's watchdog at the Exchequer), Godfrey de Lucy (a royal justice and son of a chief justiciar), and Peter des Roches (King John's and Henry III's financial expert). Godfrey de Lucy, another candidate for the authorship of the lawbook ascribed to Glanvill, was also the first bishop to date his letters systematically; the idea came from the royal Chancery, although the form of dating derived from the papal one.[112]

Conversely when bishops began to keep registers of their own, probably after the Lateran Council of 1215, the idea derived from the church, but the form of the first English registers is royal. The earliest are those made at Lincoln (starting before 1217) and York (starting in 1225).[113] Although the structure of the earliest registers is experimental and inconsistent, the documents are predominantly arranged in the format of royal Chancery rolls, that is, the parchments are stitched together head to tail to produce a long scroll. Episcopal and papal registers on the European continent, on the other hand, are usually in the form of books, as are bishops' registers in England by the latter half of the thirteenth century. In other words, the English bishops began by imitating the king's Chancery and only brought their registers into line with ecclesiastical practice elsewhere after 50 years or more.

The initiators of registers in roll format at Lincoln and York were both former royal Chancery officials, who had seen – and probably assisted in inaugurating – the system of Chancery enrolments in the early years of John's reign. Hugh of Wells, bishop of Lincoln (1209–35), described himself as 'formerly chancellor of King John'.[114] Walter de Gray, archbishop of York (1214–55) had been the first chancellor to ensure, in 1205, that his appointment to the chancellorship was itself recorded in a royal charter.[115] Former employment in the royal Chancery did not by itself guarantee that a bishop would produce a register. Hugh's brother, Jocelin, bishop of Bath and Wells (1206–42), was a Chancery official who does not seem to have made one.[116] Nevertheless this negative does not affect the validity of the general proposition that bishops' records follow the lead of the royal Exchequer and Chancery.

---

[111] *Walter of Henley*, p. 224. Cf. ch. 3, n. 46 below.

[112] Cheney, *Chanceries*, p. 87.

[113] Ibid., pp. 104–5; David M. Smith, 'The Rolls of Hugh of Wells', *BIHR* XLV (1972), pp. 168–70, argues that the Lincoln register may have been started in 1214.

[114] Cheney, *Chanceries*, p. 107, n. 1.

[115] *Foedera* I, part i, p. 93.

[116] S. Painter, *The Reign of King John* (1949), pp. 79–80.

The instance of Jocelin of Wells, who did not make a register, suggests that it is worth noticing how slowly the practice of keeping registers spread among the dioceses. Before 1250, outside Lincoln and York, no other bishop kept a register except possibly William de Ralegh, bishop of Winchester (1244–50), who likewise emanated from the king's court where he had been the principal royal justice.[117] Judging from registers known, the lead given by the great dioceses of Lincoln and York was not immediately followed. Perhaps smaller dioceses did not have the same need to keep a check on appointments of clergy through a register. Table 3 shows the dates of the earliest registers, either still extant (E) or mentioned (M) in a medieval source, for each diocese.[118]

Apart from indicating that it took a century for every English diocese to institute a register, the table confirms the generalizations underlying this chapter – that documentation did not become usual outside the king's court until the latter half of the thirteenth century, and that the reign of Edward I was the period when record-making became really extensive.

Table 3 Earliest bishops' registers

Before 1217	Lincoln	E
1225	York	E
1251–74	Rochester	M
1257–80	Exeter	E
1258–95	Coventry and Lichfield	M
1264–6	Bath and Wells	E
1266–80	Winchester	M
1268–1302	Worcester	E
1271–84	Salisbury	M
1275–82	Hereford	E
1279–92	Canterbury	E
1283–1311	Durham	M
1288–1305	Chichester	M
1292–1324	Carlisle	E
1299–1325	Norwich	E
1304–13	London	E
1316–37	Ely	M

There is a time-lag of a generation or more between a form of documentation being developed and its finding general acceptance. Not even the bishops, the most highly educated group of barons with their close connexions with the king's court and their general knowledge of the universities and papal practice, hastened to make records. It is possible that they deliberately

[117] Cheney, *Chanceries*, p. 149 argues that it is unlikely that Ralegh kept a register.
[118] Based on Ibid., pp. 147–9, and David M. Smith, *Guide to Bishops' Registers* (1981).

refrained from making registers, because they knew better than the king's clerks that records of this sort did not bring in a profitable return of information. Lists of churches in the dioceses, showing their values and the names of the patrons and incumbents, were already kept by some bishops in a *matricula* or *scrutinium*, which was easier to consult, though less detailed, than a register.[119] But there is no evidence that bishops thought about record-making as disinterestedly as that. The most academic, conscientious, and efficient bishop of the thirteenth century, Robert Grosseteste of Lincoln (1235–53), was among the first to keep a register.[120] Registers were by no means the only type of record made or kept by bishops. Nevertheless they are the best measure of the rate of episcopal record-making because they are summaries of other documents, deliberately made for future reference.

While bishops were slow to make records, when compared with the king's government, lay barons and knights were inert. They too, however, imitated royal methods and found themselves increasingly involved in the king's business, which meant using documents. An early example of imitation by a baron of a royal writ is the letter sent in *c*.1130 by Richard Fitz Gilbert of Clare to one of his tenants, ordering him to restore a tithe to Stoke priory in Suffolk.[121] The letter concludes with a warning: 'And if you do not so, Adam, my steward, is swiftly going to do it, so that I hear no plaint for want of right.' The phraseology echoes that of royal writs of right, as in a letter of Henry I protecting Ramsey abbey:[122] 'And if you do not do so, Ralf Basset is going to have it done, so that I hear no plaint about it for want or right.'

If the two passages are compared in the original Latin, the similarities and differences are more obvious. Richard Fitz Gilbert's clerk wrote: 'Et si tu non facis, Adam dapifer meus faciat cito, ut non audiam clamorem penuria recti.' Whereas Henry I's clerk wrote: 'Et nisi feceris, Radulphus Basset faciat fieri, ne audiam inde clamorem pro penuria recti.' The sense and the principal words are the same in both passages. Fitz Gilbert's clerk made some minor variations, either out of ignorance (his Latin is not so neat), or because he wanted to avoid direct imitation. It is not suggested that he copied this particular writ of Henry I's, but something very similar. A baron like Fitz Gilbert would have received such royal writs himself, admonishing him to do right to his tenants. Understandably he paid the king the compliment of imitation, when he gave similar warnings one step further down the feudal hierarchy.

The initiative in using documents came from the king and gradually made its way down the social scale – to most barons by 1200, to knights by 1250, to peasants by 1300. The proliferation of documents is regulated by this time-scale. In the words of Maitland, 'the *carta*, the written agreement, the seal, these are aristocratic forms; gradually they make their way downwards and pervade the whole community; but they begin at the top.'[123] After

119 Cheney, *Chanceries*, pp. 110–19.
120 *Rotuli Roberti Grosseteste* ed. F. N. Davis, Canterbury and York S. x (1913) or Lincoln Record S. xi. (1914).
121 Stenton, *Feudalism*, pp. 75, 269.
122 Van Caenegem, *Writs*, p. 418, no. 12.
123 *Court Baron*, p. 116.

documents begin to be extensively used, there is still a further delay before they are systematically kept in archives and registered for future reference. The king's government set an increasingly fast pace in the production of records, which left even the higher clergy, who had traditionally been the writing experts, far behind.

A final illustration of the way the proliferation of royal documents disseminated literate modes is found in the change in the meaning of the word 'record' itself. In the twelfth century to 'record' something meant to bear oral witness, not to produce a document. Thus in the civil war of Stephen's reign the earls of Gloucester and Hereford made a treaty in the form of sealed letters; yet both parties also named witnesses, who were 'to make legal record [*recordationem*] of this agreement in court if necessary'.[124] The spoken word was the legally valid record and was superior to any document. Likewise in Henry II's reign Glanvill's treatise provides the text of a writ which orders a sheriff to have a plea 'recorded' (*recordari*) in his county court, and then he is to convey this 'record' (*recordum*) to the king's court by four knights.[125] It is evident that the knights convey the record orally, as the parties to the plea are ordered to come to 'hear the record'. We have already seen instances from 1202 to 1203 of such an oral record being found to conflict with written records, and examples appear in the earliest plea rolls of sheriff and knights having to make a record in the king's court in this way.[126]

Fifty years later, however, by the time Bracton's legal treatise was taking its final shape, the procedure for making a record of this type requires the seals of the sheriff and of the coroners, which are obviously to be attached to a letter.[127] No longer are four knights required, but only two, as their word is now of secondary importance. This change, from an oral to a predominantly written procedure, appears to have occurred in John's reign. In a case in 1214 the sheriff of Cornwall is ordered to have a record of his county court at Westminster 'by four knights who were present at that record and by his sealed letters'. In other words, this instruction combines elements of Glanvill's and Bracton's procedures; in fact two knights appeared at Westminster, instead of four, similarly presaging Bracton's procedure.[128] The clearest instance of how 'record' now meant a document occurs in a similar case in 1227.[129] Four knights from the Essex county court appeared at Westminster and 'brought the record and judgement, expressed in writing, under this form'. Details of the case then follow, which have evidently been copied down by the clerk compiling the plea roll from the document handed in to the court by the knights, as he does not note everything, but says that the rest 'is more fully contained in the record'.

---

[124] *Earldom of Gloucester Charters*, pp. 95–6, no. 95.
[125] Bk viii ch. 10, p. 102. Cf. *Dialogus*, p. 116, where 'recordatio comtiatus' is used in similar context.
[126] See nn. 96–7 above; *CuriaRR* i, pp. 44, 66; ii, pp. 260, 296.
[127] Bracton, fo 149b, vol. ii, p. 423.
[128] *CuriaRR* vii, p. 169.
[129] *Bracton's Note Book* ed. F. W. Maitland (1887) ii, pp. 195–8, no. 243. Cf. the parallel text (with variants) *CuriaRR* xiii, pp. 16–17, no. 77.

Knights who bore record to Westminster, orally in the twelfth century and by letters in the thirteenth, became familiar with literate modes and learned the ways of the king's court. From such men the king increasingly drew his local officials – sheriffs, coroners, escheators and so on. The most important consequence of the proliferation of documents was that it prepared the gentry, the country-keeping knights, for literacy. Documents had to precede widening literacy. They had to have increased by accumulation in central archives and extensive distribution over the country before understanding of them became widespread in the shires. The gentry were not going to learn to read until documents were available and necessary. Necessity and availability also made for easy familiarity with writing, and from familiarity stemmed confidence in literate ways of doing business. Traditionally, literate modes had been the preserve of clerics and rulers. It took time, combined with a massive increase in the number of documents, to change traditional habits. The purpose of charting the increasing number of documents in this chapter has not been as an end in itself, but because that was the foundation on which any permanent extension of literacy had to stand.

APPENDIX

Weight of wax used in sealing Chancery writs, 1226–71

Source: *CLibR* i–vi. Up to 22 May 1250 enrolments are made at intervals of about 3–4 months, but they do not specify the period covered; this has been estimated in the table below from the dates of preceding enrolments. From 22 May 1250 enrolments specify the period in dates expressed by saints' days and regnal years; these dates have been modernized. Enrolments are missing or incomplete for those years omitted from the table.

	Volume and page nos.	Period covered	Weight of wax (in lb)	Number of weeks	Amount of wax used per week (in lb)
I:	16, 38, 44, 52, 65	18 Dec. 1226 – 29 Jan. 1228	183	58	3.15
I:	69, 78, 86, 100, 111, 115	29 Jan. 1228 – 20 Jan. 1229	158	51	3.09
I:	120, 127, 132, 138, 140, 145, 155, 162	20 Jan. 1229 – 24 Jan. 1230	242.5	52	4.66
I:	166, 175, 184	24 Jan. 1230 – 12 July 1230	89.5	24	3.72
I:	204, 215, 222, 226, 234, 239	23 Jan. 1233 – 20 Oct. 1233	169.5	39	4.35

[Handwritten marginal annotations:] increasingly / as docs became available & necessary / gentry prepared for and participated in literacy

I:	260, 274, 285, 297, 308, 314	22 Jan. 1237 – 20 Feb. 1238	245	55	4.45
I:	375, 391, 395, 421, 445	8 Jan. 1239 – 1 Feb. 1240	281	55	5.11
II:	120, 137, 149, 171, 177	8 March 1242 – 27 April 1243	425	59	7.2
II	232, 241, 265, 285	3 Feb. 1244 – 17 Jan. 1245	398	50	7.96
II:	312, III: 16	17 Jan. 1245 – 16 Dec. 1245	428	48	8.91
III:	59, 89	16 Dec. 1245 – 25 Oct. 1246	362	44	8.22
III:	385	22 May 1250 – 26 Oct. 1251	510	74	6.89
IV:	105	26 Oct. 1251 – 2 Feb. 1253	606	66	9.18
IV:	143	2 Feb. 1253 – 29 June 1253	181	21	8.62
IV:	159	29 June 1253 – 24 Feb. 1254	142	33	4.3
IV:	256	6 Jan. 1255 – 20 Nov. 1255	464	45	10.31
IV:	353	20 Nov. 1255 – 13 Jan. 1257	700	60	11.67
IV:	400	13 Jan. 1257 – 25 Oct. 1257	570	39	14.61
VI:	269	25 Oct. 1257 9 June 1258	540	32	16.87
IV:	448	9 June 1258 – 22 Jan. 1259	520	33	15.75
IV:	469	22 Jan. 1259 27 July 1259	220	27	8.15
IV:	486	27 July 1259 – 3 Nov. 1259	170	14	12.14

	Volume and page nos.	*Period covered*	*Weight of wax (in lb)*	*Number of weeks*	*Amount of wax used per week (in lb)*
IV:	532	3 Nov. 1259 – 15 Oct. 1260	584	49	11.92
V:	33	13 [*sic*] Oct. 1260 – 15 May 1261	455	31	14.67
V:	59	15 May 1261 – 13 Oct. 1261	450	22	20.96
V:	73	13 Oct. 1261 – 14 Jan. 1262	412	13	31.69
V:	96	14 Jan. 1262 – 9 June 1262	457	22	20.77
V:	116	13 July 1262 – 2 Nov. 1262	196	16	12.25
VI:	277	19 Jan. 1263 – 29 May 1263	412	19	21.69
V:	130	5 June 1263 – 30 Jan. 1264	793	34	23.32
V:	155	29 May 1264 – 5 Jan. 1265	530	31	17.09
V:	182	5 Jan. 1265 – 20 Oct. 1265	791	41	19.29
V:	295	29 Sept. 1265 – 18 Oct. 1267	1611	107	15.06
VI:	50	18 Oct. 1267 – 18 Oct. 1268	1831	52	35.21
VI:	131	18 Oct. 1268 – 6 May 1269	1786	28	63.78
VI:	160	6 May 1270 [*sic*] – 2 Feb. 1271	995	38	26.18

3

Types of Record

To appreciate the significance of the great increase in record-making in the twelfth and thirteenth centuries some scheme, classifying documents into different types, needs to be borne in mind. The elementary scheme suggested in this chapter is not intended to do more than provide an introduction to English medieval documents in this period by taking a general view over the whole area of writing activity.[1] The different classes of document proposed are not entirely mutually exclusive, nor do the examples given exhaust the variety of documents which exist. One consequence of the massive increase in the number of documents is that no individual historian today can claim to have seen all, or even most, of the evidence. Modern scholars tend to be experts in particular categories of document, such as monastic charters or royal writs or illuminated Bibles. Within these categories further specialization takes place: monastic charters from particular periods or regions are studied for instance, because the documents are so numerous and varied. Professional scholarship is necessarily based on Adam Smith's principle of the division of labour.

specialists to generalists

THE VARIETY OF WRITINGS

An educated Englishman in the thirteenth century, by contrast, would have become familiar with a variety of writings over his lifetime – charters to safeguard his landed property, royal writs for litigation, homilies for devotion, romances for entertainment, and so on. Among the 40 or so volumes which

[1] The best concise survey of the records is G. R. Elton, *The Sources of History: England 1200–1640* (1969). R. C. van Caenegem, *Guide to the Sources of Medieval History* (1978) is the best guide to medieval sources as a whole; this is updated in the French edition, *Introduction aux sources de l'histoire médiéval* (Brepols).

Guy de Beauchamp, earl of Warwick, gave by charter to Bordesley abbey in 1306 are books of the Bible, meditations and saints' lives, romances and histories, a book of physic and one of surgery, a child's primer, an encyclopae- dia, and 'a little red book in which are contained many diverse things'.[2] All the books are described as 'romances', meaning that they are in French and not Latin. A step down the social scale, the Northamptonshire gentleman, Henry de Bray of Harlestone, copied out with his own hand in Latin at the age of 52 (in 1322) a compilation for the instruction of his heirs containing a general description of the world, a more detailed description of England (its counties, bishoprics, kings and Cinque Ports), extracts from Domesday Book and other royal records, information about Northamptonshire feudal and local government, a list of his own tenants, the dimensions of Harlestone common field and the village, a table of measures, records of his expenses, and numerous copies of documents concerning his property.[3] Both Guy's charter listing books and Henry's estate book are exceptional survivals. Most of the nobility and gentry were not so careful with their documents; but they would all have come across, even if they did not possess, a comparable variety of written records during their lives.

The experience of medieval writers and makers of records cuts across the lines dividing knowledge which scholars draw today. Although writers became gradually more specialized as the demand for documents increased, in the twelfth century and earlier they tended to perform a variety of functions. One of Thomas Becket's biographers, William Fitz Stephen, describes how he was a draftsman in his chancery, a subdeacon in his chapel, a reader in his law court, and on occasions a judge.[4] In the chancery he would have been familiar with letters and literary style, in the chapel with liturgical books, and in the law court with records of pleas. Becket himself had started his career as an accountant to a London merchant and was also described as a 'clerk and accountant' of the sheriffs of London.[5] He thus had experience of financial and civic record-making before he went into Archbishop Theobald's service and thence into the king's. In the thirteenth century Matthew Paris, who was the scribe and illustrator of most of his own works, wrote the chronicles for which he is famous in Latin prose and he is associated with the making of lives of English saints in French verse for aristocratic ladies.[6] In addition he had a very competent knowledge of charters and royal writs (which he cites verbatim), Latin verse, heraldry, cartography, and an interest in natural science. His exceptionally varied activities emphasize the difficulty of classify- ing medieval writings too strictly into types.

---

[2] M. Blaess, 'L'abbaye de Bordesley et les livres de Guy de Beauchamp', *Romania* LXXVIII (1957), pp. 511–18; Legge, *Anglo-Norman*, p. 6.

[3] *The Estate Book of Henry de Bray* ed. D. Willis, Camden S. 3rd series XXVII (1916). Cf. nn. 94, 95 below concerning laymen's cartularies.

[4] *Becket Materials* III, p. 1.

[5] Ibid. III, p. 14.

[6] R. Vaughan, *Matthew Paris* (1958), pp. 168–81; Alexander & Binski, pp. 216–17, nos 38 and 39; P. Binski, 'Abbot Berkyng's Tapestries and Matthew Paris's Life of St Edward the Confessor', *Archaeologia* CIX (1991), pp. 85–100.

Even single works of Matthew's defy exclusive classification. His best-known book, the *Chronica Majora*, is in part a history copied from other sources (Matthew performed here the role of editor and scribe) and in part a contemporary monastic chronicle composed by himself. It is also an illustrated book of lively caricatures probably intended to entertain, a cartulary of documents (in the *Liber Additamentorum*), an atlas (each volume was originally prefaced with maps and itineraries), and a heraldic reference book. Matthew included in it, moreover, his famous drawing from life of the elephant given by St Louis to Henry III in 1255 (together with a discourse on elephants) and the beautiful painting of the Virgin and Child, with himself kneeling at her feet, which prefaces the final part of the chronicle.[7] In Matthew's mind history, literature, art and science were not separate realms of knowledge.

The works of Matthew Paris are an exceptional instance of a typical characteristic of medieval writings. Documents and books in manuscript tend to depart from standard forms and to contain a diversity of subject matter because there is no printing press automatically imposing uniformity. In the layout and content of their works writers and scribes aimed at the elegance which results from regularity and consistency, but personal idiosyncrasies and interests inevitably remained prominent in writings produced entirely by hand. Moreover, it is often impossible with medieval books to give an adequate single classification to an individual volume, as a modern librarian does, because a variety of works are frequently bound between the same covers. Guy de Beauchamp's 'little red book' containing many diverse things is an example of the problem. Miscellanies of this sort often reflected the interests of the compiler or owner of the book. The diverse contents had unity in his own experience and needs, rather than in any external scheme of things. An excellent introduction to the variety of works bound together into books in the thirteenth century is Oschinsky's descriptive list of the manuscripts containing treatises on accountancy and estate management.[8] For example, MS 17 includes (among other items) parliamentary statutes, cooking recipes, a lapidary (a discourse on precious stones), a glossary of measures, and treatises on management. Similarly MS 68 contains Walter of Henley's treatise on husbandry, together with Walter of Bibbesworth's poem to aid learning French, a moral poem (*La desputaisen du cors et de l'âme*), proverbs, a brief encyclopaedia called *L'image du monde*, and other works. Diverse as these subjects might appear to a modern scholar, they could all have been of interest or use to a country gentleman like Henry de Bray.

Even illuminated manuscripts, which look as if they were made exclusively for their magnificent paintings, might be seen in other ways. When in the 1180s Henry II arbitrarily gave the Winchester Bible to the ascetic St Hugh for his Charterhouse at Witham, the Carthusians were delighted because 'the correctness of the text pleased them especially, even more than the delicacy of

---

[7] Lewis, *Matthew Paris*, pp. 213, 217; Vaughan, *Matthew Paris*, frontispiece and plates; N. Morgan, *Early Gothic MSS 1190–1250* (1982), no. 92, and plate facing p. 28; Alexander & Binski, no. 437. Matthew's maps and itineraries are described in detail by Lewis, *Matthew Paris*, pp. 321–76.

[8] *Walter of Henley*, pp. 11–50. Cf. Parkes, 'Literacy', p. 562.

the penmanship and the general beauty of the work.'[9] There is likewise the remarkable case of the Sherborne abbey manuscript which is partly a cartulary of documents concerning a lawsuit in 1145 and partly an illuminated missal for use at the altar in Holy Week.[10] But enough has now been said to indicate the variety of medieval documents. Exceptions such as those described above make it all the more necessary to formulate some general rules of classification.

The most fundamental distinction to make is between primary and secondary records. A charter extant in its original form as a single piece of parchment (preferably with the seal still attached) is a primary record, whereas a copy of that charter in a monastic cartulary or in the royal Charter rolls is a secondary record. By this classification original charters, writs, chirographs, wills, court rolls, ministers' accounts and so on are primary records; whereas chronicles, cartularies, the Chancery rolls, Domesday Book and similar surveys are secondary records because they are compiled from other sources. In this sense too most medieval books, from copies of the Bible downwards, are secondary because they were made from exemplars. This distinction between primary and secondary does not readily apply in all cases. Thus the parts of Matthew Paris's chronicles which he himself composed and wrote are essentially primary records, whereas many original charters and court rolls may have been compiled from drafts which were thrown away and in that sense they too are secondary records. If this latter assumption is universally applied, however, all extant medieval documents become secondary records, which is absurd.

Taken generally, the distinction between primary and secondary is applicable and useful, because it emphasizes the difference between documents in their original form and copies or edited versions of them, whether medieval or modern. Primary and secondary records usually differ too in their format. Primary records are most often single sheets of parchment or a small stitched gathering, whereas secondary records are made up into rolls or bound books. The format of the records has affected their chance of survival over the centuries. The great majority of primary documents have been lost, because they consisted of single sheets of parchment, whereas registers and books survive in relative abundance. One purpose of copying documents into registers in the Middle Ages was to ensure that their texts did survive. To keep classifications simple, this chapter discusses only records made on parchment. Writings on paper, wood, fabric, metal and so on are discussed in the next chapter; the most common English non-parchment records were tally sticks (see plate VIII) like those used in the Exchequer.

---

[9] *The Life of St Hugh of Lincoln* ed. D. L. Douie and H. Farmer (1985), p. 86; W. Oakeshott, 'St Albans and Winchester Contributions to St Hugh's Bible' in *MSS Hunt* pp. 32–6; and see T. A. Heslop's review of Oakeshott, *The Two Winchester Bibles* in *Art History* v (1982), pp. 124–8.
[10] Zarnecki, *Catalogue*, no. 46. See also ch. 5, n. 35 below.

STATEMENTS ISSUED BY INDIVIDUALS

The primary records most commonly met with are letters of one sort or another. They are here collectively described as 'statements issued by individuals' because the generic term 'letters' is ambiguous and can mislead. A variety of descriptive terms for such written statements were used in the Middle Ages, such as *breve, carta, chirographum* and *litterae* itself. These terms were not used with strict consistency or uniformity, nor are they mutually exclusive. Nevertheless they can be adapted to create definitions which distinguish documents by their function with a fair degree of precision.

Charters

Working on this principle, a charter is a public letter issued by a donor recording a title to property (see plates i, v and vi). Charters are frequently therefore addressed to the general public – to 'those whom the present writing shall reach' or to 'all who shall hear and see this charter'. As the general public was the same as the Christian community, the donor sometimes addressed 'all the sons of Holy Church' or 'all the faithful in Christ' or 'cleric and lay'. Additionally or alternatively, he might particularize and address 'his constables and stewards and barons and all his men and friends, French and English, of Yorkshire'. All the above examples are taken from the charters of Roger de Mowbray, who died in 1188.[11] What the donor did not do in a charter was to address the beneficiary exclusively, because the charter itself was given to the beneficiary (and sometimes written by him) and served as a kind of open testimonial. Addresses have such a variety of forms primarily because standardization became usual only in the thirteenth century, when charters were issued in tens of thousands. The charter form is much older than the Norman Conquest; the main change which occurred thereafter is that their texts and format at last became stereotyped owing primarily to the increase in numbers.[12]

In practice a charter might concern any form of property, although rights over land were by far the most common conveyances in a primarily agricultural community. Of other gifts, we have already seen that Guy de Beauchamp listed books in a charter in 1306. A few years earlier John de Camoys had conveyed his wife, Margaret, with her goods and chattels to Sir William Paynel by a charter, insisting that he did this of his own free will. The ordinary formulas for conveying land, 'I have given and granted, released and quitclaimed', are used in this charter. The details survive because Margaret and William attempted to claim dower from John's lands and the case came

[11] *Mowbray Charters*, nos 31, 347, 20, 167, 166, 380. Cf. ch. 8, n. 2 below.
[12] Cheney, *Chanceries*, ch. 3, describes the development of standardized forms in charters over the period 1100–1250. A good introductory collection of texts (with English translations) is *Transcripts of Charters Relating to Gilbertine Houses* ed. F. M. Stenton, Lincoln Record S. xviii (1922). Cf. ch. 8, n. 6 below, and ch. 9, nn. 1–2 below.

before Parliament in 1300–2.[13] In 1267 or earlier Peter of Pecham wrote (in French verse) a parody of a compact with the Devil, in the form of a charter: 'Be it known to all my servants present and future that I, Prince of Greed, Pride and Envy, have given and granted to the rich, who are my retinue in chief, that they can do all that they want: by force and deceitful covetousness, by all wrong and ransom, by seizure and by false pretences, by pawn and by tallage, by privilege and by outrage, or by anything else they can think of to destroy the common people.'[14]

The amount of detail in which a conveyance is described varies according to the nature of the property, the date it was made, and the mutual trust between the parties. A later charter describing the same property might be more specific. For example, in 1209 or earlier William Blanch granted (among other lands in Ewell near Epsom) half an acre in Dunfurlong. When Gilbert son of Osbert obtained a confirmation of this grant from William Blanch's heir, John, in the 1230s, the new charter defined the half-acre in Dunfurlong more exactly as that lying 'between the land of John Skinner and of William Cupping'.[15] In this more precise description may be seen the influence of Gilbert's brother-in-law, Walter of Merton, the future chancellor who was already a royal clerk. Some attempts at definition were more amateur. A crudely written charter of the late twelfth century, issued by Jordan of Cheadle, describes the land he is giving as extending 'in length from a certain oak towards Hedilislethe, which has been uprooted there' up to another point.[16] Jordan's contemporaries in the village would have known where the remains of this oak might be seen, but not the general public, present and future, to whom this charter is addressed. Occasionally the specifications in a charter can evoke a whole landscape, as they had done so strikingly in some Anglo-Saxon charters. This is an extract from a grant of land at Lambrigg (near Kendal) in the Lake District, describing the boundaries in *c.* 1210:

> then by Sti Coleman up to the nearest pile of stones which is towards the north under the head of Langescaghe, and then rising beyond Lange-scaghe up to the little valley which is next to the upper head of Lickegile, then out across the head of Lickegile by the middle of the moor . . . [and so on].[17]

In charters there is often a contrast between the dignity and portentous language of their issuers and the pettyness of the matters they concern. In 1219 the monks of Abbey Dore obtained a confirmation in Rome of their title to a piece of land only twenty feet in width heading their millstream. Anyone 'infringing this page', Pope Honorius III warned, 'would incur the indigna-tion of Almighty God and the Blessed Apostles Peter and Paul'.[18] This

---

[13] *Rotuli Parliamentorum* (1783) I, p. 146; P & M II, pp. 395–6.

[14] D. L. Jeffry and B. J. Levy, *Anglo-Norman Lyric* (1990), p. 137 (my translation).

[15] *Fitznell's Cartulary* ed. C. A. F. Meekings, Surrey Record S. xxxvi (1968), nos 57, 62, cf. p. lxii.

[16] *Cheshire Facs*, no. 14.

[17] *Northants Facs*, no. liii.

[18] J. E. Sayers, *Papal Government and England* (1984), pp. 220–1.

illustrates very well what Max Weber meant by the 'routinization of charisma': through bureaucracy, the pope's voice as God's mouthpiece on earth was multiplied into tens of thousands of trivial pronouncements.

Chirographs

Rather similar in function to charters, though different in format, are chirographs. A chirograph recorded an agreement between two parties. The agreement might concern almost anything – matters of state, a conveyance of land, a marriage settlement, or the repayment of a loan of money to a Jew. Unlike a charter, each of the parties received a copy of the agreement, usually authenticated by the seal of the other party (see plate vii). The method is described in detail, probably because it was still relatively unfamiliar, in an agreement made before papal judges delegate between the prior of Luffield and John, vicar of Towcester, in *c.* 1215:

> This composition is reduced into a duplicate writing, made in the form of a chirograph, of which writing [*scriptura*] the prior of Luffield is to have one document [*scriptum*] sealed with the seals of the judges and of John, while John is to have the other document sealed with the seals of the judges and of the prior.[19]

The document was thus written out in duplicate and then cut in half. Across the line of the cut, before it was made, was written in capital letters a formula such as JUSTUS DOMINUS ET JUSTICIAS (an extract from Psalms xi, 7) or the word CHIROGRAPHUM (see plate vii).[20] Forgery of one part could thus be checked by aligning the severed formula with its counterpart. As a further precaution, the cut was often made by a wavy or indented line, instead of a straight one. This practice grew so common in the latter Middle Ages that chirographs became generally known as 'indentures'.

The text of a chirograph might be drafted in the form of a letter to all and sundry (like a charter), or it might be a memorandum recording that this is the covenant or final concord which has been made, at such and such a court or place, in the presence of certain persons who are named. The making of a chirograph might conclude an actual dispute between the parties, or alternatively the chirographic form was often used for amicable conveyances, because it had the advantage over an ordinary charter that both donor and beneficiary received a copy and these copies could be checked against each other. The first official records of proceedings in the king's court, extant as originals, are halves of chirographs recording agreements made in 1176 and 1182,[21] the former cut straight and the latter indented. Moreover, some chirographs were

---

[19] *Luffield Priory Charters* ed. G. R. Elvey, part i, Buckinghamshire Record S. xv (1968) or Northamptonshire Record S. xxii (1968), p. 71, no. 68. The novelty lay in the method of sealing and not in the chirographic format itself, which dated from the ninth century or earlier, B. Bischoff, *Mittelalterliche Studien* (1966) i, p. 118. Both parts of a chirograph (dated 1173) are illustrated by M. G. Cheney, *Roger Bishop of Worcester* (1980), plate facing p. 228.

[20] L. C. Hector, *The Handwriting of English Documents* (1958), plate iii.

[21] *BM Facs*, nos 55, 63.

made in triplicate: the two parties each received a copy and the third copy was deposited in an archive for safekeeping. This had been an Anglo-Saxon practice, which was revived (using a different format) by Hubert Walter when he introduced royal feet of fines in 1195. Most exceptionally, all three parts of chirographs made before royal justices survive from 1232 and 1272.[22] The practice was extended to ecclesiastical records by an interpretation of canon 38 of the Fourth Lateran Council in 1215.[23]

✳ Like other documentary forms, the chirograph made its way down the social scale. At the top it was the standard form for international treaties, of which the earliest extant exemplars are four Anglo-Flemish alliances made in the twelfth century.[24] Likewise in times of civil war magnates used chirographs to record alliances. Extant examples are two treaties made in Stephen's reign, one between the earls of Chester and Leicester and the other between the earls of Gloucester and Hereford.[25] Similarly the war between King John and his barons was concluded by a chirograph beginning, 'This is the covenant made between Lord John, king of England, for the one part, and Robert Fitz Walter, marshal of the army of God and of the holy Church in England [and other named barons] on the other.'[26] This treaty immediately preceded Magna Carta itself, which was issued in the form of an ordinary charter, presumably in order to emphasize that it was a free gift by the king and not a compromised agreement. Nevertheless when Magna Carta was reissued in 1217 by the regent, William Marshal, it too was drawn up *in modum chirographi*, according to the Waverley abbey chronicler at least.[27] At the other end of the political and social scale, we have already discussed the chirograph which the widow, Emma, made with the abbot of Gloucester in *c.* 1230 concerning ploughing and other servile duties.[28] The chirograph was a most versatile, and therefore a very common, type of document; but it is unusual for more than one of the original parts to survive to the present day.

Certificates

In addition to charters and chirographs, public statements by individuals were issued in the form of recognizances, testimonials, notifications, wills, sealed memoranda and similar records. For convenience these miscellaneous documents are here called certificates. They are often similar in form to charters, but they do not exclusively concern gifts of property. The following

[22] Illustrated by D. Crook, *Records of the General Eyre* (1982), frontispiece, and by C. Johnson and H. Jenkinson, *English Court Hand* (1915) ii, plate xviib. See also ch. 2, n. 84 above.

[23] Cheney, *Chanceries*, p. 132.

[24] P. Chaplais, 'English Diplomatic Documents' in *Study of Medieval Records*, p. 23, n. 6.

[25] Stenton, *Feudalism*, pp. 25ff, 286–8; *Earldom of Gloucester Charters* ed. R. B. Patterson (1973), plate xiv, or ed. R. H. C. Davis in *MM for Stenton*, plate xi.

[26] J. C. Holt, *Magna Carta* (1965), p. 342, plate v.

[27] *Annales Monastici* ii, p. 290; Galbraith, *Studies*, p. 13. The only extant copy of this reissue, bearing the seals of the legate Guala and William Marshal, does not look as if it is a chirograph: D. A. Carpenter, *The Minority of Henry III* (1990), plate 8 (facing p. 121).

[28] See ch. 2, n. 21 above.

extract from a testimonial by Miles earl of Hereford, probably issued shortly before he died in 1143, is exceptional in its subject matter but typical in its form:

> Miles earl of Hereford to all his friends, French and English, of England and of Wales, greeting. You are to know that this Folebarba is my jester and my man. So I entreat all my friends that they look after him, lest harm happen to him. And if anyone does him good for love of me, I will know how to thank him.[29]

Folebarba (? Funny Beard) was perhaps apprehensive of being parted from his master and hoped that this certificate of the earl's affection would help him; whether it did or not is unknown – jesters inevitably made enemies.

By far the commonest form of certificates were recognizances concerning the payment of money debts. The earliest moneylender's bonds extant in England are eight documents from the coffers of the financier, William Cade, whose archives came into the possession of the crown on his death in *c.*1166. The documents are brief and take the form of undertakings by persons named to stand surety for others, or themselves make payments to Cade or his son, Ernulf, at specified dates.[30] Documents classed here as certificates are so varied that it would be impossible to describe all types. Sometimes there is no convincing explanation as to why a particular record was ever made or preserved. Richard of Anstey's account of the protracted delays he experienced in the lawsuit he prosecuted between 1158 and 1163 has been described in numerous general histories of the period.[31] Yet why Richard made this memorandum is unclear. It begins like a solemn charter or prayer by invoking the Trinity, but it is not addressed to anyone, nor does it ask for anything or give it; it simply records his expenses and how and when they were incurred. Another form of certificate which must have been common by Edward I's reign were the testimonials which served as warrants identifying persons or their goods when moving about the country.[32]

Letters

The documents considered so far are not 'letters' in the modern sense of missives. Charters, chirographs and certificates were not usually sent by the writer to a recipient who is addressed in the document; instead they were addressed to the public and handed to the beneficiary at the time they were written. They were primarily intended to be records rather than communications. The habit of sending missives, conveying ephemeral information about day-to-day matters, developed slowly because writing in Latin was too formal a medium. 'Letters' (*litterae*) were appropriate for 'literature' to pass on to

---

[29] 'Earldom of Hereford Charters' ed. D. Walker, *Camden Miscellany* Camden S. 4th series xxii (1964), p. 15, no. 7. This document also confirms a gift of land to Folebarba.

[30] See ch. 9, n. 23 below. For Jewish moneylenders' bonds see ch. 6, nn. 17–21 below.

[31] P. M. Barnes, 'The Anstey Case' in *MM for Stenton*, pp. 1–23.

[32] See ch. 2, nn. 9–15 above.

posterity; the spoken word of messengers sufficed for conveying the ordinary business of the day. The finest letters were composed and kept as examples of style and were not necessarily sent to their addresses. In the first half of the twelfth century the art of writing such elaborate yet intimate letters reached a peak in the collections of St Bernard, Peter the Venerable, and Abelard and Heloise. This type of correspondence was exemplified in England in the latter half of the century in the letter collections of John of Salisbury and Gilbert Foliot. The best single example is John's letter to Peter abbot of Celle in *c*.1159 recalling their friendship.[33] It is often impossible to establish whether letters in anthologies like these are authentic missives; they may be literary essays, propaganda pieces, or even forgeries, as has been alleged of the correspondence between Abelard and Heloise.

In the thirteenth century more mundane letters begin to survive, which are actual missives although they are less intimate. An example are the letters written to Ralf Nevill, bishop of Chichester (1224–44), by his steward in Sussex, Simon of Senlis. These concern the management of the farms, the doings of the local clergy, arrangements for visits, request for favours, and so on. They evoke without effort a picture of country life which a rhetorician could not have bettered, yet they have survived only because Ralf was the chancellor and Simon's letters became mixed in with the royal archives.[34]

Writs

Letters first become common in England, not in the form of correspondence between individuals, but as 'writs' (*brevia*). Writs have a brevity and directness of style which contrasts with the elaboration of explicitly personal letters; as a result they can sometimes reveal more of individual attitudes. 'If we have given our peace even to a dog, it should be inviolably preserved', King John wrote in 1203 to the Londoners when reproving them for molesting the Jews.[35] The term 'writ' is used in this classification exclusively to mean a written command given by one person to another. The most frequent issuer of writs was the king, as in this example by Henry I: 'Henry, king of the English, to the abbot of Ramsey, greeting. I forbid you to do Hugh Oilard anything but right, no matter what writ might be produced. Witness: the chancellor. At Gloucester.'[36]

It is debatable whether a writ in this form is a real missive directed by the sender to the addressee. The surviving writs of Henry I are letters patent (see plates II–IV); this means that they were open documents, which were handed to the beneficiaries at the time they were made, like charters. In the writ cited

---

[33] *Letters* ed. W. J. Millor et al. (1955) I, pp. 183–4; J. McLoughlin, 'John of Salisbury and his Circle', *Fifth Harlaxton Symposium* (1988), pp. 165–181. In general see A. Morey and C. N. L. Brooke, *Gilbert Foliot and his Letters* (1965), ch. 2, and G. Constable, *Letters and Letter Collections* (1976).

[34] J. and L. Stones, 'Bishop Neville and his Correspondence', *Archives* XVI (1984), pp. 227–57.

[35] *Rot. Lit. Pat.*, p. 33.

[36] Van Caenegem, *Writs*, p. 420, no. 17. Cf. R. C. van Caenegem, *The Birth of the English Common Law* (1973), p.37.

above, it was up to Hugh Oilard, the beneficiary, to show the document to the abbot of Ramsey as evidence of the king's intervention in his case. The king took no further steps to ensure that the writ reached the abbot unchanged, nor did he require the abbot to reply to him directly. The phrase, 'no matter what writ might be produced', demonstrates that writs were already being issued in some numbers, but it also suggests that the king had no knowledge of what happened to them. If he were not ordinarily responsible for dispatching them, his ignorance is understandable.

Real missives were sent in the form of letters close. Closing up letters for confidential purposes must have been common practice for centuries, though actual examples are rare because the recipient ordinarily opened the letter up and destroyed it. Letters written on almost paper-thin slivers of wood, which closed up, have been discovered on Hadrian's Wall dating from 100 AD.[37] The next example of a letter close in England comes from 700 AD; this is a confidential letter written by the bishop of London to the archbishop of Canterbury.[38] By Henry II's reign, it can be shown that a letter close was sealed and addressed on the tie that kept it rolled up, though no such letter has been found unopened until the reign of Henry VIII.[39] Opened letters close, with their seals and ties cut off, begin to be kept from Henry II's reign because he made some categories of writ 'returnable'.[40] This meant that the addressee, usually a sheriff, was instructed to produce the writ at a subsequent time and place, most often before a royal justice. A method had therefore been devised of sending confidential instructions in writing and of checking on whether these writs were obeyed. Likewise in Henry II's reign writs begin to take common forms, both for administration (for instance the writs of summons used by the Exchequer) and for litigation. Writs in common form, available for purchase, were the framework of Henry II's legal reforms, based on the principle that no one need answer for his freehold without a royal writ.[41] Henry II had thus created a system which could potentially mass-produce documents from a few stereotypes (see p. 67 above).

This discussion has concentrated on royal writs because they set the pattern and are by far the most common. Royal practice was imitated by the magnates and by officials in the counties; we have already seen an example of a writ sent by a baron, Richard Fitz Gilbert, to his steward in *c.*1130;[42] similarly, writs sent by sheriffs to their bailiffs are extant from about a century later.[43] In due course, writs generated other letters and memoranda in the form of replies to their demands and written plaints and petitions to the king

letters close (margin annotation)

---

[37] A. K. Bowman and J. D. Thomas, *Vindolanda: The Latin Writing Tablets* (1983).

[38] P. Chaplais, in *Essays Presented to N. R. Ker* ed. M. B. Parkes and A. G. Watson (1978), pp. 3–24. S. Keynes argues that Edward the Confessor's writ (Sawyer no. 1105) is a letter close, *Facsimiles of Anglo-Saxon Charters* (1991), p. 7, no. 20.

[39] Chaplais, *Docs*, plate 25d. For seals see ch. 9, n. 56 below.

[40] Stenton, *Justice*, pp. 32–3. Chaplais, *Docs*, pp. 9–10. The earliest files of writs are listed in *Berks. Eyre*, pp. xci–xcii.

[41] Glanvill, Bk. xii, ch. 25, p. 148.

[42] See ch. 2, n. 121 above.

[43] Listed in *Berks. Eyre*, pp. cv–cvii. See ch. 8, n. 91 below.

for redress; replies to royal writs (returns of inquests) are extant in originals from Henry III's reign and petitions are extant from Edward I's.[44]

MEMORANDA KEPT BY INSTITUTIONS

Most of the documents so far described, particularly charters and chirographs, could serve as memoranda and were kept as such by the persons they benefited. Such documents differ, however, from the type of memoranda which were systematically compiled, usually by institutions, as a record of past practice for their own future guidance. Court rolls, financial accounts, cartularies and chronicles cannot be classed as single 'statements issued by individuals', because they usually form part of an accumulating series of records compiled by an authority. Although in the light of hindsight compiling memoranda seems an obvious step once the idea of writing for posterity in charters had become familiar, there is a time-lag of a century or more between the two activities. It is probable that the only type of cumulative written record used at all widely by the Anglo-Saxons was the chronicle. A century after the Norman Conquest the one continuous series of memoranda kept by the crown were the Exchequer pipe rolls; numerous additional types of Exchequer record were, however, created in Henry II's reign, for instance rolls of receipts[45] and the rolls made by Richard of Ilchester and Thomas Brown.[46] Judging by documents extant, cumulative non-financial record-keeping by the crown began during Hubert Walter's years of office between 1193 and 1205; the plea rolls of the royal courts, the coroners' and sheriffs' rolls in the counties, feet of fines, the Chancery rolls of outgoing letters, all start or are first unequivocally referred to at this time.[47]

Financial accounts

Outside the king's court, making cumulative memoranda got under way in the thirteenth century. Seignorial accounts belatedly followed the lead of the Exchequer, the earliest extant series being the pipe rolls of the bishops of Winchester starting in 1208.[48] These rolls record receipts (in money, crops, and livestock) and expenditure on the bishop's manors in detail. They are so

[44] *Guide to the Contents of the PRO*, HMSO (1963) I, pp. 27–8 (Inquisitions), 190 (Ancient Petitions).

[45] A facsimile of the receipt roll for Michaelmas term 1185 has been published by H. Hall (1899). The earliest receipt rolls are described and listed by H. Jenkinson in *Archaeologia* LXXIV (1925), pp. 298, 327–8.

[46] See ch.2, nn. 64, 61 above.

[47] See ch. 2, nn. 84–110 above.

[48] The two earliest Winchester rolls are edited by H. Hall (1903) and N. R. Holt (1964). The best introductions to manorial documents are J. Z. Titow, *English Rural Society, 1200–1350 (1969)* and P. D. A. Harvey, *Manorial Records, Archives and the User* 5 (1984). See also E. King, 'Estate Management and the Reform Movement' in W. M. Ormrod ed., *England in the Thirteenth Century* (1991), p. 6.

orderly that they must have been based on drafts or preliminary accounts in writing submitted by each bailiff. Although the earliest Winchester rolls draw up balances of receipts and expenditure, they do not aim to show profit and loss as such, but to act as a check against the bishop being cheated by his ministers. The king's Exchequer provided a model for collecting revenues rather than for running a business. The earliest records calculating the profits of manors are the Christ Church Canterbury accounts of 1224–5.[49] Manorial accounts of any sort remain very rare until the latter half of the thirteenth century and the majority of those extant were produced by the greater monasteries. Lay lords undoubtedly also possessed ministers' accounts, as some survive by chance in the Public Record Office when estates were forfeited to the crown; an example are the records of Adam of Stratton, an Exchequer official and financier, who was put on trial for corruption in 1289.[50] In addition to manorial accounts, accounts of the separate departmental heads in the great religious houses, the obedientaries, begin to be extant from the 1260s; among these are the earliest non-royal household accounts.[51] Similarly Merton College at Oxford has accounts of its administrative officers from 1277.[52] The accounts of towns follow a similar pattern to manors; the earliest continuous series are the Shrewsbury rolls of accounts of 1256 which were cast at weekly intervals.[53]

The most remarkable early accounts are the household rolls made in 1265 for Eleanor, countess of Leicester, the sister of Henry III and wife of Simon de Montfort (see plate xɪ). These record her expenditure, mainly for the supply of food and drink, under different departmental headings such as the kitchen and the marshalcy of the stables. The entries are made in a variety of cursive hands, which suggests that they were compiled by the week or fortnight. Furthermore they specify the expenditure of each day separately and thus comprise a kind of diary of expenditure. The rolls cover the period 19 February to 29 August, the latter date being nearly a month after Simon's death at the battle of Evesham. As the accounts are set out in a regular form, these rolls are evidently not the first of their kind, although they are the earliest to survive. Perhaps Eleanor retained these ones because they concerned the last weeks of Simon's life. Their chance survival suggests that by the middle of the thirteenth century many magnates' households, both clerical and lay, were keeping daily accounts of expenditure in writing on parchment.

[49] E. Stone, 'Profit and Loss Accountancy at Norwich Cathedral Priory', *TRHS* 5th series xɪɪ (1962), p. 27.

[50] *Accounts and Surveys of the Wiltshire Lands of Adam de Stratton* ed. M. W. Farr, WiltsRS xɪv (1959). Pieces of early thirteenth-century rolls, preserved in the PRO, are discussed by C.M. Woolgar, *Household Accounts from Medieval England*, ɪ (1992), pp. 10–17.

[51] Early rolls are discussed in *Compotus Rolls of the Priory of Worcester* ed. J. M. Wilson and C. Gordon, Worcestershire Historical S. (1908), p. ix, and H. W. Saunders, *An Introduction to the Obedientary and Manor Rolls of Norwich Cathedral Priory* (1930), p. 21.

[52] *The Early Rolls of Merton College Oxford* ed. J. R. L. Highfield (1964).

[53] G. H. Martin, 'The English Borough in the 13th Century', *TRHS* 5th series xxɪɪ (1963), pp. 136–7.

But because such records concerned petty expenditure only, they must usually have been treated as ephemeral and thrown away. The most commonplace records are the least likely to survive.

In 1293 Edward I's treasurer, William March, introduced into the Exchequer *jornalia* or 'journal' rolls. These were diaries ('day-books' in modern accounting terms), which showed the amount of cash in the treasury at the start of each day's business and the disbursements made during the day. As with household rolls like Eleanor de Montfort's, the purpose of the daily record was to balance income against expenditure week by week. But, in the case of an organization as complex as the royal government, 'this merely created a false sense of security, for the *jornalia* rolls took no account of the total number of wardrobe bills in circulation, or of the considerable sums paid out at source after 1298 from the county farms and taxes.'[54] Like Edward I's other attempts in the 1290s to increase royal control by doubling up on documentation, the *jornalia* rolls were a failure in practical terms, although they provide a fascinating record for posterity.

Surveys and rentals

Extant financial accounts of the thirteenth century raise the question of what type of records preceded them. Obviously the great monastic estates made some financial records before 1200. Payments (both made and received) were probably recorded on tally sticks from early in the twelfth century, although there was no conception at that time of keeping a continuous series of financial memoranda to guide the steward of an estate. A landlord in the twelfth century obtained an overall view of his property, not from account rolls, but from a survey. The typical survey was not part of an accumulating series of records, as it was made *ab initio* by the incoming lord. Jocelin of Brakelond describes how Abbot Samson conducted such a survey:

> At his order a general description [*descriptio generalis*] was made in each hundred of leets and suits, hidages and corn dues, renders of hens, and of other customs, rents and issues, which had always been largely concealed by the farmers; and he had all these reduced to writing, so that, within four years of his election [in 1182] there was no one who could deceive him even about a single pennyworth from the abbey's revenues, whereas he had received nothing in writing from his predecessors about the management of the abbey, except a little schedule containing the names of the knights of St Edmund, the names of the manors, and the rent which each farm should yield. [Abbot Samson] called this book his *kalendarium*, as individual debts which he had acquitted were also inscribed in it. He consulted this book almost daily,

[54] W. M. Ormrod, 'State Building and State Finance under Edward I' in W. M. Ormrod ed., *England in the Thirteenth Century*, Harlaxton (1991), p. 24; M. Prestwich, *Edward I* (1988), p. 536.

as if he contemplated in it the physiognomy of his own probity as in a mirror.[55]

Samson called his survey a *kalendarium* because in classical Latin that word had meant a list of debts due at the kalends of each month. Surveys and rentals of this sort, summarizing in writing the revenues due to a lord, became increasingly common. Jocelin refers in the citation above to an earlier list made at Bury St Edmunds, whose size he minimizes, as Abbot Baldwin's *Book of Feoffments* (dating from early in the twelfth century), is still extant.

The precedent for all such surveys, great and small, was Domesday Book, which had likewise been called a *descriptio*.[56] Judging by surveys known, the decade 1180–90, when Samson made his *kalendarium*, was the most productive period: from these years came the royal Assize of Arms and the *rotuli de dominabus* (lists of marriageable ladies), and inquiries conducted by Durham and St Paul's cathedrals, Glastonbury abbey, and the Knights Templar; likewise the earliest known bishop's *matricula* or *scrutinium*, that of Baldwin of Worcester, dates from this decade.[57] A remarkably detailed survey was made by Christ Church priory at Canterbury in *c*.1200. Set out in four columns, it lists each tenant, the amount of his annual rent, the date when payment is due, and the whereabouts and dimensions of the tenements. For example, the first entry describes the land of the sister of Roger son of Hamel as lying 'behind the wall of our almonry; its breadth northwards 26 feet; length from the street westwards 110 feet'.[58] In recording the dimensions of individual tenements the priory hoped perhaps to settle boundary disputes by referring to the precise evidence of writing instead of the partial recollections of neighbours.

In the thirteenth century the practice of making surveys in writing extended beyond the royal government and great religious houses to landlords in general. In the rules for estate management composed for the countess of Lincoln in the 1230s or 1240s, Robert Grosseteste recommends an incoming landlord to make a survey of his revenues in triplicate; just as Abbot Samson had consulted his *kalendarium* almost every day, Grosseteste recommends the countess to 'keep this roll by you and often look at it.'[59] In addition to serving as rentals for estates, such surveys were the basis of systematic taxation:

---

[55] Jocelin, p. 29 (my translation). A copy (dating from *c*.1230) of Samson's *kalendarium* is extant, ed. R. H. C. Davis, Camden S. 3rd series LXXXIV (1954). This text suggests that Jocelin exaggerated the scope of Samson's survey, as it had not been completed by 1190. See also D. Greenway and J. Sayers, *Jocelin of Brakelond* (1989), p. 131, n. 27.

[56] V. H. Galbraith, *Domesday Book* (1974), ch. 5, discusses Abbot Baldwin's *Book of Feoffments* and other early surveys.

[57] B. A. Lees lists the surveys in *Records of the Templars in England: The Inquest of 1185* (1935), p. xxix. For Bishop Baldwin's *matricula* see Cheney, *Chanceries*, pp. 115–16. A bishop's *matricula* differed from his *registrum*; see ch. 2, n. 119 above.

[58] W. Urry, *Canterbury under the Angevin Kings* (1967), p. 249 and map 2b, sheet 3. For the layout of this MS. see ibid., frontispiece.

[59] *Walter of Henley*, p. 388.

notable early examples are the royal subsidy assessments of 1225, Wallingford's rolls of tradesmen of 1227 and 1230 (see plates ix and x), and the well-documented valuation of the English church (diocese by diocese) for the papal tenth of 1254.[60] Impressive though surveys are as pioneers of written record and as historical documents, they cannot have been as useful to landlords as annual accounts because they soon went out of date. All surveys shared with Domesday Book the characteristic of being symbols of efficiency and authority rather than its reality.

Legal records

In courts, lists and books of rules are generally earlier than systematic memoranda of particular cases, just as surveys and rentals precede financial accounts. Thus in boroughs the oldest records, apart from the charters constituting them, are lists of guildsmen forming the corporation and custumals summarizing municipal by-laws. Leicester's guild rolls begin in 1196;[61] they are the oldest series of memoranda now extant made outside the king's court or a monastery. Northampton has a custumal of similar date, although it is not in its original form.[62] The most remarkable early custumal is a roll in French made for Exeter, which was probably compiled in the 1230s by the town clerk, John Baubi.[63] The borough court's rolls of pleas are usually of later date: 'the court's official memory still reposed in the heads of its *probi homines* [responsible men] when the guild began to commit its lists of names, fines, and vats of ale to parchment';[64] exceptionally early are the rolls of the Wallingford burghmoot which begin in 1231–2.

The records of the king's court follow a comparable pattern, with lists and books of rules preceding enrolments of actual litigation. Notes of pecuniary penalties (oblations, fines, amercements) are listed in the pipe rolls of the Exchequer from Henry I's reign and separate rolls of amercements were kept in Henry II's reign. Likewise from late in Henry II's reign comes Glanvill's treatise 'on the laws and customs of England', which is essentially a custumal for the king's court summarizing its most common rules in writing, as the author explains in his prologue.[65] Rolls of pleas, on the other hand, are not extant until 1194; their retention was perhaps due to Hubert Walter, who had been appointed chief justiciar in 1193. The making of such rolls may date back to Henry II's appointment of itinerant justices twenty or so years earlier. A

[60] C. Johnson and H. Jenkinson, *English Court Hand* (1915), plates xiia, xiib (subsidy assessments). The church valuation of 1254 is ed. W. E. Lunt, *The Valuation of Norwich* (1926).
[61] Martin, 'The English Borough', pp. 129, 132–3. Cf. ch. 2, n. 100 above and ch. 9, n. 30 below.
[62] G. H. Martin, 'The Origins of Borough Records', *Journal of the Society of Archivists* ii (1960–4), p. 152.
[63] *The Anglo-Norman Custumal of Exeter* ed. J. W. Schopp (1925). This edition has complete facsimiles.
[64] Martin, 'The Origins of Borough Records', pp. 153, 149.
[65] Glanvill, p. 3; see also p. 67 above.

Lincolnshire litigant in 1219 appealed to 'the record of the rolls of the justices itinerant' there during Henry II's reign.[66] But there is no record of these rolls being produced, and the defendant denied that this plea had ever been in Henry II's court. Court records of proceedings are essential in any modern judicial system and it is difficult to understand how Henry II's judges could have operated effectively without them. Nevertheless the judges may not have been 'modern' in this respect but traditionalist, like many lawyers. Pleas had been heard in royal courts for generations without official records of proceedings being kept, because – ideally – each case was to be judged on its merits, unrestricted by precedents in writing.

Ecclesiastical courts might be expected to have been more advanced than their royal counterparts in keeping records, since the clergy were ex officio experts in literacy. Yet the pattern and chronology of development here is much the same as in the king's court. The classic textbook of canon law, Gratian's, was composed in around 1140. But 'the earliest records of an English church court (as opposed to records of ecclesiastical litigation preserved by a party to the case)' do not appear until 1200.[67] Again it is. Hubert Walter who is responsible for this development, this time in his capacity as archbishop of Canterbury. After his death in 1205, church court records become spasmodic until rolls of suits and act books appear with regularity in the fourteenth century. But in this instance extant records are misleading, as ecclesiastical cases were usually recorded in chirographs in triplicate (for the judge and the two parties), instead of being enrolled, and consequently they have not survived as well as rolls.[68]

The pattern of making memoranda in local courts other than boroughs – hundred and manor courts for example – is less clear. Their records are more scattered and relatively few are extant, because local lordships have not had such a continuous institutional life as boroughs or the king's government. As in other courts, keeping lists of names seems to have preceded making records of proceedings. Thus Jocelin of Brakelond describes the bailiffs of the sacrist and cellarer of Bury St Edmunds enrolling men in frankpledge each year as early as 1200, whereas the first hundred court rolls date from the 1260s and they survive from no more than a dozen places before 1300.[69] Similarly the earliest manor court rolls come from the 1240s and it is unlikely that any earlier ones will be found.[70] Even plea rolls from county courts are extraordinarily rare, considering the court's importance as the principal and regular assembly of each shire. The only county court rolls extant from the thirteenth century are some from Cheshire (beginning in 1259), which are exceptional

---

[66] *Rolls of the Justices in Eyre* ed. D. M. Stenton, Selden S. LIII (1934), p. 411; R. V. Turner, *The English Judiciary in the Age of Glanvill and Bracton* (1985), p. 13, n. 45; P. Brand, 'Henry II and the Creation of the English Common Law', *Haskins Society Journal* II (1990), pp. 215–16.

[67] *Select Canterbury Cases* ed. N. Adams and C. Donahue, SS XCV (1979). p. 3.

[68] See above nn. 19, 23; J. E. Sayers, *Papal Judge Delegates in the Province of Canterbury* (1971), pp. 243–51.

[69] Jocelin, p. 102; H. M. Cam, *The Hundred and the Hundred Rolls* (1930), p. 286.

[70] *Select Pleas in Manorial Courts* ed. F. W. Maitland, SS II (1888), pp. xii–xiii. P. D. A. Harvey, *Manorial Records* (1984), p. 42.

anyway because the earldom of Chester was a privileged jurisdiction.[71] As in the development of the king's court, lists of fines from county courts are more common at first than records of pleas.[72]

Local court rolls become more common towards the end of the thirteenth century, but they remain rare compared with the plea rolls of the king's court, which exist in multiple copies in Edward I's reign. Similarly among cities and boroughs, only eleven possess extant records of any type earlier than Edward I's accession, although that figure doubles by the time of his death.[73] On the other hand, treatises written for baronial stewards in the 1260s and 1270s assume that court rolls are kept: the *Court Baron* has the bailiff say to the steward, 'By my faith, see here all that for which you ask written down in this roll' and John of Oxford's treatise advises the bailiff's clerk 'to note down everything that is done in the court as it occurs.'[74] Even if every clerk made a roll, he certainly did not note down everything. Local court rolls are usually laconic. Their main purpose was to record the names of litigants and suitors attending the court and of persons who had been fined; occasional individual items do get recorded in detail, however, when the clerk did not know how to abbreviate them. Such rolls derived their form from lists and often they are little more than that.

Year Books

Contrasting with the rigorously summarized local court rolls are the Year Books, which merit attention because they are the largest and most detailed collection of dialogue made in the Middle Ages. They are reports of court cases, beginning in the reign of Edward I, which purport to record the actual words (translated into French or Latin) of litigants, their counsel and the judges for the benefit of law students and practitioners.[75] The Year Books' practice of recording dialogue seems to have emanated from law reporters in London and not from the king's clerks. The earliest instance of such reporting occurs in London's Latin record of the royal justices' visitation of the City in 1244. Certain cases are recorded twice, first in reported speech, as is usual in plea rolls, and then again in dialogue form using the first person. For example, Alfred de Pinchbeck sued John de Coudres, a former sheriff, for wrongful imprisonment. The plea roll records in formal and general terms Alfred's complaint and John's defence that Alfred had resisted arrest and refused to find a pledge for good behaviour.[76] In the alternative version of this case, however, more circumstantial details are given: it explains that Alfred's family

---

[71] *Calendar of County Court, City Court, and Eyre Rolls of Chester* ed. R. Stewart-Brown, Chetham S. new series LXXXIV (1925), pp. 1–34. R. C. Palmer discusses early county court records in *EHR* XCI (1976), p. 777.

[72] W. A. Morris, *The Early English County Court* (1926), pp. 197–230, prints miscellaneous records of this type dating from 1258–64.

[73] Martin, 'The English Borough', p. 128.

[74] *Court Baron*, pp. 58, 72. J. S. Beckerman discusses manorial court procedure in *Law & History Review* x (1992), pp. 197–252.

[75] T. F. T. Plucknett, *Early English Legal Literature* (1958), ch. vi.

[76] *The London Eyre of 1244* London Record S. VI (1970), p. 77, no. 190.

had been imprisoned at Newgate because a Jew had accused him of killing the Jew's wife; when Alfred returned from King's Lynn fair, John, the sheriff, had demanded a pledge from him because of this charge. The alternative version then records John's cross-examination by the justices in direct speech:

> The justices said: 'For what cause did you exact a pledge from Alfred, whereas he was not in the City when the Jewess was allegedly killed?'
> John said: 'I asked him for a pledge and when he drew his knife, I seized his hand with the knife, for which cause I imprisoned him.'
> The justices said: 'You had no cause to exact a pledge from Alfred.'[77]

This version thus explains the facts of the case and the points of law involved by recording the justices' questions and comments, whereas the official plea roll is concerned only to note the procedural stages of the case in due form. This comparison between alternative versions of the same case illustrates the paradox, familiar to historians, that unofficial records are often more informative and factual than the formal texts made by professional clerks. Although formal legal records are the largest group of medieval documents extant, they are not as reliable as their orderly appearance suggests.

This description of memoranda-making has proceeded mainly by referring to the earliest extant exemplars of various types of record, and it leads to the general conclusion that outside the king's court the main series of memoranda started in the thirteenth century. Although great monastic houses had made surveys and rentals in the twelfth century and the royal Exchequer kept pipe rolls from the reign of Henry I, communal and seignorial court rolls and financial accounts are products of the thirteenth century; they were almost certainly not made before the 1190s. There are, however, two obvious objections to generalizing in this way. Firstly, the earliest records extant are not necessarily the earliest records made. For example, a Cheshire chirograph of 1228 refers to 'the authentic roll of our lord the earl' (of Chester) which preserves memory and record, whereas the earliest roll of any sort now extant from Cheshire is a plea roll from 1259.[78] The roll referred to in 1228, the 'Domesday' roll which registered covenants, existed as late as 1580 when extracts were copied from it. It was probably the first of its kind, however, as it started with a poem explaining that its 'holy page' would ensure that the agreements enrolled in it were kept.[79] Secondly and conversely, a record surviving from an early date may have always been unique and did not necessarily form part of a cumulative series of memoranda; estate surveys from the twelfth century for example, like Abbot Samson's *kalendarium*, were intended to be unique.

To sum up, the general impression left by the evidence, taking account of references to documents now lost as well as those that survive, is that the habit of making and keeping records of proceedings in continuous series stemmed

12c → 13c

---

[77] Ibid., p. 134, no. 345.
[78] *Cheshire Facs*, p. 48. Cf. n. 71 above.
[79] R. Stewart-Brown, 'The Domesday Roll of Chester', *EHR* xxxvii (1922), p. 496.

from the king's court at the end of the twelfth century and took another century to spread across the country. Hazarding a guess, manors which did not belong to the king or to ecclesiastical magnates probably only began, as a rule, to have financial accounts and court rolls in Edward I's reign.

Chronicles

One type of cumulative memorial, the chronicle, had far older origins. Not all chroniclers were monks: Ralf de Diceto and Roger of Howden were secular clerics, and Arnold Fitz Thedmar, the probable author of the London chronicle, was a layman.[80] Nevertheless the typical chronicle was monastic and had its origins in the Benedictine preoccupation with the careful regulation of time. The typical monastic chronicler distinguished his function from that of the historian: 'The historian proceeds diffusely and elegantly, whereas the chronicler proceeds simply, gradually and briefly', Gervase of Canterbury explained in *c.*1188.[81] 'The chronicler computes years *Anno Domini* and the months and kalends and briefly describes the actions of kings and princes which occurred at those times; he also commemorates events, portents and wonders. There are many, however, writing chronicles or annals who exceed their limits'.[82] Because Gervase intended to remain a humble chronicler, he insists that he wants 'to compile rather than to write' and explains that he does not write for a public library, but for his own monastic family at Christ Church Canterbury.[83] The typical chronicle was thus a dated series of events recorded for the guidance of a monastic house; it was not an interpretation of the past presented to the public by a historian. Paradoxically, but understandably, the greatest monastic chroniclers, like Matthew Paris or Gervase himself, went far beyond these narrow limits.

The chronicle is thus an unstylish production, concerned with the matter rather than the manner of presentation, and 'added to year by year and therefore composed by various people'.[84] The writer of this description, an anonymous monastic annalist of the thirteenth century associated with Winchester, advises the composer of a chronicle to see that there is always a sheet attached to the book, on which may be noted in pencil the deaths of illustrious men and other memoranda whenever the news comes to hand. At the end of each year the monk 'who has been appointed to the task, and not just anyone who so wishes, should write out briefly and succinctly in the body of the book what he thinks truest and best to be passed down to the notice of posterity'.[85] That such notes were commonly kept is suggested by John of Salisbury's statement about sixty years earlier that he had seen in the archives

---

[80] Gransden, *Historical Writing*, pp. 509ff.
[81] Gervase, I, p. 87. D. Hay, *Annalists and Historians* (1977), pp. 58–9.
[82] Gervase I, pp. 87–8.
[83] 'compilare potius quam scribere cupio,' ibid. p. 89.
[84] *Annales Monastici* IV, p. 355.
[85] Ibid Cf. Cheney, *Texts & Studies*, p. 224; Gransden, *Historical Writing* pp. 319–20.

of churches 'notes of memorable things', which would help future writers even where chronicles were unavailable.[86]

Twentieth-century historians have often distinguished between chronicle sources, which they consider biased and unreliable, and official records (such as the Chancery rolls) which they prefer. Yet the best chronicles were the official records of the monastic houses which produced them and were treated as such on occasions by the royal government. When Matthew Paris attended the ceremonies in 1247 for the Feast of Edward the Confessor, Henry III ordered him from the throne in Westminster Hall 'to write an accurate and full account of all these things and commit them indelibly to notable writing in a book, so that their memory shall in no way be lost to posterity'.[87] The king evidently knew that Matthew was writing a chronicle and invited him to dinner. Similarly when Edward I looked for historical precedents to support his claims in Scotland in 1291, he turned first to monastic chronicles and not to the royal archives. At the same time he sent monasteries information about his claims and ordered them 'to be noted in your chronicles as a perpetual memorial of the business'.[88] In Edward's time the monastic chronicle was the most ancient, but still the most secure and productive form of record in existence.

Cartularies

Like chronicles, these are monastic in origin. Hemming, a monk of Worcester who composed much of the earliest cartulary extant, describes his purpose:

> I, Hemming, monk and priest have composed this little book concerning the possessions of this our monastery, so that it may be clear to our posterity which and how many possessions in land pertain to the endowment of this monastery for the sustenance of the monks, the servants of God; or rather which [possessions] ought by right [to be ours], although we have been unjustly dispossessed of them by force and fraud.[89]

A cartulary was thus a collection of title-deeds copied into a register for greater security. Unlike chronicles, cartularies do not have ancient origins in England. They were products of the insecurity brought about by the Norman Conquest and the civil war of Stephen's reign, combined with greater competition between monastic houses to acquire and retain lands, which resulted from the increase in the number of monasteries in the twelfth and thirteenth centuries. Thus the compiler of Ramsey abbey's *Book of Benefactors* explains in *c.*1170 that the abbey had lost almost everything in the 'dark and

---

[86] 'rerum memorabilium subnotationes'. *Historia Pontificalis* ed. M. Chibnall (1956), p. 2.

[87] Matthew Paris IV, pp. 644–5; Vaughan, *Matthew Paris*, pp. 3–4.

[88] Bartholomew de Cotton, *Historia Anglicana* ed. H. R. Luard, RS XVI (1859), p. 182; E. L. G. Stones, 'The Appeal to History in Anglo-Scottish Relations', *Archives* IX (1969), pp. 12ff.

[89] N. R. Ker, *Books, Collectors and Libraries* (1983), p. 47.

gloomy days' of King Stephen, both from attacks from enemies and domestic disputes, 'and so we have collected together in one volume our chirographs and the charters of our privileges . . . as a warning for future ages and to instruct our readers.'[90] This compiler also translated the abbey's pre-Conquest documents from English into Latin to make them more acceptable. Apart from convenience and greater security, another advantage of copying records into a cartulary was that they could be modernized and improved, or even forged.

The first portion of Hemming's cartulary was not composed by him, but dates from a generation before the Norman Conquest; Hemming made his portion towards the end of the eleventh century. The only other cartulary extant from the eleventh century, the Oswald cartulary, also emanates from Worcester. It is therefore probable that the cartulary form in England was created at Worcester in the generation before the Norman Conquest and brought to fruition by Hemming as a consequence of the Conquest. English monks in the great Benedictine houses aimed to justify and explain their heritage to their Norman masters.[91] There may even be a direct connexion between Hemming's cartulary and the Normans, as V. H. Galbraith has suggested that Samson of Bayeux, the bishop of Worcester in Hemming's time, had been the compiler of Domesday Book.[92] The next oldest cartulary extant is the Rochester book *Textus Roffensis*, again from an ancient monastic house, while dates from *c*.1125. No more than half a dozen cartularies are earlier than 1150 and fewer than 30 earlier than 1200.[93] Like other series of memoranda (excepting chronicles and royal Exchequer records), cartulary-making became firmly established, not in the twelfth century, but in the thirteenth. In this century the practice spread from monasteries to laymen, although lay cartularies from the thirteenth century are very rare.[94] They seem to have been particularly prevalent in Northamptonshire; from there come Richard Hotot's estate book (see plate xv), Ralf Basset's roll, and the Braybrooke cartulary.[95] Richard Hotot was a younger brother of William Hotot, abbot of Peterborough (1246–9); so he could have learned about the importance of keeping documents from the abbot, or he may have learned from his father, Thomas Hotot. In 1322 another Northamptonshire gentleman, Henry de Bray, actually wrote his own cartulary, as we have already seen.[96]

---

[90] *Ramsey*, p. 4; Gransden, *Historical Writing*, pp. 279–80; see pp. 158, 320 below.

[91] R. W. Southern, 'The Sense of the Past,' *TRHS* 5th series xxiii (1973), pp. 247–50.

[92] *Domesday Book*, pp. 50–1. But see P. Chaplais, 'William of St Calais and the Domesday Survey' in *Domesday Studies* ed. J. C. Holt (1987), pp. 65–77.

[93] Ker, *English MSS*, p. 20; G. R. C. Davis, *Medieval Cartularies of Great Britain* (1958), p. xi.

[94] The earliest is the cartulary of the Constable family of Flamborough (dating from the 1200s), Davis, *Medieval Cartularies*, no. 1224.

[95] Ibid., nos 1256, 1188A, 1206.

[96] See n. 3 above.

Registers

In the medieval period the commonest term for a cartulary was a *registrum*. The rolls of the Chancery were likewise described as a *registrum*[97] and so was Domesday Book on one occasion.[98] This wide definition of 'register' is useful, as all these records shared the common characteristic of being edited collections, in books or rolls, which had been compiled from primary sources from separate pieces of parchment. Moreover, some of the works described as cartularies in the preceding paragraphs do not exclusively concern charters: the estate books of Richard Hotot and Henry de Bray were intended as general reference books for their families and are not narrowly legalistic. Once the idea of copying documents into books for greater security and convenience became familiar, the practice took many forms. For instance, the royal Exchequer made registers in books, like a monastic house, to provide fair copies and guides to its records and to note down miscellanea. The oldest of these Exchequer remembrance books (Domesday Book excepted) are the Red Book and the Black Book, which were compiled in the 1230s.[99] The one most commonly used by scholars today is *The Book of Fees*, containing surveys of feudal tenures between 1198 and 1293. A note on its flyleaf, probably written at the time it was compiled in 1302, reminds the user that the book is a register and not a primary source: 'Remember that this book was composed and compiled from several official inquests . . . and therefore the contents of this book is to be used for evidence here in the Exchequer and not for the record.'[100] Registers like this were guides; they did not have the authority of the original documents themselves, which were the authentic official records.

On the other hand, another class of registers were treated as official records. These were the registers which recorded copies of outgoing documents, as distinct from monastic cartularies and Exchequer remembrance books which recorded documents in the compiler's possession. The greatest series of registers of outgoing documents are the Chancery rolls of royal letters, beginning in the first three years of John's reign; the Charter roll is described as a register as early as 1201.[101] Another well-known series are the bishops' registers (starting in 1217 or a little earlier), which were modelled on the Chancery rolls.[102] Even earlier than the Chancery rolls are the provisions Hubert Walter had made in 1194 for registering Jewish chirographs of loans and receipts on rolls in designated centres throughout England.[103] The earliest local register of recognizances of debt which is extant, however, is London's

---

[97] See ch. 2, nn. 90, 92.
[98] Galbraith, *Domesday Book*, p. 105, n. 2.
[99] Described in *Dialogus*, pp. xi–xii.
[100] *Book of Fees* I, p. xx.
[101] See ch. 2, nn. 88, 90 above.
[102] See ch. 2, nn. 113–120 above.
[103] See ch. 2, n. 98 above.

Liber A beginning in 1276.[104] London also has early rolls of registered wills (beginning in 1258), and some title-deeds are enrolled in the court of Husting rolls (beginning in 1252).[105]

The practice of registering deeds of title in towns probably followed the lead of the Chancery rolls, although it could have derived from monastic practice. The earl of Chester's Domesday roll 'which preserves memory and record' is the earliest known of such registers, but it is now lost.[106] The oldest municipal register extant is a roll from Wallingford, made in 1231–2.[107] This roll is of particular interest because it appears to be a record of conveyances of small properties (houses, rents, market stalls and so on), which had been made orally in the borough court without charters. The next oldest Wallingford register, made in 1252–3, seems by contrast to be a summary of charters.[108] It looks as if in the twenty years between 1232 and 1252 the habit of conveying property in writing had become established among the Wallingford burghers.

LEARNED AND LITERARY WORKS

The increasing number of documents issued and memoranda compiled in the twelfth and thirteenth centuries is matched by a substantial upsurge in the production of 'books', in the general modern sense of learned and literary works. Yet medieval books were essentially different from modern ones because they were manuscripts. Consequently the total numbers are small by modern standards and counting them is of useful but only limited value, since individual manuscript volumes are not uniform objects like printed books. Making approximate estimates from contemporary catalogues, Durham cathedral library had about 490 volumes in the twelfth century, Rochester cathedral about 241 in 1201, and Christ Church Canterbury about 1,300 volumes in the catalogue of Prior Henry of Eastry (1285–1311).[109] These estimates are subject to every kind of qualification, because the makers of medieval library catalogues were not primarily concerned with counting their stock. The earliest Durham catalogue (from which the estimate of 490 volumes has been derived) illustrates the difficulties of counting, as various items are described as being in a certain number of 'books' (*libri*) or 'sets' (*paria*) or 'parts' (*particuli*) or 'quires' (*quaterniones*). Furthermore, books varied so much in size and in the layout of each page that the number of volumes

---

[104] Ed. R. L. Sharpe (1899).

[105] *Calendar of Wills Proved and Enrolled in the Court of Husting* ed. R. L. Sharpe (1889) I, p. xxiv.

[106] See nn. 78, 79 above.

[107] G. H. Martin, 'The Registration of Deeds of Title in the Medieval Borough' in *Study of Medieval Records*, pp. 155–6.

[108] Ibid., pp. 156–7.

[109] *Catalogi Veteres Librorum Ecclesiae Cathedralis Dunelm*, Surtees S. VII (1838), pp. 1–10. The dated catalogue from Rochester, ed. W. B. Rye, is printed in *Archaeologia Cantiana* III (1860), pp. 54ff. The size of Christ Church library is estimated by F. Wormald, 'The Monastic Library' in *English Library*, p. 22, cf. plate 10. For library catalogues see also ch. 5, nn. 53–5 below.

gives little indication of the amount of reading material available. In general, however, library catalogues show that many more books were acquired in the twelfth and thirteenth centuries, as they often list new acquisitions from particular persons.

Individuals likewise possessed few books by modern standards. Robert Grosseteste, the greatest English scholar and bishop of the thirteenth century, perhaps had about 90; John of Foxton, who gave his books on Scripture to Lincoln cathedral library in *c.* 1240, possessed about 34 volumes on that subject; Master Peter of Peckham, a lawyer, had 18 books in a coffer when he died in 1293; Guy de Beauchamp, earl of Warwick, gave away about 40 books in 1306.[110] The limitations of such fragmentary information are obvious. An inexplicable exception to the rule that neither individuals nor institutions had many books is a court case from Worcestershire in 1221, in which the toll collector of Wychbold was alleged to have impounded 'two carts which bore the books of Richard, dean of Worcester'.[111] Two carts suggests a large number of books, but whether they all belonged to Richard and where they were being taken is not specified.

Library catalogues are more informative about the types of books kept than about numbers; but there are difficulties here too, as some catalogues list only some of their books (those kept in particular places for example) and items specified can be difficult to identify because many books had no uniform titles. The library of Bury St Edmunds, which can be reconstructed with confidence for the twelfth century, indicates the main categories of books.[112] It was largely built up – by gift and purchase and by copying in the *scriptorium* – by one abbot, Anselm, between 1121 and 1148. By the end of the twelfth century Bury possessed bibles and liturgical books, texts of the main Church Fathers (largely added by Abbot Anselm), pagan Latin classics, histories both English (for example, Bede and the *Anglo-Saxon Chronicle*) and European (for example, Paul the Deacon and the *Gesta Francorum*), 'modern' (that is, twelfth-century) scholastic textbooks in divinity and law, and some 'modern' Latin literature such as the poems of Walter of Châtillon.

It would not be profitable to list in greater detail here the various books used and made in England between 1066 and 1307, as that would involve an extended essay on medieval learning and literature in Latin, Hebrew, French and English.[113] Instead, a few main types will be alluded to briefly. Unlike some of the forms of documents and memoranda already discussed in this chapter, books were not a novelty at the time of the Norman Conquest, nor is the format of the book unfamiliar to the modern reader. Although books were

[110] R. W. Hunt, 'The Library of Robert Grosseteste' in *Robert Grosseteste* ed. D. A. Callus (1955), pp. 127–9; R. M. Thomson, *Catalogue of Lincoln Cathedral Library* (1989), p. xvi and plate 6 (Foxton); *SCCKB* I, p. clxiv (Peckham). See n. 2 above (Beauchamp).
[111] *Rolls of the Justices in Eyre for Lincolnshire and Worcestershire* ed. D. M. Stenton, SS LIII (1934), p. 574, no. 1167. King John likewise had a library large enough to transport in carts: see ch. 5, n. 63 below.
[112] R. M. Thomson, 'The Library of Bury St Edmunds in the Eleventh and Twelfth Centuries', *Speculum* XLVII (1972), pp. 617–45.
[113] N. J. Morgan is editing *The Manuscript Book 1100–1400*, A History of the Book in Britain, Cambridge University Press (forthcoming).

no novelty, they do seem to have been a rarity in late Anglo-Saxon England. Or at least the prelates appointed by the Normans considered the libraries they found to be so inadequate that they restocked them on an unprecedented scale.[114] Abbot Anselm's work at Bury is an example of what was done in the main cathedrals and abbeys. Nor were the principal texts which were acquired or made in the century after the Norman Conquest new in themselves: they were the Bible, the Church Fathers, the pagan Latin classics, all works hallowed by antiquity. Scribes and illuminators wrote more accurate texts and embellished them in new ways, but they did not alter their essentials. These classics continued to be the foundation of any medieval library.

Alongside these relatively few perennials, planted by the sages of antiquity (whether Jewish, Christian or pagan), there were growing up numerous recent books by lesser men. These latter works were lesser in dignity, but not necessarily in length; the *Ormulum*, a series of homilies on the Gospels in the Missal composed in *c*.1170, numbers 20,512 short lines in Middle English in its extant form, which is perhaps one-eighth of the original.[115] Furthermore, as John of Salisbury commented in *c*.1150 (quoting Bernard of Chartres), 'modern' authors are dwarfs, but they stand on the shoulders of the giant sages of antiquity and so see more and further than their predecessors.[116] This confident attitude, combined with widening literacy caused by the dissemination of documents of all kinds in the twelfth century, produced a growing number of newly composed writings as well as further copies of the classics, both pagan and Christian. These new works are of two principal sorts. Firstly, there are the productions of the schoolmen, which aimed to cope with the increasing mass of written material by providing guides to it (in Latin) in logically organized treatises: the *Summa Theologiae* of Thomas Aquinas (composed in *c*.1260) is the best-known of such texts. Secondly, there are the very varied works composed for the book-reading or book-using public, both cleric and lay, in Latin, French and English – poems, songs, histories, romances, saints' lives, sermons, and so on.

Learned works

Taking the writings of the schoolmen first, the typical scholastic book is in the form either of a *glossa* or of a *summa*; both took definite shape in the twelfth century and aimed to cope with the increasing number of documents. The *glossa*, the 'gloss' around a text, is discussed with reference to the layout of the page in the next chapter. The *summa* is explained here. Robert of Melun, an Englishman by birth and bishop of Hereford (1163–7), defined a *summa* both as 'a concise encyclopedia of instances' and 'a compendious collection of instances'.[117] The prototype was Abelard's *Sic et Non* (composed in the 1130s),

---

[114] See ch. 1, nn. 4–5 above.
[115] Ed. R. M. White and R. Holt (1878); see also p. 131 below.
[116] *Metalogicon* Bk III, ch. 4, ed. C. C. J. Webb (1929), p. 136; Clanchy, '*Moderni*', p. 676.
[117] 'singulorum brevis comprehensio', 'singulorum compendiosa collectio', M. D. Chenu, *Nature, Man and Society in the Twelfth Century* trans. J. Taylor and L. K. Little (1968), p. 298. Robert of Melun is discussed by C. J. Mews in *Exemplaria* II (1990), pp. 486–90, 498–9.

which aimed to cut through the 'mass of words' presented to divinity students by bringing together selected apparently contradictory quotations under headings and subheadings.[118] Although many *summae* juxtaposed contradictory texts in this way, the essence of the genre was that it comprised a selection of texts organized in accordance with a logical scheme. Likewise although many *summae* contained explanatory commentaries, at the basis of the *summa* form were the quotations cited from authorities; Abelard's *Sic et Non* had no commentary apart from a prologue.

Long before the twelfth century rhetoricians had collected quotations, particularly from classical authors, into anthologies called *florilegia* (bunches of flowers), and this practice continued. As well as using such anthologies himself, Gerald of Wales presented his *Gemma Ecclesiastica* (written in *c.*1197) as a kind of *florilegium* selected from the 'mass of words': 'I am like one who with much labour extracts precious gems from the innumerable sands of the seashore, or one who, walking through spacious gardens, plucks the useful and virtuous from among the worthless and fruitless plants, separating the lilies and roses from the nettles and brambles.'[119] Such an anthology differed from a *summa* in its function: the *florilegium* provided verbal ornament to garnish a composition, whereas the *summa* invited its readers to examine the citations critically. The *florilegium* stemmed from the ancient arts of grammar and rhetoric, whereas the *summa* stemmed from 'modern' logic and dialectic.

Within the general class of *summae* there were numerous species, theological and legal textbooks being the most common. Bracton presented his treatise on English law, which was contemporary with Aquinas's *Summa Theologiae*, as a *summa*:

> I, Henry de Bracton, to instruct the lesser judges, if no one else, have turned my mind to the former judgments of just men, examining diligently their decisions . . . and have compiled whatever I found therein worthy of note into one *summa*, organized by titles and paragraphs, without prejudice to any other opinion, and committed to memory forever by the aid of writing.[120]

Bracton's description epitomizes the main elements of a *summa*: it is compiled for instruction; it is a selection of authoritative statements; it is organized systematically.

Like other writers of textbooks, Bracton can be accused of plagiarism, as the treatise to which he gave his name had been put together a generation earlier by his own masters in English law.[121] But in manuscript culture, without a distinction between hand-written and printed copy, it was harder for an author to distinguish between his own text and his notes from various sources. As a conscientious compiler and publisher, it may never have occurred to

[118] Prologue to *Sic et Non* ed. B. B. Boyer and R. McKeon (1976), p. 89.
[119] Giraldus II, p. 6. Cf. A. A. Goddu and R. H. Rouse, 'Gerald of Wales and the *Florilegium Angelicum*', *Speculum* LII (1977), pp. 489–90, and N. Hathaway, 'Compilatio', *Viator*, XXII (1989), pp. 19–44.
[120] Bracton, vol. ii, p. 19
[121] See S. E. Thorne's introduction to Bracton, vol. iii (1977).

Bracton that he was guilty of theft of intellectual property. A generation later his treatise was in its turn superseded by Fleta, who made similarly bold claims:

> To many who are in a hurry and many who are unlearned, a compendium in a brief volume of the justices' judgments may be very necessary, so that an inquirer does not have to turn over a mass of books and chapters, when he will find what he is looking for without trouble, brought together here in a brief space.[122]

A *summa* was a sort of highly organized and selective register, which aimed to instruct a wider public than one monastic house like a cartulary, or one government department like an Exchequer remembrance book. If a *summa* is defined as broadly as that, the genre includes a variety of formularies and treatises which instruct by citing examples in how to conduct law courts, draft charters, cast financial accounts, manage estates, and so on.[123] In a sense too the collections of papal decretals and parliamentary statutes (see plates XVI, XVII and XVIII) which lawyers used were *summae*. Compiling *summae* was a reaction to the proliferation of documents and books in the twelfth and thirteenth centuries; they were intended as a guide through the maze, although sometimes they added to the confusion.

Literary works

The very varied works written for, or used by, the general reader in this period are not characterized by a single dominant type like the *summa*. Old works continued to be read, particularly the pagan Latin classics, and new ones were created, in Latin and Hebrew verse and prose, and in the vernacular languages of French and English. Ideally, from the point of view of making and using documents, all works available in England in whatever language and whatever their provenance are relevant. But generalization about what was read is made difficult by the emphasis of modern scholarship, which usually concentrates on one of the languages only and is concerned primarily with linguistic development or critical assessment of newly created literature. An educated layman in 1300, by contrast, like Henry de Bray, was probably familiar with some writing in three literary languages (Latin, French, and English) and did not necessarily care whether the sermons, songs and tales he heard or read were new or old.

Scholarship in England has tended to concentrate on medieval literary works in inverse proportion to their frequency. Latin was the commonest literary language in the period 1066–1307, yet the use of Latin in England had not been surveyed until recently. English, on the other hand, which was

---

[122] *Fleta*, SS I.XXII (1953), p. 3. Fleta's claims echo the *Decretum* of Ivo of Chartres and the *Libri Sententiarum* of Peter Lombard: U. T. Holmes, 'Transitions in European Education' in *Twelfth-Century Europe and the Foundations of Modern Society* ed. M. Clagett et al. (1966), pp. 26–7.

[123] Such treatises are discussed by Oschinksy, *Walter of Henley*, pp. 3–74, 225–57.

the least used literary language (apart from Hebrew), has been intensively studied.[124] French has fared much better than Latin, but not as well as English.[125] Consequently the use of Latin works in medieval England is too large and unstudied a subject to summarize in a few pages, whereas summaries of writings in English and French are unnecessary, as excellent introductions to them already exist. The foundations have now been laid, however, for renewed study of Latin writing in England by George Rigg's encyclopedic chronological survey of authors (religious and secular, whether writing in prose or verse) and Tony Hunt's provision of authoritative texts, particularly of didactic works.[126] Most importantly, the basic materials for what was read have been listed in N. R. Ker's *Medieval Libraries of Great Britain: A List of Surviving Books*.[127]

LITURGICAL BOOKS

Books made for the church's liturgical chant and readings look at first sight an odd category of text to include in a survey of records. But to medieval Christians these were the most important records of all, because they enshrined the very words of God in script. 'Writing' (*scriptura*) essentially meant holy 'Scripture'. Throughout the Middle Ages the Four Evangelists were depicted at the opening of each Gospel as scribes, seated at their desks with pens and blank parchment at the ready, poised to record whatever the Holy Spirit dictated to them. To write or read out the words of Scripture was an act of worship in itself, because it replicated and renewed what the Evangelists themselves were believed to have done. No expenditure of effort and precious materials was therefore too great for the making of the 'sacred page'. As a consequence, illuminated Gospel Books and liturgical manuscripts are the most impressive of all medieval records. Typically they take the form of huge volumes, designed to rest on lecterns at eye level and display their texts in bold lettering (and musical notation where appropriate) enhanced by lavish illumination.

These books are described in medieval inventories by a variety of names, which reflect their contents or functions: 'psalters' (texts of the Psalms), 'missals' (texts of the service of the Mass), and many others.[128] Because they

---

[124] R. M. Wilson, *Early Middle English Literature* (3rd edn, 1968). See also W. R. J. Barron, *English Medieval Romance* (1987) and N. F. Blake ed. *The Cambridge History of the English Language*, ii, [covering the period] *1066–1476* (1992).

[125] I. Short updates Legge, *Anglo-Norman*, and makes a fundamental contribution of his own in 'Patrons and Polyglots: French Literature in Twelfth-Century England', *Anglo-Norman Studies XIV: Proceedings of the Battle Conference 1991* ed. M. Chibnall (1993).

[126] A. G. Rigg, *A History of Anglo-Latin Literature 1066–1422* (1992). T. Hunt, *Teaching and Learning Latin in Thirteenth-Century England* 3 vols (1991).

[127] 2nd edn (1964); *Supplement* (1987) by A. G. Watson.

[128] De Hamel, *MSS*, ch. 7. R. W. Pfaff, *Medieval Latin Liturgy: A Select Bibliography* (1982) and M. Huglo, *Les Livres de chant liturgique* (1988).

formed part of the service of the altar, liturgical books had to compete in magnificence with the gold and silver, jewellery, and silk amassed there. Since they embodied the most ancient and revered texts of Latin Christendom, liturgical books might be expected to undergo little development over the centuries. But this is not the case. Very old books, directly associated for example with St Augustine at Canterbury or St Cuthbert at Durham, were indeed kept as relics on the altar; but they were not used for ordinary church services. Liturgical manuscripts, like other textbooks, had to take account of frequent minor changes in regulations by producing numerous new editions. Furthermore, because these were in the texts most highly valued by the most literate persons, the monks and clergy, they had to exemplify the latest fashions in book production. Every bishop and abbot wanted the shiniest and most advanced model of liturgical book, just as every ambitious executive today wants the most luxurious limousine.

Such wants help explain why Paul of Caen, the first new abbot of St Albans after the Norman Conquest, replaced so many of the abbey's books. According to Matthew Paris, he gave 'twenty-eight notable volumes' to the abbey, as well as 'eight Psalters, a Collect, an Epistolary, a book containing the Gospel readings throughout the year, two Texts (i.e. Gospel Books) ornamented with gold, silver and gems; and other Ordinals, Custumals, Missals, Tropers and Collects'.[129] These books were kept in 'little cupboards' in the first half of the thirteenth century, when Matthew Paris wrote this description. By that time, however, they were largely obsolete, as Abbots Geoffrey and Ralph in the mid-twelfth century had replaced them, again on a grand scale, with more up-to-date books incorporating innovations in the liturgy like the feast of the Immaculate Conception of the Virgin Mary.[130] Like other medieval churches, St Albans abbey proved its vitality by renewing its books.

Liturgical manuscripts are the prime form in which the habit of using and possessing books reached the laity from the thirteenth century onwards. Everyone needed a prayer-book, their own interactive record of Scripture, whether or not they could read. Liturgical books did not make high demands on reading ability anyway, as their texts were familiar from constant repetition and they were written out in the largest lettering. Although they had originally been made for clerical and church use, liturgical books were attractive to the laity as well. Men and women who had close relatives among the clergy must have asked themselves why such covetable objects as the Psalter of Robert of Lindsey (abbot of Peterborough, 1214–22), or the Missal (dating from 1250) made for Henry of Chichester, should be the monopoly of their clerical brethren.[131] Anyone – cleric or lay, male or female, rich or poor,

[129] *Gesta Abbatum Sancti Albani* RS 28 (1867), i, p. 58; R. M. Thomson, *MSS from St Albans Abbey 1066–1235* (1982), i, p. 13.
[130] Thomson, *MSS from St Albans*, i, pp. 21–3, 28, 38–9. A 'troper' from this period with musical notation is illustrated by Thomson, ibid. ii, plate 89. See also de Hamel, *MSS*, p. 80, plate 76.
[131] R. Marks and N. Morgan, *The Golden Age of English MS Painting* (1981), plates 3 and 8; catalogue nos 47 and 100 in N. Morgan, *Early Gothic MSS 1190–1250* (1982) and *1250–1285* (1987).

saint or sinner – who saw the full-page portrait of Henry in his Missal, showing him in his best vestments offering a prayer to the enthroned Virgin and Child, might have desired such a book and such a portrait for himself or herself.[132]

An example of a liturgical book made for an identified lay person in England is the so-called 'Grey-FitzPayn Hours', which was probably presented by Richard de Grey to Joan FitzPayn as a bridal gift in 1301.[133] Husband and wife are depicted in it, in their coats of arms, kneeling beneath an image of the Annunciation of the Virgin.[134] On another page Joan is portrayed, within an initial of the text, being individually blessed by Christ in Majesty; a few lines below a young man, probably her husband, looks out from the initial 'V' of *Venite exultemus* ('Come let us rejoice', Psalm 94).[135] This portrait page may be intended to celebrate and bless their marriage. Prayer-books like this, designed for aristocrats to hold in their hands and treasure in the privacy of their chambers, retained the magnificence of ecclesiastical manuscripts while leavening the traditional recipe with witty drawings and naturalistic colour. Many of these books were made for young ladies, and it is not too fanciful to see a feminine and domestic taste in the miniatures in their borders of playful furry animals and languid damsels. In the case of the FitzPayn marriage portrait, there is potential sexual symbolism in the squirrel and the rampant goat on the borders of the page and in the beaks and tails of song-birds penetrating the body of the text.

From the aristocratic prayer-books of the thirteenth century derive the Books of Hours of the later Middle Ages. Potentially these were 'books for everybody', as C. de Hamel has characterized them. 'To the great majority of the medieval population of Europe, the first book they knew – and often the only one – must have been the Book of Hours.'[136] This form of manuscript took shape, as a portable manual of prayer for lay people – and for ladies in their private chambers in particular – in England. It looks as if it was invented in *c*.1240, possibly by William de Brailes, the Oxford illuminator, who made the first such book now extant (British Library Additional Manuscript 49,999) for the lady who is depicted in it. C. Donovan has identified half a dozen portable books of this sort, mostly having an Oxford provenance and made between *c*.1240 and *c*.1270 (dates can be no more than approximate because they depend on stylistic comparisons of the art-work).[137] These books were all made for women, and their owners are sometimes portrayed, within the illuminated initials, at their devotions. The dimensions of these books are the same as those of small modern paperbacks.

---

[132] The portrait of Henry is illustrated in colour by Alexander & Binski, p. 235.
[133] Catalogue no. 31 in L. F. Sandler, *Gothic MSS 1285–1385* (1986). Illustrated in colour by J. Harthan, *Books of Hours and their Owners* (1977), pp. 43, 45–7.
[134] Sandler, *Gothic MSS*, plate 77.
[135] Harthan, *Books of Hours*, p. 43.
[136] De Hamel, *MSS*, p. 164.
[137] Donovan, *de Brailes*, p. 183, MSS nos 1–5. N. J. Morgan, *The Lambeth Apocalypse* (1990), p. 96, n. 31, shows that these MSS were likewise made for women.

Through Books of Hours, ladies introduced their families and children to prayer – and hence to literacy – in their own homes. This domestication of the liturgical book was the foundation on which the growing literacy of the later Middle Ages was built; but that is another story.[138] Medieval lay people became functionally literate through prayer because the clergy had insisted for centuries that prayer was everyone's most important function. In liturgical books prayer was writ large: first for God and the clergy, then for ladies in their homes, and ultimately for everybody.

Although this chapter has aimed to describe the main types of record made in this period 1066–1307, and not to prescribe rules, some general conclusions about the development of documentary forms in England can be drawn. Many of the forms were ancient. The charter, the chirograph and the rhetorician's letter had been used by the Anglo-Saxons and derived from the traditions of the late Roman empire. Similarly, skills in writing and illuminating books and ensuring that posterity had a record of the past had been the preoccupation of monks for half a millenium before the Norman Conquest. What was new after 1066 was the increase in the number of documents made and the gradual extension of literate modes to more people and diverse activities. As a result old forms, like the charter and the chirograph, became stereotyped in the thirteenth century because numbers imposed standardization. The form of the letter itself, which had been used hitherto mostly as an open declaration or a literary device, became with Henry II's letters close an actual missive sent from one person to another.

The increase in the number of documents in circulation encouraged institutions to organize and record those which most concerned them in cartularies and registers, both of documents received and of documents sent out. The habit of making an accumulating series of memoranda year by year, of which the chronicle had been the forerunner, was extended first to financial accounting and then to the proceedings of law courts, from the king's court downwards. Memoranda as such were not new; the novelty consisted in annually accumulating series.

Likewise books as such were not new: the Bible, the Church Fathers, and the pagan classics were the heritage of antiquity, preserved and lovingly illuminated by monks. Innovation came from the schoolmen of the twelfth century, who provided in the *summa* a tool for cutting through the increasing mass of written words. Contrasting with the uniformity and order which the schoolmen attempted to impose on documents are the variety of literary works produced in Latin, particularly during the twelfth-century Renaissance, and in French and English from the latter half of the twelfth century onwards. In the eleventh century and earlier, making documents in England had been largely the prerogative of monks. In the twelfth and thirteenth centuries

---

[138] See my 'The Medieval Experience of Learning to Read' in my *Literacy and Law in Medieval England* (Hambledon, forthcoming), and my *Woman and the Book in the Middle Ages* (Blackwell, forthcoming); see also pp. 13 above and 251–2 below.

schoolmen and secular clerics successfully challenged this tradition. Monks and schoolmen between them created and wrote nearly all the types of document described in this chapter. Thereafter, however, the initiative lay neither with monks nor with schoolmen, who wrote in Latin, but with those who wrote in vernacular languages for a gradually enlarging public. Even so, old traditions proved resilient and the most treasured and popular of all manuscripts were those enshrining the Latin prayers in Books of Hours. Upon them the future of literacy in Western culture largely rested.

4

The Technology of Writing

The materials of which records have been made, and the methods used to transform words into symbols appropriate to those materials, have varied considerably.[1] In the Inca empire knotted cords of different colours and lengths, the *quipu*, recalled numbers and chronology and even allegedly the names and qualities of past rulers. In ancient Mesopotamia information was inscribed in clay and baked into bricks to form a durable archive. Parchment was the principal writing material in medieval Europe. Illuminated manuscripts, like the Bury and Winchester Bibles from twelfth-century England, epitomize the achievements of the Middle Ages as much as great churches in stone. Like stone, parchment was a durable material which demanded of its users an awareness of form and a consciousness of posterity. More ephemeral and less awesome writing surfaces were also used in the Middle Ages: birch bark in Novgorodan Russia, papyrus in pre-Norman Sicily and Italy, hazel wood in the English Exchequer for tally sticks, and most commonly wax tablets for making notes or drafts.

The combination of skills required to produce these diverse artefacts of written record, ranging in medieval Europe from the expertise of the tanner and the tally-cutter to that of the book illuminator and the master in the schools, constitutes a technology. A particular technology of writing shapes and defines the uses of literacy in a region or culture, just as other products, such as cloth or metalwork, depend for their forms on their technology of

---

[1] For a general introduction see A. Gaur, *A History of Writing* 2nd edn (1987) and for the Middle Ages see J. Stiennon, *Paléographie du Moyen Age* (1973) and B. Bischoff, *Paläographie des römischen Altertums* 2nd edn (1986). The fundamental works on medieval writing techniques are A. Giry, *Manuel de diplomatique* (1894) and Wattenbach, *Schriftwesen*.

manufacture. For example, because it was more difficult to write with a quill on parchment than it is with a modern ballpoint on paper, writing was considered a special skill in the Middle Ages which was not automatically coupled with the ability to read. Hence it is an anachronism, arising from a failure to appreciate technological differences, to apply modern criteria of literacy to the medieval past. A medieval historian has to be as aware of the technology of manuscripts, as a historian of nineteenth-century Europe is of industrial processes.

There was not, however, in the twelfth and thirteenth centuries a technological revolution in the means of production of writings comparable with the introduction of the codex (or book) format and of parchment in the late Roman empire or with the invention of printing in the Renaissance. The closest the twelfth and thirteenth centuries came to such technological innovation was in the increasing use of seals, since they were a precursor of printing and an accelerator of bureaucracy (as argued in chapter 9 below); but seals were not a medieval invention in themselves. Instead, the suitability of traditional materials and methods was tested by the increasing demand for documents and they were consequently modified and adapted. Thus a new style of script, the cursive, was created in the 12th century to enable scribes to write faster. New layouts were designed for greater clarity, like the glossed scholastic text, or for greater convenience, like the pocket-sized bibles made in the thirteenth century. To cope with the problem of keeping records, the king's government experimented with different formats of rolls. Although these changes are technical and detailed, they are fundamental to understanding the increasing use of written record, because the extension of literacy depended on the mastery of available writing techniques.

Medieval methods of writing have been most frequently discussed in the context of palaeography and diplomatic, particularly in works which instruct the student in how to read manuscripts and to establish their provenance and authenticity. This chapter inevitably covers some of the same ground, but with a different emphasis, as it considers documents primarily as manufactured objects and concentrates on how their makers in England reacted to the demand to produce records on an unprecedented scale. As existing methods were adapted, rather than revolutionized, our discussion begins with the scribe in his traditional posture.

THE SCRIBE AND HIS MATERIALS

The scribe sitting at his desk is depicted in numerous manuscripts in the guise of the author writing the book which is being copied. In place of the venerable author, most commonly one of the Four Evangelists, some scribes and illuminators of the twelfth century began to have themselves depicted in this way. The most remarkable example of the practice is the full-page portrait of Eadwine, monk of Christ Church Canterbury, whose picture has an inscription round the frame declaring him to be 'the prince of writers' whose praise and fame will not die.[2] Eadwine sits in the conventional pose (apart from facing to the left instead of to the right), with a quill pen in his right hand and a penknife in his left, on an elaborately carved upright chair, leaning towards a high writing desk draped with a cloth, on which is a book open at a blank page. In another unusual full-page portrait, contemporary with Eadwine's but this time of the author, Laurence prior of Durham (1149–54) sits at a desk which is shown as a folding extension of the chair, projecting out from its arms.[3]

Verbal portraits of the scribe indicate much the same features. These are found in lexicons, like Alexander Neckham's *De Nominibus Utensilium* (composed at the end of the twelfth century), which describe everyday things. A work derived from Neckham begins its picture of the scribe as follows: 'A writer of books (*librarius*), who is commonly called a scribe (*scriptor*), should have a chair with projecting arms for holding the board upon which the quire of parchment is to be placed.'[4] This work then describes the tools required for preparing the parchment – the knife or razor for scraping it, the pumice for cleaning and smoothing it, and the boar or goat's tooth for polishing the surface to stop the ink running. Then there are the tools for ruling the lines – the stylus, the pencil, the straight ruler, the plumb line, and the awl for pricking holes to mark the beginnings of the lines. Finally there is the writing equipment itself – the quill pens and penknife, the inkhorn, and the various coloured inks. This description also includes the importance of adequate heat and good light for writing, although the hot coals recommended seem mainly intended for drying the ink on damp days rather than keeping the scribe himself warm. There are some indications that in monasteries writing was a seasonal activity. Orderic Vitalis, the English historian of the Normans, says at the end of one of his books (which he penned himself) that he is so numbed by the winter cold that he is going to finish his book at this point and will relate what he has omitted when the spring returns.[5]

Writing was certainly seen as an act of endurance in which 'the whole body labours.'[6] As such, it was an appropriate theme for sermons and homilies in monasteries. A twelfth-century sermon copied into a Durham manuscript exhorts its hearers to consider how they may become scribes of the Lord,

---

[2] 'scriptorum princeps ego . . .' This inscription is compared with other self-descriptions of scribes by Wattenbach, *Schriftwesen*, p. 505; its text is given by G. Zarnecki, 'The Eadwine Portrait', *Etudes d'Art Offertes à L. Grodecki* (1981), p. 93. Zarnecki's conclusions are questioned by C. M. Kauffmann in Zarnecki, *Catalogue*, p.119. Portraits by scribe-artists are collected by J. J. G. Alexander in *Essays Presented to N. R. Ker*, ed. M. B. Parkes and A. G. Watson (1978), pp. 108–13. Eadwine's work is illustrated at plate xiv below.

[3] Boase, *English Art*, plate 53a. *English Library*, plate 6b; Zarnecki, *Catalogue*, p. 118, no. 58.

[4] C. H. Haskins, *Studies in the History of Medieval Science* (1924), p. 361. Cf. *A Volume of Vocabularies* ed. T. Wright (1857) i, pp. 116–17. Descriptions of scribes' equipment are collected by Wattenbach, *Schriftwesen*, pp. 207–61. See also U. T. Holmes, *Daily Living in the Twelfth Century* (1952), pp. 68–71, 278–9 and T. Hunt, *Teaching and Learning Latin in Thirteenth-Century England* (1991), vol. i, pp. 188–9.

[5] Orderic, Bk iv, vol. ii, pp. 360–1.

[6] Wattenbach, *Schriftwesen*, p. 495.

writing with the pen of memory on the parchment of a pure conscience, which has been scraped by the knife of divine fear, smoothed by the pumice of heavenly desires, and whitened by the chalk of holy thoughts (the chalk is a detail which Neckham's lexicon omits). The metaphors extend the theme still further: the ruler is the will of God, the bifurcated knib of the quill pen is the joint love of God and our neighbour, the different coloured inks are heavenly grace, and the exemplar is the life of our Redeemer.[7] Although the Durham sermon eulogizes monks as scribes, we should not conclude either that all monks were scribes or that all monastic books were written by the monks themselves. When Abbot Paul of St Albans (1077–93) had books made for his church, he sought out the choicest scribes 'from afar' and gave them regular ready-cooked meals so that they would not have to stop working.[8] Income was specially assigned to pay for them, their materials, and the new scriptorium in which they worked. Abbot Faricius of Abingdon (1100–17) likewise 'instituted scribes, in addition to the cloister monks' for the writing of missals and other fine liturgical books.[9]

Obviously neither visual nor verbal portraits of the scribe are drawn directly from life in all their details, as they formed part of a conventional repertoire. Since one of the functions of a lexicon like the *De Nominibus Utensilium* was to enlarge the reader's vocabulary, it tends to exaggerate the amount of equipment the scribe requires in order to present as many unfamiliar words as possible. The average scribe did not presumably sit in an elaborate chair at an elegantly draped desk; nor did he normally write on the blank pages of a bound book, as in Eadwine's portrait, but on a folded quire of parchment. Moreover, the classic portraits of the scribe are monastic in origin. They describe the traditional copyist, who wrote beautiful liturgical books from an exemplar at an even pace. In the twelfth century a new type of scribe, less worthy of a dignified portrait, came to the fore. He was the secular clerk, who rapidly wrote letters and official records from dictation. The 'scribbler' and 'petty clerk', who fawned around the king's Chancery in the thirteenth century (the description is Henry III's),[10] had little in common with Eadwine, 'the prince of writers'.

Medieval books are made up of gatherings of parchment, folded into bifolios (two large leaves, making four pages), quires (four leaves half the size, making eight pages), and so on, depending on the required size of the page.[11] The gatherings in a medieval book can therefore be of diverse character and provenance, forming distinct 'booklets' within the binding.[12] In manuscript

---

[7] R. A. B. Mynors, *Durham Cathedral MSS* (1939), p. 9. Comparable metaphorical descriptions are cited by Wattenbach, *Schriftwesen*, pp. 208–9 and Curtius, *European Lit.*, pp. 318–19. Actual writing implements, from the thirteenth century and later, are analysed by N. L. Ramsay in Alexander and Binski, pp. 382–5. Penknives are discussed by A. d'Haenens in *Mélanges Offerts à J. Stiennon* (1982), pp. 129–41.

[8] *Gesta Abbatum Sancti Albani* RS 28 (1867), I, pp. 57–8; R. M. Thomson, *MSS from St Albans Abbey 1066–1235* (1982), I, p. 13.

[9] *Chronicon Monasterii de Abingdon* RS 2 (1858), II, p. 289.

[10] 'scriptitor', 'clericulus', Matthew Paris, v, p. 374.

[11] De Hamel, *MSS*, p. 88.

[12] P. R. Robinson, 'The Booklet', *Codicologica* III (1980), pp. 46–69.

culture the coherence of the bound book was established not by the publisher's mass-production of identical units for sale but by the individual requirements of each owner or maker; each medieval book was unique. One Durham manuscript from the twelfth century, discovered in a drawer in the cathedral library in 1935, is preserved in its gatherings still unbound.[13] The great majority of medieval books have been rebound in later centuries. Nevertheless a few bindings from the twelfth century survive, in whole or in part. Winchester's 'Domesday' book retains elaborate leather work on its boards, done with metal punches. In the case of the Knights Templars' survey of their property made in the 1180s, the stitching, headbands, pegs and clasps of the bound book largely remain, as well as the ornamental leather work.[14] Ornamented bindings were expensive. More typical probably are the plain boards and spines on Cirencester abbey's twelfth-century books, now preserved at Jesus College, Oxford.[15]

Gathering writings up into books, instead of into rolls as in the ancient world, is associated with the Bible and the official reception of Christianity in Constantine's Roman Empire.[16] Books guarded, preserved and enshrined their contents between their boards more effectively and visibly than rolls. The scribe-Evangelist writing in a bound book became a medieval stereotype because he embodied this ideal of the durability of holy Scripture; such an image does not aim to portray ordinary writers in their mundane workplaces. Everything to do with writing in medieval Christendom had potential transcendent significance, and this creates difficulties for the modern historian asking utilitarian questions and looking for representations of actual daily life in medieval images.

WAX, PARCHMENT, AND WOOD

The most important equipment of the twelfth-century writer who composed for himself or wrote from dictation, as distinct from the copyist, was not the parchment book depicted in conventional portraits of scribes, but the writing tablets on which he noted down his drafts. The tablets were ordinarily made of wood, overlaid with coloured wax, and often folded into a diptych which could be worn on a belt. When something needed noting down, the diptych was opened, thus exposing the waxed surfaces, which were written on with a stylus. In two manuscripts of Boethius's *Consolation of Philosophy*, dating from the 1140s, he is depicted holding writing tablets open on his knees, a single

[13] *English Library*, pp. 38–9, plate 7.
[14] H. M. Nixon in *Winchester in the Early Middle Ages* ed. M. Biddle (1976), pp. 526–40 and plates iv and v; M. Foot in Zarnecki, *Catalogue*, pp. 342–9.
[15] De Hamel, *MSS*, p. 105, plate 102. Bindings of the thirteenth century are illustrated by: Alexander & Binski, p. 435; Donovan, *de Brailes*, p. 31; R. M. Thomson, *Catalogue of Lincoln Cathedral Library*, plate 2.
[16] The fundamental work is C. H. Roberts and T. C. Skeat, *The Birth of the Codex* (1983); see also A. Blanchard ed., *Les Débuts du Codex* (1989). Early rolls and books are illustrated by Glenisson, *Livre*, and L. Avrin, *Scribes, Scripts and Books* (1991). See also p. 139 below.

tablet in one picture and a diptych in the other.[17] In both pictures the wooden frames around the wax surfaces are clearly drawn. In one of the pictures Boethius writes with a stylus considerably taller than his hand; it tapers to a point at its writing end and is topped by a crossbar or handle. Whether this was a form of stylus in use in the twelfth century, or whether the artist intended it to appear pagan or archaic (and therefore appropriate to Boethius), awaits archaeological investigation.[18] A story by Orderic Vitalis illustrates the use of wax tablets. He was visited by Anthony, a monk of Winchester, who showed him a copy of a life of St William. Orderic wished to have a copy too, 'but in truth, since the bearer was in haste to depart, and the winter cold prevented me from writing, I made a full and accurate abbreviation on tablets, and now I shall endeavour to entrust it summarily to parchment.' This story incidentally illustrates again how writing with a pen on parchment, as distinct from making notes with a stylus on wax, was a seasonal activity for Orderic.

It seems to have been common practice for monastic authors to write on wax and then have a fair copy made on parchment. Eadmer describes the difficulties St Anselm had in writing the *Proslogion*, because the tablets on which it was written were first lost and then shattered, perhaps by diabolical intervention.[19] That wax was the normal medium for writing in the twelfth century is also indicated by other saints' biographies. The author of the life of Christina of Markyate remarks how he could not pollute 'the wax by writing' how scandalously the cleric had behaved who had been commended to Christina as her companion by Thurstan, archbishop of York.[20] On his deathbed in 1200 St Hugh dreamed that the great pear tree in his garden at Lincoln had fallen to the ground and he was worried about the waste of its timber, 'for so many diptychs could be cut from it that there would be more than enough for the scholastic studies of the whole of England and France'.[21] The tablets of Moses, on which God wrote the Ten Commandments, were likewise envisaged as a diptych: they are drawn as a pair of framed wax surfaces, in a case concerning a Jew, in an Exchequer memoranda roll of 1270.[22]

In the thirteenth century pieces of parchment were used for notes, either as a substitute for wax tablets or in addition to them. Such notes are occasionally

---

[17] Kauffmann, *Romanesque MSS*, illustration nos 136, 138. References to writing tablets are assembled by: Wattenbach, *Schriftwesen*, pp. 51–89; Hughes in *Archaeologia* LV (1897), pp. 257–82; Lalou in *Bibliothèque de l'École des Chartes* CXVII (1989), pp. 123–40; Rouse and Rouse in *Vocabulaire du livre* ed. O. Weijers (1989), pp. 220–30. Tablets with wax and writing still on them are illustrated by: Glenisson, *Livre*, p. 30; L. Webster and J. Backhouse eds, *The Making of England: Anglo-Saxon Art and Culture* (1991), p. 80.

[18] Early styluses are illustrated by Webster and Backhouse, *The Making of England*, pp. 86, 90, 100, 140, 142, 231.

[19] Orderic, Bk. VI, ch. 3, vol. iii, p. 218; Eadmer, *Vita*, pp. 30–1; Carruthers, *Memory*, p. 211.

[20] *The Life of Christina of Markyate* ed. C. H. Talbot (1959), p. 114.

[21] *The Life of St Hugh of Lincoln* ed. D. L. Douie and H. Farmer (1961) II, p. 209.

[22] Z. E. Rokeah, 'Drawings of Jewish Interest', *Scriptorium* XXVI (1972), pp. 57, 60. Wax tablets of this type are extant in the Archives Nationales in Paris, illustrated by Glenisson, *Livre*, plate 22.

referred to in the royal plea rolls.[23] Making notes on parchment had also been a practice of Robert Grosseteste. This is known because dispute arose about which of his works were authentic. The regent-master of the Franciscans stated that Grosseteste had made some marginal notes in manuscripts because 'when some noteworthy thought occurred to him, he wrote it down there so that it should not escape his memory, just as he also wrote many slips of parchment [*cedulas*] which are not all authoritative.'[24] This statement suggests that Grosseteste was not accustomed to using wax tablets for his notes and drafts, although undue reliance should not be put on an argument from silence. The practice of making memoranda, whether on wax or parchment, contradicts the common assumption that medieval people had such good memories that they required no notes. Once they were literate, they had the same needs as a modern writer. Drafts on wax or slips of parchment are the equivalent of a modern author's original manuscript, while the parchment text is comparable to a fair copy produced by a word processor.

Before discussing parchment, a few words need to be said about paper. The earliest paper documents extant in an English medieval archive are the letters sent from Italy to the Riccardi, Edward I's bankers, dating from 1296–1303.[25] The earliest records made in England on paper come most appropriately from major seaports: a register from King's Lynn beginning in 1307 and another from Lyme Regis in 1309.[26] London described its registers of apprentices, citizens, and debts as the 'paper' or 'papers' of the Chamber of Guildhall in 1300 (and perhaps as early as 1275), but its extant records from this period are in fact made of parchment.[27] Paper occurs first in seaports because it was imported. In the long term its principal advantages over parchment were that it was easier to write on and potentially cheaper. The most significant fact about paper in England in the period up to 1307 is that it was scarcely known. Consequently parchment became established for centuries to come as the appropriate material for all the most formal records, because they took shape in the twelfth and thirteenth centuries.

The commonest word for parchment was *membrana*, simply meaning animal skin. In northern Europe the skins normally used were those of cattle and sheep; goat, rabbit, and squirrel were also used. The finest parchment was vellum, made of calf skin. Thus to make the great Bury Bible in the time of Abbot Anselm (1121–48), Harvey the sacrist obtained parchment from Scotland (perhaps meaning Ireland) because he could not find calf skins locally which suited the illuminator, Master Hugh.[28] For the equally magnificent Winchester Bible it has been estimated that about 250 calf skins must

[23] C. T. Flower, *Introduction to the Curia Regis Rolls*, SS LXII (1943), pp. 9, 271.

[24] R. W. Hunt, 'The Library of Robert Grosseteste' in *Robert Grosseteste* ed. D. A. Callus (1955), p. 127; R. W. Southern, *Robert Grosseteste* (1986), pp. 37–8.

[25] R. W. Kaeuper, *Bankers to the Crown* (1973), pp. 71–3.

[26] G. S. Ivy, 'The Bibliography of the MS Book' in *English Library*, p. 36.

[27] *Calendar of Early Mayor's Court Rolls* ed. A. H. Thomas (1924), pp. 87, 163, 170; *Chronicles of Edward I and Edward II* ed. W. Stubbs, RS LXXVI (1882) I, p. 86.

[28] *Memorials of St Edmunds Abbey* ed. T. Arnold, RS XCVI (1890), II, p. 290; de Hamel, *MSS*, p. 88 and plate 80; Zarnecki, *Catalogue*, p. 108, no. 44.

have been required.[29] These 250 skins must have been selected from ten times that number, in order to find ones from healthy young animals without blemishes. Sheep-skin was the usual material for royal records, both because it was cheaper and because (according to the *Dialogue of the Exchequer*) it is not easy to make an erasure on sheep skin without it showing plainly.[30] Once parchment has been scraped and prepared for writing on, it is usually impossible to tell what species of animal skin is being used.[31]

It is frequently assumed that parchment was rare and expensive, and that its high cost obstructed the spread of literacy. Such an assumption fails to distinguish between the finest parchments, required for illuminated manuscripts like the Bury Bible, and cheaper varieties. It is also necessary to take into account the relative cost of other items, such as the scribe's time, the cost of ink and binding materials, and (in the case of letter-writing) the cost of sealing wax and delivery. These costs in their turn need to be related to the general cost of living. As no detailed study has been made along these lines, only a few indicative facts will be cited here. When Henry II asked St Hugh how much money he needed to build up a library for the new Charterhouse at Witham, Hugh replied that one silver mark would be enough for a long time.[32] The king smiled at this, saying, 'What heavy demands you make on us', and gave him 10 marks. As Adam of Eynsham, Hugh's biographer, wished to emphasize the saint's modesty, he may have minimized his requirements; even so, Adam's story assumes that 10 marks (£6 13s. 4d.) would have bought a large amount of parchment.

At the time Adam wrote this biography, the Exchequer was keeping accounts of its running costs. Although these records do not survive in complete series and some of the sums are fixed charges, which went back to Henry II's time or earlier, they do supply sufficient information to sample the relative costs of different stages in the production of documents in the 1220s and 1230s.[33] Parchment was charged for at a fixed rate of 10 shillings a year. As this sum was already customary when Fitz Neal wrote the *Dialogue of the Exchequer*, it does not indicate the real cost; but in some terms varying supplementary charges, ranging between 20 and 40 shillings a year, are recorded which presumably do indicate actual expenditure on parchment. Compared with these sums, one scribe in 1222, Robert of Bassingbourn, was paid 3s. 2d. for 10 days' work 'while he wrote summonses', and the customary charge for scribes was 5 pence per day each.[34] Similarly in Easter term of the same year the nightwatchman and lighting cost the customary 12 shillings ($1\frac{1}{2}$ pence per night) and the rushes on the floor 3s. 5d. Ink was also a notable expense, which increased in a constant ratio with the expenditure on parchment. In Fitz Neal's time 2 shillings a year had been allowed for

[29] W. Oakeshott, *The Two Winchester Bibles* (1981), p. 3.

[30] *Dialogus*, p. 31.

[31] On the making of parchment, see de Hamel, *MSS*, pp. 84–8, and R. Reed, *Ancient Skins, Parchment and Leathers* (1972).

[32] *The Life of St Hugh of Lincoln* i, p. 85; de Hamel, *MSS*, p. 84.

[33] What follows derives from *CLibR* vi, appendix i, pp. 240–84, and *Dialogus*, pp. 12–13, 31.

[34] *CLibR* vi, no. 2163; *Pipe Roll 5 Henry III*, ed. D. Crook (1990), p. xxv.

it, that is, one fifth of the cost of parchment; by the 1220s 3 shillings a year was being allowed, and by the 1230s 40 pence for the half year.[35] The cost of sealing the writs was likewise high (about 12 pence for 30 writs on average), although this sum may include the sealer's charge as well as the cost of the wax (about 7 pence per pound). An even greater expense was deliving writs to their destinations (more than 2 pence per writ in the 1220s); on 11 July 1226 the charge for carrying 6 writs to sheriffs in various counties was 3s. 6d.[36]

These figures are not presented as statistics of real expenditure, but as an indication of relative costs. As far as materials were concerned, parchment seems to have been rather cheap. Ink and sealing wax were surprisingly expensive, although all materials were relatively cheap compared with the customary charges for labour of both the unskilled, like the nightwatchman, and the skilled scribes at 5 pence per day. If parchment cost the Exchequer at the most about 50 shillings a year in the 1220s and 1230s, that is the equivalent of 4 silver marks, a negligible sum considering that the standard rate for a single fine or oblation in the king's court was $\frac{1}{2}$ mark. Like Henry II, Henry III might have smiled at the suggestion that a few marks for parchment was a heavy burden on his revenues.

It does not follow from the proposition that parchment was relatively cheap that the finished product, the manuscript was commensurately so; but the high cost of manuscripts arose primarily from their being produced by hand and not from the initial cost of animal skins. In the last decades of the thirteenth century the obedientaries' accounts of some monasteries are sufficiently detailed to distinguish between the cost of writing materials and labour costs. Like the Exchequer records, these accounts suggest that even the finest parchment was cheaper than the scribe's time. For example, at Norwich cathedral priory in 1288 12 dozen skins of vellum cost 17s. 5d., whereas the scribes were paid 20s. 5d.; similarly in 1296 12 dozen calf-skins cost £2 1s. 6d., while the scribes writing the book for which they were ordered were paid £3 6s. 10d.[37] These costs are far higher than the Exchequer's expenditure on parchment at the beginning of the century, but they are for vellum not sheep skin, and the average price of cattle (and hence of their hides) had increased by about a third since the 1220s.

The initial cost of parchment depended on the availability of animal skins. The assumption that they were scarce can be examined by relating the demand for parchment to the animal population. Although there are insufficient data to make estimates on a national scale, a sample follows which relates the number of animals in two localities at different dates in the thirteenth century to an estimate of the amount of parchment used by the king's justices when they visited those localities. On the basis of tax returns

[35] *Dialogus*, p. 12; *CLibR* vi, nos. 2169, 2259. Recipes for ink are discussed by M. Zerdoun Bat-Yehouda, *Les Encres noires au Moyen Age* (1983).

[36] *CLibR* vi, no. 2180.

[37] H. W. Saunders, *An Introduction to the Obedientary and Manor Rolls of Norwich Cathedral Priory* (1930), pp. 107, 180. The sum of £3 6s. 10d. may be an overestimate, as it includes miscellanea.

M. M. Postan has estimated that there were 14,988 sheep and 2,645 cows and calves in a group of 23 villages in south Wiltshire in 1225, and 17,059 sheep and 4,298 cows and calves in the 33 villages of Blackbourne hundred in Suffolk in 1283.[38] At the same time the king's justices and their litigants were probably the largest single consumers of parchment. When they visited a county the size of Wiltshire or Suffolk for a solemn eyre, they and the litigants would have used, on a generous average estimate, 300 membranes of parchment for their rolls and another 200 for ancillary documents. At first sight 500 membranes seems a large amount of parchment, yet 500 sheep skins comprise the flocks of 32 taxable households in south Wiltshire in 1225 or 38 in Blackbourne hundred in 1283. In Wiltshire the number of households cited comprises about three quarters of a village and in Suffolk just under one village.

These figures are not given to suggest that 500 sheep were slaughtered whenever the king's justices appeared on the scene, although large quantities of meat and corn were consumed by their entourages on these visitations, but to show that relatively few sheep skins were required for parchment even by the king's justices. The sheep of one village or less, even in a predominantly arable area like Suffolk, could supply a county's requirements. The large number of animals kept in England, particularly sheep for wool production, may have made parchment cheaper there than elsewhere. But that is a guess, as sheep skins were used for numerous purposes and the provenance of parchment is rarely specified. By 1300 the evidence does not suggest that institutions considered parchment an expense inhibiting the production of documents, although examples can be found of individual writers making economies. R. F. Hunnisett has pointed out that the parchment used for the justices' rolls markedly improves over the thirteenth century: 'almost certainly the vastly increased demand for parchment, particularly at Westminster, must have given rise to larger scale and more efficient production and supply.'[39] Perhaps the shift from memory to written record created a new industry in writing materials in England.

Apart from parchment, the most important material for making records, as distinct from ephemeral drafts written on wax, was wood. In Michaelmas term 1224 the Exchequer spent 5 shillings on rods for tallies at the same time as it spent 4 shillings on parchment.[40] Tallies were used as receipts for money or other items rendered, such as bags of corn at a mill, and also as records of obligations to make payments.[41] The appropriate sums were shown on the

---

[38] *Essays in Medieval Agriculture* (1973), pp. 227, 229.

[39] 'What is a Plea Roll?' *Journal of the S. of Archivists* IX (1988), p. 110. See also D. Crook, *Records of the General Eyre* (1982), pp. 30–3.

[40] *CLibR* VI, no. 2169. The 5s. was a customary charge, *Dialogus*, p. 12. There were also in 1224 the costs of leather for filing the tallies (9d.) and of 'a big sack' to keep them in (14d.).

[41] What follows is based on H. Jenkinson, 'Exchequer Tallies', *Archaeologia* LXII (1911), pp. 367–80 and 'Medieval Tallies, Public and Private', *Archaeologia* LXXIV (1925), pp. 289–353; M. M. Postan, *Medieval Trade and Finance* (1973), pp. 32–3; P & M II, p. 215. In general see W. T. Baxter, 'Early Accounting: the Tally and the Checkerboard', *The Accounting Historians Journal* X (1989), pp. 43–83.

tally by notches of differing widths, depths, and intervals (see plate VIII). Like a chirograph, the English tally was a bipartite record. When the notches had been cut on the stick, to the satisfaction of both renderer and receiver, the tally was split down its length so that each party had the same record. The interlocking halves were intended to act as a check against forgery. Although the numbers on the tally were cut with a knife, the names and business of the parties it concerned were written in script in ink (see plate VIII). Some tallies also bore seals like charters. Tallies were not a primitive survival from the preliterate past, but a sophisticated and practical record of numbers. They were more convenient to keep and store than parchments, less complex to make, and harder to forge. They were the foundation and origin of the royal financial system of the twelfth century and were widely adopted by private accountants in the thirteenth, who described in detail how they should be cut, just as Fitz Neal had done in the *Dialogue of the Exchequer*.[42]

Of the millions of medieval tallies made, only a few hundred survive. In 1834 the Exchequer tallies stored at Westminster were burned after the passing of the statute abolishing the Receipt of the Exchequer. The fire accidentally spread to the Houses of Parliament and thus brilliantly symbolized the abolition of the *ancient régime* and the triumph of 'reform'. The burning of the tally sticks has further ironies for the historian, because at the same time the Record Commissioners were publishing in lavish volumes with spurious Latin titles the earliest medieval records in parchment, like the Chancery rolls of King John. The Commissioners would not have dreamed of burning Domesday Book or the Chancery rolls, yet these records of the Exchequer were deliberately destroyed because they were in a medium, wood, which was too uncouth for scholars to appreciate. The fire of 1834 entered the mythology of English history. In reality the only tallies burned were the most recent ones, probably dating from after 1800. But people at the time believed them to be medieval because doing accounting with sticks looked so primitive, and even shameful, to nineteenth-century reformers. Charles Dickens for example demanded: 'What was to be done with such worn-out, worm-eaten rotten old bits of wood', which 'ages ago a savage mode of keeping accounts' had introduced into the Exchequer?[43]

Wax, parchment, and wood were the commonest documentary materials in medieval England. In addition to them, inscriptions were of course made on other materials, notably on stone, metal, bone, and fabric. Such inscriptions are too varied and scattered to discuss in detail here. The lettering of those that were cut and painted on stone monumental slabs and sculptures, or engraved and enamelled on brasses, seals, swords, rings, cups, and so on were probably designed by scribes. Their users presumably understood the significance of the Latin inscriptions, even if that were the limit of their literacy. Everyone would have seen inscriptions, or at least symbolic letters, on vestments and sacred images and utensils in churches. Similarly the Bayeux

---

[42] *Walter of Henley*, pp. 222–4, 460–1; *Dialogus*, pp. 22–4.
[43] *Speeches*, ed. Fielding (1960), pp. 204–5. See 'Burning the Tally Sticks in 1834', in my *Literacy and Law in Medieval England* (forthcoming).

Tapestry, with its summary captions in Latin (HIC HAROLD REX INTERFECTUS EST, for example), assumes an audience in which someone could read. Coins are a special case.[44] Because they were the medium in which lettering circulated most extensively among the population as a whole, their inscriptions were made by a form of mass-production. The lettering was not individually engraved on to the dies in accordance with a scribe's design; instead the letters were formed in sections by moneyers using punches of different shapes. Coins were the only form of writing which remained unaffected by the Norman Conquest; even a century later in Henry II's reign archaic lettering was still in evidence.

COMMITTING WORDS TO WRITING

How one writer went about his task is described in the prologue to Lawman's Arthurian poem, the *Brut*, which he wrote in English in the 1190s or later. Lawman was a priest at Areley on the river Severn and 'there he read books'. In order to write one of his own, he travelled widely and 'procured those noble books which he took as his exemplars'; these were three in number – in English, Latin, and French respectively. Then 'Lawman laid these books out and turned over their leaves. He beheld them lovingly; may God have mercy on him! He took quills (*fetheren*) in his fingers and applied them to parchment (literally *boc-felle*, 'book-skin') and he set down together the truer words and he compressed those three books into one.'[45] This description presents Lawman in the stereotype of the scribe-copyist working from an exemplar. In reality the process of converting the books Lawman claims to have used into over 16,000 lines of learned and original English verse must have involved more than making a précis. Why did Lawman not wish to be portrayed as a creative writer, in the modern sense of a poet and author? Perhaps because he saw himself simply as a country parson, who had put a few books together. Possibly too, putting pen to parchment is emphasized because that was such a difficult task for any medieval writer. Furthermore, Lawman was writing *historia*; his 'story' was true and, like any conscientious historian, he referred to his sources, even where he had not used them.

In reality, as distinct from the idealized and simplified description given of Lawman's writing procedure, he may have drafted his verses on wax tablets before applying quill to parchment. Or, he may have dictated them to a scribe, as this was the most professional way of committing words to writing. 'Reading and dictating' were ordinarily coupled together, not 'reading and writing';[46] the skill of writing a letter in proper form was the 'art of dictation'

---

[44] R. Brilliant, 'The Bayeux Tapestry', *Word and Image* VII (1991), pp. 98–124. For coins see the catalogues of the exhibitions on *English Romanesque Art 1066–1200* ed. Zarnecki, pp. 320–41 and *Age of Chivalry 1200–1400* ed. Alexander and Binski, pp. 313–15.

[45] *Brut*, ed. G. L. Brook and R. F. Leslie, Early English Text S. 250 (1963), p. 1; J. A. Burrow, *Medieval Writers and their Work* (1982), pp. 27–34.

[46] 'legere vel dictare', Orderic, Bk III, vol. ii, p. 2. See also p. 271 below.

(*ars dictaminis*), a branch of rhetoric. Writing was distinguished from composition because putting a pen to parchment was an art in itself. Even when an author declares that he is writing something, he may in fact be using the term metaphorically. Thus John of Salisbury remarks in a letter to Peter, abbot of Celle, in *c*.1159: 'While I was writing this (*scriberem*), the secretary was moved to laughter by the greeting at the head of the letter.'[47] His secretary (*notarius*) was presumably penning the letter and not John himself; he was evidently not a mere copyist, as he told John that the greeting was ridiculous and advised him against mixing his metaphors. Occasionally manuscripts depict the author of the work dictating to the scribe. A picture which may be of English provenance showing Peter of Poitiers dictating his *Compendium Historie* to a scribe is illustrated at plate XII. Certainly of English provenance are a miniature (dating from *c*.1130) of Josephus dictating his history of the Jewish wars to the scribe, Samuel, and a drawing (attributed to Matthew Paris) of Plato dictating to Socrates.[48]

Exceptions to the rule that authors dictated their works are usually monks, as distinct from secular clerics. Monks wrote more of their own works because they were expected to be humble and also because some had training in a *scriptorium*. We have already seen that St Anselm wrote his own draft of the *Proslogion* on wax tablets and Eadmer, his biographer, wrote in the same way.[49] As well as writing his own draft, Eadmer also penned his own fair copy on to parchment, as did the greatest monastic historians, Orderic Vitalis, William of Malmesbury, and Matthew Paris. By and large, however, the role of the composer (*dictator*) was kept distinct from that of the scribe (*scriptor*). 'The scribe must be careful not to write anything of his own in the roll', Fitz Neal advises in the *Dialogue of the Exchequer*, 'but only what the treasurer has instructed by dictation.'[50] Some scribes, like Eadwine, were supreme artists in calligraphy and presumably considered themselves superior to composers or clerks who wrote from dictation, whereas others were copyists who scarcely understood the exemplar in front of them. Lack of personal contact between editor and scribe is demonstrated by a note in one early twelfth-century manuscript addressed to: 'Scribe of this volume, whoever you are!' The note gives directions about spacing, paragraphing, capital letters, and glosses, and concludes with: 'For the rest, you will see whatever is to be written.'[51]

The style of the script depended on a variety of circumstances: the scribe's ability, the region and period in which he was working, the type of document being written, and whether the scribe was copying from an exemplar or writing from dictation. Thus Norman and English hands can be distinguished in the generation after the Conquest, as can Romanesque and Gothic by the last decades of the twelfth century.[52] Like other art forms, handwriting in England came under French influence. From the point of view of making

---

[47] *Letters* ed. W. J. Millor et al. (1955) i, p. 183.
[48] Kaufmann, *Romanesque MSS*, plate 118; Alexander & Binski, p. 331, no. 315.
[49] See n. 19 above.
[50] *Dialogus*, p. 31.
[51] R. M. Thomson, *MSS from St Albans Abbey* (1982), p. 103, no. 44, plate 92.
[52] Ker, *English MSS*, pp. 22–7 (Norman and English), 2–3 (Romanesque and Gothic).

records, the most important development was the emergence of cursive scripts in the twelfth century and their establishment in the thirteenth as the characteristic hands for writing business documents. Contemporaries, as well as modern palaeographers, distinguish between the symmetrical and closely written 'book hand', which is the predecessor of the blackletter script of the earliest printed books, and 'court hand' or cursive, which is freer and more fluent. (Plates III, V, XIV and XVIII illustrate book hands of varying dates and types, while plates IV, VI, XVI and XVII illustrate court or cursive hands.) The medieval term for book hand was *textus*, which is more appropriate as *textus* literally means a 'weave'. Thus an inventory of books in the royal treasury in *c.* 1300 describes one book of transcripts as being written *in grosso texto* (in a large or heavy weave), whereas another is *sub manu curiali* (in court hand).[53]

Gerald of Wales tells an anecdote from a century earlier which indicates a similar distinction.[54] One of his rival claimants to the bishopric of St David's, the abbot of St Dogmael, was given a reading test by the papal judges delegate. They asked the abbot to read the letter from Innocent III commissioning them to examine him. His counsel objected that it was not fair to test him on a writing of that kind, which he was not used to, and suggested church books instead. So a missal was brought 'with a large and legible script', but the abbot would not read this either. Despite the abbot's refusal, and presumed inability, to read at all, Gerald's story shows that contemporaries were already aware of the difference between the familiar book hand of a missal and the novel court hand of a papal letter.

Contemporaries also make clear that different scripts were appropriate for different kinds of document. Alexander Neckham describes three styles, one for business documents, another for books, and a third for glosses and marginalia. The glossing hand, for writing commentaries around texts, was an intermediate style between the weighty book hand and the cursive court hand (see plate XIV). Further specialized scripts become apparent in the thirteenth century, particularly among royal clerks, who developed distinctive variations of court hand for pipe rolls, Chancery enrolments, and so on. The good scribe did not therefore aim to write in a unique style distinctive to himself, like a modern writer, but to have command of a variety of scripts appropriate to different functions and occasions. 'Many writers who form a good and competent script for quires [that is, for copying books]', says one treatise, 'do not know how to adjust their hand for writing letters [in the sense of correspondence].'[55]

An Oxford manuscript, which may date from early in the fourteenth century, consists of portions of a variety of scripts suitable for the text and musical notation of liturgical books. Its publisher suggested that it was an

---

[53] Chaplais, *Docs*, p. 50 English hands of the thirteenth century are illustrated by M. P. Brown, *A Guide to Western Historical Scripts* (1990), plates 31–5. *Textus* was the term for a Gospel book; see C. R. Cheney in *BIHR* LVI (1983), pp. 9–10.

[54] Giraldus III, p. 234. Gerald gives the text of Innocent III's letter, ibid. pp. 68–9. Gerald's reliability is discussed at ch. 7, n. 104 below.

[55] Conrad of Mure, 'Summa de Arte Prosandi' in *Briefsteller und Formelbücher* ed. L. Rockinger (1863) I, p. 439; Wattenbach, *Schriftwesen*, p. 297.

advertisement by a writing master commending himself to prospective pupils.[56] Alternatively this manuscript may have functioned as a sampler which showed off the scribe's range of work, so that his customer could select the size and style of script he required. Professional scribes may have been demonstrating their skills in this way for centuries.

Because the competent scribe could write in a variety of styles, attributions of manuscripts to particular writers on stylistic grounds alone are peculiarly difficult and tend towards anachronism. Just as medieval writers did not usually aim at absolute uniformity in the spelling of proper names and the use of capital letters and punctuation, they likewise varied their scripts. For example, two charters for Robert Mauduit, King John's chamberlain, are both explicitly stated to have been written by Louis, clerk of Rockingham, as he adds the words 'who wrote this charter' after his name in the list of witnesses.[57] Yet the two charters differ so much, quite gratuitously, in their scripts and conventions that only the most expert palaeographer would have attributed them to the same scribe. Louis even varied the way he wrote his own name, as the idea of a distinctive signature was unfamiliar in England, where the authenticity of a document depended upon seals and the word of named witnesses.

Some palaeographers have attempted to create a more rigid classification of scripts than the documents warrant. Early cursive or court hands have suffered in particular, when they have been described as 'chancery hands'. The assumption behind this term is that cursive script was taught by writing masters in chancery schools. Because there is no evidence in England for the existence of such masters or schools, and little enough for organized chanceries before the last quarter of the twelfth century, some palaeographers have relied on dogmatic assertions. For example, the script of Bodleian MS Savile 21, which is alleged to be that of Robert Grosseteste, has been analysed in two palaeographical textbooks. In one the script is described as the type dominant in the chancery of Lincoln cathedral,[58] whereas in the other it is said to have been obviously learned in a chancery school but is too unclear to have satisfied any chancellor.[59] In fact it is not known where Grosseteste learned to write, nor is this writing necessarily his.[60] Other authentic exemplars of Grosseteste's handwriting do exist, however, which demonstrate that he, like other university masters, wrote in a fast cursive script.

To explain the emergence and similarity of such cursive scripts the Hungarian palaeographer, I. Hajnal, has advanced an alternative hypothesis to that of masters teaching in chancery schools.[61] He suggested that writing

---

[56] S. J. P. van Dijk, 'An Advertisement of an Early Fourteenth-Century Writing Master at Oxford', *Scriptorium* x (1956), pp. 47–64. Alexander & Binski, p. 385, no. 429.

[57] *Northants. Facs*, plates viii and x. T. A. M. Bishop illustrates the varied handwriting of one royal scribe, see n. 63 below.

[58] N. Denholm-Young, *Handwriting in England and Wales* (1954), plate 11.

[59] S. Harrison Thomson, *Latin Bookhands of the Later Middle Ages* (1969), plate 89.

[60] Hunt, 'The Library of Robert Grosseteste', pp. 133–4; R. W. Southern, *Robert Grosseteste* (1986), pp. 75–8 and 107, n. 35.

[61] *L'Enseignment de l'écriture aux universités médiévales* ed. L. Mezey (2nd edn, Budapest, 1959).

was taught in the cathedral schools and emerging universities as part of the *ars dictaminis*. Although this hypothesis is difficult to prove, Hajnal at least explains why university masters like Grosseteste wrote a cursive script. Hajnal's hypothesis also places the clerks who wrote charters and business documents in a new perspective, as it implies that many of them were university graduates or 'wandering scholars' who had at least attended a first-year course. Writing Latin from dictation was a difficult business, which required a technique different from that of monastic scribes who copied from an exemplar. University students would certainly have acquired this technique, even if it were not specifically taught, in order to write up the lectures they heard. It is possible to point to examples of university graduates, like Thomas Becket, who started their careers as secretaries, whereas an English writer trained in a chancery school has yet to be found. It used to be thought that the main volume of Domesday Book was written in a 'curial' script, distinctive to the royal writing office at Winchester. But it is now suggested that the handwriting is ecclesiastical and the Winchester official provenance is also in dispute.[62]

The most careful study of the origin of cursive script in England is T. A. M. Bishop's analysis of twelfth-century royal charters and writs. He shows that these documents were not written in a distinctly royal chancery hand, since one scribe might use a variety of forms and conversely the same scripts were used outside the royal Chancery.[63] He suggests that the cursive forms, which emerge early in the twelfth century, 'are simply the minuscule forms adapted, by the various habits of individual scribes, for the purpose of writing quickly . . . The cursive is the result of licence, not discipline; it is evidence not of a common training but of something simpler and historically more interesting: a common pressure of urgent business.'[64] Bishop thus rejects the necessity for instruction by writing masters, whether in a chancery or a university school, and argues instead that cursive is a spontaneous development resulting from the proliferation of documents. (Plates ii and iv illustrate the development of cursive hands among the scribes of Henry I and King Stephen.)

Accepting Bishop's analysis, the cursive is simply a quicker way of writing and was therefore used wherever speed was important. Hence it became the speciality of those writing offices, like the royal Chancery, which produced the most documents. Cursive was appropriately called 'court hand' by contemporaries because most rapid writing was done by courts, not because it was taught in courts or chancerics. It was not so much the distinctive mark of an official, as a practical way of getting through the business. It is consequently neither surprising, nor a contradiction in terms, to find cursive script being used for writing books from the latter half of the thirteenth century (see plates

---

[62] A. R. Rumble in *Domesday Studies*, ed. J. C. Holt (1987), p. 96, n. 76 (citing V. H. Galbraith). See also: P. Chaplais in ibid., pp. 65–77; M. Gullick and C. Thorne in *Journal S. of Archivists* viii (1986), pp. 78–80; T. Webber in *English Manuscript Studies* i (1989), pp. 1–18.

[63] *Scriptores Regis* (1961), plate v (the varied handwriting of Scribe xiii) and pp. 9, 14 (Lincoln charters). Similar suggestions had been made by Cheney, *Chanceries*, p. 54.

[64] *Scriptores Regis*, p. 13, cf. pp. 6–7.

XVI and XVII). It was quicker, and therefore cheaper, and more familiar to laymen and to those clergy who saw more of business documents than of liturgical books. Some cursive features can even be seen in earlier books, most remarkably in the manuscript in Middle English, *Vices and Virtues*, dating from *c*.1200.[65] Cursive script is thus a product of the shift from memory to written record: the demand was no longer primarily for elaborately copied monastic books, but for documents written economically yet legibly. Saving the scribe's time was a paramount consideration, because labour costs were the principal element in the price of a manuscript. Fine manuscripts written in book hand continued to be produced, however, until they succumbed in the sixteenth century to the joint attack of printing and the destruction of monasticism.

Cursive script was not an invention of the Middle Ages. It had been used in the ancient world and persisted in late Roman culture until the introduction of Carolingian minuscule. But there is a significant difference between late Roman practice and the cursive of the twelfth-century Renaissance. Medieval scribes separate the individual words from each other on the line in the way familiar to modern readers, whereas earlier writers of Latin did not. Roman cursive script abandons the dots used to distinguish one word from the next in inscriptions and runs all the letters together as if the separate words had no significance. This practice is strikingly illustrated in A. and F. N. Petrucci's enlarged facsimiles of eighth-century charters from Lucca, where even short words are arbitrarily bisected when the end of the line is reached.[66] Word separation was developed by Irish and Anglo-Saxon monks, conjecturally because their unfamiliarity with Latin made it essential for them to distinguish the words of the sacred scripture from each other.[67]

In the conventions used for abbreviating, punctuating, and making alterations or corrections, scribes in the twelfth century made minor modifications rather than any major innovation like the cursive script. A great deal of care was taken to check manuscripts for errors. Some readers emended texts as they read them.[68] In cathedrals it was the duty of such officials as the chancellor and the precentor to correct the books in their charge; at Salisbury the income from a virgate of land was assigned to this specific purpose.[69] In the Exchequer, where errors literally meant money, Fitz Neal describes the elaborate provisions for establishing accurate texts.[70] Similarly in the Chancery the senior clerks were supposed to check the writs before they were sealed,

---

[65] C. E. Wright, *English Vernacular Hands* (1960), plate 3. In general see M. B. Parkes, *English Cursive Book Hands* (1969) and Parkes, 'Literacy', p. 563.

[66] *Chartae Latinae Antiquiores*, XXXI (1989). Roman cursive from England is illustrated by A. K. Bowman and J. D. Thomas, *Vindolanda: The Latin Writing Tablets* (1983).

[67] M. B. Parkes, 'The Contribution of Insular Scribes to the Grammar of Legibility' in his *Scribes, Scripts and Readers* (1991), pp. 1–18; K. O'B. O'Keeffe, *Visible Song* (1990); P. Saenger, 'Silent Reading', *Viator* XIII (1982), pp. 377–9; J. Kittay, 'The Changing Interpretation of Writing', *Language and Society*, XVII (1988), p. 215.

[68] References to the correction of scribal errors are collected by Wattenbach, *Schriftwesen*, pp. 317–44. See also N. R. Ker in *MSS Hunt*, pp. 30–2.

[69] *Lincoln Cathedral Statutes* ed. H. Bradshaw and C. Wordsworth (1892) I, pp. 284–5; *Register of St Osmund* ed. W.H. Rich-Jones, RS LXXVIII (1883), I, p. 224.

[70] *Dialogus* pp. 18, 28–9, 31, 74, 126.

having regard to their form (*ratio*), script (*littera*), wording (*dictio*) and spelling (*silliba*).[71] Despite these checks errors in documents, as distinct from books, are quite common, particularly in the royal plea rolls. Even in the spelling of place names, where diversity was tolerated, there were rules. In the Cambridgeshire justices' visitation of 1286 one defendant objected to the plaintiff's writ because it spelt the village of Harston 'Hardlestone scilicet cum *d*';[72] so the plaintiff had to obtain another writ without the offending *d* in the middle.

An important aspect of medieval handwriting, which has not been systematically studied, is bad writing. In particular, incompetently written charters are quite common in the twelfth century and can still be found in the thirteenth (see plate vi). G. Barraclough's facsimiles of Cheshire charters provide good examples.[73] A charter for Poulton abbey in *c*.1146 is written on an irregularly shaped piece of parchment in a shaky hand which cannot keep the lines straight. The last witness, who has his name prominently in the centre of the document, is called 'Willelmus Spuens Mendacium'. Judging from the position of this name, 'William Vomiting Falsehood' was presumably the writer; the significance of the name is anybody's guess. The charter of Humfrey, lord of Bunbury, dating from 30 years later, is likewise written in a peculiar script and contains divergent spellings of common Latin words, such as *humagium* for 'homage', *harabilis* for 'arable', and *testebus* instead of *testibus* for 'witnesses'. Equally striking is the charter of Jordan of Cheadle, which was written by Roger the Chaplain, who seems to have been having trouble with his pen and decides in the second line to increase the size of his script. This charter also contains the naive drafting error of describing the boundaries of the land in relation to 'a certain oak which has been uprooted'.

Eccentrically written books, as distinct from charters, are very rare because the scribe of a book was not writing just an occasional page. The strangest book, from the point of view of physical appearance, is the *Ormulum*, which is a series of homilies on the life of Christ in the Gospels in Middle English verse. The book was probably penned, as well as being composed, over an extended period around 1170 by Orm himself, who was an Augustinian canon. He writes in an exceptionally large and heavy hand on irregularly shaped pieces of parchment, sometimes of rough quality.[74] Towards the end of the book the script becomes crowded and occasionally runs from one column into the other, with extra words fitted in vertically as well, as if the writer was preoccupied with saving parchment. Although Orm's book has an unprofessional appearance, it is obviously not the product of an illiterate. Writing in English, he had few models to follow and may not have considered appearances important anyway. His book may reflect the ideal of the Augustinian canons of teaching the Gospel in simplicity and poverty.

---

[71] Fleta, Bk ii, ch. 13, SS lxxii (1953), p. 125.

[72] *Liber Memorandorum Ecclesie de Bernewelle* ed. J. W. Clark (1907), pp. 155–6.

[73] *Cheshire Facs*, nos 1, 4(1), 14.

[74] M. B. Parkes, 'On the Presumed Date and Possible Origin of the MS of the *Ormulum*', in *Scribes, Scripts and Readers* (1991), pp. 187–200.

The problem raised by divergent and amateur documents is what kind of training and practice their writers had. It is often assumed that in the country writing was done by a local monk or clerk who was an expert. But there was little common training in writing or anything else for either monks or secular clergy before about 1200. Monasteries with great *scriptoria*, like Christ Church Canterbury, were exceptional. Not many clerks in the twelfth century could have had experience either of a cathedral school or university or of an organized writing office. By the thirteenth century, on the other hand, average standards of writing improve, presumably because more clerks were getting an appropriate education. At first many monks and secular clergy would have been unfamiliar with business documents like charters, even if they knew a little about books. Had Orm written a charter, he would no doubt have made it look as if it were produced by a semi-literate, which would be a false inference. Perhaps badly written documents principally indicate the difficulties of writing well and emphasize the professional standards of the majority of books and charters. To explain how such elegance and consistency were achieved in the majority of local documents remains an outstanding and probably insoluble problem, comparable with explaining how country churches were designed and built as microcosms of the great cathedrals.

LAYOUT AND FORMAT

The commonest sign of an amateur writer is bad layout (see plates I and VI), as the clarity of the message conveyed by the script is enhanced or obscured by this.[75] The incompetently written charters already described all have irregularities of layout. In the twelfth century and earlier some scribes of charters were understandably more accustomed to writing books. This is revealed not only by their book hands, but by their layout. One of Westminster abbey's writs of Edward the Confessor, written just before the Norman Conquest, appears to be the lower portion of a previously ruled leaf of parchment, presumably intended for a book.[76] Similarly a charter of Henry de Portu, dating from 1120–30, is written on a book-sized folio in two columns.[77] The writer was evidently uncertain about this layout and takes his text across the central space, the two columns being used only to make it easier to write in straight lines. Richard Fitz Neal in the *Dialogue of the Exchequer* is as concerned with good layout as he is with other details of office procedure. He was evidently interested in layout as an art form, as he describes a history he claims to have written himself, entitled *Tricolumnis*, because it was arranged in three columns dealing with ecclesiastical, royal,

---

[75] In general see H.-J. Martin and J. Vezin eds, *Mise en page et mise en texte du livre manuscrit* (1990), and M. B. Parkes, '*Ordinatio* and *Compilatio*' in *Essays Presented to R. W. Hunt* ed. J. J. G. Alexander and M. T. Gibson (1976), pp. 115–41.

[76] Bishop & Chaplais, plate xxiiib.

[77] *Oxford Facs*, no. 14.

and miscellaneous business respectively.[78] Tabulation by columns, distinguishing different types of subject matter, was a novelty at the time. Thus another contemporary (possibly Gervase of Canterbury) carefully explains the three-column layout he had devised for his *Mappa Mundi*, which was not a representation of the earth's surface, but a gazetteer of religious houses:

> Note that our page is divided as if into three columns. The first column contains the dignities of places, that is, archbishoprics, bishoprics, abbacies and priories. The second lists the names of the places and the saint to whom the church is dedicated. The third shows to which order and habit, and to which mother church, the inmates belong.[79]

This first attempt at a comprehensive list of religious houses was a consequence of the recent increase in their numbers combined with the growing fashion for making surveys and memoranda in writing.

Fitz Neal describes the correct layout for an Exchequer pipe roll, giving details (which can be verified from extant rolls) of how the lines should be ruled and the headings spaced out.[80] When describing how the name of the sheriff of each county should be engrossed at the head of the enrolment, Fitz Neal used the term *depingitur* (literally, 'depicted') instead of *scribitur* ('written'). The connection with painting implied by this term is appropriate, as more elaborate letters were used for headings and in some manuscripts they were picked out in red, that is, in rubrics. The use of colour was functional, as well as being an embellishment, because it helped the reader to find his place, as prologues to manuscripts point out. The author of Ramsey abbey's *Book of Benefactors* explains that he has inserted rubrics 'for the notice of readers'; similarly the Barnwell priory register exhorts the diligent reader to use its list of rubrics.[81] The functional use of rubrics, and the elegant layout of headings and paragraphs as a whole, is nowhere better exemplified than in the larger volume of Domesday Book. In manuscripts, as in medieval art in general, function and use went together.

The most elaborate layouts are found in the works of the glossators of the Bible and of Roman and canon law; the glossed Psalter of Eadwine is illustrated as an example of layout at plate xiv.[82] The gloss took definite shape in the twelfth century and grew out of the practice of lecturers and students making explanatory notes on spare space around the texts they studied. Master Vacarius, in the textbook of Roman law he wrote for English students

---

[78] *Dialogus*, p. 27. This history may have been an aspiration of Fitz Neal's rather than a reality.

[79] Gervase ii, pp. 417–18.

[80] *Dialogus*, p. 29, cf. pp. 104–5. See the facsimiles of twelfth-century pipe rolls (for the years 1130, 1156, 1167) in C. Johnson and H. Jenkinson, *English Court Hand* (1915) ii, plates iva, vb, viii.

[81] *Ramsey*, p. 65; *Liber Memorandorum Ecclesie de Bernewelle*, p. 20.

[82] Glossed texts are illustrated in colour by de Hamel, *MSS*, plates 78, 98, 106. See also C. de Hamel, *Glossed Books of the Bible* (1984), ch. 4, and Carruthers, *Memory*, pp. 215–17.

(probably while he was in the service of Roger archbishop of York, 1154–81), describes how he first put particular passages in order for the text and then he perfected the book 'by sprinkling other passages into the space for the gloss'.[83] By this means, he claims, brevity was served and the result was 'a book published at the lowest price and readable in a short time'. Glossed books – with their highly abbreviated scripts 'sprinkled' on the page – could be as bewildering to medieval readers, apart from the masters and students for whom they were intended, as they are to us today. 'The "masters of the glosses", for this is the name they have now attained', comments Robert of Melun (an English contemporary of Vacarius), 'lack understanding of their glosses as much as of the text, even if they can distinguish the glosses and separate them through punctuation marks and assign each one to the text it serves.'[84] How these punctuation marks (*puncti*) functioned as cross-references was explained by Master Herbert of Bosham in the layout he designed in the 1170s for his de luxe edition of Peter Lombard's *Great Gloss* on the Psalms.[85] The Lombard had been Herbert's own master in the Paris schools; Herbert's edition enshrined the *Great Gloss* at Canterbury.[86]

A gloss was sometimes written between the lines of the text (an interlinear gloss) as well as in the margins. By the thirteenth century some manuscripts have around their outer borders a gloss on the gloss. A special type of script, which was economical of space but quick to write, was sometimes used for glosses, as has already been mentioned. The successive series of glosses around a central text show, like tree rings, the proliferation of written record over generations of scholars. Whereas the gloss's scholastic companion, the *summa*, aimed to cut through the mass of words to the original core, the gloss did the reverse, as the commentaries swamp the main text. As examples of precise yet elaborate calligraphy, however, medieval glossed books have no rivals. They show how the technology of writing was refined in the twelfth century to meet new needs.

Turning from the layout to the format of the finished writing, changes in both the size and shape of manuscripts occurred. In general the average size of documents and books got smaller. This generalization does not imply that large charters and books were no longer produced, but only that they were no longer typical. In the latter half of the thirteenth century books of smaller size, using a more compressed script and written on thinner parchment, become relatively common. One such volume could contain the texts of three or four volumes of the preceding century. Books of the Bible, students' textbooks and other manuals (for instance, collections of English parliamentary statutes) were produced in formats small enough (15cm × 12cm or less) to be carried in

[83] *Liber Pauperum*, SS XLIV (1927), p. 1.
[84] Cited by C. J. Mews, 'Orality, Literacy and Authority in the Twelfth-Century Schools', *Exemplaria* II (1990), p. 498, n. 54.
[85] R. H. and M. A. Rouse, 'Statim Invenire', in *Renaissance and Renewal* ed. R. L. Benson and G. Constable (1982), pp. 208–9.
[86] B. Smalley, *The Becket Conflict and the Schools* (1973), pp. 82–3; C. de Hamel 'MSS of Herbert of Bosham' in *MSS Hunt*, pp. 38–41.

the pocket (see plate XVI).[87] It has been suggested that the friars were the force behind the demand for more portable books because they had to move from place to place, yet they were also expected, the Dominicans in particular, to be well read.[88] Students likewise required relatively cheap and portable books. But portability and economy are not a complete explanation for small books, as some of them are elaborately ornamented; illuminated bibles are among the works most frequently produced in pocket-sized formats, as are Books of Hours. The earliest Book of Hours extant in England, the exquisite manuscript illuminated by William de Brailes in *c*.1240, is literally a handbook: its dimensions are those of an adult's pair of hands, so that it can be used without effort by the lady who is depicted in it at her devotions.[89]

The basic explanation for books getting smaller is that they were gradually changing their function. The traditional large books were intended to be placed on lecterns and displayed or read aloud in monastic communities. The new smaller formats were designed for individual private study, if they were academic books, or meditation, if they were religious. Although the techniques had been developed for making small books by 1300, the extent of this change should not be exaggerated. Individuals still had few books of any size, and reading aloud persisted. Nevertheless, as part of the shift from memory to written record, the emphasis in production had moved by 1300 from large liturgical folios to small intelligible manuals.

In the shapes of documents, as distinct from books, greater numbers likewise brought a reduction in average size, and increasing standardization. This is most evident in episcopal charters, where by 1200 scribes almost invariably write on the longer way of an oblong parchment, whereas in the first half of the twelfth century many charters are written on the shorter way. C. R. Cheney summarizes these changes: 'For a century after 1100 we shall see a steady movement from a diplomatically crude to a finished type, from a spacious and extravagant to a small and economical format, from a normal book hand to a businesslike and distinctive charter hand.'[90] The twelfth century was the period when many forms of business document 'took shape', shapes they would retain into the sixteenth century and beyond.

ROLLS OR BOOKS?

In the format of royal documents the most far-reaching change was the use of rolls instead of books.[91] Rolls are so familiar to any medievalist who has

---

[87] Harvard Law Library has a good collection of early pocket books of English statutes: MSS 56–9, 173 5.

[88] C. H. Talbot, 'The Universities and the Medieval Library' in *English Library*, pp. 76–7. D. L. d'Avray, 'Portable "Vademecum" Books' in *MSS Hunt*, pp. 60–4.

[89] D. Diringer, *The Illuminated Book* (2nd edn, 1967), p. 267. A Dominican pocket bible is illustrated by d'Avray, n. 88 above. Donovan, *de Brailes*, colour plates 2 and 3.

[90] *Chanceries*, p. 51. Long charters of the first half of the twelfth century are illustrated in *Charters of Norwich Cathedral Priory* ed. B. Dodwell, PRS new series XL (1974), plate iii.

[91] In general see Wattenbach, *Schriftwesen*, p. 105–74; Glenisson, *Livre*, ch. 1; R. H. Rouse, 'Roll and Codex' in *Paläographie 1981* ed. G. Silagi (1982), pp. 108–23.

worked in the Public Record Office that their existence tends to be taken for granted. Yet there is no evidence that rolls were made by the royal government before the twelfth century and, in the forms they took, they are peculiar to England. Continental governments, from the papacy downwards, kept their most important records in the form of books not rolls. Consequently when William the Conqueror undertook his *descriptio* of the conquered land, the results were compiled for posterity in volumes, 'Domesday Book', not in rolls. Although some of the preliminary drafts for Domesday Book may possibly have been stitched together into rolls, they were described vaguely as *breves* or *carte* and not as rolls.[92] A special Latin word for the record in roll format came into vogue in the twelfth century at the earliest: it was a *rotulus*.

This word seems to have been brought into general use by Fitz Neal's *Dialogue of the Exchequer.* He describes a variety of types of roll – 'rolls of the treasury' or 'great annual rolls of accounts' (that is, the pipe rolls), 'rolls of the chancery', 'rolls of receipts', the 'lesser rolls of the itinerant justices', and others.[93] To Fitz Neal and his colleagues working in the Exchequer in the 1170s the roll or *rotulus* was evidently a commonplace. Nevertheless the general public were probably unfamiliar both with the name and the thing until Fitz Neal's book made the secrets of the Exchequer plain to his readers. His purpose, he explained in his prologue, was to reveal hidden treasure or the treasury (the Latin *thesaurus* means both 'treasure' and 'treasury') in ordinary language, 'even though it is permissible to invent new terms'.[94] Fitz Neal may not have been aware that *rotulus* was a new term, as it could have been part of the jargon of the Exchequer since his boyhood when his father had been the treasurer of Henry I. Rolls had certainly been made then, as Fitz Neal refers to 'the old annual rolls of that king' and furthermore much of the pipe roll for the fiscal year ending Michaelmas 1130 is still extant.[95]

The novelty of the roll in the twelfth century, outside the Exchequer that is, is suggested by the variety of forms the word takes. Fitz Neal's form, *rotulus*, took time to establish itself as the norm. A certificate confirming acquittance from paying Danegeld, dated the eight year of Henry II's reign (1162), states that the acquittance was written down at the Exchequer 'in the roll' (*in rollo*).[96] As this statement can be checked with the extant pipe roll and as the acquittance is one of a series of written privileges obtained by Ralf of Caen, who is described by Henry II as 'my clerk', the form *rollus* must have been acceptable in official circles in the 1160s. Early in the thirteenth century, on the other hand, Jocelin of Brakelond uses a feminine form, *rolla*, to describe a bailiff's roll and also to describe 'the great roll of Winchester'.[97] The latter description is strange, as the context shows that this 'great roll' is Domesday

---

[92] For the Domesday drafts see ch. 1, nn. 32–5 above. For early meanings of *breve* see nn. 100–1 below.

[93] *Dialogus*, pp. 17, 62, 70.

[94] Ibid., pp. 5, 6.

[95] Ibid. p. 42; *Magnum Rotulum Scaccarii de Anno 31 Henry I* ed. J. Hunter, RC (1835).

[96] *The Registrum Antiquissimum of the Cathedral Church of Lincoln* ed. C. W. Foster, Lincoln Record, S. xxvii (1931), i, p. 73, no. 120.

[97] Jocelin, pp. 101, 46.

Book. Perhaps Jocelin did not know that Domesday was in the form of a book, or alternatively *rolla* may have meant for him any sort of formal record. Some years earlier, in the 1180s, Alan prior of Christ Church Canterbury had likewise referred to the 'roll of Winchester', using another variant, *rotula*. Although the context is obscure, this reference may also be to Domesday Book, since Alan was arguing that the muniments and privileges of the whole English church would be subverted if they had to accord with 'that roll' (*rotulam illam*).[98] An alternative possibility is that Alan was referring to a pipe roll or some other form of Exchequer record kept at Winchester.

These rare and scattered references suggest that until the thirteenth century writers were uncertain about how a roll should be described in Latin and some of them may also have been unclear about what a roll really was in the royal bureaucratic sense. The royal records were not available for public inspection then as they are now. A sheriff answering at the Exchequer would certainly have seen the clerks writing things down, but he would not necessarily have understood how the rolls were compiled until Fitz Neal revealed these 'holy mysteries' in his book.[99] Fitz Neal implies moreover that confusion about the nomenclature of the rolls had existed even in the Exchequer itself, as he remarks at one point that the 'so called exaction roll' (*rotulus qui exactorius dicitur*) is also named *breve de firmis*.[100] The word *breve* (originally associated with 'abbreviation') came to mean a writ or short letter, as distinct from a roll, in the course of the twelfth century. It is possible that the 'exaction roll', which listed the sheriffs' farms, may have been the oldest written record used in the Exchequer and had been called a *breve* before the word *rotulus* came into vogue. Monastic obituary rolls in the late eleventh and early twelfth centuries were likewise sometimes described as *brevia* or *breves*.[101]

An apparent exception to the rule that the word *rotulus* only came into general use in Fitz Neal's time is a writ of Henry I's dating from as early as 1110. It instructs Richard de Monte to allow the abbot of Westminster 10 shillings of the royal alms, 'as it is in my rolls' (*in rotulis meis*).[102] If this writ were entirely genuine, it would suggest that the word *rotulus* and the habit of referring to the royal rolls were already established in the second decade of the twelfth century. However, the text of the writ is suspect for a number of reasons. Firstly it is in favour of Westminster abbey which was a centre of

[98] *Alani Prioris Cantuariensis Postea Abbatis Tewkesberiensis* ed. I. A. Giles (1846), p. 42, letters to Robert de Hardres. This may refer to a dispute between Canterbury and Lincoln, as Robert was a keeper of the vacant bishopric of Lincoln in 1184–6 (*Pipe Roll 31 Henry II*, p. 125; *32 Henry II*, p. 83; *33 Henry II*, p. 77), or alternatively to a dispute between the Hardres family and Christ Church, as suggested by W. Urry, *Canterbury under the Angevin Kings* (1967), p. 61. Henry II called Alan 'a second pope' because of his championship of ecclesiastical rights in 1184, Gervase I, p. 313.

[99] Among the 'sacramentorum latibula' of the Exchequer Fitz Neal includes 'rotulorum conscriptio', *Dialogus*, p. 26, cf. p. 126.

[100] Ibid., p. 62. The purpose of this record 'of farms' is explained at ibid., p. 125 and by R. L. Poole, *The Exchequer in the Twelfth Century* (1912), p. 131.

[101] *Dictionary of Medieval Latin from British Sources* ed. R. E. Latham (1975) I, p. 216.

[102] J. Armitage Robinson, *Gilbert Crispin Abbot of Westminster* (1911), p. 149, no. 32. *RRA-N* II (1956), p. 116, no. 1053.

forgery. Secondly it has a postscript saying, allow 'this also every year', whereas an authentic writ would probably have made this concession an integral part of the text. By the same token the phrase, 'as it is in my rolls', may be a later interpolation. The comparable certificate of acquittance for Ralf of Caen states that it is written *in rollo*, that is, in the roll of a specified year, and not *in rotulis* in general. It would have been tempting for a copyist – and this Westminster writ exists only in a copy – to insert the phrase 'as it is in my rolls' and the postscript into the text of a genuine writ of Henry I. Westminster abbey's dilemma may well have been that Henry I had indeed made this grant, but in subsequent reigns a writ of this sort would have required the supporting evidence of the pipe rolls. A Westminster monk therefore supplied this evidence as best he could by inserting a vague reference to 'my rolls', even though Henry I may not have had any rolls at the time the writ was issued. R. L. Poole used this Westminster writ as evidence that the pipe rolls had existed since the second decade of the twelfth century, but it could be used just as well to argue the contrary.[103]

To summarize the argument so far, the pipe rolls of the Exchequer, which were created at some unknown time by Henry I's government, seem to be the prototype for royal records in roll form in England. Whether they were started in the decade 1100–10 (as the Westminster writ implies if it is genuine) or in the decade 1120–30 (as the extant roll for 1130 might suggest) is an unresolvable problem. Either way there is no evidence of royal records in roll form before the reign of Henry I. At whatever date the Exchequer rolls were started moreover, we should not assume that their form and purpose was generally understood until Fitz Neal revealed the 'holy mysteries' of the Exchequer in Henry II's reign.

Nevertheless records in roll form were not entirely unknown in England before 1100. The earliest roll now extant was begun in the decade preceding 1088; it records professions of obedience by suffragan bishops to the archbishop of Canterbury.[104] Likewise another Canterbury roll, informing the archbishop of elections to bishoprics, contains some membranes from the 1090s.[105] As the former of these rolls dates from Archbishop Lanfranc's pontificate, it may have originated from his interest in the reform of books and records. Until they grew in length over the years, rolls like the Canterbury ones would not have been seen as startling innovations. Rolling up a membrane of parchment was the easiest and most obvious way of storing it. Moreover, the roll had ancient origins, as it had been the usual format of writings in the Graeco-Roman world. But the layout and material of ancient and medieval rolls differed, as the text was written in ancient rolls in columns on the longer way of the papyrus, whereas in medieval rolls it was written from the head to the tail of the parchment.

---

[103] *The Exchequer in the Twelfth Century*, pp. 37–8.
[104] Canterbury Dean and Chapter Archives, Chartae Antiquae C.117, described by M. Richter, *Canterbury Professions*, Canterbury and Yorks S. LXVII (1973), pp. xxvi–xxvii, and by Ker, *English MSS*, p. 17 and plate 6a.
[105] BL MS Harley Roll A.3, described by Ker, *English MSS*, p. 17 and plate 6b.

The roll was also the most convenient format for conveying a message or letter in parchment. It was customary for monasteries to send a messenger from house to house, collecting an accumulating series of obituaries forming a roll when an abbot died. A long roll of this sort, commemorating Matilda, first abbess of William the Conqueror's nunnery at Caen, was taken on an extensive tour of England soon after her death in 1113.[106] Although this roll disappeared at the French Revolution, that of Abbot Vitalis of Savigny (who died in 1122) survives and bears over 70 inscriptions from English monasteries.[107] It was perhaps an obituary roll of a comparable type that St Dunstan's biographer had in mind a century earlier when he described the saint having a vision, presaging King Edgar's death, of a man carrying a great *prolixe cartule rotella* covered all over with letters.[108] This is the earliest example of the use of the word 'roll' (*rotella* in this instance) in England. But this example also suggests that the word was unfamiliar to the biographer's readers, since he explains that the *rotella* was of *prolixe cartule*, literally meaning 'a roll of prolix little charter'. If rolls had already been common for writing purposes, it would not have been necessary to add that this one was covered with letters like a charter.

Despite the use of rolls for monastic obituaries, there was a prejudice against them which makes it surprising that the roll was adopted as the format for the most important royal records. The parchment roll was the characteristic format for the copies of the Jewish law read in synagogues and had been so since antiquity. In twelfth-century legal procedure in England the Jew was distinguished from the Christian by the fact that he took an oath 'on his roll',[109] whereas the Christian swore on the book of the Gospel. Similarly the prophets of the Old Testament were depicted in painting and sculpture holding rolls.[110] This was not an insignificant distinction, as the Bible had been written in the form of a book almost since the historical beginnings of Christianity, probably deliberately in order to distinguish it from both Jewish and pagan works in rolls.[111] In the rare instances where Christ is depicted holding a roll instead of a book in medieval manuscripts, he is usually intended to represent the God of the Old Testament. Thus the miniature in the Winchester Bible of the Christ of the Gothic Majesty, holding a rolled-up scroll in his left hand and an opened one is his right, depicts God calling the prophet Isaiah; Isaiah is appropriately shown as a Jew both by his hat and by the scroll.[112] In the Bury Bible similarly the distinction between the new dispensation and the old is made in Ezechiel's vision by depicting Christ in

[106] *Rouleaux des Morts* ed. L. Delisle, Société de l'Histoire de france cxxxv (1866), pp. 177–279. This Matilda was not a daughter of William the Conqueror, as stated by Delisle.
[107] Facsimile ed. L. Delisle (1909); Zarnecki, *Catalogue*, no. 29.
[108] *Memorials of St Dunstan* ed. W. Stubbs, RS lxiii (1874), p. 46.
[109] 'super rotulum suum', e.g. Stubbs, *Charters*, p. 256.
[110] E.g. Kaufmann, *Romanesque MSS*, plates 275–6, 279–80, 285.
[111] C. H. Roberts, 'Books in the Graeco-Roman World' in *The Cambridge History of the Bible* ed. P. R. Ackroyd and C. F. Evans (1970) i, pp. 57ff. See also p. 118 above.
[112] Fo. 131. Kauffmann, *Romanesque MSS*, plate 238.

majesty bearing a book, while Ezechiel is placed at his feet holding up a scroll.[113] Rolls bore the old law and books the new.

The faithful were reminded of the image of Christ in majesty bearing the Book of Judgement whenever they went to church, as that was how Christ was most commonly depicted in Romanesque art. William the Conqueror's book was appropriately called 'Domesday' because it reminded people of that Last Judgement.[114] Had Domesday Book been in the form of a roll, it might not have been so readily compared with holy writ. This suggestion should not be exaggerated, however, as royal rolls were themselves being compared with Scripture before the end of the twelfth century. When Fitz Neal explains that not even the king's justices may alter their rolls, once they have been delivered to the treasurer, he recalls the Gospel's warning that not one iota of the law shall pass away.[115] The Exchequer may have had the odd effect of hallowing the roll format in England.

The idea of making the pipe rolls probably originated not directly from the Jews, though that is a possibility, but from cosmopolitan arithmeticians who were familiar with Arabic practice. One suggestion is that Adelard of Bath, who introduced Arabic works on astronomy and geometry to the west, may have been an official in Henry I's Exchequer.[116] Another candidate is the royal clerk, Thurkil, who knew Hugh de Bocland, the sheriff of Essex from 1101 and perhaps earlier.[117] Thurkil's treatise on the abacus is addressed to his colleague, Simon de Rotol.[118] 'Rotol' might either be extended to 'Rotolanda', meaning 'of Rutland', or to 'Rotolis', meaning 'of the Rolls'. If the latter extension is accepted, Simon may have been the first maker or keeper of the pipe rolls. Thurkil and Simon had a common master, described only as Guillelmus R., the greatest living arithmetician; he may have been William, bishop of Syracuse in Sicily, which had just been conquered from the Arabs.[119] These scraps of information cannot satisfactorily explain the origin of the pipe rolls, but they are consistent with the hypothesis that their format was non-Christian.

The problem of origins has further complexities because the pipe rolls are in a unique format. The term *rotulus* does not describe a continuous series of membranes of parchment, which are stitched head to tail to form a length of four metres or more, like the Chancery rolls. Instead an Exchequer *rotulus* consists of two membranes only, stitched together to form a length of less than two metres.[120] Each *rotulus* comprised the account of a different county or bailiwick. When all the accounts for the year had been written, the different *rotuli* were piled one on top of another and secured at their heads with cords.

---

[113] Kauffmann, *Romanesque MSS*, plate 153, Boase, *English Art*, plate 54b.

[114] See ch. 1, n. 27 above.

[115] *Dialogus*, p. 77; Matthew, v, 18.

[116] Poole, *The Exchequer in the Twelfth Century*, pp. 56–7; Haskins, *Studies in the History of Medieval Science*, pp. 34–5; J. A. Green, *The Government of England under Henry I* (1986), p. 41.

[117] Haskins, ibid., pp. 328–9.

[118] Ibid., 327.

[119] Ibid., p. 329.

[120] *Dialogus*, p. 29.

As the lower ends are left free, referring from the face to the dorse of a particular *rotulus* is easier than on a continuous roll. Although the Exchequer had thus adopted a form of record which was easier to consult than a continuous roll, its style did not become the norm. A simplification of it, using one membrane instead of two per *rotulus* was adopted by the law courts for their plea rolls in the 1190s, but not by the Chancery in the next decade. Furthermore, when receipt rolls were introduced at the Exchequer in Henry II's reign, they were made into continuous rolls at first, as is evident from the fragments extant for Michaelmas term in 1185.[121] The consequence of these haphazard developments is that in the thirteenth century the royal government made rolls in two principal formats – Exchequer style (the membranes piled on top of each other) and Chancery style (the membranes stitched head to tail in a continuous length).

These technicalities suggest that the reason why medieval England, alone in Europe, kept its records predominantly in rolls remains largely a mystery. Convenience is not a good explanation, as continuous rolls are not convenient to consult. The folded parchment forming a quire, which was the basic component of a medieval book, was as convenient as any form of roll. Nor is economy in parchment a sufficient explanation, as the pieces from which the pipe rolls were made were of exceptional size. Economy in binding costs is a possibility, but that has to be balanced against the cost of making protective covers for the rolls. Rolls had short-term advantages, which might originally have made them attractive: the separate membranes of which they were composed could be of slightly differing sizes, and they could be compiled separately by different clerks and then stitched together in appropriate order, whereas the scribe of a book had to proceed from one page of his quire to the next. As various formats of roll were used by different departments of the royal government by the time of King John, habit and precedent seem the best general explanations, although they do not explain why certain decisions were taken in the first place. Once these distinctive formats had been established, bureaucracy ensured that they remained unchanged for centuries.

In the thirteenth century other authorities followed the lead of the royal government in keeping records on rolls (see plates IX, X and XI). Sometimes they were evidently unsure about which form of royal roll to imitate. Thus among borough records the earliest guild rolls, those of Leicester (starting in 1196), are made up in Chancery style, whereas the second earliest, those of Shrewsbury (starting in 1209), are in Exchequer style;[122] the custumal of Exeter (dating from the 1230s) combines both styles.[123] Similarly the earliest part of the first bishop's register (starting between 1214 and 1217), that of Hugh of Wells, bishop of Lincoln, is in Chancery style, but one subsequent part is in Exchequer style and the *Liber Antiquus* is in book format; contempo-

---

[121] See ch. 3, n. 45 above.

[122] G. H. Martin, 'The English Borough in the Thirteenth Century', *TRHS* 5th series XIII (1963), pp. 132, 135. Leicester's rolls begin before the Chancery rolls, but they may not have been made up into a roll until after 1200.

[123] *The Anglo-Norman Custumal of Exeter* ed. J. W. Schopp (1925).

raries probably did not think of these diverse records as forming one register.[124] By the end of the century the book format had become usual for bishops' registers, probably in order to bring them into line with continental and papal practice. Likewise the royal government itself seemed to acknowledge in the thirteenth century that rolls were not necessarily the best way to keep records. Material from rolls was copied into books, such as the remembrance books of the Exchequer, to make consultation easier.[125] Moreover, new classes of record were made into books instead of rolls; the best example are the Wardrobe books of Edward I, which contain the sort of financial details which might have gone on to the pipe rolls in Henry I's reign.[126]

Roll formats were also used for types of record other than accounts and memoranda of proceedings. A few cartularies, both monastic and lay, are in rolls, as are some monastic chronicles and narratives.[127] This practice is understandable, as such documents are akin to records. Equally understandable are those texts for which the roll format was more suitable than the book. For example, histories of the kings of England were produced in the thirteenth century in long rolls. They were perhaps intended for laymen of restricted literacy, as they depict the kings in a series of roundels with a brief commentary alongside each picture (see plate XIII).[128] When the roll is fully unfurled, the whole history of England, from its mythical foundation by the Trojans down to the reign of Edward I, is displayed as a continuous line. The most spectacular example of pictorial narrative in a roll is the life of St Guthlac of Crowland (see plate XX), which depicts the life of the saint in a series of roundels without a commentary; its precise purpose is unknown.

Occasionally ordinary texts appear in roll format.[129] One pictorial history of England has on its dorse the Anglo-Norman romance, *Amadas et Ydoine*.[130] This combination is not really strange, as history and romance were closely connected in the mind of the lay reader. More bizarre are legal and managerial textbooks in the form of continuous rolls: the Harvard Law School has a mid-thirteenth-century text of Glanvill 293 cm long, and St John's College, Cambridge, has Walter of Henley's *Husbandry* 223 cm long.[131] Here again perhaps lay landowners, who were more familiar with records than with

---

[124] *Rotuli Hugonis de Welles* ed. W. P. W. Phillimore, Canterbury and York S. I (1909) or Lincoln Record S. III (1912), I, p. iii.

[125] *Book of Fees* I, p. 20.

[126] The earliest extant Wardrobe book dates from 1285–6, ed. B. F. and C. R. Byerly, *Records of the Wardrobe and Household*, HMSO (1977), pp. 1–116. An inventory in 1300 lists 18 such books, *Book of Prests* ed. E. B. Fryde (1962), p. 228.

[127] G. R. C. Davis, *Medieval Cartularies of Great Britain* (1958), e.g. nos 407 (Flaxley abbey), 1188A (Ralf Basset). A chronicle associated with Thornton abbey (begun in ?1289) is in a roll, ed. T. Wright, *Feudal Manuals of English History* (1872), pp. 88–124, as is Durham cathedral priory's account of its litigation *v.* Bishop Anthony Bek, ed. R. K. Richardson, *Camden Miscellany* Camden S. 3rd series XXXIV (1924), pp. 1–58.

[128] Wright, *Feudal Manuals* pp. ixff; Lewis, *Matthew Paris*, pp. 140–2, 168–9.

[129] In general see R. H. Rouse, 'Roll and Codex', in G. Silagi ed., *Paläographie 1981* (1982), pp. 108–23.

[130] Wright, *Feudal Manuals*, p. xv.

[131] Harvard Law Library MS 180; St John's College MS N.13, cf. *Walter of Henley*, pp. 37–8.

traditional books, did not consider it strange or inconvenient to have texts in this form. Thus one copy (dating from early in the fourteenth century) of Walter of Bibbesworth's rhyming French vocabulary, which was intended to improve the French of the gentry, is in the form of a roll 268 cm long.[132] It is unusually narrow (10 cm wide) and the tail is slotted into a length of wood, with knobs at each end, which serves as a winder. When tightly wound up, this roll can be held in the palm of the hand.

An even smaller and earlier roll (less than 8 cm wide and 56 cm long) has written on one side of it *The Song of the Barons* in French (composed in *c.*1263) and on the other side the oldest secular play extant in English, the *Interludium de Clerico et Puella*.[133] Very probably this roll was made so small so that it could be carried by a wandering minstrel in his pouch as part of his repertoire. Its chance survival (until 1971 when it went missing from the British Museum) is a reminder of the thousands of little rolls of parchment, containing memoranda of all sorts, which supplied the material for more formal books. On the threshold of literacy, among knights and minstrels as distinct from monks and clerks, writings were perhaps at first more familiar and inviting in the form of rolls containing short vernacular texts than in the form of weighty Latin books. The contents of a little roll could be seen at a glance and readily grasped in the hand, whereas traditional liturgical books had been kept on lecterns or locked up in monastic sacristies.

In Spenser's *Faery Queen* Eumnestes, the sage of infinite remembrance, inhabits a ruined chamber which

> . . . all was hangd about with rolls,
> And old records from ancient times derivd,
> Some made in books, some in long parchment scrolls,
> That were all worm-eaten and full of canker holes.[134]

Spenser wrote when the Middle Ages were just beginning to be gothicized and made picturesque. To the Elizabethans the twin format of English parchment documents, rolls and books, seemed as old as time itself. In fact these records took their distinctive shapes in the twelfth century. A pedantic historian or archivist might also comment that, on the whole, the real records of medieval England have been preserved in better condition than Eumnestes kept his.

Although some medieval records have been attacked by vermin, and many more have been lost or damaged by neglect, parchment has proved a remarkably durable material. This particular characteristic of it was recognized from the start by medieval scribes, whose illuminated manuscripts, like the *Book of Kells* and the *Lindisfarne Gospels*, became a talisman of Christian endurance in the Dark Ages. The initial difficulty of applying script to parchment combined with the circumstances of the time to make writing the special art of monks in Anglo-Saxon England, as elsewhere in western Europe. When documents began to be required on an unprecedented scale after the

---

[132] BL MS Sloan 809. For Walter of Bibbesworth see pp. 195–200 below.
[133] BL MS Additional 23986; A. Taylor, 'The Myth of the Minstrel MS', *Speculum* LXVI (1991), pp. 68–9.
[134] Bk. II, canto ix, verse 57.

Norman Conquest, the skills of monastic scribes were adapted and extended to meet these new needs.

Surprisingly perhaps, both the traditional methods of writing and the materials, in particular parchment, showed themselves to be flexible as well as durable. It proved possible to produce parchment in varying qualities relatively cheaply and also to cut, stitch, and fold it into shapes ranging from the great Winchester Bible and the pipe rolls to pocket-sized manuals for lawyers or preachers and tightly rolled royal writs no larger than a man's little finger. Similarly the cursive script, essential to secular clerks who had to write fast from dictation, was adapted from traditional book hand and not consciously invented. The price of adaptation, as contrasted with planned innovation, was a variety of styles of writing and formats of document, which were perpetuated when they settled down into bureaucratic routine. There is more history than logic in the miscellany of styles of document preserved in the Public Record Office.

On the other hand, an advantage of adapting existing practice was that the makers of medieval records had in parchment a writing medium which was better suited to long texts than the clay bricks and stone tablets of the ancient world, yet was stronger than papyrus. Moreover, the new secular documents, from Domesday Book onwards, inherited much of the respect and even awe which had been accorded to liturgical books in the monastic tradition. Some charters at first were laid out like pages of Gospel books and the finest secular legal and literary texts continued to be indistinguishable in physical appearance from other illuminated manuscripts. The growth, from the monastic *scriptorium*, of new branches and styles of writing was probably the chief reason why documents became acceptable to the laity, and upon that acceptance the future extension of literacy depended.

It is a facile speculation to assume that paper or printing, had they been readily available in 1100, would have automatically accelerated the growth of literacy faster than parchment. The initial and most difficult task was to make the laity, knights in the countryside typically, accustomed to writing. Traditionally such men respected monks, though they did not aspire to be like them, and gave them lands on their deathbeds or in time of peril. Traditionally too the monks symbolized these gifts with Gospel books and recorded them in charters. When documents produced by the king's government began to proliferate in the twelfth century, they also were accepted because, by and large, they used traditional materials and skills. The changes which were made in the technology of writing in the twelfth and thirteenth centuries went largely unnoticed by contemporaries. They were subtle and technical and have necessitated discussion in this chapter of parchments, scripts, layouts, and so on. But because known methods of writing were adapted and extended, rather than revolutionized, fundamental changes in this most conservative area of human skills were set in motion. Techniques of writing records tended to be conservative because conservation was their main purpose.

5

The Preservation and Use of Documents

<u>Documents do not automatically become records</u>. Writing may be done for ephemeral purposes without any intention of keeping the documents permanently. In modern societies, where mass literacy is normal, most writings are made for purposes of immediate communication or short-term administrative convenience; when the message has been received or the obligation discharged, the piece of paper recording it is generally thrown away. Most people are literate, to a minimal standard, but relatively few documents are kept for long. The situation in the Middle Ages was the reverse of the modern one: there were fewer literates, but a larger proportion of their writings were intended to be preserved for posterity.

Medieval writing materials themselves made the scribe conscious of time. Because he was presented with the alternatives of wax or parchment as a medium, he made an initial choice between the ephemeral and the permanent. Notes written on wax tablets were necessarily transitory, whereas the fair copy on parchment was obviously durable. To write on parchment was therefore to make a lasting memorial: to commit 'bare and transient words' to script with its 'tenacious letters', as Adam of Eynsham says in the prologue to his life of St Hugh of Lincoln.[1] Modern paper, on the other hand, which is used for both notes and fair copies and is constantly disposed of, does not make the writer feel that he is producing a permanent record. Even when printing gives a modern work a physical permanence comparable with that of parchment manuscripts, the modern writer is more concerned with printing's ability to reach a wide audience in the present than with the transmission of his work, in a unique copy like a medieval manuscript, to posterity. Because

---

[1] Ed. D. L. Douie and H. Farmer (1961), p. 1; M. T. Clanchy, 'Archives and Memory', *Archivaria* xi (1981), pp. 115–25.

parchment manuscripts were rare and special in the eleventh century and earlier, they were valued in a way which no modern literate can fully appreciate.

MONASTIC DOCUMENTS FOR POSTERITY

The presupposition that documents were primarily records to be transmitted to posterity depended not only on the durability of parchment as a material, but on writing skills being so closely connected with monasticism. Before the Norman Conquest, and for a century after it, the majority of writers (in every sense of that word) were monks. In monasteries scribes had not been much concerned with using their skills for day-to-day business, the things of this world, but with making liturgical books for worship and with keeping in charters and chronicles a record, for future generations of monks, of the working of God's providence as revealed in gifts and portents. Documents were more often dedicated or addressed to God or to posterity than to individual contemporaries. Monasticism gave writers the humility or the arrogance, depending on one's point of view, to care about posterity. Their acute awareness of the passage of time is expressed in numerous chronicles. 'With the loss of books', says Orderic Vitalis, 'the deeds of the ancients pass into oblivion . . . with the changing world, as hail or snow melt in the waters of a swift river swept away by the current never to return.'[2] Although these phrases are variations on a theme appropriate to a chronicler's *apologia*, they probably express a point of view which was as deeply felt as it was familiar.

As most early charters concerned gifts to monasteries, they were drafted by monks in similar terms, sometimes at length, as in this notification by William de Braose of a grant to Sele priory in the mid-twelfth century: 'Since memory is frail, and as the sage has said "old age runs in from the first", it is necessary that things which are said or done be reinforced by the evidence of letters, so that neither length of time nor the ingenuity of posterity can obscure the notice of past events.'[3] A century later charters had become sufficiently commonplace for Bracton, the lawyer, to express the same idea more succinctly: 'Gifts are sometimes made in writings, that is in charters, for perpetual remembrance, because the life of man is but brief and in order that the gift may be more easily proved.'[4]

The fact that most monastic charters and chronicles are exclusively concerned with property rights and worldly events does not invalidate the rule that their makers had a religious purpose. Even Matthew Paris, whose work combines a broad and fascinated interest in English and European politics with a narrow and acquisitive concern for the aggrandizement of his house and his order, thought of his chronicle as an instrument of divine providence. In 1250 he decided to stop writing because 25 half-centuries had passed since

---

[2] Orderic, Bk. vi, ch. 9, vol. iii, p. 284.
[3] *Oxford Facs*, no. 11. Cf. ch. 9, n. 1 below and the similar preamble cited by Galbraith, *Studies*, p. 29.
[4] Bracton, fo. 33b, vol. ii, p. 108.

the Incarnation. So he wrote an endpiece to the *Chronica Majora*, which typically combines a concern for posterity with a dedication to God and his saints: 'Here end the chronicles of Brother Matthew Paris, monk of St Albans, which he has committed to writing for the use of succeeding generations, for the love of God and the honour of St Alban, protomartyr of the English, lest age or oblivion destroy the memory of modern events.'[5] Although Matthew started writing again almost immediately, there is no reason to think that his attempted ending in 1250 was insincere. He, like other chroniclers, wrote in the face of God and was motivated by the wish to give himself and his fellow monks, who lived under the protection of St Alban, a place in the divine unfolding of events.

Monks were so worldly because they considered themselves and the property of their houses to belong to God, who would support them in their battle with the 'world', which consisted of everyone else. Writings served as a memorial of their triumphs or as a warning of their difficulties: 'Because it is certain that man's memory is frail, it is a valuable labour to put some things in writing, which can be profitable and useful to our church, so that our brethren, present and future, may be assisted in their difficulties by looking at this little book.'[6] This explanation comes from the prologue to Barnwell priory's *Liber Memorandorum*, which was compiled in the 1290s to serve as a precedent book for litigation. No monastic book could be more worldly. Yet its author, like Matthew Paris, declares his place in time – the sun is setting, the world is declining into senility, charity grows cold – and proposes to help God's servants, by which he means the canons of Barnwell, in their struggle against their neighbours. For monks, writing had an ulterior motive; it was a providential instrument, rather than a merely convenient form of communication.

Monks would not have understood the modern demand for mass literacy. There was no point in teaching writing to people who would never have anything worth committing to the permanence of script. What was written down was carefully selected. The annalist should write 'what he thinks truest and best to be passed down to the notice of posterity', one monastic chronicle advised.[7] Similarly Gervase of Canterbury distinguished between memorable events (*memorabilia*) and those worth remembering (*memoranda*); only the latter which are really worthy of memory should be recorded.[8] So far from advocating the mass-production of literates or documents, the monastic writer aimed to use records to convey to posterity a deliberately created and rigorously selected version of events. Thus Eadmer, who believed it 'to be a great thing to commit to the memory of letters the events of our times for the use of students in the future', deliberately omitted many business letters from his life of St Anselm because he considered them unworthy of more than a

[5] Matthew Paris v, p. 197; R. Vaughan, *Matthew Paris* (1958), pp. 52–9. Lewis, *Matthew Paris*, pp. 104–6.
[6] Ed. J. W. Clark (1907), p. 37; see pp. 171–2 below.
[7] *Annales Monastici* iv, p. 355.
[8] Gervase i, p. 89.

mention.[9] Likewise Anselm himself would not send copies of all his letters to Theodoric, the monk of Christ Church Canterbury who was collecting them, 'because I do not think it useful for them to be preserved'.[10] Awareness of posterity made monks destroyers as well as preservers of writings.

The same preoccupation with posterity led to the forgery or alteration of documents. If a monastic house required a writing to support its title to some property in a lawsuit, an appropriate charter would be created. A historian today will say that such a charter is a forgery, as indeed it is, but its makers probably felt that it had been written just like their other charters and chronicles to justify the ways of God to men. As God and the patron saint wished the particular monastic house to flourish, they also wished to provide the means to fight the world with the world's weapons. Thus Eadmer was an accessory to forging papal bulls which supported Canterbury's claims to primacy over York.[11] The monks of Canterbury were very worried by the challenge from York, Eadmer explains, so they put their trust in God and discovered by divine revelation in some ancient Gospel books (which were sacred objects in themselves) about a dozen papal bulls, ranging in date from the seventh century to the tenth, which supported their cause. These Eadmer cites verbatim, because what had been found in the archives of the church was well worth commending to the memory of posterity. He adds that some even older documents had also been discovered but, as some of these were of papyrus and had grown illegible with age or were written in a script which he could not understand, he reluctantly refrained from citing them. Eadmer probably did not forge the papal bulls himself, but he added these corroborative details which made the story credible.

Monasteries experienced fortunate losses of documents as well as fortunate finds. The Crowland chronicle ascribed to Abbot Ingulf, which is itself a complex tissue of fact and forgery, records that a fire in 1091 destroyed the abbey's Anglo-Saxon royal charters and other muniments numbering nearly 400 documents.[12] Fortunately, however, Ingulf had removed several duplicates of these charters from the archive some years earlier in order to instruct the younger monks in Old English. These duplicates had therefore been preserved and upon them Crowland based its claims. This is an ingenious story, as there was indeed a fire at Crowland in 1091 which destroyed many books (as Orderic Vitalis attested at the time),[13] and it is probable that Crowland, like other great abbeys, made an effort to keep Old English alive after the Norman Conquest. Moreover, Crowland abbey did not claim that these charters were originals, but duplicates, and that explained any deficiencies in them. Similarly in its dispute with York, Canterbury claimed that it

---

[9] *Historia*, p. 1. *Vita*, p. 32. R. W. Southern, *St Anselm* (1990), pp. 394–403, 458–81, discusses Anselm's letters.

[10] N. F. Cantor, *Church, Kingship and Lay Investiture in England* (1958), p. 169.

[11] *Historia*, pp. 261–76; S. E. Kelly, in *Fälschungen*, pp. 347–69; R. W. Southern, *St Anselm* (1990), pp. 359–61.

[12] *Ingulph's Chronicle* trans. H. T. Riley (1854), p. 201.

[13] Orderic, Bk. IV, vol. ii, p. 346. M. Chibnall (ibid. pp. xxv–vi) discusses the authenticity of *Ingulph's Chronicle*.

had only been left with duplicates of some documents because ancient papal bulls had been destroyed in a fire in 1067.[14]

The least credible story of a document's disappearance comes from Matthew Paris.[15] He reports that in the time of Abbot Eadmer (in *c.*1012) a cache of books and rolls, written in an unfamiliar language, was discovered in a cavity in a wall among some Roman foundations at St Albans. Fortunately an old priest, named Unwona, was found who could read this ancient British language. All the texts except one contained invocations to pagan Gods, such as Phoebus and Mercury, and they were therefore burned. The remaining one turned out to be the story of St Alban himself, which the old priest translated from British into Latin for Eadmer and his brethren. But once the Latin translation had been noted down, 'the original and primitive exemplar – strange to relate – was suddenly and irretrievably reduced to dust and collapsed annihilated.' It is entirely credible that Roman remains were found at St Albans, and even possible that documents may have been preserved in a wall cavity. On the other hand, the finding of an old priest with unique knowledge of a lost language, and the initial survival of the finds when first exposed to air, strain credulity too far. Perhaps the story started with the discovery of some Roman remains which disintegrated when exposed to the air.

Monks' propensity to forgery does not imply that they are unreliable in all their statements, but only in those which particularly concern the honour of their patron saint or the status of their house. Where there was doubt, they were determined to establish the truth for posterity. By truth about the past they meant what really should have happened. For a monastic house there was a providential truth, which was higher than the random facts from which a twentieth-century historian, motivated by mere worldly curiosity, attempts to piece together what happened in the past. Essentially there is no inconsistency between Eadmer of Canterbury's or Matthew Paris's religious concern for posterity and their readiness to be accessories to forgery. The problem of forging documents is more fully discussed in chapter 9. The fact it illustrates in the present context is that for monks the primary purpose of writing was to inform, or misinform, posterity. Thus the monastic approach to records was ambivalent: documents were created and carefully conserved so that posterity might know about the past, but they were not necessarily allowed to accumulate by natural accretion over time nor to speak for themselves, because the truth was too important to leave to chance.

SECULAR DOCUMENTS FOR DAILY USE

Documents such as taxation lists or injunctions to officials, which were primarily intended for administrative use at the time they were made rather than being directed to posterity, obviously have a different function from monastic writings. The early development of such documents in medieval

---

[14] Eadmer, *Historia*, p. 296.
[15] *Gesta Abbatum Monasterii St Albani* ed. H. T. Riley, RS xxviii (1867), i, pp. 26–7.

England is hard to trace, partly because writing had been used in such a different way in the monastic tradition. Administrative documents may have been in circulation long before they were kept, since they would not have been thought worthy of preserving like monastic charters. Alternatively administrative documents may have developed only with the greatest difficulty, because writing was not considered an appropriate medium for mere secular ephemera. The skills and traditions of monastic scribes could not automatically be transferred to build up a bureaucracy, although they were successfully adapted and extended in our period. Neither monks nor laymen were literate, in the modern sense of using writing for day-to-day communication, at the time of the Norman Conquest.

Whether the Anglo-Saxon government had used documents in its daily business is a controversial question for historians, because the evidence is sparse. Some have suggested that numerous documents once existed, which were lost after the Norman Conquest because they were in English, whereas others argue that the scarcity of pre-Conquest administrative records implies that business documents were not in common use. All agree that the Anglo-Saxons were acutely conscious of the importance of writing as a way to make records, but that consciousness may have inhibited rather than encouraged the use of documents for ephemeral purposes. It does not follow from the fact that the Anglo-Saxon kings issued writs concerning property rights, which were preserved as title-deeds, that they also sent out written instructions concerning the daily routines of government. P. Chaplais has concluded that the use of the writ for injunctions pure and simple is a post-Conquest development, though he concedes that the injunction as a 'postscript to the notification of a grant was not entirely unknown in Anglo-Saxon times'.[16] His doubts, combined with the difficulties of accepting S. Harvey's hypothesis for the existence of a treasury archive earlier than the Domesday survey (which has been discussed in chapter 1), has led to the initial contention of this book that the Anglo-Saxon kings did not have a bureaucracy.[17]

The Domesday survey provides the first explicit evidence for a royal archive of administrative documents, as a writ of William Rufus refers to land 'which was written down in my writs, which are in my treasury at Winchester'.[18] But even this evidence is ambiguous, because these 'writs' (that is, the circuit returns upon which Domesday Book was based) no longer exist and some historians have argued that references to them, like the one cited above, refer to the volumes of Domesday Book and not to a separate archive of writings. Moreover, the making of Domesday Book itself, as distinct from the Domesday survey, suggests that William the Conqueror had no intention of using an archive of administrative documents. Like scribes making monastic cartularies, the compilers of Domesday Book selected information from the circuit returns and other drafts to make a fair copy for the perpetual use of posterity. Whatever his intentions, William the Conqueror had created in Domesday

---

[16] Chaplais, *Docs*, p. 5.
[17] See pp. 31–2, 66 above.
[18] *RRA-N* i, no. 468.

Book a unique record in the old monastic tradition, the *Book of Judgement* of Revelation, rather than a document of administrative value.[19]

The principal objection to this interpretation of Domesday Book is Fitz Neal's statement that it was kept in the treasury, along with the pipe rolls and many charters and writs, because such documents were required 'for daily use' in the Exchequer.[20] But the use of Domesday Book seems to have been principally symbolic, like the regalia, since it cannot be shown that it was frequently consulted at the time Fitz Neal was writing in *c*.1179. He himself was unfamiliar with its contents, as he insists that it makes no mention of 'blanch farm' (payments in assayed silver from certain counties), whereas references to such payments are quite common in Domesday Book.[21] His ignorance has puzzled editors of the *Dialogue of the Exchequer*, who have suggested as a solution that this passage about Domesday Book is an interpolation, although there is no textual evidence for that. A sufficient explanation of Fitz Neal's mistake is that neither he, nor his colleagues at the Exchequer, consulted Domesday Book at all frequently because there was scarcely any documentary continuity in administration between William the Conqueror's reign and Henry II's.

For Fitz Neal and his colleagues the pipe rolls of Henry I, rather than the Domesday survey, marked the beginning of an archive of documents which they understood and regularly consulted. One story of Fitz Neal's shows a pipe roll of Henry I being used to overrule a writ of Henry II, and another remark about what is frequently to be found 'in the old annual rolls' of Henry I suggests that a number of early pipe rolls were still extant in Fitz Neal's time.[22] The whole tone of the *Dialogue of the Exchequer*, with its meticulous regard for precedent and correct form, shows how the Exchequer was dominated by bureaucratic routines by the 1170s. Yet the writings it produced were still not systematically kept as records, as many of the types of document mentioned by Fitz Neal are not extant today, nor can they be traced in the thirteenth century. The pipe rolls of Henry I themselves have been lost, apart from the roll for 1130. That roll demonstrates, moreover, that hundreds of writs were issued each year, for such ephemeral purposes as authorizing expenditure, of which no record was kept.[23] The sparse evidence available suggests that administrative documents first came into routine use in Henry I's Exchequer, rather than at the time of the Domesday survey or earlier. Turning such documents into records for posterity took even long to develop and was far from thorough in Fitz Neal's time.

---

[19] *Dialogus*, p. 64, Cf. ch. 1, n. 29 above. For contrary arguments, see W. L. Warren, 'The Myth of Norman Administrative Efficiency', *TRHS* 5th series xxxiv (1984), p. 131, and E. M. Hallam, *Domesday Book Through Nine Centuries* (1986), ch. ii.

[20] *Dialogus*, p. 62. Cf. nn. 79, 81 below.

[21] *Dialogus*, p. 14. K. Yoshitake explains the discrepancy about blanch farm in *EHR* ciii (1988), pp. 454–5.

[22] *Dialogus*, pp. 58, 42.

[23] See ch. 2, n. 52 above. The roll for 1130 is analysed by Judith A. Green, *The Government of England under Henry I* (1986), pp. 220–5.

As discussed in chapter 2, Hubert Walter seems to have been principally responsible for making the royal government as a whole, and not just the Exchequer, begin keeping records as well as issuing documents. He laid the foundations of an accumulating archival memory, first in the law courts (in the form of the feet of fines and the plea rolls) while he was chief justiciar (1193–8), and then in the Chancery (in the form of the various rolls of outgoing letters) while he was chancellor (1199–1205). Thenceforward the Chancery rolls are extant for almost every year. Similarly the feet of fines were successfully kept in the treasury from the start, though the plea rolls proved harder to recover from the judges because they treated them as their personal property for reference purposes. To compile Bracton's *De Legibus*, for example, judges and their clerks in the 1220s and 1230s (possibly including Bracton himself as a junior) made extracts from their plea rolls and notebooks of cases.[24] Nevertheless, by the latter half of the thirteenth century, the plea rolls too were being surrendered to the treasury for preservation, as the almost complete series extant from Edward I's reign attests.

In Edward I's reign, the era of Hubert Walter began to be recognized as a turning point in the history of keeping records. By statutes in 1275 and 1293 the date of Richard I's coronation (3 September 1189) was fixed as the legal limit of memory.[25] This meant that a litigant was not required to go any further back into the past than that date when proving a claim. Fixing an arbitrary limit for claims based on precedents was not a new device, as the date of Richard I's coronation replaced Henry II's coronation and that date had replaced Henry I's death. Up until the reign of Edward I the assumption seems to have been that memory extended back for a century at the most, that is, to the earliest time which could be remembered by the oldest living persons; any period before that was considered to be 'time out of mind'. The novelty of establishing Richard I's coronation as the new legal limit only became apparent by the end of Edward I's reign, when it was left to stand instead of being updated. In retrospect the fixed limit of 3 September 1189, which continued for the rest of the Middle Ages, marked the formal beginning of the era of artificial memory. Repeated updating was no longer urgently required, because remembrance in litigation now depended primarily on documentary evidence and not on mortal memory. It was appropriate, though at first a coincidence, that Richard I's reign was acknowledged as the point in time from which it was reasonable to require proof, as Hubert Walter's reforms had made such proof possible.

Although Hubert Walter had laid the foundation of an extensive royal archive, another century elapsed before its potential was tested. In 1291, when Edward I required historical evidence to support his claims to overlordship in Scotland, he made no attempt at first to use the royal records. Instead monasteries were ordered at short notice to search their 'chronicles, registers,

---

[24] See S. E. Thorne's introduction to Bracton, vol. iii (1977). The preservation of the plea rolls is surveyed by D. Crook, *Records of the General Eyre* (1982), pp. 12–30.
[25] T. F. T. Plucknett, *A Concise History of the Common Law* (5th edn, 1956), p. 719; D. W. Sutherland, *Quo Warranto Proceedings in the Reign of Edward I* (1963), pp. 226–8.

looked to monks records over royal records.

and other archives, both ancient and modern, of whatever shape or date'.[26] The evidence adduced by this method turned out to be scrappy and unsatisfactory. For example, the treaty of Falaise of 1174 (by which King William the Lion submitted to Henry II) was cited from a monastic chronicle, whereas more accurate transcripts were to be found in both the Red Book and the Little Black Book of the Exchequer'.[27]

Belatedly in the summer of 1291, after the monasteries had submitted their evidence, Edward I wrote in haste from Scotland, ordering a chest of Chancery rolls at the New Temple to be broken open and searched.[28] Two rolls of Henry III were taken out of this chest and sent to the king – the patent roll for 1254–5 and the charter roll for 1237–8. What Edward expected to find in these rolls is not specified. As they are still extant today, however, the historian can point out that in the former roll are details of Henry III's treaty with Alexander III of Scotland in 1255 and in the latter is Henry's treaty with Alexander II in 1237.[29] Since neither of these treaties would have helped Edward's case, this preliminary attempt to use the archives for historical purposes may have temporarily discouraged further research.

Nevertheless a precedent had been established and when evidence was again required in 1300 in order to justify the English case to Pope Boniface VIII and international opinion, the royal records were ordered to be searched as well as monastic sources. The instruction was vague but comprehensive – to search all the remembrances concerning the business of Scotland – and it was coupled with a similar order 'to search all the rolls and remembrances', including all the rolls of the Exchequer and Chancery, concerning the king's forest rights.[30] Whoever ordered all the rolls to be searched, 'so that nothing is left unsearched', can have had little conception of how numerous they were, or of how inadequately they were stored and filed. This search seems to have produced no new information, presumably because it proved impossible to search the archives effectively at such short notice. But despite the ineffective nature of the searches, Edward I's claims in Scotland and the need to document them had at last made the government aware of the large historical archive it had accumulated. It is probably not a coincidence that plea rolls and other legal records likewise began to be systematically listed in detail in the 1290s.[31] In 1302 a similar attempt was made to bring together the archives of the Wardrobe, 'so that we can be advised of things at all times that we want, and these books and rolls are to remain in the Wardrobe in perpetual remembrance.'[32] To keep documents for perpetual remembrance had been the

[26] *Documents Illustrative of the History of Scotland* ed. J. Stevenson (1870) I, p. 222 (writ to the prior of Chester). Cf. E. L. G. Stones and G. G. Simpson, *Edward I and the Throne of Scotland* (1978), pp. 138ff.

[27] *Anglo-Scottish Relations*, p. 1.

[28] *Foedera* I, part ii, p. 757; *CCIR* 1288–96, pp. 245–6.

[29] *CPatR* 1247–58, pp. 421, 426; *CChR* 1226–57, p. 236; *Anglo-Scottish Relations*, pp. 30, 38.

[30] *Calendar of Chancery Warrants*, HMSO (1927) I, p. 120. Cf. n. 189 below.

[31] *SCCKB* I, pp. cxxi–cxxii.

[32] *Book of Prests*, ed. E. B. Fryde (1962) pp. 229–30.

purpose of archives for centuries; what was new was the demand that records should be readily available 'at all times'.

The aim of making the royal archives accessible for reference, initiated by Edward I in his last years, reached maturity in 1320 in Bishop Stapledon's great survey of the records. The prologue to Stapledon's commission deplores the way records had been carried about from place to place and from person to person, and frequently mislaid, whereas the frailty of the human condition requires the acts of princes and rulers to be reduced to writings as memorials, so that kings can rule their subject people justly.[33] Although Stapledon's extensive survey of the records had little immediate effect on the conduct of government, his commission marks the point at which the crown formally recognized that its administrative documents were records for posterity. The writings of kings were a bastion against human frailty and a warning or encouragement to their successors, just as their deeds had been when recorded in monastic chronicles. The gulf between records specifically made for posterity and secular documents for mundane use had been bridged. As a consequence the English government was set on the course which has produced the largest archive to survive from medieval Europe.

To sum up, administrative documents had been in routine use since Henry I's reign, they had been extensively kept since Hubert Walter's reforms around 1200, and now in the 1300s the government subjected them to comprehensive inspection. Perhaps documents had to accumulate in considerable numbers before they could be seen as an archive with a historical purpose. Searching Domesday Book, for evidence of whether land was ancient demesne of the crown or not, had followed a similar pattern; searches had started in the 1250s and only became an established routine in Edward I's reign or later, although Domesday Book had been available for two centuries.[34] Making documents for administrative use, keeping them as records, and using them again for reference were three distinct stages of development which did not automatically and immediately follow from each other.

ARCHIVES AND LIBRARIES

So far this chapter has considered when and why records began to be kept and used, but it has only incidentally answered questions concerning where and how they were deposited. It is worth attempting to answer such questions as precisely as possible, because the physical conditions in which documents were kept indicate contemporary attitudes towards them and also help explain why some types of document have survived better than others. It is also appropriate to consider archives and libraries together because, although all kinds of distinctions were made between different types of writings in the Middle Ages, the twofold modern division between books and records is an anachronism.

[33] *The Antient Kalendars and Inventories of the Exchequer* ed. F. Palgrave (1836) I, pp. 1–3.
[34] Hallam, *Domesday Book* (1986), pp. 50–73, 183–6, 199–210; see also pp. 33–4, 151 above.

At the time of the Norman Conquest documents and books had a place among the precious objects, the hoard of treasure and relics, which a ruler or the head of a religious house aimed to pass on to his successors. Documents, books, relics of the saints, and jewellery were not usually kept in places distinct from each other, because they were often physically joined together, and the difference between writings and other precious objects was not as obvious as it is to a modern literate. Books of the Bible – illuminated with gold leaf and precious paints, their bindings studded with gems or even with relics – were obviously treasure, both heavenly and terrestrial, rather than mere reading matter. A book as special as the *Lindisfarne Gospels*, for example, was itself a relic and a shrine, hallowed by its age and by its alleged association with St Cuthbert. Single documents like charters were sometimes bound or copied into such liturgical books for safekeeping. This practice has already been illustrated by Eadmer's story of finding in Gospel books ancient papal bulls which upheld Canterbury's claims over York. Although these bulls were forged, the practice of keeping documents in books was evidently commonplace enough to sound convincing to Eadmer's readers. In the Sherborne cartulary of the mid-twelfth century liturgical texts and charters (probably forged) were made into an integrated book. 'All the secular portions were placed under the protection, as it were, of the book's sacred contents and its connexion with the altar. If anyone in the future was to be so unwise as to question the validity of any of the documents, the protection and wrath of heaven could be invoked.'[35] Similarly C. R. Cheney has argued that the massive isolated pages of the so-called *Domesday Monachorum* of Christ Church Canterbury, recording estate documents of various dates in the twelfth century, originally formed part of a 'great Gospel book' (*textus magnus*), so that future violators would (in the words of Archbishop Hubert Walter) come under the 'curse of God and the saints of the church of Canterbury'.[36]

Like family bibles in later generations, liturgical books were the most obvious place in the Middle Ages to record items of importance, as they were made of the most durable materials and were likely to be solemnly handed down from one generation to the next. Where written materials were rare, these were also the texts which most readily came to hand. In *c.*1200 a Jew used the last leaves of his prayer-book to jot down (in Arabic written down in Hebrew characters) a memorandum of 'all that I have since being here in England'; his list comprises debts due from the bishops of Exeter, Bath and Winchester, from an unnamed earl, and from some lesser clerks and knights. What happened to him, or them, is unknown, as only his sacred book survives.[37] Recording items in liturgical books was made a rule by the Salisbury diocesan statutes of *c.*1217: parish priests are enjoined to 'write in missals and other books the properties and rents of the church and lists of the

[35] F. Wormald, 'The Sherborne Chartulary' in *Fritz Saxl Memorial Essays* ed. D. J. Gordon (1957), p. 109; Zarnecki, *Catalogue*, no. 46.

[36] 'Service-Books and Records', *BIHR* LVI (1983), pp.7–15.

[37] M. Beit-Arié and Z. E. Rokeah, *The Only Dated Hebrew MS Written in England* (1985), pp. 33–56,, plates 6 and 7.

books, vestments and furnishings'.[38] This was the first step in the long process of making parish priests the registrars of their villages.

As some charters were placed for safekeeping in sacred books, it comes as no surprise to find that others were put in shrines. The best-known instance of this practice is the use of the Anglo-Saxon royal *haligdom* as a place for depositing charters.[39] The *haligdom* was probably the sanctuary associated with the chapel royal. Thus a Ramsey charter (dating from the 1050s) was deposited 'by the king's order in his chapel with the relics of the saints which he has there'.[40] This chapel was probably a stone building rather than a portable altar; in that case its most likely location was either at Westminster abbey or in the ancient palace of the West Saxon kings at Winchester. It has been argued that charters had been kept at Winchester, systematically filed, since the ninth century.[41] Wherever it was situated, the *haligdom* was a depository of sacred documents for posterity and not an administrative archive.

Churches and reliquaries were the obvious place to keep documents not just because they were relatively secure, being protected by stone and iron as well as by anathemas, but also because charters were themselves relics of past gifts. Moreover, since gifts to monasteries were often made to the patron saint of the church rather than to the monks themselves, it was appropriate that the charters recording the gifts should be placed as close to the relics of the saint as possible, because they belonged to him. It was common practice to offer charters at an altar; thus the Guthlac roll depicts the benefactors of Crowland abbey presenting their charters at St Guthlac's shrine (see plate xx). Similarly one of the seals of Bury St Edmunds abbey hung from the shrine of St Edmund, presumably because it was a secure place and because the seal belonged to St Edmund in a personal sense.[42]

Together with sacred books and relics of the saints, documents came to be mixed in with cups, rings, wooden staffs, knives, and any other symbolic objects which retained the memory of past events. For example in 1096 Tavistock abbey deposited in the shrine of St Rumon the ivory knife (with an explanatory note attached) by which William Rufus had given the abbot seisin of a manor; likewise Spalding priory fifty years later put Thomas of Moulton's knife into its archive or *secretarium*.[43] As long as it remained customary to symbolize a conveyance of property by an object laid upon an altar, it was natural for such objects, whatever their form, to be kept with the sacred vessels and liturgical books which were similarly associated with the altar. To the modern eye an early medieval archive would have looked more

[38] F. M. Powicke and C. R. Cheney, *Councils and Synods*, ii (1964), p. 82, no. 67.

[39] Galbraith, *Studies*, pp. 40–1.

[40] *Ramsey*, p. 172.

[41] C. Hart, 'The Codex Wintoniensis and the King's Haligdom', *Agricultural History Review* xviii (1970) supplement (*Essays Presented to H. P. R. Finberg*), pp. 18–19, 20–3. But see the opposing comments of N. Brooks in *Anglo-Saxon England* ed. P.Clemoes (1974) iii, p. 228, and S. Keynes, *Diplomas of King Aethelred* (1980), pp. 148–9.

[42] Jocelin. p. 2.

[43] *Monasticon* ii, p. 497, no. v; ibid. iii, p. 217, no. x.

like a magpie's nest than a filing system for documents. Yet however bizarre such objects might look at first sight, the sacristan could no doubt have explained the significance as a memento of each individual object. The best modern comparison might be with an old lady's handbag, which likewise might contain symbolic rings, jewellery, miscellaneous mementoes, and a few letters and papers.

Each document or book had a special place of safekeeping, appropriate to its associations and function, but not all the documents or books were kept in one place. Liturgical books were often kept in the church, because that is where they were used, whereas other books were kept in the refectory for reading aloud, or in a chest or cupboard in the cloister for individual study.[44] At Lincoln cathedral in the thirteenth century the chancellor had charge of the scholastic books and saints' lives, the precentor kept the music books, the treasurer had the other liturgical books like breviaries and missals, and the provost looked after the charters and muniments.[45] There were good reasons for the arrangement, as the chancellor was associated with the school, the precentor with the choir, the treasurer with the safekeeping of sacred utensils, and the provost with the correspondence of the dean and chapter. The need for a centralized library or archive only became apparent if the number of books or documents increased to unmanageable proportions.

Furthermore, documents were scattered about on principle and not just from negligence. The Anglo-Saxon practice of depositing two or three copies of an agreement in different places for greater security continued after the Norman Conquest. For example, sealed copies of Henry II's will were deposited in 1182 at Canterbury, in the Winchester treasury, and in his coffers; likewise Gerald of Wales proposed in 1202 to deposit copies of his evidence concerning of the bishopric of St David's in the archives of the pope, the archbishop of Canterbury, and the bishop of St David's.[46] Similarly one reason given in 1221 for having more than one justice on the bench at a time was that each justice kept his own copy of the plea roll, whereas one roll on its own was not sufficiently secure as a record.[47] Only gradually did the crown move from the traditional notion of safety in numbers as a way to preserve its legal records to the idea of a central archive at the treasury.

To sum up, the tradition at the time of the Norman Conquest had been that documents and books were kept with other precious objects. Writings were too few and too diverse in their functions and physical formats to be treated as a special class of memento. Books and documents were not neglected, but they were kept in ways which made consultation difficult and their dispersal among various repositories meant that books belonging to an institution were not usually seen as a whole as a library, still less were documents seen as an archive.

Gradually in the twelfth and thirteenth centuries, as the number of writings increased, more specific and uniform regulations were made for their safe-keeping. The initiative in this movement seems to have come from eccle-

[44] F. Wormald, 'The Monastic Library' in *English Library*, pp. 16–18.
[45] K. Edwards, *The English Secular Cathedrals in the Middle Ages* (2nd edn. 1967), p. 211.
[46] Gervase I, p. 300; Giraldus III, pp. 230–1.
[47] *Rot. Lit. Claus*, I, p. 451.

siastics and not from the royal government. The Norman Conquest encouraged monastic houses to examine their heritage in order to justify the existence of themselves and their saints to the conquerors. Moreover, the reforming prelates appointed by Archbishop Lanfranc aimed to bring their churches into line with the best continental practice, and that meant reviewing and renewing their books and muniments. The Latin word *archiva* (neuter plural), meaning 'archives' in something like its modern sense of a safe and secret place for documents, was first used in England by Lanfranc in the early 1070s when ordering some letters concerning the bishop of the Orkneys to be preserved as a memorial for the future 'in the archives' of the churches of Worcester and Chester.[48] Examples of monasteries reviewing their muniments are numerous and relate to the beginnings of cartulary making, which has already been discussed.[49] V. H. Galbraith has pointed out that Hemming, who completed the first cartulary, also has claims to be the earliest English archivist, as he had a new lock put on Worcester's muniment chest and repaired original documents which were torn or damaged.[50] Repairing charters was closely associated with replacing them, and hence with forgery. In the monastic community archivists and forgers shared a common aim in documenting a house's titles to its property.

Archives and archivists did not originate from the requirements of disinterested historical research, but from the immediate necessity to produce documents even where none existed. This monastic movement to review and modernize records continued in the twelfth and thirteenth centuries. Thus the compiler of Ramsey abbey's *Book of Benefactors* in *c.*1170 describes the 'very ancient' charters and chirographs 'which we have found in our archives', which he claims to have translated from 'barbarous' Anglo-Saxon into Latin.[51] A decade or so later the dean of St Paul's, Ralf de Diceto, made a survey of the churches owned by the cathedral and combined this with an examination of their charters; he devised a system of cross-references between his survey and the charters by using special identification symbols.[52]

The preoccupation with making lists and surveys, which had originated with the *descriptiones* of monastic estates like Abbot Samson's *kalendarium*, also produced the first monastic book catalogues in the twelfth century. Strictly speaking perhaps these lists of books owned by particular houses should not be described as library catalogues, as most of them are simply inventories of possessions which do not indicate to the user where he will find a particular book. Such lists were not intended for the reader's use anyway, but for the librarian's. Nevertheless among the earliest half-dozen or so English library lists extant is one from Christ Church Canterbury (dating from *c.*1170) in

[48] 'in archivis', *Letters*, ed. H. Clover and M. Gibson (1979), p. 82. 'Archivum' (singular) had been used earlier in the eleventh century by Aelfric to translate the English word 'boochord', *Dictionary of Medieval Latin from British Sources* ed. R. E. Latham (1975) i, p. 120.
[49] See ch. 3, nn. 89–93 above.
[50] *Historical Research in Medieval England* (1951), p. 37.
[51] *Ramsey*, pp. 4, 65, 176. Cf. ch. 9, n. 101 below.
[52] *The Domesday of St Paul's* ed. W.H.Hale, Camden S. lxix (1857), p. 110; Gransden, *Historical Writing*, p. 234. Cf. n. 143 below.

which a series of small letters and symbols correspond with symbols on the first leaf of each book.[53] The librarian had thus marked his books in much the same way as Ralf de Diceto marked the charters of St Paul's. Such marks did not indicate where the books or charters were placed, but they did at least show which description in a list corresponded with which document in a cupboard or chest.

A good example of an early book list is the inventory, on the fly-leaves of a work of St Augustine's, made at Rochester cathedral in 1202. It begins, unusually, with a precise date and description: 'In the year AD 1202 this is the survey of our library.'[54] The use of the term 'survey' (*scrutinium*) suggests that a comprehensive review was intended. The books are listed partly under the names of authors (Augustine, Gregory, Ambrose, Jerome, Bede) which are not in alphabetical order, partly by where certain books are placed, such as those which are 'in the precentor's chest [*archa*]', and partly under special collections comprising gifts or acquisitions from named individuals. The list comprises 241 items (according to the edited text) and is evidently more complete than an earlier fragment of a list on the fly-leaves of the mid-twelfth century *Textus Roffensis*.[55]

On the fly-leaf of a copy of the sermons of St Bernard, Lincoln cathedral library has a borrowers' list (as distinct from an inventory or catalogue) dating from *c*.1220.[56] The entries are jotted down in an informal script, without ruled lines, which contrasts with the regular bookhand of the text. For example William of Avallon, the bishop's nephew, is recorded as having Bede's commentary on St Luke's gospel, the 'canonical epistles', and a *mappa mundi*. Another title has been added below these, in lighter ink: & *Ysidor*', that is, a book by Isidore of Seville, perhaps his 'Etymologies'. None of the total of fourteen titles noted on this fly-leaf are recorded as having been returned by their borrowers. To obviate loss, some Lincoln books have *Liber Sancte Marie Linc*' ('a book of St Mary's Lincoln') written on them in a bold hand.[57] A few St Albans abbey books retain a more forceful inscription of ownership: 'This is a book of St Alban's; anyone who removes it, or deletes the title, or alienates it from the church by any kind of art, fraud, or ingenuity is anathema'.[58] These inscriptions invoke the curse of the patron saint, to whom everything in the institution was deemed to belong in a personal sense. Many of 'St Mary's' books are still housed in Lincoln cathedral library, but St Alban's ones were dispersed at the Dissolution of the Monasteries. St Alban's books had been additionally protected by their physical proximity to the saints. Thus Abbot Simon (1167–83) ordered that the fine books he had had made should be kept

---

[53] Wormald, 'The Monastic Library', p. 23. Twelfth-century book lists are illustrated by de Hamel, *MSS*, p. 78, plate 73 (Reading abbey), and R. M. Thomson, *Catalogue of the MSS in Lincoln Cathedral Chapter Library* (1989), plate 3.

[54] Ed. W. B. Rye, *Archaeologia Cantiana* III (1860), pp. 54–61.

[55] Ed. R. P. Coates, *Archaeologia Cantiana* VI (1866), pp. 122–8.

[56] Thomson, *Catalogue*, plate 5.

[57] Ibid., plate 4.

[58] R. M. Thomson, *MSS from St Albans Abbey 1066–1235* (1982), II, plate 258. There are similar inscriptions on the books illustrated at plates 171, 172, 236, 237.

'in the painted chest which is up against (or "opposite", *contra*) the tomb of St Roger the hermit'.[59]

Modern libraries really started with the friars. The Dominican rule of Humbert de Romanis (dating from *c.*1260) lays down all the principal duties of a modern librarian.[60] The librarian should choose a good site for the library, secure, waterproof, and well ventilated; there should be ample shelving in the book cupboard, the shelves being designated to different subjects and having explanatory notices on them; there should be a catalogue (*charta*) of the books, which should have their titles written on the spines and an inscription inside each stating the house to which the book belongs and who gifted it; the stock should be kept up to date by replacing old books and selling duplicates; the librarian should have the key of the library and open it at specified times. Books in common use, such as the Bible, papal decretals, sermons, and chronicles were to be kept in a chained reference section, whereas less used books might be borrowed by readers provided loans were recorded in writing. A general inspection of the library was to be made once or twice a year.

If these Dominican regulations are compared with those made by Archbishop Lanfranc in his constitutions for Christ Church Canterbury two centuries earlier, the change in the use of books is striking.[61] There is a librarian (*custos librorum*) in Lanfranc's constitutions and he keeps a written list of books on loan, like his Dominican counterpart; but there the similarity ceases, as the principal duty of Lanfranc's librarian is to supervise the borrowing of books once a year on the first Monday in Lent. The books were to be laid out on a carpet and each monk was issued with one book and given the year to read it. Many books of the Church Fathers were of course long and difficult; a monk who read with attention and understanding every word of St Augustine's *City of God*, for example, had achieved a great deal in a year. Nevertheless Lanfranc's constitutions indicate a different approach to reading from the Dominican rules.

The Dominicans, like modern academics, required extensive libraries in which they could glance rapidly over a whole series of books, many of very recent authorship, in order to construct a wide-ranging argument. The purpose of the library was to ensure 'that the community of friars can have ready to hand (*in promptu*)' whatever works they required.[62] Lanfranc's monks, on the other hand, were expected to ruminate on a text which had been designated to them as a sacred task. For monks in the old Benedictine tradition, books, with their precious and brightly illuminated words, were images which produced a state of mystical contemplation and understanding. The difference in approach towards writing of Lanfranc's Benedictines and Humbert's Dominicans is so fundamental that to use the same term 'literate' to describe them both is misleading. The parallel with the change of attitudes

---

[59] *Gesta Abbatum* RS 28 (1867), I, p. 184; Thomson, *MSS from St Albans*, pp. 13, 52.

[60] K. W. Humphreys, *The Book Provisions of the Medieval Friars* (1964), pp. 32, 135–6.

[61] Ed. M. D. Knowles (1951), p. 91. Lanfranc's regulations derive from the Rule of St Benedict, ch. 48.

[62] Humphreys, *The Book Provisions*, p. 136.

towards records is evident: at the time of the Norman Conquest documents were special objects which were treasured in shrines; whereas by 1300 Edward I, like the friars, expected them all to be available for scrutiny and comparison whenever he wanted.

In fact, however, the king's books and records were less well regulated for a long period than those either of an average Benedictine house or of the friars. John is the first king since the Norman Conquest who can be shown to have owned and used books. This is surprising, as Henry I was *litteratus* and Henry II was the most educated king of his time; at his court there was 'school every day'.[63] Evidence about John's books comes from incidental references in the public records. An entry in the pipe roll of 1203, recording the cost of supplying 'chests and carts to take the king's books overseas' suggests that John had a library as large as any monastic house.[64] About the contents of this library, or where it was kept, there is only the sparsest information. In 1205 the king had 'a romance of the history of England' (that is, a text in French) sent him at Windsor by one of his stewards.[65] In 1208 'our book called *Plinius*' (that is, a Latin text of Pliny) was sent him from Reading abbey, where it had been deposited for safekeeping. A few days earlier he had obtained from Reading abbey a copy of the Old Testament, a work by Hugh of St Victor, the Sentences of Peter Lombard, and some other scholastic texts.[66] This last reference is the most interesting evidence about John's use of books, as all educated laymen of his time enjoyed history in 'romance' (in other words, in the form of vernacular stories or poems) and most *litterati* read the more obvious Latin classics like Pliny; but King John is the first king in Europe to have been interested in the theological works of the 'modern' schoolmen of the twelfth century. It is likely, however, that he required these books for a particular purpose, namely his dispute with Stephen Langton over clerical privileges; moreover, these scholastic texts probably belonged to Reading abbey rather than to the king himself.[67]

This episode showed that the king's government required a reference library, particularly for ecclesiastical business. Yet the only books possessed by John's successor, Henry III, were liturgical texts and a few romances. Henry, as a patron of artists and craftsmen rather than writers, had missals made for his and the queen's numerous chapels up and down England.[68] Queen Eleanor also used in 1250 a 'great book' in French, 'in which are contained the deeds of Antioch and of the kings', which was kept by the Knights Templar probably as part of the royal wardrobe.[69] This may be the

---

[63] See ch. 7, n. 46 below.

[64] *Pipe Roll 5 John*, PRS new series xvi (1938), p. 139; W. L. Warren, *King John* (1961), p. 157. Concerning the number of books owned by institutions or individuals see ch. 3, nn. 109–111 above.

[65] *Rot. Lit. Claus.* i p. 29.

[66] Ibid. p. 108.

[67] F. M. Powicke, *Stephen Langton* (1928), p. 99.

[68] At Hereford (*CLibR* 1240–5, pp. 29, 296), Nottingham (ibid. 1251–60, p. 11), Winchester (ibid. 1226–40, p. 419), Windsor *CIR* 1247–51, p. 162.

[69] *CIR* 1247–51, p. 283.

same as Henry's 'great book of romances', garnished with silver clasps and nails, which is mentioned in 1237.[70] Such books were evidently treasured objects, rather than a library of information, and it is therefore appropriate that they should have been kept by sacristans or by the Templars.

Similarly there is no evidence of Edward I having a library. When he wished to justify his claims to overlordship in Scotland in 1291, he had to ask monasteries to consult their chronicles (as we have already seen), presumably because he had no histories of his own, even allowing for ready access to the library of Westminster abbey. Few books are to be found in Bishop Staple-don's survey of documents in 1320. In one chest a few texts were deposited along with some seals – a book called *De Regimine Principum* (On Royal Rule) bound in red leather, a 'little book' of the rules of the Knights Templar, a quire (that is, part of an unbound book) of the life of St Patrick, another quire 'in an unknown language' (Welsh), and a book of the chronicles of Roderick archbishop of Toledo.[71] These books may have belonged to Edward I. Even if they did, they have the air of miscellaneous gifts and acquisitions rather than the foundations of a library or of a personal collection. In having no library and in leaving little evidence of possessing books, the English kings were no different from other contemporary rulers. The first pope of the period who can be shown to have had a library is Edward I's contemporary, Boniface VIII, and that was dispersed after his death.[72] The explanation for the dearth of libraries is not primarily that kings were ignorant laymen, more interested in fighting and hunting than in study. Rather it is that the business of government, whether ecclesiastical or secular, only gradually became associated with book-learning and written precedents.

THE ROYAL ARCHIVES

The development of the royal archives after the Norman Conquest requires special discussion because it is inconsistent and perplexing. The proliferation of documents beginning in the twelfth century, combined with the erratic movements of the kings back and forth across the Channel, caused records to be dispersed and frequently moved about, whereas they had been more safely preserved in the eleventh century. There is no clear line of progress from dispersal to centralization. As we have already seen, some charters which served as title-deeds before the Norman Conquest were deposited in the king's *haligdom* or sanctuary, which may have had a permanent location at either Westminster or Winchester.[73] The returns of the Domesday survey were likewise kept at Winchester in the reign of William Rufus 'in my treasury'.[74] Whether this *thesaurus*, the 'treasure' or 'treasury' of William Rufus, was the

---

[70] *CLibR* 1226–40, p. 288.
[71] *The Antient Kalendars and Inventories of the Exchequer* i, p. 106.
[72] M. Faucon, *La Librairie des Papes d'Avignon*, Bibliothèque des écoles françaises d'Athènes et de Rome xliii (1886) i, pp. 3–4.
[73] See nn. 39–41 above.
[74] See n. 18 above.

same place as the *haligdom* of the West Saxon kings is a matter for conjecture. Certainly in the twelfth century the *thesaurus* at Winchester was developing into a permanent central archive for the government, perhaps because Winchester with its access to Southampton was a good location for the capital of the Anglo-Norman lordship. Henry I's coronation charter was deposited at Winchester by his order.[75] Similarly in 1155 Henry II ordered the bull of Adrian IV giving him jurisdiction over Ireland, together with the gold and emerald ring which the pope had sent as a symbol of investiture, to be deposited 'in the archives of Winchester', according to Gerald of Wales.[76] John of Salisbury, who had brought the papal bull and ring to Henry, confirms this story by noting that the ring was deposited *in cimiliarchio publico* for safekeeping.[77] *Cimiliarchium* had been the term used by Justinian to describe the imperial archive. John had probably therefore derived the idea of a public archive from his interest in Roman law and history, rather than from English realities. Nevertheless he was at least one influential Englishman who considered that England had a public archive in a fixed place in the middle of the twelfth century.

Later in Henry II's reign, however, as the government expanded, the use of a fixed treasury and archive at Winchester was abandoned. Instead, treasure chests were constantly moved to and fro between Winchester, London, and other royal palaces, hunting lodges and fortresses.[78] The assumption has been frequently made that the treasury at Winchester was simply replaced by a similar fixed and central treasury at Westminster, but that is contradicted by the evidence. Fitz Neal's *Dialogue of the Exchequer* indicates the ambivalence of official attitudes towards the idea of one fixed place for a treasury, and hence for an archive, by the 1170s. The Pupil prompts the Master to describe the king's seal and the Book of Judgement (Domesday Book), 'the former of which, if I remember correctly, is kept in the *thesauro* and not taken out'.[79] The Master replies that the seal, Domesday Book and many other things are not taken out either. Before enlarging on this statement, he explains to the Pupil the ambiguity of the word *thesaurus*, which means both 'treasure' (such as coins, gold, silver, and vestments) and 'treasury' (a place where treasure is deposited). In reply to the Pupil's implied question, 'Where is the treasury?' the Master cites chapter vi, verse 21 of St Matthew's Gospel, 'Where your treasure is, there will your heart be also.'

Speaking through the Master, Fitz Neal thus refuses to give one geographical location to the treasury, because the king's treasure was dispersed in a number of repositories and some of it was taken about with him on his travels.[80] In the Master's words, 'plura sunt in repositoriis archis thesauri que

[75] According to Richard prior of Hexham (writing in c.1140), *Chronicles* ed. R. Howlett, RS LXXXII (1884) III, p. 142.
[76] 'in archivis Winton', Giraldus v, p. 316.
[77] *Metalogicon*, Bk, IV, ch. 42, ed. C.C. J. Webb (1929), p. 218.
[78] Galbraith, *Studies*, p. 47; R. L. Poole, *The Exchequer in the Twelfth Century* (1912) p. 72.
[79] *Dialogus* (my translation), p. 61.
[80] R. A. Brown, 'The Treasury of the Later Twelfth Century' in *Studies Presented to Sir H. Jenkinson* ed. J. Conway Davies (1957), pp. 35–49.

circumferuntur.'[81] In the English version of the *Dialogus* this passage is translated, 'There are several things in the vaults of the Treasury which are taken about.' However, *repositoriis archis thesauri* does not mean 'the vaults of the Treasury', but 'storage chests of treasure'. *Archa* is used by Fitz Neal in the sense of a 'chest' or 'archive', not in the sense of an 'arch' or 'vault': thus the *arche* containing the Exchequer rolls are mentioned earlier in his book.[82] The Master is simply informing the Pupil that 'several things' – among which are Domesday Book, the Exchequer rolls and numerous writs and charters – are locked up in treasure chests, which are taken about the country in accordance with the wishes of the king. For Fitz Neal there is no contradiction between his statement that Domesday Book is kept in the treasury and not taken out and his statement that it is taken about the country, because the treasury is in the king's heart; in other words, it is wherever he wants it to be.

Once it is understood that *thesaurus* by the late twelfth century usually meant treasure kept in portable chests, rather than a government department or a fixed place, it becomes clear why relatively few royal records of Henry II's reign (with the exception of the pipe rolls) or earlier were successfully preserved. King John likewise had no single place for his treasure.[83] In 1215 some of his treasure chests are known to have been deposited at Reading abbey, as he recovered from there jewels, relics, and 'all our rolls of our Chamber, together with our seal, and our rolls of our Exchequer'.[84] The archives in *thesauro* were evidently being 'taken about', as they had been in Fitz Neal's time a generation earlier. In addition to the records of the household and the Exchequer referred to by King John, the Chancery rolls were likewise transported from place to place by the 'portejoye' or 'serjeant of the rolls of Chancery'.[85] Some Cistercian abbeys were required in rotation to provide a strong horse to carry the rolls and books of the Chancery in the mid-thirteenth century and later.[86]

Because the royal archives had no permanent home, their safekeeping initially depended on the reliability of archivists rather than repositories. The earliest of such officials on record are William Cucuel, who had charge of the close rolls (the copies of the king's confidential letters) in 1215,[87] Roger of Whitchester, who was appointed keeper of the rolls and writs of the justices' Bench at an annual salary of £10 in 1246,[88] and John Kirkby, who held the

---

[81] *Dialogus*, p. 62.

[82] Ibid., p. 9. The translator's mistakes are compounded by giving 'Treasury' a capital letter, as if it were a modern government department.

[83] J. E. A. Jolliffe, *Angevin Kingship* (2nd edn, 1963), pp. 250–1. I have been unable to trace Joliffe's tantalizing reference to the 'arcana regni' being kept at Corfe castle (ibid., p.251, n. 9).

[84] *Rot. Lit. Pat*, I, p. 145.

[85] H. C. Maxwell-Lyte, *Historical Notes on the Use of the Great Seal* (1926), p. 293; *CPatR* 1258–66, p. 195; cf. pp. 239, 242.

[86] Maxwell-Lyte, *Historical Notes*, p. 294.

[87] Galbraith, *Studies*, p. 80; *Rot Lit. Claus* I, p. 196; *Rot. Lit. Pat*. I, pp. 137, 199.

[88] C. A. F. Meekings, 'Roger of Whitchester', *Archaeologia Aeliana* 4th series XXXV (1957), p. 106; F. Pegues, 'The *Clericus* in the Legal Administration of Thirteenth-Century England', *EHR* LXXXI (1956), pp. 546–7.

'office of the rolls of Chancery' at an annual salary of 20 marks in 1265 and was subsequently described as 'keeper'.[89] Unlike the 'portejoye', who was probably a mere porter, these men were royal clerks of education and status. They were archivists in the sense that they were in charge of *arche* of documents, but their archives were portable chests not permanent repositories.

Obviously, however, once documents accumulated, permanent repositories had to be found. Once a series of records like the Exchequer or Chancery rolls had piled up for fifty years or more, it became impractical and unnecessary to keep carting them all about in chests. Where the older royal records were kept in the thirteenth century has not been fully elucidated. In Henry III's reign London and Westminster replaced Winchester as the centre for storing royal treasure, but the repositories were scattered. Judging from later evidence, the Tower of London, the New Temple in London, and stores off the cloister of Westminster abbey were the chief repositories. The New Temple and Westminster abbey locations suggest that religious houses were still considered the most appropriate places to keep documents. Orders like one in 1257 to deposit plea rolls and chirographs 'in the king's treasury' throw no light on the location of this archive, although Westminster abbey is likely in this instance as legal records were subsequently kept in its chapter house.[90]

In Edward I's reign the largest archive in the kingdom was probably the New Temple in London.[91] In 1279 Roger of Seaton, chief justice of the Bench, kept his plea rolls there[92] and other memoranda show that the Chancery rolls were kept there: in 1289 a charter granting land to the king is described as being 'in a box in the chest in which the rolls of Chancery are kept at the New Temple';[93] in the summer of 1291, as we have already seen, Edward I ordered a chest at the New Temple to be broken open and a charter roll and a patent roll of Henry III were taken out of it.[94] The New Temple had also been a repository for books and documents of the Wardrobe, like the 'great book' which Queen Eleanor had brought from there in 1250, although in 1300 many recent books and rolls of the Wardrobe were deposited at St Leonard's hospital in York.[95]

The dissolution of the Knights Templar by papal decree in 1312 may have been an ancillary reason for reviewing the royal archives, as it deprived the king of the chief custodians of his documents. Certainly in that year new cupboards for keeping the older records were installed in the Tower of

---

[89] *CLibR* 1260–7, p. 169; *CPatR* 1266–72, p. 475.
[90] *ClR* 1256–9, p. 281; *SCCKB* i, pp. cxxiii–cxxiv. Similarly the treasury of the Wardrobe was in the crypt of the Chapter House when it was robbed in 1291, H. Harrod, 'On the Crypt of the Chapter House', *Archaeologia* xliv (1873), pp. 375–6.
[91] A. Sandys, 'The Financial and Administrative Importance of the London Temple' in *Essays in Medieval History Presented to T. F. Tout* (1925), pp. 147–62.
[92] *SCCKB* i, p. clxviii.
[93] *CClR* 1288–96, p. 56.
[94] See n. 28 above.
[95] *Book of Prests*, pp. 228–9.

London.[96] When Bishop Stapleton began his survey of the records in 1320, the White Chapel in the Tower was selected as the central repository to which all the records were brought. The idea of having a central royal archive in a fixed place under the king's direct control had at last been realized, but the government let the opportunity slip and many of the records were returned to their former repositories. The records were not again brought under a single custody until the Public Records Act of 1838.

Ideally the king's government needed archives in the localities as well as a central repository. In Anglo-Saxon England cathedrals and monasteries, which were under the king's particular protection, acted as keepers of his valuables including documents. Monks preserved royal charters because they were frequently the beneficiaries, as well as often being the writers of them. In Alfred's reign, for example, the Canterbury monks had written not only 'documents of interest to the archbishops and community, but also royal diplomas granting lands to lay nobles, private agreements between laymen, and the solemn decisions of royal councils'.[97] These practices continued intermittently after the Norman Conquest. Thus copies of Henry I's coronation charter were deposited in abbeys in each county, as well as being put in the Winchester treasury, according to later chronicle evidence.[98] One of the early copies of the reissue of Magna Carta was deposited at Lacock abbey by the knights of Wiltshire, presumably for safekeeping.[99] By the time of Magna Carta, however, sheriffs kept rolls themselves and must have been beginning to develop archives of their own. The earliest evidence of this arises from exceptional cases in which documents were mislaid. In 1212 a clerk of the sheriff of Gloucestershire explained to the king's justices that he had been obliged to go to London on the county's business and had left the sheriff's roll with 'Richard the priest of the castle'; when he returned, he found that the text of the roll had been altered.[100] In this instance Richard the priest was evidently acting as an unofficial, and inefficient or dishonest, archivist in the sheriff's castle. Past experience of documents in the sheriff's care being lost may have led the barons in 1258 to insist that copies of the letter, whereby Henry III undertook to submit to their council, should 'remain in the treasury' of each county.[101] Likewise in 1265 the letter publishing the terms of Henry III's peace with the barons was sent to every county, together with an order to keep it and accompanying documents safely as 'a memorial of the business' in the custody of trustworthy men chosen for the purpose.[102]

The precedent for regulating local archives and appointing commissioners to supervise them had been established in 1194 by Hubert Walter's statute for

---

[96] V.H. Galbraith, 'The Tower as an Exchequer Record Office' in *Essays to T. F. Tout*, p. 232. Cf. *SCCKB* I, p. cxxiv.

[97] N. Brooks, *The Early History of the Church of Canterbury* (1984), p. 168. See also Chaplais and Keynes, cited at ch. 1, nn. 20–2 above.

[98] R. L. Poole, 'The Publication of Great Charters by the English Kings', *EHR* xxviii (1913), p. 445.

[99] Ibid., pp. 451–2.

[100] *CuriaRR* vi, p. 230.

[101] *Baronial Docs*, p. 116.

[102] Ibid., p. 312.

the safekeeping of Jewish bonds. It is possible that such bonds had been kept
in chests in great churches before the statute; in the anti-Jewish riot at York in
1190 the mob broke into York Minster, seized the 'muniments of debts'
deposited there by the Jews and burned 'these instruments of profane avarice'
in the middle of the church.[103] By the statute of 1194 the bonds were to be
stored in future in designated centres in a communal archive (*in arca communi*)
or public chest, fitted with three locks.[104] The keys were to be kept by two
Jews, two Christians, and the clerk of the royal commissioners. The Jewish
and Christian key-holders are the first recorded local public archivists in
England and became known as 'chirographers'. Instances can readily be
found in the thirteenth century of the appointment of both Jewish and
Christian chirographers and of the keys being delivered to them. A chirographer was usually chosen by a jury, appointed before the justices of the
Jews, and took an oath to perform his duties faithfully.[105] As an additional
precaution, the contents of these archives were surveyed and enrolled from
time to time.[106]

As public royal archives with official archivists and writers had thus been
established in the principal towns in England by Henry III's reign, it is
surprising at first sight that greater general use was not made of them. An
exceptional instance from Oxford in 1227–8 shows a third copy of an
agreement, made by the hospital of St John the Baptist with Geoffrey Malin
and his wife, being deposited 'in the king's archive [*archa*] in Oxford'.[107] The
archive meant is presumably the chest of Jewish bonds; yet neither of the
parties is a Jew, nor does the business concern moneylending but a conveyance of land. From 1195 third copies of agreements (feet of fines) made
before royal justices were deposited in the royal 'treasury';[108] likewise third
copies of Jewish bonds were deposited in the local *arche* from at least 1205.[109] It
is possible that William, the Oxford town clerk, who was the writer of this
agreement in 1227–8, may also have been one of the keepers of the Jewish
archa and recommended his archive as a safe place for retaining a third copy of
this conveyance.

Had the procedure used in this Oxford conveyance become widespread, the
archives of the main towns of England would have developed into centres for
registering conveyances of property under the supervision of official writers
and archivists. Local royal archives thus had the potential of notarial centres
in imperial cities on the Italian model.[110] The potential was not realized,

[103] William of Newburgh, *Chronicles* ed. R. Howlett, RS LXXXII (1884), I, p. 322.
[104] Stubbs, *Charters*, p. 256; see also p. 71 above.
[105] *Calendar of the Plea Rolls of the Exchequer of the Jews* ed. J. M. Rigg (1905), I, p. 153 (Robert
le Bret), p. 135 (Jacob Copin).
[106] *Select Pleas, Starrs and Other Records of the Exchequer of the Jews* ed. J. M. Rigg, SS XV (1901), p.
50: Simon Passelewe went 'a enrouler partye de Huches de Engleterre'.
[107] *Cartulary of the Hospital of St John Baptist, Oxford* ed. H. E. Salter, Oxford Historical S, LXVI
(1914), I, p. 364 and plate iii.
[108] See ch. 2, n. 84 above.
[109] Richardson, *Jewry*, pp. 147, 264–7.
[110] Notarial practice is discussed at ch. 9, nn. 15–16, 46–50 below.

however, probably because the *arche* were too closely associated with the Jews and usury. In the eyes of Christians, depositing a Christian charter in a Jewish archive would have had the reverse effect of putting it in the shrine of a saint, as the charter would have been contaminated by the 'instruments of profane avarice' all around it. Furthermore, local *arche* may have been considered insufficiently secure despite their public supervision. In times of riots Jewish archives were burned, as happened at York in 1190 and at Bedford in the civil war between Henry III and the barons.[111]

This discussion has concentrated on the royal archives in their various forms because the king's government had the largest problems and also because, although evidence is sparse, there is sufficient to discern the outline of development. For magnates, whether ecclesiastical or lay, fewer details are available and most are of an incidental or an anecdotal type. After the king, the bishops might have been expected to accumulate business archives the fastest. Yet, just as bishops were slower than the king to make registers, their records suffered more than the king's from being carried around and having no single place of deposit in each diocese. At Rochester it was reported early in the fourteenth century that 'there never was any certain safe place appointed as a repository of muniments, but they were left about, sometimes in the cathedral church or in the manor of Halling.'[112] Some lay lords followed the king's lead and deposited documents with the Templars or at Westminster abbey.[113] Charters were also handed over to other religious persons or houses or to the village parson.[114]

Some landowners preferred to keep their own muniments, in which case they were sometimes lost or stolen. One of the earliest chirographs made before royal justices (in 1182) concerns the loss of a charter for Rochester cathedral priory by William son of Ralf of Wye.[115] The most spectacular story of a theft of charters comes from Babington in Somerset in 1201.[116] An unnamed lord was allegedly attacked in his house by a gang of eight conspirators who pulled out his tongue, broke open his chests, took out charters of Henry II, Richard I, and an archbishop of Canterbury, and burned them in his face before beheading him. Whether this allegation is entirely truthful, however, is doubtful, as the accused were allowed to make a compromise and the king did not prosecute.

Making documents, keeping them in archives, and subsequently using them again for reference were three distinct stages of development, as has already been argued.[117] Even when documents were successfully preserved

---

[111] *Select Pleas, Starrs and Other Records*, p. 49.

[112] Cheney, *Chanceries*, p. 135. For bishops' registers see pp. 74–5 above.

[113] A Sandys, 'The Financial and Administrative Importance of the London Temple', p. 148, n. 6; *CuriaRR* xiii, p. 253, no. 1152 (Westminster abbey).

[114] *CuriaRR* xiii, p. 304, no. 1415 (the anchoress of Bottisham); ibid. xi, p. 495, no. 2499 (Southwark hospital); ibid. xii, p. 72, no. 382 (Clerkenwell hospital); *Berks. Eyre*, no. 304 (the parson of Inkpen).

[115] *BM Facs*, no. 63.

[116] *CuriaRR* i, p. 395.

[117] See p. 154 above.

and kept in safe yet accessible places, it might still prove difficult to find a particular item of information within a book or roll. An example has already been given of Henry III insisting to the pope in 1272 that letters patent of his being exhibited by the prior of Christ Church Canterbury at the Roman *curia* were forgeries because they could not be found in his register.[118] In fact these letters had been enrolled in the patent rolls in 1265, but the Chancery clerks were unable to find them because they thought the letters had been issued in 1270. Without an alphabetical index of names, the clerks could not search their records thoroughly.

Searches of the rolls for particular documents were usually successful only when the record was of recent origin and its date of issue was known. For example in 1250 Walter Bloweberme, a robber who had abjured the realm after triumphing in trial by combat at Winchester in 1249, was recaptured and reconvicted by referring to the Hampshire plea roll of 1249 in which his trial had been recorded.[119] Or in the London justices' visitation of 1276 the prior of Holy Trinity at Aldgate claimed from the 'record of the Chancery rolls' that he had been authorized by Henry III to close a road; the rolls were duly searched and the record found.[120] Although it was possible to find particular cases or charters in the rolls when the exact circumstances were already known, royal records could not be effectively searched in a more general way. Thus Edward I's attempt in 1300 to search all the rolls for information about Scotland produced no new information because royal records had no indexes. Similarly the pioneering attempt of baronial commissioners in 1259 to assess from the records of the Exchequer how much money had been raised by tallages during Henry III's reign was not brought to a specific conclusion, although some information may have been gathered.[121]

The government's inability to use its archives for general guidance or for precedents in making policy decisions meant in the long term that its records were of more benefit to the governed than to the crown itself. An individual property owner or the head of a monastic house who possessed a royal charter or a transcript of litigation in the king's court could use the Chancery and plea rolls to prove his title by referring to a particular enrolment. Without systemized guides to their records the king's clerks on their side had no means of finding out whether other royal documents existed which might modify or even contradict such a claim.

A good example of the king being caught in his own bureaucratic net by insisting on written proof occurred in the *quo warranto* proceedings of Edward I. The rule had been established in 1282 that the privilege of excluding royal officers from executing writs within franchises (the franchise of 'return of writs') could be upheld only by a royal charter which made specific mention of

---

[118] See ch. 2, nn. 92–3 above.
[119] *Medieval Legal Records Edited in Memory of C. A. F. Meekings* ed. R. F. Hunnisett and J. B. Post (1978), p. 31.
[120] *The London Eyre of 1276* ed. M. Weinbaum, London Record S. xii (1976), p. 91, no. 345.
[121] *Baronial Docs*, p. 152, no. 15. A writ of a year later states that the king 'pro certo intellexit' that tallages have been excessive, *ClR* 1259–61, p. 135.

the privilege.[122] This rule was reinforced by a statute in 1285 which proposed that the treasurer should make a roll of those entitled to 'return of writs'; thenceforward any sheriff who made a return to an unenrolled franchise would be punished as a disinheritor of the crown.[123] The government's insistence on recording privileges in writing is exemplified in this dispute, both in the rule that a claimant must have a royal charter and in the proposal to make an official treasury list of franchise-holders. In the real world of practical politics, however, as contrasted with the theoretical world of Edward I's legal advisers and Chancery clerks, these rules threatened the great majority of magnates because their privileges rested on unwritten acceptance and custom rather than on royal charters or treasury lists. The roll of those entitled to 'return of writs' was consequently never made.

The story did not end there, however, as a handful of ecclesiastics, who were more concerned than lay magnates to ensure that their privileges were precisely expressed in writing, obtained new charters. Among them was the abbot of Chertsey, who appeared to comply promptly with the new rules by having a charter of Richard I, which had granted 'return of writs' to his predecessor, inspected by the Chancery and enrolled on the charter rolls in 1285.[124] What the Chancery clerks did not notice was that this charter was a daring forgery, as it was a conflation of two genuine charters of Richard I for Chertsey supplemented by interpolations. The facts can be simply proved today by looking up the Chertsey charters in the index to the printed edition of the *Cartae Antiquae* rolls which were published in 1939.[125] These rolls date from Richard I's reign and should have been known to the king's clerks in 1285. But even if they were known, they would have been difficult to search without an alphabetical index. The abbot of Chertsey had presumably taken a calculated risk that the royal archives would not, or could not, be searched for a grant which was earlier than the Chancery rolls of King John.

The Chertsey case illustrates the way powerful individuals or institutions successfully used the king's bureaucratic apparatus to benefit themselves to the detriment of the crown. Ancient monasteries like Chertsey had traditionally forged charters when they required title-deeds in writing. Now that the king was keeping copies of charters on his Chancery rolls, abbots ensured that their forged documents were reinforced by inspection in the Chancery and enrolment among the royal records. The Chancery rolls, which were intended to prevent fraud, thus became a means of making forgeries official. Once the abbot of Chertsey had got the forged charter of Richard I enrolled in 1285, his title depended on that enrolment rather than on the *Cartae Antiquae* rolls or his original charters of Richard I, which had presumably been destroyed in the process of making the forgery. Chertsey had acted in a similar way in 1256, when a forged charter of Edward the Confessor had been

[122] M. T. Clanchy, 'The Franchise of Return of Writs', *TRHS* 5th series XVII (1967), p. 71; cf. R. C. Palmer, *The County Courts of Medieval England* (1982), pp.263–81.

[123] Clanchy, 'Return of Writs', pp. 73–4.

[124] Ibid., pp. 76–7; *CChR* 1257–1300, pp. 305–6.

[125] Ed. L. Landon, PRS new series XVII (1939), pp. 65–6, nos 118, 119. Cf. S. Painter, *Feudalism and Liberty* (1961), pp. 178–84.

enrolled on the charter rolls of Henry III; the abbey had paid 100 marks for this 'confirmation'.[126]

Potentially the archives recording the acts of successive kings should have been a bastion against human forgetfulness and an assurance of just and efficient government, as Bishop Stapledon's commission claimed. If there had been an efficient filing system and indexes, royal clerks could have kept a check on fraudulent claims. In practice, however, the king's records had become so unwieldy by Edward I's reign that they constituted a largely unmapped territory. Particular monastic houses used them to their advantage by paying fees to have documents enrolled in much the same way as a modern company buys advertising space in a newspaper. As monasteries often kept careful records of these enrolments, they had better 'maps' of those parts of the royal archives which concerned them than any royal official had of the whole. For example, Bury St Edmunds abbey in 1281 paid 1000 marks to Edward I and made a gift of gold to the queen as well to have a new royal charter enrolled, which settled the division of property between the abbot and convent. This enrolment was noted in the Bury chronicle to be 'at the end of the Charter roll for the ninth year' of Edward I, where it can be duly found.[127]

The makers of monastic chronicles and cartularies had kept a watchful eye on the royal records since they had begun to expand in the 1200s. Many chroniclers cite official documents: the best example is Matthew Paris, who obtained transcripts of records through Alexander Swereford of the Exchequer and perhaps also through John Mansel of the Chancery.[128] Some of these documents may have been 'leaked' to Matthew by these officials so that he could give them wider currency and record them for posterity. In a sense a monastic chronicle like Matthew Paris's was an official record which was useful to the crown.[129] Some monasteries claimed that they had a right to make extracts of royal records which concerned them. Thus Dunstable priory submitted in 1276 that the prior was entitled to sit with the royal justices on the bench, and his 'enrolling clerk' with the justices' clerks, in order to copy the plea roll.[130]

The most remarkable collection of extracts from the royal records is Barnwell priory's *Liber Memorandorum*, which was composed in the 1290s, the most appropriate time to be compiling documents systematically as Edward I was beginning to do the same. The book contains the texts of nearly 90 official documents, ranging from citations from Domesday Book and the pipe rolls of John's reign to writs and plea rolls of Edward I. The compiler makes his purpose explicit in his extracts from a sheriff's roll at Cambridge castle: 'It will not be necessary in future to go to the castle to see the sheriff's roll, but rather the facts can be seen and learned from this book.'[131] The book was a

---

126 Clanchy, 'The Franchise of Return of Writs', p. 77.
127 *The Chronicle of Bury St Edmunds* ed. A. Gransden (1964), p.73.
128 Vaughan, *Matthew Paris*, pp. 14, 17–18.
129 See ch. 3, p. 101 above.
130 *Annales Monastici* iii, p. 272; Pegues, 'The *Clericus* in the Legal Administration', *EHR* lxxi (1956), p. 554.
131 *Liber Memorandorum*, p. 238. Cf. n. 6 above.

kind of cartulary of other institutions' records concerning Barnwell. In one citation from a Bench roll of 1288 the compiler notes that 'this record is to be found in a certain roll on the white part [that is, on the top side of the parchment] at the end of the roll where this sign [*signum*] is depicted.'[132] The *signum* is a hand with outstretched index finger, which is indeed to be found in the roll in question in the Public Record Office.[133] In this instance Barnwell priory had evidently been allowed to mark the official roll itself, as well as obtain a transcript of it. The Barnwell book is exceptional in containing so many extracts from royal records, but typical in its desire to keep pace with and master the methods of the royal bureaucracy in order to maintain the privileges gained by monks in the past. Monks had been the specialists in written record before the king's clerks appeared on the scene. Although they had lost this initiative by 1300, they fastened on the royal records like leeches and drew from them the information to sustain their privileges.

The use of a sign, like Barnwell's hand with outstretched index finger, to mark a particular item in a document was a simple way of facilitating the retrieval of information. Such signs are not essentially different from the rubrics, capital letters, running titles, introductory paragraph flourishes, and other aids to the reader which are usual in medieval manuscripts. The royal records, from Domesday Book and the pipe rolls onwards, are particularly notable for their clear and orderly layout. Marginal abbreviations and symbols were systematically used to extract payments due to the crown from a roll and to distinguish the business of one county or jurisdiction from another. It is usually easy to identify a particular item on a membrane or page of a royal document. The medieval archivist's problem lay in not knowing which page or roll to search in the first place.

WAYS OF REMEMBERING

Medieval writers were so good at layout because they were taught that ordering things on the page was directly related to ordering them in the mind.

> To fix something in the memory, it is of great value when we are reading to take pains to imprint (*imprimere*) on the memory through the imagination not only the number and order of the verses or sections in books, but also at the same time the colour, shape, position and placement of the letters: where we saw this written down and where that; in what part (of the book) and in which place (on the page) we saw it positioned – whether at the top, in the middle, or near the bottom; in what colour we discerned the shape of a particular letter or the ornament on the surface of the parchment. I think there is nothing so effective for exciting the memory as meticulously paying attention to the

---

132 Ibid., p. 114.
133 PRO (Common Pleas) CP 40/73, m. 96.

surroundings of things (*circumstantias rerum*), to those features which can occur accidentally and externally.[134]

Master Hugh of St Victor, the most influential teacher of biblical studies in Paris in the twelfth century (he died in 1142), is explaining here how to remember a text by placing it in the mind's eye and associating its abstract contents with something visible and circumstantial. In the process, he explains why scholastic books can be ornamented and illuminated as elaborately as liturgical books; the distinctive colour and shape of the words on the page helped remind the reader of where they occurred in the book. Hugh calls his memorizing techniques elementary ('puerile' is his term) and he claims no originality for them, as they derived from Greek and Roman practice.[135] Although Hugh and his contemporaries considered training the memory to be commonplace, it was none the less important because it structured the way medieval writers set out their thoughts.

'My son', Hugh of St Victor says, 'knowledge is a treasury (*thesaurus*) and your heart is its strong-box (*archa*).'[136] This is the same image and the same biblical reference ('Where your treasure is, there will your heart be also,' *Matthew* VI, 21), as the Master recommends to the Pupil in the *Dialogue of the Exchequer* to explain the meaning of 'treasury'.[137] Because the heart is a treasury of precious information, remembering is the process of extracting a particular item from it by recalling its 'colour, shape, position and placement' in the archive of the mind. Learning by heart according to Hugh's method did not mean the oral repetition of phrases until their sounds became a recording, but the visual scanning of a page until its images were imprinted in the mind's eye like a photograph. The medieval schoolmen 'printed' books, before the invention of the mechanical process of printing, by scanning texts and accessing 'through the imagination' the pages imprinted on their minds.

Because memorizing was done by associating words with their circumstantial surroundings, which 'occur accidentally and externally', medieval systems of recording and filing information can look arbitrary and strange at first sight. In *The Book of Memory* M. J. Carruthers illustrates some marginal notes drawing attention to particular passages in a text of St Augustine, such as: 'Mark (*Signa*) human benevolence!' and 'Mark (*Signa*) a most useful and brief statement!'[138] The reader's attention is drawn to the first of these notes by its being ringed by a drawing, in coloured inks, of a hound's head linked with a

---

[134] 'Liber Magistri Hugonis Sancti Victoris', ed. W. M. Green, in *Speculum* XVIII (1943), p. 490, lines 19–27. My translation is based on the translations by Carruthers, *Memory*, p. 264; G. A. Zinn, in *Viator* V (1974), pp. 211–34; C. P. McMahon, in *History of Education Quarterly* III part i (1963), pp. 33–7, as noted by J. Bowen, *A History of Western Education* (1975) II, pp. 67–72. F. Yates, *The Art of Memory* (1966) makes no reference to Hugh of St Victor.

[135] 'Ista quidem omnia puerilia sunt', 'Liber', ed. Green, p. 490, line 30; Carruthers, *Memory*, p. 95.

[136] 'Liber', ed. Green, p. 488, line 5; Carruthers, *Memory*, p. 261.

[137] *Dialogus*, p. 61, cited at p. 163 above.

[138] Carruthers, *Memory*, plates 18, 19; comment at pp.243–5.

hare's head to form a clasp. The second note is similarly ringed, by a dragon encircling the words with its sinuous tail. The book containing these notes was made for the Cistercian abbey of Holme Cultram, probably late in the twelfth century. The embellishment of the notes does not appear to form part of a coherent iconographical sequence, nor does it illustrate or echo the text. Like much embellishment in medieval manuscripts, these Holme Cultram marginalia look as if they have no purpose other than entertainment.

Cistercian monks, according to St Bernard at least, were not meant to look at images of mythical beasts, like the Holme Cultram dragon, nor admire such sports as hare coursing with hounds. The monks then and art historians since have struggled to reconcile St Bernard's strictures with actual practice.[139] Hugh of St Victor was a contemporary of St Bernard and he too was a monk, but of the Augustinian order which was less austere than the Cistercians. Hugh's remarks on memory training provide an answer to St Bernard: images in monastic manuscripts 'serve the basic function of all page decoration, to make each page memorable'; 'they also serve to remind readers of the purpose of books as a whole – that they contain matter to be laid away in their memorial storehouse.'[140] In the case of the Holme Cultram marginalia, the embellishments help to highlight and tag them, so that the reader may more readily file them away in the archive (*archa*) of his heart.

The Holme Cultram marginalia are 'signs': *signa*, as the Latin text describes them. They probably functioned in much the same way as medieval heraldry functioned, or as advertising symbols function in the twentieth century. A symbol of this sort does not necessarily illustrate the subject-matter it highlights, because memorability has to be its overriding quality. The symbol must imprint itself on the mind. In heraldry a golden circle, or a fiery dragon, on a knight's shield proved memorable primarily because it was mysterious and striking. Twentieth-century advertising uses a comparable technique in imprinting on the mind's eye the symbolic shell of Shell Oil or the tiger associated with Esso. Because the symbolic image is memorable in itself, it cues the memory, which then recalls the information required about the particular knight or brand of oil. This is the process which Hugh of St Victor describes as 'exciting the memory' (*ad memoriam excitandum*).[141]

Rationalizing the symbol – by thinking of the knight as rich in gold or fiery in temper, or of the oil as spouting from the seabed or burning bright – may help reinforce the image, but it is not essential. Effective symbols are memorable regardless of whether they make sense of the subject matter which the mind associates with them. In the Holme Cultram marginalia, the hound and hare heads clasped together may symbolize the process of hunting something down in the text, as this metaphor had been used for recollection since the time of Aristotle.[142] Even if the medieval reader knew this, however, the memorability of the image primarily depends on its strangeness: in nature,

---

139 For St Bernard, see C. Rudolph, *The 'Things of Greater Importance'* (1990).
140 Carruthers, *Memory*, p. 247.
141 'Liber', ed. Green, p. 490, line 25.
142 Carruthers, *Memory*, p. 247.

hare and hound heads do not stem from clasps. The dragon image works through a similar piece of whimsy, as its sinuous tail is the reverse of 'brief' (in contrast with the 'statement' which it encircles) and no one has seen a real dragon. It is the peculiarity of the Holme Cultram images which makes them effective as *signa*. Images from medieval heraldry and manuscript illumination can still be seen today in England acting as *signa*, when they cue the memory on public-house signs such as the 'Hare and Hounds' or the 'Green Dragon'.

Attempts were made from the end of the twelfth century to convert the use of visual signs into a system for classifying subject matter. Ralf de Diceto, dean of St Paul's, who marked charters with *signa* (as we have already seen), seems to have been the pioneer of such systems. His elaborate explanation of the *signa* used in his chronicle suggests that he had invented them himself and wished them to be appreciated. He warns the reader: 'You will find certain *signa* placed in the margin. Do not immediately conclude that this is in any way superfluous, for they are there to jog the memory more easily and are very convenient.'[143] He then explains that, because the making of a chronicle 'always runs on infinitely', the reader needs some guide to its contents. So he has devised twelve symbols (some are pictorial and some use letters of the alphabet) to indicate different subject matter, such as a sword for information about Normandy and 'PS' for persecutions of the church.[144] The phrase Ralf uses for 'jog the memory' is *ad memoriam excitandum*, the same term as Hugh of St Victor used. Furthermore Ralf cites the beginning of Hugh's treatise on memory verbatim in his chronicle and he cites Hugh also in his preamble to the statutes of St Paul's cathedral.[145] Ralf had studied at Paris and he may have 'heard with his own ears the teaching of Hugh of St Victor, which directly or indirectly impressed him so deeply'.[146] Hugh's advice to 'imprint on the memory through the imagination' (*per imaginationem*, that is, by image building) was converted by Ralf into a visible system. 'Here begin', he writes, 'the images of histories (*ymagines historiarum*), which Ralf de Diceto dean of London has put into order.'[147]

A manuscript of Ralf's work, displaying his twelve *signa* highlighted in gold, silver and colours, has annotations and drawings by the St Albans chronicler, Matthew Paris. He developed Ralf's 'rudimentary system into a complex sequence of tinted narrative drawings, painted shields and pictographic symbols'.[148] For example, Matthew used reversed shields in the margin of his chronicle to indicate the deaths of knights and reversed mitres for the deaths of bishops. For Matthew, these *signa* became an artistic device in themselves: thus the reversed and broken shield and shattered sword and banner of William Marsh, who was executed for treason in 1242, epitomize his dishonourable end.[149]

---

[143] *Radulphi de Diceto Opera Historica* ed. W. Stubbs, RS lxviii (1876), i, p. 13. Cf. n. 52 above.

[144] Ralf's *signa* are illustrated by Gransden, *Historical Writing*, plate vii; Lewis, *Matthew Paris*, p. 44; Smalley, *Historians*, p. 118.

[145] Stubbs's preface to *Radulphi de Diceto*, i, p. xxxi.

[146] Ibid., p. xxxi; B. Smalley, *The Becket Conflict and the Schools* (1973), p. 232.

[147] *Radulphi de Diceto*, i, p. 291. For meanings of *imaginatio* see R. W. Southern, *Robert Grosseteste* (1986), pp. 40–5; Carruthers, *Memory*, pp. 51–60.

[148] Lewis, *Matthew Paris*, p. 45.

[149] Matthew Paris iv, p. 196; Gransden, *Historical Writing*, plate ixf.

Matthew Paris understood that *signa* are memorable because they are rooted in feeling rather than logic. Through the sensitivity of his drawing, he made heraldry into a visual language capable of expressing emotion. As striking as the shattered insignia of William Marsh are Matthew's obituary notices for Gilbert the Marshal in 1241 and the Emperor Frederick II in 1250. The Marshal died in a tournament accident. Matthew uses his lance, drawn in the margin of the text, as a pointer to his picture at the foot of the page, where the Marshal in full armour is shown at the moment when his neck breaks as he is dragged by his horse.[150] To commemorate the portentous death of Frederick II, 'the greatest prince on earth and the wonder of the world', Matthew shows the double-headed black imperial eagle on a reversed shield hurtling down the page, while a fragile pointer makes a cross-reference to the 'Book of Additions' where Frederick's will is recorded.[151]

Ralf de Diceto and Matthew Paris shared a common inspiration for the pictographic indexing of their chronicles in the teaching of the school of St Victor. For Ralf this is explicit in the citations he makes from Hugh's treatise on memory, for Matthew the evidence is conjectural. One link with Paris is contained in Matthew's surname: he is 'the Parisian' (*Parisiensis*). Another link is the unusual number of references Matthew makes to the schools of Paris.[152] Schooling in Paris also helps explain the common features, in imagery and handwriting, which Matthew's work shares with the sketchbook of his contemporary, the Picard architect Villard de Honnecourt.[153] Both men may have been at the school of St Victor, where drawing, painting, and penmanship were integral parts of the curriculum. Hugh of St Victor had taught geometrical and figurative drawing, and the use of colours, because he believed that training the outward eye developed spiritual insight.[154] By meticulous draughtmanship, rather than abstract intellectualizing, students imprinted the meanings of things on their memories.

'Thinking (*cogitatio*)', declared one of Hugh's successors, Richard prior of St Victor, 'is without labour or fruit': understanding comes through the immediate insight of contemplation.[155] In training this faculty in his students, Hugh of St Victor explained that 'the church is the body of Christ and – to make this concept clear for you – I have depicted in visible shape (*in forma visibili depinxi*) the whole person of Christ, that is, the head and the members.'[156] In this spirit Matthew Paris treasured, and made for himself, realistic drawings of the human person of Christ. Into his 'Book of Additions' he inserted Brother William's full-page drawing of Christ; in another manuscript Matthew drew Christ enthroned, and he is likewise the painter of a striking icon of Christ (the Veronica).[157] For Matthew, as for Hugh of St Victor, artistic image, memory

---

150 Lewis, *Matthew Paris*, p. 237.

151 Lewis, *Matthew Paris*, p. 268.

152 Lewis, *Matthew Paris*, p. 3; p. 68, n. 33.

153 Lewis, *Matthew Paris*, p. 3, n. 7 (at p. 474); pp. 32, 214, 228, 240–1, 471.

154 Smalley, *Bible*, pp. 95–6. Carruthers, *Memory*, pp. 231–9.

155 'Benjamin Major', *Patrologiae* cxcvi, p. 66; G. A. Zinn, *Richard of St Victor* (1979), p. 155.

156 'De Arca Morali', *Patrologiae* clxxvi, p. 622 (my translation); Smalley, *Bible*, p. 96; H. de Lubac, *Exégèse médiévale*, part II, vol. i (1961), p. 325.

157 Lewis, *Matthew Paris*, pp. 64–5, 138–9, 128, colour plate v (between pp. 290–1).

image, and spiritual image were a single continuum advancing towards understanding.

Matthew Paris's intellectual and spiritual concerns – as much as his range of linguistic and artistic skills – exemplify at St Albans the teaching of the school of St Victor, just as Ralf de Diceto had exemplified that teaching at St Paul's in London. St Albans abbey is known to have sent monks to the school of St Victor and it took pains to obtain all Hugh's works, including the manuscript (now in the Bodleian Library) celebrating in a full-page portrait Hugh teaching some monks.[158] These contacts are documented for the period when Richard was prior of St Victor (1162–73), which may be before Matthew's lifetime (he died at an unknown age in 1259). Even so, contacts between the two houses could have continued long enough to provide Matthew with a Victorine education. He records that he took the religious habit at St Albans in 1217. How old he was in that year, how long he had been connected with the abbey, where he was born, and why he was called *Parisiensis* are details of his biography which he does not provide.[159]

From the 1290s there is evidence of a system of *signa*, similar to those devised by Ralf and Matthew, being used in the royal archives to mark particular storage chests or rolls. Thus Exchequer *Liber A*, which was completed in 1294–5, used a pictogram of a man with a lance and broadsword to indicate material which was in coffer 'T' under the title 'Scotland'.[160] Likewise, when in 1296 chests of documents and treasure were sent by Edward I from Scotland to London, the chests bore identification *signa*;[161] and in 1298 a record of a serjeanty tenure in Essex is said to be 'contained in the roll *Teste de Nevill*'.[162] This is the earliest instance of the rolls of knights' fees being identified by the 'Head of Nevill', which was probably the symbol painted on the chest containing them. As there is no evidence for the use of pictorial *signa* of this type in the royal archives before the 1290s, it is likely that they were introduced when Edward I's claims to overlordship in Scotland at last made the government aware that it needed some such system. As the king's clerks inspected chronicles for the Scottish business, they may have borrowed the idea directly from Ralf de Diceto and Matthew Paris.

WAYS OF INDEXING

Why did schoolmen as educated as Ralf de Diceto and Matthew Paris, or Edward I's clerks handling important business, use such peculiar and clumsy methods of retrieving information? Why not make an alphabetical index corresponding to numbered sections in the text? W. J. Ong provides some answers in his discussion of *Orality and Literacy*. The word 'index' is a

[158] R. M. Thomson, *MSS from St Albans Abbey* (1982), pp. 64–5, and colour plate G.
[159] R. Vaughan, *Matthew Paris* (1958), p. 1; Lewis, *Matthew Paris*, p. 3.
[160] Illustrated by E. L. G. Stones, 'The Appeal to History in Anglo-Scottish Relations', *Archives* ix (1969), plate facing p. 11.
[161] *Anglo-Scottish Relations*, p. 75, no. 25.
[162] *Book of Fees* i, p. xv.

shortened form of *index locorum*.[163] The *loci* ('places') in such an index were the 'commonplaces' or headings, under which a thinker organized various subjects for recall. These 'places' were located in the mind's eye and not in the book being read. Memorizing information by indexing it in the mind's eye was well known to Ciceronian rhetoric: 'if we want to remember a large number of items, we should equip ourselves with a large number of places (*locos*), so that we can use them to locate a large number of images (*imagines*)'.[164] The remembrancer visualizes a landscape, for example, or a chequer-board or some other pattern; then he places different images, signifying different subjects, in particular squares, rather like locating points on a map by latitude and longitude.[165]

To learn all 150 psalms in the Psalter, Hugh of St Victor recommended making a mental grid of 150 sections. This is how the schoolmen learn to quote any part of any psalm, he explains:

> For surely you don't think that, whenever they wanted to cite one of the psalms by its number, they turned over the pages (*paginas replicasse*) starting from the beginning and counting in order until they recognized the one they wanted? That would have been far too laborious a way of going about the business. Instead, they had an indexing scheme (*noticiam*) off by heart, which they retained in the memory as they learned the number and order of the individual items.[166]

As well as being quicker than thumbing through the pages, mental indexing overcame the difficulty in manuscripts that pagination might differ in a book from one copy to the next. A schoolman who knew the Psalter by heart could apply the indexing scheme he had already learned to any copy he came across. In this way he might readily find his place in an unfamiliar manuscript, or quote a psalm in an oral disputation without having to look it up. Matthew Paris describes how Abbot John of St Albans (1195–1214), who had excelled as a master in the Paris schools, could recite the psalms backwards or forwards in any order, an exercise which Hugh of St Victor recommends.[167]

Because readers indexed texts in their minds, medieval copies of the most widely studied books often have no contents tables, either at the front or the back, and no key-words or chapter numbers at the heads of the pages. To a modern eye a block of blackletter text in a medieval manuscript, differentiated only by coloured ornament and lettering in a variety of sizes from huge to minute, is bewildering and distracting. An inexperienced researcher finds his

---

[163] W. J. Ong, *Orality and Literacy* (1982), p. 125.

[164] *Ad Herennium*, ed. H. Caplan, Loeb Classical Library 403 (1954), p. 208. This text was not composed by Cicero, but medieval scholars believed that it was. Carruthers, *Memory*, p. 72.

[165] A chequer-board, with images of different animals in its squares, is illustrated by A. Piltz, *The World of Medieval Learning* (1981), p. 224. See also the illustrations in F. Yates, *The Art of Memory* (1966).

[166] 'Liber', ed. Green, p. 489, lines 42–6, my translation.

[167] T. Walsingham, *Gesta Abbatum Monasterii Sancti Albani* ed. H. T. Riley, RS 28, vol. i (1867), pp. 232, 217; 'Liber', ed. Green, p. 489, line 37.

place in it by checking a passage he can recognize against a modern printed and indexed edition. A medieval reader, on the other hand, recollected an appropriate indexing scheme, his *noticiam*, and then he found his place in the manuscript by relating the images in his mind's eye to the texture of lettering and ornament on the page confronting him. Such a reader might have found a typical modern printed page, lacking colour, ornament and different letter sizes, equally bewildering because it would not cue his memory.

A change occurs in the thirteenth century, when indexing schemes make their way from the hearts and minds of their creators, their *arche* in Hugh of St Victor's terms, on to the pages of books and documents. The *signa* of Ralf de Diceto and Matthew Paris are examples of this. These authors were not original in using *signa*, since mental indexing was routine, but in making their schemes visible to the reader. Ralf and Matthew gave the shapes in their imaginations, their 'images of histories', a local habitation and a name. R. H. and M. A. Rouse remark that indexing tools 'emerge with striking suddenness in the West, to the point that one may say that, probably before 1220, certainly before 1190, no such tools existed; and that, after the 1280s, the dissemination and new creation of such aids to study were commonplace'.[168] Essentially, this was a change in the medium rather than the message. Indexing tools had existed before 1190, as the works of Hugh of St Victor demonstrate, but they were held in the mind's eye. In the thirteenth century, *signa* make the move from memory to written record.

The proliferation of writings of all sorts, in government as much as in the schools, made reliance on identifying material solely by mental indexing less effective. The psalms might be learned by heart, but the accumulating mass of glosses on them could not. Similarly no archivist could find his way through the hundreds of membranes in the royal pipe rolls, plea rolls or memoranda rolls. To help him in his philosophical reading at Oxford around 1230, Robert Grosseteste devised a system of about 400 symbols, which he placed in the margins of texts to indicate different subject matter. An upturned 'V', for example, indicated references to 'God's wisdom' and a crescent moon pointing to the left indicates 'the dignity of man'.[169] Unlike the croziers, mitres, and other illustrative symbols used by Ralf de Diceto and Matthew Paris, Grosseteste's *signa* are abstract in form: intersecting lines, patterns of dots, and the like. They are comparable in appearance with masons' marks and other tradesmen's signs.[170] In terms of Ciceronian memorizing techniques, however, Grosseteste's *signa* are 'images' as much as those of Ralf and Matthew: Grosseteste located them on the pages he read in order to map his path through the thicket of scholastic texts.

Comparable in appearance and date with Grosseteste's *signa* are those used in Richard Hotot's estate book (see plate xv below). Their palaeography has still to be fully worked out. Three points are noteworthy: Hotot, a literate layman, may have written these *signa* himself; their form may derive directly

---

[168] *Preachers, Florilegia and Sermons* (1979), p. 4; Carruthers, *Memory*, p. 101.

[169] R. W. Southern, *Robert Grosseteste* (1986), pp 188–9; Carruthers, *Memory*, pp. 117–19.

[170] 'Craftsmen's and Merchants' Marks', *English Medieval Industries* ed. J. Blair and N. Ramsay (1991), pp. xxv–xxvii.

from Grosseteste's *signa*; Hotot's *signa* function as actual footnotes on the page, whereas Grosseteste's do not. That Hotot, a minor Northamptonshire landowner, might have borrowed a scholastic procedure from Robert Grosseteste, chancellor of Oxford university and bishop of Lincoln, is not as surprising as it looks.[171] Hotot belonged to one of those families of middle rank and independent resources, which Sir Richard Southern has described in his reconstruction of Grosseteste's educational milieu. Richard Hotot's elder brother was abbot of Peterborough. Their father, Thomas, was literate; Richard being a younger son, may have been educated as a cleric and personally known to Grosseteste. Richard is named quite often in the plea rolls of the king's courts and he may have got a living as a lawyer.[172] In that case, written records would have been very familiar to him, as would the plea roll clerks' practice of making annotations in the margins and cross-referencing entries.

Ingenious as these various systems of symbols are, the question remains: why not make an alphabetical index instead? Medieval *signa*, whether held in the mind or depicted on the page, were inevitably idiosyncratic because each person's imagination differed, as Hugh of St Victor had recognized. The alphabet, on the other hand, provided a uniform and ready-made sequence of notation. The principle of using it to classify words for reference was of great antiquity. Lists of words in Old English giving their Latin equivalents are arranged in alphabetical order in manuscripts as early as the eighth century.[173] The commonest medieval occurrence of alphabetical arrangement is St Jerome's dictionary of Hebrew names, which is appended to biblical texts.[174] In a Rochester manuscript dating from *c*.1120 the connection between alphabetical indexing and elementary schooling is made explicit: within the initial 'A' of St Jerome's dictionary is drawn a man frantically trying to teach a performing bear the ABC by beating it with a stick to make it cry out 'A'.[175] In English bibles of the thirteenth century, the list of Hebrew names is arranged in strict alphabetical order to the third or fourth letter of each word.[176]

By the end of Edward I's reign alphabetical indexes had been made to parliamentary statutes and other lawbooks. A portion of a page from such an index is illustrated at plate XIX. The layout is magnificent, the alphabetical order quite good, and the references elaborate (they use a system of roman and arabic numerals combined with letters of the alphabet). Nevertheless this index does not work properly, although the occasional reference in roman

171 E. King, 'Estate Management and the Reform Movement', *England in the Thirteenth Century* ed. W. M. Ormrod (1991), pp. 3–4, plates 1–2. Southern, *Robert Grosseteste*, p. 55.

172 P. Brand, *The Origins of the English Legal Profession* (1992), pp. 56–7, 181–2.

173 *A Second Volume of Vocabularies* ed. T. Wright (1873). In general see L. W. Daly, *Contributions to a History of Alphabetization in Antiquity and the Middle Ages* (1967).

174 Carruthers, *Memory*, pp. 115–16.

175 M. Camille, 'Seeing and Reading', *Art History* VIII (1985), pp. 29–30 and plate 2; Zarnecki, *Catalogue*, p. 107, no. 42.

176 E.g. Harvard University MS Typ 446 (a text from Bury St Edmunds) or BL Royal MS 1. D.1 (written by William of Devon).

numerals accords by chance with a folio number in the book. The index seems to have been made for another manuscript of similar contents but different pagination. The person who went to the trouble of appending this index to a book to which it does not refer precisely cannot have understood that indexes need to be exact in every detail if they are to work at all. Thus even when the principles of indexing by alphabetical order and numerical sequence had been laid down, it was still difficult to apply them widely in practice because the average reader did not expect to use a medieval manuscript as a source of ready reference. The owner of the lawbook illustrated at plate xix, probably Worcester cathedral priory, was perhaps well pleased with the index as it stood.[177] For the monks of Worcester it was valuable as an object of beauty and mystery rather than utility.[178] Medieval intellectuals were ambivalent towards alphabetical order because it militated against their sense of hierarchy. A Franciscan *Book of Examples for the Use of Preachers* dating from *c.*1270 lists the troubles of human kind alphabetically, starting with *accidia* (sloth); nevertheless its section on the heavenly beings (Christ, the Virgin Mary, angels, saints) is arranged hierarchically.[179] Of similar date is Peter of Pecham's parody of a charter, involving a compact with the devil, which lists the names of the evil spirits witnessing the deed alphabetically except for Beelzebub at their head.[180]

Instead of borrowing a primarily pictorial system of classification from traditionalist monks and their chronicles, the king's government would have done better to consult the friars, as they had the most recent experience of coping successfully with the large number of books required for their libraries, as we have already seen. Because they were the latest religious order, the friars were the most up-to-date experts in the problems posed by the proliferation of literature and documents. As early as 1239 the Dominicans in Paris had compiled an alphabetical concordance of the Bible, which was the first of its kind. It was elaborated into the dictionary entitled *Concordancie Anglicane* by a group of English Dominicans, each of whom took responsibility for a separate letter of the alphabet.[181] Probably among them was John of Darlington, who became Henry III's confessor and counsellor in the 1250s. Edward I's first archbishop of Canterbury was another Dominican friar, Robert Kilwardby (1273–8), who when teaching at Oxford had compiled an alphabetically indexed summary (a kind of *Readers Digest* guide) to the works of the Church Fathers.[182] By the end of the thirteenth century the English Franciscans were constructing a union catalogue of books in more than 180 ecclesiastical libraries.[183] Each institution was allocated a reference number in arabic

---

[177] The MS is described by S. de Ricci, *Census of Medieval and Renaissance MSS in the USA and Canada* (1935), p. 1022.

[178] Ong, *Orality and Literacy*, p. 124.

[179] Ed. A. G. Little, British Society of Franciscan Studies (1908).

[180] See p. 86 above. In general see J. Goody, 'What's in a List?' in his *The Domestication of the Savage Mind* (1977), ch. 5.

[181] Rouse and Rouse, *Preachers, Florilegia and Sermons*, p. 10.

[182] Ibid., p. 19.

[183] Rouse and Rouse in *MSS Hunt*, pp. 54–5, and their edition in the 'Corpus of British Medieval Library Catalogues'(1991).

numerals: Christ Church Canterbury is number 1, for example, and St Albans abbey is number 15. The catalogue is arranged by authors' names and, following the title of each work, is the series of reference numbers indicating which English libraries possess the work. To make this catalogue, the Franciscans gained access to the most exclusive and ancient cathedral and monastic libraries and treated the books they found in them as so many units of information. The contrast between the old Benedictine rule of mulling over a single book for a year and the friars' demand for immediate information is clear.

The Dominicans and Franciscans thus showed that they had between them the experience required to construct alphabetical indexes to particular documents and to list works scattered in numerous repositories. Moreover, some of the authors of these systems were personally known to Henry III and Edward I. To ask why these kings made no use of such expertise, when it was readily available, is to expect too much too soon of the shift from memory to written record. The friars devised new guides to ancient works, like the Bible and the Church Fathers. The only equivalent document of ancient scripture for the king's government was Domesday Book and that was being consulted regularly and systematically by Edward I's reign; it had been so beautifully designed in the first place that an index was not essential. The royal records of the twelfth and thirteenth centuries, on the other hand, were too recent and too large and diverse to be seen as a whole. Their potential was not appreciated until the last years of Edward I's reign, when the dispute over Scotland compelled the king to consider events from a historical point of view. Even then, he relied primarily on the evidence of monastic chronicles in preference to the royal archives. Although the difficulty of consulting his own records is a sufficient explanation for this procedure, there was probably political wisdom in it as well. If monasteries were asked to give evidence from their chronicles which had been compiled in the face of God, the king's case would be strengthened by this public process of consultation, whereas evidence which came exclusively from the royal archives could be said to be one-sided and clandestine.

Professional historians are bound to approach medieval archives in an anachronistic way. Their business is to hunt among documents for information and then rely on the evidence they find to construct an argument. Historians assume too readily that their medieval predecessors would have acted likewise. But in the world of thirteenth-century politics, where literate modes were relatively novel, written records were of limited value to governments. In Edward I's last years a terrible warning of what might happen to those who put their trust in written law and precedent was presented to Europe by the attack on Boniface VIII at Anagni in 1303. In a campaign of words, the pope had attempted to enforce his claims of overlordship over Philip IV of France. From the point of view of traditional ecclesiastical law Boniface's various bulls, particularly *Unam Sanctam*, were well founded. Yet in the *Dispute between a Cleric and a Knight*, which was composed as counter-propaganda, the Knight says:

I had to laugh when I heard that Lord Boniface VIII had just decreed that he is and ought to be over all governments and kingdoms. That way he can easily acquire a right for himself over anything whatever: since all he has to do is to write, and everything will be his as soon as he has written.[184]

The Knight implies that the pope could not distinguish between the theories of his chancery and *curia* and the realities of power. In reality authority depended on country-keeping knights like himself, who did not believe in the creed of writing everything down. In the *quo warranto* proceedings against the magnates, and perhaps also in his claim to overlordship in Scotland, Edward I showed that he too had been occasionally beguiled by the advice of academic lawyers with their confidence in written precedents, although by and large Edward relied on the sword rather than the pen.

Nor was it only knights and laymen who distrusted documents. In the 1180s some Parisian clerics who were going to litigate at the Roman curia were advised by the archbishop of Lyons: 'Do not confide in your decretals, for whether the pope decides for or against you, it will be said that he has decided justly.'[185] That was realistic advice, as Pope Lucius III himself admitted in 1184: 'Because of the mass of business which is referred to the Apostolic See, we cannot possibly remember the tenor of our letters and other decisions. For this reason we may be tricked into contradicting what we have written earlier.'[186] This naive and honest revelation of helplessness in the face of the mass of records, 'the inextricable wood of decretal letters',[187] would no doubt have been shared by the clerks of Edward I's Chancery *vis-à-vis* their letters, if they had dared to confess to such incompetence. A comparable statement, though it differs in being weary and cynical rather than naive, was made in 1279 about English official records by Roger of Seaton, who had recently retired from being chief justice of the Bench. When asked about the whereabouts of his plea rolls, he replied that they were deposited at the New Temple, but he added: 'Yet I cannot vouch for them for a number of reasons: because one thing is done and something else – more or less – is written in the rolls by the clerks, who are always failing to understand the litigants and disputants correctly.'[188] Thus in Seaton's opinion the plea rolls, which were the most formal and solemn records of the king's court, were fundamentally unreliable because the clerks who wrote them were too stupid or too careless to understand the business of the court.

The wheel had come full circle. Records had been made first of all by monasteries as an act of worship and to inform posterity of selected historical portents. Then in the twelfth century the king's government had begun to use

---

[184] B. Tierney, *The Crisis of Church and State* (1964), p. 201.

[185] J. W. Baldwin, *Masters, Princes and Merchants* (1970) I, p. 332.

[186] M. Bloch, 'The Suit of the Serfs of Rosny-Sous-Bois' in *Change in Medieval Society* ed. S. Thrupp (1964), p. 4.

[187] Duggan, *Decretals*, p. 26 (citing Stephen of Tournai).

[188] *SCCKB* I, p. clxviii.

documents in its daily business; intermittently these documents accumulated into an archive of potential written precedents. They were a treasure like the crown jewels. In the last decade of Edward I's reign ambitious, but largely unsuccessful, attempts were made to search among the royal records for precedents. 'Search all the rolls and remembrances', Edward ordered in 1300, 'search Domesday at the Exchequer at York and all the other rolls of the Exchequer and Chancery, so that nothing is left unsearched, then go to London to search all the other rolls there.'[189] In reality the authority of Edward I, or of any other king, depended more on his armies and castles than on his archives. The incalculable investment of time and skill in making records may not have been a benefit to the king's government. Or rather, lists of debts and the like were obviously useful for a year or two, but thereafter their only interest was historical. The government needed documents, but it did not necessarily require records. 'In fact, the sudden increase in documentation during the early 1290s seems to have been largely redundant.'[190]

Records had not originally been made for utilitarian purposes, measurable in cost-benefit terms. Rather they had been pledges to posterity and an assurance of the continuity of institutions under God's providence. Over the passage of centuries medieval royal documents have taken on the same qualities as monastic records: they have become a monument for posterity to the power and organization of the kings who persisted in making and keeping them. Whether they were profitable in the twelfth and thirteenth centuries is a question asked only by professional historians. At the time courtiers and armies, castles and palaces, gold and silk, were doubtless more potent and immediate manifestations of royal wealth and power than parchments. But now that the king's men are buried, his buildings in ruins and his treasures dispersed, the hundreds of thousands of documents survive as the best memorial to past greatness. Ironically, in attempting to make an archive for daily and practical use, the English monarchy had created one of the greatest historical monuments of all time.

How could they not be profitable?

when did this shift occur

---

[189] *Calendar of Chancery Warrants* I, p. 120. Cf. n. 30 above.
[190] W. M. Ormrod ed., *England in the Thirteenth Century*, Harlaxton Medieval Studies I (1991), pp. 24–5.

Part II

The Literate Mentality

Literacy is unique among technologies in penetrating and structuring the intellect itself, which makes it hard for scholars, whose own skills are shaped by literacy, to reconstruct the mental changes which it brings about. This difficulty has often been noticed and is most clearly put, with reference to medieval England in particular, by Maitland:

> The habit of preserving some written record of all affairs of importance is a modern one in the north and west of Europe. But it is so prevalent and so much bound up with our daily habits that we have almost forgotten how much of the world's business, even in communities by no means barbarous, has been carried on without it.[1]

Having described in the first part of this book how and when 'the habit of preserving some written record of all affairs of importance' grew up, the chapters which follow analyse developments in literate ways of thought. Because the formation of literate habits was relatively slow in England, documents from different dates can be used to pinpoint various aspects of the development. Some of these aspects are peculiar to medieval England, whereas others are common to all societies which have experienced the transition from memory to written record. Although it is difficult to reconstruct pre-literate ways of thought from historical documents, there is sufficient evidence over the two and a half centuries 1066–1307 to discern the main outlines. What is most evident is that literate habits and assumptions, comprising a literate mentality, had to take root in diverse social groups and areas of activity before literacy could grow or spread beyond a small class of clerical writers.

[1] P & M I, p. 25.

In medieval England all kinds of problems and prejudices had to be overcome before literate modes became acceptable to the rulers, and particularly to the knights in the counties upon whose lead further change depended. It was not, for example, a simple matter of writing down the language which was spoken, as a variety of languages and dialects were used, and Latin had a special status as the traditional language of literacy. To be *litteratus* meant to know Latin and not specifically to have the ability to read and write. The literacy of the laity is the most frequently discussed aspect of medieval literacy, yet that cannot be understood until the terms are defined in their medieval contexts.

The problems just described are peculiarly medieval. Added to them are the psychological differences between learning by ear and learning by looking at script. Medieval writing was mediated to the non-literate by the persistence of the habit of reading aloud and by the preference, even among the educated, for listening to a statement rather than scrutinizing it in script. Writing had the profoundest effects on the nature of proof, as it seemed to be more durable and reliable than the spoken word. On the other hand, those who valued the traditional wisdom of remembrancers within their communities had reason to distrust it. In England at least, in matters of legal proof, compromises were made which helped written modes to become more acceptable. The growth of literacy was not a simple matter of providing more clerks and better schooling, as it penetrated the mind and demanded changes in the way people articulated their thoughts, both individually and collectively in society.

Giving prominence to the term 'the literate mentality' is not intended to prejudge the question of whether literacy really does restructure thought in psychological terms, or whether a 'mentality' can exist as a separate entity in philosophical terms.[2] In order to avoid a technical language of their own, historians use common general terms as convenient descriptive labels. The records of the medieval past are cluttered with abstruse terminology, without historians adding another layer of their own. In what follows, 'the literate mentality' is used simplistically to describe the cluster of attitudes which literates in medieval England shared, and expressed in all sorts of ways in surviving records. Once these attitudes are identified and brought together, experts in a variety of sciences may address the question of whether 'the literate mentality' exists as a whole. It cannot be stressed too strongly that the discussion of 'the literate mentality' in part II of this book *follows on* from part I, 'the making of records'. Part I has as much as part II to say about 'the literate mentality', as it focuses on pre-literate collective memory (chapter I), bureaucracy (chapter 2), the typology and technology of documentation (chapters 3 and 4), and ways of recalling and classifying data (chapter 5).

To compensate for the imprecision of the term 'the literate mentality', part II of this book, like part I, proceeds by specific – and even anecdotal –

---

[2] G. E. R. Lloyd, *Demystifying Mentalities* (1990); *Literacy and Society*, ed. K. Schousboe and M. T. Larsen (1989), particularly the contributions by M. Bloch and J. P. Parry; Roy Harris, 'How Does Writing Restructure Thought?' *Language and Communication* IX (1989), pp. 99–106; D. R. Olson and J. W. Astington, 'Talking about Text: How Literacy Contributes to Thought', *Journal of Pragmatics* XIV (1990), pp. 705–21.

examples in order to show what the shift from memory to written record involved. This was a cultural shift, taking place in the imaginations and assumptions of numerous individuals. The unquantifiable sum total of these varied experiences – or rather, of those that are recorded in some form – constitute what may be described as the medieval 'literate mentality'. Historians headed by Jacques Le Goff have examined various aspects of *The Medieval Imagination*.[3] Examining 'the literate mentality', in England between 1066 and 1307, is a comparable endeavour. Like the medieval preacher's *exemplum*, anecdotal evidence can clarify and reinforce generalizations, even when the data are unverifiable or fictitious. People's beliefs and misconceptions are the historians' province as much as material facts, as the facts are insignificant without the beliefs which informed them.

Le Goff describes how in the Middle Ages 'between heaven and earth there was an incessant coming and going. The watchful choir of angels was drawn up against the cohort of demons who swooped on men whose sins called out to them. Jacob's ladder was erected between heaven and earth and on it the heavenly creatures climbed and descended ceaselessly in two columns.'[4] In one of his sermons Jacques de Vitry (who died in 1240) told the story of how a cleric in choir saw a devil weighed down with a sack.[5] The devil explained that the sack was full of 'syllables and slurred utterances (*dictiones syncopate*) and verses of the psalms' which the clergy had stolen from God when enunciating their prayers incorrectly. This devil was described in sermons across England, France, and Germany and was sometimes named 'Tutivillus'. The Oxford master and Franciscan friar, John of Wales, described in the 1280s how Tutivillus appeared in choir collecting up 'minutiae and little bits of the psalms'.[6] Judging from his concern with correct diction in choir, this devil was a product of the monastic culture of the twelfth century and earlier. Although he had an exacting ear for Latin quantities, his skills were oral rather than literate; he simply stuffed the sounds he collected into his sack, weighing himself down the more he laboured.

In addition to the sack-carrying devil (or perhaps as a metamorphosis of him), another demon makes his appearance in the thirteenth century who specialized in written record. He sat in churches like the sack-carrier, but he was equipped with pen and parchment, with which he recorded the words not of the clergy but of the laity and gossiping women in particular. In *Handlyng Synne* Robert Manning described him, sitting unseen between two women, 'with penne and parchemen yn honde' writing down everything they said.[7] V. Sekules has published a carving in the nave of Sleaford church depicting this scene: above the heads of two women squats a bat-like demon writing intently

[3] Trans. A. Goldhammer (1988).

[4] J. Le Goff, *Medieval Civilization* trans. J. Barrow (1988), p. 163.

[5] *Exempla* ed. T. F. Crane (1890), p. 6; M. Jennings, 'Tutivillus: The Literary Career of the Recording Demon', *Studies in Philology* LXXIV (1977), no. 5, p. 11.

[6] Jennings, 'Tutivillus', p. 16.

[7] Ed. F. J. Furnivall *Early English Text S.* CIX–CXXIII (1901–3), p. 291, line 9280; Jennings, 'Tutivillus', pp. 27, 42.

on a roll of parchment.[8] Sleaford is less than 15 miles from Bourne in Lincolnshire, where Robert Manning came from, and the carving is contemporary with him (he claims to have started writing in 1303). M. Camille has discussed the little scribe who sits at the foot of the demon king's throne in the Lambeth Apocalypse (painted before 1281).[9] He is tonsured like a clerk and writes on an oblong piece of parchment, shaped like a royal writ, in incomprehensible devilish script. In a contemporary picture of Edward I doing justice three little tonsured clerks sit at the foot of his throne; two of them are shown writing.[10] The scene which the scribe in the Lambeth Apocalypse is witnessing is the moment when Theophilus, the medieval Dr Faustus, shakes hands with the demon king and gives him his sealed charter, written in his own blood.

The Lambeth Apocalypse shows two types of written record in use at the court of the demon king: there is the charter which Theophilus hands over and also the writ in devilish script. This doubling-up of record-keeping accurately reflects the English royal court of Henry III or Edward I, where the charter which a litigant proffered might be copied by a royal clerk into a plea roll or Chancery record. The devil not only became literate in the thirteenth century, therefore, he also established a hellish bureaucracy to match that of the king or the pope. The bat-like demon who writes down what gossips say may not look as sinister as the scribes of the demon king, were it not that he emerges into the light of medieval art and literature at the same time as the inquisition. Ecclesiastical inquisitors, whose business was proving mortal sins, depended on written depositions of people's conversations.[11] Although the Roman Inquisition against heresy was banned in England, conscientious bishops like Grosseteste did nevertheless investigate the laity's sins (particularly fornication) in their courts.[12]

In the Lambeth Apocalypse the scene of record-making at the court of the demon king was most probably painted for Lady Eleanor de Quincy, who kneels in an accompanying picture at the feet of the Virgin Mary.[13] In the Theophilus story it is the Virgin who rescues him and his charter from Hell. A Book of Hours illuminated by William de Brailes some thirty years before the Lambeth Apocalypse shows the Virgin wresting Theophilus's charter from a

[8] V. Sekules, 'Women and Art in the 13th and 14th Centuries', in Alexander & Binski, p. 41. Cf. the misericord at Ely illustrated by G. R. Owst, *Preaching in Medieval England* (1926), p. 177, and Alexander & Binski, nos 557, 561.
[9] M. Camille, 'The Devil's Writing: Diabolic Literacy in Medieval Art', *World Art* (Acts of the 26th Annual Congress of the History of Art) ed. I. Levin (1989), p. 360, figure 4; also N. J. Morgan, *Early Gothic MSS 1250–85* (1988), ill. 139; N. J. Morgan, *The Lambeth Apocalypse* (1990), p. 55 and fo. 46.
[10] BL MS Cotton Vespasian xiii, fo. 6v; L. F. Sandler, *Gothic MSS 1285–1385* (1986), no. 9.
[11] E. Le Roy Ladurie, *Montaillou* trans. B. Bray (1978), uses Inquisition records to recreate dialogue.
[12] M. T. Clanchy, *England and its Rulers* (1983), pp. 224–6.
[13] The identity of the patron is discussed by Morgan, *Lambeth Apocalypse*, pp. 72–82. She is illustrated in colour by Morgan, *Gothic MSS 1250–85*, plate facing p. 16.

dcvil, who grasps its seal-tag with both hands.[14] The Virgin restores the charter to Theophilus by giving this devil a blow to the forehead with her enlarged fist. A caption in French alongside this scene confirms that the Virgin succeeded in recovering the complete document: *tout la chartre*. In the Lambeth Apocalypse the Virgin is similarly shown wresting the charter from a devil's grip, this time with the assistance of an angel who spears him through the throat. The Lambeth Apocalypse and the de Brailes Hours were made for ladies; indeed most of the first illustrated Apocalypses and Books of Hours in England were made for ladies.[15] They may have liked the Theophilus story because it showed the Virgin triumphing over men, in the guise of devils, including their husbands and fathers. The story's concern with written record would also have appealed, particularly to those ladies whose happiness depended on the enforcement or cancellation of written contracts. In 1302 John de Camoys conveyed his wife Margaret to William Paynel by charter.[16] In the scene in the de Brailes Hours where Theophilus does homage to the devil, his charter is labelled *Carta Theofoli* to emphasize its importance; the caption to this miniature reiterates in French that this is an *escrit chartre*.[17]

In the Lambeth Apocalypse and the de Brailes Hours, as in other books of this sort, the mixture of Latin and French on the pages raises questions about what languages their lady users understood. The practice of using French to caption illustrations goes back to the monastic books of the twelfth century; it is a convention of presentation rather than a comment on the patron's linguistic acumen.[18] Captions are written in French in order to indicate that they are not integral parts of the Latin scriptural text. In the Becket story-book (made for Isabel de Warenne under the direction of Matthew Paris), where the text is in French, the picture captions are put in Latin.[19] In the de Brailes Hours they are written in rubrics, in a smaller informal script, to distinguish them further from the blackletter Latin text. In most Books of Hours and Apocalypses the main text (whether in French or Latin) is the easiest part to read, as the lettering is large and the passages are mainly familiar prayers or liturgical readings. Even though no lady owner of a prayer book could have learned Latin in a grammar school (because schools became male preserves in the twelfth century or earlier), constant repetition and reading aloud would have made the contents of scriptural texts familiar. Furthermore women may have received some formal instruction at home, as the households of great ladies had chaplains, books, and private chambers.

The difficulty for Lady Eleanor de Quincy probably did not lie in reading (in the sense of voicing or articulating) the Latin text or the French captions in

---

[14] Donovan, *De Brailes* (1991), p. 75, figure 44; Camille, 'Seeing and Reading: Some Visual Implications of Medieval Literacy and Illiteracy', *Art History* VIII (1985), p. 40. Discussions of Theophilus are collected by Morgan, *Lambeth Apocalypse*, p. 56, n. 35.

[15] See ch. 3, n. 137 above; Camille, 'Seeing and Reading', pp. 41–2.

[16] P & M, II, p. 395.

[17] Donovan, *De Brailes*, p. 71; Camile, 'Seeing and Reading', p. 40.

[18] The French captions in BL MS Cotton Nero C. IV are listed but not discussed by K. E. Haney, *The Winchester Psalter: An Iconographic Study* (1986).

[19] J. Backhouse and C. de Hamel, *The Becket Leaves* (1988).

her book, but in comprehending the pictures. The Apocalypse or 'Book of Revelation' contained mysteries. Ladies like Eleanor, who imitated their chaplains by possessing sacred books, had to learn to read the scripture, as the clergy did, at four or more levels of meaning: historical, allegorical, tropological, and anagogical.[20] Literal construing of the Latin gave the reader no more than the 'historical' or contextual meaning of the text, which was merely the first step. 'The letter killeth, but the spirit giveth life' (2 Corinthians, III, 6) was well understood by medieval readers. The letters of scripture were illuminated and embellished in medieval books in order to give them greater significance and memorability. From embellishing initial letters and the margins of pages, it was a relatively short step to presenting half pages, or even whole pages, in pictures as in Eleanor's book. Precedents for making picture-pages existed from the earliest Romano-Christian and Irish books.

In a de luxe book like the Lambeth Apocalypse the pictures are undeniably ornate; they glow with gold-leaf and expensive pigments. At the same time they are functional, as they illustrate the scriptural text page by page. For the pious user of a book like the Lambeth Apocalypse, moreover, beyond ornament and illustration lay the inviting realm of contemplation, where the reader sought for visionary meanings, which transcended the literal interpretation of the text and the representations in the illustrations. The Apocalypse was peculiarly well suited to this sort of reading, as it announced in its first chapter:

> *Beatus qui legit et audit verba prophetiae hujus*: Blessed is he that readeth and they that hear the words of this prophecy, and keep those things which are written therein; for the time is at hand.

Whereas the prophets of the Old Testament were extinct volcanoes now that Christ had come, the Apocalypse still held its promise of imminent doom for some and salvation for others. It had been much resorted to in the eleventh and twelfth centuries, judging by the use of its imagery in Romanesque art. What is new in the thirteenth century is lay people, and ladies in particular, getting Apocalypses for their own private use.[21] The pictures in them vividly portray the scenes described by the author: earthquake and massacre, the seven-headed dragon, the beast, the great harlot, and so on. In their sensationalism these 'Doomsday Books' are the equivalent of the tabloid press of the twentieth century. Eleanor de Quincy was countess of Winchester; English aristocratic ladies still enjoy the same sort of reading material, much of it pictorial, in daily newspapers.

---

[20] J. Pelikan, *The Growth of Medieval Theology 600–1300* (1978), p. 40.
[21] English illustrated Apocalypses are listed with a summary bibliography by Morgan, *Lambeth Apocalypse*, pp. 271–2. See also M. Camille, 'The Book of Signs', *Word and Image* I (1985), pp. 133–4.

WHAT READING MEANT

Pope Gregory the Great had justified the use of images in worship by arguing that pictures let the illiterate 'read by seeing (*videndo legant*) on walls in churches what they are unable to read in books'.[22] This idea soon became a commonplace, which allowed the literate clergy to patronize the laity and justified the veneration of images, though Pope Gregory himself – by using the word *legere* of pictures – had been hinting at something more profound about the relationship between images and writing. As a commonplace, Gregory's words were recalled in another de luxe book made for an English lady, Christina of Markyate, a century and more before the Lambeth Apocalypse. In addition to over 200 picture initials, Christina's Psalter has 40 full-page pictures showing the progress of the Christian dispensation from the Garden of Eden to Pentecost. Following these pictures is a page citing Pope Gregory's justification of images, written in both Latin and French.[23] The editors of Christina's Psalter thought its scribe was responsible for this citation, but the decision to provide such a large number of picture pages and to justify their use by papal authority probably came from a more exalted source in the ecclesiastical hierarchy. The most likely candidate is Geoffrey, abbot of St Albans (1119–46), who was an entrepreneur of book production as well as being Christina's patron.[24] Christina, who was a visionary like her contemporary Hildegard of Bingen, presumably 'read' the pictures by meditating on them. The translation of Pope Gregory's words into French suggests that Christina read French rather than Latin, though her biographer says nothing about her literacy or linguistic abilities. (Hildegard came to understand Latin by divine inspiration at the age of 43 in 1141.[25]) Christina had been born into the Anglo-Danish patriciate of Huntingdon, and English was presumably her mother tongue.

The full-page Annunciation scene in Christina's Psalter is the earliest representation to show the Virgin Mary unequivocally as a reader meditating on a text.[26] The language of the text is unspecified, as the pages are blank,

---

[22] C. M. Chazelle, 'Pictures, Books, and the Illiterate: Pope Gregory I's Letters to Serenus of Marseilles', *Word and Image* vi (1990), p. 139; Carruthers, *Memory*, p. 222.

[23] O. Pächt, C. R. Dodwell and F. Wormald, *The St Albans Psalter* (1960), plate 37; Camille, 'Seeing and Reading', p. 26; L. G. Duggan, 'Was Art Really the "Book of the Illiterate"?' *Word and Image* v (1989), p. 230.

[24] R. M. Thomson, *MSS from St Albans Abbey*, i, pp. 21–7. The best introduction to Christina of Markyate is C. J. Holdsworth in *Medieval Women: Dedicated to R. M. T. Hill* ed. D. Baker (1978), pp. 185–204.

[25] Hildegard, *Scivias* Corpus Christianorum (1978), p. 3. In general see B. Newman, *Sister of Wisdom: St Hildegard's Theology of the Feminine* (1987).

[26] Pächt, Dodwell and Wormald, pp. 63–7, plates 15, 116, 117, 118. There are Carolingian and Anglo-Saxon representations of the Virgin Annunciate with an open book on a lectern, and eleventh-century ones of her with a closed book on her lap. Christina's Psalter is the first representation to combine the open book with the lap, i.e. it shows the Virgin in a domestic setting.

though late medieval representations of the Virgin had no hesitation in showing her with a Latin or vernacular text. In Annunciation scenes before the thirteenth century, the Virgin is ordinarily shown spinning, without a book in sight, whereas in the fourteenth and fifteenth centuries she is often depicted as a pious reader in an oratory with up to half a dozen books.[27] In keeping with the shift from memory to written record, the clergy made the Virgin into a reader in their own image, much as they made the devil into a writer. Both ideas were disseminated to the laity by sermons. A sermon by Ailred, abbot of Rievaulx (1147–67), describes how, at the moment of the Annunciation, the Virgin held the book of Isaiah in her hands and read the verse: 'Behold a virgin shall conceive.'[28] This may be what the Virgin is doing in Christina's Psalter: the book is open on her lap and she raises her eyes from it to the Angel Gabriel at the door, as if she had been interrupted in her reading. This representation of the Virgin absorbed in her studies provided a role model for Christina herself, as she sat in her busy hermitage (by Watling Street on the London road) interrupted by her own visions and passing visitors. Abbot Geoffrey of St Albans, who had been a master in the schools before becoming a monk, may have designed this studious image of the Virgin for her. It became, in the Books of Hours of the later Middle Ages, the most popular of all images of the Virgin.

Pope Gregory's 'read by seeing' is rendered into English in an early fourteenth-century prologue to an Apocalypse, addressed to *Who redes this boke of ymagerie* – 'Whoever reads this book of imagery'.[29] In the Lambeth Apocalypse one full-page picture specifies by numerous captions in French how it should be 'read'.[30] In the bottom left-hand corner of this page sits a lady, a younger and prettier version of Eleanor de Quincy, on a wooden chair carved with the elaboration of a royal or episcopal throne. A caption at her head explains: *par la Dame est signifie repentant* – 'by the Lady is signified the penitent'. On the finial on the back of her chair perches a dove symbolizing the Holy Spirit, who expounds the scripture to the Lady. The Lady defends her front with the shield of faith, which has three bosses at its corners, spelling out the persons of the Trinity and meeting in a central boss marked *deu* – 'God'. Her shield is directed at a devil, who shoots arrows of evil suggestions at her; in appearance he is like the demons who beguile Theophilus in the same book. Above the Lady's head circle large bluish flies, signifying those empty thoughts which disturb the penitent at prayer. Many other features in this picture of the Lady Penitent are similarly explained by captions, and on other folios in the Lambeth Apocalypse there are pictures with explanations almost as elaborate. Their interest in the present context lies in the questions they raise about the medieval literate mentality.

---

[27] K. Schreiner, 'Marienverehrung, Lesekultur, Schriftlichkeit', *Frühmittelalterliche Studien* XXIV (1990), pp. 314–68.

[28] Pächt, Dodwell and Wormald, p. 64. See also the sermon by Odilo of Cluny, ibid., p. 66.

[29] R. H. Robbins ed. *Secular Lyrics of the 14th and 15th Centuries* 2nd edn (1955), p. 93, no. 100; S. Lewis, 'The English Gothic Illuminated Apocalypse, *Word and Image* VII (1991), p. 1.

[30] Morgan, *Gothic MSS 1250–85*, ill. 141; Morgan, *Lambeth Apocalypse*, pp. 258–9, fo. 53.

Was Lady Eleanor de Quincy *alias* the Lady Penitent literate? In the Lambeth Apocalypse she is depicted holding it, or another prayer-book, open while she prays to the Virgin and Child. Was a lady's ability to recite daily prayers, in Latin or French, literacy? There is no evidence that Lady Eleanor, or Christina of Markyate, could write. Nor is the Virgin Mary ever depicted in an Annunciation scene making a note of the Angel Gabriel's message, though in Virgin and Child scenes the Child is sometimes shown writing. The Virgin was expected to remember the angelic message by taking it into her innermost being: 'Mary kept all these words and pondered them in her heart' (Luke, II, 19). In his treatise on memory Hugh of St Victor explained how knowledge is a treasury and 'your heart is its strong-box' (*cor tuum archa*).[31] He recommended remembering what one read, rather than depending on the written text. This was prudent in manuscript culture, when no two books were exactly alike and books were hard to come by anyway. But, in emphasizing the priority of memory, Hugh's concern was probably religious and ideological rather than utilitarian.

The danger with writing was that it implanted forgetfulness in the soul, as Socrates had said, preventing people from recalling the truth from within themselves. Writing anything down externalized it and – in that process – changed it and falsified it to some extent. 'Writing restructures consciousness', as W. J. Ong has put it.[32] Throughout twelfth-century Europe charters and title-deeds were frequently forged by monks, the experts in writing. They understood very well, from their experience in expounding and copying holy scripture, that a document which stated something untrue or unverifiable would continue to state it – and make it look authentic and proven – as long that document existed. In all societies literates face problems about whether writing is true or not. In modern western culture the primary meaning of 'writer' is a creator of fiction. Unaccustomed to the convention of the fictitious narrator in the modern novel, twelfth-century readers were unsure whether Geoffrey of Monmouth or Walter Map was a historian or a liar. Writing was untrustworthy in itself, and furthermore its use implied distrust, if not chicanery, on the part of the writer. An honest person held to his word and did not demand written proof. It was appropriate that the devil should become a writer. The recording demon consumed rolls of parchment noting down people's sins and made himself ridiculous, according to the preachers, by trying to stretch the parchment with his teeth to accommodate his screeds.[33] (The skin is stretched in the process of manufacturing parchment, but the finished product has little elasticity.) Likewise the ugly little clerk in the Lambeth Apocalypse, who sat at the foot of the demon king's throne writing in his devilish script, was no more to be admired by noble people than the scriveners of the king's Chancery or the law clerks in Westminster Hall.

Writing was a very necessary activity, but it was not to be done by great ladies like the Virgin Mary, Christina of Markyate and Eleanor de Quincy. They were its beneficiaries, not its makers. They understood the significance

---

[31] See p. 173, n. 136 above; Carruthers, *Memory*, p. 261.
[32] *Orality and Literacy* (1982), pp. 78–80. See also Carruthers, *Memory*, pp. 30–1.
[33] Jennings, 'Tutivillus', pp. 25, 27–8, 44–5.

of writing and enjoyed its fruits, in the form of their splendid books and of documents (whether true or false) entitling them to their material privileges. The illuminated and gem-encrusted books of the Middle Ages were indeed made for the glory of God and his saints, but equally they were made to glorify their owners and donors. Christina's and Eleanor's books were designed for conspicuous display as much as any piece of jewellery. They are akin to the large enamelled brooches and golden torques, which in the Celtic world had distinguished aristocrats from their social inferiors for a millennium. Abbot Geoffrey of St Albans headed one of the richest and most exclusive corporations in medieval England; in the name of piety and learning he conferred the distinction of its wealth, in the form of a Psalter, on Christina of Markyate. Her Psalter and the Lambeth Apocalypse show that lady readers might enjoy both a heavenly and an earthly reward.

The reading ability of these ladies was not the equivalent of modern reading. In many ways it was more demanding. It was not sufficient simply to read the mother tongue. Ideally ladies (and gentlemen) in twelfth- and thirteenth-century England should be able to read in three languages at least: Latin, French, and English. In their religious devotions they had also 'to read the book of imagery', that is, to understand through the labour of meditation the forms and signs of divine revelation. In the Lambeth Apocalypse one picture-page illustrates the story of the monk who kept the face of the Virgin Mary so successfully in his mind's eye that the Virgin appeared to come alive and the holy Child gestured towards him.[34] This was a model for the level of concentration that Lady Eleanor should have in her study of the book. People who succeeded in doing this and who became visionaries, like Christina of Markyate, won prestige and wealth. Christina's Psalter is one of the most expensive artefacts made in twelfth-century England. Another very rich manuscript, originating from St Albans and identified with the Winchester Bible, was arbitrarily given by Henry II to Hugh of Lincoln; the king believed that Hugh's power of prayer had saved him from shipwreck when crossing the Channel.[35]

The profits of literacy, in terms of both heavenly and earthly advantage, were therefore best sought in religious reading. Skill in writing (which was taught separately from reading) could be rewarding for scribes working in rich monasteries and professional ateliers, like Eadwine 'the prince of writers', but such men were the exceptions. Most writing involved repetitive manual labour of the type done by the recording demons and the king's clerks. Neither for reading nor for writing were materials readily available in domestic settings. Consequently the relatively few books that there were, of which Christina's Psalter and Eleanor's Apocalypse are outstanding examples (by and large only the finest manuscripts have been preserved), were studied by their owners intensively and repeatedly, over years or decades, in order to seek out their deeper levels of meaning. This involved a variety of reading strategies: hearing the text read aloud while looking at the lettering and images on the pages; repeating the text aloud with one or more companions,

---

[34] Lewis, 'English Gothic Illuminated Apocalypse', pp. 7, 10.
[35] *Life of St Hugh of Lincoln* ed. D. L. Douie and H. Farmer 2nd edn (1985), p. 86.

until it was learned by heart; construing the grammar and vocabulary of the languages of the text silently in private; translating or transposing the text, aloud or silently, into Latin, French, or English; examining the pictures and their captions, together with the illuminated letters, as a preparation for reading the imagery.[36]

The ultimate stage of reading was contemplation, when the reader 'saw with his heart', like St John the author of the Apocalypse, the truth of hidden things. In this stage, text and image combined with the reader's own perceptions and feelings to produce enlightenment. Richard, prior of St Victor, who is contemporary with Christina of Markyate and had contacts with St Albans, described how 'contemplation endures (*permanet*) without labour but with fruit', whereas thinking on its own was fruitless.[37] Such a non-utilitarian approach to reading is alien to modern western culture. Richard of St Victor would be more at home now in a Buddhist community than in his native Scotland or in the University of Paris. Similar reading strategies were applied to secular romances and other forms of vernacular literature, which were rendered into fine manuscripts from the thirteenth century onwards. Often they were bound into books alongside religious texts. For many medieval readers, tales of King Arthur or Alexander the Great were not essentially different in their structure and content from tales of King David or Jesus Christ.

Medieval texts were designed to be read in a variety of ways – orally or silently, by one person or in a group – and at different levels of meaning, taking account of word and image and a variety of linguistic registers. Even common law writs, the most mundane of business documents, were embellished in that they bore on them the great seal of the king, with its two-sided image signifying laws (the king enthroned in majesty) and arms (the king riding as a knight). Most exceptionally, the text of a charter of Edward I's, granting hunting rights to Roger of Pilkington in 1291, is surrounded on all four sides with good coloured drawings of animals, birds, and trees, as if to embody the privileges it grants.[38] The charter may have been granted in this form as a sign of royal favour, as the realistic depiction of birds in particular is characteristic of the finest illuminated manuscripts associated with Edward I's family, like the Alphonso Psalter and the Ashridge *Historia Scholastica*.[39] Medieval users of books understood very well that picturing and writing are connected. 'Writing stands at the basis of the picture just as much as the picture stands at the basis of writing.'[40]

Enough has been said by way of introduction to show that medieval attitudes to literacy differed in a variety of ways from our own. Our modern

---

[36] R. Muir Wright, 'Sound in Pictured Silence: The Significance of Writing in the Illustration of the Douce Apocalypse', *Word and Image* VII (1991), pp. 239–74.

[37] *Patrologiae* CXCVI, pp. 66–7. See also ch. 5, n. 155 above, and Richard's commentary on the Apocalypse, cited by Lewis, 'English Gothic Illuminated Apocalypse', p. 5.

[38] See p. 292 below.

[39] B. Yapp, *Birds in Medieval MSS* (1981), colour plates 1, 21, 22, 23, 35.

[40] Roy Harris, *The Origin of Writing*, (1986), p. 156.

literate mentality makes it difficult to understand theirs. Ideally and traditionally, medieval readers were concerned with quality in their literacy rather
than quantity. Similar criteria applied to writing. Soon after the invention of
printing in the fifteenth century, the abbot of Sponheim commented contemptuously that paper books would only survive a couple of centuries, whereas
parchment manuscripts had been made to last for a thousand years.[41]
Medieval owners of books like Christina of Markyate and Eleanor de Quincy
may not have known how to write, but they did know what good writing
should be like: it should be magnificent and awe-inspiring. How much
responsibility these ladies had for the design of the books they owned is
unknown. Any medieval book owner, however, had a more personal relationship with his books than a modern literate who buys a mass-produced item in
a bookstore.

Although the modern literate receives his books in mass-produced and
stereotyped forms, he has a more individualistic approach to handwriting
than his medieval predecessor. Literates reacted to the mechanization of
writing, after the invention of printing, by cultivating their own distinctive
and idiosyncratic writing styles. In the form of personal signatures on credit
cards, these are accepted in modern societies as warrants of authenticity.
Medieval people, on the other hand, warranted documents with their seals or
by a notary's mark; handwriting was the business of professionals, who aimed
to make it as uniform and impersonal as possible. The ability to write well, in
the sense in which Eadwine 'the prince of writers' wrote well (see plate xiv), is
as alien to the average modern literate as the ability to read a text at different
levels of meaning. Our twentieth-century western form of literacy is not an
invariable norm; it is as culture-bound and shaped by available technologies
as medieval manuscript literacy was. Comparing medieval norms with
modern ones puts current questions about literacy in perspective. The best
way of understanding the modern western literate mentality is to see where it
came from. The abbot of Sponheim looked back on a tradition of manuscript
writing which had lasted for a thousand years (over the medieval millennium
500–1500 AD) and repeatedly renewed itself. Twentieth-century planners and
educators, on the other hand, have found it difficult to provide even for a
decade in advance.

---

[41] *De Laude Scriptorum*, ch. 7, ed. K. Arnold (1974), p. 63; M. T. Clanchy, 'Looking Back from
the Invention of Printing', in *Literacy in Historical Perspective* ed. D. P. Resnick (1983), p. 10.

6

Languages of Record

Before the formation of literate habits can be analysed the languages in use, whether oral or written, need to be described, since language is necessarily prior to literacy. After the Norman Conquest the way languages were used in England became extraordinarily complex, primarily because of the introduction of French as a spoken language and the decline of Old English as a written one. For the next two centuries at the very time that documents came into common use, Latin, French, and English had to compete with each other to establish themselves as written languages. Whether the growth of literacy was obstructed or encouraged by such competition is difficult to establish; certainly literacy cannot have remained unaffected. In addition, Hebrew was used as a language of record by the Jews who arrived in the twelfth century. These problems of diversity of language and of the differences between written and spoken language are approached in this chapter by starting with a specific example of a book which aimed to help the English gentry improve their French.

      lippe   *the hare*
Vous avez la levere et le leverer.
   the pount   *book*
La livere et le liv(e)re,
La levere c'est ke enclost les dens,
Le levere ki buys se tent dedeins,

La livere sert de marchaundie,
Le livere nous aprent clergie.[1]

These lines come from Walter Bibbesworth's rhyming French vocabulary with occasional English interlineations. Walter was a knight from Essex (with some interests in Hertfordshire), who participated in the county's business and served Henry III in the 1250s and 1260s.[2] He wrote his work for 'ma dame Dyonise de Mountechensi'.[3] There were a number of ladies called Denise de Montchensy in the thirteenth century; the one most probably known to Walter is the Lady Denise who was the wife and widow (after 1255) of Warin de Montchensy.[4] Walter explains that he wrote the book to enable Denise to teach her children the vocabulary of 'husbandry and management', which they would require when they grew up.[5]

The extract cited from Walter's work introduces all the principal problems concerning the use of languages in medieval England. Walter assumes for a start that Lady Denise can read in both English and French. He explains that he is not teaching elementary French, 'which everyone knows how to speak', but something 'not so common'.[6] By distinguishing in this extract between words of similar sound in French but different meanings in English (*la levere* 'the lip', *le leverer* 'the hare', *la livere* 'the pound', *le livere* 'the book'), Walter emphasizes the need for accurate reading and grammar beyond the colloquial French 'which everyone knows'. He aims to teach good French, the king's French of the court of Henry III, and not the French of Marlborough or of Stratford-atte-Bow.[7] The existence of 'Anglo-Norman' features in the language of Walter and other English writers of French does not imply that they thought their French a different language from the French of France.

Although Lady Denise can already speak French, like everyone of her class in Walter's opinion, his work makes it clear that English is her mother tongue, as much as it is his. As Denise was the daughter of Nicholas Ansty of Hertfordshire and had been the widow of Walter Langton at the time she married Warin de Montchensy in *c*.1235, it is likely that she was not a native French speaker.[8] The English interlineations which distinguish the masculine and feminine meanings of *levere* and *livere* would only be helpful to someone who knew English better than French. These interlineations were designed by

---

[1] *Le Traité de Walter de Bibbesworth* ed. A. Owen (Paris, 1929), pp. 50–51, lines 61–6. Errors in this edition are listed by W. Rothwell in *The Modern Language Review* LXXVII (1982), pp. 282–93. See also T. Hunt, *Teaching and Learning Latin* (1991), vol. i, p. 12.

[2] Walter's career has not been thoroughly studied. There may have been two persons, father and son, of the same name. J. C. Russell, *Dictionary of Writers of Thirteenth-Century England* (1936), pp. 175–6, provides an introduction.

[3] *Le Traité*, p. 43.

[4] G. E. Cokayne, *The Complete Peerage* (2nd edn) IX (1936), pp. 421–2 (Munchensy).

[5] 'husbondrie e manaungerie', *Le Traité*, p. 43.

[6] Ibid., pp. 52–3, lines 82, 86.

[7] For these derogatory terms see G. E. Woodbine, 'The Language of English Law', *Speculum* XVIII (1943), p. 413.

[8] *The Complete Peerage* IX, p. 421.

Walter as an integral part of his work – 'You will find first the French and then the English above it', he says[9] – in order to assist those who could not have coped with improving their French entirely by his direct method. The way Walter and his readers think in English is best illustrated by his use of single English words as a starting point for building up vocabulary in French. Thus he gives the example of a handsome knight whose hair is red (*rous* in French), whose horse is red (*sor*), whose shield is red (*goules*), whose lance is red (*rouge*) and so on.[10]

For Walter and his audience English is assumed to be the mother tongue, but they need to know good French as well because it is the language of the gentry, the *gentils hommes* (as Walter calls them), and of the king's court. 'For unless a man knows French, he is thought of little account' is an affirmation of another of Walter's contemporaries.[11] Because in Walter's time French was just beginning to come into common use as a written language, ambitious men and women in England required a more accurate knowledge of it than would have been necessary in the twelfth century. Walter catered for their needs by providing a practical vocabulary for those who wished to get on in society, including – as in our extract – the parts of the body ('the lip which encloses the teeth'), hunting ('the hare which hides in the wood'), weights and measures ('the pound which is used in trade') and learning ('the book which teaches us *clergie*').

In this last reference, to the book which teachers us *clergie*, Walter reminds his audience that they will have already learned some Latin, the language of the 'clergy', as well as English and French. The difference for Walter between learning French and learning Latin is that French is initially learned colloquially by hearing and then improved by using his treatise, whereas Latin is primarily and essentially book learning. The book which teaches us *clergie* is the Latin primer, which Walter assumes his readers, including Lady Denise, are familiar with from their childhood. Latin was taught systematically by tutors, using grammar as a basis, whereas French was often more informally acquired. At the same time as Walter was writing, however, other works were being composed which treat French grammatically and proceed from Latin.[12] They presumably catered for the minority of lower-class clergy who had not been exposed to French while they grew up.

Walter assumes that it is possible to teach yourself French but not Latin. Although cases can be found of Latin being learned without formal instruction, they are exceptions which prove the rule that it was difficult. Gerald of Wales has a story about a hermit, Wecheleu, whom he met near the river Wye in *c*.1193, who had acquired Latin miraculously while on a pilgrimage to Jerusalem. He used only infinitives and substantives, explaining to Gerald

---

9 *Le Traité*, p. 44.
10 Ibid., p. 75, cited by W. Rothwell, 'The Role of French in Thirteenth-Century England', *BJRL* LVIII (1976), p. 464.
11 *Metrical Chronicle of Robert of Gloucester* ed. W. A. Wright, RS LXXXVI (1887), II, p. 544, line 7542.
12 Rothwell, 'The Role of French', pp. 458ff.

that 'the Lord who gave me the Latin tongue, gave it not me by way of grammar and cases, but only that I might be understood and understand others.'[13] In Wales of course the language problem was even more complex than in England, as a man like Gerald needed to know some Welsh as well as Latin, French, and English.

The knowledge of languages which Walter expected upper class English men and women of his day to have was: some acquaintance with Latin and the book learning of the clergy, a knowledge of colloquial French which required extending and refining, and an effortless facility in English because it was the mother tongue. Walter's work underlines generalizations which characterized English culture in the thirteenth century. By his time the gentry were not usually illiterate; rather, their reading ability was taken for granted, as was a little Latin. Nor were many of them native French speakers. Walter and his like were Englishmen who learned French because it was the most influential language in Europe, as it was spoken by their Plantagenet kings as well as by St Louis. Moreover, some of the English magnates, as distinct from knights like Walter, were native French speakers; the most famous example in Walter's time was Simon de Montfort. A combination of social and political pressures thus encouraged both Lady Denise and her children and knights like Walter to master languages.

Walter of Bibbesworth was not unique in being a relatively obscure knight who had a good knowledge of written and spoken French. Comparable with him is his namesake, Walter of Henley, who a generation later advised another great dowager, Isabel de Forz, and wrote his treatise on farm management, *Husbandry*, in French.[14] Both Walters were typical of the educated gentlemen of each county who acted as stewards and managers for royal and baronial enterprises. Walter of Bibbesworth was described as a 'discreet knight' of Essex in a royal writ in 1254.[15] Although such men were usually essentially English, they knew French because it was the language of management (*manaungerie*) and lordship, and they were familiar with Latin because it was the language of the schoolmen and of the older branches of the royal administration.

THE VARIETY OF LANGUAGES

English, French and Latin performed distinct social and intellectual functions in twelfth- and thirteenth-century England.[16] No one language could serve all the diverse purposes required because their struggle for dominance was still undecided. English appeared to have given way to Latin as the standard written language of government in the century after the Norman Conquest.

[13] Giraldus I, p. 91. M. Richter, *Sprache und Gesselschaft im Mittelalter* (1979), p.79.
[14] *Walter of Henley*, pp. 147–8.
[15] *ClR* 1253–4, p. 42.
[16] In general see P & M I, pp. 80–7; R. M. Wilson, 'English and French in England', *History* XXVIII (1943), pp. 37–60; E. Salter, *English and International* (1988), part I, pp. 1–100; N. Morgan, *The Lambeth Apocalypse: A Critical Study* (1990), pp. 91–7.

But just as the renewed vigour of Latin was sweeping all before it in the latter half of the twelfth century, the time of John of Salisbury and Richard Fitz Neal, French began to flourish as a literary language. A century later, in Edward I's reign, it looked as if French might replace Latin as the commonest written language in England. Yet throughout the whole period from 1066 to 1307 English had remained the commonest spoken language, and this is probably the reason why it emerged in the fourteenth century, transformed and fortified, to take its place as the principal language of literature and ultimately of record.

In addition to English, French, and Latin, writings survive in Hebrew. The first Hebrew writings extant in England are notes on moneylenders' bonds. The earliest of such bonds were written in Latin with the Hebrew notes appended to them in the form of endorsements or additions on the face of the document. Thus one of the earliest Jewish bonds extant is a Latin letter patent of Aaron of Lincoln, stating that the men of Barton have paid £10 10s. at Michaelmas in 1182. To this letter is appended a note of receipt in Hebrew by Aaron's agents, which can be translated as follows:

> This my signature attests that I have received £10 10*d*. [*recte* 10*s*.] of the Barton tax at Eckel 143. And I the undersigned have received one half on behalf of Dom R. Isaac, son of Dom R. Joseph. And what I have received I have written and signed: Berechia son of R. Eliahu.[17]

The date 'Eckel 143' refers to Michaelmas (transliterated into Hebrew as 'Eckel') in the year of the foundation of the world 4800 + 143, which accords with 1182 AD.[18] Jews usually authenticated such documents with their signatures, although seals were also sometimes used. A Hebrew note of acquittance of a debt by Jacob son of Aaron, which is appended to a Latin charter dating from 1238–9, is written on the parchment tag bearing his seal.[19]

About half a dozen Hebrew writings appended to Latin documents survive from the 1180s, including two receipts and some miscellaneous notes recording the contents of bonds or the names of Jews who acquired interests in the property they concerned.[20] The latter notes were presumably made so that a Jew could readily see in his own language which bond he required when it was deposited in a chest. In the thirteenth century, up to the expulsion of the Jews in 1290, the number of such bilingual Latin–Hebrew documents increases. Moreover, from the 1260s similar documents are drawn up in French and Hebrew because French was by then competing with Latin as the language of

---

[17] *Starrs and Jewish Charters Preserved in the BM* ed. I. Abrahams et al. (1930) I, p. 117. This is not the earliest moneylender's bond extant, as those of the Fleming, William Cade, date from the 1160s.

[18] Ibid., pp. xxii–xxiii.

[19] Ibid., plate iii facing p. 81.

[20] Ibid., p. 119; *Shetaroth: Hebrew Deeds of English Jews before 1290* ed. M. D. Davis, Publications of the Anglo-Jewish Historical Exhibition II (1888), p. 289; Richardson, *Jewry*, p. 256; *Oxford Facs*, no. 85; *Northants. Facs*, p. 120, plate xlv.

title-deeds.[21] In addition to writings on parchment, Hebrew was also used on the wooden tallies which were kept by the Exchequer and other accountants.[22]

When Jews made written agreements with each other, as distinct from making them with Christians, they used Hebrew throughout instead of mixing Hebrew with Latin or French. The earliest English documents entirely in Hebrew survive from the 1230s.[23] Among the most evocative of such documents are: the arrangements made by three sons for the well-being of their mother and sister at Norwich in 1251; correspondence to and from Rabbi David, bailiff of the Nottingham Jews, in the same period; a betrothal contract made at Lincoln in 1271.[24] In the Lincoln contract part of the gift made by the future bride to the groom is a precious Massoretic Bible. It was evidently normal for both male and female English Jews to be literate in Hebrew. The men, and a notable number of women, who had business dealings with Christians had to understand Latin, French, and English as well. Although the total number of Jews was small and they were mainly concentrated in towns, all large property-owners, particularly the lay barons and great monasteries, must have seen, even if they did not understand, Hebrew writings when they borrowed money. Some indebted magnates of the thirteenth century would probably have come across more writing in Hebrew than in English.

This discussion of Hebrew has been confined to legal documents because they are extant in originals and can be precisely dated. It would be a false inference, however, to conclude that medieval English Jews were concerned only with moneylending or that they used Hebrew primarily for that purpose. There was a renaissance of Hebrew in the twelfth century just as there was a renaissance of Latin. C. Roth argued that prominent Jewish religious authors worked in England and that original studies of Hebrew grammar and punctuation were written by Londoners around 1200.[25] If these latter writings can be identified with Jews named in English royal records, it is not too fanciful to surmise that such work was stimulated by the proliferation of documents and the precise regulations imposed on Jewish scribes by Hubert Walter in 1194. More Jews were influenced by Christian works than vice versa because many of them spoke French or English and read Latin, whereas only a handful of Christian biblical scholars knew Hebrew, though Englishmen like Herbert of Bosham and Roger Bacon were prominent among them.[26]

This excursus on the use of Hebrew emphasizes how no one language could serve all purposes because different languages were associated with particular persons and functions. It is an anachronism to attempt to identify one language as the general language of the population. Nor is the problem

[21] *Starrs and Jewish Charters*, pp. 12–13, 124–5.

[22] H. Jenkinson, 'Exchequer Tallies', *Archaeologia* LXII (1911), p. 378, plate li.

[23] *Shetaroth*, pp. 222–5 (Nottingham AD 1233), pp. 312–15 (Canterbury AD 1230).

[24] Ibid., pp. 43–6 (Norwich), pp. 275–7 (Nottingham), pp. 298–302 (Lincoln)

[25] *A History of the Jews in England* (3rd edn, 1964), pp. 126–7. M. Beit-Arié, *The Only Dated Medieval Hebrew MS Written in England* (1985), pp. 1–9, is doubtful about Hebrew works being written in England.

[26] Smalley, *The Bible*, pp. 186ff, 329ff.

resolved by assuming instead that there was complete bilingualism in English and French.[27] The statements made particularly by poets writing in French that their work is expressed in that language so that everyone, 'great and small' (*li grant e li mendre*), can understand should not be taken at their face value.[28] They do not mean that all classes knew French; rather, they are typical of the explanations which authors of French works had to make to justify not writing in Latin. Conversely the remark of Hue de Rotelande in *c.*1180 (in his prologue to the romance, *Ipomedon*) that, 'if the Latin is not translated, there will scarcely be anyone who understands it', is not sufficient evidence that a knowledge of Latin was rare.[29] It was a polite convention for romancers like Hue to claim that their works were based on ancient Latin books because fiction as such was unacceptable. Such explanations by authors throw little light on how widely either French or Latin was known, but they do show that the status of French as a literary language was not yet firmly established.

The relative dignity and status of the three principal languages (Latin, French, and English) was a favourite subject of debate among writers at the time and has remained so with modern scholars.[30] Latin was argued to carry greater weight than its rivals. Thus Peter of Blois apologized for a sermon, which lacked the 'dignity of eloquence', because it had been translated from a 'vulgar' tongue which preferred brevity.[31] The 'vulgar' tongue referred to here was probably Peter's native French, though it may have been English, as he admits elsewhere that he had difficulty understanding English.[32] Similarly in the thirteenth century the translator of a Latin sermon on Antichrist into French rhyming couplets assured his hearers that it was 'a very great thing in Latin', although it seemed so slight in French.[33]

The best-known variation on this theme of rival languages is Walter Map's remark in one of his prologues that, instead of Latin epics like the *Aeneid* which celebrated the heroes of antiquity, 'only the trifling of mummers in vulgar rhymes' celebrates for his contemporaries the achievements of the Charlemagnes and Pepins.[34] Walter wrote in the last two decades of the twelfth century when the *Chanson de Roland* and other works concerning the 'Matter of France' were well known. He purports to ignore the writers of his own day, particularly the non-Latin ones, as he asks the reader: 'Is there anyone who would dare to put upon a page what is happening nowadays, or to write down

---

[27] I. Short, 'On Bilingualism in Anglo-Norman England', *Romance Philology* xxxiii (1980), pp. 467–79, brings together objections to this assumption.

[28] Rothwell, 'The Role of French', *BJRL* (1976), p. 453 (citing Denis Piramus, line 3270).

[29] Ibid., p. 450 (citing *Ipomedon*, lines 28–9).

[30] R. Wright ed., *Latin and the Romance Languages in the Early Middle Ages* (1990); W. Rothwell, 'Language and Government in Medieval England', *Zeitschrift für Französische Sprache und Literatur* xciii (1983), pp. 258–70; J. Frankis, 'The Social Context of Vernacular [English] Writing', in P. R. Coss and S. D. Lloyd eds, *Thirteenth-Century England* i (1986), pp. 175–84.

[31] *Patrologiae* ccvii (1855), col 751; Richter, *Sprache und Gesellschaft*, p. 63, n. 33.

[32] Ibid., p. 67, n. 44.

[33] Legge, *Anglo-Norman*, p. 235.

[34] 'nobis divinam Karolurum et Pepinorum nobilitatem vulgaribus ritmis sola mimorum concelebrat nugacitas'. Walter Map, Bk. v, ch. 1, p. 404.

even our names? Certainly if any novel orthography [*aliquis novus karacter*] were to put upon record "Henry" or "Walter", or even your own name, you would deride it and laugh at it.'[35] By calling vernacular authors 'mummers', implying that they are performers in vulgar dumbshows, and by discounting the success of innovation in writing in vernacular scripts, Walter suppresses the voice of vernacular literature by ignoring its existence.

Yet Walter himself may have been teasing his Latin readers, or have been unconscious of his own inconsistencies. His question, 'Is there anyone who would dare to put upon a page what is happening nowadays?' can be readily answered by citing contemporary works in French. Thus at the time Walter was writing, Jordan Fantosme composed his verse chronicle of the war in 1173–4 between England and Scotland.[36] Like Walter's learned readers, Jordan was a graduate of Paris, a bishop's clerk and a master in the schools (at Winchester), yet he chose to write in French, not Latin. Likewise in Walter's time Wace wrote (in French) the *Roman de Brut*, a history of England based on Geoffrey of Monmouth, and the *Roman de Rou*, a history of Normandy which was commissioned by Henry II.[37] Furthermore, as Walter probably knew well, other educated clerics were writing in English. In the 1190s or later Lawman, the Worcestershire priest, procured books in English, French, and Latin in order to write his English version of the *Brut* story.[38] The outstanding example of literary composition in English from this period is the debate poem between *The Owl and the Nightingale*, but its exact date and provenance are hard to establish. It may have been composed by Master Nicholas of Guildford as early as Henry II's reign, though it could date from a century later and be the work of nuns.[39]

In asking who would dare to write non-Latin literature, Walter Map was contributing to the debate on the relative status of languages in a character-istically facetious and ambivalent way. Gerald of Wales reports that Walter told him that *dicta* in the vernacular were more profitable than *scripta* in Latin because knowledge of Latin was declining.[40] Walter was therefore well aware that the Latinists had to make a spirited attack, if they were to compete with the trifling 'mummers' who were busy composing in 'vulgar rhymes' the greatest literature of the Middle Ages. His own *De Nugis Curialium* (*Courtiers' Trifles*) was a flashy attempt to make modern Latin literature attractive.[41]

[35] Walter Map, pp. 404–6.

[36] *Jordan Fantosme's Chronicle* ed. R. C. Johnston (1981).

[37] Gransden, *Historical Writing*, pp. 202, 219.

[38] See ch. 4. n. 45 above. Lawman's *Brut* is discussed by L. Johnson, in, *Leeds Studies in English* xxii (1991), pp. 139–65 and by R. Allen in her translation (1992).

[39] J. Coleman, '*The Owl and the Nightingale* and Papal Theories of Marriage', *Journal of Ecclesiastical History* xxxviii (1987), pp. 517–68; A. Barratt, 'Flying in the Face of Tradition: A New View of *The Owl and the Nightingale*', *University of Toronto Quarterly* lvi (1987), pp. 471–85.

[40] Giraldus v, pp. 410–11. See also ch. 8, nn. 55–6 below.

[41] K. Bate in *Cahiers de civilisation médiévale* xxxiv (1991), pp. 15–21, questions whether *De Nugis Curialium* is the work of a single author.

Despite Walter, however, the classicists had already been as summarily dismissed by the greatest composer in 'vulgar rhymes', Chrétien de Troyes:

Car de Grezois ne de Romains
Ne dit an mes ne plus ne mains,
D'ax est la parole remese
Et estainte le vive brese.[42]

[For of the Greeks and Romans no one now says either much or little; there is no more word of them, and their glowing embers are extinguished.]

Another of Walter's contemporaries, Jocelin of Brakelond, likewise enjoyed the languages debate and treated it humorously in his account of the election of Herbert as prior of Bury St Edmunds in 1200.[43] Herbert objected that he was insufficiently learned in Latin to preach a sermon in the monastic chapter. In reply, 'to the prejudice of the literate' (that is, the Latinists), Abbot Samson condemned rhetorical ornament and told Herbert that he could preach 'in French or better still in English'. The 'illiterate' monks were delighted and teased their 'literate' brethren with such puns as 'they have declined *musa, muse* so often that they are all bemused.' Samson himself was exceptional in steering a middle course between learning and action and in rejecting the conventional hierarchy of languages, which placed Latin at the top, French in the middle, and English at the bottom. For him their different merits were not mutually exclusive. According to Jocelin, Samson was a graduate of Paris and 'was eloquent in French and Latin'. In addition, he knew 'how to read literature written in English most elegantly (*elegantissime*) and he used to preach in English to the people, but in the speech of Norfolk where he was born and bred.'[44]

In this passage Jocelin emphasizes the dual status of English: there is spoken popular English (with its diverse dialects) in which Samson preaches to the people, and there is written English in which he reads *elegantissime*. Jocelin thus takes it for granted that English is a language of educated men in which elegance of expression is appreciated. The literature (*scriptura*) which Samson read so elegantly was probably Anglo-Saxon; Aelfric's *Passion of St Edmund*, for example, would have been an appropriate text for an abbot of Bury to read aloud.[45] Samson may also perhaps have enjoyed twelfth-century homiletic literature in English, or even the witty legalistic debate of *The Owl and the Nightingale* (though its southern diction might have struck him as novel), as he was a fine debater in the county court.[46] Samson's trilingual mastery of Latin, French, and English was probably shared by many of the

[42] *Cligés*, lines 39–42, ed. A. Micha (Paris, 1957). Chrétien's *Arthurian Romances* are translated by D. D. R. Owen (1987).
[43] Jocelin, pp. 128–30.
[44] Ibid., p. 40. Richter, *Sprache und Gesellschaft*, p. 63.
[45] *Lives of Three English Saints* ed. G. I. Needham (1966).
[46] Jocelin, p. 34.

energetic men who ran England in 1200, but it would not have been typical of the population as a whole. When half a century later Roger Bacon remarks that 'we speak English, French and Latin', he means by 'we' his educated readers and not the masses.[47] Nor probably were the great majority bilingual either, as English was their mother tongue.

SPOKEN AND WRITTEN LANGUAGE

The way languages were used in medieval England can be difficult to understand, because in modern received English the hiatus or disjuncture between the spoken and the written word is not usually obvious. Academic lectures are read from texts verbatim, or conversely talks are presented in writing in an informal style recalling the register in which they are spoken. Although medieval vernacular literary texts often reflect oral diction, in business documents by contrast not only the style and register but even the language itself might change in the process of transforming the spoken into the written word. A statement made in court in English or French, for example, might be written down in Latin, or conversely a Latin charter might be read out in English or French. Men like Abbot Samson evidently interchanged languages effortlessly, using whichever one was appropriate for the occasion. The fact that a statement is recorded in a certain language does not mean that it was originally made in that language. Latin had served traditionally as the common medium of literacy in a multilingual and predominantly oral society. A royal message to a sheriff in the thirteenth century might have been spoken by the king in French, written out in Latin, and then read to the recipient in English. Although this conjecture cannot be conclusively proved, because only the language of record survives, some explicit evidence of such inter-changeability of languages begins to appear by the end of the thirteenth century.

A good example is the Latin notarial instrument recording the act of homage of John Balliol as king of Scots to Edward I in 1292.[48] John uttered the words of homage 'with his own mouth in the French language', but to give them full legal force they were recorded by Edward's notary, John of Caen, 'literally' (*litteraliter*). This did not mean that Balliol's words were transcribed verbatim, but that they were translated into Latin for the record. According to the notarial instrument Balliol says: 'Devenio vester homo ligeus' (I become your liegeman). By contrast, in the less solemn letters patent recording the similar acts of homage of the Robert Bruces and others in 1296, the same words are written down in French: 'Jeo devenk voster home lige.'[49] The oath of homage actually spoken on the two occasions would not have differed, but the notarial instrument required the words of the king of Scots to be written down in Latin, whereas the letters patent of the earls and barons were expressed slightly less formally in French. The language of record depended

---

[47] *Rogeri Bacon Opera* ed. J. S. Brewer, RS xv (1859), p. 433.
[48] *Anglo-Scottish Relations*, p. 63.
[49] Ibid., p. 69.

on the status of the persons concerned and the nature of the document and not on the language actually spoken on the occasion.

Another example, illustrating interchangeability between French and English instead of French and Latin, is provided by the procedure for recording the *veredicta* of juries in the Kent justices' visitation of 1313–14. The jurors' answers or 'true sayings' (*veredicta*), which were presented to the court in reply to the justices' questions, were written down in a roll and, when the justices arrived, the chief clerk of the crown 'began to read the first presentments as they were entered on the roll in French'.[50] The jurors were then required to present the same answers orally at the bar of the court in English. If there were any deviation between the French and English versions, the jurors were liable to imprisonment. Latin was involved in this change of language as well as French and English, since early *veredicta* (the first dating from Kent in 1279) are in Latin and the first account of the procedure (dating from *c*.1240) precisely describes how they are to be written in Latin.[51]

As Latin was involved, the following changes of language took place, if the jurors' procedure is examined in detail. First of all, the jurors were presented with the justices' questions (the 'articles of eyre' technically) in writing in either Latin or French. They replied orally, probably in English, although their answers were written down as *veredicta* by an enrolling clerk in Latin. When the justices arrived in court, the chief clerk read out the enrolled presentments or *veredicta* in French, mentally translating them from Latin as he went along. On behalf of the jurors, their foreman or spokesman then presented the same answers at the bar in English. Once the presentments, in both their French and English oral versions, were accepted by the court, they were recorded in the justices' plea rolls in Latin. Thus, between the justices' written questions being presented initially to the jurors and the final record of the plea roll, the language in use changed at least five times, although it begins and ends with writings in Latin.

This commonplace procedure has been analysed in detail because its implications are far-reaching. It is obvious that the foreman of the jurors, if not his fellows, would need to be able to read French and preferably also Latin. If the oral English statement, which he presented at the bar, deviated in any detail from the written statement, the jurors faced imprisonment. The foreman may also have had this statement at the bar written out in English to ensure that there were no deviations, although it is as probable that he memorized it verbatim. The linguistic ability he required was of a high standard. To find such a man to head every jury must sometimes have been difficult. Yet that was probably not an insuperable problem, as every county had its group of 'discreet and lawful knights', like Walter of Bibbesworth, who were masters of languages and were accustomed to this sort of business.

Although by 1300 lawyers' manuals were usually written in French, it does not follow that French was the spoken language of the court, any more than

[50] *The Eyre of Kent* ed. F. W. Maitland et al., SS xxiv(1909), pp. 20–1.

[51] Early *veredicta* are listed by R. E. Latham and C. A. F. Meekings in *Collectanea* ed. N. J. Williams et al. WiltsRS xii (1956), p. 52, n. 1. Procedure in *c*.1240 is described in *SCPWW*, p. cciii. Cf. Bracton, fo. 116, vol. ii, p. 329.

Bracton's use of Latin conversation in his *De Legibus* in the 1250s implies that Latin was being spoken in the courts then.[52] There was probably no marked change in the spoken language of the courts during the thirteenth century. What did change was the language of record. From the middle of the thirteenth century, in both England and France, French became acceptable as a forensic language. Thus the earliest petitions to St Louis in 1247 are written in Latin, whereas those of two decades later are in French.[53] Legal records in England were affected by the same linguistic development. Thus the Provisions of Oxford of 1258, which inaugurated the baronial revolution, are recorded in a novel mixture of Latin and French.[54] The explanation is not that there had been a sudden influx of French-speaking laywers who displaced Latin speakers in the 1250s, nor had the barons learned to write French overnight. What had happened was that French had at last achieved literate status for legal purposes.

For the next 100 years writs, charters, petitions, memoranda, and lawyers' textbooks were increasingly written in French, though Latin also continued. The fact that more French was being written down in England from the middle of the thirteenth century does not mean that more was being spoken. The relative number of documents extant in Latin, French, and English is an indicator of the uses of literacy, but it bears no relation to the number of words spoken in each language at the time. If documents were the measure of speech, we would be obliged to conclude that French was not spoken at all in England in the reigns of William the Conqueror and William Rufus, whereas it had become very common two centuries later in Edward I's reign, which is absurd.

It might be objected that, as lawyers' manuals in French report court proceedings in the form of dialogues, it must be accepted that their authors presented them in the language in which they took place. At first sight such dialogues look convincing. For example, in a manual from the 1270s Hugh is accused by John of stealing a horse:

'Hue', fet la justice, 'avez entendu ce ke Johan ad vers vous conte?'
['Hugh', says the judge, 'have you heard what John recounts against you?']
'Sire, oyl.'
['Yes, sir.']
'Ore li respones solom ce ke vous quidez ke bon seit.'
['Then answer him as you think good.']
'Sire, pur Deu, je su un simples homs et nynt ay geres use playe de terre . . .'

---

[52] Woodbine, 'The Language of English Law', p. 429, n. 2. J. H. Baker, *Manual of Law French* (2nd edn, 1990), pp. 2–3.
[53] A. Harding, 'Plaints and Bills in the History of English Law', *Legal History Studies 1972* ed. D. Jenkins (1975), pp. 74–5.
[54] *Baronial Docs*, pp. 96–112.

['Sir, God knows, I am a simple man and have scarcely ever made a plea (by the law) of the land . . .'][55]

At this point the reader may begin to doubt. Hugh is a 'simple man', yet he speaks and understands French. Either we accept the unlikely proposition that poor villagers knew French, or we choose the simpler alternative that the writer of this treatise retails dialogue in French just as a monastic chronicler like Matthew Paris retails it in Latin. It is not even evident that the judge is really speaking French either. His aim is to trap Hugh into confessing his guilt by cross-examining him, which would probably be most effectively done in Hugh's own language. Even in Henry III's reign the judges were native Englishmen and there is sufficient evidence to show that English was their mother tongue.[56] Like most texts, this manual is addressed to its readers. Its language, the French used for study by English students, is attuned to them and not to the real protagonists in the court.

This example does not mean that French was never really spoken in English courts, but it emphasizes that there is the same hiatus or disjuncture between spoken and written language in French records as there is in Latin ones. The formal pleadings were certainly made in French in Edward I's reign, since one lawyer's manual describes them as being 'uttered by narrators in Romance words and not in Latin ones'.[57] Nevertheless the language of the formal pleadings was not necessarily that of cross-examinations and forensic dialogue. The use of French and English in ecclesiastical courts is mentioned by William of Drogheda, and in the Canterbury court in 1271, where Latin was the language of record, but French and English were used orally.[58] It is probable that the king's court did likewise. Although the Year Books (the law reports which begin in Edward I's reign) record all conversations in the court in French, it cannot be proved that French was the language actually being spoken. In some instances, as when a 'simple man' is being cross-examined, commonsense militates against it. Moreover, the earliest of all such actual reports of a cross-examination by a judge (from the London justices' visitation of 1244), as distinct from a hypothetical dialogue like that with Hugh, is reported in Latin because that was the appropriate language of record in the 1240s.[59]

From such an instance scholars do not immediately jump to the conclusion that Latin was actually being spoken in the court, because Latin can readily be recognized by its standardized form as a language of script rather than of speech. Many early French manuscripts, on the other hand, reveal such a diversity of orthography and syntax that they give a superficial impression of

---

[55] *Placita Corone* ed. J. M. Kaye, SS supplementary series IV (1966), pp. 16–17. The names of Hugh and John are muddled up in this text. For a comparable dialogue from *Court Baron* see ch. 8, n. 113 below.

[56] Woodbine, 'The Language of English Law', p. 431.

[57] See ch. 8, n. 98 below.

[58] R & S, p. 278, n. 2; R. H. Helmholz, *Marriage Litigation in England* (1974), p. 119, n. 18.

[59] See ch. 3, n. 77 above.

having been written by naive semi-literates, who simply aimed to reproduce the spoken word as faithfully as possible. Because dialect has been used in novels since the nineteenth century to indicate *ipsissima verba*, we tend to assume that medieval writers used it likewise. In fact medieval writing in dialect arose primarily from the lack of a generally accepted standard in a vernacular, rather than from a meticulous attempt to record speech as such.

In their search for a standard, some twelfth-century vernacular writers devised consistent and individual systems of orthography from their own dialects, whereas other works reveal a mixture of regional speech patterns. Examples of writings in consistent dialects are the *Ormulum*, which was probably composed and penned by its author in his own diction, and the *Ancrene Wisse*, which uses standard spellings even though it was penned by a number of different scribes.[60] A good example of a work revealing diverse regional speech patterns, on the other hand, is the Anglo-Norman *Romance of Horn* by Master Thomas. Its editor argues that its diversity of language is a product of Thomas's diverse personal experience, hypothetically as a child of immigrants from the Loire valley who was educated in England and at the schools of Poiters.[61] But in this case it should not be assumed that a composer of romances, like Thomas, had either the intention or the ability to reproduce in script every nuance of his own speech, as Orm seems to have aimed to do in his eccentric *Ormulum*.

A professional medieval author, which is what Thomas appears to be, did not necessarily compose in his mother tongue, but in whichever language was appropriate to his theme and his audience. Thomas is just as likely to have been a native English speaker as a French one, as the story of *Horn* is English or Scandinavian in origin. Judging from the prefix 'Master', he was also a Latinist and a schoolman like his contemporary Nicholas of Guildford, the putative author of *The Owl and the Nightingale*, who composed in English. Numerous examples can be cited from the thirteenth century of clerics, like Matthew Paris and Robert Grosseteste, who composed in both Latin and French, and there is at least one instance, the Franciscan Thomas of Hales, of a trilingual author who wrote in Latin, French, and English.[62]

Thomas begins the *Romance of Horn* by addressing his audience: 'Seignurs, oi avez le vers del parchemin' (Lords, you have heard the lines of parchment).[63] When composing his *vers del parchemin*, Thomas would aim to write in a way which was generally acceptable to the *seignurs* of his audience, rather than to reproduce the idiosyncrasies of his own diction. A sufficient explanation of the composite character of the language of the *Romance of Horn* is that the mixture of western, south-western and Anglo-Norman French combined some of the speech traits of Thomas with those of the original scribe (to whom he probably dictated the work) and his potential audience. Among the *seignurs* of Angevin England the amalgam served up by Thomas was probably accept-

---

[60] For *Ormulum* see ch. 4, n. 74 above. For *Ancrene Wisse* see *Passiun of St Juliene* ed. S. R. T. O. d'Ardenne, Early English Text S. CCXLVIII (1961), p. xxix.

[61] Ed. M. K. Pope, Anglo-Norman S. XII-XIII (1964), II, p. 122.

[62] Legge, *Anglo-Norman*, pp. 227–8. Cf. Wilson, 'English and French in England', p. 59.

[63] *The Romance of Horn* IX-X (1955), I, p. 1.

able as the best French they knew. They expected their jongleurs and entertainers to have the gift of tongues. 'Scribal practice, of course, does not so much directly reflect any linguistic milieu as represent a compromise between various constraints.'[64] The relationship between spoken and written language is complex in any linguistic community; in post-Conquest England it was peculiarly so, because of the variety of languages and the experimental uses of literacy.

CHRONOLOGICAL DEVELOPMENT

At the time of the Norman Conquest the languages in use in England, for written purposes at least, are relatively easy to identify. They were Latin and Anglo-Saxon or Old English. Both were literary languages with centuries of development behind them. Although the form of Old English used in the Anglo-Saxon Chronicle and royal writs had derived from West Saxon, it was not a spoken dialect but a standard literary language which extended as far as the authority of the English kings.[65] (Henceforward in this discussion this standard form of Old English will be called 'Anglo-Saxon' to distinguish it from other forms.) Like Latin on the continent of Europe, Anglo-Saxon was closely associated with monasticism and royal power. Any standardized language needs a powerful authority, whether political or cultural, behind it in order to maintain uniformity. The existence of a standard written Old English language does not imply that spoken Old English was equally uniform. The predecessors of Middle English regional dialects already existed in 1066, although they had rarely yet been committed to writing. In some parts of England written Anglo-Saxon, which was as much a royal and clerical language as Latin was, may have appeared almost as foreign and archaic to local people. Anglo-Saxon cannot be described as the popular vernacular in 1066 in contrast to Latin, as both were literary languages.

For a few years after 1066 Anglo-Saxon continued to be used in royal writs (assuming that they are authentic). Moreover, a bilingual notification dating from the 1070s, addressed by William the Conqueror's half-brother, Odo bishop of Bayeux and earl of Kent, to Archbishop Lanfranc and the sheriff of Kent, marks the transition from Anglo-Saxon to Latin in business documents.[66] This notification, which was probably written by a scribe of the beneficiary (Christ Church Canterbury) has the Latin text at the top and the Anglo-Saxon below it. Perhaps Odo wanted Latin used because it seemed absurd to address Lanfranc in a language which neither of them knew, while the Christ Church scribe favoured Anglo-Saxon because that was the traditional language of English writs. Although Canterbury produced other

---

[64] C. Clark, 'People and Languages in Post-Conquest Canterbury', *JMH* ii (1976), p. 24 (commenting on the trilingual *Eadwine Psalter*, see plate xiv below).
[65] D. G. Scragg, *A History of English Spelling* (1974); W. Hofstetter, 'Winchester and the Standardization of Old English Vocabulary', *Anglo-Saxon England* xvii (1988), p. 161.
[66] *Sir Christopher Hatton's Book of Seals* ed. L. C. Loyd and D. M. Stenton, Northamptonshire Record S. xv (1950), no. 431 and plate viii.

comparable bilingual charters in the twelfth century (see plate III), royal
clerks soon wrote exclusively in Latin. This change in the written language
does not imply that royal writs ceased to be proclaimed in English in the
county court, but only that a text in Anglo-Saxon was no longer provided. The
clerk of the court was presumably as capable of translating from Latin into the
appropriate regional dialect, as he had been of making Anglo-Saxon fully
comprehensible in his locality. For governmental purposes the language of
script did not need to be the same as the language of speech.

Although Anglo-Saxon was not used after the 1070s by the king's government or by the clergy as a whole, it found defenders in the monastic
antiquarian reaction which maintained English ways in the face of the
Norman conquerors. Those monastic houses like Worcester and Rochester
which produced the first cartularies were also among those which were most
concerned to preserve a knowledge of Anglo-Saxon. Anglo-Saxon texts
continued to be copied for a century after the Conquest and some works
survive only in copies made in the twelfth century.[67] As we have seen in Odo
of Bayeux's notification, the reaction at Canterbury took the form of
producing bilingual Latin and Anglo-Saxon documents, including a manuscript of the *Anglo-Saxon Chronicle* in this form and a number of royal charters
written by scribes at Christ Church (see plate III).[68]

The most remarkable product of this movement at Canterbury is the
trilingual psalter written under the direction of Eadwine in the middle of the
twelfth century. The beautifully written and illustrated text gives three Latin
variant versions of the Psalms in parallel, together with explanatory glosses in
Latin, Anglo-Saxon, and French (see plate XIV). The French gloss is the
earliest French version of the Psalms extant and is written in good prose,
whereas the Anglo-Saxon one is an archaic and corrupt text going back to the
tenth century. In the famous full-page portrait of Eadwine at the end of the
manuscript, he is described as the 'prince of writers' whose fame will not die.[69]
He had good reason to be proud of the calligraphy and layout of the Psalter,
but not of the Anglo-Saxon gloss if that also was his. The way in which the
Anglo-Saxon and French glosses are interlined could suggest that they are
slightly later additions, although it is more likely that their placing indicates
the relative status of the three languages in Eadwine's mind: Latin was the
true language of holy writ; English and French could only be subordinate
aids.[70]

The future of English as a written language was assured not by scribes like
the Canterbury monks who attempted to perpetuate Anglo-Saxon, but by less
conservative writers who gradually promoted various forms of spoken English
to the rank of a literary language. The displacement of Anglo-Saxon as the

[67] C. E. Wright, *English Vernacular Hands* (1960), pp. x-xi.
[68] Ibid., p. x. The bilingual charters of Henry I and Henry II for Canterbury (written
between 1107 and 1155) are listed by T. A. M. Bishop, *Scriptores Regis* (1961), nos 95, 97, 101,
103–5, 107, 335, 344, 390–1, 399–402, 406.
[69] Zarnecki, *Catalogue*, p. 119.
[70] G. Shepherd, 'English Versions of the Scriptures before Wyclif' in *The Cambridge History of
the Bible* ed. G. W. H. Lampe (1969) II, p. 370.

language of government caused written English to diversify into regional dialects and simplify its noun endings, much as the collapse of Roman power had accelerated the breakaway of the Romance languages from Latin. The diversification of written English can be precisely traced and dated in one instance in the Peterborough abbey continuation of the *Anglo-Saxon Chronicle*.[71] Up to and including the year 1121 this manuscript is written in Anglo-Saxon. The annal for 1122 is written by the same scribe; but, because he no longer has an exemplar to copy from, his writing begins to show east Midlands forms. Thirty years later another scribe wrote up the annals for the years 1132–54, using spelling and script which are even further removed from the standard Anglo-Saxon of the annals before 1122. As a postscript to this development, the Peterborough manuscript has on its concluding folios a crude rhyming chronicle in French which is written around the twelfth-century text in the form of a gloss. This seems to have been done in the reign of Edward I, presumably by a monk who either could not understand the English of the original or who thought the manuscript too old-fashioned to be useful for anything except spare parchment. The Peterborough manuscript illustrates the difficulties inherent in using English as a written language in preference to Latin. If Anglo-Saxon were perpetuated, the text became archaic, yet colloquial forms with their diverse usages might be just as incomprehensible to subsequent generations.

The profound changes in how English was written down which occurred in the twelfth century do not imply that spoken English changed as dramatically. The real change was that colloquial English now affected the written language, because the old standard was no longer being maintained by a public authority. Nor does the relative reduction in the amount of English used for literary purposes imply in any way that it was ceasing to be the ordinary language of oral discourse. There is no explicit evidence that the Norman Conquest caused French to become an alternative to English as the mother tongue of the mass of the people. Numerous words of French origin ultimately entered the English language and French personal and place names became relatively common, but these changes originated from French being the language of the rulers rather than of the people. French remained the language of the influential group immediately around the king for more than two centuries, as each 'new French queen brings with her a new swarm of Frenchmen'.[72] Nor were these later immigrants often Normans; in the century after the accession of Henry II in 1154 they tended to come from the west and south: they were Angevins, Limousins, Poitevins, Provençals and so on. It has never been convincingly shown that 'Anglo-French', which has been called 'Anglo-Norman' by twentieth-century scholars for convenience, was decisively shaped by the dialect of Normandy. 'Anglo-Norman' was not a vernacular, in a dictionary's sense of being the language or dialect of the country, because 'Anglo-Normandy' never existed as one homogeneous

---

[71] *The Peterborough Chronicle 1070–1154* ed. C. Clark (2nd edn. 1970); facsimile ed. D. Whitelock, *Early English MSS in Facsimile* iv (Copenhagen, 1954); R. N. Bailey, 'The Development of English' in *The Medieval World* ed. D. Daiches and A. Thorlby (1973), pp. 148–9.

[72] P & M i, p. 83.

country and it ceased altogether with King John's loss of Normandy in 1204. Yet French only became a common written language in England for business purposes fifty years or so later.

At all social levels except that of the king's court native French speakers seem to have been rapidly and repeatedly assimilated into the local population. The only exception to this rule are the Jews, who remained separate because of their different religion and scriptural language and not because of their French origins. The remark of Richard Fitz Neal, that English and Normans were so intermarried by his time (*c.*1179) that they were indistinguishable, has often and rightly been cited.[73] Just as significant in the testimony of Orderic Vitalis a century earlier.[74] He was born near Shrewsbury in 1075, the eldest son of a priest from Orléans and of an English mother. Although his father was one of the counsellors of the Norman magnate, Roger II of Montgomery, Orderic learned no French from his family but only his mother tongue. Nor apparently had he ever heard French spoken in England, as he remarks that when he was sent to Normandy to be a monk at the age of 10, he felt an exile, like Joseph in Egypt, because he heard a language which he could not understand. Yet his father had been concerned about Orderic's education, as he was put into the charge of a priest, Siward, who started to teach him the ABC and Latin at the age of five. The conclusion to draw is that in Orderic's time a basic education did not include French, as it would do in Walter of Bibbesworth's time two centuries later, because French had not yet acquired sufficient prestige with its native speakers. For the Norman conquerors, Latin not French was the indispensable language of lordship and management. It was not primarily the Norman Conquest but the advance of French as an international literary and cultural language, particularly in the thirteenth century, which caused its increasing use as a written language for English records.

French could never compete with English as the mother tongue of those outside the king's court, nor at first could it compete with Latin as a written language. Latin was at its strongest at this time. When Richard Fitz Neal's pupil urged him in *c.* 1179 not to write a prolix book but to explain the workings of the Exchequer in 'common words', the ordinary language they both had in mind was Latin, not French or English; Fitz Neal describes the Latin Domesday Book similarly as being written in 'common words'.[75] Thanks to the Latin renaissance of the eleventh and twelfth centuries, which had first reached England with Archbishops Lanfranc and Anselm as an indirect consequence of the Norman Conquest, Latin became capable of serving a variety of purposes. There was the simple narrative Latin of monastic chroniclers, the ornate and antiquarian style of rhetoricians like John of Salisbury, the expressive hymns and songs of the wandering scholars, and the precise legal language of Domesday Book or Magna Carta. Twelfth-

---

[73] *Dialogus*, p. 53.
[74] Orderic's early life is discussed by M. Chibnall, Orderic II, pp. xiii–xiv; *The World of Orderic Vitalis* (1984), ch. 1.
[75] *Dialogus*, pp. 6, 63.

century Latin was the language of Abelard and Bernard, of Gratian and the Archpoet; so far from being dead, it was still creating new forms

Yet this new Latin was associated not so much with the monks and prelates who had been the transmitters of the Romano-Christian heritage, as with the secular *moderni* of the schools. The schoolmen, the 'masters' of Paris and Bologna and then of Oxford, were a novel phenomenon of the twelfth century. Latin was their primary language, whether they were lawyers, academics, or royal officials. They were responsible for ensuring that Latin could cope with the new demands made on it by the schools, city communes, religious orders, and royal lordships which took shape in the twelfth century and produced documents in unprecedented numbers. Although England was only on the periphery of this Latin renaissance, its effects were sufficient to inhibit the wide use of either English or French as a written language in the twelfth century.

Paradoxically the schoolmen and clergy, the masters of Latin, were also the pioneers of writing in vernaculars. Master Nicholas of Guildford is associated with the writing in English of *The Owl and the Nightingale*. Master Thomas names himself as author of the *Romance of Horn* in French. Jordan Fantosme names himself in his French verse chronicle and he is identified with the Master of that name. The Augustinian canon Orm pioneered Middle English verse in his *Ormulum*, as did Lawman the priest in his *Brut* story. The monk Benedict and the cleric Philip de Thaon wrote in French for Henry I's queen, Adeliza of Louvain. In the thirteenth century Matthew Paris (who was probably a product of the Paris schools) composed saints' lives in French verse for ladies, as well as his chronicles in Latin prose. There is no real contradiction in this paradox, as the basic training of the schools was in the use of language, and the techniques learned there could be applied from Latin to the more difficult task of creating styles for writing vernaculars. Often perhaps it was the most sophisticated and not the most primitive authors who experimented with vernaculars. We should not be misled by the prefatory apologies in vernacular works, or by their unusual orthography, into thinking that they were composed by the less educated.

THE WRITING DOWN OF FRENCH

A fundamental question is whether the Norman Conquest helped develop French as a written language.[76] The only form of French surviving as literature before the twelfth century is the writing in Occitan (the southern French of the Languedoc) attributed to the troubadour poet, Duke William IX of Aquitaine (1071–1127). The *Chanson de Roland* (in northern French) had

[76] In general see M. D. Legge, 'La Precocité de la littérature anglo-normande', *Cahiers de civilisation médiévale* VIII (1965), pp. 327–49, and I. Short, 'Patrons and Polyglots: French Literature in Twelfth-Century England', *Anglo-Norman Studies* XIV: *Proceedings of the Battle Conference 1991* ed. M. Chibnall. See also p. 18, n. 47 above.

certainly been composed by this date, as some form of it was sung at the battle
of Hastings in 1066 to urge the Norman knights to follow Roland's example in
fighting against desperate odds in a foreign land. William of Malmesbury
describes it in this context by name as the 'song of Roland' (*cantilena
Rollandi*).[77] As a consequence of their victory, the Normans came into contact
with the only culture in Roman Christendom which possessed heroic vernacular verse in writing, sustained over the centuries from *Beowulf* to *The Battle of
Maldon*. This confrontation with Anglo-Saxon literature may have inspired the
Norman conquerors to have the *Chanson de Roland* written down, in order to
commemorate their victory at Hastings and show that the 'French' (as *The
Anglo-Saxon Chronicle* called the Normans) had something as good in their
language. This is no more than a conjecture, but it has the merit of explaining
why the earliest manuscript (dating from the twelfth century) of the *Chanson de
Roland* is preserved in England and probably originated there.[78]

Exceptionally early literature in French is associated with the court of
Henry I in England and particularly with his queen consorts, Edith or
Matilda (who died in 1118), and Adeliza of Louvain (whom he married in
1121). At Edith's 'command', possibly as early as 1106 (and again at
Adeliza's commission according to reliable manuscripts), the monk Benedict
rendered a Latin text of the *Voyage of St Brendan* into French rhyming couplets.
Benedict's identity is obscure and his work has been considered uninspired,
though it proved popular. Nevertheless it inaugurates three characteristic
features of medieval French romantic literature: it is commissioned by a great
lady, presumably for reading aloud at her court; its subject is a quest or
journey in which the hero is tested by a series of adventures; its inspiration
and location are Celtic, like the Arthurian and Grail romances which follow
on in the twelfth century. Benedict describes his task as the process of
'putting' the story of St Brendan down 'in letter and in romance' (*en letre mis e
en romanz*).[79] Benedict cannot simply say 'I am writing this in French' because
he does not think of the language as 'French', and 'writing' essentially meant
putting something down in Latin. So he says instead that he is putting his text
into the letters (*en letre*) of the Latin alphabet, even though the words are *en
romanz*.

The use of the term 'romance' makes clear how Benedict and his contemporaries distinguished between the written language of Latin and its various
spoken forms, which were thought to be 'Roman' or at least 'Romanic'. Since
there was no sense of disjuncture from ancient Rome until the Italian
Renaissance, twelfth-century users of Latinate languages may well have
believed that they spoke the language of the Romans, just as they acknowledged the German emperor to be king of the Romans. Latin was a uniform
prescribed language, articulated by its grammar and learned through

---

[77] *Gesta Regum* ii, p. 302; C. Morton and H. Muntz eds, *The Carmen de Hastingae Proelio* (1972),
pp. 82–3.
[78] Coloured facsimile page in P. Wolff, *Western Languages A.D. 100–1500* (1971), p. 153. This
MS is discussed from a different but equally radical viewpoint by H. E. Keller, *Autour de
Roland* (1989). See also M. B. Parkes, *Scribes, Scripts and Readers* (1991), pp. 86–9.
[79] *The Anglo-Norman Voyage of St Brendan* ed. I. Short and B. Merrilees (1979), line 11.

schooling, whereas 'Roman' or 'romance' diction had as many and varying forms as living speech. To write anything down in its colloquial 'Roman/ romance' form was therefore novel and difficult. Many authors before the twelfth century must also have thought it unnecessary, since Latin sufficed for writing. The writing down of French 'romance' literature was so successful and pervasive, however, that the description 'romance' was applied to the content of this literature, as much as to the language in which it was expressed. Once this began to happen in the twelfth century, a new word had to be found to distinguish the language from the content. The word that ultimately prevailed was of course 'French', but it took a century or more to find acceptance.

One of the earliest instances of the use of the word 'French', instead of 'romance', to describe the written form of the language comes from England, and this is probably not a coincidence. Because the Anglo-Saxons called their Norman conquerors the 'French', this generic term could be applied just as well to their language, which was immediately distinguishable in England from both Anglo-Saxon and Latin. In France itself, on the other hand, the difference between 'French' and other vernaculars was less clear because there were so many varieties of speech, ranging from Latinate forms in the south to Germanic ones in the north. Isolation and separation, compounded by the Norman conquest, made languages in England easier to categorize. For Henry I's queen Adeliza, Philip de Thaon reduced the Latin *Bestiary* (the standard book of beasts, mythical and real) into French rhyming couplets. He describes this process as 'extracting' the *Bestiary* 'in French': *en franceise raisun*, literally meaning 'in French reasoning' or 'discourse'.[80] Philip sees Latin likewise as a language or 'discourse' (*Latine raisun*) and not simply as the written form of speech.[81]

These inchoate and perplexing descriptions of the process of writing something down in French reveal their authors' difficulties with the shift from memory to written record. By the end of the twelfth century thousands of lines of rhyming couplets had been composed and written in French for patrons in England, from Henry I's Queen Adeliza downwards. Judged as poetry, by comparison with the *Chanson de Roland* or the works composed by Chrétien de Troyes in France, most of the early French written in England is of indifferent quality and unattractive to modern critics. In the history of record-making, however, as distinct from the history of literature, this early French writing in England is extraordinary, not least Philip de Thaon's *Bestiary*. Why did Queen Adeliza want him to write it down at all? If she wanted the *Bestiary* explained, she could readily have sent for a copy of it and got her chaplain or another cleric to translate the Latin orally while she looked at the pictures of the animals described. Did she perhaps admire Philip de Thaon's extempore French translation on such an occasion so much that she commissioned him to immortalize his achievement by writing it in verse? Is this why Philip did not write in prose, which would have given a more accurate translation? Or did

---

[80] *Le Bestiaire* ed. E. Walberg (1900), lines 2, 4.
[81] Ibid., line 2015.

Philip write in verse because there were no models for writing (as distinct from speaking) French, other than verse ones like the *Chanson de Roland?*

Did Queen Adeliza want the *Bestiary* written down in French because she could not read Latin? But in that case, she would not have been able to read the French version either. Or was she on the contrary an accomplished reader, who observed that whereas Latin and English had literatures, her native French did not and she therefore commissioned her clerks to make a start? Perhaps she wished to instruct her English courtiers (male and female, cleric and lay) in the finer points of French. Alternatively, Adeliza's French may have been poor; coming from Louvain in Flanders, her mother tongue may have been Germanic rather than French. In that case, she may have commissioned Philip and the other writers to improve her spoken French by writing rhyming couplets, which she could read aloud to perfect her pronunciation and enlarge her vocabulary. This would explain why she commissioned work which is pedestrian from the point of view of literary quality. There are no satisfactory answers to such questions as these. Nevertheless they are worth asking, as they show how much remains speculative about the beginnings of writing down vernacular languages in Europe. The hardest question to answer precisely is why a growing number of patrons and writers in the twelfth century ceased to be satisfied with Latin as the medium of writing and experimented with 'romance' and 'French' instead.

Of Philip de Thaon's writings in French rhyming couplets, the strangest to a modern eye is the *Comput*, which is probably the earliest of his works.[82] This is a poem constructed from Latin sources on how to calculate the movable feast days which governed the church's year. The poem, Philip claims, enables priests to keep ecclesiastical law. Village priests may well not have had the Latin texts to hand, such as Bede, by which to calculate dates. On the other hand, country priests in England would not have found French any easier to read than Latin. As with Philip's *Bestiary*, there is also the problem of why he wrote in rhyme, when prose would have made better sense of such a technical matter. Philip dedicates the *Comput* to his uncle, Humfrey de Thaon, who was chaplain to an identifiable person in England, Eudo the Steward of Henry I. M. D. Legge therefore suggested that the *Comput* was not intended for English country priests, but for the French-speaking clergy of the king's household. Under the direction of the steward, they organized the king's itinerary and supplies and they would indeed have needed to be experts in calculating dates and numbers.[83] This suggestion has far-reaching implications. The *Comput* may have been written as early as 1113. If written French was being used in the royal household at this early date, why could it not replace Latin (which had itself replaced Anglo-Saxon in the 1070s) as the official language of the king's administration?

That it was possible to write administrative documents in French prose in the first half of the twelfth century is demonstrated by the existence of the *Leis Willelme*.[84] This is a text of the so-called 'Laws of William the Conqueror', a

---

[82] Ed. I. Short, Anglo-Norman Text S. (1984).

[83] Legge, *Anglo-Norman*, pp. 21–2.

[84] P & M I, pp. 102–3. I. Short provides an update on the *Leis Willelme* in 'Patrons and Polyglots', *Anglo-Norman Studies* n. 72.

miscellaneous and unofficial collection of decrees which probably do stem from William the Conqueror. The French text may reflect an earlier state of these decrees than the Latin version; in others words, these decrees could have been drafted in French before being put into Latin. The earliest charter in French, dating from *c.*1140 and granting land to the Knights Hospitaller, is copied into their cartulary, presumably from an original likewise in French.[85] The earliest administrative document in French existing in its original form comes from Henry II's Inquest of Sheriffs in 1170. This is a reply to the Inquest and is written in an untidy semi-cursive script on an irregular shaped piece of parchment with no sign of a seal.[86] It is presumably a draft which was returned in mistake for the Latin fair copy. Its chance survival suggests that thousands of such informal documents once existed which were discarded when their usefulness was over.

Likewise in the 1170s Jordan Fantosme describes Henry the Young King (the eldest son of Henry II) composing a letter in French and sealing it with a ring.[87] Jordan gives the contents of this letter, which offered Northumberland and Westmorland to William the Lion of Scotland; but the text Jordan gives is not intended to be an authentic document, as he recounts it in verse as part of his narrative.[88] The earliest letter in French to be enrolled in the royal records, as distinct from being accidentally kept like the reply to the Inquest of Sheriffs, is a charter of Archbishop Stephen Langton's in 1215.[89] This letter was not given the same status as the royal letters in Latin, however, as it is written on the back of the charter roll instead of the front. It is an example not of the government experimenting with French, but of an important person being permitted to use the royal records to guarantee his private deeds. A few early copies of Magna Carta written in French are known, together with an explanatory royal letter addressed to the sheriff of Hampshire and dated 27 June in the 17th year of John's reign (i.e. 1215) at Odiham (in Hampshire).[90] This is the oldest authentically dated royal letter extant in French. Perhaps copies of Magna Carta and of this letter were sent out in French, as well as Latin, to the sheriffs of every county. These texts are not recorded in an English source; they come from the cartulary of the leper hospital at Pont-Audemer in Normandy.

All these instances of administrative documents being written down in French are best interpreted as exceptions proving the rule that French was not yet a language of record for royal government in England. There is no real

---

[85] *Cartulary* ed. M. Gervers (1982), pp. 169–70, no. 272. I owe this reference to Professor Ian Short.

[86] H. Suggett (née Richardson), 'A Twelfth-Century Anglo-Norman Charter', *BJRL* xxiv (1940), plate facing p. 168, and *BJRL* xxvii (1942), pp. 179–81. See also ch. 2, n. 70 above.

[87] 'En romanz devise un brief, d'un anel l'enseele', *Chronicle* ed. Johnston (1981), p. 18, line 245; Galbraith, 'Literacy', p. 221.

[88] *Chronicle*, p. 20, lines 254–70.

[89] *Rotuli Chartarum*, RC (1837), p. 209 and plate at p. xli; F. M. Powicke, *Stephen Langton* (1928), p. 215.

[90] J. C. Holt, 'A Vernacular-French Text of Magna Carta', *EHR* lxxxix (1974), pp. 346–64, reprinted in his *Magna Carta and Medieval Government* (1985) where the letter to the sheriff of Hampshire is at p. 257. See also I. Short in *Semasia* iv (1977), pp. 53–63.

contradiction between the rapid advance of French as a literary language and its slow acceptance as a language of record. French may have been used for drafting documents as early as William the Conqueror's reign. But the fair copies were rendered into Latin because that was the essence of 'letters' in the Norman government's view. Literary French, on the other hand, was being written down in fair copies at this same time in order to record the metres and rhymes of verses and songs, which could not be preserved by rendering them in Latin. Nothing was lost (except to philologists and antiquarians) by translating a reply to the Inquest of Sheriffs from French into Latin because it was in prose. Indeed something was gained, since Latin was considered a stronger preservative for legal purposes. Different conventions therefore applied to writing verse and prose. Verse had to be rendered in something like its original diction and language, whereas that was not necessarily appropriate for prose. Unlike verse, French prose writing did not attain a dignity and authority of its own until the end of the twelfth century.[91] This explains why much inappropriate subject matter (in the eyes of modern critics), like Philip de Thaon's *Comput*, had been put into verse. As importantly, it explains why drafts of documents in French prose were, throughout the twelfth century and beyond, discarded in favour of fair copies in Latin.

ROYAL DOCUMENTS IN LATIN, FRENCH, AND ENGLISH

In their written forms, Latin, French, and English ran on non-convergent lines of development. Latin was very old and therefore had a fixed orthography and learned rules. French was new and flourished in various forms, primarily in verse. English was peculiar; like Latin, it had been a standard for government business and it possessed centuries of literature, but the Norman conquerors rejected it. Consequently it absorbed numerous words from French and developed peculiar local forms (in Middle English). As a fixed language of record (Anglo-Saxon), it ceased to function. No text of Magna Carta or royal writ is extant in English to match the French versions. But this does not mean that Magna Carta was not written down in English in 1215. As it was ordered (in a letter to all the king's sheriffs, foresters, gamekeepers, watermen, and other bailiffs) to be read out in public, numerous copies of Magna Carta must once have existed.[92] To have the effect the barons wanted, these public readings were probably made in vernaculars. It is certain that readings of it later in the century were made in *patria lingua* or in English and French.[93] Such a procedure may have been taken for granted in 1215. It was no more necessary to note it specifically in the royal records than for the former British imperial government in Africa or India to specify to its own officials every native language in which government regulations were to be announced. Just as English was the official language of the British empire,

---

[91] J. Kittay, 'Thinking about Literacies' in *Literacy and Orality* ed. D. R. Olson and N. Torrance (1991), p. 169. See also W. Godzich and J. Kittay, *The Emergence of Prose* (1987).
[92] J. C. Holt, *Magna Carta* (1965), p. 345.
[93] See ch. 8, nn. 51, 54 below.

Latin was the language of government and record in King John's England. His sheriffs and other officers did not need to be reminded in writing that it was not the spoken language of themselves or their people.

An English monastic scribe, who wished to record Magna Carta for posterity, would not have thought it proper to copy it in any form less solemn than the Latin in which the authentic text was written and sealed. If he heard or came across a public crier's version, in either French or English, his probable reaction would have been to reject it in preference for the Latin text. He was not aiming to record vulgar forms of French or English for the benefit of modern philologists, but to make a fair copy of the charter in its most lawful form. Why then did the Norman scribe at Pont-Audemer record Magna Carta in French? This copy seems to be a casual interpolation in the cartulary, inserted in the early 1220s. For this scribe and his fellows in Normandy, which was now under the rule of the French crown, the charter had curiosity value only, so that it did not matter if it were expressed in a form which lacked the fullest legal authority. This Norman scribe thus unwittingly preserved a text of much more interest to posterity now than the numerous identical Latin copies of Magna Carta in English monastic cartularies. Unfortunately no scribe of 1215 has yet to come to light who was ignorant enough of the law of the land to think that an English version of the charter was worth copying down. Writers of English were probably too well educated for that.

Although Magna Carta was officially issued only in Latin, in the next baronial rebellion in 1258 letters patent in French and English (and Latin as well, according to the Burton annalist) were sent in the king's name to every county. There were two sets of letters, dated 18 and 20 October respectively – first, an undertaking by Henry III to abide by the rulings of his new baronial council; secondly, the Ordinance of Sheriffs which proposed to investigate their misconduct.[94] No satisfactory contemporary explanation is given for issuing these letters in languages other than Latin, but it can be inferred that the reason for this unprecedented action was that Henry's sheriffs and other officials could not be relied upon to have them publicly read in the usual way because the letters were explicitly critical of their own conduct. Unlike John's letters in 1215, Henry's letters in 1258 were not addressed to the sheriffs themselves but to all the king's subjects. The Burton and Dunstable annalists are mistaken to suggest that these letters were dispatched to sheriffs,[95] as the official texts deny that, as does a note in the liberate rolls which records that the letters 'are being sent throughout all our counties'.[96]

This note also records that the composer and writer of the English and French letters was Robert of Fulham, who was paid 50 shillings because this was not his usual work. He was a constable (debt collector) of the Exchequer and was subsequently its remembrancer and a justice of the Jews. Thus the writer of these non-Latin letters was not a baronial nominee from outside the administration, but a clerk who had been in the king's service before the civil

---

[94] *Baronial Docs*, pp. 116–23, and *English Historical Documents* iii *1189–1327* ed. H. Rothwell (1975), pp. 367–70.
[95] *Annales Monastici* i, p. 453, iii, p. 210.
[96] *CLibR* 1251–60, p. 440; R. F. Treharne, *The Baronial Plan of Reform* (1932), p. 120, n. 1.

war and remained so afterwards.[97] Robert is the prime example of the multilingual competence of English administrators at the time, since he must have known Latin to perform his ordinary duties and he probably understood some Hebrew too as he was a justice of the Jews. His mastery of English and French is clear from the fact that he composed and wrote the letters in both those languages. Whether his starting point was Latin or French or English is anybody's guess.

In the period before 1258 Henry III had made numerous proclamations on a variety of subjects which, if they were to be effective, cannot have been announced in the Latin forms in which they are summarized in the Chancery rolls or in Matthew Paris.[98] They were presumably proclaimed by criers in whatever vernaculars were appropriate.[99] Whether such criers translated *viva voce* from the Latin text, or whether they provided themselves with 'stage scripts' like jongleurs, is a matter for conjecture.[100] In 1258 the barons apparently distrusted the sheriffs, including their criers, and resorted instead to writing down in languages other than Latin precisely what they wanted to say. Exceptional circumstances temporarily caused both English and French to be treated as languages of record.

The barons' action implies distrust of the spoken word and a preference for the precision of writing. The non-Latin letters of 18 and 20 October were not primarily proclamations, though they have been repeatedly described as such by historians. They were letters patent which were enrolled in the Chancery rolls and were intended to serve as permanent records, not transient spoken words, in the counties. The letter of 18 October was 'to remain in the treasury' of each county, although only Oxfordshire has retained its copy to the present day.[101] (The surviving copy addressed to Huntingdonshire is not that county's actual copy, but the specimen enrolled for reference on the Patent Rolls.) This letter's concern with written record was further emphasized by its being sent 'all in the very same words' (*al on tho ilche worden*) to each county.[102] As so few copies survive, we cannot be certain that this phrase means that a uniform orthography was adopted in every county's copy, although that is the obvious inference. If a uniform orthography were used throughout, this royal letter of 18 October 1258, the work of Robert of Fulham, marks the precocious beginning of London English as the new written standard. The letter of 20 October (the Ordinance of Sheriffs) was likewise directed primarily at readers, as it is addressed to 'all people of the county who shall see these letters', not to those who hear them proclaimed.[103] These letters reached out

---

[97] Robert's career can be traced in the indexed references to him in *CLibR* 1251–72, *ClR* 1254–68 and *CPatR* 1247–72.

[98] See ch. 8, nn. 37–41 below.

[99] Criers are not well documented because their art was speech, but they are referred to in 1248 (see ch. 8, n. 88 below) and in the surname 'Crier': B. Thuresson, *Middle English Occupation Terms* (Lund, 1950), p. 153.

[100] E. Auerbach, *Literary Language and its Public in Late Antiquity and in the Middle Ages* (1965), p. 288.

[101] *Royal Letters Addressed to Oxford* ed. O. Ogle (1892), p. 12. Cf. ch. 5, n. 101 above.

[102] *English Historical Documents* ed. Rothwell, p. 368.

[103] *Baronial Docs*, p. 118.

beyond the sheriff and the traditional non-literate procedures of the county court to the new reading public in the shires. That public consisted of knights, like Walter of Bibbesworth, who were familiar with written English and French but found Latin or *clergie* rather more difficult.

The letters in English and French of 1258, written by Robert of Fulham 'by ordinance of the magnates of our council',[104] showed that either language or a combination of them could have been used henceforward as the language of government and record. But this innovation of the barons had been no more than a temporary expedient. When they got fuller control of the administration after the battle of Lewes, Latin was restored to its former dignity as the medium of literacy. The rebels needed to invest their victory with the greatest legality possible, and that meant using Latin rather than French or English for making records. The letters patent of 14 March 1265, which publish Henry III's oath to keep peace with the barons, are comparable in their purpose with those of 18 October 1258. Like those of 1258, the letters of 1265 indicate a residual distrust of the sheriffs specifically. But this time the letters were issued in Latin only and were ordered to be 'published' (*publicari*) in the county courts.[105] Publication presumably took the traditional form of vernacular announcements by criers working without official non-Latin texts.

The history of Henry III's non-Latin letters of 1258 forms an appropriate conclusion to this discussion. It illustrates how written language was not usually derived directly from the speech of the majority of the people but from tradition, political authority, and social status. The mother tongue of ordinary discourse was normally entirely distinct from the languages of script. Those who read or wrote had to master a variety of languages. They passed from English to French or Latin, and some to Hebrew as well, frequently without comment and perhaps without effort. Knowledge and familiarity with these languages, or variants of them, depended on each individual's social status, age, domicile, and personal ambitions and experience of life. Generalizations, such as that everybody was bilingual in English and French in 1200 or that only the clergy knew Latin, are pointless and misleading apart from being unprovable. Although it is impossible to reconstruct in detail the values and knowledge of men of intermediate social class, like Walter of Bibbesworth and Robert of Fulham, the evidence available suggests that in order to rule their fellow Englishmen they must have been lords of language in both speech and script.

[104] *CLibR* 1251–60, p. 440.
[105] *Baronial Docs*, pp. 312–15.

7

Literate and Illiterate

In the summer of 1297 some jurors from Norfolk came to the court of King's Bench to attest that Robert de Tony was twenty-one years of age and was therefore entitled to have his wardship terminated. Proving the age of feudal heirs by sworn testimony was a routine procedure at the time, in which each juror attempted to recollect some memorable event which coincided with the birth of the child in question. Jurors might recall, for example, specific gifts or public events or accidents to themselves or their neighbours.[1] Thus in a case in 1304 at Skipton in Yorkshire Robert Buck, aged 41, remembered being at school at Clitheroe where he had been so badly beaten that he ran away and that was twenty-one years ago.[2] Such a cumbersome system was required because births were only rarely recorded in registers. This customary method of establishing the age of individuals by collective oral testimony is a good example of the medieval reliance on memory rather than written record.

The case from Norfolk in 1297 is exceptional in that the proof primarily depended not on the usual personal recollections, but on a record of the date of Robert de Tony's birth (4 April 1276), which had been written down in the chronicles of West Acre priory.[3] This record had not been made at the time of Robert's birth, as he was born in Scotland, but a year or more later when he was brought down to West Acre priory, of which the de Tony family were the founders, by his mother. She seems to have been seeking the protection of the

---

[1] S. S. Walker, 'Proof of Age of Feudal Heirs in Medieval England', *Medieval Studies* (Toronto) xxxv (1973), pp. 316–20.
[2] *Calendar of Inquisitions Post Mortem* iv, pp. 171–2, no. 239.
[3] *Placitorum Abbreviatio*, RC (1811), p. 293 (text incomplete); *Coram Rege Roll for Trinity Term 1297* ed. W. P. W. Phillmore, British Record S. Index Library xix (1897), pp. 241–3; G. E. Cokayne, *The Complete Peerage* (2nd edn) xii, part i (1953), p. 773. No chronicle of West Acre Priory is extant.

priory on her son's behalf and had his date of birth written down there to establish that he was the lawful de Tony heir. Because the circumstances of Robert's birth could not have been known to the Norfolk jurors from personal experience in the customary way, resort had to be made to the West Acre chronicle.

The first juror, William de la Sale of Swaffham, therefore gave evidence that he had seen the chronicle and read it and was thereby certain of Robert's age. Six other jurors agreed with William without exception or addition, that is, they too claimed to have read the chronicle and understood its significance. Three more likewise agreed and added ancillary recollections: Robert Corlu said his younger brother was born in the same year who was now twenty-one; John Kempe said his father had died five years after Robert had been brought down from Scotland. The eleventh juror, John Laurence, agreed with William 'with this exception, that he had not read the aforesaid chronicles because he is *laycus*'. The twelfth, Roger of Creston, attested the same. A thirteenth juror (why evidence was taken from thirteen men instead of twelve is not explained), Thomas of Weasenham, said that he had neither seen nor read the chronicle, but he had learned of its contents from the prior. Thomas was not necessarily incapable of reading like John and Roger. He may have presented his evidence in this form simply because he had not been present on the day his fellow jurors saw the chronicle.

Thus, of the thirteen men examined, ten swore that they could read the entry in the chronicle, an eleventh may have been able to read, and two were unable to do so. The latter two were described as *layci* (laymen) presumably because they had no 'clergy' in the sense of a reading knowledge of Latin. We have already seen that Walter of Bibbesworth took it for granted in the 1250s or 1260s, the time when these Norfolk jurors were growing up, that the gentry usually had experience from childhood of the 'book which teaches us *clergie*'.[4] Those without this knowledge were 'laymen' in the modern sense of being inexpert. The other jurors were 'clergy' only in the sense of knowing some Latin. William de la Sale and his fellows were no churchmen. They were knights and freemen of the neighbourhood, approximately the social equals of the heir in question, as required in jury trial procedure.

This case therefore shows that from a random sample of thirteen gentlemen of Norfolk at the end of the thirteenth century, ten could read an entry in a chronicle, two could not, and one's ability is unrecorded. Those who swore that they had read the chronicle were presumably telling the truth, as they risked being cross-examined in the King's Bench, and they had no apparent motive for perjuring themselves since they were not claiming benefit of clergy. The statement that two of the jurors were incapable of reading, together with the unspecific testimony about Thomas of Weasenham, adds credibility to the contrasting testimony of the rest. Although evidence of proof of age was sometimes falsified, there is no reason to reject the essential facts of this testimony. Obviously no generalizations about levels of literacy can be made from a unique case. On the other hand, the evidence of this case, that the great majority of the jurors examined were capable of reading one line of Latin in a

---

[4] See ch. 6, n. 1 above.

chronicle, need cause no surprise. We have already seen that the procedure for giving juries' verdicts in royal courts, which depended on documents written in Latin and perhaps also in French and English, demanded a higher level of literacy among jurors than that.[5] By 1297 the two who were unable to read at this elementary level are more surprising than the ten who could do so.

MEANINGS OF 'CLERICUS' AND 'LITTERATUS'

The fact that most of these Norfolk gentlemen could read conflicts in appearance only with the medieval axiom that laymen are illiterate and its converse that clergy are literate. The terms cleric and lay, literate and illiterate, were used in ways which preserved intact the appearances of these fundamental axioms while acknowledging the realities of daily experience, where some clergy were ignorant and some knights knew more of books than brave deeds. Traditional roles had become confused, as Nigel de Longchamp of Canterbury observed with regret in *c.*1192: 'In the church today there are clergy without knowledge of letters, just as there are many knights without skill and practice in arms, who for that reason are called "Holy Mary's knights" by the others.'[6] This discrepancy between theory and practice, between literature and life, did not of course mean that the ideals were immediately altered to fit the facts. On the contrary, the ideals of the learned cleric and the valorous knight became reinforced as fantasies, which had three or four centuries of vigorous life before them in literature and academic treatises.

The axiom that laymen are illiterate and its converse had originated by combining two distinct antitheses:

clericus: laicus
litteratus: illitteratus

The latter antithesis derived from classical Latin, where *litteratus* meant 'literate' in something like its modern sense and also (in the most classical usage of Cicero) described a person with *scientia litterarum*, meaning a 'knowledge of letters' in the sense of 'literature'.[7] The former antithesis derived from the Greek *kleros*, meaning a 'selection by lot' and hence subsequently the 'elect' of God in terms of Christian salvation, whereas *laos* meant the 'people' or crowd.[8] Gradually in the process of Christian conversion those who were specially consecrated to the service of God, the *clerici* or 'clergy', became distinct from the mass of the people, the *laici* or 'laity'. The antithesis *clericus: laicus* was thus a medieval creation, while *litteratus: illitteratus* was of Roman origin. In the half-millennium 500–1000 AD the reduction of the number of learned men in the west coincided with the expansion of Christianity

---

[5] See ch. 6, nn. 51–2 above.
[6] Nigellus de Longchamp dit Wireker, *Tractatus Contra Curiales et Officiales Clericos* ed. A. Boutemy (1959), I, p. 204.
[7] H. Grundmann, *'Litteratus-Illitteratus'*, *Archiv für Kulturgeschichte* XL (1958), p. 17.
[8] *Dictionaire du droit canonique* ed. R. Nax (1935–65) III, col. 828; VI, col. 328.

by the conversion of the barbarians. As a consequence *clerici* began to be associated with *litterati*, although the two concepts had originally nothing in common. This association of ideas reflected the fact that outside the Mediterranean area nearly all Latinists were churchmen and most were monks. As academic standards declined, *litteratus*, which had meant 'lettered' or 'learned' for Cicero, more often came to mean 'literate' in the sense of having a minimal ability to read Latin. Such *litterati* were still learned compared with the great majority, who had no Latin or book learning at all.

These first clerical *litterati*, whose sparse knowledge had scarcely anything in common with the Latin scholars either of ancient Rome or of the twelfth-century Renaissance, established a privileged status for themselves in society by despising non-Latinists as an ignorant crowd of *laici*. In reality the *clerici* were unsure of their status, as Europe was dominated not by them but by warriors with a non-literate sense of values. Charlemagne and Alfred were exceptional in wanting the nobility to be better Latinists; their examples were lauded by the clergy to encourage the others. Dark-Age Europe was far from unique in creating an elite of priests who monopolized writing, yet who were constantly aware of their impotence *vis-à-vis* the dominant warlords. The supposed gulf between cleric and lay, between the elect and damned, was some compensation to the clergy, although not even Pope Gregory VII could make it a reality for long in the terrestrial world.[9]

Thus by constant repetition the pairs of antitheses, *clericus: laicus* and *litteratus: illitteratus*, were coupled in the mind. The terms of each antithesis became interchangeable and ultimately synonymous. By the twelfth century *clericus* meant *litteratus*, *laicus* meant *illitteratus*, and vice versa. The case from Norfolk has already illustrated *laicus* being used to mean *illitteratus*. The converse (*clericus* meaning *litteratus*) was discussed in detail in the 1170s by Philip of Harvengt, who observed that a person was not called a cleric unless he was 'imbued with letters', and hence:

> A usage of speech has taken hold whereby when we see someone *litteratus*, immediately we call him *clericus*. Because he acts the part that is a cleric's, we assign him the name *ex officio*. Thus if anyone is comparing a knight who is *litteratus* with a priest who is ignorant, he will exclaim with confidence and affirm with an oath that the knight is a better *clericus* than the priest . . . This improper usage has become so prevalent that whoever gives attention to letters, which is clerkly, is named *clericus*.[10]

Philip, like Nigel de Longchamp and other writers on the state of the clergy, deplored the way real knights and clergy no longer fitted the traditional roles assigned to them. More important in the present context is his observation

---

[9] In general see the contributions by L. Prosdocimi and Y. Congar to *I laici nella societas christiana dei secoli XI e XII* ed. G. Lazzati and C. D. Fonseca (1968), pp. 56–117.
[10] 'De Institutione Clericorum', Bk. IV, ch. 110, *Patrologia* CCIII (1855), col. 816; cf. n. 30 below. P. Riché, 'Recherches sur l'instruction des laïcs du IX au XII siècle', *Cahiers de civilisation médiévale* v (1962), p. 181.

that a learned knight would be called a *clericus*, because that implies that a person described as *clericus* in a document was not necessarily a member of the clergy. Such a person is just as likely to have been an educated layman.

Philip of Harvengt's comments are best illustrated in England by Matthew Paris's obituary of Paulin Peyver or Piper, a steward of Henry III who died in 1251. He is described as *miles litteratus sive clericus militaris*, 'a literate knight or knightly clerk'.[11] Matthew thus emphasized that these terms were interchangeable in Paulin's case. Paulin was a cleric only in the learned sense, as he had numerous knights' fees and a wife and legitimate children. Similarly the Northamptonshire knight, Henry de Bray, who was born in 1269 and wrote his own cartulary, noted that his maternal grandfather, Richard lord of Harlestone, 'was called Ricardus Clericus because he was *litteratus*'.[12] The most familiar example of this usage is the nickname 'Clerk' or 'Beauclerk' given to Henry I. How learned Henry really was is a separate and controversial question; certainly he was described by Orderic Vitalis as *litteratus* and 'nurtured in natural and doctrinal science'.[13] A *clericus* in common parlance was therefore a person of some scholarly attainments, regardless of whether he was a churchman. As early as the third decade of the twelfth century a polemic of English origin, commenting on the large number of schoolmasters, asked rhetorically: 'Are there not everywhere on earth masters of the liberal arts, who are also called *clerici*?'[14] Peter the Chanter summarized the situation in around 1200: 'There are two kinds of *clerici* and in both there are good and bad, namely those who are ecclesiastics and those who are scholastics.'[15]

The use of *clericus* and *litteratus* as interchangeable terms, both meaning 'learned' or 'scholarly', is clearest in Jocelin of Brakelond's descriptions of the debates within Bury St Edmunds abbey over the election of Abbot Samson in 1182 and Prior Herbert in 1200. On each occasion the more scholarly monks argued that they must be governed by *litterati* and not by the ignorant. Their opponents teased them with a new litany. 'A bonis clericis, libera nos, Domine!' (From good clerics, good Lord, deliver us),[16] and with puns about learning Latin grammar, 'Our good *clerici* have declined so often in the cloister that now they themselves have declined.'[17] *Clericus* was a relative term. Thus Jocelin has one monk say: 'That brother is something of a cleric [*aliquantulum clericus*], although much learning [*littere*] doth not make him mad.'[18] On another occasion Jocelin told of how Hubert Walter, the archbishop of Canterbury, had to admit that Abbot Samson was a better *clericus* than he

---

[11] Matthew Paris v, p. 242; N. Denholm-Young, *History and Heraldry* (1965), pp. 32–4.

[12] *The Estate Book of Henry de Bray* ed. D. Willis, Camden S. 3rd series xxvii (1916), p. 79.

[13] Thompson, *Literacy*, p. 170, n. 40. For a contrary view see Galbraith, 'Literacy', pp. 201–2, 211–12.

[14] R. W. Southern, 'Master Vacarius and the Beginning of an English Academic Tradition' in *Medieval Learning and Literature: Essays Presented to R. W. Hunt* (1976), p. 268, n. 1, citing *Studia Anselmia* xli (1957), p. 65. Cf. R & S, p. 270, n. 4.

[15] J. W. Baldwin, *Masters, Princes and Merchants* (1970) ii, p. 51, n. 57.

[16] Jocelin, p. 12.

[17] Ibid., p. 130.

[18] Ibid., p. 12. *Acts* xxvi, 24.

was, meaning that Samson was the better scholar.[19] The way Jocelin uses *clericus* is explained by Philip of Harvengt, who notes that when we meet a monk of humanity and charity,

> We ask him whether he is a *clericus*. We don't want to know whether he has been ordained to perform the office of the altar, but only whether he is *litteratus*. The monk will therefore reply to the question by saying that he is a *clericus* if he is *litteratus*, or conversely a *laicus* if he is *illitteratus*.[20]

It might be added that a monk who aspired to Christian humility would not call himself *litteratus*, even if he were of scholarly inclinations. Thus Adam of Eynsham, in his life of St Hugh of Lincoln, claims not to know how to satisfy the *litterati*, who will cavil at his style and simple narrative.[21] Adam is using here the hagiographer's common device of making his story appear more truthful by being naive.

As *clericus* and *litteratus* both meant learned, it followed that a person of no great book learning was a *laicus*, a 'layman', even if he were a monk or a priest. Thus Archbishop Hubert Walter was described by the chronicler of St Augustine's abbey at Canterbury as *laicus et illitteratus*.[22] Hubert was not of course a layman in the ecclesiastical sense, nor was he illiterate in any modern sense, as he was the chief justiciar and chancellor who did more than any other individual to create the royal archives. The St Augustine's abbey chronicler was using *laicus* and *illitteratus* as terms of abuse – he also called Hubert a legal *ignoramus*[23] – but he was not using these terms inaccurately. Hubert was a *laicus* in Philip of Harvengt's sense and *illitteratus* in Jocelin's, as he lacked the academic learning of Bologna or Paris. That academic snob, Gerald of Wales, alleged that Hubert's Latin was shaky and that his only school had been the Exchequer.[24]

Like *clericus*, *litteratus* was a relative term. Whether a particular individual was appropriately described as *litteratus* was a matter of opinion, since essentially it meant 'learned'. The same man might be *litteratus* in one assessment and *illitteratus* in another. Thus Ralf Nevill, Henry III's chancellor and bishop of Chichester, was certified by a papal legate as *litteratus* when elected dean of Lichfield in 1214, but *illitteratus* by another papal adviser in 1231 when his candidature for the archbishopric of Canterbury was rejected.[25] Conscientious churchmen considered Ralf to be a worldly administrator. Like Hubert Walter, he was no *clericus* or *litteratus* in the ideal sense of being either the elect of God or a scholar. On this occasion in 1231 the successful candidate for Canterbury, St Edmund of Abingdon, was both. Hubert and Ralf were not

[19] Ibid. p. 84.
[20] *Patrologiae* cciii (1855), col. 816.
[21] Ed. D. L. Douie and H. Farmer (1961) i, p. 43.
[22] *Historiae Anglicanae Scriptores Decem* ed. R. Twysden (1652), col. 1841.
[23] 'juris ignarus', ibid., col. 1841.
[24] See ch. 2, nn. 103–5 above.
[25] *The Great Register of Lichfield Cathedral* ed. H. E. Savage, The William Salt Archaeological S. (1924), p. 341, no. 713; Matthew Paris iii, p. 207 (citing Roger of Wendover). I owe these references to Dr Jeanne Stones.

the only distinguished churchmen and administrators to be described as *illitteratus*. To their company should be added Roger, bishop of Salisbury, Henry I's chief justiciar, and the controversial Abbot Ording of Bury St Edmunds.[26] In the exalted view of John of Salisbury, who aspired to Ciceronian standards, all those who are ignorant of the Latin poets, historians, orators, and mathematicians should be called *illitterati* 'even if they know letters.'[27]

John's contention is taken for granted by Walter Map when he described a boy he had known, who was a paragon and was 'educated among us and by us'; yet 'he was not *litteratus*, which I regret, although he knew how to transcribe any series of letters whatever.'[28] Walter would have liked to have described this boy as *litteratus*, since he was one of his kinsmen, but he had to admit that nice penmanship was no substitute for scholarship. He adds that the boy left England and became a knight of Philip of Flanders (1168–91). At his learned court, where many of 'the order of laymen' knew 'letters' (according to Philip of Harvengt), this boy would presumably not have been numbered among the *milites litterati*.[29] The ability to write well comprised the technical skill of an artist and was not an integral part of the science of letters. Writing is not included among the skills which cause Philip of Harvengt's knight who is *litteratus* to be described as a *clericus*. In Philip's opinion the essential abilities are to read, understand, compose by dictation, make verse, and express oneself in the Latin language.[30] The medieval *miles litteratus* was thus a gentleman educated in the classics; he embodied a recurrent ideal in European culture.

The way the words *clericus* and *litteratus* were used has been discussed in detail here because such examples demonstrate that neither word, when applied to an individual, can be accurately translated by its modern equivalent. A *clericus* was not necessarily either a 'cleric' or a 'clerk', although he was someone with a reputation for erudition. Likewise a person described as *litteratus* was much more than 'literate' in the modern sense. Counting the number of persons called *clericus*, or making lists of knights described as *litteratus*, provides examples of persistent and characteristic medieval ways of thinking, but it throws no light on whether such persons, whether designated cleric or lay by ecclesiastical law, were 'literate' in a twentieth-century sense of that word.[31]

---

[26] William of Newburgh, *Chronicles* ed. R. Howlett, RS LXXXII (1884), I, p. 36; Jocelin, p. 11.

[27] *Policraticus*, Bk. VII, ch. 9, ed. C. C. J. Webb (1909) II, p. 126. Cf. Grundmann, '*litteratus-Illitteratus*', p. 52 and Riché, 'Recherches sur l'instruction des laïcs', pp. 180–1.

[28] Walter Map, Bk. IV, ch. 1, p. 278.

[29] *Patrologiae* CCIII (1855), cols 148–9; Thompson, *Literacy*, pp. 139–41.

[30] 'miles legit, intelligit, dictat, versificatur et inter clericos linguam Latinam proferens', *Patrologiae* CCIII (1855), col. 816. Cf. n. 10 above.

[31] In general see J. Dunbabin, 'From Clerk to Knight: Changing Orders' in *The Ideals and Practice of Medieval Knighthood II* ed. C. Harper-Bill and R. Harvey (1988), pp. 26–39.

THE QUESTION OF THE LITERACY OF THE LAITY

Discussions of medieval literacy have been bedevilled by the difficulty of distinguishing between the modern 'literate' and the medieval *litteratus*. When a knight is described as *litteratus* in a medieval source, his exceptional erudition is usually being referred to, not his capacity to read and write. Such knights were rare because good Latin scholars have always been rare among country gentry and government officials in England. A few existed even in this period. Thus shortly after the Conquest a Norman called Robert, *miles ille litteratus*, endowed St Albans abbey with an income to provide books for the church.[32] He probably had a greater interest in books than most of the monks. About a century later Gerald of Wales tells how a *miles litteratus* appeared as a ghost, demanding to play a game of capping Latin verses with a learned master, for that had been his 'social recreation' when he was alive.[33] Similarly Matthew Paris is recording his admiration for the learning and not the elementary schooling of John of Lexington, when he describes him as *miles elegans* (refined) *et facundus* (eloquent) *et litteratus*, or of Roger de Thurkelby, *miles et litteratus*.[34] John was the keeper of the royal seal, whose obituary Matthew was writing in 1257, while Roger was one of the few royal judges who possessed legal wisdom in Matthew's opinion.

The historian's initial difficulty, when discussing the literacy of the laity, is to avoid anachronisms. Medieval ideas of literacy were so different from those of today that some modern questions are meaningless. To ask, 'Were laymen illiterate?' is a tautology: of course *laici* were *illitterati* because these terms were synonyms. Faced with the question another way round, 'Were laymen literate?' a medieval schoolman might have thought that he was being invited to take part in an exercise in elementary dialectic. Asking whether laymen were literates was like asking whether evil was good or black was white. Every bachelor of arts knew that the validity of axioms such as these was not affected by individual cases of moral imperfection or greyness in this imperfect world. The axiom that *clerici* were *litterati* and its converse belonged to the same order of thinking. Contemporaries, like Philip of Harvengt or Jocelin of Brakelond, knew of numerous exceptions in their daily experience, but they saved the appearances of the rules by calling learned knights *clerici* and ignorant monks *laici*. Such axioms cannot be equated with twentieth-century historians' generalizations, which derive from an assessment of a multitude of individual cases. Scholastic axioms derived their validity not from individual experience but from universal rules, which were superior and prior to particular cases because they were part of a divine order of things. When explaining medieval ways of thought it is correct to say that all laymen were considered illiterate, yet it would be mistaken to conclude from that proposition that in any

---

[32] *Gesta Abbatum Monasterii S. Albani* ed. H. T. Riley, RS xxviii (1867), i, p. 57; R. M. Thomson, *MSS from St Albans Abbey* (1982), i, p. 13.

[33] Giraldus viii, p. 310; R & S, p. 273, n. 8.

[34] Matthew Paris v, pp. 610, 317.

particular time or place all non-churchmen were unable to read or write. Scholastic axioms differ from real cases.

Another anachronism is the assumption that the capacity to read and write is a simple and constant measure which readily applies to medieval cases. The automatic coupling of reading with writing and the close association of literacy with the language one speaks are not universal norms, but products of modern European culture.[35] Literacy in this modern sense is so deeply implanted from childhood in every twentieth-century scholar that it is difficult to liberate oneself from its preconceptions, or to avoid thinking of it as an automatic measure of progress. Over the last two centuries medievalists have painfully learned to overcome anachronisms when discussing feudal society or scholastic philosophy. Yet, when they reach elementary education and literate skills, they tend to assume that these problems can be readily understood by applying modern criteria and experience to the medieval past.[36] Past ideas must be analysed in their own terms before they are addressed in modern ones.

As the citations from Walter Map and Philip of Harvengt have already illustrated, reading and writing were not automatically coupled at the end of the twelfth century, nor was a minimal ability to perform these actions described as literacy. Writing was a skill distinct from reading because the use of parchment and quills made it difficult. Likewise the traditional emphasis on the spoken word caused reading to be coupled more often with speaking aloud than with eyeing script. Although the average medieval reader may have been taught to form the letters of the alphabet with a stylus on a writing tablet, he would not necessarily have felt confident about penning a letter or a charter on parchment. Scholars and officials employed scribes, particularly for drafting formal legal documents, just as typists and word processors are employed today. To this rule there are exceptions, of which the most spectacular is the beautifully written will of Simon de Montfort, as it states in its text that it is written in the hand of his eldest son, Henry.[37] Wills were unusually personal documents, intimately associated with the family circle, because their main purpose was to ensure the testator's state of grace at death rather than the worldly disposition of his property; hence Henry was performing a special act of filial devotion in writing his father's will.

Another fundamental difference between medieval and modern approaches to literacy is that medieval assessments concentrate on cases of maximum ability, the skills of the most learned scholars (*litterati*) and the most elegant scribes, whereas modern assessors measure the diffusion of minimal skills among the masses. Consequently modern assessments of literacy have been primarily concerned with the minimal ability of persons to sign their own names and the development of elementary schools in which this ability is taught as the basic educational skill. In twelfth- and thirteenth-century

---

[35] H. J. Graff, *The Legacies of Literacy* (1987), pp. 373 ff.

[36] These assumptions are discussed by K. O'B. O'Keeffe, *Visible Song: Transitional Literacy in Old English Verse* (1990), pp. 9–10.

[37] Facsimile, ed. C. Bémont, *Simon de Montfort* trans. E. F. Jacob (1930), pp. 276–8 (the will is in French and was written in 1258); M. M. Sheehan, *The Will in Medieval England* (1963), pp. 260–1, nn. 128, 131.

England the ability to sign one's name was likewise considered important, but it was not directly associated either with writing or with schools. The personal signature or sign manual was not accepted by itself as a lawful symbol of authentication on a document unless the signatory were a Jew. A Christian was required either to sign with a cross, indicating that he was making a promise in the sight of Christ crucified, or more commonly he affixed to the document his *signum* in the form of a seal.[38]

In medieval England possession of a seal bearing the owner's name comes closest to the modern criterion of making the ability to sign one's own name the touchstone of literacy. Although the possessor of a seal might not be able to write, he or she was a person familiar with documents and entitled to participate in their use. Neither the medieval seal nor the modern sign manual on a document indicates that the signatory has anything more than a minimal competence in the skills of literacy. Such a person need not be *litteratus* in a medieval sense nor 'educated' in a modern one. If possession of a seal is taken as the medieval equivalent of the modern sign manual as a measure of minimal literacy, the growth of literacy (in this modern sense) can be approximately assessed. Scarcely anyone apart from rulers and bishops possessed seals in 1100, whereas by 1300 all freemen and even some serfs probably had them. Thus the statute of Exeter of 1285 expected 'bondsmen' to use them when they authenticated written evidence.[39] How far the expectations of this statute reflected actual practice is a matter for conjecture, although instances can be readily cited as early as the 1230s of smallholders and tenants owing labour services affixing their personal seals to charters.[40] The extent of minimal literacy in this sense among the peasantry by 1300 has been underestimated because historians have been reluctant to allow such competence even to the gentry.

The discrepancies between modern and medieval conceptions of what constituted literacy go deeper than differences in minimal requirements. The variety of languages in which spoken and written thoughts were formulated in medieval England made any capacity to read or write an intellectual achievement. This variety also obstructed the rapid spread of literacy, in the modern sense of the majority of people acquiring a minimal ability to read and write the language they spoke. Elementary instruction in reading and writing started from Latin because that was the traditional language of literacy and sacred Scripture. Those who wrote in vernaculars, whether in Middle English or French, were building novel and complex structures on a foundation of Latin. Neither Middle English nor French was sufficiently standardized, or well enough established as a literary language, to become the basis of elementary instruction in reading and writing until well after 1300. If a person in Edward I's reign or earlier had learned to read in English or French but not in Latin, he could never have become *litteratus*, nor could he have understood the majority of writings circulating in his own lifetime because these were in Latin. English and French had to have become common business and literary

---

[38] The symbolism of seals and crosses is discussed at ch. 9, nn. 53–90 below.

[39] *Statutes*, p. 211. See ch. 2, n. 24 above.

[40] See ch. 2, nn. 21–2 above.

languages before it was practical or desirable to initiate literate skills with them.

Nevertheless by 1300 the supremacy of Latin, and the privileges of the *clerici* and *litterati* who upheld it, was increasingly being challenged, both by writings in vernaculars and by anti-clericalism. Boniface VIII introduced his bull *Clericis Laicos* in 1296, directed primarily at Edward I and Philip IV of France, with the provocative words: 'That laymen are notoriously hostile to clerics antiquity relates and recent experience manifestly demonstrates.'[41] Yet English non-churchmen were slower than their French counterparts to abandon Latin as the basis of literate skills, probably because of the competition between English and French as alternative literary languages. In general from *c.* 1300, lawyers and government officials preferred French, while creative writers favoured English. Moreover, in the later Middle Ages an elementary reading knowledge of Latin became a matter of life and death for Englishmen. Any person charged with felony, who could read a prescribed verse from the Psalter, was theoretically entitled to benefit of clergy and hence escaped the death penalty.[42] Now that middle-class laymen were beginning to assert themselves, they took over the old association of *clericus* with *litteratus* and turned it to their own advantage in order to save themselves from hanging. *Litteratus* was thus reduced from meaning a person of erudition to meaning a person with a minimal ability to read, albeit in Latin. A *clericus* was still a *litteratus*, but he was now neither a churchman nor a scholar: he was anyone who was literate in this minimal sense. By the middle of the fifteenth century London tradesmen are being described as *litterati*.[43] Consequently after 1300 it became relatively common to be literate. What had changed, however, was not necessarily the proportion of persons in the population who had mastered reading and writing, but the meanings of words. A *clericus* was now a common clerk and a *litteratus* was a minimal literate. The literacy of the laity had been achieved, perhaps not so much by the efforts of schoolmasters and the mysterious forces of progress, as is sometimes alleged, as by the method which Humpty Dumpty explained to Alice in *Through the Looking-Glass*: 'When *I* use a word, it means just what I choose it to mean, neither more nor less . . . The question is which is to be master – that's all.' Verbally at least, the *laici* had mastered the *clerici* and *litterati*; and from that mastery the modern concept of literacy, meaning a minimal ability to read, was born.

KNOWLEDGE OF LATIN AMONG NON-CHURCHMEN

To avoid ambiguities the question, 'Were laymen literate?' needs recasting. A more productive question to ask is, 'Did non-churchmen know any Latin?' since Latin was the foundation of literacy in England in this period. The latter

[41] P. Dupuy, *Historie du differand d'entre le Pape Boniface VIII et Philippe le Bel* (1655), p. 14; G. de Lagarde, *La Naissance de l'esprit laïque au déclin du Moyen Age* (1948) I, ch. 12.
[42] L. C. Gabel, *Benefit of Clergy in England in the Later Middle Ages* (1928–9), pp. 68–78. J. H. Baker, *Reports of Sir John Spelman* II, ss XCIV (1978), pp. 327–31.
[43] Gabel, pp. 82–4.

question has been progressively answered in the affirmative by scholars over the past fifty years. Starting at the top of the social hierarchy, historians have demonstrated that at least an acquaintance with Latin became increasingly widespread over the two centuries 1100–1300.

Independently of each other in the 1930s, V. H. Galbraith in Britain and J. W. Thompson in California demonstrated that the kings of England from Henry I onwards were instructed in Latin and that Henry I and Henry II were even considered *litterati* by some contemporaries.[44] More importantly, Henry II showed his mastery of written instruments in a series of judgements concerning the charters of the abbeys of St Albans in 1155, Battle in 1157 and 1175, and Bury St Edmunds in 1187.[45] He evidently enjoyed presiding over legal wrangles between abbots and bishops in his court, as it gave him an opportunity to scrutinize their charters and demonstrate that he was their master in intellect and legal wisdom as well as in material power. Peter of Blois was probably not exaggerating when he states that among Henry's commonest forms of relaxation were private reading and working with a group of *clerici* to unravel some knotty question: at his court there was 'school every day'.[46] By 'school' Peter did not mean an elementary school, but a circle of learned schoolmen discussing *questiones* as they did at Paris or Oxford. From King John's reign onwards elementary instruction in Latin was taken for granted: 'Henceforth all our kings were taught letters in their youth, and their literacy, as distinct from their culture, has no particular importance.'[47]

The example set by the kings inevitably gave the baronage and gentry a motivation to learn some Latin, both to avoid looking foolish at court (where there was school every day), and to have sufficient understanding of the written demands, expressed in Latin, which began to pour from the royal Chancery and Exchequer. For these reasons H. G. Richardson and G. O. Sayles in 1963 widened the range of those who had 'a limited knowledge of Latin, a knowledge to be easily and rapidly acquired by any intelligent youth', from kings to the baronage and gentry of twelfth-century England.[48] Their conclusion concerning the baronage is cautious and unexceptionable: 'Without rashly generalizing from what may perhaps be called a handful of cases, it may fairly be said that they create a presumption that a man of noble birth will in his youth have had the opportunity of learning something of Latin letters.'[49] Richardson and Sayles also suggested that even some of the lesser knights read and wrote Latin. This suggestion is based on the written replies to Henry II's inquest into knights' fees in 1166 and his Inquest of Sheriffs in 1170. The argument is that 'the more informal documents, those that have no

---

[44] Galbraith's lecture to the British Academy (Galbraith, 'Literacy', pp. 201–38) was published in 1936. Thompson's *The Literacy of the Laity in the Middle Ages* (Thompson, *Literacy*, ch. 7) was completed in the same year, but was not published until 1939.

[45] *Gesta Abbatum Monasterii S. Albani* I, pp.1 50–4; *Battle*, pp. 154–6, 280; Jocelin, p. 51. Cf. Galbraith, 'Literacy', p. 222, n. 46.

[46] *Patrologiae* CCVII (1855), col. 198; *Becket Materials* VII, p. 573.

[47] Galbraith, 'Literacy', p. 215.

[48] R & S, p. 278 and (more generally) pp. 269–83.

[49] Ibid., p. 273.

marks of clerkly skill' were written by the knights themselves.[50] Although the assumption that such men would or could write on parchment is contentious, the lesser conjecture that many knights read the royal writs themselves and drafted their own replies is possible.[51]

The strongest argument of Richardson and Sayles for a relatively wide acquaintance with Latin is that royal officials like sheriffs and judges, most of whom were non-churchmen, had to have a working knowledge of Latin because they performed offices 'demanding the use of written instruments'.[52] Although such officials usually employed clerks to do their writing, and to read letters aloud to them, they had to understand enough Latin to master the business in hand and not be misled by their clerks or by the litigants' lawyers. At least one of Henry II's lay sheriffs, Richard, sheriff of Hampshire, wrote as well as read in Latin, as his holograph acknowledgement of a debt to William Cade is extant.[53]

The presumption that officials knew some Latin, which applies to officers of the central government by 1200, extends to manorial and village stewards, bailiffs, beadles, and reeves by 1300.[54] On the basis of this evidence M. B. Parkes, in his contribution to the literacy of the laity question, argues that historians should allow for an 'extent of pragmatic literacy among the peasantry'.[55] His arguments are strengthened by the instances of peasants using seals and charters which have already been discussed. Parkes cites Walter Map, who took it for granted that 'serfs [*servi*], whom we call peasants [*rustici*], are eager to educate their ignominious and degenerate children in the [liberal] arts.'[56] Walter deplored this because a liberal education was appropriate only for freedom. The question had arisen one day when he and the chief justiciar, Ranulf de Glanvill, were discussing why it was that the clerical judges of Henry II were harsher than the lay ones. Walter's explanation was that the clerics did not behave like gentlemen because they were serfs in origin. Although Walter was only expressing a personal opinion, and his opinions were often perverse and ironical (Walter was a clerical justice himself), his remarks had some basis in fact.

Starting at the top of the hierarchy with kings and descending through barons and knights, historians of medieval literacy have reached the peasants at the bottom and are suggesting that even some of them were acquainted with Latin. N. Orme has surveyed literacy (mainly in the later Middle Ages) from the top of society to the bottom as an introduction to his study of medieval schools.[57] He divides people into seven classes – clergy; kings and princes; nobility and gentry; administrators and lawyers; merchants, craftsmen, artisans; villeins; women. For the twelfth and thirteenth centuries a

---

[50] R & S, p. 275.

[51] W. L. Warren, *Henry II* (1973), pp. 276–7.

[52] R & S, p. 274.

[53] Parkes, 'Literacy', p. 558, n. 20.

[54] See pp. 46–7, nn. 3–9 above.

[55] Parkes, 'Literacy', p. 560.

[56] Walter Map, Bk. I, ch. 10, p. 12.

[57] N. Orme, *English Schools in the Middle Ages* (1973), ch. 1.

fourfold classification into kings and princes, nobility or baronage, gentry or knights, and peasantry (both free and unfree) is more appropriate. Neither the clergy nor women were separate social classes, as they derived their place in society from their families. Nor were administrators and lawyers yet a distinct class, as the legal profession (in a literate sense) emerged only in the late thirteenth century.

It might be thought that merchants are worth distinguishing as a group, as their families were at the forefront of education in the city states of Flanders and northern Italy. In England, however, merchant dynasties like those of London took on the social colouring of the landed gentry and were not, in the thirteenth century anyway, a distinct 'bourgeoisie'. Knightly merchants were as educated as other knights. With lesser merchants, it is doubtful whether literacy in Latin was yet an essential skill, as they worked from memory and tally sticks. Book learning and book keeping became crucial to lesser merchants only when they ceased to travel with their wares and sat in offices instead. On the whole, that is a development of the fourteenth century rather than the twelfth, as far as England is concerned. St Godric, who mastered the *mercatoris studium* without any formal education, is probably typical of eleventh- or twelfth-century experience.[58] Financiers, on the other hand, like Osbert Huitdeniers (Eightpence) of London, who employed the young Thomas Becket as a clerk and accountant, needed as much Latin as the judicial side of their business (writing and enforcing bonds for loans) required.[59] But financiers are not a sufficiently homogeneous group to constitute a social class, as many of them were Jews; they were literate in Hebrew and often in Latin as well.

The knowledge of the peasantry (both free and unfree), at the bottom of the social pyramid, remains to be discussed. The suggestion that some peasants were acquainted with Latin is not implausible when the role of the church in village life is considered. Theoretically at least every adult in England should have known some Latin because of its use in the liturgy. The attitude of the western church towards Latin was ambivalent. The identification of *clerici* with *litterati*, which implied that only Latinists were the elect of God, was counterbalanced by the perennial message of the Gospels insisting that Christian teaching should be conveyed to everybody, and therefore to the crowd of *laici*. Various attempts had consequently been made to translate prayers, Scripture and the church's teaching into vernacular languages. The works of Alfred and Aelfric are obvious examples of such attempts in pre-Conquest England.

By the eleventh century an uneasy compromise seems to have been reached whereby, for the people at large, the irreducible minimum of Christian teaching – namely the Lord's Prayer and the Creed – was to be recited in Latin, while sermons, homilies and the like were expressed in the vernacular. Thus a law of Cnut enjoined every Christian to apply himself until he could at

---

[58] See n. 63 below.
[59] Clanchy, '*Moderni*', p. 681 and *Becket Materials* II, p. 361. F. Barlow, *Thomas Becket* (1986), pp. 26–7.

least 'understand aright and learn the *Pater Noster* and the *Credo*'.[60] Although this law does not mean that everybody is to read Latin, they are to recite these two Latin texts by heart. Hence one of the glosses accompanying this law adds that Christ himself first recited the *Pater Noster*. That Latin texts are meant and not English translations is suggested by the use of the Latin names for the texts and also by the glosses which describe the penalties for failing to learn them. If the texts had been in the vernacular, there would presumably have been no problem about learning them.

As it was, most people probably did not find this minimal amount of Latin overwhelmingly difficult because they were accustomed to using their ears to learn and furthermore they heard these texts recited whenever they went to church. Assuming that most of the population were minimally conscientious about their religious duties, we are led to the conclusion that most people could recite a little Latin. They had thus taken the first step towards literacy, as paradoxically they could speak *litteraliter*. Those who reached slightly greater competence, in other words, those who understood what they recited and could perhaps also distinguish the letters of the alphabet, would not have been altogether at a loss if they were required to sign their names with seals on Latin charters.

A conjecture of this sort, concerning the level of education of the mass of medieval people, is impossible to prove because evidence of any sort about elementary instruction, and particularly about that of ordinary people, is rare. The biographies of saints sometimes provide glimpses of childhood, but the only detailed description of an English saint of this period of undoubted peasant origins is the life of St Godric, which was written (in various versions) from his own recollections.[61] Although he features in numerous social histories, because he is the first English example of the Dick Whittington type who made his fortune as a merchant, Godric's story is worth examining again from the point of view of what sort of education he acquired.

Godric was born in Norfolk in *c.*1065 of parents who were good, though poor and ignorant. Since he had no wish to remain a peasant, but to exercise his mind, he exerted himself to study.[62] So he strove to learn to be a merchant (*mercatoris studium*), first by selling things locally, then by joining travelling chapmen and ultimately by becoming an international shipman.[63] As merchants travelled with their wares, he mastered navigation and practical maritime astronomy.[64] Business combined well with religion, as he journeyed to the shrines at Lindisfarne and St Andrews, and beyond Britain to Rome, Santiago, and Jerusalem.[65] For a while he returned to Norfolk and became

[60] I Canute 22, ed. A. J. Robertson, *The Laws of the Kings of England from Edmund to Henry I* (1925), p. 170. Cf. n. 77 below.
[61] *Libellus de Vita et Miraculis S. Godrici* ed. J. Stevenson, Surtees S. (1845); T. A. Archer, 'Godric' in *The Dictionary of National Biography* VIII, pp. 47–9. M. Richter, *Sprache und Gesellschaft* (1979), pp. 80–6.
[62] *Libellus de Vita*, ch. 2, p. 25.
[63] Ibid., p. 25.
[64] Ibid., ch. 4, p. 30.
[65] Ibid., ch. 6, pp. 34, 36.

steward and general manager to a certain rich man.[66] Godric was a pious but not yet a bookish man, although he had known the Lord's Prayer and the Creed 'from the cradle' and he often pondered them on his journeys.[67] At about the age of 40 a kinsman in Carlisle gave him a Psalter, from which he learned the Psalms most diligently, retaining them in his memory.[68] This was an abbreviated version of the Psalter, commonly called 'St Jerome's Psalter'. The book must have been quite large, as Godric permanently distorted his little finger by carrying it around, even to bed.[69] After further travels he came to Durham, where he learned more Psalms 'and afterwards he learned the whole Psalter'.[70] By staying around St Mary's church at Durham, where 'boys were learning the first elements of letters', he tenaciously applied his memory to 'hearing, reading and chanting' and thus became 'firm and certain' in the liturgy.[71] Finally he settled at Finchale, near Durham, as a hermit.

Because Godric was self-educated, both the devil and the monks of Durham adopted a patronizing attitude towards him. The twelfth-century devil shared Walter Map's opinion of serfs who had advanced in the world and called Godric a 'stinking old peasant',[72] while his chief biographer, Reginald of Durham, quite often describes him without malice as *laicus, illitteratus* and *idiota*.[73] Technically Reginald was correct, as Godric was not a *clericus* and *litteratus*. Nevertheless Reginald revealed his own ignorance of the effects of travel on an intelligent man, when he considered it miraculous that Godric understood 'French or Romance', even though his mother tongue was English.[74] Reginald likewise considered that it was the Holy Spirit, rather than his native wit, which enabled Godric to understand the Latin conversation of four monks from Durham, who had been sent to cross-examine him.[75] By these means Godric was able to give an impressive exposition of the Scriptures to them (in English), 'as if he were an outstanding *litteratus*'.[76] The information provided by Godric's biographers about his knowledge was not recorded for its own sake, as it was intended as evidence of his religious devotion and of those miraculous powers which were the indispensable sign of a saint. Nevertheless the various versions of the life are sufficiently circumstantial and consistent to provide a historical record of one man's self-education and rise from the mass.

Godric's life story provides numerous correctives to the modern tendency to assume that schools are the beginning and end of education. He received his instruction in the Lord's Prayer and the Creed 'from the cradle', presumably

---

[66] Ibid., ch. 6, p. 35.

[67] Ibid., ch. 4, p. 28.

[68] Ibid., ch. 9, pp. 41–2.

[69] Ibid., ch. 92, pp. 200–1.

[70] Ibid., ch. 16, p. 59.

[71] Ibid., pp. 59–60.

[72] O rustice decrepite! O rustice stercorarie!' ibid., ch. 38, p. 93.

[73] Ibid., ch. 38, p. 94; ch. 47, p. 110; ch. 87, p. 192; ch. 161, p. 306.

[74] Ibid., ch. 94, pp. 203–4; ch. 96, p. 206.

[75] Ibid., ch. 79, pp. 179–80.

[76] Ibid., p. 179.

meaning from his parents. He is therefore an example of Christian law being applied in practice, as it was the duty of every parent to teach his child the *Pater Noster* and the *Credo*.[77] Thereafter Godric was self-taught. He learned numeracy and navigation, the *mercatoris studium*, by experience. Literacy obviously presented greater problems. Godric may never have learned to write and his knowledge of Latin depended primarily on hearing and memorizing. Although he could never become *litteratus* by this method, he could evidently cope with the normal uses of Latin in ecclesiastical circles. Gerald of Wales gives an example of another hermit and travellers, Wecheleu, who had likewise miraculously learned Latin by ear.[78] The fact that such knowledge was considered miraculous suggests, however, that Latin was thought difficult to learn without formal instruction in grammar. Nevertheless even Latin was in its rudimentary stages primarily a spoken language, to which children were introduced by the church's liturgy and prayers in the home.

Although a man like Godric, who had memorized whole portions of the liturgy, could not pass as a Latinist among the *litterati*, he could probably make as good a show of Latin as some clergy. His self-taught Latin became a problem only when he wanted to be accepted as a conscientious churchman and monk. In lay society Godric's lack of a formal education had not prevented him from mastering the *mercatoris studium*, or from becoming a rich man's steward. In the latter capacity tally sticks and a trained memory were more useful than parchments, although if Godric had lived a century later, he might have found it more difficult to conduct business without writing. Yet before deciding that Godric could not have succeeded a century later, it is worth recalling that the greatest of all medieval stewards and business managers, Hubert Walter, was likewise described as *laicus et illitteratus*.[79] Like Godric, he had little or no formal schooling and was ignorant of elementary Latin grammar, if Gerald of Wales is to believed. A little Latin, like a little literacy in more recent times, could get a man a long way in ordinary business, deplorable as that was in the eyes of scholars.

THE ACQUISITION OF CLERICAL EDUCATION

Godric's life shows that a little Latin, and a great deal of education in the broader sense of understanding and mastering one's environment, could be acquired by a determined peasant without any formal schooling. Nevertheless those children of serfs whom Walter Map had in mind who became royal justices had probably risen through some clerical training in childhood, as Latin could only be superficially acquired by self-education. The commonness of such instruction has probably been underestimated, both in terms of the number of children involved and of the social classes from which they came. A

[77] *Wulfstan's Canons of Edgar* ed. R. Fowler, Early English Text S. cclxvi (1972), pp. 6–7. Cf. n. 60 above.
[78] See ch. 6, n. 13 above.
[79] See n. 22 above, and ch. 2, nn. 103–5 above.

polemicist of the early twelfth century argued that there were numerous *clerici*, just as there were numerous royal tax collectors and officials, since highly expert schoolmasters existed 'not only in cities and boroughs, but even in little villages [*in villulis*]'.[80] Even if this were not exaggerated, however, the problems for a serf's family were paying for instruction and doing without the labour of the child concerned.

As a solution of these problems, the role of the church in disseminating free instruction in villages through its priests may have been as underestimated as its role in familiarizing people with Latin through the liturgy. Village priests became increasingly common from the eleventh century onwards, as a network of parish churches gradually replaced and supplemented the centralized minster churches of the missionary period. Henceforward priests and their books were more widely and permanently distributed over the country-side. 'By 1154 the existence of elementary education was taken for granted: that is to say, there was basic education available for everyone who wanted and could afford it; and the clever poor would often be educated free.'[81] Isolation in villages and local recruitment, compounded after 1066 by the alienation of the Normanized prelates from the Anglo-Saxon lower clergy, may in the short term have caused the educational standards of some priests to deteriorate. Nevertheless most scholars agree that by the thirteenth century, when information becomes sufficiently abundant to make generalizations, parish priests were often of peasant, even servile, origins and also that the standard of learning of the priesthood was on the whole quite high.[82] The latter generalization is the more controversial, as a handful of cases of priestly ignorance have been repeatedly cited against it. The most frequently quoted report is from the dean of Salisbury's visitation of Sonning in 1222, where some of the vicar's chaplains' ignorance of Latin grammar was exposed.[83] Yet this case does not suggest that such ignorance was normal, as the incompetent chaplains were suspended or dismissed as a consequence of this visitation.

Cases of priestly ignorance, when recorded in detail in bishop's registers, indicate not that priests were generally ignorant but that reformers were requiring higher standards. Thus it has been calculated from the earliest bishop's register, that of Hugh of Wells, concerning the largest diocese, Lincoln, over a period of a quarter of a century (1209–35) that out of 1,958 institutions to benefices only 101 candidates were recorded as deficient in learning and most of these cases arose from candidates not having completed

---

[80] Cited by R. W. Southern, see n. 14 above.

[81] F. Barlow, *The English Church 1066–1154* (1979), p. 229; W. J. Blair, 'Local Churches in Domesday Book and Before' in *Domesday Studies* ed. J. C. Holt (1987), pp. 265–78, and *Minsters and Parish Churches* ed. Blair (1988), p. 192.

[82] Gabel, *Benefit of Clergy*, p. 75 gives instances of priests of servile origin. Absentee rectors should be distinguished from the poor priests who performed their duties: G. C. Homans, *English Villagers of the Thirteenth Century* (1941), pp. 388–90. J. R. H. Moorman, *Church Life in England in the Thirteenth Century* (1945), p. 93, points out that whether one thought the priesthood sufficiently learned depended on one's point of view.

[83] *The Register of St Osmund* ed. W. H. Rich Jones, RS LXXVIII (1883), I, pp. 304ff. First publicized by G. G. Coulton, *Life in the Middle Ages* (2nd edn, 1928) II, no. 21, pp. 39–41.

their education; only four deficient candidates were already priests.[84] If most parish priests were of peasant origins, and if by 1230 many were sufficiently instructed, it follows that a number of persons of peasant origins had been efficiently instructed in Latin, with a view to becoming priests, even in the twelfth century.

How was the initial instruction of peasants achieved? Not often presumably through schools in towns because of the expense, either of travel or of lodging. Certainly would-be clergy lodged in town schools after they had shown sufficient ability to learn reading and elementary Latin grammar, but their initial instruction and selection must have taken place in the villages themselves. If, as has been argued, parish priests were themselves sufficiently instructed, they could perform this function. Indeed it was required of them by canon law, reiterated in numerous manuscripts. Thus the ninth-century provision of Theodulf, bishop of Orléans, that 'priests should have schools throughout the villages [*per villas*] and teach children free of charge' was translated into English and copied into ecclesiastical compilations of the eleventh century.[85] Of course the repetition of such rules implies that some priests failed to comply. Moreover, a village priest, who was relatively poor and ignorant himself, could not have instructed many children at a time, nor have got them much beyond the ABC and the bare elements of reading Latin. Many priests probably performed these duties to a minimal level at least, as incidental references to them can be found. Thus in one of the fables attributed to Marie de France, which may be of English origin, a priest is pictured teaching a wolf the ABC.[86] The wolf is the rarity and not the priest. Among the miracles of St Edmund, recorded by Hermann in *c*.1095, is the cure of a man who had been so ill that the parish priest named Goding, immediately 'coming with his scholars', rushed to give him the last rites.[87] The elementary teaching duties of priests were so commonplace that they seem only to be mentioned in exceptional circumstances like these.

Even if the average parish priest taught only one poor boy a year, a boy for example who served him at the altar, and if only one such boy in ten proceeded beyond the ABC, nine sons of peasants in the village had acquired a little familiarity with letters and one had advanced into the lowest ranks of the clergy. Perhaps only one in ten of these boys rose to be a parish priest, and only one in a hundred became a *litteratus*, because the course grew progressively more difficult. Such speculations – and they are no more than that – suggest that each prelate and *litteratus* of humble origin whose name has come down to history (Robert Grosseteste is the obvious example) was the one in a thousand who achieved his objective.[88] Although it was difficult therefore for a poor boy to rise through the church, some succeeded, and the difficulties

[84] Orme, *English Schools*, p. 17.

[85] *Patrologiae* cv (1864), col. 196; *Ancient Laws and Institutes of England* ed. B. Thorpe, RC (1840) p. 475, ch. 20.

[86] U. T. Holmes, *Daily Living in the Twelfth Century* (1952), p. 230.

[87] *Memorials of St Edmunds Abbey* ed. T. Arnold, RS xcvi (1890), i, p. 81.

[88] R. W. Southern, *Robert Grosseteste* (1986), p. 63, suggests medieval hagiographers may have exaggerated Grosseteste's humble birth.

ensured that many who were disappointed in their expectations had at least learned the ABC. Famous prelates of humble origin stood at the visible apex of a pyramid of peasant education extending deep into the villages.

More specific information about peasants' sons rising through a clerical education is difficult to find, however, because childhood is rarely described and the social origins of particular persons are often a matter of subjective judgement. Either poverty or gentility may be misleadingly reported by a biographer wishing to demonstrate his subject's sanctity or success. Auto-biographical information is even rarer and no easier to assess. Thus John of Salisbury, who may have been a peasant as his parentage is very obscure, remarks that he learned Psalms from a priest, and he was presumably first taught to read in this way.[89] Yet this instance does not indicate John's confidence in such instruction, as he only mentions it because the priest had tried to teach him sorcery as well. A clearer case of a country boy rising to be a *litteratus* is Jocelin's account of Abbot Samson, although that also illustrates the difficulties of assessing social class. Samson may even have been the model for Walter Map's remarks about Henry II's clerical judges of servile origins being harsher than the lay ones, as he 'exalted justice over mercy' according to Jocelin.[90]

Jocelin reports that, although he had heard Samson say that he had kinsmen of noble blood, 'he had no kin within a third degree, or at any rate pretended that this was so.'[91] It is possible that Samson's reticence concealed servile origins. He seems to have been brought up by his mother, who introduced him to the shrine of St Edmund at the age of nine.[92] Instead of kinsmen, Samson rewarded those 'who had treated him as their kinsmen when he was a poor cloister monk'. Thus he gave benefices to the sons of the man 'of no high birth' who had preserved his patrimony, to the chaplain who sold holy water to maintain him as a student at Paris, and to the son of Master William of Diss who let him enter his school out of pure charity.[93] Whatever Samson's origins, he is certainly an example of a promising country boy who was picked out for training as a *clericus* and owed his rise primarily to ecclesiastical charity.

Samson's career also illustrates another important aspect of clerical educa-tion. He once confided to Jocelin that he would never have become a monk if he had possessed sufficient money to remain at the schools.[94] It was therefore only chance which confirmed him in his ecclesiastical vocation. Some *clerici* abandoned ecclesiastical life and traded their skills in the world, even becoming knights. This was another way in which literate education was integrated into lay society. Among the miracles of St Godric is one in which he identified one of the household knights of Bertram of Bulmer (in the middle of the twelfth century) as a *clericus* and *litteratus*, even though the knight had

---

[89] *Policraticus*, Bk. ii, ch. 28, vol. ii, p. 164.
[90] Jocelin, p. 34.
[91] Ibid., p. 43.
[92] Ibid., p. 37.
[93] Ibid., pp. 43–4.
[94] Ibid., p. 36.

grown his hair to conceal his tonsure.[95] This young knight had been sent to
Godric on his lord's business on a Sunday. Godric made him reveal his
clerical upbringing by compelling him to read the lesson at Mass, which he
did 'not at all like a *laicus*, but rather as a *litteratus*'. So Godric gave him a good
talking to, telling him that he was making unworthy use of his education in
not going on to be a priest. A century later John of Gaddesden, a cleric with
numerous benefices who had been the queen's chamberlain, renounced his
ecclesiastical status with more ceremony. He was belted as a knight by Henry
III on Christmas Day 1244 and married a lady's daughter.[96] Matthew Paris
reported that this gave rise to envious gossip, which he thought misplaced, as
John had willingly given up all his benefices. More scandalous presumably in
Matthew's view were those clerics who, instead of acknowledging their lay
status, maintained spouses and illegitimate children from their benefices.

The rule of clerical celibacy, which had long been an ideal of the church,
was given new force by the Gregorian reformers of the eleventh century and
had come near to being the norm among the higher clergy by the thirteenth.[97]
Ironically, this rule may have been the chief cause of the dissemination of
clerical skills in literacy among all classes of the laity. If the Gregorian
reformers had not intervened, the *clerici-litterati* might well have become a
hereditary caste, like priestly scholars in some other cultures. Knowledge of
Latin would then have been restricted to a self-perpetuating elite. Instead,
clerical celibacy drove trained men who could not accept it back into lay
society, thus disseminating literate skills, and it also made the production of
future clergy depend initially and primarily on the laity. Priests found it
increasingly difficult to hand on their benefices to their sons, as they were
deemed illegitimate. Opportunities consequently increased for non-clerical
families to get a clerical training.

A text of the mid-twelfth century, extant only in England though connected
with the school of Abelard, comments that Christian families unlike Jewish
ones educate one son only, 'not for God but for gain, in order that the one
brother, if he be a cleric, may help his father and mother and his other
brothers'; because a cleric has no heir, any acquisitions will return to the
family.[98] That this selective attitude prevailed in the twelfth century, even
among the nobility, is suggested by the childhood of Gerald of Wales. He was
the youngest (born in *c*.1147) of four brothers and showed his suitability for
the clergy at an early age by building sand churches and monasteries at the
seaside while his brothers built castles.[99] His father was pleased and called the
boy his 'bishop'. So Gerald was put in the charge of his uncle, David, who was
the real bishop of St David's. In due course Gerald was himself twice a
candidate for the bishopric of St David's, though his election was quashed.

---

[95] *Libellus de Vita*, ch. 109, pp. 226–8.
[96] Matthew Paris IV, p. 403; F. Pegues, 'The *Clericus* in the Legal Administration of
Thirteenth-Century England', *EHR* LXXI (1956), pp. 556–7.
[97] C. Brooke, 'Gregorian Reform in Action: Clerical Marriage in England', *Medieval Church
and Society* (1971), pp. 69–99.
[98] *Commentarius Cantabrigiensis* ed. A. Landgraf, cited by Smalley, *The Bible*, p. 78.
[99] Giraldus I, p. 21; R. Bartlett, *Gerald of Wales* (1982), pp. 27–8.

Gerald's family had a hereditary interest in the bishopric of St David's. Clerical celibacy at least ensured that offices now passed from uncle to nephew instead of father to son, and hence initial recruitment depended on laymen like Gerald's father.

Before Gregorian reform became effective, many future *clerici* must have been introduced to Latin and formal education by their own parents. Thus Orderic Vitalis's father, who was a priest, knew that Latin should be started young and had him instructed by another priest from the age of five.[100] As hereditary priests grew rarer, the responsibility for inaugurating children in Latin became the duty of parents who were technically *laici* and *illitterati*. They thus became familiar with the problems of learning, even if they remained uninstructed themselves. As clergy were required at all social levels, ranging from a noble bishop like Gerald's uncle to peasant parish priests, an increasing number of families began to have experience of education. *Clerici* and *laici* were united in the closest kinship by celibacy, not set apart. Literacy ceased to be a high arcane mystery when a younger brother was obliged to acquire it because he had no patrimony.

Among the nobility, pious mothers who read the Psalter and lives of the saints often perhaps took an active role in educating their children, as in the uniquely documented case of Guibert de Nogent.[101] At a humbler social level in England, it may have been Samson's mother who arranged for his schooling, when she showed off her precocious son of nine at the shrine of St Edmund. A century later Walter of Bibbesworth assumes that it will be the mother, albeit a widow, Denise de Montchensy, who improves her children's French.[102] 'Woman teacheth child on book' is put forward as a statement commanding general assent in an English poem (dating from c.1300) associated with Walter of Bibbesworth.[103] Walter assumes furthermore that both mother and children are familiar with the Latin primer, the 'book which teaches us *clergie*', because by the thirteenth century, among the nobility at least, all children both male and female were usually taught a little formal Latin and hence initiated into 'clergy'. A little *clergie* had the advantage of keeping children's options open. From inclination or necessity, boys or girls could subsequently join the 'religious', provided they had a grounding in Latin and some local influence. From the fourteenth century, moreover, a little Latin, 'benefit of clergy', was also an insurance against being hanged. Thus by 1300 conscientious or ambitious parents of all social classes had strong motives for seeing that their children were *clerici* and *litterati* in the new minimal sense of being capable of reading a verse from the Bible.

Real *litterati*, in the old sense of 'scholars', of course remained rare. Those who were totally ignorant, that is, those who could not pass a Latin reading test, were perhaps as rare. Detailed cases of failure to read are thought amusing, particularly by academics, and have therefore been repeatedly cited. Repetition gives the false impression that such cases were typical and

---

[100] See ch. 6, n. 74 above.
[101] *Self and Society in Medieval France* ed. J. F. Benton (1970).
[102] See ch. 6, nn. 1–5 above.
[103] N. Orme, *From Childhood to Chivalry* (1984), p. 16, n. 80.

commonplace. The description by Gerald of Wales of the abbot of St Dogmael's inability to read a papal letter, or even a missal, has already been cited.[104] But Gerald's numerous and lively descriptions of clerical ignorance are difficult to generalize from, as he even alleged that Hubert Walter was ignorant of elementary grammar. Possibly that was so, yet it did not prevent Hubert mastering the royal archives. Gerald's anecdotes, like other detailed reports of illiteracy among churchmen, suggest that normal expectations were relatively high.

Total inability to read was likewise the exception and not the rule among knights by 1300. Examples of such knights are as difficult to find as their converse, the *milites litterati*. Certainly there were some, like the two jurors in the de Tony case who were described as *laici*, though the use of the word 'layman' in this context implies that *clerici* were now the norm. One example of a really ignorant and boorish knight is a certain Hugh, who was charged with rape in 1293.[105] He had pleaded benefit of clergy and, when this plea was disallowed, he wished to challenge some of the jurors, which required reading out their names. At this point he had to admit that he was unable to read. But Hugh's predicament does not suggest that he was typical in being unable to read. On the contrary, it emphasizes how important it was by 1300 for a man in trouble to have sufficient *clergie* to get himself out of it. Even a century earlier in 1198 an illiterate landlord in Oxfordshire, Alan Fitz Roland, had found himself arraigned before the king's justices when he had failed to act on a writ brought against him in his court by his serfs; Alan's excuse was that he had no clerk who could read the document.[106] Thus sometimes by 1200 and invariably by 1300 a landlord, on however small a scale, needed sufficient *clergie*, in the sense of a personal knowledge of Latin, to assess, if not fully to understand, the written demands made upon him.

EDUCATED KNIGHTS

Knights who were able to read a little Latin, sufficient to get the gist of a royal writ or to understand a line in the Bible or in a chronicle, were literate in something like a modern minimal sense. By 1300, it has been argued in this chapter, such an ability was common among the gentry and may not have been rare among peasants. The conclusions to be drawn from this extension of minimal literacy are more problematical, however. In the modern world a little literacy enables a person to begin to cope with the mass of written instructions and bureaucratic demands which are a commonplace of daily experience. Further ability opens to the private reader, for recreation or self-improvement, the thousands of printed books available in his own language. A person who cannot read and write is therefore at a disadvantage in the mastery of daily life and he is also excluded from those areas of culture which depend on the printed word. These truisms are stated here only

[104] Giraldus III, p. 234; see ch. 4, n. 54 above.
[105] See ch. 8, n. 103 below.
[106] *CuriaRR* I, p. 46; cf. ibid., p. 203.

because they did not apply with equal force in the Middle Ages. A knight of the eleventh century who learned the rudiments of Latin in childhood would not have found this skill had much application in daily life, nor did it open to him the cultural heritage of his people, because Latin was a foreign language and books were not generally available.

By 1300 the situation had changed, though not radically. Bureaucratic demands in Latin were now sufficiently common to make it useful for any landowner to be able to understand them. 'Pragmatic' literacy, defined by Parkes as 'the literacy of one who has to read or write in the course of transacting any kind of business',[107] thus became usual. Literacy for purposes of recreation or self-improvement, the literacy of 'the cultivated reader', was still not very useful, although that too was beginning to change as more was being written down in vernacular languages. The books given by the earl of Warwick to Bordesley abbey in 1306, or the various late thirteenth-century manuscripts containing treatises on accountancy and estate management, indicate the kind of literature which might be found in a nobleman's, or even a gentleman's, household by 1300. On the whole, however, private reading must still have been a luxury, largely confined to retiring ladies and scholars. Books were scarce and it was ordinary good manners to share their contents among a group by reading aloud.

The increase in the number of persons who could read, at a minimal level, over the period 1066–1307 was thus a consequence of the demands of the 'pragmatic' rather than the 'cultivated' reader. That is why this book has approached literacy from record-making, instead of from the usual standpoint of an advance in culture and education. 'Documents had to precede widening literacy . . . The gentry were not going to learn to read until documents were available and necessary.'[108] Although a little Latin had become an essential of business and a commonplace of gentlemanly education by Walter of Bibbesworth's time, it was still something alien, and even contrary, to traditional knightly culture. Hence Latin was learned from the 'book which teaches us *clergie*'. An aspiring knight of the thirteenth century did not become a cultivated gentleman primarily by being a reader, necessary as that now was. He had to master the skills of combat, hunting, hawking, and chess, and know the vernacular languages, law, traditional oral 'literature', and music of his people. Such knowledge was not primarily to be found in Latin books, but in speech, gesture, and memory.

The biography of William Marshal (who died at an advanced age in 1219) is a unique recollection of knightly life in this period. It was written not in Latin but in French rhyming couplets (19,254 lines survive in the manuscript), so that it could be readily understood and remembered by the Marshal's family and retinue. His senior knight, John of Earley, supplied the information and he too may have been the composer of the verse. The biography says nothing about the Marshal's abilities in literacy. 'His accomplishments in Latin were probably no more than the basics required of a layman: the Lord's Prayer, the Ave Maria, and the Creed, which he would

[107] Parkes, Literacy', p. 555.
[108] See p. 78 above.

have learned, as like as not, from his mother or the household chaplains.'[109] Nevertheless it can be shown from the Marshal's charters that he, like other great men, had a clerical staff of three or more persons to keep accounts and do correspondence, together with household chaplains to look after his travelling chapel and its furnishings including prayer books.[110] When he became regent of England after the death of King John, the Marshal headed a bureaucratic administration which differed in scale rather than in substance from what he was already used to as an earl and a courtier. It was not reading and writing that made the life of knights like the Marshal so challenging, as he had his own clerks, but the unpredictability of his lay peers, particularly the Angevin royal family. Judging from the Marshal's biography, understanding what a horse and its rider might do under stress was a more precious form of knowledge than *clergie*.

Clerici and *litterati* might claim that book learning was the only intellectual and noble pursuit. Yet the slighest consideration of the languages an English knight needed to know, or any knowledge of the subtleties of heraldry or hawking, suggests that knightly education was equally demanding intellectually though in a different way. This suggestion cannot be incontrovertibly proved, however, because knightly culture before the fourteenth century has been largely lost to posterity, as it was primarily oral. Lack of written record did not of course make knightly culture any less real or less demanding for contemporaries. Indeed it may have been more lively than later literate culture, because knightly culture depended on the immediacy of speech. Judging from the romances, intellect and wit were prized among knights. A knight of advanced oral education was expected to contribute towards the knowledge and entertainment of his fellows instead of being a passive and silent recipient of book learning. The *clerici* might claim to be the elect of God, but the knights or warriors (*bellatores*) were as powerful and as venerable an elite. In the extension of medieval literacy the *clerici* did not impose their culture on ignorant and passive *laici*. Rather, clerical skills were gradually absorbed, in so far as they were useful, and an amalgam was formed over generations of literate and pre-literate habits of thought.

To give substance to generalizations which may seem vague and romanticized, this chapter will conclude with a look at two small incidents concerning knights recorded by Jocelin of Brakelond. Samson's first action after being inaugurated as abbot in 1182 was to turn away all suitors except one man. This was a knight (Jocelin does not record his name), 'eloquent and expert in law' (*juris peritus*), who was retained because Samson had no experience of business in secular courts.[111] After a while Samson began to master secular law, just as he mastered canon law, and the services of this knight presumably then became less essential. According to Jocelin, everyone marvelled at Samson's new expertise and the under-sheriff, Osbert Fitz Hervey, said: 'This abbot is a debater [*disputator*]; if he goes on as he has begun, he will dazzle us

---

[109] D. Crouch, *William Marshal* (1990), p. 23, cf. p. 3.
[110] Ibid., pp. 142–5. Gransden, *Historical Writing*, pp. 345–55, provides an excellent introduction to the biography of William Marshal.
[111] Jocelin, p. 24.

all, every one of us.'[112] Soon, 'having proved himself in cases', Samson's competence in secular law was officially recognized by his being appointed a royal justice in eyre.[113]

In these two incidents (first Samson's initial appointment of the anonymous knight and then the remark of Osbert Fitz Hervey on Samson's progress) Jocelin introduces his hero and his readers to an uncharted intellectual world, for which Samson's training as a *clericus* and *litteratus* had not explicitly prepared him. As it turned out, Samson mastered this world of secular law in due course, as he mastered everyone and everything in Jocelin's opinion. Yet this was a cause for surprise. Fitz Hervey had evidently not assumed that Samson's clerical education would make him a good debater in the county court. Knights like Fitz Hervey, who mastered county business, had learned their skills which were predominantly oral by years of attendance at the court, first by listening and then by speaking. About 30 years earlier in the same county court (again in a case concerning Bury St Edmunds) one of its 'proved and prudent men', Hervey de Glanvill, recalled how he had attended county and hundred courts first with his father and then as a householder in his own right for over fifty years.[114] His ancient wisdom had been duly heeded on that occasion.

From knights like Osbert Fitz Hervey, who learned their business orally, the king chose most of his justices and sheriffs, and litigants chose their advocates. Such expert knights were those 'greater men of the county, who are called *buzones*, on whose nod the views of the others depend', according to Bracton.[115] The *buzones judiciorum* are recorded giving judgement in a case in 1212.[116] Samson was not the only abbot to take legal advice from knights. In 1201 the abbot of Crowland had relied on the counsel of 'the wise and discreet knight, Reynold surnamed de Argento', in his litigation with the prior of Spalding.[117] Reynold in the 1190s had been a sheriff, a justice in eyre and an attorney of the bishop of Ely among others.[118] Osbert Fitz Hervey himself served as a justice in eyre in Richard I's reign and also on the Bench at Westminster between 1192 and 1206.[119] As a judge he achieved exceptional distinction, since he is one of only seven judges (including three chief justiciars) whose opinions on points of law are referred to in manuscripts of *Glanvill*.[120]

---

[112] Ibid., p. 34.

[113] Ibid., p. 34. Cf. n. 90 above.

[114] *English Lawsuits from William I to Richard I*, ed. R. C. van Caenegem, i, SS cvi (1990), p. 290; Clanchy, 'Remembering', p. 174. J. C. Russell suggests that Hervey may have been the father of Ranulf de Glanvill, the justiciar, *Speculum* xlv (1970), p. 71.

[115] Bracton, fo. 115b, vol. ii, p. 326.

[116] *CuriaRR* vi, p. 231; G. Lapsley, 'Buzones', *EHR* xlvii (1932), pp. 179ff; R & S, p. 94, n. 1; p. 183, n. 10.

[117] Stenton, *Justice*, p. 192.

[118] *Pleas before the King or his Justices* ed. D. M. Stenton, SS lxxxiii (1966), iii, pp. ccxcvi–ccxcvii.

[119] Ibid., p. cccxxx (indexed references under 'Osbert Fitz Hervey').

[120] Glanvill, pp. xliv–xlv.

Although knights like Fitz Hervey were experts in law (*juris periti*), their expertise was not in book learning but in oral advocacy. Skilful pleading in courts, the mastery of the spoken word, has been admired in many non-literate societies and is best exemplified in medieval Europe from those two extreme geographical points of medieval culture, the Iceland of the sagas and the crusader Kingdom of Jerusalem. From Iceland the best known example is the story in *Njal's Saga* of how Gunnar tricked the expert, Hrut, into summoning himself.[121] In the Kingdom of Jerusalem its knightly jurists (Ralf of Tiberias, John of Beirut, and Balian of Sidon) were the contemporaries of Osbert Fitz Hervey and Reynold de Argento. Although their opinions were subsequently written into the law books of the Kingdom, there is no doubt that they themselves learned their art, like the English jurists of the county court, from vernacular practice and not from ecclesiastical Latin schools.[122]

It is a mistake to regard knightly jurists as amateurs and clerical ones as professionals. Both knights and clergy contributed skills which shaped the legal profession. Pleading had been developed by knights as an alternative to private warfare, both as an honourable profession and as an intellectual pastime. When Henry the Young King and his companions spent a year in England in 1175 under the guardianship of that model of chivalry, William Marshal, they did nothing 'except pleading, hunting and fighting in tournaments'.[123] Clerics were trained in a comparable, though more book-centred, form of intellectual warfare by the disputations of the schools. Peter Abelard, the prototype of scholastic masters, in his autobiography saw his whole life in terms of warfare with other masters. The schools of Paris had probably taught Abbot Samson more than Osbert Fitz Hervey realized about how to be a *disputator*. In the twelfth century, when literate and pre-literate ways of thought were beginning to penetrate each other and interact, strong and novel institutions were formed by drawing on both traditions. Thus English common law benefited from the clerical training of scholastics like Samson and the oral lore of knights like Osbert. Whether royal judges were technically clergy or laymen seems to have had no bearing either way on their professional competence, although Walter Map thought it affected their severity. Once the judiciary becomes sufficiently documented in John's reign, it can be shown that of his 15 regular judges (that is, those who served for 10 or more terms) only four were clergy.[124] Similarly in Henry III's reign some judges, like Bracton, were clergy whereas others of equal distinction at the time, like Thurkelby, were knights.

The knights of English county courts, like knights all over Europe, were educated and cultured men regardless of whether they were literate. Perhaps by 1200, and certainly by 1300, they had usually learned enough Latin to cope with the documents which came their way. But this restricted knowledge of

---

[121] See ch. 8, n. 96 below.

[122] J. Riley-Smith, *The Feudal Nobility and the Kingdom of Jerusalem* (1973), pp. 123ff.

[123] 'A nule riens fors a pleidier ou a bois ou a torneier', *L'Histoire de guillaume le Maréchal* ed. P. Mayer, Societé de l'Histoire de France (1891–1901), lines 2393–4.

[124] R. V. Turner, 'The Judges of King John: their Background and Training', *Speculum* LI (1976), p. 454.

literacy was a pragmatic convenience, rather than a positive contribution to their intellectual education. A little Latin, learned from a relatively ignorant priest, did not educate a man in the culture of imperial or of Christian Rome, and hence it did not make him a *litteratus* in the traditional sense. Literacy became something more positive for non-churchmen only when writing recorded a substantial part of their own heritage in vernacular languages. That is a development of the later Middle Ages and not of the period 1066–1307.

Yet the twelfth and thirteenth centuries are crucially important because these are the years in which the traditional division between cleric and lay, literate and illiterate, was broken down. Gradually, by all sorts of avenues, a little literacy, in the sense of minimal Latin or *clergie*, became commonplace until 'benefit of clergy' came to mean the ability to read a few words of Latin. Because literacy had been identified with Latin for a thousand years, it had first to be learned by the laity in this clerical and alien form. Those old rivals, the *clerici-litterati* and the *laici-illitterati*, had to come to terms and absorb each other's thought processes before literacy could become a common vernacular habit. The extension of literacy was therefore a complex social problem in the Middle Ages and not a simple matter of providing more educational facilities. Knights absorbed clerical culture and clergy lived alongside knights. That archetypal *clericus*, Gerald of Wales, recounts how in 1188 his nephew, William de Barri, was committed at the age of 12 to Gerald's care for his education. This accorded with the custom whereby aristocratic boys were educated in a household other than their own. The boy was set 'continually to riding' in the retinue of Baldwin archbishop of Canterbury, whom Gerald was accompanying in the preaching of the Third Crusade in Wales and England. William grew up to become a knight and not a cleric, a knight who had acquired both book learning ('doctrine') and 'courtliness' under Gerald's direction.[125]

A fundamental question which has not been addressed here is the role of women in the dynamics of medieval literacy.[126] This is too large and complex a problem to discuss as an endpiece to this chapter. I hope to consider it in a subsequent study, ranging over a wider area and longer time-span than England between 1066 and 1307.[127] The subject also requires a different approach, using the evidence of imagery as much as written sources, because

[125] *Speculum Duorum* ed. Y. Lefèvre and R. B. C. Huygens (1974), p. 52. On the literacy of knights see also: R. V. Turner, 'The *Miles Litteratus* in Twelfth and Thirteenth-Century England: How Rare a Phenomenon?' *American Historical Review* LXXXIII (1978), pp. 928–45; F. H. Baüml, 'Varieties and Consequences of Medieval Literacy and Illiteracy', *Speculum* LV (1980), pp. 237–65; D. H. Green, 'Orality and Reading: The State of Research in Medieval Studies', *Speculum* LXV (1990), pp. 267–80.
[126] In general see the following authors cited below in 'Further Reading on the History of Literacy' (pp. 337–9 below): Alexandre-Bidon, Bell, Dronke, Ferrante, McKitterick, Rezak, Schreiner, Shahar, Swanson.
[127] *Woman and the Book in the Middle Ages* (Blackwell, forthcoming): part I, 'Women and Latin Literacy'; part II, 'Changing Images' (of the Virgin Mary and of ladies with books); part III, 'Domesticating the Book'. See also p. 13, n. 34 and p. 112, n. 138 above.

explicit references to women's literacy are rare. The best-documented literate women are nuns and anchoresses, like Christina of Markyate, but they are the least significant as far as female literacy is concerned because their rules and way of life were modelled on male monasticism. Nuns can be classified either as honorary males or as of neuter gender like all clergy. More significant in the history of literacy are the ways in which clerical habits and values were absorbed into the households of the aristocracy through ladies acquiring prayer books for their own use and commissioning or owning other works.[128] It has already been shown that liturgical books, in the form of Books of Hours, begin to be made for lay people in the thirteenth century and that the earliest English examples were made for women rather than men.[129]

Ladies with their own households and withdrawing chambers could conduct themselves like groups of male clergy: reciting prayers, reading silently, and looking at and listening to – and perhaps even writing – their own books, whether religious or secular. Within such female households, too, children acquired familiarity with books at an early age, and habits of literacy were thus transmitted from one generation to the next. By these means literate skills were extended beyond the caste of *clerici*. The 'domestication' of ecclesiastical books by great ladies, together with the ambitions of mothers of all social classes for their children, were the foundations on which the growth of literacy in fourteenth- and fifteenth-century Europe were constructed. This shift in the focus of literacy from monastic church to noble household was perhaps as significant a cultural change as the shift from memory to the written record, but it lies beyond the scope and period of this book.[130]

---

[128] See the discussion of the Lambeth Apocalypse and Christina of Markyate's Psalter at pp. 188–94 above.

[129] See pp. 111–12, nn. 136–7 above.

[130] M. T. Clanchy, 'Looking Back from the Invention of Printing', in *Literacy in Historical Perspective* ed. D. P. Resnick (1983), p. 14; N. Orme, *From Childhood to Chivalry* (1984).

8

Hearing and Seeing

'Fundamentally letters are shapes indicating voices. Hence they represent things which they bring to mind through the windows of the eyes. Frequently they speak voicelessly the utterances of the absent.'[1] In these antitheses John of Salisbury's *Metalogicon* grapples with the basic problems of the relationship between the spoken and the written word. The difference between sounds or voices (*voces*) and things or realities (*res*) was complicated for him, writing in the mid-twelfth century, by the controversy between Nominalists and Realists, between those who argued that universals were mere names and those who claimed they were real things. This philosophical controversy is not our concern here. John's remarks are relevant because, like much of *Metalogicon*, they seem to reflect his own experience as a secretary and drafter of letters as well as exemplifying current scholastic thought.

Numerous charters of the twelfth century are addressed to 'all those seeing and hearing these letters, in the future as in the present' or to 'all who shall hear and see this charter'; these two examples come from the charters of Roger de Mowbray who died in 1188.[2] The grantor of another charter, Richard de Rollos, actually harangues his audience, 'Oh! all ye who shall have heard this and have seen!'[3] Early charters likewise quite often conclude with 'Goodbye' (*Valete*), as if the donor had just finished speaking with his audience.[4] Documents made it possible for the grantor to address posterity ('all who shall hear and see') as well as his contemporaries. In the opening words of the

---

[1] 'Littere autem, id est figure, primo vocum indices sunt; deinde rerum, quas anime per oculorum fenestras opponunt, et frequenter absentium dicta sine voce loquuntur', *Metalogicon*, Bk. I, ch. 13, ed. J. B. Hall and K. S. B. Keats-Rohan (1991), p. 32.
[2] *Mowbray Charters*, nos 92, 347. Cf. ch. 3, nn. 11–12 above.
[3] Stenton, *Feudalism*, pp. 111, 273, no. 27.
[4] E. g. *Oxford Facs*, nos 7, 38, 54, 56, 60, 62, 72, 74.

Winchcombe abbey cartulary, 'when the voice has perished with the man, writing still enlightens posterity.'[5] Writing shifted the spotlight away from the transitory actors witnessing a conveyance and on to the perpetual parchment recording it. By the thirteenth century, when charters had become more familiar to landowners, donors cease addressing their readers, as Richard de Rollos did, and likewise they no longer conclude with *Valete*. Once it was understood that charters were directed to posterity, it must have seemed foolish to say 'Goodbye' to people who had not yet been born. In place of such conversational expressions, thirteenth-century charters are more stereotyped; they are often impersonally addressed in some such form as 'Let all persons, present and future, know that I, A of B, have given X with its appurtenances to C of D.'[6]

A comparable change occurs in wills. Until the thirteenth century the will was an essentially oral act, even when it was recorded in writing. The persons present witnessed the testator making his bequests 'with his own mouth'; they 'saw, were present, and heard' the transaction.[7] By the end of the thirteenth century a man's final will no longer usually meant his wishes spoken on his deathbed, but a closed and sealed document. The witnesses no longer heard him; instead they saw his seal being placed on the document. When wills were first enrolled, as they were in London from 1258, the formula of probate still put emphasis on the witnesses who had seen and heard. But a generation later, by the 1290s, the London roll often omits the names of the witnesses, presumably because the written will was the preferred evidence.[8] The validity of the will now depended primarily upon its being in a correct documentary form and not on the verbal assurances of the witnesses. This is another illustration of the shift from memory to written record between 1100 and 1300. Wills had been made in writing by the Anglo-Saxons; the novelty lay in their being closed and sealed documents.

SYMBOLIC OBJECTS AND DOCUMENTS

Before conveyances were made with documents, the witnesses 'heard' the donor utter the words of the grant and 'saw' him make the transfer by a symbolic object, such as a knife or a turf from the land. William the Conqueror went one better and jokingly threatened to make one donee 'feel' the conveyance by dashing the symbolic knife through the recipient abbot's hand saying, 'That's the way land ought to be given.'[9] Such a gesture was intended to impress the event on the memory of all those present. If there were

---

[5] *Landboc sive Registrum de Wincehlcumba* ed. D. Royce (1892) I, p. 17.

[6] C. A. F. Meekings analyses conveyancing forms in *Fitznell's Cartulary*, Surrey Record S. XXVI (1968), pp. cxliff.

[7] M. M. Sheehan, *The Will in Medieval England*, Pontifical Institute of Medieval Studies: Studies & Texts VI (1963), pp. 186–7.

[8] Ibid., pp. 192; 188, n. 90.

[9] P & M II, p. 87, n. 4. In general see J. Le Goff, *Time, Work and Culture in the Middle Ages* (1980), pp. 244–8, 354–60.

dispute subsequently, resort was had to the recollection of the witnesses. Similar rules applied to the oral 'records' of courts, which were retained (in theory at least) in the memory of those present. For example, if the record of the county court were disputed, the aggrieved litigant brought forward two witnesses who each gave evidence of what they had heard and seen. In such a case in 1212 the prior of Ware (in Hertfordshire) defended himself by 'one hearing and one understanding', namely Jordan of Warew and Robert of Clopton; Robert also offered to prove the prior's allegation by battle, 'as he was present and heard this'.[10] In this case some distinction is evidently being made between the knowledge of the two witnesses: Jordan had heard, or at least understood, less of the preceedings than Robert. Likewise at Cheshunt (in Hertfordshire) in a seignorial court in 1220 a litigant challenged the record by 'one person hearing and another seeing'.[11] Which testimony was thought preferable in this instance, that of the person who heard or of the other who saw, is unclear. These cases suggest that the legal commonplace of making a record by 'hearing and seeing' was not a mere formula made meaningless by repetition.

Documents changed the significance of bearing witness by hearing and seeing legal procedures, because written evidence could be heard by reading aloud or seen by inspecting the document. In John of Salisbury's definition, letters 'indicate voices' and bring things to mind 'through the windows of the eyes'. Once charters were used for conveyances, 'hearing' applied to anyone hearing the charter read out loud at any time, instead of referring only to the witnesses of the original conveyance. From there it was a short step to substitute 'reading' for 'seeing', as one of Roger de Mowbray's charters does, which is addressed to 'all his own men and to the rest, *reading* or hearing these letters'.[12] This phrase plays also with the ambiguity of the word 'letters', which in Latin (as in English) means both alphabetic symbols and missives.

A curiously worded grant for St Mary's priory at Monmouth is addressed to the donors, Richard de Cormeilles and Beatrice his wife, instead of to the recipients.[13] The charter rewards Richard and Beatrice with divine bliss because they have given the tithes of Norton-Giffard to Mary the mother of God. She is the ostensible grantor of the charter, though the document itself was presumably written by a monk of St Mary's priory which was the terrestrial beneficiary. The writer's Latin is eccentric – for example he spells *uxor* (wife) as *hucxor* – but revealing in its phraseology. He includes the phrase *sicut presens breve loquitur* (as the present writing speaks), whereas ordinary usage would have *dicitur* (says) or *testatur* (attests) in place of *loquitur*. The writer also makes it clear that the named witnesses, who 'saw and heard the gift solemny exhibited by the book upon the altar', are 'subsequent' and therefore secondary to the evidence of the writing itself. In making the writing 'speak' and in putting the pre-literate witnessing ceremony of seeing and

---

[10] *CuriaRR* vi, p. 230. See also ibid. xiii, p. 405, no. 1926; and p. 77 above.
[11] *SPC*, pp. 124–5, no. 192.
[12] *Mowbray Charters*, no. 98.
[13] *BM Facs*, no. 16.

hearing into a subsidiary role, the naïve writer of this charter has exemplified John of Salisbury's scholastic definition (which is contemporary with the charter) that letters 'speak voicelessly the utterances of the absent', the absent in this instance being the grantor, Mary the mother of God.

Once property was conveyed in writing, it would have seemed logical for the charter to supersede the symbolic object, such as the knife or turf, which had formerly been used in the witnessing ceremony. As the grant to Monmouth priory shows, that object had sometimes itself been a writing – a book solemnly exhibited upon an altar. Traditionally the book used for this purpose was the text of the Gospels. For example a gift of a saltpan was made to St Peter's priory at Sele in Sussex in 1153 'by the text of the Holy Gospel upon the altar of St Peter, many persons hearing and seeing'. The Gospel book was used because it was customary to reinforce oaths with it (as is still the practice in law courts); thus in Edward I's wardrobe there was kept 'a book, which is called *textus*, upon which the magnates were accustomed to swear'.[14] To replace a Gospel book by a charter in a conveyancing ceremony was a relatively small change in appearance (it was simply substituting one document for another), but a large one in substance. The charter in its text actually 'represented' (in John of Salisbury's definition) in a durable record the terms of the conveyance, whereas the Gospel book merely symbolized the solemnity of the occasion for the witnesses. The Monmouth priory charter therefore distinguishes the written grant (*breve*), which 'speaks' to the hearers, from the symbolic book (*liber*) which is 'exhibited' to the viewers. Nevertheless, although it seemed logical to dispense with symbols and make full use of the potentialities of writing, contemporaries continued with their pre-literate habits long after charters had become common. In the rare instances where the conveyance appears to be made by the written document itself (as in the Monmouth priory charter), we should probably assume that the document is serving the ancient function of a symbolic object, rather than being considered primarily for its contents in a modern literate way.

There are examples of the conveyancing document being presented on the altar like a Gospel book. In a charter of 1193 the abbot of Glastonbury states that 'the present charter was placed on the altar of St Mary by me as an offering, the clergy and people of the same vill [of Street in Somerset] standing round.' In his *Life of St Alban* Matthew Paris portrayed King Offa of Mercia on bended knee before the altar of the saint handing his charter of gift to a monk, who stands facing him vested for Mass, while a servant rings the great bells of the abbey church.[15] Although Matthew showed some of the ancient features of St Albans in his drawings, like the Roman bricks and the round arches, the form in which he drew Offa's charter is as anachronistic as the bells. It has prominently ruled lines and the seal looks like the Great Seal (introduced in the eleventh century). These anachronisms may be deliberate, however, as Matthew's purpose was not to teach archaeology but to instruct his contemporaries in 1250 about the endowments of the abbey. Multiple

---

[14] *Oxford Facs*, no. 9; Chaplais, *Docs*, p. 50, n. 2. C. R. Cheney discusses the meaning of *textus* in *BIHR* LVI (1983), pp. 9–10.

[15] C. R. Cheney, *Notaries Public in England* (1972), p. 7, n. 4; Lewis, *Matthew Paris*, p. 113.

time-frames are also contained in the roundel portraying the principal benefactors of Crowland abbey at the altar of their patron, St Guthlac (see plate xx). King Ethlebald of Mercia at the front is eighth-century, Abbot Thurketel in the centre is tenth-century, and some of the other benefactors are eleventh-century or later. Each one holds open a scroll recording his gift in abbreviated Latin. Thus the scroll of the bearded figure on the extreme left says: 'I Alan de Croun give you, Father Guthlac, the priory of Freiston with appurtenances.'[16] Scrolls were used iconographically to indicate speech. The Crowland artist, like an artist portraying an Old Testament prophet, turns speech-acts into scripture: each benefactor presses forward to lay his scroll on St Guthlac's altar, as if it were a charter. This roundel is both a work of art and an artifice, which gives written form to gifts for which Crowland abbey had inadequate documentary proof. The benefactors' scrolls are letters which 'speak voicelessly the utterances of the absent'.

An explicit instance of a conveyance by the charter itself is a gift made by William of Astle in *c.* 1200 to the Knights Hospitaller. The last witness is Ivo, clerk of Stafford, representing the Hospitallers, 'in whose hand I, William, have made scisin with this charter in the church of Alderly'.[17] The usual rule was that a conveyance could not be made by a document alone, but depended on the recipient having 'seisin' (meaning actual possession of the property). Nevertheless the exception to this rule in William of Astle's charter may merely prove it, as the charter, conveyed from hand to hand, is a substitute for the usual object symbolizing the transaction. The unfamiliar idea of a writing being interpreted primarily as a symbolic object, rather than as a document- ary proof, is most clearly evident when the object written upon is not a parchment, but something else. Thus an ivory whip-handle found at St Albans abbey had an inscription on it stating that 'this is the gift from Gilbert de Novo Castello of four mares.'[18] The object, a whip, appropriately symbolized the gift of horses; the writing was ancillary. In 1266 an inquiry about the forest of Bernwood in Buckinghamshire attested that John Fitz Nigel held it from the king 'by a horn, which is as a charter (*quod est charte*) for the aforesaid forest'.[19] An appropriate symbolic object, a hunting horn, was allowed to stand in this case as the equivalent of documentary proof because the tenure dated from before the Norman Conquest, through a gift allegedly made by Edward the Confessor to his huntsman Nigel. The 'Boarstall Horn' in Buckinghamshire Record Office, dating in its present mounting from the fifteenth century, may be the same horn as that referred to in the inquiry of 1266.

---

[16] For this gift see *Monasticon*, IV, p. 125. For scrolls see F. Garnier, *Le Langage de l'image au Moyen Age*, vol. ii (1989), pp. 229–44, 394–400.

[17] *Cheshire Facs*, no. 13 (2).

[18] H. Ellis, 'Observations on Some Ancient Methods of Conveyance in England', *Archaeologia* XVII (1814), p. 313. I have not been able to trace this whip-handle.

[19] *The Boarstall Cartulary* ed. H. E. Salter, Oxford Historical S. LXXXVIII (1930), p. 170, no. 562; Patent Rolls 1266–72, p. 15; J. Cherry, 'Medieval Horns of Tenure', *The Antiquaries Journal* LXIX (1989), p. 113, plate xix.

Most remarkable is a knife preserved at Durham, which symbolizes Stephen of Bulmer's agreement (made in the second half of the twelfth century) with the monks of the Holy Island of Lindisfarne about the chapel of Lowick. Its haft is inscribed, which makes it comparable with the St Albans whip-handle and the hafts of other inscribed knives no longer extant.[20] Whereas the hafts of these other knives were made of ivory, Stephen's is of hard horn (perhaps a deer's) and the inscriber has had difficulty making much impression on it. He was not perhaps an experienced carver but a scribe, possibly a monk of Lindisfarne, who only had a pen knife readily available. Although the lettering of the inscription is shaky and uneven, it is conceived in a bold monastic hand. Along one side of the knife's haft is written *Signum de capella de lowic* (the sign of the chapel of Lowick) and on the other side *de capella de lowic & de decimis de lowic totius curie & totius ville* (for the chapel of Lowick and for the tithes of Lowick from the whole court and the whole vill). As well as this inscription on the haft, a parchment label is attached (written in a comparable bold monastic hand), which gives fuller details of the agreement. This label cannot be described as a charter, as it is irregular in shape and is written on both sides. A statement on its dorse helps explain the purpose of the knife. It records that Stephen of Bulmer had not come in person to make the agreement at Holy Island, but sent Lady Cecily and Aschetin, the *dapifer* or steward, in his place. Probably Aschetin brought the knife with him as a symbol of Stephen's consent. It may well have been Stephen's own carving knife; the haft is heavy and shows signs of use and, although the blade is broken near the top, what remains of the knife still measures $13\frac{1}{2}$ cm. It would thus have been an appropriate object for a steward, who probably carved at his lord's table, to bring as durable and substantial evidence that he truly represented his master.

Why go to the trouble of trying to write on a knife, when pen and parchment did the same job more efficiently? Ordinary writing materials were evidently available, as Stephen's knife has the parchment label on it as well as the inscription. The explanation may be that the parties to this agreement had more confidence in the evidence of the knife than in writing. Knives were traditional symbols for conveyances, perhaps going back as far as the discovery of metals, whereas charters authenticated by seals were a novelty (although seals in themselves were ancient). Of particular interest and obscurity is what breaking the knife signified in the conveyancing ceremony. A charter dating from early in Henry I's reign records a gift made by William Fitz Baderon to the monks of St Florent for their priory of St Mary's at Monmouth. The gift was 'made by a knife', the charter says, but there was a mishap when Bernard the king's chaplain 'could not break the knife with his hands' and had to 'break it

---

[20] Ellis, 'Observations', pp. 313, 315–16, gives examples of inscribed knives. Bulmer's knife is best illustrated in the engraving in J. Raine, *History and Antiquities of North Durham* (1852), appendix, p. 135; M. T. Clanchy, 'Reading the Signs at Durham Cathedral', in *Literacy and Society* ed. K. Schousboe and M. T. Larsen (1989), pp. 175–7.

beneath his foot' instead.[21] The charter records this mishap presumably because breaking the knife with the hands was an essential part of the conveyancing process, which had not been complied with in this instance. Bernard the king's chaplain was curator of the diocese of Hereford, in which Monmouth lay. Why it was his responsibility to break the knife is obscure, as he was neither the donor nor the recipient of the land. Possibly he personified the authority of the bishop or the king. If the symbolism of knives were understood, much might become clearer about pre-literate property law in Europe. As well as being traditional, some contemporaries may have thought that a knife was more durable than, and therefore preferable to, parchment and sealing wax. It was true that only the sparsest details of a conveyance could be engraved on the handle of a knife or a whip, but the tradition had been that the true facts of a transaction were engraved on the hearts and minds of the witnesses and could not be fully recorded in any form of writing however detailed. The symbolic knife would have been retained regardless of whether it had anything written on it, because it preserved the memory of the conveyance.

Only literates, who could interpret the 'shapes indicating voices' (in John of Salisbury's definition of letters), were going to be convinced that the writing was superior to the symbolic object. Such objects, the records of the non-literate, were therefore preserved along with documents. Another example is the knife by which Thomas of Moulton gave the church of Weston in Lincolnshire to Spalding priory, which was deposited in its archive (*in secretario*) according to the charter confirming the gift.[22] This latter knife is no longer preserved. To later archivists, knives and other archaic relics meant nothing unless they had inscriptions connected with them; such things were thrown away as medieval rubbish, because the language of memory which they expressed had no significance for literates.

It is possible that the seals, *signa* in Latin, attached to charters were seen by many contemporaries in a similar way as inscribed 'signs'. To students of diplomatic today, seals are a method of authenticating documents which preceded the sign manual or written signature. To medieval people they may have appeared rather as visible and tangible objects symbolizing the wishes of the donor. The seal was significant even without the document. Early seals (that is, twelfth-century ones) tend to be disproportionately large compared with the writings to which they are attached (see plate 1). John of Salisbury, writing on behalf of Archbishop Theobald of Canterbury about the safekeeping of seals, says that 'by the marks of a single impress the mouths of all the pontiffs may be opened or closed.'[23] Just as letters 'speak voicelessly the utterances of the absent', seals regulate that speech. Emphasis on the spoken word remained.

---

[21] J. H. Round, *Calendar of Documents Preserved in France* (1899), p. 409, no. 1138. Latin text ed. P. Marchegay in *Bibliothèque de l'École des Chartes* XL (1879), p. 179, no. 16 (I owe this reference to Dr J. Barrow). 'Bernard the Chaplain' is different from 'Bernard the King's Scribe'. Breaking is discussed by Le Goff, *Time*, p. 360.

[22] *Monasticon* III, p. 217, no. x. See also p. 156, n. 43 above.

[23] *Letters* ed. W. J. Millor et al. (1955) I, p. 109.

The 'signs' attached to documents, whether they took the form of inscribed knives or impressed wax or even ink crosses made by the witnesses, all helped to bridge the gulf between the traditional and the literate way of recording transactions. Pre-literate customs and ceremonies persisted despite the use of documents. The doctrine of livery of seisin – the rule that a recipient must have the property duly delivered to him and enter into possession (that is, seisin) of it, whether there was a document of conveyance or not – became a fundamental principle of the common law; but there are exceptions to it, like the charter of William of Astle to the Knights Hospitaller which has already been discussed. The treatise ascribed to Bracton insists (in the first half of the thirteenth century) that 'a gift is not valid unless livery follows; for the thing given is transferred neither by homage, nor by the drawing up of charters and instruments, even though they be recited in public.' Written words were thus entirely inadequate, and even spoken ones were insufficient, without physical symbols: 'If livery is to be made of a house by itself, or of a messuage for an estate, it ought to be made by the door and its hasp or ring, by which is understood that the donee possess the whole to its boundaries.' It followed also that a gift 'may be valid though no charter has been made . . . and conversely the charter may be genuine and valid and the gift incomplete.'[24] The physical symbol, the door hasp or ring in Bracton's example, continued to epitomize the whole gift better than any document.

Likewise the drafting rule became general that the past tense should be used in charters for the act of giving: 'Know that I, A of B, *have* given', not simply 'I give'. This emphasized that the ceremonial conveyance was the crucial transaction, whereas the charter was merely a subsequent confirmation of it. This rule became firmly established only in the thirteenth century. Numerous charters of the twelfth century depart from it, presumably because their more amateur draftsmen did not appreciate the relationship between written record and the passage of time. Similarly a generation or two after Bracton the need for the livery of seisin rule was not apparent to ordinary people. Some Derbyshire jurors, who had supposed in 1304 that a charter might suffice without it, were described by a second group of jurors as 'simple persons who were not cognizant with English laws and customs'.[25] The doctrine of seisin, which had once been a self-evident and commonsense rule, had become with the spread of literacy one of those technical mysteries in which the common law abounded.

THE SPOKEN VERSUS THE WRITTEN WORD

The increasing use of documents created tension between the old methods and the new. Which was the better evidence, for example, seeing a parchment or hearing a man's word? How was the one to be evaluated if it conflicted with the other? A good illustration of this particular dilemma is Eadmer's account of the investiture controversy between St Anselm, archbishop of Canterbury,

---

[24] Bracton, fos 39b–40, vol. ii, pp. 124–5; ibid., fo. 11b, p. 50.
[25] *Calendarium Genealogicum*, RC (1865) ii, p. 659; P & M ii, p. 89.

and Henry I.[26] Both Anselm and the king had sent envoys to Pope Paschal II; Anselm sent two monks of Canterbury, while the king sent the archbishop of York and two other bishops. The envoys returned to England in September 1101 with papal letters addressed to the king and to Anselm, prohibiting royal investiture of churches and exhorting resistance to them. When the pope's letter to Anselm had been publicly read out, Henry's envoys objected. They claimed that Paschal had given them a purely verbal message that he would treat the king leniently on the investiture question and would not excommunicate him; the pope had added that he did not wish this concession to be put in written form (*per carte inscriptionem*) because others rulers would use it as a precedent. Anselm's envoys replied that the pope had given no verbal message which conflicted in any way with his letters. To this Henry's bishops answered that Paschal had acted in one way in secret and another in public. Baldwin of Bec, Anselm's chief envoy, was outraged at this allegation and said that it was a calumny on the Holy See.

Dissension then arose in the audience. Those favouring Anselm maintained that credence should be given to 'documents signed with the pope's seal (*scriptis sigillo pape signatis*) and not to 'the uncertainty of mere words'. The king's side replied that they preferred to rely on the word of three bishops than on 'the skins of wethers blackened with ink and weighted with a little lump of lead'. They added further venom to the argument by alleging that monks were unreliable anyway, as they should not be engaged in worldly business. Eadmer puts the controversy into dialogue form:

> *Anselm's monks:* 'But what about the evidence of the letters?'
> *Henry's bishops:* 'As we don't accept the evidence of monks against bishops, why should we accept that of a sheepskin?'
> *Anselm's monks:* 'Shame on you! Are not the Gospels written down on sheepskins?'

Obviously the conflict could not be quickly resolved. In Lent 1102 Anselm set out for Rome and opened on his way another letter from the pope, in which Paschal denied that he had ever given contradictory verbal instructions to the bishops or said that he was reluctant to set a precedent in writing.[27] Who was telling the truth is of course impossible to resolve. Paschal was attempting to make peace and settle the investiture controversy by diplomacy. He may well therefore have said something off the record to the bishops which they had possibly exaggerated. Like all statesmen, the pope obviously had to make a formal denial of such secret negotiations once they became public.

The substance of the story is not our concern here, but the attitudes it reveals towards documentary evidence. Papal letters, sealed with the leaden bull and bearing the symbols and monograms of curial officials, were the most impressive documents produced in medieval Europe, their only rival being Byzantine imperial letters. Yet in Eadmer's story the papal bull is disparagingly described as a sheepskin blackened with ink with a bit of lead attached

---

[26] *Historia*, pp. 132–40.
[27] Ibid., pp. 149–51. R. W. Southern, *St Anselm* (1990), p. 295, n. 17.

to it, an extreme example of a document being treated simply as a physical object rather than for its contents. Anselm's supporters were entitled to riposte that the Gospels too were written on parchment – in other words, that Christianity was essentially the religion of a book. At Orléans in 1022 a group of heretics had been burned for disparaging the book learning of the clergy cross-examining them, which they had called human fabrications 'written on the skins of animals', whereas the heretics claimed to believe 'in the law written in the inner man by the Holy Spirit'.[28] The heretics had therefore been arguing that the true written law (*lex scripta*) was not canon law nor Justinian's code, but inspiration retained in the mind alone; real writing was not man-made script on animal parchment. Such an idea may well have derived from the Scripture itself, most probably from St Paul's Second Epistle to the Corinthians, 'written not with ink, but with the spirit of the living God . . . for the letter killeth, but the spirit giveth life.'[29] Early in the thirteenth century St Francis was to take up this theme as part of his revolt against the spiritually empty book learning of some monks: 'Those religious have been killed by the letter who are not willing to follow the spirit of the divine letter, but only desire to know words and interpret them for other men.'[30] As so often in his work, Francis blended orthodox and heretical viewpoints in an insight of his own. Literacy was not a virtue in itself. Emphasis on the word inscribed spiritually on the minds of men, as contrasted with letters written on parchment, retained its strength in the Christian message as it did in secular conveyancing ceremonies.

The argument of Henry I's envoys, that their word was better evidence than a papal bull, would not in fact have appeared as outrageous or surprising to contemporaries as Eadmer suggests in his account of the controversy with Anselm. The principle that 'oral witness deserves more credence than written evidence' was a legal commonplace. It was cited for example by Hubert Walter, archbishop of Canterbury, in a letter to Innocent III in 1200 controverting Gerald of Wales's well-documented claim to be bishop-elect of St David's.[31] Gerald conceded the point in his reply to the pope, but added that he had brought both documents and witnesses. Behind this principle lay the correct assumption that numerous documents used in legal claims, from the Donation of Constantine downwards, were forgeries. Not all those who relied on the traditional use of the spoken word, rather than parchments, were necessarily therefore obscurantist conservatives. The technology of written record was insufficiently advanced to be efficient or reliable. As a consequence, documents and the spoken word are frequently both used in a way which appears superfluous to a modern literate. To make a record often meant to bear oral witness, not to produce a document. For example, in the civil war

---

[28] *Recueil des historiens des Gaules* ed. L. Delisle (1869–) x, p. 539; R. I. Moore, *The Birth of Popular Heresy* (1975), pp. 10–15. The author of this account is discussed by B. Stock, *The Implications of Literacy* (1983), pp. 107–15.

[29] 2 *Corinthians*, iii, 3, 6. Cf. Smalley, *The Bible*, ch. 1 ('The Letter and the Spirit').

[30] R. B. Brooke, *The Coming of the Friars* (1975), p. 126.

[31] 'testibus et non testimoniis credi oportet,' Giraldus iii, pp. 14, 21, H. E. Butler, *The Autobiography of Giraldus Cambrensis* (1937), pp. 168, 175–6.

of Stephen's reign Robert earl of Gloucester and Miles earl of Hereford made a treaty of friendship in writing, in the form of a sealed letter; yet both parties in this document also name witnesses, who are 'to make legal record of this agreement in court if necessary'.[32]

The rule that oral witness is preferable to documents, like the rule that seisin is superior to a charter, shows how cautiously – and perhaps reluctantly – written evidence was accepted. Much important business continued to be done by word of mouth. Bearers of letters were often given instructions which were to be conveyed *viva voce*, either because that was convenient and traditional or because the information was too secret to write down. Twice, for instance, in March 1229 Henry III sent messengers to the count of Toulouse. In their mouths, the king wrote, he had put matters which they would disclose more fully to the count, since the business (presumably concerning a truce with Louis IX) could not be committed to writing because of the dangers of the roads.[33] Similarly in the period of the baronial rebellion, when Henry was in France in 1260, he wrote to the earl of Gloucester instructing him to report on the state of the kingdom by Gilbert Fitz Hugh, the king's serjeant, who would tell the earl more fully *viva voce* about the king's situation.[34] In such negotiations the letter itself did not convey essential information but, like a modern ambassador's letter of credence, was a symbolic object replacing the messenger's ring or other *signum* which had formerly identified him as a confidential agent of his master.

Oral messages were also used to give instructions which later generations would have put in writing. For example, in 1234 John le Franceis and John Mansel were authorized by royal letters of credence to conduct inquiries concerning Jews in certain counties and give instructions to sheriffs *viva voce*.[35] An interesting but non-English case of oral delivery is the poem which the troubadour, Jaufre Rudel, lord of Blaye in the Gironde, sent to the Comte de Marche in *c.*1150 'without a parchment document' (*senes breu de parguamina*) by the mouth of the jongleur, Filhol.[36] The jongleur is thus being used as a kind of living letter. There is, however, a paradox in all such evidence, since historians can only know of the survival of oral ways of conveying information by extant written evidence. Jaufre Rudel's poem, once sent without a script, is written down none the less.

Much business was still done by word of mouth for the obvious reason that documents were bound to be relatively rare until printing made their automatic reproduction possible. The usual way of publishing new laws and regulations was by proclamation. The following instances from the Chancery records of Henry III for 1234 are typical.[37] On 28 August the sheriff of Northumberland and some others were ordered to have it proclaimed (*clamari facias*) that pleas were to be adjourned until the coming of the eyre justices. On

---

[32] See p. 77, n. 124 above.
[33] *ClR* 1227–31, p. 233.
[34] Ibid., 1259–61, p. 281.
[35] Ibid., 1231–4, p. 586.
[36] A. E. van Vleck, *Memory and Re-Creation in Troubadour Lyric* (1991), p. 41.
[37] *ClR* 1231–4, pp. 592–3.

29 August all sheriffs were to proclaim the regulations for supervising hundred courts in accordance with the revision of Magna Carta in 1234. On 1 September the sheriff of Norfolk and Suffolk was to proclaim throughout the two counties that no Jew was to lend money to any Christian in the king's demesne.[38] Matthew Paris suggests that Henry III pursued a policy of legislating by proclamation: in 1248 the people were harassed by diverse precepts promulgated 'by the voice of a crier' (*voce preconia*) throughout the cities of England; the king established a new fair at Westminster, for example, in this way.[39] The proclamation to which Matthew gives most attention likewise occurred in 1248, when the king 'ordered it to be proclaimed as law by the voice of a crier' that henceforward no man might castrate another for fornication except a husband in the case of his wife's adulterer.[40] The reason for this was that John le Bretun had castrated the Norfolk knight, Godfrey de Millers, for lying with his daughter.

How extensively or frequently proclamations of this sort were made is not clear. Proclamations were a quick and effective way of conveying information in crowded cities like London, but were obviously less practical in the countryside. Most references to proclamations concern cities. For example, in 1252 Henry III had it proclaimed throughout London that no one should lend money to the abbot of Westminster; or in the preceding year a proclamation had been made against the royal judge, Henry of Bath, in London and in the king's court.[41] One consequence for the historian of Henry III's government's use of the spoken word for legislation is that all trace of it is lost, unless a chronicler happened to record it or the Chancery rolls refer to it incidentally. Edward I is considered a great lawgiver partly because the legislation of his time is preserved in the statute rolls. In Henry III's reign less was written down, though a comparable amount of legislative activity probably took place.

Magna Carta became the great precedent for putting legislation into writing. Yet even it was not officially enrolled in the royal archives, although it was proclaimed extensively and repeatedly. Within a few days of King John's assent to it letters were sent to all his sheriffs, foresters, gamekeepers, watermen, and other bailiffs informing them of the agreement between the king and the barons, 'as you can hear and see by our charter which we have had made thereon', which they were ordered to have read publicly throughout their bailiwicks.[42] As a result, in theory at least, everyone in England should have heard Magna Carta read out, although it is unlikely that a sufficient number of copies were available.[43] Similarly when the barons again had the upper hand in 1265, they ordered the terms of Henry III's oath to keep peace with them to be published in the full county court at least twice every year, at

---

[38] Ibid., p. 592; C. Roth, *A History of the Jews in England* (1941), p. 53.

[39] Matthew Paris v, pp. 18, 29.

[40] 'voce preconia iussit pro lege acclamari,' ibid., p. 35; *CIR* 1247–51, pp. 139, 394; *CPatR* 1247–58, p. 387.

[41] Matthew Paris v, pp. 305, 223; *CPatR* 1247–58, p. 101.

[42] J. C. Holt, *Magna Carta* (1965), p. 345.

[43] F. Thompson, *The First Century of Magna Carta* (1925), p. 94.

Easter and Michaelmas.[44] In 1300 transcripts of Magna Carta and the Charter of the Forest were delivered to every sheriff to read out 'before the people' four times a year, at Christmas and Midsummer as well as at Easter and Michaelmas.[45] Nevertheless by 1300 there had been a significant change, as considerable emphasis was now being put on seeing the document as well as hearing it. Sealed transcripts of Magna Carta were sent to all judges, sheriffs, and civic officials and also to all cathedral churches.[46] A precedent for the latter had been made in 1279 when Archbishop Pecham's council at Reading had ordered a copy of Magna Carta to be posted up in every cathedral and collegiate church in a public place 'so that it can be clearly seen by the eyes of everyone entering'; in the spring of each year the old copy was to be taken down and a new fair copy substituted for it.[47] The royal government was sufficiently alarmed to make Pecham have all these copies removed from church doors shortly afterwards.[48]

By 1300 there should have been hundreds of copies of Magna Carta in existence, some transcribed into books of statutes and others circulating in individual exemplars. Not all those who saw them were able to read Latin, but they could be assured of Magna Carta's main points by oral explanations and be confident that the document existed. In modern society similarly it is only lawyers who understand the full texts of legislation; the literate public are generally satisfied with newscasts and press summaries. The copies of Magna Carta which have survived from the thirteenth century are not all identical in their texts, even those of the same redaction, which they would be if they had been printed or photocopied like modern statutes. Not only did scribes make mistakes which were overlooked, they also inserted emendations which in their judgement made better sense of the text. They wrote the words *in capite*, for example, into clause 34 of Magna Carta in order to update it, even though there was no textual warrant for this. 'Most scribes were not tremendously concerned to follow their exemplars exactly. The charter mattered, but what mattered to both compilers of statute books and writers of chronicles was its gist, not its exact words.'[49] Manuscript culture put the emphasis in any text on its current presentation rather than its archaeological correctness. This was because reading aloud compelled both reader and listener to make immediate sense of the text. Insistence on absolute literal accuracy is a consequence of printing, compounded by photocopying and computing. As Ong points out, the mechanization of letter formation disengages words entirely from speech and living thought; writing takes on an independent existence in typographic space.[50] Operatives of printers and photocopiers can produce texts which have

---

[44] *Baronial Docs*, pp. 312–15.

[45] *Statutes*, p. 136.

[46] *Chronicle of Bury St Edmunds* ed. A. Gransden (1964), p. 154; Stubbs, *Charters*, pp. 490–1.

[47] 'Omnium intrantium oculis', D. L. Douie, *Archbishop Pecham* (1952), p. 113, n. 2; M. Prestwich, *Edward I* (1988), pp. 250–1.

[48] *ClR 1272–9*, p. 582.

[49] S. Reynolds, 'Magna Carta 1297 and the Legal Use of Literacy', *BIHR* LXII (1989), p. 241.

[50] *Orality and Literacy* (1982), ch. 5 ('Print, Space, and Closure').

not passed through their minds at all, which was impossible in manuscript culture.

Public readings of documents were done in the vernacular as well as in Latin and might reach a wider audience that way. Thus in 1300, according to the chronicler Rishanger, Magna Carta was read out at Westminster 'first in Latin (*litteraliter*) and then in the native tongue (*patriae lingua*)'.[51] Similarly a year earlier letters of Pope Boniface VIII about the peace between England and France had been read out in Parliament 'in Latin for the literate and in the native tongue for the illiterate'.[52] Also in 1299, according to the Worcester annals, royal letters concerning a new perambulation of the forests were 'proclaimed in the city of Worcester in the mother tongue (*materna lingua*)'.[53] The 'paternal' or 'maternal' language might mean either English or French. Thus in 1254 the papal excommunication of infringers of Magna Carta was ordered to be published 'in the English (*Anglicana*) and French (*Gallicana*) tongues' whenever and wherever appropriate.[54] The use of English and French in this instance was probably a reiteration of existing practice, rather than an innovation, as it is likely that Magna Carta itself had been proclaimed throughout the land in both English and French in 1215.

The distinction the chroniclers wished to emphasize in the citations above was between the language of literacy (Latin) and spoken language; they were less concerned with which vernacular was used. To pedantic Latinists vernacular simply meant the spoken language. Gerald of Wales hoped that someone would translate his work into French and claimed that Walter Map used to tell him that he (Gerald) had written much, whereas Walter had said much.[55] Although Gerald's writings (*scripta*) were more praiseworthy and durable than Walter's speeches (*dicta*), Walter had the greater profit because his *dicta* were accessible, since they were expressed in the common idiom, while Gerald's *scripta* were appreciated only by the declining few who knew Latin. In fact the distinction Gerald drew here between himself and Walter Map was misleading, as Walter also was a precocious Latinist. Possibly Gerald felt that Walter had been a more successful preacher and *raconteur* in the vernacular than he was. The point of the story from our angle, regardless of whether it is true or not, is that Gerald felt that the spoken vernacular brought greater prestige than written Latin.

LISTENING TO THE WORD

Whatever the language,[56] and whether the record was held solely in the bearer's memory or was committed to parchment, the medieval recipient

---

[51] *Willelmi Rishanger Chronica* ed. H. T. Riley, RS xxviii (1865), p. 405.
[52] Ibid., p. 389.
[53] *Annales Monastici* iv, p. 541. For the meaning of *materna lingua* see C. Clark, 'Women's Names in Post-Conquest England', *Speculum* liii (1978), pp. 224–5.
[54] *Annales Monastici* i (Burton, Annals), p. 322.
[55] Giraldus v, pp. 410–11.
[56] In general see P. Zumthor, *La Poésie et la voix dans la civilisation médiévale* (1984).

prepared himself to listen to an utterance rather than to scrutinize a document visually as a modern literate would. This was due to a different habit of mind; it was not because the recipient was illiterate in any sense of that word. In his account of his claim to be bishop-elect of St David's Gerald of Wales describes a private audience in the pope's chamber with Innocent III in 1200, when the pope looked up a register listing all the metropolitan churches of Christendom and went through the rubrics until he found Wales.[57] But when at a subsequent private audience Gerald showed the pope a transcript of a letter of Eugenius III which Gerald had found in another papal register, Innocent handed the transcript to Cardinal Ugolino and told him to read it; 'and when it had been read and diligently heard, the pope replied that he was well pleased with it.'[58] Gerald's account of the earlier audience depicts the pope browsing through a reference book as a modern literate would do; but when at the subsequent audience the pope needs to absorb carefully the details of a letter, he has it read to him instead of scrutinizing it. Reading aloud in this case is not being done to enable everyone present to learn the contents of the letter, as the only persons at this private audience are Innocent, Gerald, and Ugolino who is supporting him. Nor obviously was Innocent incapable of reading the script of papal registers. Yet he evidently found it easier to concentrate when he was listening than when he was looking; reading was still primarily oral rather than visual.

Indications of the same habit of mind appear in the 'auditing' of monetary accounts. Abbot Samson of Bury St Edmunds 'heard' the weekly account of his expenditure, yet he obviously could have consulted such a document (if the account were in documentary form at all), as his biographer Jocelin says that he inspected his *kalendarium* (his register of rents and so on) almost every day 'as if he contemplated in it the physiognomy of his own probity as in a mirror'.[59] The modern word 'audit' derives from a time when it was the habit to listen to, rather than to see, an account. Thomas of Eccleston in his description of the arrival of the Franciscan friars in England in 1224 records that when the superior heard the first annual account of the London friars and realized how little they had to show for such lavish expenditure, he threw down all the tallies and rolls and shouted, 'I'm caught', and 'he never afterwards wanted to hear an account.'[60] In this instance accounts in writing existed, in the form of both wooden tallies and parchment rolls, yet the superior 'heard' them none the less. H. J. Chaytor points out, however, that one must be careful of colloquial speech in such an instance as this. For example modern English uses the phrase 'I have not heard from him for some time' to mean 'I have had no letter'.[61]

Similarly in law courts, 'inspecting' a document might mean hearing it read aloud. Thus in 1219 in an action of warranty of charter in Lincolnshire William of Well, the defendant, is reported in the plea roll to 'have come and

---

[57] Giraldus III, p. 165. R. L. Poole, *Lectures on the Papal Chancery* (1915), pp. 150–1, 194–6.

[58] Ibid., p. 182.

[59] See p. 95, n. 55 above.

[60] *Monumenta Franciscana* ed. J. S. Brewer, RS IV (1858), I, p. 8.

[61] *From Script to Print* (1945), p. 145.

claimed a hearing (*auditum*) of his father's charter' and it was duly heard.[62] A generation later, in a similar action in Berkshire in 1248, the abbot of Beaulieu who was the defendant claimed that the plaintiff should 'show' him the charter by which he should warrant her.[63] The contrasting emphasis on hearing and seeing in these similar claims only thirty years apart may indicate a general change of attitude developing within this period, if only in the minds of the enrolling clerks; or more likely the two cases show the differing approach to documents of a knight, William of Well, and a monk, the abbot of Beaulieu.

Literary works, especially vernacular ones, were frequently explicitly addressed by the author to an audience, rather than to readers as such. Thus the nun of Barking in her French version of Ailred's life of Edward the Confessor in *c.*1163 requests 'all who hear, or will ever hear, this romance of hers' not to despise it because the translation is done by a woman.[64] In the *Romance of Horn* by Master Thomas the author begins by addressing his audience: 'Lords, you have heard the lines of parchment' (*Seignurs, oi avez le vers del parchemin*).[65] The parchment is evidently thought of here as a direct substitute for a jongleur; it speaks and is heard, like the charter of Richard de Cormeilles for St Mary's priory at Monmouth.[66] Likewise in the *Estoire de Waldef* (dating from *c.*1190) the author refers to the *Brut* story:

> If anyone wants to know this history
> Let him read the *Brut*, he will hear it there
> (*Qui l'estoire savoir voldra*
> *Lise le Brut, illoc l'orra*)[67]

A modern literate would not say 'he will *hear* it there', but 'he will *find* it' or 'see it there.' The emphasis in such works on hearing does not necessarily mean that their contents stem directly from oral tradition, but that reading continued to be conceived in terms of hearing rather than seeing. Until cheap printing supplied every 'reader' with his own book, this emphasis on hearing was understandable.

Latin works too were generally intended to be read aloud – hence the speeches and frequent use of dramatic dialogue in monastic chronicles. Eadmer concludes the first book of his *Life of St Anselm* with an interval, as in a play: 'But here, lest our unpolished speech (*oratio*) weary our readers or hearers by being too long drawn-out, we shall make our first halt in the work.'[68] Traditional monastic reading in particular bore little relation to a

---

[62] *Rolls of the Justices in Eyre* ed. D. M. Stenton, SS LIII (1934), p. 300, no. 630.
[63] *Berks. Eyre*, p. 150, no. 354.
[64] Legge, *Anglo-Norman*, p. 65. Other examples in H. J. Chaytor, *From Script to Print*, pp. 11–12, 144–7. In general see R. Crosby, 'Oral Delivery in the Middle Ages', *Speculum* XI (1936) pp. 90–102.
[65] See ch. 6, n. 63 above.
[66] See n. 13 above.
[67] Legge, *Anglo-Norman*, p. 143.
[68] *Vita*, p. 62.

modern literate's approach to a book. *Lectio* was 'more a process of rumination than reading, directed towards savouring the divine wisdom within a book rather than finding new ideas or novel information'.[69] The process is well illustrated by St Anselm's *Meditation on Human Redemption*: 'Taste the goodness of your redeemer . . . chew the honeycomb of his words, suck their flavour which is sweeter than honey, swallow their wholesome sweetness. Chew by thinking, suck by understanding, swallow by loving and rejoicing.'[70] Reading was a physical exertion, demanding the use not only of the eyes, but of tongue, mouth and throat. Writing was a similar act of endurance, requiring three fingers to hold the pen, two eyes to see the words, one tongue to speak them, and the whole body to labour.[71] For these reasons some monks argued that work in the *scriptorium* was an adequate substitute for manual labour.

The system of punctuating and abbreviating words in Latin works was likewise intended primarily to assist someone reading aloud, rather than a person silently scrutinizing the page. N. R. Ker cites the case of a manuscript where the Latin word *neque* (neither), which is written out in full, has been amended throughout to *neq*; he suggests that writing *neque* out in full was likely to mislead an oral reader into stressing the second syllable; writing out the word in full was an error on the scribe's part which has been duly corrected.[72] The earliest printed book, the Gutenberg Bible, reproduced the medieval standard abbreviations as if they were additional letters of the Latin alphabet, which they had indeed become. Occasionally manuscripts have stress-marks on particular syllables to help a reader pronounce the Latin correctly. As medieval Latin was an artificial language without any native speakers, an agreed correct pronunciation – and hence correct punctuation – helped to make sense of it, for both reader and listener.[73] Roger Bacon in 1267 discussed the correct pronunciation of words in the Bible, particularly those with Hebrew or Greek roots. He placed accentuation and punctuation under the heading of music 'because all these things consist in the raising and lowering of the voice and are therefore like some kind of chant, it is obvious that the explanation of all these matters pertains to music.'[74] Bacon was correct, as the scholastic art of music centered on the mathematical analysis of sound. But his strident tone suggests that he also knew very well that punctuation articulated the meaning of a statement as much as its sound, and that it therefore belonged to the art of grammar as well as music. Following Isidore

---

[69] C. J. Holdsworth, 'John of Ford and English Cistercian Writing', *TRHS* 5th series xi (1961), p. 124.

[70] *Opera Omnia* ed. F. S. Schmitt (1938–61) iii, p. 84.

[71] A description repeated by various scribes but originating in the eighth century, Wattenbach, *Schriftwesen*, p. 495.

[72] *English MSS*, p. 51.

[73] R. W. Southern explains the punctuation system in Eadmer, *Vita*, pp. xxv–xxxiv. Stress-marks are being studied by L. E. Boyle. In general see M. B. Parkes, *Pause and Effect: an Introduction to the History of Punctuation in the West* (1992).

[74] 'Opus Tertium', ch. 62, *Fratris Rogeri Bacon Opera* ed. J. S. Brewer RS xv (1859), p. 256. Bacon discusses the pronunciation of Biblical words at ch. 60.

of Seville, John of Salisbury (a century before Bacon) had discussed punctuation under the heading of grammar. For him punctuation marks indicate different breathing intervals when speaking, as well as distinguishing the clauses of a sentence.[75]

Ideally a 'reader' was expected to look at the text as well as listen to it, but that was the exception and not the rule. In the *Life of St Margaret* of Scotland the author considered it a point worth remarking that Margaret's daughter, Matilda (Henry I's queen), 'desired not only to hear, but also to inspect continually the impress of the letters' of her mother's life.[76] A school manual, not English and later than our period, sums up in a dialogue the medieval meaning of 'reading' (*lectio*):

'Are you a scholar, what do you read?'
'I do not read, I listen.'
'What do you hear?'
'Donatus or Alexander, or logic or music.'[77]

Donatus's *Ars Minor* and Alexander's *Doctrinale* were Latin textbooks. The term 'reading' a subject has been preserved at Oxford and Cambridge; whereas some undergraduates think that 'reading' implies studying books instead of hearing lectures, medieval students understood *lectio* primarily to mean that the master read while they listened. Whole books were published by being read aloud. Gerald of Wales says that he published his *Topography of Ireland* in this way in *c.*1188 by reading it at Oxford to different audiences on three successive days. But Gerald's action was not typical, as he boasts that 'neither has the present age seen, nor does any past age bear record of, the like in England.'[78] The normal way of disseminating scholarly works, as distinct from popular romances, was by the modern method of circulating copies. For instance Herbert of Bosham assumed in his life of Becket that his readers will be able to study Becket's correspondence, which he omits for the sake of brevity, 'because that book of letters is already in the possession of many persons and churches'.[79] If Becket is thought too exceptional an example because of his extraordinary popularity, Eadmer mentions in his appendix to St Anselm's *Life* that he intends to make a new start, because the *Life* has already 'been transcribed by many and distributed to various churches'.[80] Distributing copies did not of course rule out public readings; on the contrary, as more books became available, the practice may have grown even more widespread.

Just as reading was linked in the medieval mind with hearing rather than seeing, writing (in its modern sense of composition) was associated with

---

[75] *Metalogicon* Bk. I, ch. 20, p. 46.
[76] Thompson, *Literacy*, p. 171, n. 46.
[77] F. M. Powicke, *The Christian Life in the Middle Ages* (1935), p. 88; C. H. Haskins, *Studies in Medieval Culture* (1929), p. 83.
[78] Giraldus I, pp. 72–3.
[79] *Becket Materials* III, p. 396.
[80] *Vita*, p. 153.

dictating rather than manipulating a pen. Reading and writing were not inseparably coupled with each other, as they are today. A person might be able to write, yet not be considered literate. As we have seen, Walter Map mentions a boy 'who was not *litteratus*, although he knew how to transcribe any series of letters whatever'. Literacy involved being learned in Latin, whereas writing was the process of making a fair copy on parchment, which was the art of the scribe. Some authors (notably the great monastic historians Orderic Vitalis, William of Malmesbury, and Matthew Paris)[81] did their own writing, but they are the exceptions and they distinguished that activity from composition.

Medieval distinctions are well illustrated by Eadmer. He explains that he had to conceal from St Anselm that he was 'writing' his biography. When he had begun the work 'and had had already transcribed on to parchment a great part of what I had composed (*dictaveram*) in wax', Anselm asked 'what it was I was composing and copying' (*quid dictitarem, quid scriptitarem*).[82] The process of composing on wax tablets is thus described in Latin by the word *dictitare* (literally, 'to dictate'), even though in Eadmer's case he was dictating to himself. The use of 'writing' (*scriptitare*) is confined to making the fair copy on parchment. Similarly when Orderic Vitalis wishes to say that before the time of William the Conqueror the Normans had concentrated on war rather than reading and writing, the phrase he uses is *legere vel dictare*, not *legere vel scribere*. Numerous other examples of using 'dictate' where a modern literate would use 'write' could be given.[83] Dictating was the usual form of literary composition and the *ars dictaminis*, taught in the schools as part of rhetoric, was the skill governing it. Letter writing was thus an intellectual skill using the mouth rather than the hand. Peter of Blois, a busy secretary of state like John of Salisbury, boasted that the archbishop of Canterbury had seen him dictating to three different scribes on diverse subjects, while he dictated and wrote a fourth letter all at the one time.[84]

Reading aloud and dictating permit the non-literate to participate in the use of documents, whereas reading and writing silently exclude the illiterate. When the voice is used, the clerk or scribe becomes no more than a medium between the speaker or hearer and the document. Neither the hearer of a book nor the *dictator* of a letter needs to be a master of every detail of the scribal technique himself, just as modern managers are not required to type or to programme computers. Obviously it is helpful if the manager understands how these things are done and has some experience of them, but this experience is not indispensable. For these reasons medieval kings and their officials, such as sheriffs in the counties, did not need to be literate in the modern sense. Lack of literacy did not mean that they were ignorant or incapable of coping with business; they were as literate as the tasks required. As the number of documents increased and habits of silent visual reading

---

[81] Their holographs are illustrated by Gransden, *Historical Writing*, plates iv, v, x.

[82] *Vita*, p. 150; Carruthers, *Memory*, p. 195.

[83] Orderic, Bk. iii, vol. ii, p. 2. Cheney, *Texts & Studies*, pp. 246–7, gives excellent examples from a letter of the Englishman, Gervase abbot of Prémontré, who died in 1228.

[84] Southern, *Medieval Humanism*, p. 119.

became more common, levels of literacy (in the modern sense) presumably increased also; but there is no evidence of a crisis suddenly demanding numerous literates. Because the pre-literate emphasis on the spoken word persisted, the change from oral to literate modes could occur slowly and almost imperceptibly over many generations.

The text usually quoted to show that medieval attitudes towards literacy were similar to modern ones is John of Salisbury's quotation in *Policraticus* that 'Rex illitteratus est quasi asinus coronatus' (an illiterate king is like a crowned ass).[85] In this passage John is primarily concerned that the prince should have wisdom, which is gained by reading the law of God daily. For that reason, and not for administrative requirements, the prince needs skill in letters. John concedes moreover that it is not absolutely necessary for the prince to be *litteratus*, provided he takes advice from *litterati*, that is, from priests who, like Old Testament prophets, will remind the prince of the law of God. 'Thus the mind of the prince may read in the tongue of the priest. For the life and tongue of priests are like the book of life before the face of the peoples.'[86] John is obviously thinking here of the spiritual, and not the worldly, value of reading. His discussion emphasizes that an illiterate prince can participate in wisdom through the medium of the priest's voice. The prince is not excluded by being illiterate: 'nor is he altogether destitute of reading (*lectionis*) who, even though he does not read himself, hears faithfully what is read to him by others.' John thus shows that in his day non-literates could participate in literate culture; he is not arguing for the absolute necessity of rulers being literate in either the medieval sense of being learned in Latin or the modern sense of having a minimal ability to read and write. Ironically the king of England at the time, Henry II, was literate in every sense of the word; yet he was not a good king by John's definition, as he refused to listen to the lectures of priests and was responsible for the murder of Becket.

THE SPOKEN WORD IN LEGAL PROCEDURE

The persistent emphasis on the spoken word, despite the growing use of documents, is best illustrated by the evolution of legal procedure. The forms which had been suited to a purely oral procedure were preserved and ossified when documents were introduced. Before the thirteenth century parties were given notice to appear in law courts, not by having a writ served on them, but by an oral summons. Fitz Neal describes the summons to the county court 'by the crier's voice' and Glanvill explains in detail how the sheriff must ensure that the summoners are instructed in a public place and that the summons itself is publicly proclaimed.[87] In one list of summoners and jurors surviving from the Berkshire justices' visitation of 1248 the pair of summoners are appropriately, but exceptionally, called 'criers' (*criatores*)[88] their function was

---

[85] Bk. IV, ch. 6, C. J. Webb (1909) I, p. 255; Galbraith, 'Literacy', pp. 212–13.
[86] *Policraticus*, p. 255.
[87] *Dialogus*, p. 116; Glanvill, Bk. i, ch. 30, pp. 17–19.
[88] *Berks. Eyre*, p. 474, no. a175.

to voice the oral summons in due form. In the city of London, and in other places where population was concentrated, persons were summoned to the court of Husting not by the sound of a voice, but by a bell. If anyone claimed that he had not been duly summoned, 'the beadle has no other witness, nor ought to have, than the great bell which is rung for the folkmoot at St Paul's.'[89] Emphasis thus remained on hearing a sound, rather than seeing a document, whether the summons was made by a bell or the voice of a crier.

Nevertheless, once the rule had been established in Henry II's reign that 'no one is bound to answer for any freehold of his in his lord's court without a royal writ',[90] a document (a royal writ), instead of a voice, became the basis of legal procedure for all important land transactions in seignorial courts as well as royal ones. By Edward I's reign at the latest it had become usual for the sheriff to execute a royal writ in the first instance, not by instructing summoners orally as had been the practice in the twelfth century, but by sending a written precept to the appropriate local bailiff ordering him to execute the writ. The earliest sheriffs' precepts actually extant date from the 1240s and 1250s.[91] Yet the requirement to have oral summoners continued; by the later Middle Ages they had become fictitious persons, 'John Do' and 'Richard Ro' and the like, because their ancient function had been superseded by writing.

Just as summoners continued long after their usefulness had disappeared, common law procedure once the parties had come into court was likewise modelled on non-literate practices. Before the development of authenticated documents, courts were most reluctant to allow a litigant to be represented in his absence. Elaborate regulations were developed governing 'essoins' or excuses for non-appearance made by a third party. The assumption was that where possible a litigant must speak on his own behalf in court, because only words from his own mouth were authentic.[92] It is true that a few references will be found from Alfred's reign onwards to litigants having an advocate, who is described as a *forespeca* in Anglo-Saxon documents and a *perorator* in the Latin *Leges Henrici Primi*.[93] But, as the *Leges* makes clear, the advocate is not a true representative of the litigant as he may be corrected by him. The purpose of having an advocate was to allow for mistakes in the oral pleading, 'for it often happens that a person sees less in his own case than in someone else's and it is generally possible to amend in another person's mouth what may not be amended in his own.'[94] The advocate was thus a dispensable mouthpiece. His function was to make the litigant's formal claim, his 'tale' (*talu* in Anglo-Saxon), in due form.[95] The Anglo-Saxons had evidently put consider-

---

[89] Stubbs, *Charters*, p. 313.

[90] Glanvill, Bk. xii, ch. 25, p. 148.

[91] *Berks. Eyre*, pp. cv–cvii.

[92] P & M i, pp. 211–12.

[93] The instance from Alfred's reign (concerning the litigant Helmstan) is printed by F. E. Harmer, *Select English Historical Documents* (1914), pp. 30–2. Later examples in D. Whitelock, *Anglo-Saxon Wills* (1939), references indexed under 'advocate'.

[94] *Leges Henrici Primi*, ch. 46, ed. L. J. Downer (1972), p. 156.

[95] A. J. Robertson, *Anglo-Saxon Charters* (2nd edn, 1956), pp. 366–7 explains *talu*.

able emphasis on correct enunciation (*ryhtracu*) in their legal procedures. They may even have rivalled the Icelanders who insisted (in theory at least) on word-for-word accuracy, as is illustrated by the passage in *Njal's Saga* where the uninitiated litigant, Gunnar, tricks the expert, Hrut, into summoning himself by pretending to admire Hrut's verbal expertise.[96]

A person similar to the *forespeca* or *perorator* reappears in thirteenth-century documents, where he is called a *narrator* in Latin or a *conteur* in Anglo-Norman. Direct links between the *forespeca* and the *narrator* or *conteur* are lacking, but as they all performed similar functions, the supposition of continuity is reasonable. The *narrator* or *conteur* made the formal claim or pleading on the litigant's behalf. The pleading was called a 'tale' (*narratio* in Latin or *conte* in French) just as it had been in Anglo-Saxon. The earliest written collection of common law pleadings, the *Brevia Placitata* dating from the mid-thirteenth century, calls them *les contes en romancees*.[97] Another early tract (date *c*.1285) records that the pleadings 'are uttered by narrators in romance words and not in Latin ones'.[98] The 'narrator' was thus a 'romancer', a professional teller of tales in the vernacular, but his 'tales' were legal pleadings and not romances in the modern sense. Yet in origin the technique of the legal narrator was probably similar to that of his namesake, the Singer of Tales, studied by Milman Parry and A. B. Lord.[99] A narrator, whether of common law pleadings or of epic and romance, had originally reconstructed his tale in due form on the basis of a few remembered formulas. He was a professional oral remembrancer, very necessary before law and literature were committed to writing.

The interesting question is why narrators continued to flourish in English legal procedure once documents had become common. By the reign of Edward I a litigant required both a narrator and an attorney. The narrator was a layman, expert in oral pleadings, whereas the attorney was often a cleric and expert in written ones. The two functions remained distinct: from narrators derived the serjeants-at-law and barristers, who dominated the legal profession, while attorneys became associated with the humbler solicitors.[100] Both narrator and attorney were necessary because the narrator could not represent the litigant; that was the attorney's function, as he was appointed 'to win or lose' (*ad perdendum vel lucrandum*). Like an Anglo-Saxon advocate, the narrator spoke on the litigant's behalf in his presence; his words were not binding on the litigant, who could 'disavow' them. Behind the narrator's inability to be a true representative remained the ancient assumption that a litigant must speak on his own behalf. In fact the narrator spoke for him; but in theory at least the narrator remained no more than a spokesman, an extension of the litigant's faculty of speech.

---

[96] Trans. C. F. Bayerschmidt and L. E. Hollander (1955), p. 59. W. I. Miller, *Bloodtaking and Peacemaking* (1990), pp. 247–57, discusses Icelandic law.

[97] Ed. G. J. Turner, SS LXVI (1947), pp. xxxv, 153.

[98] 'per narratores in romanis verbis et non in latinis pronunciantur', *Four Thirteenth-Century Law Tracts* ed. G. E. Woodbine (1910), p. 162.

[99] *The Singer of Tales* (1960); Clanchy, 'Remembering', p. 175; R. Finnegan, *Oral Poetry* (1977) and *Literacy and Orality* (1988) has a different point of view.

[100] See in general P. Brand, *The Origins of the English Legal Profession* (1992).

One consequence of the litigant having to speak for himself was that the deaf and dumb seem to have had no legal rights in thirteenth-century England. Whether they were considered insane, as in Roman law, is unclear. In 1210 in a case in which one of the plaintiffs, Agnes, was a deaf mute the defendant, William de Schegetun, objected that Agnes could undertake nothing binding because she was unable to speak. When the plaintiffs' attorney asked the bench whether Agnes ought to lose her rights merely because she was a mute, the royal judges ruled that she must drop out of the case.[101] In 1224 when knights were sent to William Maufre to hear whom he wished to appoint as his attorney because he was ill, they found that he could not speak clearly owing to paralysis 'but in so far as he could speak, he appointed Reynold, his son, as his attorney.'[102] Nevertheless Reynold was not admitted by the court, because his father could not speak, and was told that he must produce his father in person.

Writing shifted the emphasis in testing truth from speech to documents and sometimes made the ancient rule that a litigant must speak on his own behalf look rather absurd. In 1293 a certain Hugh was charged with rape.[103] He first of all claimed benefit of clergy. When this was rejected by the judge because Hugh was married to a widow, Hugh claimed that he was a knight and should be tried by a jury of his peers. This was allowed, but Hugh then wanted to challenge some of the jurors as being prejudiced against him. The judge agreed and asked the challenges to be read out. At this point Hugh admitted that he did not know how to read and asked for his counsel. When this was refused, Hugh said to the judge: 'You have the challenges, you may read them.' The judge answered: 'No, because they must be propounded by your mouth.' When Hugh again said: 'I don't know how to read them', the judge told him that he should not have claimed benefit of clergy if he were unable to read. Hugh stood silent and confused, but the judge told him not to be discomforted and that now was the time to speak. He turned to Nicholas of Leicester, Hugh's counsel, and asked: 'Do you wish to read Sir Hugh's challenges?' Nicholas replied: 'Yes, my lord, if I may have his list which he has in his hands.' Having been allowed the list, Nicholas then asked: 'My lord, the challenges here are named against numerous persons, do you wish me to read them publicly?' The judge: 'No, no! You are to read them to the prisoner secretly, because they must be taken to come from his mouth.' Prompted by his counsel, Hugh duly made his challenges and was acquitted. This courtroom farce shows how by 1290 the oral procedure of challenging jurors had become in reality a written one. Hugh had to read from a list; he could not simply declare his challenges. On the other hand, the survival of oral procedure still required that he voice the challenges himself and so he had now to be able to read. In this case writing has made Hugh incapable of speaking and has reduced the voice of his counsel to a whisper.

---

[101] *CuriaRR* vi, p. 13. Cf. a similar case in 1230, ibid., xiv, p. 31, no. 161.

[102] Ibid., xi, p. 557, no. 2768.

[103] *Year Books of 30–31 Edward I* ed. A. J. Horwood, RS xxxi (1863), pp. 530–2. BL Add. MS 31826, ff. 206–7; JUST/1/1090, mm. 76–7. I owe these MS references to Dr H. R. T. Summerson.

In the long term the use of documents was bound to change the old way of pleading. Narrators survived throughout the Middle Ages, but by the fifteenth century 'counting' was no longer done orally but on paper. Cheap paper had completed the revolution begun by writing on parchment. 'But, now', regrets Roger North in the seventeenth century, 'the pleadings are all delated in paper.'[104] The forms, which the non-literate pleader had learned by listening, and the first literates by reading, are now, says North, 'better understood and learned by writing'. Nevertheless North records that a vestige of the old count survived: 'When causes, which they call real, come on, and require counting, and pleading at the bar, it is done for form, and unintelligibly; and whatever the serjeant mumbles, it is the paper book that is the text.' The use of documents had ultimately reduced the ancient art of pleading to an unintelligible mumble.

Gradually formal speech began to be learned by studying books instead of hearing the words of others. Handbooks for this purpose begin in England in the middle of the thirteenth century. An Anglo-Norman manual, *The Court Baron* composed in *c.*1265, instructs a seignorial steward in 'how he ought to speak' by giving a series of dialogues, like a modern conversation primer for learning a foreign language.[105] Likewise in the *Rules* of estate management, which Robert Grosseteste wrote for the countess of Lincoln in the 1240s, the lady is instructed in how to address her steward: 'Good sir, you see plainly that I have had these inquiries and enrolments made to shed light on my rights . . .' and so on.[106] A schoolman like Grosseteste probably derived the idea of writing hypothetical speeches from the *ars dictaminis* taught in the universities, where students were shown how to write letters for all occasions in this way.[107] Most English legal treatises of this sort contain the texts of oaths – a witness's oath to tell the truth, a vassal's oath of homage to his lord, a bailiff's oath to act honestly, and others; these examples are taken from *How to Hold Pleas and Courts* composed in *c.*1272 by John of Oxford.[108] It is possible that John taught seignorial administration and elementary legal procedure at Oxford.[109] Knowledge which a century before had been passed on by word of mouth from father to son, or learned from the old wise men of the court, was now part of an academic curriculum.

Similarly the texts of speeches, which chroniclers had formerly been obliged to invent or borrow from Roman historians, were sometimes now put in writing. Thus Edward I's envoys to France in 1294 were instructed (in French in the original) as follows: 'Our messengers shall say to the king of France: "Our lord the king of England, lord of Ireland, and duke of Aquitaine, does you homage on condition . . ."' and so on.[110] A year earlier when John Balliol,

[104] *The Lives of the Norths* (1826) i, p. 30. Cf. *Novae Narrationes* ed. S. F. C. Milsom, SS lxxx (1963), p. xxvi.

[105] *Court Baron*, p. 49.

[106] *Walter of Henley*, p. 390.

[107] C. H. Haskins, *Studies in Medieval Culture*, chs 1, 9.

[108] *Court Baron*, pp. 77–8.

[109] Clanchy, '*Moderni*', p. 686.

[110] P. Chaplais, 'English Diplomatic Documents' in *Study of Medieval Records*, p. 35.

king of Scots, personally protested to Edward I about his claim of overlord-ship, John delivered to the king and his council the text of the speech he made (in French) written on a schedule, perhaps by his own hand.[111] By far the largest collection of speeches and dialogues surviving from the reign of Edward I are the Year Books, which purport to record the actual words (translated into French or Latin) of litigants, their counsel, and the judges in royal courts.[112] The case already cited of Hugh, who was unable to read his challenges, is a meagre example of a Year Book's quality of dialogue.

The makers of the Year Books appear to record actual speech, whereas the writers of handbooks for speaking in court set out hypothetical conversation as in a play. Under the heading, 'Ici comence le play de la coroune' (here begin the pleas of the crown), *The Court Baron* presents a dialogue between a steward and his bailiff.[113] (The use of 'play' in the French is a coincidence and has no connexion with 'play' in English.)

The steward speaks first:

'Bailiff!'
'Sir!'
'Bring up the prisoners.'
'Willingly, sir. See they are here.'
'Why is this man under arrest?'
'Sir, for a mare which he took in the field in another way than he should have.'

The steward then proceeds to examine the prisoner; the dialogue vividly creates a courtroom scene. Some protagonists are even given star roles, like the naive poacher, Walter de la More, who begins his explanation (beautifully translated by Maitland) as follows:

Sir, for God's sake do not take it ill of me if I tell thee the truth, how I went the other evening along the bank of this pond and looked at the fish which were playing in the water, so beautiful and bright, and for the great desire that I had for a tench I laid me down on the bank and just with my hands quite simply, and without any other device, I caught that tench and carried it off . . .[114]

The poacher then tries a hard-luck story about how his wife had been ill and off her food for a month, but she had a great yearning to eat a tench. There is obviously a large element of imaginative licence in this presentation of the poacher's statement; apart from anything else, a poor peasant would have spoken in English and not in the French in which the speech is written.

Lawbooks like *The Court Baron* were not written to entertain, yet they have similarities with the use of dialogue in romances and with the earliest English

[111] *Anglo-Scottish Relations*, p. 66.
[112] See ch. 3, n. 75 above.
[113] *Court Baron*, p. 62.
[114] *Court Baron*, pp. 54–5.

drama in French.[115] The idea of each protagonist having a set part written down verbatim, which he must adhere to, was unfamiliar to the non-literate and presented actors, whether in law courts or on stage-sets outside churches, with common problems. In a religious drama, the *Play of Adam* dating from the middle of the twelfth century, how the words are to be spoken is described in detail. M. D. Legge suggests that writing set parts may have been new; that is why the actors are instructed not to add or omit anything, to speak clearly, and to say their lines in the right order.[116]

It would be tempting to see the lawyers' Year Books and handbooks as having something in common with the jongleurs' 'stage scripts', in which the vernacular romances are thought to have been first recorded in writing.[117] Scripts, whether for jongleurs or lawyers, enabled 'a young man to see (*veer/vere*) how he ought to speak with subtlety' and 'see the manner distinctly' (in the words of *The Court Baron*.)[118] A student now learned the rudiments of public speaking by reading, by seeing the 'shapes indicating voices' (in John of Salisbury's phrase) in a book, instead of hearing the words of his master. Yet we should not exaggerate the speed of this development; as long as writing depended on manuscripts alone, the change from oral to literate modes was gradual. Dependence on symbolic gestures and the spoken word persisted in law and literature, and throughout medieval culture, despite the growth of literacy.

WRITINGS AS WORKS OF ART

Writing has the power to change the way words are perceived by the senses, because it shifts the emphasis in communicating language from hearing to seeing. The language of script can be received 'through the windows of the eyes' by silent reading, or it can be transmitted 'voicelessly', even to people not yet born, by shaping letters with the hand. In non-literate cultures the skills of eye and hand are associated primarily with craftsmanship and the visual arts, while the skills of language which depend on the transmission of sound are identified with mouth and ear. Although writing had the potential, in medieval England as elsewhere, to change the perception of language by making it visual as well as auditory, it has been argued already in this chapter that pre-literate habits of mind persisted long after documents became common. Books and letters continued to be read aloud and listened to, instead of being silently scrutinized by the eye, and authors went on thinking of composition in terms of dictation rather than of manipulating a pen. The skills of reading and writing therefore remained separate, because reading was part

[115] Examples of dialogue in Legge, *Anglo-Norman*, pp. 92 (by Hue of Roteland), 256 (by William of Barnwell). Drama in ibid, pp. 311–31.
[116] Ibid., pp. 318–9; R. Axton, *European Drama of the Early Middle Ages* (1974), p. 115.
[117] E. Auerbach, *Literary Language and its Public in Late Antiquity and in the Middle Ages* (1965), p. 288.
[118] *Court Baron*, pp. 49, 20.

of the mastery of speech whereas writing was one of the manual and visual arts.

Early medieval civilization shared with other ancient cultures of the world an approach to writing which was non-utilitarian. The skills of the scribe were primarily devoted not to transmitting mundane information in an economical and straightforward way, but to making illuminated manuscripts which were masterpieces of calligraphy, painting, jewellery, and metalwork. In such works as the *Book of Kells* or the *Lindisfarne Gospels* the text was of secondary importance. It was there to remind the chanter of the familiar phrases of the liturgy, if he did not immediately recall them, and to serve as an act of worship in itself by catching the words of God in sacred script and displaying them on the page like butterflies in a showcase. Writing was aimed at God's eye more often than at communicating information to fellow human beings. For that reason books were kept on the altar or in a sacristy rather than in a library. Because illuminated manuscripts appealed primarily to the eye, like pictures, they could be understood almost as well by the non-literate as by the literate. To appreciate their finer points required expertise, but the knowledge needed was that of the artist and craftsman rather than that of the linguistically educated. As we have seen, Walter Map distinguished the good scribe, who 'knew how to transcribe any series of letters whatever', from the *litteratus*. The scribe was expert in calligraphy, whereas the *litteratus* was expert in Latin.

The separation of the skills of reading and writing continued up until the invention of printing and was not immediately affected by the proliferation of documents in the twelfth and thirteenth centuries. Gutenberg himself, the inventor of printing, had not aimed to supersede the illuminated book, but to improve it and make it more readily available. The earliest book to come from his press, the 42-line Bible, is indistinguishable at first sight from an illuminated manuscript. Similarly the first dated book (18 November 1477) printed by Caxton, *The Dictes and Sayengs of the Philosophers*, was copied and illuminated by hand from the printed text for presentation to Edward IV and his family, presumably because the printed version was thought too poor-quality a product to present at court. Caxton states proudly that the book had been 'sette in forme and emprynted in this manere as ye maye here in this booke see', but the king might not have been so pleased by an untried technology which produced inferior goods.[119] He and his kind were not going to benefit from mass-production anyway. Writings continued to be works of art, embellished in a variety of ways, as long as they were produced by hand. However humble a scrivener he was, the medieval scribe was an individual artist, who had to discipline himself to achieve anonymity and uniformity, whereas printing imposes uniformity automatically and excludes ornamentation except when it has been deliberately planned in advance.

At the very time that documents were beginning to be used in greater numbers for business purposes, in the middle of the twelfth century, some of

---

[119] L. Hellinga, *Caxton in Focus* (1982), p. 77, colour plates I, III. In general see M. T. Clanchy, 'Looking Back from the Invention of Printing', in *Literacy in Historical Perspective* ed. D. P. Resnick (1983), pp. 7–22

the most elaborately written and illuminated manuscripts were produced. In pride of place stand the glossed texts of scripture, such as the Psalter inscribed *Johannes me fecit Rogerio* ('John made me for Roger'), the double-glossed Epistles of St Paul, and the Eadwine psalter.[120] Eadwine's work (see plate XIV) is clearly in the old tradition of emphasizing form in writing rather than literal meaning, as elegant design takes precedence over textual accuracy. His Anglo-Saxon text is peculiarly corrupt and his Latin has unnecessary errors. The scribe and the *litteratus* were not invariably at odds, however, as the Winchester Bible (which is contemporary with Eadwine's Psalter) has a good text as well as magnificent calligraphy and illuminations. In the unusually purist opinion of St Hugh's Carthusians, the correctness of the text was its best feature.[121] A rigid distinction between an artistic and a practical manuscript is often impossible to make, because a synthesis of the beautiful and the functional is a general characteristic of medieval art, as churches and castles make abundantly evident.

Even the most businesslike manuscripts required some embellishment, in the form of rubrics and enlarged initials, to enable the user to find his place in the book. Thus the larger volume of Domesday Book uses vermilion paint for three distinct types of rubrication – capital letters for the names of shires and other headings; shading for the initial letter of each paragraph and certain abbreviations; underlining for the names of places and tenants.[122] The rubrication contributes to making Domesday Book a masterpiece of functional layout, which is a form of abstract art in itself. Subsequently, however, the embellishment of the Domesday text was taken much further when multi-coloured copies were made from it: one in the twelfth century (*Herefordshire Domesday*) and another in the thirteenth (the Exchequer Breviate).[123] Unlike the original, these manuscripts are primarily ornamental. They show that Domesday Book had achieved the status of a revered text, which was worthy to be beautified and embellished like a Gospel book. The name 'Domesday', recalling the book of Revelation, had already associated it with Holy Writ.

Most manuscript books show a similar mixture of the pictorial and the functional. A representative small collection are the dozen English lawyers' manuals, containing parliamentary statutes and other texts for ready reference (dating from a decade or so on either side of 1300), which are now preserved at the Harvard Law School.[124] Lawyers' textbooks might be expected to be severely practical and economical in format. A few are, notably MS 36 in the Harvard collection, which uses rubrics sparingly and is written

[120] These three MSS are illustrated by de Hamel, *MSS*, pp. 83, 103, 77.

[121] See ch. 3, n. 9 above.

[122] V. H. Galbraith, *Domesday Book* (1974), frontispiece in colour. The design of Domesday Book is discussed by M. Gullick in *Domesday Book Studies* ed. A. Williams and R. W. H. Erskine (1987), pp. 93–7.

[123] See ch. 1, nn. 30–2 above. These MSS are illustrated by E. M. Hallam, *Domesday Book Through Nine Centuries* (1986), pp. 41–7.

[124] Harvard Law Library MSS 12, 33, 36, 39, 49, 56–9, 173–5. In general see A. Bennett, 'Anthony Bek's Copy of Statuta Anglicana' in *England in the Fourteenth Century: Proceedings of the 1985 Harlaxton Symposium* ed. W. M. Ormrod (1986), pp. 1–14, figures 1–15.

rather untidily, like a plea roll, in a rapid business hand (see plate XVII). By contrast, MS 173 has initials illuminated in blue, green and gold leaf, in addition to the usual rubrics; while MS 12 has broad margins, pictorial initials, and other drawings illustrating the subject matter of the statutes; for example, a boar and a deer in a wood and a man shooting a deer with a longbow accompany the text of the charter of the Forest (see plate XVIII). English canon lawyers' books of decretals of a century earlier show similar contrasts between plain working copies, presumably used by practitioners and teachers, and illuminated fair copies intended for presentation or as show pieces.[125]

At the opposite poles of writings intended to catch the eye of God with their illuminations and writings intended for mundane consultation are liturgical manuscripts on the one hand and the public records (particularly legal and financial documents) on the other. Yet here also some exceptions can be found. The Sherborne cartulary of the mid-twelfth century integrates royal charters and illuminated liturgical texts into one book intended for the altar.[126] Conversely the most mundane public records are occasionally illustrated. Thus an Exchequer receipt roll for 1233 has at its head an elaborate drawing caricaturing prominent Jews of Norwich, and a plea roll for 1249 depicts trial by combat and the hanging of the loser.[127] Much more common throughout the royal records are amateurly foliated initials and caricatured heads in profile, which seem to be doodles made by bored enrolling clerks. In a plea roll from 1249, which has a friendly-looking devil at the foot of one membrane, the clerk admitted his boredom by cancelling an enrolment and replacing it with what may have been a snatch from a French popular song, which in translation reads: 'It's my little loves that keep me cheerful and give me fun.'[128] Traditional scribal habits made rigorous formality and a total lack of personal embellishment difficult to impose. In private business documents minor embellishments are even more common, as scribes were less constrained by bureaucratic standards. For example, the earliest account roll of Crowland abbey (dating from 1258–9) is ornamented with foliations, animal heads and what seem to be facetious portraits.[129] Although to a modern eye such amateur ornament detracts from a document's dignity, the monastic writer even of an account roll may have felt obliged to give his work some embellishment to make it look authoritative.

The continuing emphasis on the visual aspects of writings, despite the increasing number of business documents (which grew more uniform and economical of materials and time in the thirteenth century), helped to bridge

---

[125] Duggan, *Decretals*, pp. 81–2, plate ii.

[126] See ch. 5, n. 35 above.

[127] The roll of 1233 is illustrated by V. D. Lipman, *The Jews of Medieval Norwich* (1967), p. 33. Other caricatures in Exchequer rolls are gathered by Z. E. Rokéah, 'Drawings of Jewish Interest', *Scriptorium* XXVI (1972), pp. 55–62. The roll of 1249 is illustrated by R. F. Hunnisett and J. B. Post, *Medieval Legal Records Edited in Memory of C. A. F. Meekings* (1978), frontispiece, comment at pp. 32–4; illustrated also by Lewis, *Matthew Paris*, p. 34.

[128] *Crown Pleas of the Wiltshire Eyre* ed. C. A. F. Meekings, Wilts RS XVI (1961), p. 25.

[129] F. Page, *The Estates of Crowland Abbey* (1934), plate v.

the gap between non-literate and literate, just as the persistence of reading aloud and listening did. Before writing became common, people were accustomed to use knives, or even Gospel books, as symbolic objects which could be transferred in the presence of witnesses as a sign that property had been duly conveyed. As has been suggested earlier in this chapter, conveyances by charter may have been made acceptable to non-literates by the seals attached to them. Like illuminated manuscripts embellished with precious stones and relics, seals were visible and tangible symbols of a donor's wishes.[130] Neither clergy nor laity would have trusted or admired documents which were writings pure and unadorned, because they would have been inadequate as symbols of a person's wishes. It is true, however, that the modern belief that medieval books were invariably magnificently illuminated is a misconception, which has grown up because – generally – only the most lavish manuscripts are exhibited or made into facsimiles.

To knights, who were on the threshold of literacy in the twelfth century, writings may have appeared attractive as another system of signs. Their capacity to devise and understand a complex system of pictorial signs is shown by the development of heraldry, which is contemporary with the shift from memory to written record. The first recorded rolls of arms were illustrated and written in the language of blazon in the middle of the thirteenth century, although heraldry had been developing visually and orally for more than a century before that.[131] Whether the growth of recorded heraldry and the contemporaneous spread of literacy among knights are coincidental or connected developments is a matter for conjecture. Inauguration into literate ways of thought through pictorial manuscripts and visual symbols like seals may have caused knights to create an alternative system of 'shapes indicating voices' in heraldry. Traditionally 'letters' were the clergy's symbolic way of indicating their superior status, since a *clericus* was a *litteratus*. Heraldry originated as an alternative language of signs. Clerics intoning the Latin liturgy at the altar from great illuminated manuscripts wore embroidered vestments bearing sacred scenes and insignia: the Holy Cross, the Lamb of God, Alpha and Omega, and many others. The knights, who were their brothers both spiritually and in fact, responded with a liturgy and learned language of their own. Their silken coats of arms displayed the insignia of their calling and their families in the form of stylized animals, birds, plants, and geometric shapes.[132]

In England heraldic shields are first found depicted in a series on the pages of a Psalter, which may date from the 1230s and contains work by the

---

[130] See ch. 9, 'The Symbolism of Seals and Crosses', pp. 308–17 below.
[131] G. J. Brault, *Early Blazon* (1972), p. 8. In general see A. Ailes, 'Heraldry in Twelfth-Century England: The Evidence' in *England in the Twelfth Century: Proceedings of the 1988 Harlaxton Symposium*, ed. D. Williams (1990), pp. 1–16; J. Cherry, 'Heraldry as Decoration in the Thirteenth Century' in *Proceedings of the 1989 Harlaxton Symposium* ed. W. M. Ormrod (1991), pp. 123–34.
[132] Ecclesiastical and heraldic embroidery is discussed by K. Staniland, *Embroiderers*, BM Medieval Craftsmen (1991).

illuminator William de Brailes.[133] The shields were probably included on the instructions of the knightly family who commissioned this book. Shields are first found massed on the page in order of rank of the persons concerned, as if recorded by a herald, in Matthew Paris's 'Book of Additions' to his chronicles.[134] The heraldic drawing on these shields is very similar in style to the shields in the margins of Matthew's chronicles, which he devised as a finding system (as we have already seen in chapter 5).[135] Thus the traitor William Marsh's broken shield and Frederick II's reversed imperial eagle stand in the margins of the page alongside the notices of their deaths. Matthew was the greatest all-round writer in the monastic tradition in thirteenth-century Europe. Throughout his work he shows that the ideal of making a synthesis of the visual and the intellectual in writing was still alive, as he composed and penned his own works and illustrated them with line drawings, maps, diagrams, and more formal paintings. Nor did he ignore the need for accurate texts, although like other scribal artists he considered himself entitled to make variations and embellishments of his own. Matthew Paris is exceptional in his abilities, but not in his approach to his art, which treats writing as a visual skill inseparable from pictorial values.

WORD AND IMAGE

In Matthew Paris's history of Edward the Confessor, which he wrote in French rhyming couplets probably in the 1240s for the royal family, he provided illustrations (*portraiture figurée* is his term). 'For I desire and wish', he explained, 'that what the ear hears the eye may see.'[136] In writing in French for the aristocratic laity Matthew was in line with current fashion. Another schoolman and contemporary of Matthew's, Richard de Fournival, wrote in northern France a popularizing work which he entitled *Li Bestiare d'Amours*, 'The Bestiary of Love'. Bestiaries, describing animals real and imaginary, were a familiar genre of picture-book which introduced the laity to natural history and mythology. Among the earliest writings in French is Philip de Thaon's bestiary, composed for Henry I's queen Adeliza in the 1120s.[137]

One of the pictures which Richard de Fournival designed for his bestiary is an image of Lady Memory, standing in a niche like the statue of a saint,

---

[133] N. J. Morgan, *Early Gothic MSS 1190–1250* (1982), p. 114.

[134] *The Matthew Paris Shields* ed. T. D. Tremlett, *Aspilogia* II (1967). One page is reproduced in colour by M. Keen, *Chivalry* (1984), plate 32, and by Lewis, *Matthew Paris*, plate facing p. 291.

[135] See pp. 175–6 above.

[136] *Lives of Edward the Confessor*, ed. H. R. Luard, RS III (1858), p. 136; Lewis, *Matthew Paris*, pp. 49, 481, n. 156; M. Camille, 'Seeing and Reading', *Art History* VIII (1985), p. 41. For the attribution and date see: Alexander & Binski, no. 39 (by N. J. Morgan); P. Binski, 'Abbot Berkyng's Tapestries and Matthew Paris's Life of Edward the Confessor', *Archaeologia* CIX (1991), pp. 89–95.

[137] See p. 217, n. 80 above.

flanked on her right by a gigantic disembodied eye and on her left by an ear.He explains the symbolism: 'Memory has two doors, sight and hearing'; the paths to these doors are imagery (*painture*) and speech (*parole*); imagery serves the eye and speech the ear.[138] 'When I am not present', he adds, 'this writing – by its *painture* and by its *parole* – will bring me back to your memory as though I were present.'[139] The supposedly ignorant vernacular reader thus has the commonplaces of medieval psychological theory presented to him, or rather her, in dramatic form. Like Matthew Paris, Richard de Fournival thinks of the text (his 'writing' – *escrit*) entering the intellect primarily through the ear. 'All writing', he comments, 'is done to signify *parole* so that one may read it; and when one reads it, it reverts to its nature as *parole*.'[140] The typical medieval reader therefore reconstituted the script before his eyes as speech (*parole*) by spelling it out, either silently in his mind or pronouncing it aloud. Richard does concede, however, that writing is not purely auditory; it also has the quality of *painture* 'because a letter does not exist unless one depicts it'.[141]

Comments of this sort by medieval authors suggest that they questioned the value of writing and that neither they nor their readers took its significance for granted. Did writing exist independently of speech? Was it heard or seen? Was it a record or a picture? The paradoxes of writing are pointed up in the portrait of Eadwine of Canterbury 'the prince of writers' in the Eadwine Psalter (see plate XIV). This portrait may have been made as an obituary for him in the 1160s.[142] The inscription round its frame takes the form of a dialogue in Latin rhyme between the 'writer' and the 'letter'. The 'writer' poses a riddle: 'Ask my letter who I am.' The 'letter' answers: 'You whom the painted image shows, your writing declares to be Eadwine, living by your fame through the ages.' The 'letter' of the inscription speaks out loud; it reverts to its nature as *parole* in Richard de Fournival's terminology. Nevertheless the 'letter' identifies Eadwine not by reading the words of the inscription, but by looking at his 'writing' (*tua scriptura*). Its style 'declares' him to be Eadwine, just as the 'painted image' (*picta figura*) of the portrait does. There is *painture* in the *scriptura* of Eadwine as much as in the *figura* of him. To emphasize the closeness of hearing and seeing, the inscription uses derivatives of *dico* ('I speak') to describe what the 'letter' perceives: Eadwine's script 'declares' (*predicat*) who he is and likewise the 'beauty of this book demonstrates (*indicat*) his genius'. (This is an obituary in the spirit of Christopher Wren's *Si monumentum requiris, circumspice*.)

Latin letters were a cue for speech, not a substitute for it. When people spoke in vernaculars but wrote in Latin, the disjuncture between speech and script was obvious. Furthermore, as Walter Ong points out:

---

[138] Illustrated by: V. A. Kolve, *Chaucer and the Imagery of Narrative* (1984), p. 25; H. Solterer in *Word and Image*, V (1989), p. 142; S. Lewis in *Word and Image*, VII (1991), p. 17. See also Carruthers, *Memory*, pp. 223, 341, n. 12.

[139] Carruthers, *Memory*, pp. 223–4, 341, n. 12.

[140] Ibid., pp. 223, 341, n. 11.

[141] Ibid., pp. 223, 341, n. 11.

[142] G. Zarnecki in *Etudes Offertes à L. Grodecki* (1981), pp. 93–100; Kauffmann in Zarnecki, *Catalogue* (1984), p. 119, no. 62; Heslop in Gibson, Heslop, Pfaff (1992).

Written words are isolated from the fuller context in which spoken words come into being . . . In oral speech, a word must have one or another intonation or tone of voice – lively, excited, quiet, incensed, resigned, or whatever. It is impossible to speak a word orally without any intonation . . . Actors spend hours determining how actually to utter the words in the text before them.[143]

The medieval reader sounded out or read aloud the text in front of him in order to hear its significance: 'quiet, incensed, resigned, or whatever'. The modern reader may still be taught to do this in the special circumstances of reading a play. Its text may contain directions in parentheses about the tone of particular statements (*excitedly*, *quietly*, or whatever), by contrast with modern novels which leave the reader to infer the tone from the dialogue on the page. Advanced modern readers go to 'see' plays being performed, particularly classics like Shakespeare, even though they can read these texts for themselves. Victorian audiences crowded to hear Dickens read aloud from his novels, even though they could listen to these texts at home in hearthside readings. The intonation and body language of the actor or author reinforce the meaning and authenticity of the text for the audience. Without voices and gestures to articulate it, a Shakespearian text remains a closed book to most modern literates.

What applies in modern English-speaking society to Shakespeare applied in the Middle Ages to all texts. Medieval texts were more difficult for their readers than Shakespeare is for modern ones because most texts were expressed in an archaic language, Latin, which was over 1,000 years old and alien in its structures to speakers of Germanic languages like English. Hearing the text read aloud in a performance – even if the sole performer was the reader himself – was therefore the rule rather than the exception. A possible analogy is with musical literacy. Only a minority of the modern population reads music, and those who do so go to concerts, listen to records, or play instruments as well. The paper text of the music is not felt to be a substitute for its performance, even though an expert reader may hear the music in his mind. Like musical notation, medieval letter script was understood to represent sounds needing hearing.

This is why John of Salisbury called letters 'indicators of voices' (*vocum indices*).[144] In this respect he altered Isidore of Seville's definition (*indices rerum*, 'indicators of things'), which had been made six hundred years earlier when the Roman tradition of literacy was still strong.[115] The medieval reader liked to hear a word's 'voice' before he sensed the 'thing' it meant; he combined its *painture* on the page with the *parole* in his ear in order to open the doors of his mind, in Richard de Fournival's terms. That John of Salisbury was not merely theorizing is shown by the way his contemporaries among the higher clergy 'audited' texts, rather than scrutinizing them silently. What appears to the

[143] *Orality and Literacy* (1982), pp. 101–2. See also n. 155 below.
[144] *Metalogicon* Bk. 1, ch. 13; see n. 1 above.
[145] *Etymologies* Bk. 1, ch. 3, ed. W. M. Lindsay (1911), line 7.

modern reader to be mindless verbosity in medieval letters was designed for the recipient as a listener. At the papal chancery

> the emphasis on listening to the written word encouraged the use of set phrases and forms. The mind was allowed to relax while the familiar formulas were employed. This must have made the special information more obvious and arresting and there is no doubt that the essence of the document would have been retained more easily in the memory.[146]

John of Salisbury himself, in the opening of his poem *Entheticus*, prays that his 'little book' may be guided well in 'tongue and mind' in its journey to its public.[147]

When discussing punctuation marks and accents in *Metalogicon*, as part of his insistence on correct grammar, John of Salisbury remarked that the ancients had used certain 'notations' (*notae*) to distinguish the 'modes' (or 'moods') of writings, 'so that it may be grasped which bit in them is clear and which obscure, which certain and which dubious, and many other things of this sort'.[148] As John singled out Isidore of Seville for praise in this chapter, he probably had his description of grammatical terms in mind. Isidore says that the most celebrated classical authors used such symbols as asterisks and obelisks to indicate omissions in a text or corrupt readings or other editorial difficulties.[149] Nowhere in Isidore's detailed discussion does he describe notations which distinguished clarity from obscurity or certainty from doubt. But John of Salisbury was enthused by this idea and he berated his predecessors for allowing this 'notarial art' (*artem notariam*) to perish. 'It is not surprising', he adds, 'that there was such power in tiny notations (*notulis*), when singer musicians may indicate many variations in the highness or lowness of the voices by a few marks.'[150] (John probably refers to notations of pitch here.) Liturgical manuscripts of the eleventh and twelfth centuries, with their 'tiny notations' of the chant in the form of superscripts and marginations, confirm the accuracy of John's description.[151] He then takes up the idea that, just as the notes are the keys to music, so there once existed great keys to knowledge in the lost 'notarial art'. Seneca and Cicero undertook to impart this knowledge, John adds, but they failed to do so.[152]

[146] J. E. Sayers, *Papal Government and England* (1984), p. 97. See also nn. 57, 58, above.

[147] *Patrologiae* CXCIX, 965–6; R. M. Thomson, 'What is the *Entheticus*?' in *The World of John of Salisbury* ed. M. Wilks (1984), p. 293.

[148] 'Ut deprehendatur quid in eis lucidum, quid obscurum, quid certum, quid dubium, et in hunc modum plurima, *Metalogicon* Bk. I, ch. 20, p. 47.

[149] *Etymologies*, Bk. I, ch. 21.

[150] 'Nec miretur quis tantam vim fuisse in notulis, cum et musici cantores paucis caracteribus multas acutarum et gravium differentias indicent vocum', *Metalogicon* Bk. I, ch. 20, p. 47. Carruthers, *Memory*, p. 113.

[151] For musical notation in England, see: I. Fenlon ed., *Cambridge Music MSS 900–1700* (1982); S. Rankin, 'From Memory to Record', *Anglo-Saxon England* XIII (1984), pp. 97–112, plates ix, x, xi.

[152] *Metalogicon* Bk. I, ch. 20, p. 47.

The history of musical notation in the Middle Ages has been seen in terms of a cumulative increase in controls: 'controls, that is, as against the habits and constraints that the performer brought to the performance'.[153] Ultimately, the number of controls may increase to the point where they 'operate so closely and so constantly that the notation becomes in actuality a system of direct representation rather than of controls'.[154] Neither twelfth-century musical notation nor Latin letters were seen as systems of direct representation. John of Salisbury may have thought that the 'tiny notations' of the chant, which he described, came closer to the representation of voices than letters did. On the other hand, he conceded that letters are more than 'indicators of voices', since they can speak 'voicelessly' (*sine voce*). The grammar of Latin letters (in every sense of 'letters'), as perceived by John of Salisbury and Isidore of Seville and other medieval commentators in the Roman rhetorical tradition, was valued as a uniform system of controls, external to the habits and constraints which the individual reader or writer brought to his work. This is why it was the foundation of the liberal arts. Through the teaching of Hugh of St Victor, Peter Abelard, William of Conches, and other masters in the French schools in his formative years (starting in 1135), John of Salisbury may well have been led to hope that there were keys to knowledge still to be recovered from antiquity, even keys which would unlock the clear from the obscure and the certain from the dubious. His metaphor of a key was enshrined in the New Testament in the warning, 'Woe unto you, lawyers, for ye have taken away the key of knowledge' (Luke, xi, 52). John's dual professional experience, as a teacher of linguistic logic and a confidential clerk to the archbishop of Canterbury, combined to make the meaning of writing an important question for him.

An alphabetic script, particularly in a language as archaic as Latin, might indeed benefit from having a supporting system of notations, in addition to the letters, in order to restore to the discourse some of the intonation and imagery which writing eliminated. Probably, however, John was thinking of something less ambitious for his 'notarial art'. His contemporaries, the glossators of lawbooks and scripture, already used annotations to comment on what was obscure or dubious in a text. At Canterbury, the Eadwine Psalter was being completed at about the time John was writing (his *Metalogicon* was finished in 1159). A glossed book presented to the reader's eye at a glance a multiplicity of texts (see plate xiv), ranked in importance by the size, style and positioning of the lettering and by its colouring (as in rubrics). Bringing various texts together all on one page was wise practice in manuscript culture, when books were hard to come by; it accorded likewise with the doctrine that scripture was to be read at different levels of meaning. The Eadwine Psalter presents seven texts at once: three Latin versions of the psalms, an English version, a French version, a Latin interlinear commentary, and a fuller Latin commentary in the margins. The lettering varies in size between these, from the largest to the smallest, in a ratio of one to eleven.

---

[153] L. Treitler, 'Oral, Written, and Literate Process in the Transmission of Medieval Music', *Speculum* LVI (1981), p. 488.

[154] Ibid., p. 489.

However many explanations and versions of a text a scribe as expert as Eadwine could fit on to a single page, difficulties remained with any statement in writing even for the most expert reader. Writing, like all language, has the capacity to mislead, either unintentionally (when the reader misunderstands it) or by the author's design. Doubt remains, moreover, even when the tone of an author's statement can be established and his sources verified. Writing is so attractive a medium for the artist precisely because of its disjuncture from speech. The writer (in the modern sense of a creator of fiction) makes imagined voices ring true; he takes the word from 'its natural, oral habitat' (in Ong's metaphor) and sounds it out in the solitude of his study.[155] No 'notarial art', in John of Salisbury's sense, could ever have distinguished the certain from the dubious in the writings of such contemporaries of his as Geoffrey of Monmouth and Walter Map. They divided and fascinated readers then, just as they perplex medievalists now.[156] John of Salisbury himself produced doubt and ambiguity in his own writings, deliberately 'manufacturing pseudo-antiques' in the opinion of one modern critic.[157] Even the tone of his description of the lost 'notarial art' is difficult to gauge, as his references to Seneca and Cicero are flawed. Whether John misquoted classical texts because he could not get better copies of them, or whether he did it deliberately, remains a matter of opinion. Before the Italian Renaissance, even scholars as learned as John had a less literal attitude towards texts. They were not going to let 'the industry of the ancients', as Walter Map called it (perhaps facetiously), bury their own creations.[158]

Before John of Salisbury, Gilbert Crispin abbot of Westminster (*c*.1085–*c*.1117) had taken up the same subject of 'notations' (using Isidore of Seville's *Etymologies*, as John had done), in order to argue that 'just as letters stand in one way as images and notations of words, so also pictures exist as likenesses and notations of things written.'[159] Gilbert did not mean this was invariably the case, but that it applied in the particular context he was discussing, which was the controversy about images in Christian worship. The passage occurs in Gilbert's *Dispute of a Jew with a Christian*, where the Christian argues that a sculpture of Christ in Majesty surrounded by the four Evangelist symbols (a recurrent theme in Romanesque art) is justifiable because this image occurs in the Old Testament itself. 'Therefore what Isaiah saw, said and wrote, what Ezechiel saw, said and wrote, may after them be

[155] *Orality and Literacy*, p. 101.
[156] J. Gillingham, 'The Context and Purposes of Geoffrey of Monmouth's "History of the Kings of Britain"', *Anglo-Norman Studies* XIII (1990), ed. M. Chibnall, pp. 99–118; R. Levine, 'How to Read Walter Map', *Mittellateinisches Jahrbuch* XXIII (1988), pp. 91–105.
[157] J. Martin, 'John of Salisbury as a Classical Scholar' in *The World of John of Salisbury* ed. Wilks, p. 194.
[158] Walter Map, Bk. V, ch. 1, p. 404.
[159] 'Sicut enim littere quodam modo fiunt verborum figure et note, ita et picture scripturarum rerum existunt similitudines et note', *The Works of Gilbert Crispin Abbot of Westminster* ed. A. S. Abulafia and G. R. Evans (1986), p. 52; M. Camille, 'The Book of Signs', *Word and Image* I (1985), p. 135.

said and written and signified by some pictorial notation.'[160] Gilbert traces an unbroken line from seeing through saying to writing, because medieval readers of the Bible believed that the sacred page of scripture was literally what the prophets themselves had written down. As Gilbert's Christian explains in the passage above, there are three stages in approaching Isaiah or Ezechiel: first there is 'saying' (that is, reading the text aloud), secondly there is 'writing' (as in the penning of the sacred page in a monastic scriptorium), and finally there is 'signifying' pictorially (by painting or otherwise giving visible shape to the text in question). As the starting point of Isaiah or Ezechiel had been a vision, not a text, the reader's ultimate aim must be to reconstruct that vision.

But Gilbert Crispin was being disingenuous, as it cannot have escaped his notice that a great deal of imagery in Romanesque art, in sacred manuscripts as much as in churches, did not explicitly signify or illustrate things in Scripture. Gilbert might have replied that illustrating the mysteries of Scripture was best done implicitly, through symbolism, rather than explicitly. In the example he gives of the four Evangelist symbols described in the prophecy of Ezechiel, the reader has to know that the man's face in Ezechiel's vision prefigures the Evangelist Matthew, the lion prefigures Mark, the ox Luke, and the eagle John. The image of the eagle, for example, can therefore be read as the name of the Evangelist John, like a pictogram in a non-alphabetic script. This accords with Pope Gregory the Great's justification of 'reading by seeing' and it accords too with Gilbert's description of pictures as 'notations' (*note*), just as letters are 'notations'.[161] Once the symbolism is understood, such grotesque images as the Evangelist Luke seated with pen and parchment facing backwards on an ox, or Mark seated with a portable writing-frame but having the head of a lion, make sense (these examples are taken from English books of Gilbert's time).[162] Since symbolic imagery was drawn from a mass of Christian and pagan sources, what looks like monstrous ornamentation in manuscripts can sometimes be due to a modern reader's ignorance of its meaning rather than to its maker's lack of religious fervour. 'Few habits of the medieval mind are as foreign to the modern Western world as the impulse to take symbolism seriously.'[163]

When prayer-books begin to be made for the laity – mainly for aristocratic ladies – in the middle of the thirteenth century, they too often have what looks like monstrous ornamentation. This appears peculiarly irreligious when grotesque figures are detached from the text and begin to enjoy a life of their

---

[160] 'Quod ergo Isaias vidit, dixit et scripsit, quod Ezechiel vidit, dixit et scripsit, licet post eos dici et scribi et picture nota aliqua signari', *The Works*, p. 52. Possibly Gilbert had a particular sculpture at Westminster in mind, C. N. L. Brooke and G. Keir, *London 800–1216* (1975), p. 305.

[161] For Gregory see C. M. Chazelle in *World and Image* vi (1990), p. 139, and pp. 191–2 above. For Gilbert see n. 159 above.

[162] Kauffmann, *Romanesque MSS*, illustration nos 58, 76.

[163] T. A. Heslop, 'Brief in Words but Heavy in the Weight of its Mysteries', *Art History* ix (1986), p. 2.

own, as it were, on the border bars and margins of the page. The earliest and
best example of an English book of this sort is the Rutland Psalter. As it
records the death of Edmund de Lacy, earl of Lincoln, in May 1258, it was
presumably made before this date, possibly for his wife or mother. Prominent
in the borders of its pages are a brilliant repertoire of grotesques, of the sort
that will be repeated and varied in prayer-books made for the aristocracy
during the next 100 years, most famously in the Luttrell Psalter.[164] Some idea
of what the Rutland Psalter's grotesques are like is conveyed by N. J.
Morgan's summary description of a few of them in his analysis of the artists
involved. 'Artist A', for example, produced the following series of figures:
'hybrid musician, semi-nude man dancing, Marvel of the East with pickaxe,
shepherd with dog, rabbit in landscape, female centaur suckling her child,
griffin holding head of man, dragon, cat approaching mouse on sheaf of
wheat, man pointing to woman crawling with devil on back'.[165] Explanations
may be found for some of these subjects in classical mythology or medieval
folklore, and perhaps they can also be related to Christian symbolism. Even
then, however, it is difficult to show what relevance they have to the text of the
psalm on each page.

Like any form of notation, the grotesques in the borders of a manuscript
provide some sort of commentary on its text, even if they do no more than
distract the reader. As 'likenesses of things written', it might be possible to
read them like glosses. But what they signify is a perplexing problem, to which
there is no single answer. As far as the relationship of hearing and seeing is
concerned, grotesques are *painture* in Richard de Fournival's terms, though
they do not necessarily accord with Matthew Paris's wish 'that what the ear
hears the eye may see'.[166] The difficulty of interpreting them is well illustrated
by an example from the Egerton Hours, a little prayer-book (contemporary
with the Rutland Psalter) made for an unknown lady. She is depicted in a
miniature, kneeling beneath the enthroned Virgin and Child.[167] She holds her
prayer-book up with both hands, so that she can read the text (this is a mirror
image: an open book within an open book). But her prayer may be disturbed
by a monkey with a gittern and a hare, standing on his hindlegs, equipped
with a pipe. This pair are tuning up, to a handbell held by the hare, on the
border-bar a little to the left of the Virgin's head. Even if the lady depicted in
the miniature cannot see them from beneath the Virgin's throne, they are
distractingly visible to the actual user of the Egerton Hours. Possibly they are
contributing to the prayer set out on the page, 'My mouth will announce thy
praise' (the opening response in the Matins of the Virgin), as the hare blows
his pipe while the monkey prepares to sing. Further along the border-bar a
crane or stork is feeding something (quite a common motif) to a hybrid

---

[164] J. Backhouse, *The Luttrell Psalter* (1991).

[165] 'The Artists of the Rutland Psalter', *British Library Journal* xiii (1987), pp. 176–7. See also
N. J. Morgan, *Early Gothic MSS 1250–85* (1988), pp. 78–82, no. 112.

[166] See n. 136 above.

[167] Donovan, *de Brailes*, pp. 133–4, 186–7; Morgan, *Early Gothic MSS 1250–85*, illustration no.
304, catalogue no. 161. Another image of this lady owner is illustrated by Alexander &
Binski, p. 217, no. 41.

creature with a dog-like body and human face. The prayers for Matins begin with the words 'Lord, open my lips', and this is precisely what the crane is encouraging the hybrid to do.

Grotesques like this appear in the margins of books made for scholastics, as well as in prayer-books for the laity.[168] The fashion originated in Paris, possibly in the schools, and it appears first in England in manuscripts associated with Oxford. Margins were an 'extra-textual realm, where both artist and reader sought evocative escape from the wearisome codification of the *logos* and its illustration'.[169] Grotesques also served as memorizing images, whether pictured in the mind or painted on the page, as M. Carruthers has demonstrated.[170] The scholastic reader used the grotesques, in the margins and at the head and foot of the page, to find his place in the book. The Oxford philosopher Thomas Bradwardine described memorizing images more bizarre than anything on the pages of manuscripts, such as a bright red bull with bleeding and swollen testicles confronting a woman in labour with her womb ripped open.[171]. Bradwardine was not intending to be obscene or sadistic, but to create unforgettable images to which his students could attach abstract propositions for memorizing purposes. Even when grotesques in scholastic texts are explained as aids to relaxation or memorizing, their presence in prayer-books remains disturbing. Perhaps the monkey and the hare in the Egerton Hours, and even the crane and the hybrid, are reverencing the text as best they can. Nevertheless these creatures have lascivious associations in medieval symbolism. The monkey and the hare may be about to start such a cacophony that the lady in the miniature will be unable to hear herself pray.

On this interpretation, grotesques are jesters who make a nonsense of the text. They do indeed provide a commentary, as they demonstrate through their antics the difference between the chaos on the edge of the page and the stability at the centre. Where grotesques penetrate the body of the text (which they do often), they challenge writing's function as a system of controls. In John of Salisbury's or Isidore of Seville's terms, they undermine the grammar of the Latin letters. Occasionally grotesques mock writing explicitly, like the monkeys in a French manuscript who tease the scribe by imitating his gestures.[172] By drawing the eye away from the body of the text to the surrounding pictorial forms of penmanship, grotesques remind the reader that letters themselves are not the truth. Primarily the letters, like the grotesques, are 'shapes' (*figure*, as John of Salisbury called them); they are 'indicators of voices' and not their reality.[173] In that case, what are the grotesques indicators of? The short answer is: equivocation. The hybrids in particular make a nonsense of John's hopes for an art which will distinguish the clear from the

---

[168] Morgan, *Early Gothic MSS 1250–85*, no. 145 (Aristotle).

[169] Camille, 'The Book of Signs', p. 142. In general see M. Camille, *Image on the Edge: The Margins of Medieval Art* (1992).

[170] Carruthers, *Memory*, pp. 245–7.

[171] Ed. Carruthers, in *Journal of Medieval Latin* ii (1992), p. 37.

[172] Camille, 'The Book of Signs', p. 143; *Image On the Edge*, p. 25.

[173] See nn. 1, 144 above.

obscure and the certain from the dubious.[174] The realism of much grotesque
ornament compounds the problem of ambiguity. In the Egerton Hours the
hare musician, standing on his hindlegs, is as life-like a figure (though
miniaturized) as Tenniel's March Hare in *Alice in Wonderland*. Through skilful
penmanship the scribe artist, whether painter or writer, created the illusion on
the page that 'the fiction is not a fiction'.[175] Like Alice, the lady kneeling in the
Egerton Hours is in wonderland: letters metamorphosize into mythical
creatures, animals change size and act like human beings, sacred words
become the playthings of equivocators and blasphemers.

The best example of fictitious realism in an English manuscript from this
period is the depiction of birds in the margins of the Alphonso Psalter (begun
for Edward I's son Alphonso, who died in 1284).[176] 'From an ornithological
point of view', comments B. Yapp, 'I do not think such good pictures were
drawn again until the nineteenth century.'[177] In Yapp's opinion such drawings were done from actual specimens and not from model-books.[178] A
generation earlier Matthew Paris had almost certainly drawn the king's
elephant from life.[179] Realistic miniatures of birds occur principally in
manuscripts of royal or East Anglian provenance. One link is Roger of
Pilkington, who was squire to Master William of Louth, treasurer of the
Wardrobe and bishop of Ely.[180] As officers of the Wardrobe (which
administered the royal household), Roger and his master may have had some
part in commissioning the Alphonso Psalter. In 1291 Roger was granted a
royal charter, which is most exceptional in being ornamented on all four sides
with animals, birds, and trees.[181] The birds are similar to those in the
Alphonso Psalter, though they are not done by such a good artist. This
ornament is descriptive, as it shows the flora and fauna which Roger will
encounter when enjoying the hunting rights granted by the charter. This
realistic art-work enhances the document's authority. As real animals and
birds frame the words of the charter, so real rights are conveyed by its text.
Painter and writer are both illusionists in shapes (*figure*), reaching the minds
of readers of the charter by the devious paths of imagery and speech (*painture*
and *parole*).

The way manuscripts were made as splendid visual objects, rather than
mundane communications, ensured that there was no irreconcilable division

---

[174] See nn. 148–50 above. Numerous types of hybrid are listed by L. M. C. Randall, *Images in the Margins of Gothic MSS* (1966), pp. 111–28.
[175] F. H. Bäuml, 'Varieties and Consequences of Medieval Literacy and Illiteracy', *Speculum* LV (1980), p. 262.
[176] L. F. Sandler, *Gothic MSS 1285–1385* (1986), no. 1; Alexander & Binski, p. 355.
[177] *Birds in Medieval MSS* (1981), p. 80 and colour plates 1, 21, 22, 23.
[178] Ibid., pp. 73–8.
[179] Lewis, *Matthew Paris*, pp. 212–16.
[180] *Records of the Wardrobe and Household 1285–6* ed. B. F. and C. R. Byerly (1977), nos 100, 115; ibid. *1286–89* (1986), nos 1234, 2324.
[181] Illustrated in colour by Camille, *Image on the Edge*, p. 121. See also C. Clay in *Antiquaries Journal* XI (1931), pp. 129–32; G. E. Hutchinson in *Isis* LXV (1974), pp. 14–15; Sandler, *Gothic MSS 1285–1385*, plate 43.

between writers and non-writers when documents began to be used more widely in the twelfth and thirteenth centuries. Many manuscripts continued to be lavishly embellished and all were read aloud so that the non-literate could participate in their use. There was no conscious or deliberate attempt to integrate literate and non-literate – indeed the clergy wanted to remain a class apart – but change was sufficiently slow to make gradual adaptation possible. As long as all writings were manuscripts, that is, as long as they were made exclusively by hand, old habits of mind persisted. Throughout the Middle Ages the writer remained a visual artist and the reader a specialist in the spoken word. Medieval reading (*lectio*) was primarily something heard rather than seen until the invention of printing, and writing (*scriptura*) often continued to be admired for its calligraphy rather than its textual accuracy. The laity were gradually coaxed towards literacy by ensuring that it changed the old ways of hearing and seeing as little as possible.

9

Trusting Writing

Documents did not immediately inspire trust. As with other innovations in technology, there was a long and complex period of evolution, particularly in the twelfth century in England, before methods of production were developed which proved acceptable both to traditionalists and to experts in literacy. There was no straight and simple line of progress from memory to written record. People had to be persuaded – and it was difficult to do – that documentary proof was a sufficient improvement on existing methods to merit the extra expense and mastery of novel techniques which it demanded.

A modern literate tends to assume that statements in writing, especially if they are in print, are more reliable than spoken words. This assumption is the result of schooling in reading and writing from an early age and the constant use of documents, such as bills, for even the smallest transactions. The obvious advantage to a modern literate of documentary proof is that it cannot be as easily or as readily changed as a person's word. But this advantage of writing was less obvious in medieval England, since even literates did not use documents in ways which assured their effectiveness as proof. Most charters of the twelfth century were neither dated nor autographed, nor were they copied into registers for future reference. In the earliest private charters draftsmen and scribes give the impression that, instead of sharing a common training in the drawing up of instruments, they are each making a personal and individual but necessarily amateur effort to master the complexities of documentary proof for the first time.

A charter whereby Ralf of St Audoen gave a salt-pan to Sele priory in Sussex illustrates the work of an amateur draftsman very well, even though it is dated (1153 *Anno Domini*) and autographed, which is unusual.[1] The draftsman or scribe, who was probably one of the monks of Sele, begins with a

---

[1] *Oxford Facs*, no. 9. Cf. other Sele priory preambles at ch. 5, n. 3 above.

justification for written record: 'Because, it is appropriate that this should be brought to reach the notice of many, it is committed to the muniments of letters by provident deliberation, lest in the process of time it be destroyed by ruinous oblivion.' The gift itself was publicly symbolized not by this charter, however, but by a more traditional form of writing – a Gospel book which was laid on the beneficiary's altar. The monks of Sele seem to have been determined to ratify the gift in as many ways as possible, both traditional and novel. Ralf's lord, William de Braose, made his autograph sign of the cross on the charter twice, once in the priory and again when the document was exhibited and ratified at his court in Bramber castle. Ralf also put his seal on the charter. Those who trusted the sign of the cross and those who favoured the more modern wax seal, which with its device of a knight on horseback was a symbol of feudal lordship, could therefore both be satisfied. (See plate 1 where a charter is authenticated in a similar way.) For those who trusted neither, lists of witnesses were specified for both transactions. As F. M. Stenton commented of a Lincolnshire charter of similar date, 'the transaction is unusually complicated, but it is probable that the expression of a grant in writing was often less important to the parties than the performance of ceremonial acts of which the charter itself makes no record.'[2] The writing was of secondary importance, and was hedged about with repetitious clauses, because less confidence was placed in it than in the oaths and public ceremonies which had traditionally sanctioned conveyances. For example, a signatory who put his sign of a cross on a charter would also have made a ceremonial sign of the cross across his body with his right hand touching his forehead, heart, left shoulder and right shoulder.

At first, each charter tended to differ in its phraseology, because every document was felt to be an individual affirmation fixing human relationships at a certain point in time and space. Doubts about whether such stability was possible or appropriate may explain why early drafters of charters are often reluctant to state the time and place of writing and why they invoke the aid of God and his saints so frequently. The advantage to the historian today, though not to the property-owner at the time, of this diversity of practice is that it provides a record, like an archaeological stratification, of how a literate mentality developed over generations. Information, which students of diplomatic have accumulated in order to date charters and identify forgeries, can be used to illustrate how attitudes to writing changed over the twelfth and thirteenth centuries. The evolution of common form is not commonplace, as it marks the stages in the gradual acceptance of literate ways of doing business.

MEMORY AND WRITING

Before documents were used, the truth of an event or transaction had been established by personal statements, often made on oath, by the principals or witnesses. If the event were too far in the past for that, the oldest and wisest men were asked what they could remember about it. Numerous examples

---

[2] *Transcripts of Charters Relating to Gilbertine Houses*, Lincolnshire Record S. XVIII (1922), p. xxx.

could be cited of collective oral testimony being given from memory, particularly in cases involving the proof of age of feudal heirs. The example which follows illustrates the method in answer to a less routine question. In 1127 a writ of Henry I ordered a jury to be chosen of twelve men from Dover and twelve from Sandwich to settle a dispute between St Augustine's abbey at Canterbury and Christ Church about customs dues at the port of Sandwich. The jurors were described as 'twenty-four mature, wise seniors of many years, having good testimony'.[3] Each in turn then swore on a Gospel book in public that the tolls belonged to Christ Church, saying: 'this I have received from my ancestors, and I have seen and heard from my youth up until now, so help me God and these Holy Gospels.'

Whether in circumstances like these the jurors really told the historical truth is impossible to establish, since the past events in question were recorded only in people's living memories. As the jurors had publicly sworn on the Gospels that they were telling the truth, no more could be said, unless their Christian principles were to be impugned. Thus, without documents, the establishment of what passed for truth was simple and personal, since it depended on the good word of one's fellows. Remembered truth was also flexible and up to date, because no ancient custom could be proved to be older than the memory of the oldest living wise man. There was no conflict between past and present, between ancient precedents and present practice. Customary law 'quietly passes over obsolete laws, which sink into oblivion, and die peacefully, but the law itself remains young, always in the belief that it is old.'[4] Written records, on the other hand, do not die peacefully, as they retain a half-life in archives and can be resurrected to inform, impress or mystify future generations.

Those who objected in the Middle Ages to the literate preference for the artificial memory of written record, instead of the living memory voiced by wise men of age and experience, were in a long tradition – had they known it – which extended back to myths about the invention of writing. According to Socrates, the god who invented writing had been rebuked by the king of Egypt, Thamuzz, who said:

> If men learn this, it will implant forgetfulness in their souls: they will cease to exercise memory because they rely on that which is written, calling things to remembrance no longer from within themselves, but by means of external marks; what you have discovered is a recipe not for memory, but for reminder.[5]

Both to ignorant illiterates and to sophisticated Platonists written record was a dubious gift, because it seemed to kill living eloquence and trust and substitute for them a mummified semblance in the form of a piece of

---

[3] Stenton, *Justice*, p. 118.

[4] F. Kern, *Kingship and Law in the Middle Ages* trans. S. B. Chrimes (1939), p. 179; Clanchy, 'Remembering', p. 172.

[5] Plato, *Phaedrus*, 274–5, trans. R. Hackforth (1952). Cf. Curtis, *European Lit.*, p. 304; Goody, *Literacy*, p. 50; Carruthers, *Memory*, pp. 30–1, 296–7.

parchment. Henry I's partisans in the dispute with Anselm, who had called a papal bull a sheepskin 'blackened with ink and weighted with a little lump of lead', were arguing for the priority of the personal testimony of the three bishops who exercised memory over the mere 'external marks' of a writing.[6] Those medieval Christians who recalled St Paul's warning, 'the letter killeth, but the spirit giveth life', were in a similar long tradition.[7] Likewise perhaps the Earl Warenne himself, when he allegedly produced before Edward I's judges the 'ancient and rusty sword' of his ancestors, was appealing to a sign which was superior to any letters because it lived in people's memories. Warenne's rusty sword might have appealed to medieval intellectuals as much as to ordinary people, since the schoolmen were trained to make physical objects create graphic images in the memory to which they attached their abstract ideas. Hugh of St Victor taught that 'there is nothing so effective for exciting the memory as meticulously paying attention to the surroundings of things.'[8]

Objectors to written record had a case which was strong in substance as well as in sentiment, since numerous medieval charters were forged and the authenticity of the genuine ones was difficult to prove. Such a bewildering variety of 'external marks' had been used in idiosyncratic attempts to demonstrate the authenticity of charters that written record was highly suspicious. There were thousands of authentic charters without dates or places of issue, some of them written by scribes who seem never to have wielded a pen before (see plates I and VI).[9] Although most English charters had seals attached to them, a few were authenticated by inked crosses (some autographs and others not), or by other symbolic objects signifying the donor's wishes such as rings or knives. Nearly all charters listed witnesses to the transaction, ranging in numbers from the king's unique *Teste me ipso* (witness, myself) to the 123 individuals named in an agreement in Kent in 1176.[10] It was common for a scribe to conclude his list of witnesses with some such phrase as 'and many others who would take too long to enumerate',[11] a description which was useless for future identification, although it recorded the impressiveness of the occasion at the time. The scribe of an Oxfordshire charter dismissed the witnesses to the deed with the phrase: 'whose names we have been prevented by tedium from writing'.[12] Witnesses soon died anyway and some, like the saints who witness a Christ Church charter of *c.*1200, may never have lived.[13] Sometimes the scribe of the charter identifies himself as the last witness, offering a test of authenticity, but more often he does not.

In these circumstances, where practice was so varied and even eccentric, both literate and illiterate were entitled to distrust charters. Authentic-looking

[6] See ch. 8, n. 27 above.
[7] See ch. 8, nn. 28–30 above.
[8] Cf. ch. 5, n. 134 above; Carruthers, *Memory*, p. 264.
[9] See ch. 4, n. 73 above.
[10] Chaplais, *Docs*, p. 16; *BM Facs*, no. 57.
[11] *Mowbray Charters*, p. 17, no. 13.
[12] *The Sandford Cartulary*, II, Oxfordshire Record S. xxII (1941), p. 181; D. Postles, 'Choosing Witnesses in Twelfth-Century England', *The Irish Jurist* xxIII (1988), p. 344.
[13] Galbraith, 'Literacy', p. 222.

documents might well be forged, or conversely amateur scrawls might turn out to be genuine. In addition to inconsistencies and lack of uniform scribal training, the principal difficulty was that monks, who were the traditional experts in writing, were also the greatest forgers. The more powerful and ancient the house, the more likely it was that its documents would be forged in a professional manner. Of the seals used by Christ Church Canterbury, Archdeacon Simon Langton wrote to Gregory IX in 1238: 'Holy Father, there is not a single sort of forgery that is not perpetrated in the church of Canterbury. For they have forged in gold, in lead, in wax, and in every kind of metal.'[14] Much the same, of course, could be said of the papal *curia* in an earlier period, when it had used the Donation of Constantine and other forged decretals.

Yet in theory at least it would have been relatively easy for English medieval writers to make documents whose authenticity could normally have been proved. Although no system of safeguards could cover all cases, the great majority could certainly be guaranteed. All that was required was to follow elementary principles of Roman legal practice, which were familiar in twelfth-century Italy and throughout the *pays du droit écrit* bordering on the Mediterranean, and ensure that each document was precisely dated and written by an authorized scribe or notary. Ideally, in addition, the notary needed to register a copy of the document in a record kept by a public authority. As is well known, these elementary principles were not followed in medieval England, nor elsewhere at first in northern Europe. Although some notaries practised in England in the thirteenth century, their activities were normally restricted to a few types of ecclesiastical business. Similarly public registers of certain types of property transactions existed in England by 1200, in the Jewish *arche* and the royal feet of fines established by Hubert Walter, but there was no comprehensive system of registration.[15] Sometimes the king's government could not trace its own documents, let alone other people's.

The reason why England did not develop a notarial system on the Roman model is generally thought to be simple and obvious: 'customary law prevailed.'[16] Although correct, this explanation is inadequate, as customary law did not prevail in other areas of bureaucratic activity because twelfth-century England had been opened to Italian and other European influences, first by the Norman Conquest and then by the Angevins. Thus the accounting system of the Exchequer, which Richard Fitz Neal thought to be largely a product of immemorial custom when he wrote his *Dialogue of the Exchequer* around 1179, had in fact been created in Henry I's reign by French (and perhaps also Arabic) arithmetical expertise. The common law itself, as articulated by Henry II's writs, owed more to deliberate legislative thought than to custom. From the latter half of the twelfth century, English royal officials were sufficiently influenced by the canon and civil law schools of Bologna to know that custom by itself was inadequate. Fitz Neal himself evoked Roman law, when he credited William the Conqueror with the

---

[14] Cheney, *Texts & Studies*, p. 104.
[15] For these registries see ch. 2, nn. 84–98 above.
[16] Cheney, *Notaries* p. 6.

intention of bringing 'the conquered people under the rule of written law'.[17] Although Fitz Neal's remark has elements of anachronism when applied to William the Conqueror, it reflects the assumption of contemporary administrators in Henry II's reign that Roman *jus scriptum* could be applied to England.

Why England remained largely unaffected by the Roman notarial system, while being influenced by other continental bureaucratic procedures, is therefore a question worth pursuing further, as it goes to the roots of the non-literate's lack of understanding and consequent distrust of written modes of proof. Without documents, memory had stemmed from the living wisdom of the local community whereas the dead hand of writing, the 'mortmain' of the monks and clergy, defined and extended boundaries by its 'external marks' across both time and space.

DATING DOCUMENTS

The difficulties experienced by English writers of the twelfth century, when confronting problems they felt to be novel, are well illustrated by their variety of approaches to dating documents, ranging from those who omit the date altogether to others who use more than one system of computation on the same document. To write out the date at the head of a letter is an elementary routine for a modern literate and was relatively simple likewise for a trained medieval notary. Thus an imperial notary, Henry of Asti, wrote the date as follows on an instrument drawn up in London: 'Anno a nativitate Christi millesimo ducentesimo sexagesimo octavo, indictione undecima, die Mercurii xviii intrante mense Januraii, pontificatus domini Clementis papae iiii anno tercio'.[18] This date, Wednesday 18 January 1268 AD, is expressed in a way which is familiar to a modern European, although the papal year (the third of Clement IV) and the reference to the eleventh indiction are Roman notarial refinements which now seem superfluous. For some transactions notaries were expected to record the hour as well as the day. Thus an episcopal notification from Lincoln in 1228 specifies times of dispatch and receipt of letters, as well as verifying the sender's seal.[19] Even a common law judge, Roger of Seaton, followed notarial practice in 1279 when he acknowledged receipt of one letter from the Chancery 'at about the ninth hour' and another 'just a little after dark'.[20] These times are not more precise presumably because Seaton was estimating the hours by daylight and not by a clock.[21]

---

[17] *Dialogus*, p. 63 and ch. 1, n. 1 above.

[18] Cheney, *Notaries*, p. 168. *Handbook of Dates for Students of English History* ed. C. R. Cheney (1945), is a concise introduction to dating problems.

[19] *Rotuli Hugonis de Welles* ed. W. P. W. Phillimore, Canterbury & Yorks S. I (1909) or Lincolnshire Record S. III (1912), II, pp. 145–6.

[20] *SCCKB* I, pp. clxvii (s), clxviii (t).

[21] An early example of recording time by a mechanical clock is Richard II's abdication in 1399 at 'circiter nonam pulsationem horologii', Cheney, *Notaries*, p. 137.

The purpose of being precise about the year, month, day, and even hour at which a document was issued or received was in order to settle subsequent disputes about its authenticity by checking the time. Thus Henry III assured Gregory X in 1272 that some royal letters patent, which were being exhibited at the papal *curia*, were forgeries because 'we were not at Canterbury on that day and year'; in fact Henry was mistaken, but that is another story.[22] Dates and places of issue had the added advantage of putting documents and their makers in a temporal and geographical perspective, which extended over centuries if the Christian system of years of grace *Anno Domini* was used.

Despite the advantages of stating when documents were issued, most twelfth-century charters do not do so. The eight extant bonds (the earliest of their kind) of the Flemish financier, William Cade, are significant in this respect, as it might be expected that records of debts would be drafted as precisely as possible.[23] Yet none of the bonds bears a date of issue and three of them (nos 2, 5, 8) do not even specify the year in which the debt is to be paid, but only a day in relation to feast days of the church. Although the other five do specify the year, it is expressed in ways which are clumsy and could be ambiguous in the long term:

1   After Henry, the king of England's son, espoused the daughter of the king of France [1160];
3   after the espousal of the king of England's son and the king's daughter;
4   after the king and Count Thierry of Flanders had talks together at Dover before the count went to set out for Jerusalem [1157];
6   after the king's great council at London [1163];
7   after Gilbert Foliot was received into the bishopric of London [1163].

Cade evidently did not expect his debts to be outstanding for long and so it was appropriate to date repayments in relation to current events.

More precise forms of dating begin in the last decade of the twelfth century. Royal letters are uniformly dated (by place of issue, day of the month, and regnal year) from the accession of Richard I in 1189.[24] Influenced by royal rather than papal practice, English bishops begin to date their solemn *acta* with regularity from the end of the twelfth century, although their secular enfeoffments and administrative precepts went on being undated until the end of the thirteenth century.[25] Books and similar scribal work are likewise usually undated and unautographed, although there are notable exceptions like the chronicles of Matthew Paris or Domesday Book, one of those volumes states that 'this *descriptio*' was made in 1086 AD.[26] Other than Domesday, the earliest

---

[22] See ch. 2, nn. 92–3 above.
[23] H. Jenkinson, 'A Moneylender's Bonds' in *Essays to Poole*, pp.205–10; C. Brooke and G. Keir, *London 800–1216* (1975), plate 36 facing p. 139.
[24] Chaplais, *Docs*, p. 14.
[25] Cheney, *Chanceries*, pp. 83ff.
[26] For Matthew Paris see ch. 5, n. 5 above. For Domesday Book see Galbraith, *Studies*, p. 93; *descriptio* refers to the Domesday survey as a whole rather than to the writing of this particular volume.

extant English book dated by its scribe is a text of St Augustine, which is stated to have been written at the Cistercian abbey of Buildwas in 1167 AD; another book from Buildwas is similarly dated 1176 AD.[27]

Why not always give the date on a document in a precise and uniform way, if only as a routine precaution? Various explanations can be suggested for not doing so. One sometimes mentioned is that charters were seen as mere confirmations of transactions which had already taken place, and there was therefore no point in dating them. The difficulty with this explanation is that even when a charter was written after the event, it would still have been prudent, if the draftsman really had that regard for posterity which his preamble claimed, to specify in the text the date of the transaction itself and distinguish that from the date on which the charter was written. To specify both dates was good notarial practice. Another possible explanation for omitting dates is that they were difficult to compute without printed diaries. Gervase of Canterbury describes some of the problems: when exactly was the Crucifixion (in 32, 33 or 34 AD)? When should the year begin – at the Annunciation (25 March), the Passion (a movable feast), Christmas Day, or the Circumcision (1 January)?[28] Yet these difficulties were surmountable and since most early charters were written by monks, who were the experts in chronology, their lack of dates is still mysterious.

Other reasons for not dating documents are more profound. Until putting the date on a document became a mindless routine, dating required the scribe to express an opinion about his place in time. In relation to which persons, human or divine, and over what length of time was the date to be computed? A Jew might date his bond 'from the Creation' and think of a continuum 'from the beginning of time up to the end of the world', because the temporal order proceeded without intermission.[29] For the pope, on the other hand, it was appropriate to begin a new era with the birth of Christ and to date letters *Anno Domini*, since the pope was Christ's vicar in unbroken succession from St Peter. A bishop or a monastic chronicler might likewise compute by years of grace, since bishops too were successors of the Apostles and monks had an accepted place in the Christian dispensation. Yet ecclesiastics did not date all their documents: enfeoffments and precepts were usually left undated, as has already been mentioned. In such instances omission of the date may not have been due to negligence, but to conscientiousness. Perhaps it was thought presumptuous or even blasphemous to associate worldly business with the time of Christ's incarnation. To record the year *Anno Domini* on a document was to give it a place in the chronology of Christian salvation in past, present, and future time, as expounded by St Augustine in the *City of God*. Paradox-ically, monks may have so rarely dated documents in the twelfth century or earlier because they were too conscious of the significance of time and of their place in posterity.

The non-religious, by contrast, had such a personal and short view of time that they too found it difficult at first to specify a numerical year on a

---

[27] Ker, *English MSS*, p. 21; Cheney, *Texts & Studies*, p. 331, n. 1; de Hamel, *MSS*, p. 92.
[28] Gervase I, p. 88.
[29] Examples cited by F. A. Lincoln, *The Starra* (1939), pp. 30, 32, 57.

document. Everyone knew which year was meant, the present one, and if there were doubt, some notable event could be referred to. Examples have already been given of William Cade dating his bonds in this frame of mind. The richest variety of memorable events in an early record appears in the guild rolls of Leicester (the earliest of their kind), which extend over the period 1196–1232.[30] The first year is specified in relation to the release from captivity in France of the earl of Leicester (in 1196) and the second 'after the death of the emperor of Germany' (Henry VI in 1197). Thereafter other events of national or international importance, such as the Interdict in John's reign or the death of William Marshal and the capture of Damietta by the crusaders (both in 1219), are interspersed with local events in Leicester, such as the dedication of St Nicholas's church (in ?1221) and the deaths or terminations in office of town worthies like aldermen. Only three times are English regnal years referred to, and years *Anno Domini* are not used at all. Evidently the Leicester town clerks were uncertain of what standard to adopt for dating their rolls. By their variety of practices the rolls give an indication of how events, in Leicester and beyond, were viewed by the local community.

The earliest extant final concord made before royal justices is similarly dated not by a numerical year, but at the feast of Peter and Paul (29 June) 'after the king took the allegiance of the barons of Scotland at York'.[31] This refers to the homage done to Henry II in York Minster in August 1175 after his defeat of King William the Lion. This concord, which concerns a lawsuit in Oxford between the canons of Osney and a widow and her daughters, has no direct concern with Anglo-Scottish politics. Nevertheless it was evidently assumed that the time when Henry II formally exhibited his superiority over the Scots would be remembered for at least as long as the settlement of this lawsuit at Oxford. Whether the drafters of this concord thought that their document would last only for a generation or so, or whether conversely they thought that Henry II's triumphant ceremony in York Minster would be remembered for centuries, is impossible to establish. Probably they had not given the matter much thought either way. They dated the concord not in relation to a documented time continuum stretching over centuries, but, as a non-literate might, in relation to a recent famous event. Despite their appeals to posterity, medieval writers seem to have found it difficult to imagine that their work might survive for centuries and that a time would come when only a professional historian knew when 'the king took the allegiance of the barons of Scotland at York.'

Even when a year is given *Anno Domini* on a document, a memorable event is sometimes specified as well, as if years of grace were too alien (except to the professionally religious) to inspire personal confidence. Thus a gift by the wife of Roger de Mowbray to Fountains abbey is dated 1176 AD, 'the year in which the fortresses of Thirsk and [Kirkby] Malzeard were razed'.[32] This event likewise concerns Henry II's defeat of William the Lion, as Roger de

---

[30] *Records of the Borough of Leicester* ed. M. Bateson I (1899), pp. 12–35; G. H. Martin, 'The English Borough in the Thirteenth Century', *TRHS* 5th series XIII (1963), p. 133.
[31] *BM Facs*, no. 55.
[32] *Mowbray Charters*, p. 101, no. 131.

Mowbray had been among the rebels whose castles were demolished. The Mowbrays here recalled their personal humiliation by Henry II instead of the larger submission in York Minster. A concord made in the court of William de Ferrers is dated comparably by the fortunes of the local lord – 'the year 1192 AD, namely the year in which Earl William de Ferrers took to wife Anneis, sister of Ranulf earl of Chester'.[33] Enough has been said to show that traditionally, before documentation was properly understood, the measurement of time was related to a variety of persons and events and not to an external standard.

The novelty of dating documents, and the variety of ways in which it might be done, is best summarized by the unnecessarily elaborate datary which Ralf de Diceto gave for his survey of the manors of St Paul's cathedral. His invention of distinctive *signa* for his chronicle and the St Paul's charters suggests that he was extraordinarily sensitive to modes of documentary proof. He therefore intended there to be no doubt about the year in which he made his survey. It was:

> The 1181st year AD, the 21st year of Pope Alexander III, the 27th regnal year of King Henry II of the English, the 11th regnal year of King Henry the son of the king, the 18th year that time has passed since the translation of Bishop Gilbert Foliot from Hereford to London, when this inquest was made by Ralf de Diceto, dean of London, in the first year of his deanship.[34]

Ralf thus computes the year by six different systems which he arranges hierarchically, from years *Anno Domini* through the pope and the kings down to himself at the bottom in his first energetic year of office as dean of St Paul's.

In the thirteenth century, when charters were written in tens of thousands, methods of dating become less self-conscious and more uniform. A parody of a datary in French, purporting to be written in a letter to the noble Lady Desire, sets out the commonest rules: 'Given within the four seas of England, on the eve of St John the Baptist, in the 27th year of the reign of King Edward the son of King Henry.'[35] The eve of St John Baptist is 23 June (Midsummer's Eve) and the 27th year of Edward I's reign in 1299. Between the various possible ways of recording the year, month and day the commonest procedure adopted in England was to relate the day within each year to a feast of the church and to express the year in terms of regnal years. This compromise between church and state, which rejected years *Anno Domini* (as used in episcopal chanceries), and Roman calendar months (as used in the royal Chancery) probably seemed the most appropriate to knightly landowners. They trusted regnal years more than years *Anno Domini* because there was a more immediate point of reference in the king's coronation, which was a publicly remembered event. The growth of dating by regnal years, rather than by more personal events or by the regimes of lesser lords, also suggests that the king was becoming

---

[33] Stenton, *Feudalism*, p. 54, n. 3.
[34] *The Domesday of St Paul's* ed. W. H. Hale, Camden S. LXIX (1857), p. 109.
[35] Legge, *Anglo-Norman*, p. 342.

accepted as the head of the English community. Some knights were beginning, moreover, to learn the lengths of reigns of their kings from illustrated rolls which set them out in succession (see plate XIII).[36]

Although after 1300 many private charters still bear no date, forms of dating had become firmly established and commonplace. In general, after much preliminary hesitation, writers had got the measure of time. But because dating had evolved at the slow pace at which literate habits became acceptable, rather than being arbitrarily imposed by Roman law, English methods of dating documents remained complex and inconsistent. From a historical point of view, this variety of methods is a memorial to the formation of literate habits reflecting both feudal and Christian ways of thought. The evolution of the dating of documents is a measure of growing confidence in their usefulness as records.

SIGNING DOCUMENTS

Everyone agreed that legal documents like charters must be signed, but there was as much diversity of opinion about what constituted a valid signature as there was about what made a date appropriate. As with dating, this diversity suggests that ways were being sought which would prove acceptable both to non-literate traditionalists and to experts in records. By and large in Mediterranean Europe notarial practice was preferred for authenticating documents as for dating them. A notary provided safeguards against forgery usually by writing the document in his own hand and by appending to it his name and an individual *signum* which he drew with a pen. If dispute arose, the notary could be cross-examined or, if he were dead, reference could be made to other documents signed by him or to a register in which an exemplar of his style and *signum* was recorded.

Examples of notarially authenticated parchments can be found in England, though they are not abundant, from the latter half of the thirteenth century onwards, usually among ecclesiastical documents.[37] Most exceptionally Edward I had notarized parchments drawn up in the 1290s, when he had to justify his actions in Scotland by the standards of international jurisprudence instead of English common law. For this reason John Balliol's homage in 1292, his renunciation of that homage in 1296, and his statement when Edward's prisoner in 1298 were all written up for the record by a notary, John of Caen. Thus Balliol's letter renouncing his homage in 1296 was authenticated as follows:

> And I, John Arthur of Caen, notary public by authority of the Apostolic See, have written a faithful copy, word for word, in order as I have found it, of the text of the letter, and have drawn it up in the form of this public instrument with the mark of my *signum*, at the command and

---

[36] Smalley, *Historians*, p. 178.
[37] Notaries' *signa* are illustrated by Cheney, *Notaries*, plates 1–6, and by J. S. Purvis, *Notarial Signs from the York Archiepiscopal Records* (1957).

request of the king of England, as fuller evidence of the foregoing matters.[38]

This formula illustrates the main elements of authenticity in a notarial instrument. The notary states his name and authority, he pens the document in his own hand, and he authenticates it further with a distinctive *signum*. The fact that a document is signed by a notary does not mean that the statements in it are true in themselves, but that they are true in law. John of Caen altered one of the documents in the Scottish case some years after it was made. The ink has now faded slightly, so that the place where he made his erasure and substitution can be clearly seen.[39] Allegedly the most important point in the whole process against John Balliol had been left out. This was that the king of Scotland had acknowledged that the king of England's 'hand of direction' should be placed in future over the Scottish kingdom. Whether Balliol had ever made such an acknowledgement officially is impossible to know. As an accredited writer, John of Caen's remit was not historical fact but legal evidence. In altering this document – and in prejudicing the Scottish case elsewhere in his record – 'at the command of the king of England', he provided Edward I with the proof he required in international law. Like the master craftsman employed by Edward I's court to paint the realistic birds in the Alphonso Psalter, John of Caen created through his notarial art the illusion on the page that 'the fiction is not a fiction.'[40]

The Roman system of authorizing notaries was a relatively simple and normally effective way of coping with the problems of authenticating documents in the Middle Ages. Not every party to a document, even if he were able to read, could be expected to sign personally with a distinctively penned signature of his own, as in modern western culture, because writing on parchment was a business for specialists. Confining signing to professional scribes had other advantages. It imposed uniform standards on the production of documents and it restricted writers to a manageable number, whose credentials could be checked. A notary signed documents with his *signum* in much the same way as a master mason marked the stones he cut before they were built into a permanent fabric. Despite these advantages, qualified notaries were not much used in England.

Scribes of English charters identify themselves only in a minority of cases, and the variety of ways in which they do so suggests that there was no uniform purpose or training behind such identifications.[41] Some writers were aware, however, that their name served as an additional form of attestation, as in the following two instances from the twelfth-century Mowbray charters:

[38] *Anglo-Scottish Relations*, p. 72.
[39] E. L. G. Stones and G. G. Simpson, *Edward I and the Throne of Scotland* (1978), vol, i, pp. 50–2 and plate ii.
[40] See p. 292, n. 175 above.
[41] J. H. Hodson, 'Medieval Charters: The Last Witness', *Journal of the Society of Archivists* v (1974), p. 71.

Witness, Dom Samson d'Aubigny, by whose hand this composition was made;

And I, John the chaplain, have written this writ [*breve*] because I was present.[42]

The declared 'maker' of another twelfth-century charter, Walter the Chaplain, appended to his attestation a curse to 'confound in eternity whoever wishes to destroy' the charter.[43] On the other hand, the scribe of another charter from the mid-twelfth century, 'Herbert the clerk who wrote this well [*bene*]', was drawing attention, like the portrait of Eadwine of Canterbury, to his ability as a scribal artist rather than his importance as a witness, assuming (that is) that *bene* is not a mistranscription of *breve* (a writ).[44] Even writers of royal writs do not usually identify themselves until the latter half of the thirteenth century, when the practice began in the Chancery of the scribe writing his surname in a corner of the document.[45] For private charters it never became the rule in medieval England that the writer had to identify himself.

Some scribes seemed ambitious to follow notarial practice, but because there was no uniform training nor regulations their efforts are haphazard. For example, in an Oxford charter of 1277 the last witness is a certain Philip 'the notary' (*notarius*) and the concluding formula of the charter is embellished in a way which may have been intended to serve as his individual *signum*.[46] Yet Philip does not consistently place his name last in the charters he writes and, although he was generally known as 'the notary' (as his family charters attest), his status was probably no different from that of another professional writer of charters in Oxford at the time, Richard of Eppewelle.[47] Neither Philip nor Richard was probably a notary in any Roman sense. Similarly a century earlier a Cheshire charter appears to be 'signed' by its last witness, William Legat, as his surname is written out in capitals and his forename in full, unlike those of the other witnesses.[48] Yet William's practice is inconsistent, as in another charter his 'signature' is less prominent, though still evident, and in a third it is written no differently from that of the other witnesses.[49] Another writer, Robert Carpenter, who was not a professional scribe at all but an aspiring freeman of the Isle of Wight active in Hampshire

---

[42] *Mowbray Charters* p. 72, no. 97; p. 245, no. 381. In no. 97 the word 'compositio' could refer to the 'agreement' itself rather than to its 'composition'. However Hodson, 'Medieval Charters', p. 71, n. 3, cites another example of a charter's 'compositor' naming himself.

[43] *Northants. Facs*, plate xviii.

[44] Hodson, 'Medieval Charters', p. 71, n. 2.

[45] 'in quolibet brevi debet scribentis nomen inbreviari', Fleta, Bk. ii. ch. 13, p. 126. Chaplais, *Docs*, p. 52.

[46] *Cartulary of the Hospital of St John Baptist* ed. H. E. Salter, Oxford Historical S. LXVI 91914), i, plate xiv.

[47] Philip's family and property: ibid., nos 114, 127–36; Richard of Eppewelle: ibid., pp. vi–vii and plates xv, xvi.

[48] *Cheshire Facs*, no. 9.

[49] *Cheshire Facs*, nos. 6, 2. Cf. Hodson, 'Medieval Charters', p. 74.

legal business, nevertheless followed notarial practice when he gave details of his work:

> In the 49th year of the reign of King Henry son of King John and 1265 *Anno Domini*, at Whitsun, the following page was written in St Edward's chapel at Westminster and extracted from the chronicles in a small roll by the hand of Robert Carpenter of Hareslade, and he wrote this here.[50]

Robert only needed to have added a *signum* to rival the precision of a professional notary, like Henry of Asti or John of Caen.

These examples suggest that English writers had the knowledge and capacity, and some even the wish, to draw up instruments like notaries, although they were not officially accredited by public authorities. Why English common law did not develop public notaries is a complex problem, which reflects the way literate modes developed. Once documents began to proliferate, English men of business needed reliable forms of written instruments just as Italian merchants did. This need was first acknowledged by the royal government in Hubert Walter's statute of 1194, which provided for the official writing of Jewish moneylenders' bonds in designated centres. The chirographers established by this statute served much the same purpose as notaries. For example, in a dispute in 1218 between a Jew, Samuel son of Aaron of Colchester, and a Christian, Sewal son of William de Spineto, about a bond made by Sewal's father, Sewal denied that the seal on the chirograph was his father's. Samuel insisted that the chirograph was genuine and appealed to the testimony of both Christians and Jews, 'who know the handwriting of the clerk who was chirographer when it was made'.[51] Samuel was therefore arguing that the handwriting of bonds could be attributed to individual scribes, whose script was a better mark of authenticity than a seal; for, as Samuel also argued, a knight might have more than one seal. Although this case was adjourned and no decision is on record, it shows that notarial principles were understood, at least by Jews who were literate and preferred to ratify documents with their signatures and not with seals. Samuel's private opinion may have been that seals were mere lumps of wax, whose use typified Christian ignorance and chicanery.

A more ambitious attempt at laying down standards for authenticating bonds was made by the Statute of Merchants in 1285.[52] This required all merchants (excluding Jews) to have their debts recorded before the mayor of London, or before similar designated authorities in other cities and towns. The test of distinctive handwriting was acknowledged, as bonds were to be enrolled 'in the hand of one of the [town] clerks who is known' and each bond was likewise to be written by a designated clerk. Yet the statute did not

---

[50] N. Denholm-Young, 'Robert Carpenter and the Provisions of Westminster', *EHR* L (1935), p. 22. Cf. C. A. F. Meekings, 'More about Robert Carpenter of Hareslade', *EHR* LXXII (1957), pp. 260–9.

[51] *Calendar of the Plea Rolls of the Exchequer of the Jews* ed. J. M. Rigg I (1905), p. 7, cf. p. 14.

[52] *Statutes*, p. 99 (amending the statute of Acton Burnell of 1283).

require the clerk to put either his name or his scribal signature on the bond like a notary. By 1285 English legal practice was probably too accustomed to seals to replace them by notarial *signa*. Nevertheless the possibility of forging seals was recognized by the statute, as royal seals were to be made in two interlocking parts, one part to be kept by the mayor and the other part by the authorized clerk. The Statute of Merchants thus came close to the essentials of notarial practice, while avoiding the name: bonds were to be written by authorized writers, enrolled in official registers and authenticated by a *signum* (in the form of a special seal) in the writer's charge. If these rules had been enforced and extended from money bonds to all written conveyances of property, England would have had official writers and registries on a scale superior to any in Europe.

THE SYMBOLISM OF SEALS AND CROSSES

The reasons why England did not develop a uniform scribal system for authenticating documents seem to centre on the use of seals. Although medieval seals varied considerably in size, materials, and design, they had two typical elements – a device or pictorial symbol in the centre, such as a knight on horseback (see plates I and v) and a legend or inscription around the circumference bearing the sealer's name. Exceptions to this rule are signets on finger rings, which had no space for an inscription, and personal seals which might display apophthegms in place of the owner's name. For example the signet of Isabella countess of Gloucester (1189–1217) announces (in Latin) 'I am an eagle, guardian of my lady'; or a matrix from *c*.1300, with a squirrel on it, is inscribed 'I crake nutis swete.'[53] The typical seal, combining a device or *signum* with the signatory's name, functioned in much the same way as a notarial form of authentication. Moreover, in one way a seal was more efficient than a notary's manual *signum*, as every seal in wax from the same matrix was identical. Because seals reproduced script, they enabled people to sign their names in an acceptable form without labour or skill. In effect every possessor of a seal could be his own notary, as he could authenticate documents with his individual *signum* and name, even if he were unable to manipulate a pen. Like the practice of reading documents aloud, seals helped to bridge the gap between the literate and the non-literate. For the possessor of a seal the scribe who wrote the document, like the clerk who read it aloud, was a mere intermediary, an artisan of script. Perhaps English scribes were not required to identify themselves, not to put their *signa* on the documents they wrote, because writers were of little significance. Instead, the donor and witnesses themselves authenticated the documents with their own *signa* in the ready-made form of seals.

[53] In general see M. Pastoureux, *Les Sceaux* (1981). For England see T. A. Heslop, 'English Seals from the Mid-Ninth Century to 1100', *Journal of the British Archaeological Association* CXXXIII (1980), pp. 1–16. Heslop is likewise the author of the sections on seals in Zarnecki, *Catalogue*, p. 306, no. 337, and Alexander & Binski, p. 277, no. 201. Cf. also A.B. Tonnochy, *Catalogue of British Seal-Dies in the British Museum* (1952), no. 754: 'I krak nuts.'

Not only by intent but also in practice a seal does exactly the same as the printing press: it reliably copies and multiplies information by mechanical means – in this case information of ownership. This information can consist of a picture (illustration), one single sign (movable type), or a short text (block print). We have here in embryo all the basic elements of printing. The reason for the long hiatus between the first Mesopotamian seal, the first Far Eastern block print and the Gutenberg Bible must not be sought in a lack of creative ability.[54]

The European type of printing invented by Gutenberg in the fifteenth century depended on technologies of metallurgy – in engraving, punching, casting, and compressing – which had been developed for coins and seals centuries earlier. For example, a screw-press similar in form to the earliest printing-press was made for Canterbury cathedral in *c*.1232, where it was used to fix the church's double-side seal to documents.[55] Every possessor of a large double-sided seal (which was the form favoured by the royal Chancery and great churches) required a press of this sort. The smaller and more usual medieval seals, on the other hand, had much in common with other inscribed objects designed for carrying on the person, particularly coins, message-sticks and wax tablets. Whereas coins have survived in relatively large numbers, because they are durable and valuable, seals (meaning the wax impressions as distinct from their matrixes) are not extant in England until the eleventh century and are not common until the thirteenth. Similarly the earliest extant message-sticks are the thirteenth century tally-sticks of the Exchequer, and the earliest English wax tablets are of similar date. With perishable objects like these, which were used for ephemeral purposes, the date from which an article first survives is no guide to the date of its first use.

The seals from ordinary medieval letters (as distinct from solemn charters intended to posterity) have almost all been destroyed, presumably when the letters were opened. They are even rarer than unopened franked letters from the first years of postage stamp production in the nineteenth century. From England the earliest unopened royal 'letter close' dates from Henry VIII's reign, but it has no seal. A portion of the royal seal survives on a letter close of Edward III preserved by Oxford University.[56] Seal impressions could be produced in malleable metals, like gold and silver, which are more durable than wax. An old practice, exemplified by the papacy, was to use a seal of lead – the *bulla*. But an advantage of sealing-wax over metal was that it could be stuck on to the document itself, whereas the papal *bulla* had to be attached with string. Sealing-wax was therefore used, like glue on an envelope, to close up a letter. When and from where the recipe for sealing-wax was introduced into England is not known. The medieval form was an amalgam of beeswax,

---

[54] A. Gaur, *A History of Writing* (1984), p. 194.

[55] Illustrated in Alexander & Binski, pp. 399–400, no. 460. Cf. the printing press of 1499 illustrated by V. Scholderer, *Johann Gutenberg* (1963), plate xiv.

[56] Chaplais, *Docs*, plate 25, d, e. The form of a 'letter close' is explained at p. 91 above.

which becomes malleable under gentle heat, and resin, which acts as a solvent and adhesive.[57] In an often quoted remark King Alfred wrote: 'Consider now, if your lord's letter (*aerendgewrit*) and his seal (*insegel*) came to you, whether you could say that you could not recognize him by this means.'[58] As no writs or seals are extant from Alfred's reign, it is difficult to know what he meant in material terms. The lord's *aerendgewrit* may have taken the form of a message-stick, though a letter written on parchment is more likely. His *insegel* may either have been stamped in metal and detached from the stick or letter, or it may have consisted of wax impressed on the parchment to seal it up into a letter close.

The earliest English seals made of wax and still fixed to their documents are on charters of Edward the Confessor, dating from the middle of the eleventh century (150 years after King Alfred).[59] These documents prove nothing about earlier practice regarding the sealing and sending of letters in England, as they are a deliberate innovation and they are not letters in the ordinary sense of missives. As Gervase of Canterbury noted in his chronicle, Edward the Confessor was 'the first of the kings of England who appended pressed wax on his charters as testimony of the truth'.[60] Gervase did not mean that Edward was the first English king to use sealing-wax for sending letters, but that he was the first to apply it to 'charters', which was a novelty. Charters conveyed property in perpetuity, as distinct from the day-to-day mandates sent out as letters close. For seals to stand permanently 'as testimony of the truth' necessitated devising a method of preserving the wax impression on the charter, instead of destroying it as happened when a letter close was opened. This is why Gervase explains that Edward the Confessor, or rather the official who later became known as the spigurnel, 'appended' the wax to the charter. The seal hung ('appended') from a tongue of parchment or on strings, instead of being stuck tightly to the document (see the mark of the seal on the writ of Henry I in Plate ii). Instead of using the adhesive quality of the wax to show the recipient that the document had reached him unopened, Edward the Confessor's innovation made the hardened adhesive itself a symbol of the royal will. The seal was intended to stick to the charter in perpetuity in validation of the grant. Henceforward a charter without a seal was not acceptable as evidence in the king's court.

The new seal of Edward the Confessor was much larger and heavier than ordinary seals and it was also double-sided, in imitation of papal and imperial seals; this was made possible by its hanging freely, instead of sticking to the body of the document. The apparatus like a printing press for producing these double-sided seals was not easily portable, as the seal-press (judging by

[57] H. Jenkinson, *Selected Writings* (1980), pp. 28, 156.

[58] S. Keynes and M. Lapidge, *Alfred the Great* (1983), p. 141; P. Chaplais, 'The Anglo-Saxon Chancery', in *Prisca Munimenta* ed. F. Ranger (1973), pp. 51–3; S. Keynes, in R. McKitterick ed., *The Uses of Literacy in Early Medieval Europe* (1990), pp. 244–7.

[59] Zarnecki, *Catalogue*, p. 301, no. 328; Bishop & Chaplais, plates iii and xviii; F. Barlow, *Edward the Confessor* (1970), plate 5 (facing p. 100).

[60] 'Hic est primus regum Anglie qui in cartis suis ad testimonium veritatis ceram impressam appendit', *Gesta Regum* RS lxxiii (1880), vol. ii, p. 59.

the one at Canterbury) required two people to lift it. The king or his chancellor could not put the new seal in his pocket; but it was not intended to facilitate the ordinary business of government anyway. The 'great seal' of Edward the Confessor was not designed for everyday use. It was a portentous object which gave weight, physically and symbolically, to the king's most solemn grants. Judging by its size and appearance, the great seal has more in common with the Earl Warenne's rusty sword and Stephen of Bulmer's broken knife-handle than it does with the mechanisms of bureaucracy. Its wax impression was a visible sign of the king's will, which could be transferred from hand to hand at the charter conveyancing ceremony like a symbolic knife or rod. It had the advantage over other symbolic objects that it was harder to forge and easier to fix securely to the charter because it adhered to the parchment. Another advantage was that it printed out the king's name, titles and icons of authority automatically, whereas the monks of Durham had had great difficulty inscribing Stephen of Bulmer's knife-handle. The great seal also automated and depersonalized the signing process, as it had a little cross at its head which made the king's sign of the cross on his behalf and even in his absence. The seal's icon of the king enthroned in majesty made his authority present wherever his image was present, like Christ in Majesty.

Edward the Confessor's innovation of the great seal had far-reaching consequences, partly because it coincided with the Norman Conquest. It invalidated all Anglo-Saxon charters which had been authenticated by the sign of the cross alone. Consequently in the eyes of nostalgic monks, the Anglo-Saxon past became that 'simple olden time' (*simplex illa antiquitas*) before the growth of malice and cunning, when 'golden crosses depicted by the hands of kings' (this is Matthew Paris's description) authenticated charters.[61] The Ramsey chronicler (writing in c.1170) described the great seal as a 'two-faced image' of duplicity.[62] The chronicle ascribed to Abbot Ingulf of Crowland repeats that the charters of the Anglo-Saxons were graced by golden crosses and other sacred signs. As this chronicle was forged (or confected from earlier sources) in the fifteenth century, it marks a stage in the growth of the myth of the noble but primitive Anglo-Saxon.[63] Charters are the principal administrative documents to survive from Anglo-Saxon England and, because they are not sealed, it came to be believed that the Anglo-Saxons had not possessed seals. Similarly, because they signed their charters with crosses (which were not even autographs), they were believed to be illiterate.

V. H. Galbraith refuted the former of these beliefs in his Raleigh Lecture to the British Academy in 1935 by citing King Alfred's remark about the lord's *insegel*, which had been brought to his attention by F. M. Stenton.[64] But in the same lecture he reinforced the myth of the primitive Anglo-Saxon by equating literacy with 'civilized government' and insisting that the charters signed with crosses show that 'the written word had no intelligible meaning' for the kings

---

[61] *Ramsey*, p. 65; Matthew Paris, *Gesta Abbatum* RS xxviii (1867), i, p. 151.

[62] 'inversivas huiusmodi figurarum facies', *Ramsey*, p. 65.

[63] Gransden, *Historical Writing*, ii (1982), pp. 490–2. See also p. 148, nn. 12–13 above.

[64] Galbraith, 'Literacy', p. 218, n. 41. Cf. n. 58 above.

before Alfred, who lived in 'stark illiteracy'.[65] In the Ford Lectures delivered at Oxford in 1941 Galbraith again equated the use of seals with being 'relatively literate and not uncivilized', whereas the charters signed with crosses are unprofessional and 'primitive'.[66] Galbraith allowed his experience as an officer in the Public Record Office to overshadow his historical judgment here. To Anglo-Saxons, charters signed with crosses probably looked more authentic than writs with seals because each cross, written alongside a witness's name by a priestly scribe, recorded the subscription of a solemn oath made in the presence of Christ crucified. The value put on oaths is reiterated throughout the Anglo-Saxon law codes, and the charters often spell out that the subscription is the sign of the Holy Cross of Christ. Seals, on the other hand, were probably not associated in Anglo-Saxon England with religious or public undertakings. Judging from King Alfred's remark, they were common enough but their use was confined to messages about the business of lordship.[67] To have used a seal on a solemn grant to the church would have been inappropriate if not sacrilegious. As has already been argued, Edward the Confessor's great seal was an extraordinary innovation.

William the Conqueror took over the great seal because he claimed to be Edward the Confessor's lawful successor. Indeed he improved on it, by having his image as a knight on horseback (the first such image on a seal) placed on its obverse and by using the two-sidedness of the seal to emphasize his dual authority in Normandy and England.[68] The seal's inscription in Latin hexameters spelt out its function as an icon: 'By this, recognize William guardian of the Normans, and [turn over the seal] by this sign, acknowledge the same, king over the English.' The extravagant titles which earlier kings had claimed in the preambles to their charters were now subsumed by the seal. Nevertheless these efforts to give prestige to the great seal were not sufficient to make it an immediate substitute for the king's personal sign of the cross. Plate I shows a charter bearing the crosses of Ilbert de Lacy and his wife and of their lord, King William Rufus. Whereas Ilbert's seal was attached to this charter, there is no sign that a royal seal ever was. Rufus's sign of the cross appears also on a charter for Peterborough abbey.[69] His signature differs from that on the Lacy charter, but no significance was probably attached to consistency in the exact shape of the cross. The Peterborough charter does carry the great seal, but it is fixed by silk cords in the French style instead of being stuck directly to the parchment. As this charter was written by a royal scribe and signed by the chancellor, its irregularities cannot mean that it was an unofficial production. Its unusual form may reflect a compromise between the Anglo-Saxon conservatism of the Peterborough monks, who demanded signs of the cross from the king and his officers, and their Norman abbot,

[65] Galbraith, 'Literacy', pp. 216–17, 206.
[66] Galbraith, *Studies*, pp. 36, 32.
[67] Anglo-Saxon seals are discussed by Heslop, 'English Seals', pp. 2–8, and Keynes, 'Royal Government', pp. 246–7. Matrixes are illustrated by J. Backhouse, D. H. Turner and L. Webster eds, *The Golden Age of Anglo-Saxon Art* (1984), pp. 112–14.
[68] Chaplais, *Docs*, p. 2; Heslop, 'English Seals', p. 10.
[69] Bishop & Chaplais, plates XIX, XX; E. King, *Peterborough Abbey* (1973), p. 19.

Turold, who wanted something more modern and French to impress his rival, Robert, bishop of Lincoln. In addition to the silk cords, the great seal on this charter was provided with a bag of embroidered silk.

When charters are authenticated by signs of the cross as well as seals, it is likely that their makers had doubts about whether the seal alone could signify a sacred undertaking. A charter for Chester abbey makes this explicit:

> I, Earl Hugh, and my barons have confirmed all these things in the presence of Archbishop Anselm [of Canterbury] not only by my seal but also by the seal of Almighty God, that is the sign of the holy cross, so that each of us makes a sign of the cross with his own hand as evidence for posterity.[70]

To emphasize that the sign of the cross was the 'seal' (*sigillum*) of God, the charter pens a cross on God's behalf before the crosses of the other signatories. In modern terms this charter is a forgery, as all the purportedly autograph crosses on it were probably written after the signatories were dead; it may date from fifty years after the death of Anselm of Canterbury in 1109. The monks of Chester were perhaps so insistent on the authenticity of the signs of the cross because they had written them themselves. They considered themselves qualified to sign on behalf of their benefactors – and of God himself – because they were protecting their benefactors' interests. There is a comparable case from Durham, where the charter entitling the cathedral to its properties bears what look like the individual autograph crosses of Lanfranc of Canterbury and other prelates, even though half of them had died before its ostensible year of issue in 1093 (this was the year in which the foundation stone of the cathedral was laid). As in the Chester charter, the principal signatory spells out the value of the sign of the cross:

> May anyone who gives some benefit in alms merit, here and in the future, the blessing of Almighty God and St Cuthbert the reverend confessor, and may he be a participator in all the benefits of the church of Durham. Amen. I, William bishop of Durham, have been the first to subscribe this sign of the cross in testimony of this charter and in eternal memory of me.[71]

A number of Durham's twelfth-century charters are authenticated in peculiar ways. Mention has already been made of the two knife-handles preserved at Durham. The Durham monks may have been deliberately old-fashioned in their public acts because they were newcomers, who had to convince the Northumbrians that they were guardians and not usurpers of the heritage of Cuthbert at Lindisfarne and Bede at Jarrow.[72]

---

[70] *The Charters of the Anglo-Norman Earls of Chester* ed. G. Barraclough, Record S. of Lancs. and Cheshire cxxvi (1988), p. 7.

[71] *Durham Episcopal Charters* ed. H. S. Offler, Surtees S. clxxix (1968), pp. 58–9.

[72] A. J. Piper, 'The First Generations of Durham Monks and the Cult of St Cuthbert' in G. Bonner, D. Rollason and C. Stancliffe eds, *St Cuthbert* (1989), pp. 437–46. For the knife-handles see ch. 1, nn. 51, 58 above.

In addition to documents authenticated by crosses as well as seals, there is a charter sealed by God, like the Chester charter, though in the Durham case the *signum* is in the form of a wax impression instead of a sign of the cross. This charter (made in the 1150s) records Ralf de Gaugy's surrender of the church of Ellingham to Durham.[73] Instead of Ralf's seal, it carries a seal with the inscription SIGNUM CLEMENCIE DEI ('Sign of God's Clemency') around an image of the dove bringing the olive branch to Noah (Genesis, VIII, 11). Excavations at Jarrow in 1971 turned up a seal matrix in the form of a pendant bearing the same inscription and image, though the design is more fluid and a bit smaller. Another pendant seal matrix with a bird on it was excavated at Jedburgh in 1984, but it has no inscription and the bird looks like a hawk.[74] These pendants emphasize that seals were intimately personal objects, which functioned as jewellery and charms as well as badges of identity. The power of a seal emanated from the material of which the matrix was made as well as from the message it bore. The Jarrow pendant is made of translucent amber. Its wearer presumably hoped to profit spiritually and materially from wearing this 'sign of God's clemency' next to his heart. Possibly the Durham monks gave these pendants to their devotees, just as they gave Richard the Engineer some texts and relics of St Cuthbert to hang round his neck to guard against falling off the scaffolding.[75]

Ralf de Gaugy was an important landowner in Northumberland. His sealing this charter with SIGNUM CLEMENCIE DEI does not necessarily mean that he had no seal of his own, but that this was the 'sign' required in this instance. The Durham monks conducted a running battle with the de Gaugy family about the church of Ellingham and they may have thought this 'sign of God's clemency' was the best way of sealing their pact. In the 1170s the elder son of this Ralf de Gaugy, also called Ralf, again confirmed the surrender of Ellingham. His charter too was authenticated in an unusual way. He subscribed a sign of the cross, but the parchment was folded over it while the ink was still wet so that it smudged.[76] An explanation is provided by the seal which reads: TEGO SECRETA FRANGE L[EGE] ('I cover secrets. Break [me and] read'). Seals which say they keep secrets are quite common. For example a matrix of jasper reads: CLAUSA SECRETA TEGO ('I cover closed secrets'); a silver one reads: FRANGE LEGE LECTA TEGE ('Break. Read. Cover what is read'); a gold and sapphire signet ring reads: TECTA LEGE LECTA TEGE ('Read what is covered. Cover what is read').[77] These matrixes date from the thirteenth century and probably belonged to women. An undertaking to keep secrets was appropriate for sealing up a personal

---

[73] E. Bateson, *History of Northumberland* (1895), II, p. 228; M. T. Clanchy, 'Reading the Signs at Durham Cathedral' in *Literacy and Society* ed. K. Schousboe and M. T. Larsen (1989), p. 178. I am grateful to Professor R. Cramp for showing me the Jarrow matrix.

[74] J. Higgitt, 'The Jedburgh Comb' in *Romanesque and Gothic: Essays for G. Zarnecki* (1987), pp. 120–1.

[75] See ch. 10, n. 5 below.

[76] Bateson, *Northumberland*, II, plate between pp. 228–9.

[77] Alexander & Binski, p. 276, no. 198; Tonnochy, *Seal-Dies*, p. 145, nos 705, 706. Alexander & Binski, p. 486, no. 654.

letter. It was not suited to a charter of gift, which was a public declaration. The legal value of Ralf de Gaugy's subscribing his cross was nullified, if it were immediately concealed under the fold of the parchment. Nevertheless this had to be done, presumably because somebody felt that a seal which said 'I cover secrets' was valid only if it had a secret to cover.

Both these de Gaugy charters suggest that seals had not traditionally been the impassive legal instruments which they became once they were used on impersonal and formal statements in charters. Seals were designed for personal correspondence. Like the message-stick in the Anglo-Saxon poem now called 'The Husband's Message', a seal carried its owner's bidding.[78] This is why it might speak in the first person. Another Durham charter (dating from early in the twelfth century) bears a seal inscribed: THOR ME MITTIT AMICO ('Thor sends me to a friend'). This is attached to a letter to Thor's 'dearest lord', Earl David of Scotland, concerning a gift to St Cuthbert.[79] Thor issued a confirmatory charter, which has no seal, addressed to 'all the sons of holy church'.[80] The seal carrying Thor's message 'to a friend' would not have made sense on the charter addressed to the general public. Gradually over the twelfth and thirteenth centuries landowners followed the king's lead in having two seals: a great seal for authenticating public statements and a private or 'privy' seal for sending letters. In 1230 a minor Somerset landowner, William, son of John of Harptree, acknowledged before the king's justices that he would seal a charter of gift 'with his great seal' and replace the 'private seal' with which it had been temporarily sealed.[81] In reality only the king and the aristocracy can have had much use for a great seal, as minor landowners and burgesses did not issue public statements and neither did they often make deeds of gift.

A great seal was a desirable object in its own right, however, irrespective of whether it was useful, because it was a symbol of status and power. This is precisely what the seals of Edward the Confessor and William the Conqueror had been. The silver matrix made for Exeter in the first decade of the thirteenth century has inscribed on its back in Latin: 'Luke made me'; 'William Prudum gave me to the city of Exeter, God have mercy on his soul.'[82] This seal has therefore been endowed with a sacred personality, as invocations to God were normally inscribed only on vessels made for the altar. A sacred charge may also be seen in the great seal of Robert Fitz Walter, the 'Marshal of God's Army' in the barons' war against King John. This magnificent matrix is made of silver and shows Robert on his warhorse bestriding a dragon.[83] Another matrix, the size of the royal great seal but triangular in

---

[78] J. C. Pope, 'The Husband's Message' in *Medieval Scribes: Essays Presented to N. R. Ker* ed. M. B. Parkes and A. G. Watson (1978), pp. 56–9.

[79] Heslop, 'English Seals', pp. 15–16; Zarnecki, *Catalogue*, p. 317, no. 370; A. C. Lawrie, *Early Scottish Charters* (1905), pp. 25–6, 274.

[80] Lawrie, *Early Scottish Charters*, p. 19.

[81] *CuriaRR*, xiv, p. 132, no. 664.

[82] M. Campbell, 'Gold, Silver and Precious Stones' in *English Medieval Industries* ed. J. Blair and N. Ramsay (1991), p. 145; Zarnecki, *Catalogue*, p. 319, no. 378.

[83] G. Henderson, 'Romance and Politics on Some Medieval English Seals', *Art History* i (1978), 34–42; Alexander & Binski, p. 397, no. 454.

shape and made of lead, was found at Dunwich in Suffolk and has been dated
to the second quarter of the thirteenth century. It has a floral device and an
inscription in Latin declaring it to be the 'seal of Benedict the Baker'.[84] This
object is crude by comparison with Robert's matrix, emphasizing the gulf in
rank and style between a baron of England and a tradesman of Dunwich.
What Benedict the Baker used this seal for is unknown; perhaps it concerned
the assize of bread.

   To those who were not familiar with documents, seals may have been
attractive because they looked as if they had a better chance of surviving the
rigours of time than a piece of parchment. (In fact, seals and parchment have
both turned out to be resilient materials.) In order to justify the use of seals in
place of signs of the cross, phrases begin to be used in charters in the twelfth
century explaining that the seal gives dignity and strength to the document.
The two examples which follow are typical of thousands:

> And so that this gift of mine may be permanent, stable and unshaken, I
> have esteemed it worthy to be strengthened with my seal.

> And so that this gift and grant of mine and confirmation of my charter
> may last in perpetuity, I have reinforced the present writing with the
> impress of my seal.[85]

Although such phrases soon become common form, their variety suggests that
abstract documentary proof without the physical reinforcement of symbolic
objects was widely and deeply felt to be inadequate. When fixed to a charter,
the seal became a relic which could be seen and touched, in order to obtain
from it that authentic knowledge of a donor's wishes which no writing could
adequately convey. The seal was a message from the past. Many early seals
were made from Graeco-Roman gem stones, which were valued as talismans
associating their medieval users with the great and mysterious men of
antiquity. Gem seals (intaglios) very occasionally turn up in Anglo-Saxon
settings and it is possible that this was the means by which the practice of
sealing was carried over from Roman Britain to Anglo-Saxon England.[86]
Antique seals become common in the twelfth century. Usually the engraved
gem was reset in a ring or pendant of precious metal. Thus Thomas Becket's
personal seal, presumably impressed from a gold or silver ring, is inscribed in
Latin 'the seal of Thomas of London' and it has as its device a man naked
except for a helmet.[87] The original Roman owner of this seal may have
described this figure as Mercury or Mars. Becket probably did not identify it

---

[84] Tonnochy, *Seal-Dies*, p. 25, no. 161. My thanks to Dr. Emma Mason.
[85] *Luffield Priory Charters* ed. G. R. Elvey, Buckinghamshire Record S. xv (1968), p. 98, no. 98
and p. 75, no. 72.
[86] *Anglo-Saxon Art and Culture* ed. L. Webster and J. Backhouse (1991), pp. 23–4, no. 5h;
Anglo-Saxon Art ed. Backhouse, Turner and Webster (1984), pp. 98–9, no. 90.
[87] F. Barlow, *Thomas Becket* (1986), plate 2 and pp. 38–9, 286.

so precisely. If the device were mysterious, that added to the seal's attraction. A cornelian engraved with a figure now identified as Dionysus, is inscribed on its silver pendant setting IGNOTA NOTO ('I know the unknown'), which was appropriate too for an ancient deity.[88]

Antique gems were thought to have various curative and magical properties, depending on the type of stone used and the figure engraved on it. A seal of red jasper, for example, with an armed man on it, eliminated fear if worn as a pendant. Or a seal in firestone, with a dove holding an olive branch in its mouth, brought many invitations to dinner if worn in a silver finger ring.[89] (This is the same image as on Ralph de Gaugy's SIGNUM CLEMENCIE DEI, but that seal was made of amber and in the form of a pendant.) In some cases it was necessary to form the impression in wax to harness the seal's power. To make discord between people, the user of one seal was recommended to touch them with the wax image, and another wax seal did the reverse by preventing people speaking ill of the person holding it.[90] The seal matrix's ability to reproduce itself through a mirror image inevitably associated it with magic and the occult. Four elements combined to give a seal matrix its power: the material of which it was made, the device engraved on it, the inscription surrounding it, and the manner in which it was worn on the body (whether as a pendant, ring, or brooch).

The seal was indeed a 'two-faced image', as the Ramsey chronicler had called it, though not because it was specially deceptive; indeed seals were harder to forge than the signs of the cross penned on charters. Metaphorically it was two-faced. In the formation of a literate mentality the seal looked back over centuries – or even millennia – to message-sticks, charms, and traditional symbols of conveyance like knives and rods. At the same time it looked forward to the automation of writing and government. The mass production of the king's image on sealed writs was the basis of the English Exchequer and common law system of bureaucracy from the twelfth century onwards. Although the writing process itself was not automated until the invention of printing, sealing resolved the problem which was prior to that of reproducing books for the literate public. Before being offered printed books, the public had to be persuaded of the value of writing itself. Sealing resolved this problem in terms which were acceptable both to chanceries and to non-literates. The seal was the harbinger of literacy, as it was the device which brought literate modes even into remote villages, particularly in the form of taxation demands from the Exchequer sealed with the hated green wax. Sealing was a labour saving technology, both at the exalted level of the royal Chancery and at the humble level of the peasant who could sign his name with his seal without being able to write.

---

[88] Tonnochy, *Seal-Dies*, pp. 154–5, no. 765.

[89] Treatise on stones in BL Harley MS 80, ed. T. Wright in *Archaeologia* xxx (1844), pp. 451–2, nos 2, 11.

[90] Ibid., pp. 452–3, nos 12, 20

FORGING DOCUMENTS

Although it has long been known that many early medieval documents
(particularly monastic charters) are forgeries, the connection between forgery
and the growth of literacy has not been extensively explored. In England the
greatest period for forging documents was the century after the Norman
Conquest, when the old houses of Black monks had to convince the incomers
of their ancient dignities and privileges. 'No document coming from such
centres of proved fabrication as Westminster, Evesham, Winchester
cathedral, Chertsey and Malmesbury should be accepted at its face value
without close examination.'[91] This list of monasteries is cited by F. M. Stenton
in his summary of the critical work of W. H. Stevenson at the beginning of this
century. Many more centres of proved fabrication could now be added to this
list, such as Christ Church and St Augustine's abbey at Canterbury and
Gloucester and Ramsey abbeys. Nor was the Norman Conquest the root cause
of the problem, since houses founded after the Conquest, notably Battle
abbey, likewise forged audacious title-deeds.[92] Even the estimate made by C.
N. L. Brooke, that about 17 out of 30 pre-Conquest monastic houses 'tolerated
forgery on a fair scale', may be an under-assessment.[93] Recent research may
ultimately lead to the conclusion that in England in the century after the
Norman Conquest forgery of charters was the rule rather than the exception.

The extent of forgeries can be approximately gauged by the figures in table
4, which estimate the number of authentic documents extant in the name of
Edward the Confessor (1042–66).[94] In the greatest monastic houses documents of his were specially valued because William the Conqueror claimed to
be his lawful successor. The figures are subject to every kind of qualification
because opinions will always differ about what makes a document authentic.
Many of the problematical charters about which scholars are undecided may
never be satisfactorily resolved. Allowing, however, for all such qualifications
and for the possibility that Edward the Confessor's writs were forged more
than those of any other king, the conclusion to draw is that most documents
extant in his name are of doubtful authenticity. Medieval forgeries are
extraordinarily difficult to evaluate because a document like a charter of
Edward the Confessor may be spurious, in the sense that it was written after
his death, and yet be accurate in the essentials of the information it records.
Forged charters were often based on earlier authentic documents or on good
oral traditions. The purpose of forgery was to produce a record in a form
which was acceptable, particularly in courts of law, at the time it was made.
Forgery was necessary because contemporaries had no historical sense. A

---

[91] F. M. Stenton, *The Latin Charters of the Anglo-Saxon Period* (1955), p. 11.
[92] M. Chibnall, 'Forgery in Narrative Charters'. *Fälschungen*, pp. 342–3; M. T. Clanchy,
review of *Chronicle of Battle Abbey* ed. E. Searle, in *American Journal of Legal History* xxv (1981),
pp. 252–3; J. C. Holt, 'More Battle Forgeries', *Reading Medieval Studies* xi (1985), pp. 75–86.
[93] *Gilbert Foliot and his Letters* (1965), pp. 128–9.
[94] The figures have been estimated by me from P. H. Sawyer, *Anglo-Saxon Charters* (1968),
pp. 298–343.

Table 4 Charters of Edward the Confessor

Total extant	164	100
Authentic	64	39%
Undecided	56	34%
Spurious	44	27%

good oral tradition or an authentic charter of an early Anglo-Saxon king might be rejected by a court of law because it seemed strange, whereas a forged charter would be acceptable because it suited contemporary notions of what an ancient charter should be like.

Forgers re-created the past in an acceptable literate form. They are best understood not as occasional deviants on the peripheries of legal practice, but as experts entrenched at the centre of literary and intellectual culture in the twelfth century. The most influential historical writer of the century, Geoffrey of Monmouth, probably invented most of the *History of the Kings of Britain* (written in *c.*1136), although scholarly opinion will always differ about that.[95] Similarly, in order to give verisimilitude to the Arthurian legend which Geoffrey had made popular, Glastonbury abbey in 1191 exhumed the bodies of King Arthur and Queen Guinevere. Here again, scholars differ as to whether this was a deliberately staged forgery or a genuine discovery of ancient tombs.[96] Judging by some other forgeries of the time, the Glastonbury monks would certainly have been capable of creating such an ambitious deception. Forgery succeeded because it was ordered or condoned by the greatest scholars, prelates and administrators. Walter abbot of Battle, who was responsible for the Battle forgeries, was the brother of Richard de Lucy, Henry II's chief justiciar, and Walter presumably acted with his brother's knowledge. The former head of Henry I's writing-office, Robert de Sigillo, seems to have been responsible for forging a royal charter for Reading abbey after he became a monk there.[97] Among scholars responsible for forgeries were Osbert de Clare, prior of Westminster, who created charters of Edward the Confessor in Stephen's reign, and Gilbert Foliot, who was an accessory to forgery when abbot of Gloucester.[98]

Those monastic writers, who are most insistent in the prologues to their works on the importance of telling the truth, are often those who were involved in fabricating charters. Thus Eadmer of Canterbury, who affirmed

---

[95] J. Gillingham, 'The Context and Purposes of Geoffrey of Monmouth's "History of the Kings of Britain";, *Anglo-Norman Studies* xiii (1990) ed. M. Chibnall, pp. 99–118, is an introduction to Geoffrey. See also J. C. Crick on Geoffrey's *Dissemination and Reception* (1991).
[96] A. Gransden, 'The Growth of Glastonbury Traditions and Legends', *Journal of Ecclesiastical History* xxvii (1976), p. 352, reasserts that the exhumation was 'bogus, a spectacle put on for the credulous public', whereas L. Alcock, *Arthur's Britain* (1971), pp. 73–80, argues that the exhumation has authentic features.
[97] See n. 106 below.
[98] For Osbert see P. Chaplais, in *MM for Stenton*, pp. 91–5. Two forgeries associated with Osbert are illustrated in *Facsimiles of Anglo-Saxon Charters* ed. S. Keynes (1991) plates 38, 39, comment at p. 11. For Gilbert see Morey and Brooke, *Gilbert Foliot*, pp. 124–7.

'that it is a shocking thing for anyone knowingly to write what is false in sacred histories, for the soul of the writer is slain every time they are read or listened to', was an accessory to the Canterbury forgeries in 1121–2.[99] Similarly 'it is hard to exonerate William of Malmesbury from the charge of knowingly including forged material in his history', despite his precocious concern with evaluating evidence.[100] In general, twelfth-century writers protest too much about their veracity to inspire confidence. For example, the compiler of Ramsey abbey's *Book of Benefactors* insists that his purpose is to translate charters from Old English into Latin, so that the Normans will understand them, and also to retain the record of oral gifts in the memory of writing 'so that all falsehood and controversy may be removed'.[101] Yet two of the royal charters he cites were certainly forged, although it is possible that the compiler himself was ignorant of this.[102]

The distinction between fact and fiction was sometimes so finely drawn by twelfth-century writers as to be impossible to see. Occasionally authors may have misled themselves as well as their readers. Not only monastic chroniclers but literary historians, like Geoffrey of Monmouth, and composers of vernacular romances insisted that their works derived from ancient books. Thus the Anglo-Norman poet, Hue de Rotelande (writing in *c*.1180), assures his audience that his story of *Ipomedon* comes from a Latin text, although he is surprised that 'those wise clerks who understand many languages have not put it in memory.'[103] Hue's audience were presumably intended to appreciate the irony of referring to the authority of a Latin text which probably did not exist. Likewise in *Ipomedon* Hue is able to describe for his secular audience the writer's craft with greater frankness than a self-righteous monk like Eadmer can:

> Now understand this very well, my lords,
> Hue says that he never tells a lie in it,
> Well, hardly ever, and then not much;
> No one can keep himself entirely from it.[104]

To a modern reader Hue de Rotlande is a composer of creative literature, a writer of fiction or romance, who therefore has no need to excuse himself for telling untruths to his audience. Hue himself, however, apparently felt that some explanation was required, perhaps because poetic licence or unadorned fiction was difficult for his 'lords' to accept, particularly when authors were just developing into writers on their own account instead of being reciters of traditional tales. Unlike Hue, a monastic chronicler or composer of charters is expected by a modern reader to record the literal truth, and furthermore the chronicler will often assure the reader in his prologue that this is precisely

[99] Eadmer, *Vita*, p. 149.
[100] Gransden, *Historical Writing*, pp. 177–8.
[101] *Ramsey*, pp. 161, 243.
[102] Sawyer, *Anglo-Saxon Charters*, nos 798, 1109.
[103] Ed. E. Köbling (Breslau, 1889), lines 21–4; Legge, *Anglo-Norman*, p. 95.
[104] Ibid., lines 7173–6; Legge, *Anglo-Norman*, p. 94.

what he intends to do. Nevertheless the distinction between fact and fiction in writing, which leads the modern reader to think of Walter, abbot of Battle, or Osbert de Clare as forgers and Hue de Rotelande as an entertaining romancer, would not have been as sharp to medieval people, although they were very conscious of the moral difference between truth and falsehood and of the penalties, both material and spiritual, for fabricating seals or documents.

The fundamental difficulty was that literate criteria for making or criticizing documents had not usually been applied in the first place. Even the English royal government, which was a pioneer of chancery procedure, did not consistently date its charters until Richard I's reign and began to keep regular copies of them only in John's reign. Nor was keeping registers of documents much use unless they could readily be referred to. We have already seen that neither Henry III's government nor Edward I's had foolproof means of searching their own rolls; Edward I's Chancery was deceived by a forged charter of Richard I even though an authentic copy was in the government's possession. Up to Henry II's reign the practice had continued of the royal seal being affixed to documents written by the beneficiaries' scribes (see plate III), although gradually this practice became the exception rather than the rule. From the king's point of view, the procedure whereby a royal officer fixed the royal *signum* to a writing made by the beneficiary was essentially oral and manual rather than literate. The document was presumably read out aloud to the king or his delegate, perhaps only in a translated and summarized form, and then authenticated by the touch of the seal. In these circumstances the difference between a document which had received the royal touch and one which had not, between 'authentic' and 'forged' by modern criteria, was a fine one.

Often documents were produced in duplicate or triplicate for greater security, and occasionally alternative texts seem to have been prepared by the beneficiary, probably in the hope that the seal would be affixed to the more advantageous one. This hypothesis seems the most plausible explanation for the existence of two parallel charters in King Stephen's name, both dated Christmas Day (1139) and written by the same scribe, who had probably been a clerk of Roger, bishop of Salisbury, the chief justiciar.[105] As Roger had just died, the purpose of the charters was presumably to ensure that Salisbury cathedral retained the property they concerned. Both charters quitclaim royal rights in lands and churches, which Roger had given to Salisbury, but the second charter adds that King Stephen had given 10 pounds' worth of his own demesne lands as well; the place in which this demesne lies is left blank. H. A. Cronne, who published these two charters (though with a different explanation), has drawn attention also to a charter in King Stephen's name for Reading abbey, which is written by a known royal scribe although it bears a forged seal.[106] He suggests that Robert de Sigillo, who had been the master of

---

[105] *RRA-N* IV (1969), p. 6 and plates xlviii, xlix. Multiple copies are discussed by R. Mortimer, 'The charters of Henry II', *Anglo-Norman Studies* XII (1989), ed. M. Chibnall, pp. 128–9.

[106] *RRA – N* IV, pp. 5–6 and plate x. *Reading Abbey Cartularies*, ed. B. R. Kemp, Camden S. (1986), I, p. 44, no. 13.

Henry I's writing-office and had become a monk at Reading, may have been behind this forgery. These instances show that documents might be unauthentic even when they were written by official scribes. Indeed, to think of writs produced by the royal Chancery as official and other documents bearing the royal seal as unofficial is an anachronism until the last decade of the twelfth century. Without defined standards of authenticity, there could be no definite criteria for distinguishing forgeries from authentic documents.

The apparently careless attitude of even the king's government towards its written *acta* was not a product merely of incompetent administration, nor of the special circumstances of Stephen's reign when so many forgeries seem to have been made. Stricter procedures were not followed because written record itself was unfamiliar and abnormal outside a small circle of royal officers and old monastic houses. Despite the growth of the Exchequer and the proliferation of writs, the emphasis in royal government remained largely oral until Henry II's reign at least. Henry himself was an energetic legislator, yet even his decrees were not written down in authoritative and officially authentic statutes. They seem to have been promulgated orally and then noted haphazardly by chroniclers. There was no *Liber Augustalis* of the common law. This lack of a *jus scriptum* so troubled the author of *Glanvill* (writing at the very end of Henry II's reign), who wished to harmonize his knowledge of English and Roman law, that he felt obliged to begin by arguing that it is not absurd to speak of English 'laws' even though they are unwritten because 'what pleases the prince has the force of law.'[107] With this nod towards Roman principle, the author then hopes that it will not be considered presumptuous on his part, 'but rather very useful for most people and highly necessary to aid the memory', if he commits at least the commonest rules of the king's court to writing.[108]

Like the author of *Glanvill*, monastic charter makers and chroniclers had to set about filling the gaps and correcting the anomalies in written record which kings and other past benefactors appeared to have negligently left. It was the responsibility of the beneficiaries and not of the donor to see that adequate documents were supplied. In the non-literate past, people had been accustomed to the flexibility of speech and memory and they applied similar criteria at first to written record. A charter was inaccurate and should be corrected if it failed to give the beneficiary a privilege which the donor had obviously intended it to have, had he still been alive to express his wishes. Writing, or the lack of it, should not be allowed to annul or invalidate previous pious gifts. From this point of view 'forgery' is an inappropriate term to apply to renewals of evidence which were intended to ensure that a monastic house was adequately provided with charters to defend its patrons and saints against rivals. Even a charter which a modern critic would consider perfectly genuine did not record the complete and precise wishes of the donor himself, as these had been expressed orally and physically by oaths and symbolic gestures at a public ceremony in the presence of witnesses and not by any form of writing. The charter could not record the donor's exact words, because it was written

107 Glanvill, p. 2.
108 Ibid., p. 3.

in Latin, and furthermore it was often expressed in the past tense – 'Know that I, A of B, have given . . .' – which made it clear that it was an afterthought.

In these circumstances the distinction between a 'genuine' and a 'forged' charter depended on what interval of time between giving and writing, and what mark of approval by the donor, was generally considered allowable. To a modern critic a charter of Edward the Confessor, if written by Osbert de Clare seventy years or more after the king's death and sealed with a new seal, is a forgery. To Osbert, on the other hand, who composed a life of the Confessor and was pressing for his recognition as a saint, Edward was immortalized by his sanctity and still lived in the church where his relics were preserved. In his capacity as prior of Westminster, Osbert may have thought that writing a charter in the dead king's name was essentially no different from writing on behalf of a contemporary ruler. Osbert was fulfilling Edward's pious intentions and assuring him his place in heaven by restoring the evidence of his endowments. Discussing Osbert's work, Brooke comments:

> There had been forgery in England before the Conquest, and it may even be the accidents of survival which lead us to suppose the twelfth century to be its golden age. Yet there is clearly a sense in which the spread of literacy and of written instruments of land tenure made the eleventh and twelfth centuries, in a special sense, *the period of the shift from oral to written testimony*. The opportunities, the temptations, and the urgent calls of duty in such a period were quite exceptional.[109]

Galbraith, referring to 'this slow evolution from oral to written government', made a comparable observation twenty years earlier: 'Written evidence was still the exception rather than the rule, and, as a novelty, was apt to be accepted without very close scrutiny. It is scarcely surprising, then, to find that the twelfth century was the golden age of forgery.'[110] The forgery or renewal of documents was essentially a product of the movement from memory to written record and is best understood in that context.

In theory it would have been as easy to eliminate forgeries as to produce charters which were uniformly dated and signed. Reliable criteria for detecting forgeries had been developed by canon lawyers in Italy, just as Roman law prescribed rules for the production of notarially authenticated instruments. The *summa* (dating from the last quarter of the twelfth century) of the best canonical authority on forgeries, Huguccio, was known in England. He recommended that, where there was doubt about the authenticity of a decretal, resort should be had first of all to the papal registers.[111] If the document were not found there, other tests should be applied regarding the style and substance of the text and the physical characteristics of the parchment, the *bulla* and its attaching thread. In short, the document should

---

[109] 'Approaches to Medieval Forgery', *Medieval Church and Society* (1971), p. 115 (my emphasis).
[110] *Studies*, pp. 40–9.
[111] Duggan, *Decretals*, p. 41, n. 1.

be examined as a whole from as many aspects as possible. These were sound rules, which were subsequently promulgated generally by Innocent III, who had been Huguccio's pupil at Bologna.[112]

Nevertheless the gulf between theory and practice was enormous, because these rules were as difficult to enforce as those governing the drawing up of written instruments. When discussing forgery, the English canonist glossators were obliged to ignore Huguccio's advice to resort first of all to registers, presumably because there were no systematic registers of English ecclesiastical documents. Instead, they recommended testing forgeries by the customary oral method of swearing oaths and producing witnesses.[113] In other words, the validity of documents was primarily assessed by the pre-literate wager of law and not by tests using writing.

Similarly Innocent III himself, when he came to practice as distinct from laying down rules, could be as easily deceived by a forged papal bull as anyone else. Thomas of Marlborough, abbot of Evesham (1229–36), gives a first-hand account of how Evesham forgers deceived Innocent and his cardinals in a case in the Roman *curia* in 1205.[114] Thomas was at that time Evesham's principal advocate in its claim to be exempt from the jurisdiction of the bishop of Worcester. Among other documents adduced as evidence by Thomas were two bulls in the name of Constantine I, who had been pope from 708 to 715. Worcester counter-claimed that these documents were forgeries 'in parchment and script, thread and *bulla*', and stated that privileges of Constantine I were entirely unknown in England.[115] So the bulls were handed to the pope, who 'felt them with his own hands and pulled on the *bulla* and the parchment to see if he could separate the *bulla* from the thread, and he examined them most diligently.' He then passed them round the circle of cardinals, while Thomas admits to being worried about the outcome. However, when the bulls were passed back to the pope, he held the documents up and magisterially pronounced: 'Privileges of this sort, which are unknown to you, are well known to us, and they cannot be forged. These are genuine.' Although Thomas perhaps exaggerated the forthrightness of Innocent's opinion, there is no reason to doubt the substance of this story. The papal judgement in Evesham's favour encouraged Thomas to copy the bulls of Constantine I, which had released Evesham from the 'Egyptian slavery' of Worcester, into his chronicle for future reference.[116] The copies demonstrate that the bulls were undoubtedly forged and, as Thomas 'improved' Evesham's chronicle as well to suit the dispute with Worcester,[117] it is likely that he had played a major part in deceiving the pope.

This case suggests that, although by 1200 the papal *curia* had developed rules for detecting forgeries of recent decretals, it had no effective means of

---

[112] Ibid., p. 41, n. 2; Brooke, 'Approaches to Medieval Forgery', p. 108, n. 18.
[113] Duggan, *Decretals*, p. 42.
[114] *Chronicon Abbatiae de Evesham* ed. W. D. Macray, RS xxix (1863), pp. 160–1; J. E. Sayers, 'The Case of the Abbey of Evesham', *Fälschungen*, pp. 371–96.
[115] nam carta et stylus, filum et bulla', *Chronicon Abbatiae de Evesham*, p. 160. For variations on this phrase see Duggan, *Decretals*, p. 41, n. 2.
[116] *Chronicon Abbatiae de Evesham*, pp. 171–3.
[117] Gransden, *Historical Writing*, pp. 112, 519.

checking documents which claimed to be hundreds of years old. By fingering the parchment and pulling the thread, Innocent III was applying elementary physical tests and not the canons of careful textual criticism which would have revealed the bulls to be forgeries. But it would be anachronistic to expect even Innocent III to have shown a sharper awareness or a deeper understanding of the development of papal documents than he did in this case. Scientific historical criticism was first applied to early papal documents by Renaissance humanists of the fifteenth century, and it revealed that the pope's own title-deeds, the Donation of Constantine, were themselves forgeries. Of course Innocent III was highly educated and learned in law, yet he and his cardinals were not accustomed to the careful scrutiny of documents.[118] Their training in the schools had been predominantly oral in character and caused them to prefer touch, speech, and hearing to intensive literate study.

Moreover, neither the papal *curia* nor lesser courts had anything to gain by scrutinizing forged charters with strict regularity. Decisions had to be reached in cases even when both parties produced forged documents. Conventions seem to have existed among the higher clergy within which forgery, while not being openly approved of or acknowledged, was at least tolerated. Every ruler in Europe, from the pope downwards, had suspect title-deeds if historically authentic writings were to become the yardstick of authority. Medieval criticism of charters was quite sophisticated compared with general standards of historical criticism. The fictions or half-truths of Geoffrey of Monmouth and other creators of political myths were often accepted as historically reliable. Thus Geoffrey's *History of the Kings of Britain* was used by Edward I (though admittedly as an afterthought) in his letter to Boniface VIII in 1301, setting out the precedents for English overlordship in Scotland going back to the days of the prophets, Eli and Samuel, and the fall of Troy.[119] Nor in their reply did the Scots deny the historicity of such myths, but only the English interpretation of the evidence.[120] Although by 1300 governments and owners of property had begun to use documents on a scale unprecedented since the fall of the Roman empire, they still approached the past through hearsay and myth.

This is not to suggest that literate standards of documentation were unknown, but rather that they could not be uniformly or readily applied to particular cases, because literate ways of doing business were still too novel. In exceptional cases, where the opposing parties were unequally matched and unprotected by clerical conventions, forgery could be systematically revealed. Thus Galbraith has described a case in 1220 in the Jewish Exchequer where a bond attributed to the prior of Dunstable was shown to be a forgery on numerous counts – its unusual form of date, ungrammatical Latin, unauthorized handwriting, false chronology and peculiar physical condition (it had been washed and whitened).[121] Nevertheless it is a mistake to conclude that

---

[118] Gerald of Wales shows Innocent III scrutinizing a register in an exceptional instance, see ch. 8, n. 57 above.

[119] *Anglo-Scottish Relations*, pp. 97 ff.

[120] Ibid., pp. 113ff.

[121] Galbraith, *Studies*, pp. 51–2; *Select Pleas etc. of the Exchequer of the Jews* ed. J. M. Rigg, SS xv (1901), pp. 4–5; *Annales Monastici* iii, p. 66.

this case shows how skilful the English courts had become in the detection of forgery, as these points of criticism were made not by the court but by the plaintiff, Master Richard de Morins, the prior of Dunstable, who was a canonist and a graduate of Bologna.[122] He was able for once to put legal theory into practice because his opponent was a Jew and the bond was evidently an amateur forgery. Had Richard been facing an opponent of his own expertise and status, like Thomas of Marlborough, he might have found that his allegations of forgery received no more sympathetic a hearing than Innocent III had given to Worcester in its plea against Evesham. Successful forgery was the business of monks and *magistri*; amateurs, still less Jews, were ill-advised to try it.

The Dunstable case, like the exceptional instances (which have already been discussed) of documents being dated with simplicity and consistency or of English scribes authenticating charters with the precision of Roman notaries, shows that principles of good documentary procedure were known to experts. The problem lay in putting academic theory into general practice. Landowners, whether cleric or lay, were just as likely to distrust genuine charters as to be suspicous of forged ones. Not even the greatest experts, like Innocent III or Edward I's Chancery officials, could be relied upon to detect forgeries. The monks who had the temerity or desperation to deceive them must have learned that forgery was the best course, provided it was competently done.

Cases of simple deception with a document, as distinct from the complex forgeries done by monks, are rarely recorded. One came up in the justiciar's visitation of Surrey during the baronial revolution of 1258. Peter le Templer showed that Walter Kardun had altered the amount of a payment from 2 shillings a year to one clove of garlic (a peppercorn rent).[123] Walter had 'confected' the charter and read its terms out to Peter as a rent of 2 shillings. Peter 'being ignorant' failed to check the text before sealing it. Whether Peter was unable to read or merely ignorant of the law is impossible to know. He had legal experience as a bailiff in Kingston-on-Thames and he had been involved in litigation before. Furthermore, he allowed Walter to deceive him a second time. Walter had him summoned into the ecclesiastical court of Master Rostand, the papal nuncio, a hundred miles away in Suffolk. The sting took the form of Walter getting the vicar of Kingston to tell Peter that he no longer intended to prosecute. Walter then went ahead with the prosecution, so that Peter was excommunicated in his absence and had to pay Walter 40 shillings. Possibly Walter was something of a scoundrel and an expert in legal procedure, like Chaucer's Summoner who was also partial to garlic and knew how to punish a man through his purse.

In this bewildering world, where holy men forged documents and writers of fiction were concerned to tell the literal truth, it may seem surprising that written record ever got a good name át all or established itself as a reliable form of communication. Perhaps it did so not for the practical and progressive reasons which a modern literate would expect, but because of the prestige

---

[122] Cheney, *Texts & Studies*, p. 221.
[123] JUST 1/873, m. 7d. I owe this reference to Dr A. Hershey.

which writing had acquired in the centuries before the Norman Conquest from its use by monks in liturgical books. The Gospel book placed on the altar had been used as a symbol of conveyance by laymen long before they became accustomed to charters. Although it is true that monks were commonly forgers, they compensated for this by imbuing script with sacred associations. All writers of the twelfth century – whether forgers, romancers, or simple scribes – drew on this rich reserve of awe and faith.

Faith was needed because most twelfth-century documents, whether forged or not, were not trustworthy in the strict sense of that word, as they did not state precisely when they had been written, nor were they penned by authorized and professionally trained scribes. Effective precautions against fraud were not taken, because they demanded extensive professionalism and because writings seemed to have been thought of at first as subsidiary aids to traditional memorizing procedures and not as replacements of them. A new technology usually adapts itself at first to an existing one, camouflaging itself in the old forms and not immediately realizing its potential. By the thirteenth century documentary proof had become more familiar and routine. Nevertheless throughout the Middle Ages many common forms of document, particularly charters for conveyances of property, retained in their physical format and set phraseology numerous reminders that they had been developed in an earlier period when more reliance had been put on living memory than on parchment.

10

Practical Literacy

The theme of this book has been the growth of literacy for practical purposes. Laymen became more literate in order to cope with written business, initially in England with writs from the royal government demanding information or money. Knights involved in county business, and even peasants who acted as manorial reeves, needed to be able to read the warrants presented to them and to keep records themselves in order to make adequate answers. According to the *Anglo-Saxon Chronicle* William the Conqueror in the Domesday survey had made a list of every ox and cow and pig in the land; two centuries later bailiffs were recommended to record in writing in the autumn of the year each tool and horseshoe and everything that remained on the manor, great and small. Although these schemes were too ambitious and can never have reached the point of listing every person, animal and thing in up-to-date inventories, the idea of such lists was a continuing aspiration between William the Conqueror's Domesday Book and the series of inquests undertaken by Edward I's government which culminated – and collapsed under their own weight – in the *quo warranto* proceedings.

The first part of this book, 'The Making of Records', has described the proliferation of business documents and the development of skills to produce them and of archives to make them of lasting use. Judging by documents now extant, the output of the royal government increased more than tenfold in the century spanning the reigns of William the Conqueror and Henry II (see figure 1 at p. 60). In the thirteenth century this geometric progression continued, with the royal Chancery using 3.63 lb of sealing wax per week in the late 1220s and 31.9 lb by the late 1260s (see table 2 at p. 59). Such increases necessitated the creation of a bureaucracy, which can be seen in embryo in Fitz Neal's *Dialogue of the Exchequer* (written in *c.*1179). During the years 1193–1205 when Hubert Walter dominated the royal administration, written record was effectively extended to nearly every sphere of government, both central and local. Hubert Walter's achievement was to put theory into practice. It is possible that Chancery rolls, plea rolls, feet of fines, Jewish *archa*, and the rest had been thought of before he appeared on the scene; but he first gave them continuing life. His influence on county and village record-making was as important as his effectiveness at the centre, although local records took another century before they were established as a norm. By Edward I's reign serfs possessed seals to sign their names and they recorded their property transactions in writing. Thus the *nativi* – the natives, naifs, villeins, or serfs – who had thought Domesday Book to be the Last Judgement (according to Fitz Neal in the twelfth century) had charters of their own (the *Cartae Nativorum*) by the 1300s.

The types of writing which were done became increasingly more practical. The sacred Scriptures, which had dominated literate culture before 1066, still stood in pride of place of course, but they were surrounded and overlaid from the twelfth century onwards by the glosses and summaries of the schoolmen. The scholastic *summa*, 'a concise encyclopedia of instances', was intended as a short cut through the mass of words for the 'many who are in a hurry and the many who are unlearned'. The written statements of individuals likewise became more immediately practical in purpose and format. Although solemn charters (which had often been written by monastic beneficiaries after the event) were still produced, less portentous and more sophisticated forms of document increased in numbers. Sealed chirographs in particular emphasized the equal status of the two contracting parties and required both of them, together with their witnesses, to participate with their seals in the making of the written instrument. Similarly in the late twelfth century letters, in the modern sense of missives sent by one individual to convey confidential information to another, came into more general use. Previously letters had usually been either writs patent, which were open declarations or title-deeds, or 'literature' composed by rhetoricians and preachers.

Gradually too the idea of accumulating memoranda for future reference became established, first with the pipe and plea rolls of the king's court and then with comparable documents produced by bishops, barons, and boroughs. By the 1260s the countess of Leicester, and presumably other great housekeepers also, were keeping diaries of their daily expenditure (see plate XI). At a similar date records begin in the Year Books which purport to record every word spoken by learned counsel and judges in royal courts. Even the art of speech itself was taught in books of hypothetical dialogues (like the *Court Baron*) for students of law and estate management.

The traditions and techniques of monastic writing, which had been created to produce illuminated liturgical manuscripts, had to be adapted to the utilitarian demands made on them by secular writs and rolls. It was relatively easy to economize on materials by omitting coloured inks and using thinner and smaller pieces of parchment. Although most business documents continued to have enlarged initial letters and some still had rubrics and even illustrations (see plate XVIII), they were generally on a far less lavish scale than Gospel books. Even the scriptures themselves were presented in cheaper and more accessible formats. Orm, who wrote his Gospel homilies or *Ormulum* probably with his own hand in *c*.1170, seems to have cared little about its

untidy and unprofessional appearance. As an Augustinian canon he exemplified the new ideal of simplicity in spreading the Gospel, instead of treasuring
it in precious manuscripts as the Black monks did. Illuminated manuscripts
themselves began to be produced in more economical formats so that they
could be put in the pocket or held in the hands while at prayer. Likewise
students' and lawyers' textbooks of the thirteenth century use smaller and
more economical formats (see plate XVI).

Even more pressing than the need to economize on parchment and
pigments was the need to save the scribe's time, as the application of his skill
was the most expensive element in the production of documents. To meet this
need, secular scribes learned to write faster in cursive hands instead of the
traditional monastic book hands. Contrary to former palaeographical teaching, cursive script is not evidence of special training in chanceries but of 'a
common pressure of urgent business'. Hence in the thirteenth century cursive
scripts began to be used for writing books as well as writs and rolls (see plate
XVII). The new pressures of secular business, as contrasted with the studied
calm of the monastic tradition, are most strikingly conveyed in the contrast
between royal writs in cursive hands and liturgical manuscripts in book hands
(compare plates IV and XIV). The royal administration even automated
writing, at least to the point of producing stereotyped documents (like
common law writs) and of authenticating them with a seal instead of with the
king's sign manual. The seal was the forerunner of printing as it reproduced
script from a metal exemplar in a repeatable series.

Speeding up the production of documents was easier than organizing
archives and reference systems to make good use of them. There was nothing
new about keeping precious writings in treasuries or reliquaries. The novelty
lay in getting into the habit of referring to a book or archive for information
instead of seeking oral testimony. Domesday Book seems rarely to have been
consulted in the century after it was made; only in Edward I's reign did
regular consultation begin. Gradually Edward I's government began to
realize that it possessed an archive of information which could be used in
disputes with opponents. As late as 1290 when the king first called for
historical information about the claims of the English crown in Scotland,
resort was made to the monasteries, as the traditional remembrances and
chroniclers, and not the royal archives. A year later, however, Edward I
hurriedly sent a message from Scotland, ordering a chest of Chancery rolls to
be broken open and searched, and thus inaugurated systematic searches of the
archives.

The reasons for not regularly consulting records hitherto had been mixed.
Even when officials had learned that documentary evidence could be more
advantageous than oral testimony (which was not invariably the case of
course), archives and the collections of documents within them had to be
arranged in ways which made consultation possible. Edward I's instructions
in 1300 to search all the rolls and remembrances 'so that nothing is left
unsearched' was absurd, when chests of documents were scattered in a variety
of repositories and their contents unlisted. The surveys of the records in
Edward I's last years, which culminated in Bishop Stapledon's array in 1320,
mark the point at which the royal government at last recognized the

usefulness of its archives. Archives had become a department of government instead of a treasury of relics. Libraries likewise, owing to the initiative of the friars, began to be arranged systematically so that readers could have books 'ready to hand' (*in promptu*), just as Edward I wanted his archives available 'at all times'. Hurriedly extracting information from quantities of books was a different kind of literate activity from meditating on a single text for a year, as the Black monks had done in the old Benedictine tradition.

In establishing literacy as a practical convenience, much in the inheritance of the past had to be overcome. The second part of this book, 'The Literate Mentality', has indicated some of the problems. Most fundamental was the problem of language itself. After the Norman Conquest written Old English became an archaic language like Latin, with which it had competed for so long. Neither English nor Norman administrators could use the language of everyday speech in business documents, because they did not share a common language and also because written English and French were still in a fluid stage of development. Both languages, moreover, were for long overshadowed and beguiled by the ancient dignity of Latin. In these circumstances the linguistic skill required of a local man doing a practical task, like a foreman of a jury or a knight collecting testimony for the county court, was unusually demanding. In the thirteenth century such a man needed to speak English and French and to read in English, French, and Latin. In this multilingual society people switched languages often probably without comment. the practice of writing documents in a particular language for the record, usually Latin (or French by 1300), does not mean that Latin (or French) was necessarily the language in which the business was done. By and large the knights of thirteenth-century England, and their families too, probably had a wider and deeper knowledge of language than those historians who have adopted a patronizing tone towards them because they were not highly literate.

The variety of languages in use made literacy difficult both to acquire and to define. Traditionally a person who was *litteratus* had been learned in Latin literature and of a clerkly disposition. Such a *litteratus* had little in common with the average modern literate, who has learned to read and write his own language for pragmatic purposes. It is probably not a coincidence that the royal officials who pioneered the use of writing in government – Roger bishop of Salisbury (Henry I's chief justiciar), Hubert Walter (Richard I's chief justiciar and King John's chancellor), Ralf Nevill (Henry III's chancellor) – were all described as *illitterati* by contemporaries. What was meant was that they were administrators, rather than good churchmen of scholars. According to Gerald of Wales at least, Hubert Walter's school had been the Exchequer and not the university.

The question, 'Were laymen literate?' cannot be answered directly from contemporary sources because it is a contradiction in medieval terms. A layman (*laicus*) was unclerkly by definition, whereas a literate (*litteratus*) was clerkly even if he were a knight. Leaving these scholastic subtleties to one side, it is probable that a minimal knowledge of Latin among the population at large has been underestimated. A little Latin was the broad but shallow foundation from which men of peasant origin rose to be clerics, and it was also indispensable for literacy in vernacular forms. Gradually 'clergy' in common parlance came to mean a little Latin instead of meaning an estate of the church. From the fourteenth century a person who knew a little Latin had 'benefit of clergy'.

This minimal knowledge of Latin did not make a person educated in any real sense, but it was of practical use. It could save a man accused of felony from being hanged and it gave him sufficient knowledge to cope with government business. Thus in a case in 1297 ten jurors were able to read the entry of Robert de Tony's birth in a monastic chronicle and those who were unable to do so were described as *laici*, meaning that they were non-readers rather than 'laymen' in a more general sense. Such minimal skill did not make a man either *litteratus* or educated in the traditional sense. Knights had been educated in the skills of language long before they were required by the growth of documentation to learn a little Latin or 'clergy'. Traditionally they had learned to speak well and to give counsel to clergy as much as to kings. Thus the judges who shaped the English common law in the twelfth and thirteenth centuries were drawn indifferently from knights and clergy. For laymen, literacy was a practical convenience long before it became an education. Although the Scriptures might teach religion, wisdom in the worldly sense did not depend on writings.

Because writing was only an ancillary aid at first for laymen, it did not immediately sweep away traditional non-literate ways of doing business. Reliance upon symbolic objects and 'livery or seisin' in conveyances of property persisted. Writing was converted into the spoken word by the habitual practice of reading aloud and of listening to or making an 'audit' of a statement, rather than scrutinizing its text on parchment. Clerks and scribes themselves were slow to comprehend the full potentialities of documentary proof, as their inconsistencies in dating and signing documents demonstrate. Writing was distrusted and for good reason, as numerous charters of the twelfth century in particular were forgeries. Paradoxically the continuance of non-utilitarian and primarily visual forms of writing, especially in liturgical manuscripts, may have helped to persuade the laity that literacy was valuable because of its long association with sacred Scripture. Writers of the twelfth and thirteenth centuries – whether they were composers or copyists of texts, or clerks making business documents – drew on the reserves of awe and faith with which monks had imbued writing in the half millennium before 1066.

The growth of literacy for practical purposes, which has been the theme of this book, was not necessarily an inevitable process. Emphasis on practical literacy is a commonplace of twentieth-century culture because we have inherited the values of the utilitarians. In nineteenth-century Europe and North America mass literacy was promoted by governments for the first time in the history of the world in order to ensure that populations could cope with the growing written demands of daily life – in railway trains, factories, conscript armies, and so on. Opponents of government policy were worried that schools might succeed in educating people to a point where there would be a surplus of scholars and critics who might undermine the social hierarchy. Such fears were allayed by reformers emphasizing elementary practical literacy and numeracy (the three Rs of reading, writing, and arithmetic) rather than a liberal education in the classical tradition, which remained as much the preserve of an elite of *litterati* in 1900 as it had been in 1200. The twentieth century assumption that literacy is primarily utilitarian in purpose and character is a product of recent history and not an invariable norm.

Although practical or utilitarian literacy only became a mass movement in Europe in the nineteenth century, this book has argued that it had its origins in the twelfth and thirteenth centuries in the shift from memory to written record. That change might alternatively be described as a shift from sacred script to practical literacy. In Anglo-Saxon England, and generally in early medieval Europe, writing had been primarily associated with monasticism, sacred Scripture, and the liberal arts of antiquity. Only in the twelfth century did the number of documents, and the number of persons who understood them, begin to increase at a fast rate under the pressures of emerging bureaucracy. Practical business was the foundation of this new literacy.

'The old literacy of the village had no implication for the art of government and politics and the transmission of manual skills ... The recording of disputes, collection of village statistics, transmission of government orders to villagers are tasks that require literacy, but this is a feature of the new literacy.' This contrast between old and new uses of literacy is not made by a medieval historian, but by an anthropologist, S. J. Tambiah, in a study of the uses of writing in a village in Thailand.[1] In the village temple Buddhist monks have been skilled in writing from time out of mind and they have been in direct contact with the people of the village, from whom their numbers are drawn and to whose community many of them return to marry. Writing has been used (in three scripts) by a variety of specialists in the village – monks, lay officiants, physician, astrologer, and folk-opera entertainers.[2] Nevertheless, although a fair number of people in the village have been acquainted with writing in one form or another perhaps for centuries, literate skills were not applied to pragmatic purposes until the Thai government began to promote the 'new' or practical literacy under European influence.

The recording of disputes, collection of village statistics, transmission of government orders to villagers are essentially the uses to which literacy was applied in England by William the Conqueror in his Domesday survey. Thereafter his successors, because they were foreigners ruling in a tradition of conquest, bombarded local officials with one inquest after another. Landlords, clerical and lay, followed suit. From that momentous new start – *Doomsday* to the 'natives' and a Roman triumph of *jus scriptum* to court functionaries like Fitz Neal – documents proliferated and accumulated in archives until lay literacy became the basis of the culture which produced our own.

Writing takes many forms and has been used for diverse purposes in different societies. Ashanti warriors covered their war-coats with written charms to ward off bullets.[3] Likewise medieval knights has their swords

---

[1] 'Literacy in a Buddhist Village in North-East Thailand' in Goody, *Literacy*, p. 122, cf. p. 93. A comparable situation is described by Goody, 'Restricted Literacy in Northern Ghana', ibid., pp. 216ff.

[2] Ibid., pp. 128–9.

[3] Goody, *Literacy*, p. 202.

inscribed with prayers or mysterious letters[4] and Richard the Engineer (who may have been one of the architects of Durham cathedral in the twelfth century) carried around with him numerous names of Christ and extracts from the Gospels on slips of parchment, which he kept in a small silken bag with some relics of St Cuthbert.[5] Warriors and builders were in perilous professions where they needed charmed lives. Technologies are created or adapted to suit the requirements of different societies. The Tibetans used rotary motion solely for prayer wheels, and their monks used block printing to make charms and to write invocations on the surface of the water to acquire merit.[6] In early medieval Europe the skills of scribes were likewise primarily applied to acts of worship through the production of liturgical manuscripts like the *Lindisfarne Gospels*.[7] Gradually, however, despite Christianity being a religion of a book and medieval culture being shaped by monks, writing on parchment was adapted and applied to mundane purposes of government, property-owning and commerce. The beginnings of this growth of practical literacy, of depending for daily business on written record instead of the living memory, have been the subject of this book.

---

[4] R. E. Oakeshott, *The Archaeology of Weapons* (1960), plates 6d and 7b.
[5] *Reginaldi Monachi Dunelmensis Libellus* ed. J. Raine, Surtees S. I. (1835), ch. xlvii, pp. 94–7 and ch. liv, pp. 111–12.
[6] Goody, *Literacy*, p. 16 (citing R. B. Ekvall).
[7] This generalization is brought into doubt by R. McKitterick ed., *The Uses of Literacy in Early Medieval Europe* (1990).

Further Reading on the History of Literacy

This bibliography, selected primarily from work published since the completion of the first edition of *From Memory to Written Record* in 1977, provides an introduction to the history of literacy in general and medieval literacy (over the millennium 500–1500 AD) in particular. Preference has been given to publications in the English language.

BL – British Library publication

LITERACY IN HISTORY IN GENERAL

P. Attewell, 'The clerk deskilled', *Journal of Historical Sociology* 2 (1989), pp. 357–88.

L. Avrin, *Scribes, Script and Books: The Book Arts from Antiquity to the Renaissance* BL (1991).

G. Baumann ed., *The Written Word: Literacy in Transition* (1986).

W. T. Baxter, 'Early Accounting: The Tally and the Checkerboard', *The Accounting Historians Journal* 10 (1989), pp. 43–83.

A. K. Bowman and J. D. Thomas, 'Vindolanda 1985: The New Writing Tablets', *Journal of Roman Studies* 76 (1986), pp. 120–3.

G. Brooks and A. K. Pugh eds, *Studies in the History of Reading* (1984).

P. Burke, 'The Uses of Literacy in Early Modern Italy' in P. Burke and R. Porter eds, *The Social History of Language* (1987), pp. 21–42.

R. Chartier ed., *The Culture of Print* (1989).

R. Chartier, 'The Practical Impact of Writing' in P. Ariès and G. Duby eds, *A History of Private Life* 3 (1989), pp. 111–59, 615–17.

F. Coulmas, *The Writing Systems of the World* (1989).

D. Cressy, *Literacy and the Social Order: Reading and Writing in Tudor and Stuart England* (1980).

O. A. W. Dilke, *Roman Books and their Impact* (1977).

E. L. Eisenstein, *The Printing Press as an Agent of Change* (1979).

M. Finlay, *Western Writing Implements in the Age of the Quill Pen* (1990).

R. Finnegan, *Oral Poetry: Its Nature, Significance and Social Context* (1977).

R. Finnegan, *Literacy and Orality: Studies in the Technology of Communication* (1988).

G. Flegg, *Numbers: Their History and Meaning* (1983).

J. M. Foley, *Traditional Oral Epic* (1990).

K. E. Foote, 'Archives, Memory and Culture', *The American Archivist* 53 (1990), pp. 378–92.

W. Ford, 'The Problem of Literacy in Early Modern England', *History* 78 (1993), pp. 22–37.

F. Furet and J. Ozouf, *Reading and Writing: Literacy in France from Calvin to Jules Ferry* (1982).

A. Gaur, *Writing Materials of the East* BL (1979).

A. Gaur, *A History of Writing* BL 2nd ed (1987).

J. Goody ed., *Literacy in Traditional Societies* (1968).

J. Goody, *The Domestication of the Savage Mind* (1977).

J. Goody, *The Logic of Writing and the Organization of Society* (1986).

J. Goody, *The Interface between the Written and the Oral* (1987).

H. J. Graff, *The Literacy Myth: Literacy and Social Structure in the Nineteenth-Century City* (1979).

H. J. Graff ed., *Literacy and Social Development in the West: A Reader* (1981).

H. J. Graff ed., *Literacy and History: An Interdisciplinary Research Bibliography* (1981).

H. J. Graff, *The Labyrinths of Literacy* [essays] (1987).

H. J. Graff, *The Legacies of Literacy* [history] (1987).

N. Gray, *A History of Lettering* (1986).

A.-G. Hamman, *L'Epopée du livre* (1985).

Roy Harris, *The Origin of Writing* (1986).

William V. Harris, *Ancient Literacy* [Greece and Rome] (1989).

F. D. Harvey, 'Greeks and Romans Learn to Write' in E. A. Havelock and J. P. Herschell eds, *Communication Arts in the Ancient World* (1978), pp. 63–78.

E. A. Havelock, *The Literate Revolution in Greece and its Cultural Consequences* (1982).

J. F. Healey, *The Early Alphabet* BL (1990).

B. J. Hibbitts, 'Communication and Legal Expression in Performance Cultures', *Emory Law Journal* 41 (1992), pp. 873–960.

R. A. Houston, *Literacy in Early Modern Europe 1500–1800* (1988).

I. M. L. Hunter, 'Lengthy Verbatim Recall' in A. Ellis ed., *Progress in the Psychology of Language* (1985), vol. i, pp. 207–35.

J. M. Hurwit, Orality, Literacy and Early Greek Art', *Word and Image* 6 (1990), pp. 180–97.

E. Johansson, *The History of Literacy in Sweden* (1977).

E. R. Kingten, 'Literacy', *Visible Language* 22 (1988), pp. 149–68.

J. Kristeva, *Language the Unknown: An Initiation into Linguistics* (1989).

J. P. Losty, *The Art of the Book in India* BL (1982).

D. F. McKenzie, *Bibliography and the Sociology of Texts* (1986).

H.-J. Martin, *Histoire et pouvoirs de l'écrit* (1988).

M. Meek, *On Being Literate* (1991).

D. R. Olson, 'From Utterance to Text', *Harvard Educational Review* 47 (1977), pp. 257–81.

D. R. Olson and J. W. Astington, 'Talking about Text: How Literacy Contributes to Thought', *Journal of Pragmatics* 14 (1990), pp. 705–21.

D. R. Olson and N. Torrance eds, *Literacy and Orality* (1991).

W. J. Ong, *Orality and Literacy: The Technologizing of the Word* (1982).

J. Oxenham, *Literacy: Writing, Reading and Social Organization* (1980).

M. B. Parkes, *Pause and Effect: An Introduction to the History of Punctuation in the West* (1992).

R. Pattison, *On Literacy* (1982).

J. Poucet, 'L'Ecrit et l'écriture dans la Rome, *Latomus* 48 (1989), pp. 285–311.

M. A. Powell, 'Three Problems in the History of Cuneiform Writing', *Visible Language* 15 (1981), pp. 419–40.

S. Rassekh, *Regards sur l'alphabétisation: sélection bibliographique mondiale* UNESCO (1990).

B. Reay, 'The Context and Meaning of Popular Literacy: *Past and Present* 131 (1991), pp. 89–129.

D. P. Resnick ed., *Literacy in Historical Perspective* (1983).

D. P. and L. B. Resnick, 'The Nature of Literacy: An Historical Explanation', *Harvard Educational Review* 47 (1977), pp. 370–85.

G. Sampson, *Writing Systems: a Linguistic Introduction* (1985).

A. Schimmel, *Calligraphy and Islamic Culture* (1984).

K. Schousboe and M. T. Larsen eds, *Literacy and Society* (1989).

S. Scribner and M. Cole, *The Psychology of Literacy* (1981).

W. M. Senner ed., *The Origins of Writing* (1989).

W. A. Smalley, C. K. Vang and G. Y. Yang, *Mother of Writing* (1990).

J. V. Smith, 'Reading, Writing and Reification', *Scottish Educational Review* 13 (1981), pp. 25–35.

John D. Smith, 'How to Sing a Tale' in J. B. Hainsworth and A. T. Hatto eds, *Traditions of Heroic and Epic Poetry* (1989), vol. ii, pp. 29–42.

T. C. Smout, 'Born Again at Cambuslang: New Evidence on Popular Religion and Literacy in Eighteenth-Century Scotland', *Past and Present* 97 (1982), pp. 114–27.

M. Spufford, 'First Steps in Literacy', *Social History* 4 (1979), pp., 407–35.

B. V. Street, *Literacy in Theory and Practice* (1984).

M. Stubbs, *Language and Literacy* (1980).

G. Sutherland, 'Education' in F. M. L. Thompson ed., *The Cambridge Social History of Britain 1750–1950* (1990), vol. iii, pp. 119–69.

C. J. Swearingen, *Rhetoric and Irony: Western Literacy and Western Lies* (1991).

Keith Thomas, 'The Meaning of Literacy in Early Modern England' in G. Baumann ed., *The Written Word* (1986), pp. 97–131.

Keith Thomas, 'Numeracy in Early Modern England' *TRHS* 5th series 37 (1987), pp.103–32.

Rosalind Thomas, *Oral Tradition and Written Record in Classical Athens* (1989).

Rosalind Thomas, *Literacy and Orality in Ancient Greece* (1992).

R. F. Tomasson, 'The Literacy of the Icelanders', *Scandinavian Studies* 47 (1975), pp. 66–93.

M. Twyman, *Early Lithographed Books* (1990).

D. Vincent, *Literacy and Popular Culture. England 1750–1914* (1989).

T. Watt, *Cheap Print and Popular Piety 1550–1640* (1991).

S. West, 'Archilochus's Message-Stick', *Classical Quarterly* 38 (1988), pp. 42–8.

READERS AND WRITERS IN MEDIEVAL EUROPE

D. Alexandre-Bidon, 'Apprendre à lire à l'enfant au Moyen Age', *Annales* 44 (1989), pp. 953–92.

F. H. Bäuml, 'Varieties and Consequences of Medieval Literacy and Illiteracy', *Speculum* 55 (1980), pp. 237–65.

R. Beaton, 'Was "Digenes Akrites" an Oral Poem?' *Byzantine and Modern Greek Studies* 7 (1981), pp. 7–27.

S. G. Bell, 'Medieval Women Book Owners' in M. Erler and M. Kowaleski eds, *Women and Power in the Middle Ages* (1988), pp. 149–87.

C. Brett, 'Breton Latin Literature as Evidence for Literature in the Vernacular', *Cambridge Medieval Celtic Studies* 18 (1989), pp. 1–25.

Elizabeth A. R. Brown, 'Medieval Forgers and their Intentions' in *Fälschungen* i, pp. 101–19.

R. Browning, 'Literacy in the Byzantine World', *Byzantine and Modern Greek Studies* 4 (1978), pp. 39–57.

R. I. Burns, *Society and Documentation in Crusader Valencia: the Charters of Jaume I 1257–1276* (1985).

M. Camille, 'Seeing and Reading', *Art History* 8 (1985), pp. 26–49.

M. Camille, 'The Book of Signs', *Word and Image* 1 (1985), pp. 133–48.

M. Camille, 'Visual Signs of the Sacred Page', *Word and Image* 5 (1989), pp. 111–30.

M. J. Carruthers, *The Book of Memory: A Study of Memory in Medieval Culture* (1990).

C. M. Chazelle, 'Pictures, Books and the Illiterate', *Word and Image* 6 (1990), pp. 138–53.

M. T. Clanchy, 'Looking Back from the Invention of Printing' in D. P. Resnick ed., *Literacy in Historical Perspective* (1983), pp. 7–22.

G. Constable, 'Forgery and Plagiarism', *Archiv für Diplomatik* 29 (1983), pp. 1–41.

G. Constable, 'Forged Letters in the Middle Ages' in *Fälschungen* v, pp. 11–37.

M. Curschmann, 'Hören – Lesen – Sehen', *Beiträge zur Geschichte der deutschen Sprache und Literatur* 106 (1984), vol. ii. pp. 218–57.

D. d'Avray, *The Preaching of the Friars: Sermons Diffused from Paris Before 1300* (1985).

P. R. Denley, 'Governments and Schools in Late Medieval Italy' in T. Dean and C. Wickham eds, *City and Countryside: Essays Presented to Philip Jones* (1990), pp. 93–107.

P. Dronke, *Women Writers of the Middle Ages* (1984).

J. J. Duggan, 'Performance and Transmission', *Romance Philology* 43 (1990), pp. 49–58.

L. G. Duggan, 'Was Art Really the "Book of the Illiterate"?' *Word and Image* 5 (1989), pp. 227–51.

J. Dunbabin, 'From Clerk to Knight: Changing Orders' in C. Harper-Bill and R. Harvey eds, *The Ideals and Practice of Medieval Knighthood* 2 (1988), pp. 26–39.

J. M. Ferrante, 'The Education of Women in the Middle Ages in Theory, Fact, and Fantasy' in P. H. Labalme ed., *Beyond their Sex* (1980), pp. 9–43.

J. M. Ferrante, 'Was Vernacular Poetic Practice a Response to Latin Language Theory?' *Romance Philology* 35 (1982), pp. 586–600.

J. M. Foley ed., *Oral Traditional Literature: A Festschrift for A. B. Lord* (1981).

S. Franklin, 'Literacy and Documentation in Early Medieval Russia', *Speculum* 60 (1985), pp. 1–38.

J. Fried ed., *Schulen und Studium im sozialen Wandel des hohen und späten Mittelalters* (1986).

P. F. Gehl, 'Latin Readers in Fourteenth-Century Florence', *Scrittura e Civilità* 13 (1989), pp. 387–440.

J. M. Gellrich, *The Idea of the Book in the Middle Ages* (1985).

R. Gibbs, 'Images of Higher Education in Fourteenth-Century Bologna' in E. Fernie and P. Crossley eds, *Medieval Architecture and its Intellectual Context: Studies in Honour of P. Kidson* (1990), pp. 269–81.

M. T. Gibson, 'Boethius in the Carolingian Schools', *TRHS* 5th series 32 (1982), pp. 43–56.

W. Godzich and J. Kittay, *The Emergence of Prose* (1987).

D. H. Green, 'Orality and Reading: the State of Research in Medieval Studies', *Speculum* 65 (1990), pp. 267–80.

P. F. Grendler, *Schooling in Renaissance Italy: Literacy and Learning 1300–1600* (1989).

A. Harvey, 'Early Literacy in Ireland: The Evidence from Ogam', *Cambridge Medieval Celtic Studies* 14 (1987), pp. 1–15.

N. Hathaway, '"Compilatio": from Plagiarism to Compiling', *Viator* 20 (1989), pp. 19–44.

T. A. Heslop, 'Brief in Words but Heavy in the Weight of its Mysteries', *Art History* 9 (1986), pp. 2–11.

S. Huot, *From Song to Book: The Poetics of Writing in Old French Lyric and Lyrical Narrative Poetry* (1987).

J. K. Hyde, 'Some Uses of Literacy in Venice and Florence in the Thirteenth and Fourteenth Centuries', *TRHS* 5th series 29 (1979), pp. 109–28.

H. Keller, K. Grubmüller, N. Staubach eds, *Pragmatische Schriftlichkeit im Mittelalter* (1992).

W. Klein, H. Günther, U. Maas [and others], 'Schriftlichkeit', *Zeitschrift für Literaturwissenschaft und Linguistik* 59 (1985), pp. 1–115.

A. B. Langeli and A. Petrucci eds, *Notizie: Alfabetismo e Cultura Scritta* [occasional series] (1978–).

R. McKitterick, *The Carolingians and the Written Word* (1989).

R. McKitterick ed., *The Uses of Literacy in Early Medieval Europe* (1990).

R. McKitterick, 'Frauen und Schriftlichkeit im Frühmittelalter', in H. W. Goetz ed., *Weibliche und Lebensgestaltung im Frühen Mittelalter* (1991), pp. 80–145.

R. McKitterick, 'Nuns' Scriptoria in England and Francia in the Eighth Century', *Francia* 19 (1992), pp. 1–35.

C. J. Mews, 'Orality, Literacy and Authority in the Twelfth-Century Schools', *Exemplaria* 2 (1990), pp. 475–500.

L. Miglio, 'Leggere e scrivere il volgare: sull' alfabetismo delle donne nella Toscana tardo medievale', *Atti della Società Ligure di Storia della Patria*, 103 (1989), pp. 355–83.

A. J. Minnis, *Medieval Theory of Authorship* 2nd ed (1988).

M. Mullett, 'Aristocracy and Patronage in the Literary Circles of Comnenian Constantinople' in M. Angold ed., *The Byzantine Aristocracy* (1984), pp. 173–201.

W. J. Ong, B. Stock, F. H. Bäuml, A. J. Gurevich [and others], 'Oral and Written Traditions in the Middle Ages', *New Literary History* 16 (1984), no. 1, pp. 1–206.

W. D. Patt, 'The Early "Ars Dictaminis" as Response to a Changing Society', *Viator* 9 (1978), pp. 133–55.

A. Petrucci, 'Modello notarile e testualità', *Studi storici sul notariato italiano* 8 (1985), pp. 125–45.

A. Petrucci, 'Pouvoir de l'écriture, pouvoir sur l'écriture dans la renaissance italienne', *Annales* 43 (1988), pp. 823–47.

B. B. Rezak, 'Women, Seals, and Power in Medieval France' in M. Erler and M. Kowaleski eds, *Women and Power in the Middle Ages* (1988), pp. 61–82.

P. Riché, *Ecoles et l'enseignement dans le haut Moyen Age* (1979).

P. Saenger, 'Silent Reading: Its Impact on Late Medieval Script and Society', *Viator* 13 (1982), pp. 367–414.

P. Saenger, 'Books of Hours and the Reading Habits of the Later Middle Ages' in R. Chartier ed., *The Culture of Print* (1989), pp. 141–61.

M. G. Scholz, *Hören und lesen: Studien zur primären Rezeption der Literatur im 12 und 13 Jahrhundert* (1980).

K. Schreiner, 'Marienverehrung, Lesekultur, Schriftlichkeit', *Frühmittelalterliche Studien* 24 (1990), pp. 314–68.

S. Shahar, *Childhood in the Middle Ages* (1990).

L. Smith, 'Lending Books: the Growth of a Medieval Question', in L. Smith and B. Ward eds, *Intellectual Life in the Middle Ages: Essays Presented to M. Gibson* (1992), pp. 265–80.

G. M. Spiegel, 'History, Historicism, and the Social Logic of the Text in the Middle Ages', *Speculum* 65 (1990), pp. 59–86.

J. Stevenson, 'The Beginnings of Literacy in Ireland', *Proceedings of the Royal Irish Academy* 89 (1989), pp. 127–65.

B. Stock, *The Implications of Literacy: Written Language and Models of Interpretation* (1983).

B. M. Tock, 'Auteur ou impétrant? Réflexions sur les chartes des évêques d'Arras au douzième siècle', *Bibliothèque de l'Ecole des Chartes* 149 (1991), pp. 215–48.

L. Treitler, 'Oral, Written, and Literate Process in the Transmission of Medieval Music', *Speculum* 56 (1981), pp. 471–91.

L. Treitler, 'Reading and Singing: On the Genesis of Occidental Music Writing', *Early Music History* 4 (1984), pp. 135–208.

A. E. van Vleck, *Memory and Re-creation in Troubadour Lyric* (1991).

J. C. M. Vigueur, C. Pietri and J.-P. Genet eds, 'L'Etat et l'écrit' in *Culture et idéologie dans la genèse de l'état moderne* Collection de l'école française de Rome 82 (1985), pp. 9–131.

Roger Wright, *Late Latin and Early Romance in Spain and Carolingian France* (1982).

Roger Wright ed., *Latin and the Romance Languages in the Early Middle Ages* (1991).

P. Zumthor, *La Poésie et la voix dans la civilisation médiévale* (1984).

METHODS OF WRITING AND MAKING BOOKS IN MEDIEVAL EUROPE

J. J. G. Alexander, *Medieval Illuminators and their Methods of Work* (1992).
J. J. G. Alexander, *The Decorated Letter* (1978).
D. H. Banks, *Medieval Manuscript Bookmaking: A Bibliographic Guide* (1989).
L. J. Bataillon, B. G. Guyot and R. H. Rouse eds, *La Production du livre universitaire au Moyen Age* (1988).
R. Bergeron and E. Ornato, 'La Lisibilité dans les manuscrits et les imprimés de la fin du Moyen Age', *Scrittura e Civiltà* 14 (1990), pp. 151–98.
B. Bischoff, *Latin Palaeography* trans. D. O'Croinin and D. Ganz, corrected edn (1992).
A. Blanchard ed., *Les Débuts du codex* Bibliologia 9 (1989).
L. E. Boyle, 'Diplomatics' in J.M. Powell ed., *Medieval Studies: an Introduction* 2nd edn (1992).
L. E. Boyle, *Medieval Latin Palaeography: A Bibliographical Introduction* (1984).
Michelle P. Brown, *A Guide to Western Historical Scripts from Antiquity to 1600* BL (1990).
L. L. Brownrigg ed., *Medieval Book Production: Assessing the Evidence* (1990).
M. Camille, *Image on the Edge: the Margins of Medieval Art* (1992).
C. F. R. de Hamel, *Glossed Books of the Bible and the Paris Book Trade* (1984).
C. F. R. de Hamel, *A History of Illuminated Manuscripts* (1986).
A. C. de la Mare, 'Humanistic Script: The First Ten Years' in F. Kraft and D. Wuttke eds, *Das Verhältnis der Humanisten zum Buch* (1977), pp. 89–110.
D. Ganz and W. Goffart, 'Charters Earlier than 800 from French Collections', *Speculum* 65 (1990), pp. 906–32.
P. F. Ganz ed., *The Role of the Book in Medieval Culture* Bibliologia 3 and 4 (1986), 2 vols.
L. Genicot ed., *Typologie des sources du Moyen Age occidental* 1–55 (1972–90) [in progress].
Margaret Gibson, *The Latin Bible* (1993).
J. Glenisson ed., *Le Livre au Moyen Age* (1988).
J. F. Hamburger, *The Rothschild Canticles* (1990).
A. Henry, *Biblia Pauperum: A Facsimile Edition* (1987).
M. Huglo, *Les Livres de chant liturgique* (1988).
K. W. Humphreys ed., *The Friars' Libraries* BL (1990).
E. Lalou, 'Tablettes de cire', *Bibliothèque de l'École des Chartes* 147 (1989), pp. 123–40.
J. Lemaire, *Introduction à la codicologie* (1989).
A. Maieru ed. *Grafia e interpunzione del latino nel medioevo* (1987).
H. J. Martin and R. Chartier eds, *Le Livre conquérant*: Histoire de l'édition française (1982).
H. J. Martin and J. Vezin eds, *Mise en page et mise en texte du livre manuscrit* (1990).
M. B. Parkes, 'The Influence of the Concepts of "Ordinatio" and "Compilatio" on the Development of the Book' in J. J. G. Alexander and M. T. Gibson eds, *Medieval Learning and Literacy: Essays Presented To R. W. Hunt* (1976), pp. 115–41.
A. Petrucci, *Brevia Storia della Scrittura Latina* (1989).
C. Questa and R. Raffaelli eds, *Il libro e il testo* (1982).
C. H. Roberts and T. C. Skeat, *The Birth of the Codex* (1983).
R. H. Rouse, 'Roll and Codex in G. Silagi ed., *Paläographie 1981* (1982), pp. 108–23.
R. H. Rouse and M. A. Rouse, *Preachers, Florilegia and Sermons: the 'Manipulus Florum'* (1979).
R. C. van Caenegem, *Guide to the Sources of Medieval History* (1978).
O. Weijers ed., *Vocabulaire du livre et de l'écriture au Moyen Age* (1989).
R. S. Wieck ed., *Time Sanctified: The Book of Hours in Medieval Art and Life* (1988).
M. Zerdoun Bat-Yehouda, *Les Encres noires au Moyen Age* (1983).

READERS AND WRITERS IN MEDIEVAL ENGLAND

M. Aston, 'Devotional literacy' in her *Lollards and Reformers* (1984), pp. 101–33.
J. H. Baker, *The Third University of England* Selden Society Lecture (1990).
A. Bammesberger ed., *Old English Runes and their Continental Background* (1991).
A. Barratt ed., *Women's Writing in Middle English* (1992).
P. Brand, 'Courtroom and Schoolroom: the Education of Lawyers in England prior to 1400', *BIHR* 60 (1987), pp. 147–65.
R. Brilliant, 'The Bayeux Tapestry: A Stripped Narrative for their Eyes and Ears', *Word and Image* 7 (1991), pp. 98–124.
Julian Brown (ed. J. Bately, M. P. Brown, J. Roberts), *A Palaeographer's View* (1993).
Michelle P. Brown, 'The Lindisfarne Scriptorium' in G. Bonner, D. W. Rollason and C. Stancliffe eds, *St Cuthbert: His Cult and his Community* (1989), pp. 151–64.
J. A. Burrow, *Medieval Writers and their Work* (1982).
M. Camille, 'The Language of Images in Medieval England, 1200–1400' in Alexander & Binski (1987), pp. 33–40.
J. I. Catto ed., *The Early Oxford Schools* History of the University of Oxford, 1 (1984).
J. I. Catto and T. A. R. Evans eds, *Late Medieval Oxford* History, 2 (1992).
M. T. Clanchy, 'Literacy, Law and the Power of the State' in J.-C. M. Vigueur, C. Pietri and J.-P. Genet eds, *Culture et idéologie dans la genèse de l'état moderne* Collection de l'école française de Rome, 82 (1985), pp. 25–34.
M. T. Clanchy, 'Power and Knowledge' in W. M. Ormrod ed., *England in the Thirteenth Century* (1985), pp. 1–14.
M. T. Clanchy, 'Reading the Signs at Durham Cathedral' in K. Schousboe and M. T. Larsen eds, *Literacy and Society* (1989), pp. 171–82.
M. T. Clanchy, *Literacy and Law in Medieval England* [collected articles, forthcoming].
C. H. Clough ed., *Profession, Vocation and Culture: Essays for A. R. Myers* (1982).
J. Coleman, *English Literature in History 1350–1400: Medieval Readers and Writers* (1981).
P. R. Coss, 'Aspects of Cultural Diffusion in Medieval England', *Past and Present* 108 (1985), pp. 35–79.
William J. F. Davies, *Teaching Reading in Early England* (1973).
M. Denley, 'Elementary Teaching Techniques and Middle English Didactic Writing' in H. Phillips ed., *Langland: Essays in Honour of S. S. Hussey* (1990), pp. 223–40.
D. Dumville, *English Caroline Script and Monastic History 950–1030* (1992).
J. Frankis, 'The Social Context of Vernacular Writing' in P. R. Coss and S. D. Lloyd eds, *Thirteenth-Century England* 1 (1986), pp. 175–84.
C. Franzen, *The Tremulous Hand of Worcester* (1991).
V. H. Galbraith, *Kings and Chroniclers* [collected articles] (1982).
A. Gransden, *Historical Writing in England* (1974 and 1982) 2 vols.
Richard F. Green, *Poets and Princepleasers* (1980).
T. J. Heffernan ed., *The Popular Literature of Medieval England* (1985).
L. Hellinga, *Caxton in Focus* BL (1982).
J. Higgitt, 'The Stone-Cutter and the Scriptorium: Early Medieval Inscriptions in Britain and Ireland' in W. Koch ed., *Epigraphik 1988* (1990), pp. 149–64.
W. Hofstetter, 'Winchester and the Standardization of Old English Vocabulary', *Anglo-Saxon England* 17 (1988), pp. 139–61.
A. Hudson, *Lollards and their Books* (1985).

R. W. Hunt (ed. M. Gibson), *The Schools and the Cloister: Alexander Nequam* (1984).

A. M. Hutchison, 'Devotional Reading in the Monastery and in the Late Medieval Household' in M. G. Sargent ed., *De Cella in Saeculum* (1989), pp. 215–27.

M. Jennings, 'Tutivillus: The Literary Career of the Recording Demon', *Studies in Philology* 74 (1977) no. 5, pp. 1–95.

L. S. Johnson, 'The Trope of the Scribe and the Question of Literary Authority in the Works of Julian of Norwich and Margery Kempe', *Speculum* 66 (1991), pp. 820–38.

R. W. Kaeuper, 'Two Early Lists of Literates: 1334, 1373', *English Historical Review* 99 (1984), pp. 363–9.

S. Kelly, 'Anglo-Saxon Lay Society and the Written Word' in R. McKitterick ed., *The Uses of Literacy in Early Medieval Europe* (1990), pp. 36–62.

N. R. Ker, (ed. A. G. Watson) *Books, Collectors and Libraries* (1983).

M. Lapidge, 'Schools, Learning and Literature in Tenth-Century England' in *Il Secolo di Ferro* Settimane di Studio del Centro Italiano di Studi sull'Alto Medioevo' 38 (1991), ii, pp. 951–1005.

S. Lerer, *Literacy and Power in Anglo-Saxon Literature* (1991).

S. Lewis, 'The English Gothic Illuminated Apocalypse: "Lectio Divina" and the Art of Memory', *Word and Image* 7 (1991), pp. 1–32.

C. M. Meale ed., *Women and Literature in Britain 1150–1500* (1993).

D. Moffat, 'Anglo-Saxon Scribes and Old English Verse', *Speculum* 67 (1992), pp. 805–27.

J. A. H. Moran, *The Growth of English Schooling 1340–1548* (1985).

N. Morgan, 'Texts and Images of Marian Devotion' in W. M. Ormrod., *England in the Thirteenth Century* (1991), pp. 69–103.

K. O'B. O'Keeffe, *Visible Song: Transitional Literacy in Old English Verse* (1990).

N. Orme, *From Childhood to Chivalry: Education of the Kings and Aristocracy 1066–1530* (1984).

N. Orme, *Education and Society in Medieval and Renaissance England* [collected articles] (1988).

M. B. Parkes, *Scribes, Scripts and Readers* [collected articles] (1991).

M. B. Parkes and A. G. Watson eds, *Medieval Scribes, Manuscripts and Libraries: Essays Presented to N. R. Ker* (1978).

D. Pearsall ed., *Manuscripts and Readers in Fifteenth-Century England* (1983).

M. Richardson, 'Henry V and Chancery English', *Speculum* 55 (1980), pp. 726–50.

C. Richmond, 'Hand and Mouth': Information Gathering and Use in England in the Later Middle Ages', *Journal of Historical Sociology* 1 (1988), pp. 233–52.

M. Richter, *Sprache und Gesellschaft im Mittelalter* (1979).

A. G. Rigg, *A History of Anglo-Latin Literature 1066–1422* (1992).

J. T. Rosenthal, 'Aristocratic Cultural Patronage and Book Bequests 1350–1500', *Bulletin of the John Rylands Library* 64 (1982), pp. 522–48.

J. T. Rosenthal, 'English Medieval Education' [review], *History of Education Quarterly* (1982), pp. 499–511.

W. Rothwell, 'Language and Government in Medieval England', *Zeitschrift für französiche Sprache und Literatur* 93 (1983), pp. 258–70.

E. Salter (ed. D. Pearsall and N. Zeeman), *English and International: Studies in the Literature, Art and Patronage of Medieval England* (1988).

W. Scase, 'St Anne and the Education of the Virgin' Proceedings of the 1991 Harlaxton Symposium *Harlaxton Medieval Studies* 3 (1993).

I. Short, 'On Bilingualism in Anglo-Norman England', *Romance Philology* 33 (1980), pp. 467–79.

I. Short, 'Patrons and Polyglots: French Literature in Twelfth-Century England', *Anglo-Norman Studies 14: Proceedings of the Battle Conference 1991*, ed. M. Chibnall.

Jeremy J. Smith and M. L. Samuels, *The English of Chaucer and his Contemporaries* (1988).

R. W. Southern, *Robert Grosseteste: The Growth of an English Mind in Medieval Europe* (1986).

A. Taylor, 'The Myth of the Minstrel Manuscript', *Speculum* 66 (1991), pp. 43–73.

R. M. Thomson, 'England and the Twelfth-Century Renaissance', *Past and Present* 101 (1983), pp. 3–21.

R. M. Thomson, *William of Malmesbury* (1987).

R. V. Turner, 'The "Miles Literatus" in Twelfth- and Thirteenth-Century England: How Rare a Phenomenon?' *American Historical Review* 83 (1978), pp. 928–45.

C. P. Wormald, 'The Uses of Literacy in Anglo-Saxon England and its Neighbours', *TRHS* 5th series 27 (1977), pp. 95–114.

RECORDS AND MANUSCRIPT-MAKING IN MEDIEVAL ENGLAND

Editions of documents are included in this section only when their editors discuss how and why they were made.

N. W. Alcock, 'The Catesbys in Coventry: A Medieval Estate and its Archives', *Midland History* 15 (1990), pp. 1–36.

J. Backhouse and C. de Hamel, *The Becket Leaves* BL (1988).

M. Beit-Arié, *The Only Dated Medieval Hebrew Manuscript Written in England* (1985).

A. Bennett, 'Anthony Bek's Copy of "Statuta Angliae"' in W. M. Ormrod ed., *England in the Fourteenth Century* (1986), pp. 1–27.

J. Boffey, *Manuscripts of English Courtly Love Lyrics* (1985).

P. Brand, 'The Drafting of Legislation in Mid-Thirteenth-Century England', *Parliamentary History* 9 (1990), pp. 243–85.

J. Campbell, 'The Significance of the Anglo-Norman State in the Administrative History of Western Europe' in his *Essays in Anglo-Saxon History* (1986), pp. 171–89.

P. Chaplais, 'The Royal Anglo-Saxon "Chancery" Revisited' in H. Mayr-Harting and R. I. Moore eds, *Studies in Medieval History Presented to R. H. C. Davis* (1985), pp. 41–51.

C. R. Cheney, 'Service Books and Records', *BIHR* 56 (1983), pp. 7–15.

J. Cherry, 'Symbolism: Horns of Tenure', *The Antiquaries Journal* 69 (1989), pp. 111–18.

C. P. Christiansen, *London's Early Book Trade* (1989).

M. T. Clanchy, 'Archives and Memory', *Archivaria* 11 (1981), pp. 115–25.

J. C. Crick, *The "Historia Regum" of Geoffrey of Monmouth: Dissemination and Reception* (1991).

D. Crook, *Records of the General Eyre* HMSO (1982).

W. J. Dohar, 'Medieval Ordination Lists: the Origins of a Record', *Archives* 20 (1992), pp. 17–35.

C. Donovan, *The de Brailes Hours: Shaping the Book of Hours in Thirteenth-Century Oxford* BL (1991).

C. Donovan, *The Winchester Bible* BL (1993).

A. Duggan, *Thomas Becket: A Textual History of his Letters* (1980).

I. Fenlon ed., *Cambridge Music Manuscripts A.D. 900–1700* (1982).

R. C. Finucane 'Two Notaries and their Records 1282–1307', *Journal of Medieval History* 13 (1987), pp. 1–14.

T. Foulds, 'Medieval Cartularies', *Archives* 18 (1987), pp. 3–35.

M. Gibson, T. A. Heslop, R. W. Pfaff eds, *The Eadwine Psalter* (1992).

J. R. Gilleland, 'Eight Anglo-Norman Cosmetic Recipes', *Romania* 109 (1988), pp. 50–67.

A. Gransden, 'The Chronicles of Medieval England and Scotland', 2 parts, *Journal of Medieval History* 16 (1990), pp. 129–50; 17 (1991), pp. 217–42.

Judith A. Green, 'The Earliest Surviving Pipe Roll', *BIHR* 55 (1982), pp. 1–17.

J. Griffiths and D. Pearsall eds, *Book Production and Publishing in Britain 1375–1475* (1989).

R. A. Griffiths, 'Public and Private Bureaucracies in England and Wales in the Fifteenth Century', *TRHS* 5th series 30 (1980), pp. 109–30.

E. M. Hallam, *Domesday Book through Nine Centuries* (1986).

[handwritten marginal note:] Clanchy art. pp. 201–5.

P. D. A. Harvey ed., *Manorial Records of Cuxham* Oxfordshire Record Society 50 (1976).

P. D. A. Harvey, *Manorial Records* Archives and the User 5 (1984).

P. D. A. Harvey, 'Personal Seals in Thirteenth-Century England' in I. Wood and G. A. Loud eds, *Church and Chronicle: Essays Presented to John Taylor* (1991), pp. 117–27.

G. Henderson, *From Durrow to Kells: The Insular Gospel Books 650–800* (1987).

T. A. Heslop, 'English Seals from the Mid-Ninth Century to 1100', *Journal of the British Archaeological Association* 133 (1980), pp. 1–16.

T. A. Heslop, 'The Production of De Luxe Manuscripts and the Patronage of King Cnut and Queen Emma', *Anglo-Saxon England* 19 (1990), pp. 151–95.

J. C. Holt ed., *Domesday Studies* (1987).

R. F. Hunnisett, 'What is a Plea Roll?' *Journal of the Society of Archivists* 9 (1988), pp. 109–14.

R. F. Hunnisett and J. B. Post eds, *Medieval Legal Records Edited in Memory of C. A. F. Meekings* HMSO (1978).

T. Hunt, *Popular Medicine in Thirteenth-Century England* [texts] (1990).

T. Hunt, *Teaching and Learning Latin in Thirteenth-Century England* [texts] (1991), 3 vols.

P. R. Hyams, 'The Charter as a Source for the Early Common Law', *Journal of Legal History* 12 (1991), pp. 173–89.

D. L. Jeffrey and B. J. Levy, *The Anglo-Norman Lyric* (1990).

S. Keynes, *A Handlist of Anglo-Saxon Charters* (1993).

S. Keynes, *The Diplomas of King Aethelred 'the Unready'* (1980).

S. Keynes, 'Regenbald the Chancellor' in R. Allen Brown ed., *Anglo-Norman Studies* Proceedings of the Battle Conference 10 (1987), pp. 185–222.

S. Keynes, 'Royal Government and the Written Word in Late Anglo-Saxon England' in R. McKitterick ed., *The Uses of Literacy in Early Medieval Europe* (1990), pp. 226–57.

S. Lewis, *The Art of Matthew Paris in the 'Chronica Majora'* (1987).

W. H. Monroe, 'Two Medieval Genealogical Roll-Chronicles in the Bodleian Library', *Bodleian Library Record* 10 (1981), pp. 215–21.

N. J. Morgan, *Early Gothic Manuscripts 1190–1250* (1982).

N. J. Morgan, *Early Gothic Manuscripts 1250–1285* (1988).

N. J. Morgan, *The Lambeth Apocalypse: A Critical Study* (1990).

J. Morrish, 'Dated and Datable Manuscripts Copied in England during the Ninth Century', *Mediaeval Studies* 50 (1988), pp. 512–38.

R. Mortimer, 'The Charters of Henry II: What are the Criteria of Authenticity?' *Anglo-Norman Studies* 12 (1989) [ed. M. Chibnall], pp. 119–34.

D. A. E. Pelteret, *Catalogue of English Post-Conquest Vernacular Documents* (1990).

D. Postles, 'Manorial Accountancy at God's House', *Archives* 18 (1987), pp. 36–41.

S. Rankin, 'From Memory to Record: Musical Notations in Manuscripts from Exeter', *Anglo-Saxon England* 13 (1984), pp. 97–112.

S. Reynolds, 'Magna Carta 1297 and the Legal Use of Literacy', *BIHR* 62 (1989), pp. 233–44.

F. Riddy ed., *Regionalism in Late Medieval Manuscripts and Texts* (1991).

P. R. Robinson, 'The "Booklet": A Self-Contained Unit in Composite Manuscripts', *Codicologica* 3 (1980), pp. 46–69.

R. H. and M. A. Rouse, *Registrum Anglie de Libris* [Franciscan union catalogue] (1991).

L. F. Sandler, *Gothic Manuscripts 1285–1385* (1986) 2 vols.

J. E. Sayers, *Papal Government and England during the Pontificate of Honorius III* (1984).

E. Searle ed., *The Chronicle of Battle Abbey* (1980).

M. M. Sheehan, 'English Wills', *Journal of Medieval History* 14 (1988), pp. 3–12.

R. A. Skelton and P. D. A. Harvey eds, *Local Maps and Plans from Medieval England* (1986).

R. C. Stacey, *Receipt and Issue Rolls 26 Henry III* PRS 49 (1992).

E. L. G. Stones and G. G. Simpson eds, *Edward I and the Throne of Scotland* [texts] (1978).

J. and E. L. G. Stones, 'Bishop Ralph Neville, Chancellor to Henry III, and his Correspondence', *Archives* 16 (1984), pp. 227–57.

K. J. Stringer, 'The Charters of David Earl of Huntingdon and Lord of Garioch' in K. J. Stringer ed., *Essays on the Nobility of Medieval Scotland* (1985), pp. 72–101.

J. Taylor, 'Letters and Letter Collections in England 1300–1420', *Nottingham Medieval Studies* 24 (1980), pp. 57–70.

A. T. Thacker, ed., *The Earldom of Chester and its Charters* Journal of the Chester Archaeological Society 71 (1991).

R. M. Thomson ed., *The Archives of the Abbey of Bury St Edmunds* Suffolk Record Society 21 (1980).

R. M.Thomson, *Manuscripts from St Albans Abbey 1066–1235* (1982), 2 vols.

R. M. Thomson, 'The Norman Conquest and English Libraries' in P. F. Ganz ed., *The Role of the Book in Medieval Culture* (1986) vol. i, pp. 27–40.

R. M. Thomson, *Catalogue of the Manuscripts of Lincoln Cathedral Chapter Library* (1989).

R. V. Turner, 'Changing Perceptions of the New Administrative Class in Anglo-Norman England', *Journal of British Studies* 29 (1990), pp. 93–117.

T. Webber, 'Salisbury and the Exon Domesday', *English Manuscript Studies* 1 (1989), pp. 1–18.

T. Webber, *Scribes and Scholars at Salisbury Cathedral 1075–1125* (1992).

J. K. Weber, 'The Power of Judicial Records', *Journal of Legal History* 9 (1988), pp. 180–200.

L. Webster and J. Backhouse eds, *The Making of England: Anglo-Saxon Art and Culture A.D. 600–900* [charters and books] BL (1991).

A. Williams and R. W. H. Erskine eds, *Domesday Book Studies* (1987).

C. M. Woolgar, *Household Accounts from Medieval England* (1992), 2 Vols.

B. Yapp, *Birds in Medieval Manuscripts* BL (1981).

Plate I: Charter and seal of Ilbert de Lacy

This charter of one of the Norman conquerors records the gift of the manor (*mansio*) of Tingewick (*tinduicz*) in Buckinghamshire to the abbey of La Sainte Trinité du Mont at Rouen. It is authenticated by the crosses, presumably autographs, of King William Rufus, Ilbert and Hawise (*Haduidis*) his wife. In addition to these *signa*, Ilbert's seal used to be attached to the charter (at the hole below Hawise's cross). This SIGILLUM ILBERTI DE LACEO, in brown wax with the obverse blank, is one of the earliest knightly seals in existence. The apparently long pointed nose of Ilbert on the seal may in fact be the nasal piece of a helmet of the type depicted in the Bayeux Tapestry. The writer of the charter, perhaps a monk at Rouen, seems unaccustomed to producing this sort of document. He is inconsistent in his spacing and size of script and eccentric in his spelling, for example *Wiliel-mi* for King 'William'. Also his *m*'s and *n*'s with initial descenders and his tall embellished *s*'s are peculiar. The concluding words *& decimam de Fraite villa* ('and the tithe of Freteval') look as if they have been added by someone else, possibly with the donor's approval. The writing upside down at the bottom is an archivist's finding aid, dating probably from the fourteenth century.

Winchester College Muniments 11334. Reduced in size. Date *c*.1090 (*VCH Bucks*. i, p. 212). Transcript: *Archaeological Journal* iv (1847), pp. 249–51. Comment: W. E. Wightman, *The Lacy Family in England and Normandy* (1966), pp. 11, 56–7, 60.

Notum sit omnibus Xpi [Christi] tam presentibus quam futuris qd [quod] ego hubt [Hubertus] de lascio

... cu [cum] hiduide [H]illuide uxore mea do maisilloie [maisill...] ... sce [sancte] Trinitati de

... monte rotomagensi [Rotomagensi] ... scilicet cu [cum] aqua q̄ [que] pr[a]tis q̄ siluis omnibus q̄

ad ipsam maisiloiem [maisillonem] ... p[ro] anima mea atq̄ [atque] dni [domini] mei Willel

... regi ... p̄ [pro] ... p[ar]entib[us] q̄ amicos meos ... p[ro] anima

q̄ uxoris mee ... filio mea hugon[is] ... p[ro] eo q̄d [quod] et ipse

supradictu filius m... loco requiescit e[t] decima in de

fraxce uilla

ʃ [signum] Willelmi regis

✝

ʃ [signum] h. Alba   ʝ [signum] hilduidis uxoris ca

... ...

... ...

ʃcp̄

Plate II: Early writ of Henry I

This plate shows the typical form of a royal letter patent, penned on thin parchment in the assured hand of a king's scribe. The narrow tag at the bottom of the document served as a tie to secure the writ when it was folded up. On the broader tag in the middle was fixed the king's seal: the burn mark, made by the hot wax, can be seen. The text is neatly and economically written on ruled lines. It grants Bernard abbot of Ramsey the right to tax his own knights (*vavasores*) and to recover the land which his deposed predecessor, Abbot Aldwin, had alienated. The writ is addressed to the lords of the region – Robert bishop of Lincoln, Simon the earl (of Huntingdon) and Roger the sheriff. Although this document looks as if it were a letter sending information to the addressees, that is not its real purpose. The first of the addressees, Bishop Robert, already knew what it said, as he is also named as the first witness. The purpose of this writing was not primarily to convey information but to provide Abbot Bernard with evidence that the king supported his cause. Essentially this document is a title-deed.

BL Add. Charter 33642. Actual size. Date 1103 (*RRA-N* II, p. 33, no. 650). Transcript: *Ramsey*, p. 220. The handwriting is identified as that of Scribe I by T. A. M. Bishop, *Scriptores Regis* (1961), p. 52, no. 316.

Henr(icus) rex Angl(orum) . Rob(erto) epo(scopo) lincol(niensi) . 7 Iustic(iariis) . 7 uicecom(itibus) . 7 om(n)ib(us) . 7 ba-
ronib(us) . 7 om(n)ib(us) . seruientib(us) . 7 fidelib(us) suis franc' 7 Angl' salt'm . Sciatis q(uod) uolo 7 p(re)cipio
ut abb(a)s Bernard(us) de ramesia 7 monachi . fac' h(ab)eant om(n)es suas consuetud(ines) . Sicut eas hab(uer)unt temp(or)e
Henr(ici) regis aui mei . 7 sicut m(eli)us 7 plenius habuer(unt) . T(este) . . . .

Plate III: Bilingual writ of Henry I

By contrast with the writ illustrated in plate II, this one was probably written not by a king's scribe but by a monk of Canterbury. Its ostensible purpose is to confirm to Archbishop Anselm and to the monks of Christ Church their ancient rights of sac and soc, toll and team, etc. The text is in both Latin and English (the English starts at line 8). As much of the Latin text consists of English formulas (*on strande & streame, on wudu & felde*, etc., line 3), the bilingualism is largely superfluous. These alliterative formulas derive from the oral recitations of remembrancers. Canterbury's bilingual writs seem to be an attempt to put this traditional lore, superficially Latinized, into a written form acceptable to the Norman government. The reasons for thinking that this writ is not a product of the royal Chancery are that the seal is eccentrically attached on the left-hand side (where the tag projects), the parchment is too thick, and the style of script is book hand. A note on another exemplar of this writ states that it was originally produced in quadruplicate. It is thus a throwback to pre-Conquest practice, when great monastic houses (occasionally at least) wrote out for themselves copies of title-deeds in the king's name and then got the royal seal affixed to them.

BL Campbell Charter xxix. 5. Reduced in size. Date *c*.1107 (*RRA-N* II, p. 72, no. 840). Transcript: *Journal of the British Archaeological Association* xxix (1873), p. 242. Comment: D. A. E. Pelteret, *Catalogue of English Post-Conquest Vernacular Documents* (1990), p. 73, no. 46.

Plate IV: Writ of King Stephen

This writ is an unusually early example of cursive script in England. The writing is controlled and professional but rushed. It suggests the urgent pressure of business which caused the king's scribes to write as fast as they could. T. A. M. Bishop considers this 'the most fluent of twelfth-century Chancery hands' (*Scriptores Regis*, plate xxia). The change of style can be readily seen by comparing this hand with that of Henry I's scribe in plate II and with the book hand in plate III. Nevertheless the way the letters are formed in this writ of King Stephen is not a fundamental departure from the minuscule of Henry I's scribes. The differences stem from the need to write fast rather than from special training. This writ is addressed to Henry of Essex and Adam of Belnai and all the king's officers in Essex. It acquits William Fitz Robert of a forfeiture. Like the writ benefiting Bernard abbot of Ramsey (see plate II), this one would have been obtained and kept by William, the beneficiary, and shown by him to the king's officers in Essex when and if evidence was demanded of Stephen's judgement on his behalf. The document is in the form of a letter patent, with two tags to enable it to be opened and closed repeatedly (as illustrated in plate II).

BL Add. Charter 28319. Actual size. Date 1135–41. Transcript: *RRA-N* III, p. 120, no. 318. Other facsimiles of this hand are shown in *RRA-N* IV, plates xvii and xviii.

Si vox dming h. se effecit. & de detrac̃ oing Mim̃fact fuit. se effect. &
clamo gere Willm At Ẽot fauessarim, ung̃ splaciar̃ fuit̃ sa effarof ing
fug̃ de Barhestera, ia se ani sude gēõ fit nec ude angli fu splaciartauf̃
si anigli n luĉ fuerit falda effarca õr fug̃ de Barhestera. & Ẽds se
ei Ay werthn.

Plate V: Charter and seal of William del Turp

This charter is typical of many non-royal documents produced in the latter half of the twelfth century. Written on ruled lines in a confident hand, its purpose is to serve as proof for the future that the beneficiary, Simon son of Robert, holds his land (2 bovates in Eden in county Durham) by hereditary right and honourably as a free tenant, quit from any servile conditions. The grantor, William has a fine seal, showing him as a knight advancing on horseback from left to right (compare the more static image of a knight on the seal of a century earlier in plate I). William wears a conical helmet and holds his shield in front of him; his right arm brandishing a drawn sword is stretched back, ready to strike. Other charters of a William de Thorp are preserved at Durham cathedral, and it is possible that this one also is a Durham product, though none of the ten witnesses (named in the last three lines of the charter) tally with those in William de Thorp's charters. Most early charters record gifts to religious houses and were written by the monks who benefited from them (as in plate I), whereas this one benefits a lay tenant. The writing could be that of the first of the named witnesses, Ralf the priest (*Rad' p[re]sbit[er]*). Whoever the scribe was, he has produced an elegant and professional piece of work – consistent in its layout and script, and generous in its use of parchment – which contrasts with the charter of William Benedict which follows (see plate VI).

Harvard Law Library MS 87, 2. 012. 5. Reduced in size. No certain date (?last quarter of the twelfth century). Seven charters of William de Thorp of Eden are printed by W. Greenwell in *Feodarium Prioratus Dunelmensis* Surtees S., LVIII (1871), pp. 132–4.

Witts deltcir̄ p̄ oib; uidentib; ⁊audientib; has l̄ras sal·Sciatis me dedisse ⁊ꝯcessisse ⁊ p̄senti

karta ꝯfirmasse Simoni filio Robʼti ⁊heredib; suis duas bouatas t̄re in eden q̄s pat̄ suus Robʼ

de me tenuit·scilicet ut Simon ⁊ heredes sui teneant eas ī feudo ⁊ hereditate de me ⁊

heredib; meis libe ⁊q̄ete ⁊ honorifice· in ꝑtis ⁊ pascuis ⁊ uiis ⁊ semitis ⁊ exitib; ⁊oib;

libʼtatib; faciendo ꝑ eis libum forense suum duar̄ bouatar̄ in eden· ⁊ ꝯrq̄ Simon ⁊

heredes eiꝰ d̄ pdictis duab; bouatis ab oib; aliis suitiis ⁊ꝯsuetudinib; libi ⁊q̄eti· Testes· Rad̄

pʼbr̄· Higellus· Iohis d̄ cadredesaceʼs ⁊adā filiʼ eʼ· Wittms d̄ elletun· Rob̄ d̄ pouuitt· Rob̄ d̄ hefeld·

walt̄us d̄ querenduir̄· Aledui d̄ herdwic· walt̄us fr̄ Simonis· Samel d̄ cadredesaceʼs·

Plate VI: Charters of William Benedict and Walter Deyville

These two little charters, both dating from the first half of the thirteenth century, contrast with each other and with the preceding one (see plate v), although all three serve a common purpose in providing written evidence that their beneficiaries hold by hereditary right as free tenants. The top charter is untidily written in uncouth script (possibly that of the first witness, John the chaplain of Irnham), whereas the lower one is in a tiny and assured cursive hand similar to that of royal writs of the period. This contrast may reflect the different rank of the persons concerned. Walter Deyville (*Daivill'*), the grantor of the lower charter, was lord of Stoke in Coventry, and the beneficiary, Walter son of Terry of Coventry, likewise came from a known family (*Warwickshire Feet of Fines*, Dugdale S, xi (1932), p. 17, no. 83). The grantor of the top charter, on the other hand, William Benedict of Boleby (*Boleb'*) in Lincolnshire is obscure, and so is the beneficiary, Henry son of Thomas of Hawthorpe (*Huvartorp'*). Henry was perhaps a smallholder of relatively low status, comparable with the fenland peasants of the *Carte Nativorum* (see chapter 2, nn. 18–19 above). Despite these differences, both charters concern small properties: William's grants four strips in an open field and Walter's grants a croft. Both charters therefore show how documentary evidence was increasingly used in the thirteenth century, even for small properties and even by peasants.

Harvard Law Library MS 87. 2. 012. 4 and 2. 013. 8. Both actual size. The seals are not illustrated because they are damaged; William's is a floral seal (befitting a peasant), whereas Walter's is armorial. Comment: charters of a Walter d'Eyvill are published by P. R. Coss, *Early Records of Coventry* (1986), pp. 250–1.

Plate VII: Agreement between Colchester abbey and the burgesses

This plate illustrates a precisely dated piece of writing and the typical format of a chirograph. The date is given in the first line as the 39th year of King Henry son of King John on Sunday after the feast of St Edmund (22 November 1254). In an agreement by chirograph each party received a matching copy of the document authenticated by the seals of the other party (see chapter 3, nn.19–26 above). Thus at the top of this document can be seen where the word CYROGRAPHUM has been cut across by a wavy line to match its counterpart. This is Colchester's abbey's copy, as it bore the seals of the 12 burgesses of Colchester who are named in lines 2 and 3 (there are 12 slits for seals, although only 5 survive). The document is written in a formal cursive or business hand, comparable with the cursive book hands illustrated at plates XVI and XVII, either by a monk of Colchester or by a clerk of the town. The agreement concerns hunting rights: the abbey is to have free warren 'on the left side of the path which leads by the stile (*scalario*, line 5) next to the house which was Hamo de Campo's', while the burgesses 'can lawfully hunt hare, fox and cat' (*leporem, wlpem & catum*, line 11) on the right. Putting this agreement in writing was evidently intended to prevent disputes in future; yet the terms of the settlement are conceived for the present only, as posterity might soon forget which house had been Hamo de Campo's.

Harvard Law Library MS 87, 2. 254. Reduced in size. Transcript: *Cartularium Monasterii St Johannis Baptiste de Colecestria* ed. S. A. Moore (1897), ii, p. 505. Translation: *The Red Book of Colchester* ed. W. G. Benham (1902), pp. 162–3.

Plate VIII: Tally sticks of Robert of Glamorgan

These tallies were issued by the Exchequer to Robert of Glamorgan, sheriff of Surrey and Sussex, as receipts for payments into the treasury in the financial year 1293–4. Like a chirograph (see plate VII), a tally stick was a bipartite record. When completed it was split down its length; the larger part (the stock) was issued as a receipt, while the smaller part (the foil) was kept by the Exchequer. The sticks in the photograph are all stocks. Sums of money are shown on them by notches of different depths and shapes. Thus the stick at the top, with a pair of deep triangular notches at the right-hand end, is a receipt for 2 × £20. The next stick has a single triangular notch (for £20) on the lower side and 7 × £1 and 8 × 1 shilling notches on the upper side. On the third stick 19 × 1 shilling notches are visible and on the bottom stick there are eight narrow notches (for 1 penny each) on the upper side and a single notch for 1 shilling on the lower side. The tallies were written on in pen and ink in order to identify them. They were not designed for illiterates, as they could not be lawfully identified without the writing on them. Thus the sticks illustrated all bear the sheriff's name and county, the regnal year and term, and details of what the payments are for. These notes are not all visible in the photograph because they are written on different sides of the sticks. As the photograph shows, tallies were an intricate but robust form of record, which could not be readily replaced until the invention of carbon copying.

PRO E. 402/2. Actual size. Illustrated by M. H. Mills, *The Pipe Roll for 1295, Surrey Record S. VII* (1924), p. x. See also pp. 123–4 above.

Plate IX: Wallingford's first roll of tradesmen

This short roll lists people by trades, recording how much each person owes for the year to practise his trade in the town. The portion illustrated lists, under headings in the left-hand margin, the glovers (*Wa[n]ti[ere]s*) and mercers (*Mercat[iari]i*) or general traders. Other portions list butchers, carpenters, hosiers, smiths, weavers, etc. After each person's name is entered the sum due from him, followed by details of payment. For example the second enrolment in the list of glovers states that from Roger the Clothier (*D[e] Rog[er]o Parme[n]tario*) 16 pence (*xvi.d.*) are due. To the right of this sum follow receipts by instalments in three distinct hands: received 4 pence (*r. iiij. d.*); received 6 pence; received 6 pence, *quit.* The roll thus served both as a list of traders and as a record of receipts for licences to trade. The royal Exchequer had kept rolls of receipts since Henry II's reign, but this is the first example of such a record from an English town. Possibly the clerks who wrote it had worked for the government, as the roll is dated by the regnal year (11 Henry III, that is, 1226–7) and Wallingford was usually held by a royal nominee or kinsman. The parchment is thin, causing the enrolments on the dorse to show through on the right-hand side.

Berkshire Record Office W/FC 1. Portion of the face of the roll, which is headed *Rotulus de pactionariis in Walingeford.* Reduced in size. Comment: N. M. Herbert, *The Borough of Wallingford* (unpublished PhD thesis, University of Reading, 1971).

Plate X: Wallingford's second roll of tradesmen

This roll contrasts in appearance with its predecessor (see plate ix). The portion shown lists the glovers and mercers, as in the previous roll. But the names are written more boldly and lines are ruled to separate the enrolments and to make vertical columns. The receipts are likewise more clearly set out, so that there is no mistake about which sum refers to which person. The roll is dated 14 Henry III (that is 1229–30) at its head. The clerk who designed it also wrote Wallingford's roll of rents (W/FT 1) for the preceding year, which is laid out in the same way. In each case the receipts are entered in a different hand from the names. It will be noticed that the names appear in much the same order in both rolls of tradesmen (see plate ix), although some of the assessments differ and there are four extra names (one of which is cancelled) concluding the list of glovers in the second roll. The order seems to be one of precedence or seniority rather than financial means. The greater formality of this second roll, compared with its predecessor, suggests that the Wallingford clerks were now thinking in terms of rolls being permanent records rather than casual memoranda supplementing receipts on wooden tallies. A trades-man who saw his name engrossed, as if in a liturgical book, and his payments accumulating from left to right on the parchment until they culminated with his acquittance in the right-hand margin, should have been impressed by the dignity of written record.

Berkshire Record Office W./FC 2. Portion of the face of the roll. Reduced in size.

Plate XI: Household roll of Eleanor de Montfort

This roll records Eleanor's daily expenditure and itinerary during the last months of Simon de Montfort's life. The portion illustrated concerns the week 19–26 February 1265, when Eleanor proceeded southwards from Wallingford to Odiham via Reading. Each day is enrolled separately, sometimes by a different clerk. Thus the first three enrolments illustrated appear to be in different hands. The entry for Saturday marked *Rading'* (that is, at Reading) in the margin, is typical. It notes expenditure on bread, wine, beer, and cups, which is followed by kitchen expenses on herrings, fresh fish, peas, and dishes. Finally comes the expenditure of the marshalcy on hay for 65 horses, oats, bedding straw (*litere*), charcoal (*carbonibus*, possibly coal), barley, and black-smithing. To conclude the enrolment the day's expenditure is totalled, amounting in this instance to 44 shillings and $6\frac{1}{2}$ pence. Each day's expenditure could thus be seen at a glance by running the eye down the sums on the right-hand side of the roll. The initiator of detailed accounts like these was the king's government. As Eleanor was Henry III's sister, she would probably have been familiar with written accounts from childhood.

BL Add. MS. 8877. Reduced in size. Transcript: *Manners and Household Expenses of England*, Roxburghe Club LVII (1841), pp. 3–5. Comment: M. W. Labarge, *A Baronial Household of the Thirteenth Century* (1965), pp. 189–201. In general see: C. M. Woolgar, *Household Accounts from Medieval England* (1992).

Plate XII: Peter of Poitiers dictating to a scribe

As Peter explains in the prologue to his *Compendium* or *Tabula Historie* reproduced here, he devised a time chart which overcame the 'prolixity of sacred history' by encouraging students to learn with their eyes through simple diagrams which 'commend themselves to the memory by habit'. The figure in the central roundel is God as Christ in Majesty. In the roundels at his feet are Adam and Eve, and from them stems the genealogical tree of man's history. The author is himself depicted in the roundel on the left at the top. He holds open a book while dictating to the scribe on the right. The matter being dictated is presumably the text of the prologue which is set between them. The book (represented as open pages with ruled blank lines) on the author's lectern must be one of the prolix histories which Peter aimed to simplify. The scribe turns towards the author in order to catch his words. In this contorted posture he dips his quill into an extravagantly large inkhorn, while holding a penknife of comparable dimensions in his left hand. He is bald but not clearly tonsured like the author, as a scribe was not necessarily of clerical status. Dangling over his lectern is the blank membrane of parchment on which he is about to write. Peter's text was designed to form a continuous roll displaying man's unfolding history from Adam to Christ.

Harvard University, Houghton Library fMS. Typ 216. Reduced in size (actual size of roll 354 cm × 35 cm). Date *c*.1210. Comment: Carruthers, *Memory*, pp. 250–1; H. E. Hilpert, 'Geistliche Bildung,' *Journal of Medieval History* xi (1985), pp. 315–31; N. Morgan, *Early Gothic MSS 1250–1285* (1988), pp. 180–1, and ibid., *1190–1250* (1982), pp. 91–2.

Plate XIII: Genealogical history of England

Just as biblical history was presented in a sequence of diagrams by Peter of Poitiers (see plate XII), so the roll format was used from the middle of the thirteenth century to schematize the history of England. This plate shows the portion depicting William the Conqueror (*William Bastard*) from a genealogical history of the kings of England down to Edward I. William sits in state, like Christ in Majesty (see plate XII) and like the image on the king's seal. The text in French on the left records that William conquered England from Harold, reigned 21 years, died in his 59th year in 1087, and had been crowned by the archbishop of York on Christmas Day 1067 (1066 by modern reckoning). From William stem his nine children – Robert *Cortehuse* duke of Normandy, William *le Rous* (Rufus), Richard (who died in *c.*1075), Henry I, Ela (or Adela) duchess (or countess) of Blois, Cecily abbess of Caen, Constance countess of Brittany, and two unnamed daughters. The countesses wear coronets and the abbess a nun's veil. This pictorial scheme with captions thus provides an elementary but precise chronology of the rulers of England, together with an explanation of their relationship to each other. The design attracts the eye, like Peter of Poitiers's (see plate XII), and it can be understood by someone of restricted literacy. A knightly family possessing a roll of this sort therefore had the means to master chronology, which had hitherto been the preserve of monks.

Harvard University, Houghton Library MS Typ 11. Reduced in size (actual size of roll 403 cm × 26 cm). Date *c.*1300. See also B. Smalley, *Historians in the Middle Ages* (1974), pp. 178–9; Alexander & Binski, pp. 200–1, no. 10 (by L. F. Sandler); Lewis, *Matthew Paris*, pp. 140–2.

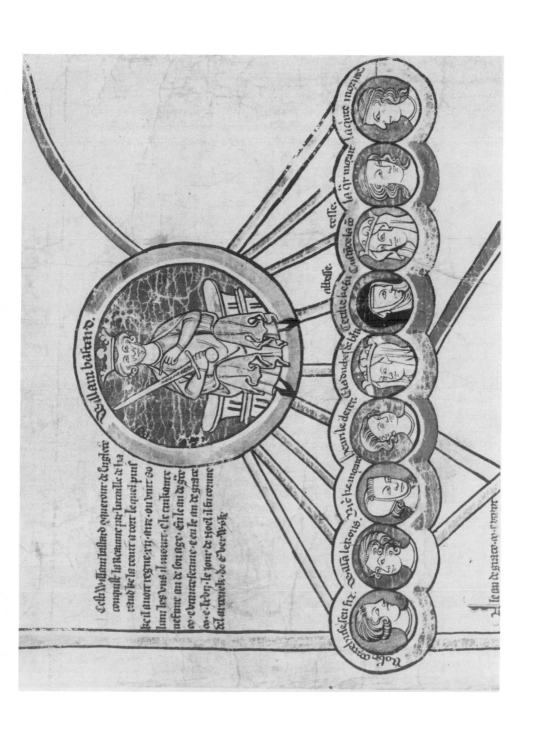

Plate XIV: The Canterbury or Eadwine Psalter

This masterpiece of calligraphic design was probably made at Canterbury under the direction of Eadwine, 'the prince of writers'. The layout makes it possible to show all on one page the three versions of St Jerome's Latin text of the Psalms, side by side in parallel columns, together with Latin glosses and Anglo-Saxon and French translations. The main text, the 'Gallican', is in the largest script towards the left of the page. Its marginal and interlinear glosses, in miniature abbreviated script, comprise a commentary derived from the Church Fathers. For example in the margin to the left of the capital Q is written: *Dilexi l[egem] q[u]i dilig[it] q[uo]d iub[et] d[ominu]s* ('I loved the law who love what the Lord commands'). Similarly to the right of the Q is immediately above *dilexi* ('I loved') is interlined: *non timui* ('I did not fear'). The pair of slimmer columns on the right of the page show the 'Roman' and 'Hebrew' variant texts. Between the lines of the 'Roman' text is the Anglo-Saxon translation, written in a style derived from insular minuscules, and between the lines of the 'Hebrew' is the French translation.

Trinity College Cambridge MS R.17.1. Lower portion of fo. 219b: Psalm 118 (*QUOMODO dilexi legem tuam, Domine*), that is, Psalm 119, verses 97–100, in the Authorised Version. Date 1145–1170 (Zarnecki, *Catalogue*, p. 119). Facsimile ed. M. R. James (1935). Comment: *The Eadwine Psalter*, ed. M. Gibson, T. A. Heslop and R. W. Pfaff (1992). See also pp. 115–16, 212, 284, 287 above.

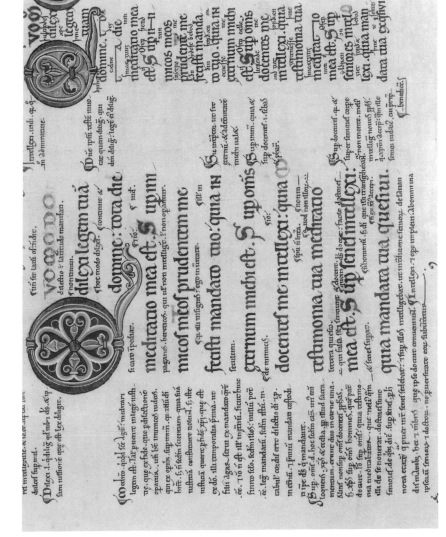

dilexi legem tuam domine: tota die meditatio mea est.

Super inimicos meos prudentem me fecisti mandato tuo:

Super omnes docentes me intellexi: quia testimonia tua meditatio mea est.

Super senes intellexi: quia mandata tua quesivi.

Plate XV: Estate book of Richard Hotot

Richard was a landowner in Northamptonshire and Bedfordshire in the 1240s. The book associated with him contains a family chronicle, details of his properties, and copies of Magna Carta and the Charter of the Forest. The opening folios are generously laid out and illuminated in green (showing up as a lighter tone in the photograph) with red embellishment, which gives the book a bucolic air. The page illustrated is headed on the left (in green): *Redditus et f[ir]me de Torveye ad festum s[anc]ti Micael[is]* ('Rents and farms from Turvey at Michaelmas'); the year is not specified. Beneath are listed in two columns the tenants' names and their annual rents, starting with: *De Will[elm]o Martel. iii d[enarii]* ('From William Martel – 3 pence'). The writing may be the work of clerks, comparable with those who wrote Wallingford's lists of dues at about the same time (see plates IX and X). An alternative possibility is that Richard's father, Thomas (who died in ?1212), inaugurated this book and wrote some of it in his own hand; Richard also may have been taught to write, as his elder brother was abbot of Peterborough. A notable peculiarity are the symbols preceding most of the names. These tally, though in a different order, with the footnotes (in smaller more cursive script) specifying the size of each tenant's holding. Thus the symbol preceding William Martel's name indicates that his rent is *pro dimidia v[ir]gata* ('for half a virgate'). In appearance the symbols are similar to those used by Robert Grosseteste (see chapter 5, nn. 169–71 above).

BL Add. MS 54228, fo. 6b. Reduced in size (actual size 28 cm × 18 cm). Transcript: *A Northamptonshire Miscellany*, ed. E. King, Northants. Record S., XXXIII (1983), pp. 24–5. Comment: T. Foulds, 'Medieval Cartularies', *Archives* XVIII (1987), p. 26 and E. King in *England in the Thirteenth Century* ed. M. Ormrod (1991), pp. 1–4.

Reddit' de Firma de Turri

de Willo marcel — iiij d
de radulfo chico — viij d
de robto germ — iij d
de Willo fil ade — ix d
de rogo filio strnoy — vj d
de walto le packere — iiij d
de ric de la leye — iij d
de henr fil willmi — j d
de rad donoldis — iij ob
de augu'ce le chaf — iiij d
de ... — v d
de hug le corset — vj d
de galfrido de boteo — iiij d
de Willo le macon — iiij d
de amicia cunas — j d
de Abbate de ... — j d
de ... fil ... — j d
de Willo le packere — j d
de michel de ... — iiij d
de robto mand alle — iiij d
de ... briet — ix d
de ada piset — iiij d
de ada fil — ix d
de henr vert de gand — iiij d
de ... penal — vij d
de gilbto baylel — iij ob
de ... — iiij d
de ... ourcel — iiij d
de Willo de ... — j d

de valeo de pila bulle — j ob
de thoma fra — ... de ...
de Willo le huhere — ij d
de radulfo de noche — xiij d
de Willo g ... vnam acram

de ... le pakker — iiij ob
de galf fil le ... — j gr
de ... flex — j gr

pd amid actu Assalt de ra sibbe

de Willo fil flex — v d
de henrico de hardmad — viij d

de Willo fil dni vnam libr in cumi
de stefano lauke — j ob

pro dimidia acra
pro duob' acris
pro tribz acris
pro sex acris
pro tribz acris
p uno q'to trre
p una acra
p mess' agr eratsto
p medietate feod de ben'
pro tribz acris
p tribz acris
p vn acr de feod
p tcia p'te
p tcia p'te

Plate XVI: Pocket book of statutes

This is an example of a book which is small enough to carry in the pocket of a robe. As it is shown actual size and fully open, its compactness when closed can be appreciated. The growth of formal legislation in Edward I's reign, culminating in the confirmations of Magna Carta in the 1290s, encouraged the production of handbooks of parliamentary statutes (usually starting with Magna Carta) in various shapes and sizes. Thus the text illustrated here on the right-hand page is the beginning of the statute of Merton of 1235 (headed *Mertone*) and that on the left is the ecclesiastical condemnation issued in 1297 of infringers of Magna Carta (headed *Sentencia sup[er] cartas*). As is usual in manuscript books, the two sentences written boldly at the bottom of the left-hand page point out where one text ends and another begins: *Explic[it] sente[n]c[ia] lata s[upe]r cartas* ('Here ends the sentence imposed on the charters') and *Incipiunt p[ro]visiones de M[er]tone* ('Here begin the provisions of Merton'). This book was probably written shortly after 1297, perhaps for a practising lawyer and presumably by a professional scribe. Manuscripts like this, which emphasize the text rather than scribal ornament, were often written in a distinctive type of cursive script which is analysed and described as 'Anglicana' by M. B. Parkes, *English Cursive Book Hands* (1969), plate 4.

Harvard Law Library MS 175. Small books are discussed at pp. 134–5 above.

Plate XVII: Larger book of statutes

This manuscript was presumably made for a practising lawyer who was primarily concerned with its content rather than its appearance. It is written in a faster cursive script than the pocket book just illustrated (see plate XVI) and pays less regard to pleasing layout. Thus the letter 'p' at line 11 on the left has never been completed by the rubricator, by contrast with the similar 'p' on the right-hand page of the pocket book (see plate XVI). There are also cancellations and interlineations, which are acceptable in plea rolls but not usually in books: for example d[o]m[ini] is crossed out in line 11, because it is written twice, and an ampersand is interlined at line 13. The texts on this page are the end of the Charter of the Forest (Stubbs, *Charters*, pp. 347–8) and the beginning of the statute of Merton (*Statutes*, pp. 1–2). The symbols in the margin on the right point out where each numbered clause of the statute of Merton begins, so that a user of the book can readily find his place. Similarly the headlines (*de foresta/M[er]ton*) indicate the contents of the page. Although such an untidy-looking book might have disgusted a monk trained in a traditional *scriptorium*, it is a professional piece of work none the less. Lawyers, who were accustomed to working with the plea rolls and writs of the royal courts, would probably have found it easier to read than something in book hand like the page which follows (see plate XVIII).

Harvard Law Library MS 36. Reduced in size. Date *c.*1300.

2

Explicit carta de foresta. Incipit provisio de Merton

a.2

Plate XVIII: Illustrated book of statutes

Unlike the books just illustrated (see plates xvi and xvii), this one seems to have been made for someone who primarily wanted a manuscript which was pleasing to look at, even if it was a lawbook. It was probably written for the child bride, Philippa of Hainault, to present (in 1326) to her future husband and king, Edward III. The two columns, precisely ruled both horizontally and vertically, and the generous margins contrast with the cramped layout of the page in the preceding illustration (see plate xvii). Moreover, the text is written in a formal hand, which gives the page a more settled and liturgical appearance than the urgent cursive script of the preceding one. Originally this book had no headlines (the heading *Stat. de Merton* is a later addition), which suggests that the reader was not intended to flick rapidly through it. But it does use rubrics (they show up in a lighter tone in the photograph) and illuminated capital letters (*E* in the left column and *C* in the right) introduce each statute. The line drawings in the margins, which illustrate the subject matter of the statutes, are exceptional. The one on the left, showing a man with a longbow shooting at a deer, is placed alongside Edward I's ordinance of 1306 against trespassers in forests. Similarly the drawing on the right, showing a widow, veiled and in black, pointing towards a French text of the statute of Merton, is appropriate because its first chapters concern the rights of dowagers. Illustrations like these could therefore help a reader to find his place, but they are not used consistently in this way throughout the book.

Harvard Law Library MS 12. Reduced in size (actual size 34 cm × 24 cm). Comment: M. A. Michael, 'A Manuscript Wedding Gift from Philippa of Hainault to Edward III', *Burlington Magazine* cxxvii (1985), pp. 582–98.

Plate XIX: Alphabetical index

This is a portion of a folio from a large lawbook made in the 1290s. The book contains Bracton's treatise together with statutes and some other texts. The index refers both to Bracton and the statutes (Magna Carta is mentioned, for example, under the heading *scutagium* on the left). As the illustration shows, the index is arranged in columns with subject headings in approximate alphabetical order. Thus subjects beginning with *S* appear on the left and those beginning with *T* in the centre, but the sequence is not strictly alphabetical within these columns. On the right *W* (*Warentu*[*m*] 'warranty'), *U* (*Utlagaria*, 'outlawry') and *V* (*Vent*[*er*]*i*[*n*]*spiciend*[*us*], 'womb inspection') are all treated as one letter for alphabetical purposes. The references following the subject headings are elaborate. For example, after *Submersus* ('drowning') in the bottom left-hand corner is written *xli.* ('41' in Roman numerals) *3.* ('3' in Arabic numerals) *f.* (the letter 'f'). The Roman numerals should refer to folios, the Arabic ones to numbered articles or chapters, and the letters to subsections. In practice, however, this index fails to work consistently. Although it sometimes refers to the correct folio number in Roman numerals, the Arabic ones and the letters have no equivalents throughout the text. The index was evidently made not for this particular manuscript but for another one of similar contents. It works only by chance. The reasons for giving this book an elaborate yet unreliable index are discussed at ch. 5, pp. 180–1 above.

Harvard Law Library MS 1. Unnumbered preliminary folio. Actual size of complete folio 40 cm × 26 cm. In general see: Carruthers, *Memory*, p. 120; R. H. and M. A. Rouse, 'Concordances & Index', in *Mise en page et mise en texte du livre manuscrit*, ed. H.-J.Martin and J. Vezin (1990), pp. 219–28.

Supplicacio. xxij. 7. b.

<table>
<tr><td>

Sokemanni. iij. 7. b.
item. Lxxxiij. g. a.

xbij. z. a.
Sokagiu in ast. Alxg. ig. cd.
item. Alxvij. de cj ctoiz.

Scutagiu. ? max cait. g6. cd.
fte. Alxxxx. i. c.

Subtractio hedis. xix. 7. e.

Suspensio. Alxxxij. z. e.

Successio herd. xxxiij. z. d.
item. xxxd. zj. b.

Suggestio falsa. Alxxxix. e. f.

Summoniao justic gehal.
xxxvj. 7. f.
item m oiert. Alxj. 76. a.

Submersus. xlj. z. f.

</td><td>

Tradicio. xij. e. b.

Titlarpti. Alxxviij. z. c.

Terminar. vij. ei. e.

Terre. ? oiert. Alxg. 1d. 7 10. d.

Tenementu. Alxxx. 1. c.

Testes i cartis agend.
Lxxxv. z. f.

Tenetes medii. 7 Weftm.
Alxix. z. cd.

Theolonium. xxxj. e. b.
item. Alxxxviij. e. f.

Thesauru. xlj. e. b.

Turn vic ? oiac cait. gz. cd.
item m oiert. Alxj. 76. cd.
item. Alxxxd. g. d.

</td><td>

Warentu. ftat oldud. Alxg.
1. cd.
item Alxxvj. ki. cd.
item 7 Weftm. Alxviij. e. f.
item. Alxxvj. 7. e.
item. Alxxxij. 1. cio. f. 7. 7.
a. fore p totum.

Vtlagaria. xlij. 7. f. A
fte. delj. ftr. 1a. cd. &c. xlvo. 7. c.
tam. Alxlvij. g. d.
fte. Alxxxij. v. c.

Veut inpiciend. xxxvj. e. f.

Vertii namiu. Lvj. e. c.
item. 7 Weftm. 7. cd.

Vretii aaris. xlj. 1. b.
fte. i p. Weftm. Alxj. g. cd.

Veyfii. xlj. g. f.

Venditio ? max cait. gq. cd.
item ? cate. gg. cd. 2. xl. cd.
item fta cloud. Alxvj. e. e. 7.
item. Alxvj. de oiercioiz.
item. 7. Weftm. Alxxxiij. 1. a.

</td></tr>
</table>

Plate XX: Benefactors of Crowland abbey

This roundel is one of a series illustrating the life and miracles of St Guthlac, the Anglo-Saxon founder of Crowland. The abbey's most important bene-factors, headed by King Ethelbald (716–57), proceed towards the altar in front of St Guthlac's shrine. Beside the shrine (on the extreme right) a miraculous cure is taking place. An epileptic, his wrists still bound together, ejects a devil from his mouth during a fit so strong that it lifts him off the ground and thrusts his head almost out of the frame. His individual frenzy contrasts with the massed determination of the benefactors, each of whom displays a scroll specifying his gift in Latin. The king has one foot on the top step of the altar, across which he lays his scroll as a symbolic offering. The tenth-century Abbot Thurketel stands, holding his crozier, ready to follow him. Old Testament Prophets display similar scrolls on the roundel of an altar cross now in The Cloisters, New York (illustrated in colour in Zarnecki, *Catalogue*, p. 70; see also B. R. Jones in *Gesta* xxx 1991, p. 77). Like the Prophets, Crowland's benefactors are old wise men testifying to the truth. There may also be an allusion here to Christ and his Apostles, as twelve benefactors are shown with a king at their head. On a mundane level, the scene is reminiscent of a law court where remembrancers give testimony. This image encapsulates the transition from memory to written record: the scrolls of Crowland's Anglo-Saxon benefactors represent their remembered voices, which become written records by being sanctified on St Guthlac's altar.

BL Harley Roll Y6. Actual size of roundel: 16 cm in diameter. Date ?*c.*1200. Comment: G. Henderson, 'The Imagery of St Guthlac of Crowland', in *England in the Thirteenth Century* ed. W. M. Ormrod (1985), p. 85; Alexander & Binski, p. 35 (by M. Camille) and pp. 215–16 (by N. Morgan). See also ch. 8, p. 257 above.

Index

Medieval persons are indexed by forename and modern persons by surname.